ECONOMICS AGAINST THE GRAIN
VOLUME TWO

ECONOMISTS OF THE TWENTIETH CENTURY

General Editors: David Colander, *Christian A. Johnson Distinguished Professor of Economics, Middlebury College, Vermont, USA* and Mark Blaug, *Professor Emeritus, University of London, Professor Emeritus, University of Buckingham and Visiting Professor, University of Exeter, UK*

This innovative series comprises specially invited collections of articles and papers by economists whose work has made an important contribution to economics in the late twentieth century.

The proliferation of new journals and the ever-increasing number of new articles make it difficult for even the most assiduous economist to keep track of all the important recent advances. By focusing on those economists whose work is generally recognized to be at the forefront of the discipline, the series will be an essential reference point for the different specialisms included. Wherever possible, the articles in these volumes have been reproduced as originally published using facsimile reproduction, inclusive of footnotes and pagination to facilitate ease of reference.

A list of published and future titles in this series is printed at the end of this volume.

Economics Against the Grain
Volume Two

Julian L. Simon
Formerly College of Business and Management
University of Maryland, USA

ECONOMISTS OF THE TWENTIETH CENTURY

Edward Elgar
Cheltenham, UK • Northampton, MA, USA

Published by
Edward Elgar Publishing Limited
Glensanda House
Montpellier Parade
Cheltenham
Glos GL50 1UA
UK

Edward Elgar Publishing, Inc.
6 Market Street
Northampton
Massachusetts 01060
USA

A catalog record for this book is available from the British Library

Library of Congress Cataloging in Publication Data
Simon, Julian Lincoln, 1932–1998
Economics against the grain / Julian Simon.
(Economists of the twentieth century)
A collection of his articles previously published from 1965 to 1995.
"Writings of Julian Simon"
Includes bibliographical references and index.
Contents: v. 1. Microeconomics, industrial organization, and related themes — v. 2. Population economics, natural resources, and related themes.
1. Microeconomics. 2. Industrial organization. 3. Population–
–Economic aspects. 4. Natural resources. I. Title. II. Series.
HB172.S565 1997
330—DC20 96–27070
CIP

ISBN 1 85898 170 0

Printed and bound in Great Britain by Biddles Ltd, Guildford and King's Lynn

Contents

PART III INDIVIDUAL BEHAVIOR

PART IV POPULATION ECONOMICS

Acknowledgements

The author and the publisher wish to thank the following who have kindly given permission for the use of copyright material.

American Journal of Agricultural Economics for article: 'Price Elasticity of the Demand for Cigarettes in the United States,' with Herbert L. Lyon, **50** (4), November 1968, 888–95.

Blackwell Publishers for the following chapters from *Theory of Population and Economic Growth*, 1986: 'A Micro-Model of Invention and its Relation to the Technical Progress Function,' 22–44; 'Are Natural Resources an Increasing Constraint Upon Growth?' 184–215.

Econometric Society for article: 'The Price Elasticity of Liquor in the U.S. and a Simple Method of Determination,' *Econometrica*, **34** (1), January 1966, 193–205.

Elsevier Science for articles: 'Why Don't State Incomes Converge? Effective Worker Pay Does Not Differ Among States,' *Economics of Education Review*, **12** (2), 1993, 105–15; 'Phelps' Technical Progress Model Generalized,' with Gunter Steinmann, *Economics Letters*, **5**, 1980, 177–82; 'The Economic Implications of Learning-by-Doing for Population Size and Growth,' with Gunter Steinmann, *European Economic Review*, **26**, 1984, 167–85; 'Forecasting the Long-Term Trend of Raw Material Availability,' *International Journal of Forecasting*, **1**, 1985, 85–93.

Illinois Business Review for article: 'Cigarette Advertising and the Nation's Welfare,' **21**, May 1964, 6–8.

JAI Press for article: 'A Theory of Effort as an Economic Variable,' *Journal of Socio-Economics*, **20** (2), 1991, 105–23.

Mathematical Association of America for article: 'Probability and Statistics: Experimental Results of a Radically Different Teaching Method,' with David T. Atkinson and Carolyn Shevokas, *American Mathematical Monthly*, **83** (9), November 1976, 733–9.

National Council of Teachers of Mathematics for article: 'A New Way to Teach Probability Statistics,' with Allen Holmes, *The Mathematics Teacher*, **LXII** (4), April 1969, 283–8.

Population Association of America for articles: 'Puzzles and Further Explorations in the Interrelationships of Successive Births with Husband's Income, Spouses' Education and Race,' *Demography*, **12** (2), May 1975, 259–74; 'The Welfare Effect of an

Additional Child Cannot be Stated Simply and Unequivocally,' *Demography*, **12** (1), February 1975, 89–105.

The Population Council for article: 'Immigrants, Taxes, and Welfare in the United States,' *Population and Development Review*, **10** (1), March 1984, 55–69.

The Population Investigation Committee for articles: 'The Effect of Income on Fertility,' *Population Studies*, **XXIII** (3), November 1969, 327–41; 'The Mixed Effects of Income Upon Successive Births May Explain the Convergence Phenomenon,' *Population Studies*, **29** (1), March 1975, 109–22, erratum.

Princeton University Press for the following chapters from *Population and Development in Poor Countries*, 1992: 'An Integration of the Invention-Pull and Population-Push Theories of Economic-Demographic History', 43–77; 'The Effects of Population Size, Growth, and Concentration on Scientific Productivity,' with Douglas O. Love, 317–33; 'Population, Natural Resources, and the Long-Run Standard of Living,' with Gunter Steinmann, 89–121.

Random House Inc. for the following chapters from *Basic Research Methods in Social Science: The Art of Empirical Investigation*, 1969: 'Statistics of Probability: Part I,' 'Statistics of Probability: Part II' and 'How Big A Sample?', 362–432, references.

Sage Publications for articles: 'The Theory of Binding Commitments Simplified and Extended, with Generalization to Interpersonal Allocation,' *Rationality and Society*, **2** (3), July 1990, 287–309; 'Lebensraum: Paradoxically, Population Growth May Eventually End Wars,' *Journal of Conflict Resolution*, **33** (1), March 1989, 164–80; 'Interpersonal Allocation Continuous with Intertemporal Allocation: Binding Commitments, Pledges, and Bequests,' *Rationality and Society*, **7** (4), October 1995, 367–92.

Springer Verlag for articles: 'Resampling: A Tool for Everyday Statistical Work,' with Peter Bruce, *Chance*, **4** (1), 1991, 22–32; 'City Size, Prices, and Efficiency for Individual Goods and Services,' with Douglas O. Love, *The Annals of Regional Science*, **24**, 1990, 163–75.

Transaction Publishers for article: 'Shakespeare, Procreation, and Progress,' *Society*, **28** (5), July/August 1991, 58–62.

University of Chicago Press for articles: 'The Effect of Income on the Suicide Rate: A Paradox Resolved,' *American Journal of Sociology*, **74** (3), November 1968, 302–3; 'The Effect of Foster-Care Payment Levels on the Number of Foster Children Given Homes,' *Social Service Review*, **49** (3), September 1975, 405–11; 'Doctors, Smoking, and Reference Groups,' *Public Opinion Quarterly*, **31**, Winter 1967–1968, 646–7; 'The Effect of Population Density on Infrastructure: The Case of Road

Building,' with Donald R. Glover, *Economic Development and Cultural Change*, **23** (3), April 1975, 453–68.

Western Economic Association for article: 'A Specification Bias Interpretation of Cross-Section vs. Time Series Parameter Estimates,' with Dennis J. Aigner, *Western Economic Journal*, **VIII** (2), June 1970, 144–61.

Every effort has been made to trace all the copyright holders but if any have been inadvertently overlooked the publishers will be pleased to make the necessary arrangements at the first opportunity.

Introduction

I What is this book?

Heaven's refusals are often our greatest gifts. (On a parochial school blackboard.)

The proper attitude is gratitude. (Posted outside a church in a poor Hispanic town in New Mexico.)

The publishers ask each author of a book in this series to write a short autobiographical sketch of 'your career and intellectual development.' That delightful invitation – complicated only by the fact that I have never had (or thought of myself as having) a 'career' – set me to doing the usual, churning out so many words that the project outgrew all reasonable bounds.

So I scrapped that enterprise, and went back to the pages I wrote years ago when I was in a different professional situation to now, and in a different frame of mind. (Nowadays, as the first quotation suggest, I believe that most of my failures have led to better things than otherwise would have happened, and hence I am grateful for those fortunes, as the second quotation advises.)

This introduction is likely to seem peculiar. But what makes it peculiar may also make it interesting, and perhaps more valuable in the long run than a better-graced description. Furthermore, some of the specifics of my intellectual life as an economist may be found in the forewords to the individual articles.

As to the title of these volumes: When I was a boy, my father advised me that when cutting a board with a hand saw (he had no power tools because he believed that they were dangerous and unnecessary), one should always try to cut with the grain rather than across it. Sawing with the grain gives you a sweet, harmonious sound, and a sense of swift progress. In contrast, cutting across the grain is always hard work, and makes a rasping sound that sets your teeth on edge.

I have always yearned for the pleasantness of working with the grain. Nevertheless, much of the time I have seemed to be working against it, and that may be a big reason for the troublesome results that I have obtained. My sound is seldom harmonious, and often grates on the reader. The work seldom soars effortlessly, though it is often enormously enjoyable struggling across the grain. Sometimes the vibration knocks my tools out of my hand.

The key fact is that, with my work as with a board, mostly it is not possible to choose whether to cut with the grain or across it. Rather the course of the saw is guided mainly by what one is trying to do and by the materials at hand.

Most of the text which follows was written in the 1970s, and subsequent amendments are within brackets. Amendments written in 1983 are within single brackets, those written in the 1990s are within double brackets. Dates are inserted occasionally as reminders.

Most of my best articles in population economics have been reprinted in the volumes *Theory of Population and Economic Growth* (1986) and *Population and*

Development in Poor Countries (1992). I shall therefore include here mostly my work on other subjects.

What is this ungraceful book, with its ridiculous subtitle? [It then was subtitled 'Economic Essays Making Large Assertions But Going Widely Unread.']

It is a collection of articles that I believe present new and useful ideas, but that have been widely or totally unread. The book also contains this introduction explaining the unusual mode of publication, wherein I tell some of my experiences, background, and psychology. (If personal exposure makes you uncomfortable, I hope you will turn now to the articles themselves.)

As to the ridiculous subtitle: if I were to present these essays to you straightforwardly, you would not be likely to pay any attention to them, let alone take them seriously. But if I present them to you as a joke (though not a lighthearted joke, I confess), a few of you about whose opinions I care may give some serious attention to an essay or two. The title seeks to attract your attention even at the cost of your disdain. This tactic runs counter to my lifelong professional and personal style, though I now notice that the titles of my articles have become more strident with time and neglect.

[The above paragraphs, and almost all of the Introduction except the portions surrounded with brackets, were originally written in the summer of 1979 when I was particularly discouraged about my work making any difference to economists or others. I felt as David Hume once wrote: 'It would have been very silly for me ... to continue writing any more.'[1] I was sufficiently desperate in 1979 that I identified with the Dutch art forger Han van Meegeren, who decided that if he could not reach people with work over his own name, he would reach them with work over the names of others (Kilbracken, 1951). I fantasized performing a hoax that, after attracting interest and being unmasked, would draw attention to my ideas. And I made half-serious plans to stand in LaGuardia or O'Hare airports with a signboard, handing out pieces of my work.][2]

[[1990: My original plan was to have the book printed privately and then distribute it myself, on the assumption that no commercial or university press would publish it. Publishing would not have been a sound business decision for a publisher, because the expected sales at that time surely were somewhere between low and zero; I had no reputation to create interest in the book, and its varied contents would not appeal to any group of specialists. I calculated that I might sell enough copies to university libraries to recoup most of my expenses. The amount that I would be out of pocket would simply be in place of cars, clothes, and other forms of consumption for which my wife and I have very plain tastes. Over the years, other expenditures on our research have been a relatively large part of our budget.]]

[1983: I was bitter, as you can tell. But I was not depressed, because four years earlier, in 1975, I learned how to keep depression at bay after an unusually long and constant depression (about which more later, and in Simon, 1993). Then luck changed in 1980, and my work on population and resources succeeded beyond my dreams. It reached a considerable audience, was praised by some, and has even been accepted and built upon by a few writers within economics and without (in both senses of the word). I am grateful for this new professional fortune. Perhaps the unusual before-and-after, rags-to-prosperity nature of this introduction will create interest in the book.]

[My bitter views about the sociology of economic and demographic knowledge remain unchanged, however. I still think that the structure of university departments, funds-granting organizations, and – most important of all – the professional journals considered as a set, are mostly impregnable to people who have new ideas that are out of the mainstream, yet wish their work to affect thought and policy. Luck seldom comes as suddenly as it did for me in cracking through this wall. I am *not* bitter that I have not managed to achieve the symbols and rewards of success in the academic life. Rather, I am grateful for the miracle that finally enabled me to have my ideas heard, for my freedom to use my time mostly as I wish, for being able – because of the kind of work I do, and the way I do it – to get along without much research support, and for the personal blessings of health, family, and friendship. And I shall never again be bitter at professional fortune; I have been too lucky for that.]

The criteria for essays to be included in these volumes are: (a) that they have been ignored, and in many cases unpublished; (b) that they are unconventional; and (c) that they are of more than transient interest, in this author's unbiased judgment. I have not included work that is traditional in subject and method, or that has received a modicum of attention from workers in the field.

Many of these essays also have the following characteristics: (a) they use whichever method offers an answer to the question at issue, rather than sticking to the theoretical and econometric methods that are tradition in economics; and (b) many of them offer solutions to economic and social *problems*, rather than being *explanations* of economic phenomena. The spirit of that sort of reseach is closer to engineering and business research for solving operational problems than to the Western scientific tradition of striving to understand nature and uncovering its secrets. Several of the essays inquire into the philosophical foundations of economics – for example, causality, utility, and interpersonal comparisons – and they use some devices drawn from the Einstein–Bohr philosophical view in order to unlock paradoxes and resolve confusions.

(Curiously, though economists often pride themselves on their subject's philosophical likeness to physics, their model usually is the physics of the years before Einstein and Bohr rather than the physics that these two created. The operational definition of time, a linguistic matter, is at the heart of Einstein's relativity discovery. And Bohr never ceased to emphasize the primacy of linguistic questions in physics and elsewhere in science. But economists are impatient with such philosophical and linguistic discussions – consider the lack of interest in Machlup's work on economic semantics [1967] – though such work can resolve many wasteful arguments that swallow up talent and human energy, and crowd into scarce journal space. Economics therefore continues to work with constraining notions of fundamental properties and ideal qualities (for example, utility, as discussed in Volume One, Chapter 3). By analogy, instead of insisting that the world 'is' round, we should understand that the world can best be *viewed* as flat by a carpet layer, out of round by a geologist, and jagged to an airplane pilot.[3] More about this later.)

Benefits for the reader?

For an advertising man – which is how I started professional life, though the poor quality and small quantity of my self-promotion [until 1981] calls into question my advertising skills – the first rule is to study the benefits of the good you wish to sell, and then promise those benefits to the potential customer. As Samuel Johnson put it long ago, 'Promise, large promise, is the soul of an advertisement.' (*The Idler* 41, via Oxford Dictionary of Quotations.) But the potential benefits of this book to the reader are, in truth, fewer than I would like to advertise. It may serve for graduate students as an instruction manual of the kind of work that one should not do if one is to get ahead in the profession. It may provide a useful acquaintance with the negative referees' reports included here, without suffering their pain at first hand. It may afford some sensitive souls the opportunity to feel the uplifting sentiment, 'There but for the grace of God go I,' or give to some persons with high self-regard the gratifying feeling that he or she has been sufficiently perspicacious to succeed where I have not. Beyond that, there may be some entertainment value in my slant on the profession, slightly morbid though the entertainment may be. [There also may be some unusual insights because it was mainly written before subsequent events put a gloss upon the successless past. Few successless persons ever are heard from in print.] And yes, maybe someone will find a basic idea of value here. I hope so.

II Why is the screwball author doing this?

If personal revelations embarrass you, please stop reading this introduction, and move on to the articles themselves.

You – and probably I, too, if I were faced with a document like this – are likely to ask: 'Why is he doing this?', meaning by 'this' something strange, quirky, excessive, and not sensible by everyday professional and career criteria. The simplest explanation is straightforward 'profit' maximization: I have spent years working on these ideas and trying to get people to believe them, and I have a large inventory of unused material. This volume is another way of trying to sell the stuff off, like a 'Fire Sale' except that the fire is real. And playing the clown is an attempt to draw customers to the sale. (There are additional explanations that I will go into below.)

So, what do I want to achieve with this volume? I want a few readers whose judgment matters to say 'Hey, this guy makes some sense. Let's try looking at it his way,' the 'it' being one idea or another, and 'some' being the key word in 'some sense.' If you now proceed to look at a piece or two, I will have done as much as I can with this introduction and with the volume.

At a deeper level, the explanation for this volume lies in an observation of von Hayek's: 'There is perhaps no more poignant grief than that arising from a sense of how useful one might have been to one's fellow men and of one's gifts having been wasted' (1960, p. 80).

You may feel that an academic who produces a volume like this one must be exhibitionistic, a person with an overdeveloped need for attention. Well, maybe. I think the record will show that such is not the case with me. More to the point, however: it is easy to be gracefully modest when one's ideas attract attention; there is then no pay-off to clumsy repellent hollering for more attention. But if one's ideas do *not* attract attention through the usual channels of scholarly publication, then one must choose between (a) gracefully accepting non-existence, and swallowing the fact that all one's best efforts come to naught; and (b) trying in an unpleasant and socially-unacceptable manner to draw the attention of at least a few people, for a little while, to one or more of the ideas that you believe are valuable. In other words, the choice is between going quietly to your demise, or going kicking and screaming. The end result is probably the same, but I think there is more honor in trying to make a fuss, at least once, though it goes against my everyday nature.

Is all this *just* a self-indulgent cry for help and pity? There is no way I could argue to the contrary – especially since there is *some* amount of cry in this. But does it matter? Maybe it does. Ultimately you will judge this for yourself, of course. This part of the introduction will go more fully into why I am doing all this.

A more interesting question is: Why am I doing this *now*? ['Now' meaning 1979]. One answer: Whatever response I get to this volume may help me evaluate the extent to which I am unrealistic, foolish, or just plain nuts [by 1983 the 'nuts' element is less of an issue], and/or why the fate of my best work is what it is. And that response may help me decide how best to spend the rest of my writing life. That is one reason for doing the volume now.

[[A note about the word 'screwball' in the title above: A screwball may be an 'erratic' or 'unpredictable' pitch, according to the dictionary, but there is nothing *crazy* about the pitcher or the pitch.]]

Another reason: By nature, I am a scribbler rather than a talker, and it is fun for me (I smile with pleasure as I write these sentences) to indulge myself in writing down some loose thoughts and favorite contentions. As John Locke wrote in the introduction to *An Essay Concerning Human Understanding*

> [If] thou has but half so much pleasure in reading as I had in writing it, thou wilt as little think thy money, as I do my pains, ill bestowed.

Locke went on to say, however, as I would also say,

> Mistake not this for a commendation of my work; nor conclude, because I was pleased with the doing of it, that therefore I am fondly taken with it now it is done.

Those of you who also express yourselves more comfortably and more clearly in writing than in speech will understand this motive. A less sympathetic description might be 'ego trip.'

As to costs: I have little to lose by doing this [[still mostly true in 1994]]. These volumes cannot turn off a flow of honors, research funds, flattering job offers, opportunities to give talks at the American Economic Association and to contribute to volumes of essays, invitations to serve on prestigious boards of editors and directors, or even invitations to review important books in powerful media (some of which I would not want even if offered the opportunity); there is no flow to staunch. On my vita I mention no honors or awards or offices, in the thin hope that the scanner of the vita will think I am a modest fellow; the better explanation is that there are no honors to speak of.[4]

Letting it all hang out – writing what is on your mind and in your heart, without worrying about referees, editors, and publishers – is a once-in-a-lifetime pleasure. Few can afford such a pleasure more than once, and most feel they cannot afford it even once. Luckily I can afford the money cost once in a lifetime [1994: I had expected to have to pay for printing and distributing it by myself] thanks to my working wife, a couple of multi-edition books, and cheap tastes.

This is being written [in 1979] under the influence of the rejection of a research proposal seeking support of my work on population and growth theory. The rejection notice was negative to the point of contempt, agreed to by all hands on the review panel, and without a redeeming word. What I am doing here is saying: Ladies and gentlemen, you tell me very clearly what you think of my ideas (and my style of presenting myself). Now I will tell you what *I* think about my work, rather than just letting the work speak for itself in journals (or not speaking at all in my large footlocker of unpublished manuscripts).

[1984: And, of course, this introduction was a cry for help when I wrote it. Characteristically, the pages uttering that cry remained in my drawer, and perhaps would have stayed there forever if the conditions of my life had not changed and I luckily came not to need help in the way that I did when I wrote it.]

[[1994: After all this talk about why I was going to publish this work myself, why did I never do so? Simply the shortage of time and energy. I kept procrastinating publishing not only this work but two other books, also, for which I could not find publishers. It was always 'I've got to do it next year,' but other tasks were always much more appealing than the labors of self-publishing, or more pressing, or both.]]

Why do I go on doing the kind of work I do?

Why does an otherwise-sensible person go on spending time developing ideas that are out of the mainsteam, when one's profession does not give positive recognition (and/or gives negative recognition) to one's past efforts that also are out of the mainstream? And, how can one go on believing that one's ideas are valuable in the face of colleagues mostly saying they are not valuable? I wonder about this when others do it as well as when I do it.

A possibility, of course, it that one is (a) very sure of oneself, or (b) good at making excuses, or (c) both. And excuses aplenty there are, a favorite being that 'they' are too stupid (conventional, socialized, hidebound, unimaginative, moved by self-interest, or whatever) to appreciate one's ideas. Add to this the belief that in the future the wheel may turn in a more appreciative direction, and the combination of self-assurance and facile excusing may get one by – for a while, anyway.

Another possibility is that at least some support is given by a few people [[for example, the letter from von Hayek in Note 4 had a huge effect]]. Several decades ago a psychological experiment showed how much more tenaciously a person will hold to a judgment about the arrangement of spots on a wall, despite massive contradiction from the experimenter, when one other person supported the subject's view as compared to when no one did; one other person's agreement makes you feel that you are not crazy. The importance of my getting *some* confirmation that an idea makes sense from persons I respect is told in the preface to the article about interpersonal comparisons (see Volume One, Chapter 3).

Some people are good at building coteries whose members act as claques for one another, and thereby provide mutual reinforcement.[5] I have not done so, perhaps because of social ineptitude or because of lack of willingness to ask others to invest a part of their lives into a line of research on the basis of my personal belief.

My ability to hold a view in the absence of support has always been quite considerable. And I have greater willingness than most people to go about my business quite on my own (I worked totally without professional contact for my first three years as a professor, following two years out of the university starting and operating my own business) and without institutions and colleagues giving evidence that they value me (though in my personal life I crave love as much as the next person). These traits surely have kept me going longer in the directions I have gone than otherwise would have been the case.

Finding out that the same ideas that you have had are well-received when published *by others* can reinforce your belief in yourself; this has happened to me on a good many occasions. But this is double-edged and bitter-sweet, of course – one then asks: 'Why do I fall short in the communication and persuasion process?' and, 'How can I do it better?'

A very strong reinforcement is having one or more of your ideas actually tried out successfully, after it was generally said that it could not be successful. That was the case with me and the airline overbooking auction scheme (see Volume One, Chapters 2 and 22, and Simon, 1994).

[[The fact that the forecasts explicit and implicit in my work on resource availability in connection with population growth have been entirely consistent with subsequent events has strengthened my resolve, of course. The fact that the doomsayers whose prophecies have been falsified by events continue to make just the same prophecies as before, yet have lost no credibility with the press or public, bewildered me at first; now I have grown accustomed to the phenomenon.]]

However, I believe that the reason that most fully explains my work behavior and my continuing to do what I do is this: I want to be useful to the community, and I do not know of any other way that better promises to take advantage of what talents I may have than what I am now doing, thinking, and writing. During 1964 and 1965, after I came to believe that study of the economics of advertising is not very important (even though advertising itself is important), I spent some time almost every day assessing the potential contribution of work I might do in various fields of economics and business. Eventually I decided that the economics of population and the marketing of birth control offered the best opportunity. It is ironic that I came to this conclusion because I saw population growth (along with war) as one of the two main threats to mankind, because later, as a result of my reading and investigations, I concluded that there is more truth in the opposite viewpoint, that population growth is a boon in the long run.

There is also a secret personal reason why I do not turn my back on economics and move into academic or business or consulting work in fields I know rather well – advertising, managerial economics, marketing research, mail-order – or even start a new career studying the relationship of living patterns to disease (which attracts me and which I think I could do well using tools I already have): I love economics! Even though I never studied in an economics department and have no degree in the subject,[6] I am in awe of the power and the subtlety of the great ideas that have come from great minds: Petty's analysis of division of labor and other effects of population size, and his genius (and that of Graunt and now Kuznets) at scientifically estimating such quantities as life expectancy and national income that had never before been estimated; Smith's and von Hayek's understanding of the mystery of spontaneous order and economic coordination across markets and over time without central direction; the great simultaneous discoveries of modern value theory, Marshall's scintillating insights and encyclopedic knowledge of the working of an economy; Walras's vision of general equilibrium as a matrix for our thought; Pareto's optimum and other speculations about welfare economics; a host of clever scholars finding ways to measure quantities such as bootleg liquor and illegal gambling and the price of copper in the year AD1; and (as the television commercials for mail-order record albums say) lots, lots more. I cannot easily pull out the wires that connect me to this marvelous body of ideas and information – that is perhaps the most painful part of my situation. I am an unrequited lover who feels that even being in the presence of the uninterested beloved is better than the affection of one who does not excite you with the same passion.

Often I have speculated on the personal and professional qualities that have helped some of our best writers to make a large impression on the profession. Chances are too high that these guesses are not sound, but I will hazard them anyway about a few economists about whom I have some information: Gary Becker has personally inspired with his approach many students who have become professors in well-known universities; the ex-students have built a large self-reinforcing literature. Much the same seems true of Theodore Schultz with special emphasis on foreign students. Milton Friedman has taught many students and non-students, both in person and with his books, who implemented his ideas through governmental monetary agencies. In contrast, Kenneth Arrow and George Stigler have written articles that seem to call out for the kind of mathematical development which promises career advancement (though the articles that follow often share little of the importance of the founding articles). Samuelson simply dazzles, and attracts as other stars do. Simon Kuznets produces raw material which is indispensable to a wide range of scholars; even those who lack appreciation of him cannot do without him. (It should also be noted that Kuznets gets amazingly widespread praise for his skill as a developer of projects and organizations.) Similarly, there is no alternative to Wassily Leontief's input–output work; but without heavy government support, that work might never have made a large impression.

How important are charm, charisma, ability to inspire students, capacity to attract research grants, and a place in a first-class department among other scholars who can help sharpen your ideas? I cannot guess; perhaps you will try.[7] Can you point to fundamental bodies of thought which have been kept from the profession for lack of these personal–institutional factors? Maybe none, except for the 'Austrians' Ludwig von Mises and Friedrick von Hayek. But what about important though not fundamental advances? (The very worst part of my writing life is to feel that the more important and useful the topic, the broader the understanding of the economic and social world, and the more innovative the techniques used [unless they are innovations in the mainstream of technique], (a) the more difficult it will be to get the article past referees and into print, and (b) the less likely it is that economists will read it. Every deviation from the form of a utility-maximizing model of resource allocation, with or without data to test the model, reduces the work's prospects. And discussion of the deviations from orthodox method so as to 'justify' them to the reader makes economists impatient, apparently because methodological discussion seems so unnecessary to them; in their minds, perhaps, all the relevant methodological issues have been discussed and settled long ago. This is a classical case of paradigm-blindness, and it is rather sad all round. For me personally, it means that after the joy of getting what I think is a particularly good idea, I want to cry.)

On quacks, quackery, and the author

[This section may now seem inappropriate, because the recent turn in my fortunes has given me some legitimacy. Nevertheless, I include it as originally written because I believe it is helpful in understanding what someone on the outside feels like, and is up against.]

If you are still reading, you are probably weighing the likelihood that the writer is a quack. By 'quack' I mean a person outside the established intellectual order whose ideas are demonstrably vacuous. The odds *must* be high that a person is a quack if he or she embarks on a venture such as this, and writes such an introduction; to a prudent person this is prima-facie evidence that it pays to read no further. But perhaps curiosity will lead you to check the evidence of the work itself, though of course as you read you will continue to update your estimates about whether the work is quackery. Therefore a few words about the identification of quacks and quackery may be in order.

1. One way to identify a quack – or to dismiss a non-quack who expresses unconventional views – is to determine that even if the assertion of the writer is correct, acceptance of the assertion would not make much difference to anyone. Indeed, people occasionally complain that their fundamental ideas are ignored when what they are really offering is an alternative language or set of concepts that, though logically correct and perhaps more attractive, would not yield different conclusions about important theoretical or policy issues. One might conclude that even if I am right in my argument in Volume One, Chapter 2, that the concept of product differentiation is worthless, there would be no policy ramifications; one might note that mainstream economic theory has mostly dropped the term and concept (though in fact the term continues to be used in a variety of contexts, including major anti-trust cases). But for others among my ideas there are undeniable implications of importance. For example, if I am right about the connection of population growth to productivity change, then Western countries should not discourage births or immigration. If I am right about its relevance and learnability, the marginal-revenue-equal-to-marginal-cost analysis should be stripped out of textbooks. And if I am right about the usefulness of Monte Carlo methods [now called *resampling*] in elementary statistics, the basic statistics course, and much of statistical practice, should be radically altered. So triviality is not a reasonable ground for dismissal of most of the ideas in these essays.
2. Quacks tend to be impractical or very abstract. But it is important to guard against judging that a person is not a quack in one field because he or she is a practical person in another. That is, it does not follow that I am not an economic quack because I have written well-accepted practical books on how to run a mail-order business and how to do empirical research, as well as articles that have led to practical results toward resolving the airline overbooking problem to everyone's benefit, and setting advertising budgets profitably. There are too many examples in the economics section of the library stacks of otherwise-practical people – businessmen and engineers, especially – who have written high-order economic quackery.

Practicality in other endeavors cannot be considered a reliable safeguard against quackery.

3. Somewhere (perhaps in one of C.P. Snow's books) I have read a physicist asserting that one can always understand what a quack is saying about physics, whereas if one cannot understand the writer there is a good chance that the work is valuable. In my experience, however, it is often tedious and difficult to determine what economic quacks are trying to say, making this particular quack-identification system ineffective for economics.
4. A persuasive reason to assume [as of 1979] that I am a quack is that there are – to my knowledge – few cases of scientists who have several times come up with sound fundamental ideas that have gone nowhere. I do not know of any such cases in the social sciences today. And as becomes apparent in the process of faculty recruiting, there do not seem to be many productive talented people languishing in obscurity. Of course it could be that we do not know about them just because they *are* obscure. But at the institutions where I have taught, I have not met any such productive talented people who are widely ignored; that is a small sample, but something of a check. I conclude that few first-rate or close-to-first-rate people remain unknown to their contemporaries. (If you know of any such languishers, please drop me a line, and I will pass their names on to the recruiting committee.) Therefore, if one feels that a substantial body of one's own work *is* first-rate or close to it yet cannot interest people in the work or persuade them of its value, and if one thinks that the consensus of experts' judgments usually contains useful information, one must wonder whether one is a megalomaniac. Yet I say it: I think that the economic profession is not correct in its implicit judgment that these essays are wrong-headed or unimportant.
5. But, does not the act of spending money and energy reproducing this material that will still go largely unread *prove* that this author's judgment is poor? Well, though the expected pay-off is small, the cost in money and time also is small, and hence the net present value of the endeavor to this writer is fairly high.

Why does my work meet the fate it does?

Over the years I have speculated a lot about why the corpus (corpse?) of the work I consider my best meets the fate that it does. The simplest and most obvious hypothesis is that the work is no good. I discussed earlier why the evidence on the matter is somewhat less than conclusive. Therefore I have cast around for other explanations.

For a while I thought that it was my mode of presentation that was at fault – too staid, or not well-enough organized, or too lengthy. The results of that speculation can be seen in my shift to big-claim titles for articles, so that no eye could miss what I am trying to say, as in the titles of several chapters in these volumes. But that tactic did not work either, and hence I concluded that it is not merely my mode of presentation that is at fault. Another hypothesis is that I have worked in too many areas, spreading myself too thin and weakening my credibility. I cannot believe this is the main explanation, however.

Yet another hypothesis is that I have not been a member of a group of people working in a shared tradition on a related set of problems in which the profession at large is interested. Maybe. Yet the successful innovators do not confine themselves in such a fashion, and they manage to get their ideas across anyway. Perhaps such successful innovators have greater force of personality than I do, and are supported by more confidence in themselves and their ideas, which shows up as infectious enthusiasm.[8] But this cannot be the whole answer, either. Certainly my reluctance to employ the framework of the optimizing allocation decision – with full mathematical regalia – where I consider that framework unnecessary or inappropriate, has not helped. Much of my work deals with very long run economic development, a context in which the creation of new technology is the most important element. Often that process is better not treated with the logic of profit maximization.

About ideology: Joan Robinson may or may not be correct when she wrote that 'Economics has mixed its ideology into the subject so well that the ideologically unconventional usually appear … to be scientifically incompetent' (1977, p. 1319). But my economic and social ideology are quite in the mainstream of Anglo-Saxon economics, and hence cannot explain the fate of my work. Rather, it is my approach to the craft of science, and my philosophical approach to scientific method, that are out of the mainstream. Yes, on grounds that *seem* ideological some economists and almost all demographers vigorously disagree with the view about population growth that I (though not I alone) espouse. But my work on subjects other than population also evokes chilly reactions, with no such ideological explanation.

It may be a crippling defect that I digress too much (see how I grasp at straws?), perhaps because I think about the underlying meaning of each word, and that leads to side thoughts. (I am the sort of person that, when I write a note to someone I am not too fond of, wonders whether I will be true to myself if I begin with 'Dear ...' And when someone asks me 'How are you?' I sometimes scratch my head and think about it – though I almost always give the stock answer 'Fine.' If I am feeling loose I say, 'In the long run fine; in the short run, I don't know.') And I have a variety of inconsistent reactions to the same stimulus: When writing an article, at one moment I may think I am writing to a reader who can understand any nuance, and at the next moment I may assume that without a cannon going off the reader will pay no attention to the article or to any of its main points.

Also I write at too-great length, being by nature an encyclopedist (or, as you like, a pack rat) who hates to leave out a good quote or display of data. It hurts me that many of my most useful thoughts about method will likely be counter-productive if I include them, just as simplicity of style is counter-productive. This is true cynicism. Yet I continue to write mostly the way I want to, foolishness though it may be. I suppose it is because I am anxious to avoid the shame I would feel if people detected me doing otherwise, taking shortcuts or building on a shoddy foundation or being purposely obscurantist. Generally, I believe that my foundation is much more solid than the facade is pretty.

The absence of steady demeanor in my writing mirrors my behavior in person. Though I have a very large intellectual confidence, I am confusingly self-effacing with most people, and I seldom talk about my work. If asked what I am doing, I am likely to say 'The same old thing – scribbling and trying to get my desk clear. What are you doing?' But if I think that the person I am with is able and willing to appreciate what is on my mind, I come on too strong and say too much. Yet, I cannot believe that this defect, either, accounts for the failure of my best work.

The pro-technique tendency of the profession is a disaster for me professionally because I have an irrational distaste for unnecessary flourish. I grew up seeing how the desire for proper front can destroy a person's self-respect, and keep a family from getting a living; therefore I hated it. I have always thought that the jingle 'Simple Simon' fitted me nicely. Nowadays I no longer actively hate front, but only despise it; that attitude shows through. For a long time I was taken (or better, taken in) by the notion that simplicity is an ideal in science. (I even titled two of my early articles 'A Simple Method ...') It took me years to appreciate that T.S. Eliot's remark about poetry applies also to scientific writing: It must be easy enough to understand, but hard enough so that it cannot be understood immediately. Simplicity fails because, as Stigler puts it, 'The form of work takes on a value independent of its content: a scholar should be literate, and his work should be pursued with non-vulgar instruments' (quoted by Fisher, 1986, p. 78). And as Goodwin (quoted by Fisher, 1986, p. 80) put it, 'It is the essence of a profession that the skills required therein are not possessed by those without.' This has led my work to take some bumps. For example, I wished to compare the areas between two empirical curves showing sales responses to advertising over time, and I simply counted the squares under the curves on graph paper. A referee was horrified at the 'primitiveness' of this mode of integration, and at the ignorance of the author. A more important example is the resistance that my method of teaching and doing probability and statistics by Monte Carlo methods arouses in those who prefer formulae, despite the experimentally-proven large pedagogical advantage of the Monte Carlo method (see Volume Two, Part I).

Also, my early experience as a writer of advertisements and magazine articles taught me skills counter-productive in economics. In those media one tries to be as interesting and clear and simple in one's prose as possible. But in academic writing these qualities are taken to be the signs of a lightweight who is nether serious nor dignified. This, for example, was in a referee's report I received last week: 'The prose style must conform to expository standards. At present the style is that of conversation or a very informal seminar presentation.' And another: '[T]he writing style was inappropriate for an academic conference.' And a third: 'The paper is very simplistically written ... It needs to be ... rewritten with a more sophisticated presentation.'

Like engineers and business people, I intend my work to fill a need and do a job, rather than to be a work of art. This inevitably makes it more difficult to attract the interest and attention of colleagues in economics and demography. The devices I regard as desirably simple as tools in business decision-making – for example, tabular and total analysis (as distinguished from the marginal analysis) – are seen as undesirably crude by colleagues.

Speaking of engineers and business people, I share with them a dominant interest in the independent variables rather than in the dependent variable. That is, usually economists (and scientists generally) want to know the causes of the variation in the dependent variable, for example, the birth-rate, and the movements of the stars. In contrast, business people and engineers want to know how a particular independent variable (say income or education) changes a dependent variable such as consumption of alcohol, or the birth-rate.

The most flattering speculation is that I fail because my ideas run against common beliefs – that is, against the grain. I believe that, as information theory teaches, information contributes most to knowledge if it is dissimilar to other information presently in the system (and, of course, if the information is correct). As it is said, 'If the two of us agree, one of us is unnecessary.' Indeed, much of what I write does not simply bill itself as new, but begins by saying that the conventional view is wrong. However, I cannot convince myself that this is a major explanation, much as I would like to believe it. Others also offer unpopular or unconventional ideas, and yet they get people to pay attention to those ideas.

[As of 1983 [[even more so, as of 1994]], I have solid – and slightly painful, though not entirely unwelcome – evidence that my ideas simply rub people the wrong way. The wider audience that my most recent book (*The Ultimate Resource*) and articles have reached has responded in some extraordinary and ugly fashions. I will spare you the details here because you can find them in an Epilogue to the 1995 edition of *The Ultimate Resource* and in my 1990 *Population Matters*.]

[All this attention, I am quick to say, is music to my ears, in welcome contrast to the deafening silence that for more than a decade enveloped this work on the rare occasions when any of it found its way into print. But this open hostility to my recent writing aimed at a wider audience makes it more believable that there is also latent hostility to my technical work, and also makes it more plausible that my ideas somehow rub people the wrong way even on less emotional topics simply because the ideas are not conventional.]

So, again, why *is* my work received as it is? After years of thought, I can only be sure that – aside from issues of the pure quality of the work – there is something about my favorite ideas and ways of expressing them, my interests, my philosophical point of view and methods of work, and my need to do different things and do them differently – which intersects with the economics profession's ways of thinking and behaving in a manner that just does not click; the merchandise just does not sell, but I do not know why. There is just something about me that goes against the grain.

Without doubt I have misunderstood what the academic fields of economics, demography, and even marketing generally want. Earlier I mentioned how I mistakenly believed that scientists want simplification and simplicity. I also mistakenly believed for a long time that scientists want a reconciliation of opposing views; in fact, they tend to prefer continued controversy, with its attendant crowd-pleasing interest. But there surely are other misunderstandings that I have not yet identified.

In brief, I have not done the proper market research on what these disciplines want. And even when I have correctly understood what the colleagues want, and how they want it packaged, I have refused (or have been unable) to prepare my best work in that fashion. That is a perfect prescription for failure in a consumer goods industry. Whether that also is enough to ensure failure in the knowledge industry, or whether it must be accompanied by low quality work to ensure failure, I still do not know.

[There is one more element, and while good fortune still smiles on me as it does in 1983, it will not seem like sour grapes to mention it: Luck. Popper says:

> I think that success in life is largely a matter of luck. It has little correlation with merit, and in all fields of life there have always been many people of great merit who did not succeed. Thus it is only to be expected that this happened also in the sciences and in the arts (1974/1976, p. 70).

Or read Read:

> The element of chance therefore plays a considerable part in the achievement of success … But this is to consider only happy chances; the phenomenon also has its negative aspects. The lack of success during their lifetimes of many artists who are posthumously recognized may be due to personal qualities of diffidence, as I have already suggested, or to incompetent methods of salesmanship, but it may be just bad luck. Apart from the bad luck of being born in a remote province, or a small country (chances which afflict the poet much more severely than the painter); apart from the bad luck of being born to poverty or with physical defects (such as bad eyesight), there is an element of fatality in any artist's career which cannot be controlled. So much depends, in what is at all times a game of chance, upon the people we meet and the places we visit (1963, p. 109).

I think Popper and Read put *too* much weight on luck. But it certainly is not unimportant. I rejoice with gratitude at what seems to me a miracle, that a series of events which flowed from a single article in *Science* – an article which for a year and a half was on the brink of not being published at all due to a staff member's sabotage (as described in Simon, 1990) – enabled my work to make an impression upon the thinking of a fair chunk of the public. If the first domino had not toppled, the rest probably would not have happened either. Of course the material was there. But I believe that, though there was a body of good work, in the chance that one event had gone the other way the body of work by itself would not have found the light.]

III How did I get to be this way?

If one is out of step with the rest of the world, one wonders why.

One important cause of my writing what and how I do is that I was not trained as an economist. I studied experimental psychology as an undergraduate, then (after three years in the Navy and a year in business) I took a four-quarter masters degree in business administration, plus one more quarter of courses to study for prelims in marketing. I then wrote a thesis on optimal storage of books in university libraries, based on surveys of book use that I did in conjunction with Herman Fussler. After that I went into the mail-order business on my own. I never expected to be an academic, let alone an economist. (One of the reasons I intended not to be an academic was that I knew myself unsuited for the kinds of politics found in universities. As it is said, the politics in universities are so vicious because the issues are so trivial.)

I only began to teach after I realized that scribbling is the work I enjoy best. I began in the department of advertising in 1963 at the University of Illinois, but was kicked out in 1966 by the department head ostensibly for lack of research (see my vita re the plausibility of this assertion). I then moved to the department of marketing which later became part of business administration, still at the University of Illinois. In 1969 I became a half-time member of the department of economics. I have also taught business for two and a half years in three stretches at Hebrew University. [[In 1983, I moved to the University of Maryland by way of an open-ended appointment in the Division of Social Sciences. As part of complex administrative reorganization, my services (that is, an additional budget line, in academic lingo) were twice offered (without my knowledge) to the economics department for free, a deal that any department would avail itself of if the professor in question is capable of doing long division and reading at the eleventh grade level. But the Maryland economics department turned down the offer, mobilized by a professor who regards my work on population as akin to the seductions of the devil. The College of Business and Management was happy to get my services, and I am happy to be in it.]]

When I was young I wrote some non-fiction articles for mass magazines and fiction for 'little' magazines. I also did legal and engineering work as (mainly) line officer's work aboard a Navy ship and while attached to the Marines and I have always read about philosophical methods.

All this means that my head is a ragbag. In academic terminology, my thinking is 'eclectic,' than which nothing is thought to be worse. Many economists have opined that such diversity makes for good economics. Marshall quoted Mill with approval: 'A person is not likely to be a good economist who is nothing else' (1920, p. 771). Von Hayek expressed it in stronger terms:

> The physicist who is only a physicist can still be a first-class physicist and a most valuable member of society. But nobody can be a great economist who is only an economist – and I am even tempted to add that the economist who is only an economist is likely to become a nuisance if not a positive danger (quoted by Machlup, 1976, p. 49).

Or as Hutchinson quoted Viner:

> Men who have been trained to think only within the limits of one subject, or only from the point of view of one subject, will never make good teachers at the college level even in that subject. They may know exceedingly well the possibilities of that subject, but they will never be conscious of its limitations, or if conscious of them will never have an adequate motive or a good basis for judging as to their consequences or extent (1977, p. 7).

Diversity may be good for one's understanding, but it may also be disastrous for one's ability to relate (in both senses of the word).

But my thinking may not be as scattered as it seems on the surface. Von Hayek writes of some scholars that 'many of their particular ideas in different fields may spring from some single more general conception of which they are themselves not aware but which, like the similarity of their approach to the separate issues, they may much later discover with surprise' (1978, p. 54). And indeed, a few years ago I noticed that underlying all of my work on population, resources, and environment (though not most of the work in this volume) is the idea of progress, that as individuals and as groups people gradually and erratically, but surely, move toward greater efficiency, a higher standard of living, and a better living environment. This theme is discussed in Volume One, Chapter 38.

Lack of training as an economist has meant that I am without some technical skills which help one pass for an economist. Once in a while this lacuna has even slowed up my work. I have also remained unacquainted with various standard concepts and chunks of literature, though I have tried piecemeal to learn what seemed valuable; therefore I have sometimes reinvented old ideas, but this happens to many.

On the positive side, this lack of training has saved me from getting stuck with some conventional ideas which are wrong, especially the conviction that allocation of fixed resources should be the central interest of economists, and that all speculation should be done within closed systems (of which more below). It has also led me to use a variety of empirical methods rather than just regressions based on published economic data; some of these other methods are illustrated in the articles collected here.

A shortcoming of the socialization that comes with graduate training in economics is that people begin their inquiry into puzzling real-world situations with standard concepts, rather than with more primitive unstructured curiosity. For example, if one asks: 'Why does competition produce more effort than monopoly?', the trained economist is likely to begin with demand functions, cost functions, and utility functions, rather than wondering: 'If I were a business person, what would the situation look like, and how would I view it, with one competitor compared to no competitor?' The former mental habit constrains the imagination from dreaming up radically new analytic approaches which – though *usually* not warranted – may *sometimes* be crucial. As Buchanan says about the conventional thinking:

> Economics seems unlikely to escape from this chaos for many years, if indeed it survives at all as an independent discipline. Few economists are wholly free of the confusions that I have discussed. For myself, I advance no claim that my own thinking has yet fully rid itself of the paradigms of neoclassical orthodoxy (1979, p. 63)

The other side of the matter is that many of my colleagues in economics – and even more astonishing, many of my colleagues who teach business administration – have never worked in business. Many have never in their whole lives even worked at any job such as the armed services or school-teaching or the Peace Corps or anything else; they have never been away from school for more than a summer. And yet they teach about business, even how to practice 'business policy.' (First-hand experience in business would produce unwelcome confusion to most economists, and would undoubtedly interfere with the practice of conventional career-oriented allocation-of-resources article writing. But it would lead to better economics.)

My personality surely is also important in determining how I got to be the way I am professionally. I am comfortable neither as follower nor as leader. I am best suited by nature to be a freelance prospector for semi-rare metals, the kind of person who will not stop with small veins but rather keeps trying to trace back the veins to the mother lode. Sometimes when I have what seems to me a really good fundamental idea I feel like a prospector who has found the mother lode but cannot find a way to transport it out of the jungle and into the market. Nowadays, though, I am rather glad when a small vein peters out before it leads me to chase after a more fundamental idea where I will again feel stuck out in the jungle without transport to the market. I get into the same sort of difficulty as those who have the tastes of the rich but the pocketbook of the poor; I have the aspirations and the intellectual habits but not some other powers of the great social scientists.

I grew up thinking that no one – and certainly not the world as a whole – has a burning need of my work or of me personally, other than as a member of a family and as a friend. And a fair amount of evidence in adulthood – in my relations with institutions, groups, and professions – has tended to confirm that childhood view. I expect to lose out in whatever the competition is, and I go quietly – up to a point. But at some point I go to the mat, and I will not give up until the time is up (or sometimes even after the time is up, as these volumes show). Then the guerrilla side of me emerges.

A key element in my thinking, in which respect I differ from most (but not all) economists, is that I believe (along with diverse writers, the most famous of which are Einstein and Bohr) that scientific propositions are inventions that arise from the interaction of human imagination with natural and social reality, rather than being 'laws' which the scientist 'discovers' that inhere in the natural and social reality. In the latter view, the world is a system having inherent order, and the task of the scientist is to uncover the 'true' propositions and relationships in that system. For example, one may think that the speed with which a body falls due to gravity is one of the underlying propositions that characterize our world, and if we diligently seek after such propositions and relationships we can discover them all and then have a complete understanding of the universe. To put this view another way, at the beginning the universe was created or evolved according to a set of equations, and it is our job to discern the equations. White notes that

> The consistency with which scientists during the long formative centuries of Western science said that the task and the reward of the scientist was 'to think God's thoughts after him' leads one to believe that this was their real motivation (1967, p. 1206).

The other view – the one which I find more helpful – is to assume only that the universe is not perfectly formless or chaotic – though it may once have been – and the regularities and generalizations which we discover follow from our interests and perceptions as well as from the 'out there' features of the world. That is, we invent and develop the relationships we find, rather than merely discovering them. Again, what shape is the earth? To a firm that manufactures cheap globes it is round and smooth, but it is bumpy to a manufacturer of more expensive globes. To a surveyor or farmer, it is flat. For geologists, its circumference is greater at the equator than elsewhere. To an aviator, it is an unsmooth, unround set of upcropping mountains. And so on. The earth does not have one shape but rather many, and the relevant 'model' – flat, round, bumpy, or whatever – depends upon your needs and interests. No 'model' of the earth captures all its features, because then it would not be an abstracted model, but the earth itself. As Georgescu-Roegen put it:

> [A]ctuality is a seamless whole we can slice ... wherever we may please. And, Plato to the contrary, actuality has no joints to guide a carver ... Only our particular purpose in each case can guide us in drawing the boundary of a process. So, every scientist slices actuality in the way that suits best his own objective – an operation that cannot be performed without some intimate knowledge of the corresponding phenomenal domain (1970, p. 3).

It follows from this latter view that when systems are logically closed, they are so because we close them for our convenience, rather than because they are 'naturally' so. The mathematics and the other logical techniques we apply to these systems result in approximations – good approximations if we close the systems sensibly, and silly approximations otherwise. This is quite the opposite of the view that God (or an original force) made the lawful universe, and left it to us to discover the laws, the view that Keynes attributes to Newton:

> He regarded the universe as a cryptogram set by the Almighty – just as he himself wrapt the discovery of the calculus in a cryptogram when he communicated with Leibnitz. By pure

> thought, by concentration of mind, the riddle, he believed, would be revealed to the initiate (1963/1951, p. 314).

The view I hold is consistent with Einsteinian operationalism. Bridgman,[9] the explicator of the latter concept, put it this way: 'The proper definition of a concept is not in terms of its properties but in terms of actual operations' (pp. 6–7). He pointed out that definitions in terms of properties constituted the barrier that held physics back and took Einstein to crack through.[10]

Related to the closed-system way of thinking is the notion that available resources are finite and countable. Chapter 4 in Volume One argues at length that this is simply a prejudice, and a prejudice which leads to unsound long-run forecasts. For now I wish only to note that, in Einstein's words, 'Even scholars of audacious spirit and fine instinct can be obstructed in the interpretation of facts by philosophical prejudices' (quoted by Clarke, p. 90). And elsewhere Einstein wrote:

> Concepts which have proved useful for ordering things easily assume so great an authority over us, that we forget their terrestrial origin and accept them as unalterable facts. They then become labelled as 'conceptual necessities,' 'a priori situations,' etc. The road of scientific progress is frequently blocked for long periods by such errors. It is therefore not just an idle game to exercise our ability to analyze familiar concepts, and to demonstrate the conditions on which their justification and usefulness depend, and the way in which these developed, little by little (as quoted by Holton, 1973).

Of course I, too, am constrained by predispositions and prejudices, but at least mine have the virtue that they differ considerably from the consensus of the economics profession.

Notes

1. I do not wish to leave the impression that some kind and flattering things have not been said about me too. My lament, however, was that people paid no attention to what I wrote, whereas Hume lamented the 'Treatment I have met with [due to] the Prejudices of a stupid, factious Nation, with whom I am heartily disgusted' (quoted p. 26 of the Introduction to his 1965 *Essential Works*). If the genial Hume, with the sweet nature all his friends loved, could arrive at such sentiments, it should not be surprising if we lesser minds and natures are not serene when we think we have failed to do what we sought to do.
2. If you find this fantasy disturbing, consider Margaret Sanger's reaction to her frustration at not being able to carry out her work as she desired to: 'I was reminded of the story of a Spaniard who had become so desperate over the injustice meted out to innocent prisoners that he had taken a revolver into the street and fired it at the first person he met; killing was his only way of expressing indignation. I felt like doing the same thing' (1938, p. 214). My sense of the ridiculous prevents me from taking things so seriously.
3. The word 'is' is [sic] a semantic trap, because it implies identity between the words connected by 'is', but *also* implies something *other than* identity. Attempting to write without using the word 'is' is an instructive exercise.
4. To disprove any charge of modesty, I include here a letter from von Hayek which begins:

   > Dear Professor Simon,
   > I have never before written a fan letter to a professional colleague, but to discover that you have in your *Economics of Population Growth* provided the empirical evidence for what with me is the result of a life-time of theoretical speculation, is too exciting an experience not to share it with you …

   I would not swap that letter for a bunch of other honors.
5. Popper has this to say on a related subject:

> The theory that art advances with the great artists in the van is not just a myth; it has led to the formation of cliques and pressure groups which, with their propaganda machines, almost resemble a politicial party or a church faction (1974/1976, p. 71).

6. It is a pleasure to acknowledge the economics learned in business school courses with Jack Hirshleifer and Garfield Cox, however.
7. Von Hayek remarks that 'it is almost never possible to determine what part of a successful career has been due to superior knowledge, ability, or effort and what part to fortunate accidents' (1960, p. 82).
8. Read's discussion of the importance of charm in the art world may apply to academic science, too:

   > In achieving success, almost as important as genius or long study, is what we might call charm (though some artists can exploit a reputation for being 'difficult' – anti-charm). This quality is perhaps too obvious to be worth mentioning, but from one's own observation of the world of art one sees what a difference an artist's personality can make (1963, pp. 106–7).

   I think I am not usually the complete opposite of charming, except in my dealings with anyone who has any authority or influence over my life. In those situations I expect unfeeling treatment, and I am so frightened of complaining that the relationship invariably goes sour.
9. Quotation of Bridgman here does not constitute endorsement of his general program. We have learned much in the past 50 years about the limitations of this idea, as well as its strengths.
10. The two views are seen in the following exchange. Robert Solow, commenting on a paper by Guy Orcutt and Alice Rivlin: ' What is required is that the *residuals* from the "true" structural automobile demand function be uncorrelated with the family's income' (1961, p. 321). Orcutt and Rivlin: 'We would be curious to see what kind of an operational definition Solow would give to the notion of, "the 'true' structural demand function" (p. 323). I share the Orcutt–Rivlin view that the notion of a "true" function is meaningless scientifically, and counter-productive. However, this is a minority view.

References

(Details of Julian Simon's own works cited in the Introduction are in the Appendix)

Buchanan, T. (1979), *What Should Economists Do?*, Indianapolis, Liberty Press.

Hayek, F.A. von (1960), *The Constitution of Liberty*, Chicago: University of Chicago Press.

Hayek, F.A. von (1978), *Tiger by the Tail: A 40 Years' Running Commentary on Keynesianism by Hayek*, London: Institute of Economic Affairs.

Holton, G.J. (1973), *Thematic Origins of Scientific Thought*, Harvard University Press.

Hume, David (1964), *The Philosophical Works*, Thomas Hilbreen and Thomas Hodge Grose (eds), Scientia Verlagen.

Johnson, Samuel (1761), *The Idler*, quoted from *The Oxford Dictionary of Quotations*, 2nd edition, Oxford University Press, 1953.

Keynes, J.M. (1951), *Essays in Biography*, W.W. Norton.

Kilbracken, John Raymond Godley, Baron (1951), *Master Art Forger: The Story of Han van Meegeren*, W. Funk.

Locke, John (1959), *An Essay Concerning Human Understanding*, 2 volumes, Dover Publications.

Machlup, F. (1967), *Essays in Economic Semantics*, Merton Miller (ed.), Norton.

Popper, K. (1976), *Unended Quest: An Intellectual Autobiography*, Open Court.

Robinson, Joan (1977), 'What Are the Questions?,' *Journal of Economic Literature*, **15**(4), December, 1318–39.

Sanger, Margaret (1938), *Family Limitation*.

The Introduction and reference list were not finalized at the time of Julian Simon's sudden death in February 1998 and have been completed, as far as possible, with the assistance of Rita J. Simon.

PART I

STATISTICS AND PROBABILITY

[1]

Foreword

This article, written for a lay audience, serves as an introduction to the articles on resampling in this section.

Using the data to "simulate" sampling from a population offers a powerful heuristic for solving statistical problems.

Resampling: A Tool for Everyday Statistical Work

Julian L. Simon and Peter Bruce

Probability theory and its offspring, inferential statistics, constitute perhaps the most frustrating branch of human knowledge.

Right from its beginnings in the seventeenth century, the great mathematical discoverers knew that the probabilistic way of thinking—which we'll call "prob-stats" for short—offers enormous power to improve our decisions and the quality of our lives. Prob-stats can aid a jury's deliberation about whether to find guilty a person charged with murder . . . reveal if a new drug boosts survival from a cancer . . . help steer a spacecraft to Saturn . . . inform the manager when to take a pitcher out of the baseball game . . . help a wildcatter to calculate how much to invest in an oil well . . . and a zillion other good things, too.

Yet until very recently, when the method of resampling came along, scholars were often unable to convert this powerful body of theory into a tool that laypersons could and would use freely in daily work and personal life. Instead, only professional statisticians felt in comfortable command of the prob-stats way of thinking. The most frequent applications are by social and medical scientists, who know that prob-stats is indispensable to their work yet too often fear and misuse it.

Prob-stats continues to be the bane of students, most of whom consider the statistics course a painful rite of passage—like fraternity paddling—on the way to an academic degree. At the end of the semester, most of those who study it happily put prob-stats out of their minds forever.

The statistical community has made valiant attempts to improve this sad situation. Great statisticians have struggled to find interesting and understandable ways to teach prob-stats. Learned committees and professional associations have wrung their hands in despair, and spent millions of dollars creating television series and textbooks. A few publications, including *Chance*, imaginatively demonstrate and explain the exciting uses and benefits of prob-stats.

Despite successes, these campaigns to promote prob-stats have often ended in failure. The enterprise smashes up against an impenetrable wall—the body of complex algebra and tables that only a few understand right down to the foundations. For example, almost no student can write the formula for the "Normal" distribution that is at the heart of most statistical tests. Even fewer understand its meaning. Yet without such understanding, there can be only rote learning.

Most students of probability and statistics simply memorize the rules. Many users of prob-stats select their methods blindly, understanding little or nothing of the basis for choosing one method rather than another. This often leads to wildly inappropriate practices, and contributes to the damnation of statistics. Indeed, in the last decade or so, the discipline's graybeards have decided that prob-stats is just too hard to learn, and have concluded that students should be taught mainly descriptive statistics—tables and graphs—rather than how to draw inferences probabilistically, which is really the heart of statistics.

The newly resurgent methods of resampling, in combination with the personal computer, promise to change all this. It is our belief that resampling may finally realize the great potential of statistics and probability. Resampling estimates probabilities by numerical experiments instead of with formulae—by flipping coins or picking numbers from a hat, or with the same operations simulated on a computer. And a computer program, such as our own RESAMPLING STATS, can perform these operations in a transparently clear and simple fashion.

The mathematical statisticians have now developed a statistical theory for resampling methods. And controlled studies show that people ranging from engineers and scientists down to seventh graders quickly handle more problems correctly than with conventional methods. Furthermore, in contrast to the older conventional statistics that is a painful and humiliating experience for most students at all levels, the published studies show that students enjoy resampling statistics.

The Reappearance of Resampling in the History of Statistics

Resampling returns to a very old tradition. In ancient times, mathematics in general, and statistics in particular, developed from the needs of governments and rich men to count their armies and flocks, and to enumerate the taxpayers and their possessions. Up until the beginning of the twentieth century, the term "statistic" meant "state-istics," the number of something the "state" was interested in—soldiers, births, or what-have-you. Even today, the term "statistic" usually means the quantity of something, such as the important data for the United States in the *Statistical Abstract of the United States.* These numbers are now known as "descriptive statistics," in contrast to "inferential statistics" which is the science that tells us how reliable is a set of descriptive statistics.

Another stream of thought appeared by way of gambling in France in the 17th century. Throughout history people had learned about the odds in gambling games by experimental trial-and-error experience. To find the chance of a given hand occurring in a card game, a person would deal out a great many hands and count the proportion of times that the hand in question occurred. That was the resampling method, plain and simple.

Then, in the year 1654, the French nobleman Chevalier de Mere asked the great mathematician and philosopher Blaise Pascal to help him deduce what the odds ought to be in some gambling games. Pascal, Pierre Fermat, and others went on from there to develop analytic probability theory, and Jacob Bernoulli and Abraham DeMoivre initiated the formal theory of statistics. The experimental method disappeared into mathematical obscurity except for its use when a problem is too difficult to be answered theoretically, as happens from time to time in the development of statistical tests—for example, the development of the famous *t*-test by "Student," the pen name of William S. Gosset, and the World War II "Monte Carlo" simulations for complex military "operations research" problems such as how best to search for submarines with airplanes.

Later on, these two streams of thought—descriptive statistics and probability theory—were joined together. Users of descriptive statistics wondered about the accuracy of the data originating from both sample slrveys and experiments, so statisticians applied the theory of probability to assessing the accuracy of data, thereby creating the theory of inferential statistics.

How This Approach to Resampling Developed

It was the spring of 1967 at the University of Illinois, in my (Simon's) course in research methods with four graduate students working toward their Ph.D.'s. I required each student to start and finish an empirical research project as a class project. Now the students were presenting their work in class. All used wildly wrong statistical tests to analyze their data. It was a case of too much book-learning and too little understanding. The students had swallowed but not digested a bundle of statistical ideas which now misled them, taught by professors who valued fancy mathematics even if useless or wrong.

"Why do you use the technique of cluster analysis?" I asked Moe Baher (a pseudonym).

"I want to be up-to-date," said Baher.

"How much statistics have you studied?" I asked.

"Two undergraduate and three graduate courses," Baher answered proudly.

It was the usual statistical disaster. A simple count of the positive and negative cases in Baher's sample was enough to reveal a clear-cut conclusion. The fancy method Baher used was window-dressing, and inappropriate to boot. It was the same sad story with the other three students.

All had had several courses in statistics. But when the time came to apply even the simplest statistical ideas and tests in their research projects, they were lost. Their courses had plainly failed to equip them with basic usable statistical tools.

So I wondered: How could we teach the students to distill the

The RESAMPLING STATS Language and Program Compared to BASIC and Other Languages

The computer language and program RESAMPLING STATS enables the user to perform experimental trials in the simplest, as well as more complex, Monte Carlo simulations of problems in probability and statistics. Most of the 20 or so commands in RESAMPLING STATS mimic the operations one would make in conducting such trials with dice or cards; for example, SHUFFLE randomizes a set of elements. (The rest of the commands are IF, END, PRINT, and the like.) This correspondence between the computer operations and the physical operations that one would undertake in a simulation with an urn, playing cards, or other object that corresponds to the physical elements in the real situation being modeled, greatly helps the user to understand exactly what needs to be done with the computer to arrive at a sound answer.

RESAMPLING STATS employs a fundamentally different logic than do standard programming languages such as BASIC and PASCAL. (APL is the only language with a similar logic.) Standard languages imitate mathematical operations by making a variable—one number at a time—the unit that is worked with. In contrast, RESAMPLING STATS works with a collection of numbers—a vector. This enables each operation to be completed in one pass, whereas in other languages there must be repeat loops until each element in the vector is processed, which complicates matters.

Furthermore, whereas other languages name variables, RESAMPLING STATS names locations, and moves otherwise nameless collections of numbers from location to location. In computer logic this may not be a meaningful distinction. But it is as much a working distinction as between a) a set of instructions that tell how to process tourist group 37—first show them where the hotel bar is, have their suitcases put away, and get them onto the bus, and b) instructions that tell what to do with whomever is in hotel A on January 1 and move them to hotel B, then process whomever is in hotel B on January 2 and then move them to hotel C, and so on.

RESAMPLING STATS programs are much shorter and clearer than BASIC programs. Typically, only about half as many instructions are needed. Here is an example of the same problem written in the two languages, selected for illustration because it is the first problem in the 1987 book *The Art and Techniques of Simulation*, by Mrudulla Gnanadesikan, Richard L. Scheaffer, and Jim Swift, prepared by the American Statistical Association for use in high schools.

"*Outcomes with a Fair Coin*: What are the numbers of heads (or tails) you can expect to get if you flip a given number of coins?" (Please notice that there is a statistics problem closely related to this probability problem, with the same program used to solve it. For example: "You have a device that produces (say) a sample of 15 successes in 20 attempts. How likely is it that the long-run ("true") rate for the device is 50% successes (or less)?")

The BASIC program of Gnanadesikan et al. is as follows:

```
80 INPUT "ENTER THE NUMBER OF KEY COMPONENTS";N
100 INPUT "ENTER THE NUMBER OF TRIALS";NT
120 DIM T$(NT,N),C(2*N)
140 FOR I = 1 TO NT
150 LET NH = 0
160 FOR J = 1 TO N
170 LET X = RND (1)
180 IF X < .5 THEN 220
190 T$ (I,J) = "H"
200 NH = NH + 1
210 GOTO 230
220 T$ (I,J) = "T"
230 IF J = N THEN 260
250 GOTO 270
270 NEXT J
280 C(NH + 1) = C(NH + 1) + 1
290 NEXT I
330 FOR K = 1 TO N + 1
350 NEXT K
360 END
```

The BASIC program is written in general form and does not specify a particular number of coins and heads, as RESAMPLING STATS does. (It has been simplified here by removing the many "print" statements.)

Here is the RESAMPLING STATS program that does the same job, for a sample of five coin tosses:

```
REPEAT 100               Run a hundred simulation trials
   GENERATE 5 1,2 A      Generate randomly a sample of five "1"s and "2"s
   COUNT A=1 B           Count the number of "1"s in this trial sample
   SCORE B Z             Record the results in vector Z
END                      End the repeat loop
HISTOGRAM Z              Graph the results, and also produce a table of results with the
                         relative and cumulative frequencies
```

Continued next page

The results of this RESAMPLING STATS program are in the following figure.

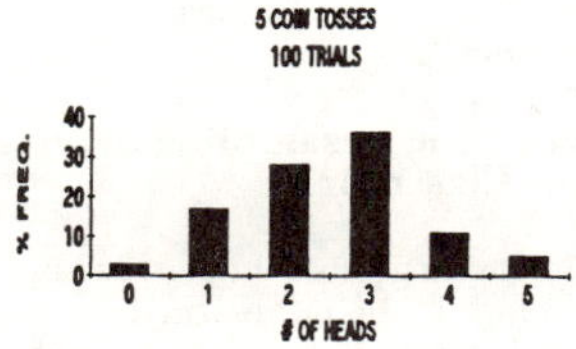

Do you agree that the RESAMPLING STATS program is not only much shorter and easier to write, but also is much more obvious to your intuition?

Even more important, the above program in the RESAMPLING STATS language is written by the user, which leads to learning about both statistics and computers. In contrast, the BASIC program given by Gnanadesikan et al. is pre-written by the authors, and all the user does is fill in the parameters. The students therefore do not learn what is necessary to develop an abstract model of the real-life situation, or write a computer program to simulate that model, both of which are crucial steps in the learning process.

meaning from their data? Simple statistical methods suffice in most cases. But by chasing after the latest sophisticated fashions the students overlook these simple methods, and instead use unsound methods.

I remembered trying to teach a friend a concept in elementary statistics by illustrating it with some coin flips. Given that the students' data had a random element, could not the data and the events that underlie the data be "modeled" with coins or cards or random numbers, doing away with any need for complicated formulas?

Next class I shelved the scheduled topics, and tried out some problems using resampling (though that label had not yet been invented). First the students estimated the chance of getting two pairs in a poker hand by dealing out hands. Then I asked them the likelihood of getting three girls in a four-child family. After they recognized that they did not know the correct formula, I demanded an answer anyway. After suggesting some interesting other ideas—we'll come to them later—one of the students eventually suggested flipping coins.

With that the class was off to the races. Soon the students were inventing ingenious ways to get answers—and sound answers—to even subtle questions in probability and statistics by flipping coins and using random numbers. Next students rediscovered an advanced technique originally invented by the great statistician Ronald A. Fisher.

Resampling had earlier been suggested for one particular case in inferential statistics in technical articles in the *Annals of Mathematical Statistics* by Meyer Dwass in 1957, and in the *Journal of the American Statistical Association* by J.H. Chung and D.A.S. Fraser in 1958. These papers applied sampling methods to the problem of deciding whether two sample means differ from each other, basing the procedure on Fisher's famous "randomization" test. A similar approach might handle *all* (or at least most) problems by resampling. And to that end, I taught a systematic procedure for carrying out resampling procedures and illustrated it for a wide variety of problems.

Could even children learn this powerful way of dealing with the world's uncertainty? Max Beberman, the guru of the "new math" who then headed the mathematics department in the University of Illinois High School, agreed that the method had promise and suggested teaching the method to a class of volunteer juniors and seniors. The kids had a ball. In six class hours they were able to discover solutions and generate correct numerical answers for the entire range of problems ordinarily found in a semester-long university introductory statistics class. Furthermore, the students loved the work.

A semester-long university class in statistics came next, with resampling and the conventional method taught side by side. But students complained that dealing cards, flipping coins, and consulting tables of random numbers gets tiresome. So in 1973 I (Simon) developed a computer language that would do with the computer what one's hands do with cards or dice. The RESAMPLING STATS program, which handles all problems in statistics and probability with only about 20 commands that mimic operations with cards, dice, or random numbers, is a simple language requiring no computer experience. Even seventh graders quickly understand and use it, though it is powerful enough for scientific and industrial use. (It also provides a painless introduction to computers, which is a valuable educational bonus.)

Recent interest in resampling comes in large part from the development of statistical theory for one aspect of resampling—the "bootstrap"—by Bradley Efron in the late 1970s. The bootstrap has now swept the field of statistics to an extraordinary extent. The *New York Times* had this to say:

> A new technique that involves powerful computer calculations is greatly enhancing the statistical analysis of problems in virtually all fields of science. The method, which is now surging into practical use after a decade of refinement, allows statisticians to determine more accurately the reliability of data analysis in subjects ranging from politics to medicine to particle physics . . .
>
> "There's no question but that it's very, very important" said Frederick Mosteller, a statistician at Harvard University . . . Jerome I. Friedman, a Stanford statistician who has used the new method, called it "the most important new idea in statistics in the last 20 years, and probably the last 50." He added, "Eventually, it will take over the field, I think." (Nov. 8, 1988)

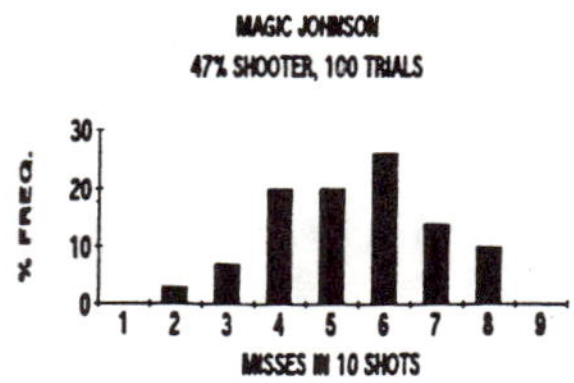

Figure 1.

Learning Resampling in the Classroom

Resampling is best understood by seeing it being learned. The teacher walks into a new class and immediately asks, say, "What are the chances that if I have four children that three of those children will be girls?" Someone says, "Put a bunch of kids into a hat and pick out four at a time." After the laughs, the teacher says, "Nice idea, but it might be a bit tough to do. . . . Other suggestions?"

Someone else says, "Have four kids and see what you get." The teacher praises this idea because it points toward learning from experiment, one of the key methods of science. Then the teacher adds, "But let's say you have four children once. Will that be enough to give you an acceptable answer?" So they discuss how big a sample is needed, which brings out the important principle of variability in the samples you draw. The teacher then notes that to have, say, a hundred families could take quite some time, plus some energy and money, so it doesn't seem to be practical at the moment. "Another suggestion?"

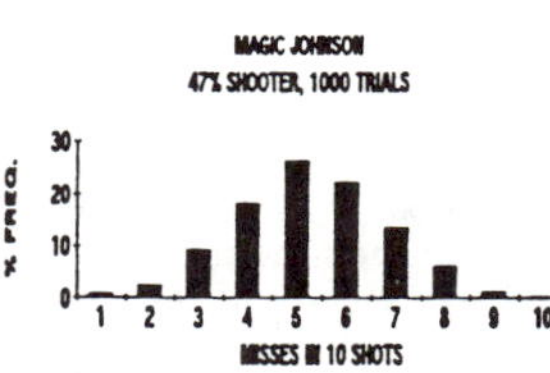

Figure 2.

Someone suggests taking a survey of families with four children. The teacher applauds this idea, too, because it focuses on getting an answer by going out and looking at the world. But what if a faster answer is needed?

A student wonders if it is possible to "do something that is *like* having kids. Put an equal number of red and black balls in a pot, and pull four of them out. That would be like a family." This kicks off discussion about how many balls are needed, and how they should be drawn, which brings out some of the main concepts in probability—sampling with or without replacement, independence, and the like.

Then somebody wonders whether the chance of having a girl the first time you have a child is the same as the chance of pulling a red ball from an urn with even numbers of red and black balls, an important question indeed. This leads to discussion of whether 50-50 is a good approximation. This brings up the question of the purpose of the estimate, and the instructor suggests that a clothing manufacturer wants to know how many sets of matched girls' dresses to make. For that purpose, 50–50 is okay, the class says.

Coins are easier to use than balls, they concur. Someone wonders whether four coins flipped once give the same answer as one coin flipped four times. Eventually all agree that trying it both ways is the best way to answer the question.

The teacher commissions one student to orchestrate the rest of the class in a coin-flipping exercise. Then the question arises: Is one sample of, say, 30 coin-flip "families" enough? So the exercise is repeated several times, and the class is impressed with the variability from one sample of 30 to the next. Once again the focus is upon variability, perhaps the most important idea inherent in prob-stats.

Or another example: The teacher asks, "What are the chances that basketball player Magic Johnson, who averages 47% success in shooting, will miss 8 of his next 10 shots?" The class shouts out joking suggestions such as "Go watch Magic," and "Try it yourself on the court." The teacher responds, "Excellent ideas, good scientific thinking, but not feasible now. What else could we do?"

The students discuss a coin-flipping experiment, but someone complains that flipping coins or dealing cards would be wearisome. Aha! Now the teacher breaks out the computer and suggests doing the task faster, more accurately, and more pleasurably with the following computer instructions:

REPEAT 100 obtain a hundred simulation trials
GENERATE 10 1,100 A generate 10 numbers randomly between 1 and 100, put them in A
COUNT A between 1 53 B count the number of misses in the trial (Magic's shooting average is 47% hits, 53% misses.)
SCORE B Z record the result of the trial
END end the repeat loop for a single trial
COUNT Z ≥ 8 K count the number of trials with 8 or more misses

The histogram (Fig. 1) shows the results of 100 trials, and Fig. 2 shows the results of 1000 trials. The amount of variability obviously diminishes as the number of trials increases, an important lesson.

Then the teacher asks: "If you see Magic Johnson miss 8 of 10 shots after he has returned from an injury, should you think that he is in a shooting slump?" Now the probability problem has been inverted into a problem in statistical inference—testing the hypothesis that Magic is in a slump. And with proper interpretation the same computer program yields the appropriate answer—about 6.5% of the time Magic will miss 8 or more shots out of 10, even if he is not in a slump. So you probably don't take him out or stop him from shooting. Understanding this sort of variability over time is the key to quality control.

Now the instructor changes the question again and asks: "If you observe a player—call him Houdini—succeed with 47 of 100 shots, how likely is it that if you were to observe the same player take a great number of shots—a thousand or ten thousand—his long-run average would turn out to be 53 per cent or higher?" A sample of 47 baskets out of 100 shots could come from players of quite different "true" shooting percentages. Resampling can help us make transparent several different approaches to this problem in "inverse probability."

We need to have some idea of how much variation there is in samples from shooters like Houdini. If we have no other information, we might reasonably proceed as if the 47/100 sample is our best estimate of Houdini's "true" shooting percentage. We could take repeated samples from a 47% shooting machine to estimate how great is the variation among shooters with long-run averages in that vicinity, from which we could estimate the likelihood that the "true" average is 53%. (This is the well-known "confidence interval" approach. In truth, the logic is a bit murky, but that is seldom a handicap in daily practice.)

Alternatively, we might be interested in a particular shooting percentage—say, 53%, Houdini's lifetime average before a shoulder injury. In such a case, we might want to know whether the 47 for 100 is just a spell of below-average shooting, or an indication that the injury has affected his play. In this situation, we could repeatedly sample from a 53% shooting machine to see how likely a 47/100 sample is. Using this "hypothesis-testing" approach, if we find that the 47/100 sample is very unusual, we conclude that the injury is hampering Houdini; if not, not.

Consider still another possibility: If Houdini is a rookie with no history in the league, we might want to apply additional knowledge about how often 53% shooters are encountered in the league. Here we might bring in information about the "distribution" of the averages of other players, or of other rookies, to learn the likelihood of a 47/100 sample in light of such a distribution—a "Bayesian" approach to the matter.

The resampling approach to problems like this one helps clarify the problem. Because there are no formulae to fall back upon, you are forced to think hard about how best to proceed. Foregoing these crutches may make the problem at hand seem confusing and difficult, which is sometimes distressing. But in the long run it is also the better way, because it forces you to come to terms with the subtle nature of such problems rather than sweeping these subtle difficulties under the carpet. You are in a better position to choose a step-by-step logical procedure that fits the circumstances.

To repeat, in the absence of black-box computer programs and cryptic tables, the resampling approach forces you to directly address the problem at hand. Then, instead of asking "Which formula should I use?" students ask such questions as "Why is something 'significant' if it occurs 4% of the time by chance, yet not 'significant' if a random process produces it 8% of the time?"

A Definition for Resampling

Let us define resampling to include problems in inferential

statistics, as well as problems in probability, with this "operational definition": *Using the entire set of data you have in hand, or using the given data-generating mechanism (such as a die) that is a model of the process you wish to understand, to produce new samples of simulated data, and to examine the results of those samples.* That's it in a nutshell. In some cases, it may also be appropriate to amplify this procedure with additional assumptions.

Problems in pure probability may at first seem different in nature from problems in statistical inference. But the same logic as stated in this definition applies to both varieties of problems. The only difference is that in probability problems the "model" is known in advance—say, the model implicit in a deck of poker cards plus a game's rules for dealing and counting the results—rather than the model being assumed to be best estimated by the observed data, as in resampling statistics.

The General Procedure

The steps used in solving the particular problems in the previous section have been chosen to fit the specific facts. We can also describe a more general procedure that simulates what we are doing when we estimate a probability using resampling operations.

Step A: Construct a simulated "universe" of cards or dice or some other randomizing mechanism whose composition is similar to the universe whose behavior we wish to describe and investigate. The term "universe" refers to the system that is relevant for a single simple event. For example:

a) A coin with two sides, or two sets of random numbers "1–105" and "106–205", simulates the system that produces a single male or female birth, when we are estimating the probability of three girls in the first four children. Notice that in this universe the probability of a girl remains the same from trial event to trial event—that is, the trials are independent—demonstrating a universe from which we sample with replacement.

b) An urn containing a hundred balls, 47 red and 53 black, simulates the system that produces 47% baskets.

Hard thinking is required in order to determine the appropriate "real" universe whose properties interest you.

Step B: Specify the procedure that produces a pseudo-sample which simulates the real-life sample in which we are interested. That is, specify the procedural rules by which the sample is drawn from the simulated universe. These rules must correspond to the behavior of the real universe in which you are interested. To put it another way, the simulation procedure must produce simple experimental events with the same probabilities that the simple events have in the real world. For example:

a) In the case of three daughters in four children, you can draw a card and then replace it if you are using a deck of red and black cards. Or, if you are using a random-numbers table, the random numbers automatically simulate replacement. Just as the chances of having a boy or a girl do not change depending on the sex of the previous child, so we want to ensure through replacement that the chances do not change each time we choose from the deck of cards.

b) In the case of Magic Johnson's shooting, the procedure is to consider the numbers 1–47 as "baskets," and 48–100 as "misses."

Recording the outcome of the sampling must be indicated as part of this step (e.g., "record 'yes' if a girl or a basket, 'no' if a boy or a miss").

Step C: If several simple events must be combined into a composite event, and if the composite event was not described in the procedure in step B, describe it now. For example:

a) For the three girls in four children, the procedure for each simple event of a single birth was described in step B. Now we must specify repeating the simple event four times, and counting whether or not the outcome is three girls.

b) In the case of Magic Johnson's ten shots, we must draw ten numbers to make up a sample of shots, and examine whether there are eight or more misses.

Recording of "three or more girls" or "two or less girls", and "8 or more misses" or "7 or fewer", is part of this step. This record indicates the results of all the trials and is the basis for a tabulation of the final result.

Step D: Calculate the probability of interest from the tabulation of outcomes of the resampling trials. For example: the proportions of a) "yes" and "no", and b) "8 or more" and "7 or fewer", estimate the probability we wish to estimate in step C.

There is indeed more than one way to skin a cat (ugh!). And there is always more than one way to correctly estimate a given probability. Therefore, when reading through the list of steps used to estimate a given probability, please keep in mind that a particular list is not sacred or unique; other sets of steps will also do the trick.

Let's consider an extended example, my (Simon's) study in the 1960s of the price of liquor in the 16 "monopoly" states (where the state government owns the retail liquor stores) compared to the 26 states in which retail liquor stores are privately owned. (Some states were omitted for technical reasons.) This problem in "statistical hypothesis testing" would conventionally be handled with Student's t-test, but with much less theoretical justification than the resampling method possesses here.

These were the representative 1961 prices of a fifth of Seagram 7 Crown whiskey in the two sets of states:

16 monopoly states:
$4.65, $4.55, $4.11, $4.15, $4.20, $4.55, $3.80, $4.00, $4.19, $4.75, $4.74, $4.50, $4.10, $4.00, $5.05, $4.20
Mean: $4.35

26 private-ownership states:
$4.82, $5.29, $4.89, $4.95, $4.55, $4.90, $5.25, $5.30, $4.29, $4.85, $4.54, $4.75, $4.85, $4.85, $4.50, $4.75, $4.79, $4.85, $4.79, $4.95, $4.95, $4.75, $5.20, $5.10, $4.80, $4.29
Mean: $4.84

A social-scientific study properly begins with a general question about the nature of the social world, such as: Does state monopoly affect prices? The scientist then must transform this question into a form that can be studied scientifically. In this case, the question was translated into a comparison of the above two sets of data for a single brand as collected from a trade publication. If because of variation within the two samples the answer is not completely obvious from casual inspection of the data—as in the case here, where the two samples overlap—the researcher may turn to inferential statistics for help.

The first step in using probability and statistics is to translate the *scientific* question into a *statistical* question. Once you know exactly which prob-stats question you want to ask—that is, exactly which probability you want to determine—the rest of the work is relatively easy. The stage at which you are most likely to make mistakes is in stating the question you want to answer in probabilistic terms. Though this step is difficult, it involves no mathematics. Rather, this step requires only hard, clear thinking. You cannot beg off by saying "I have no brain for math!" The need is for a brain that will do clear thinking, rather than a brain for mathematics. People who use conventional methods can avoid this hard thinking by simply grabbing the formula for some test without understanding why they chose that test. But resampling pushes you to do this thinking explicitly.

The *scientific* question here is whether the prices in the two sets of states are systematically different. In *statistical* terms, we wish to "test the hypothesis" that there is a "true" difference between the groups of states based on their mode of liquor distribution—that is, a difference that is not just the result of happenstance—or whether the observed differences might well have occurred by chance. In other words, we are interested only in whether the two subgroups of states are "truly" different in their liquor prices, or whether the difference we observe is likely to have been produced by chance variability.

The resampling method proceeds as follows: We consider that the entire "universe" or "population" of possible prices consists of the set of events that have been observed, because that is all the information that is available about the universe. We therefore write each of the 42 observed state prices on a separate card, and shuffle the cards together; the deck simulates a situation in which each state has the same chance as any other state of being dealt into a given pile. We can now examine, on the "null hypothesis" assumption that the two groups of states do not really reflect different price-setting mechanisms but rather differ only by chance, how often that universe produces by chance groups with results as different as those we actually observed in 1961. (In this case, unlike many others, the states constitute the entire universe we are interested in, rather than being a sample taken from some larger universe, as is the case when one does a biological experiment or surveys a small sample drawn from the entire U.S. population.)

From the simulated universe we repeatedly deal groups of 16 and 26 cards *without replacing the cards*, to represent hypothetical monopoly-state and private-state samples. We sample without replacement (and for convenience we could look only at the 16-state set, since, once it is chosen, the average of the remaining 26 is also fixed), because there are only 42 actual states for which data is available, and hence we are not making inferences about a much larger or infinite universe. Instead, we have the entire universe at hand.

The probability that prices in the monopoly states were "really" lower than those in the private-enterprise states may be estimated by the proportion of times that the difference between the averages of those randomly chosen 16 and 26 prices is less than (or equal to) the difference between the observed 16 and 26 prices. If we were often to obtain a difference between the randomly chosen groups equal to or greater than that actually observed in 1961, we would conclude that the observed difference could well be due to chance variation.

This logic may not be immediately obvious to the newcomer to statistics. It is subtle, and requires a bit of practice, even with the resampling method, to bring it to the fore. But once you understand this way of thinking, you will have reached the heart of inferential statistics.

The steps again:

Step A: Write each of the 42 prices on a card and shuffle.

Steps B and C (combined in this case): Deal the cards into groups of 16 and 26 cards. Then calculate the mean price difference between the groups, and compare the simulation-trial difference to the observed mean difference of $4.84 – $4.35 = $.49; if it is as great or greater than $.49, write "yes," otherwise "no."

Step D: Repeat step B-C a hundred or a thousand times. Calculate the proportion "yes", which estimates the probability we seek.

The estimate—not even one "success" in 10,000 trials (see Fig. 3)—shows that it would be very unlikely that two groups with mean prices as different as were observed would happen by chance from the universe of 42 observed prices. So we "reject the null hypothesis" and instead accept the proposition that the type of liquor distribution system influences the prices that consumers pay.

Under the supervision of Kenneth Travers and Julian Simon at the University of Illinois during the early 1970s, Ph.D. candidates Carolyn Shevokas and David Atkinson studied how well students learned resampling, working with experimental and control groups of junior college and four-year college students. Both found that with resampling methods—even without the help of computer simulation—students produce a larger number of correct answers to numerical problems than do students taught with conventional

Figure 3.

methods. Furthermore, attitude tests as well as teacher evaluations showed that students enjoy the subject much more, and are much more enthusiastic about resampling than conventional methods.

It is an exciting experience to watch graduate engineers or high-school boys and girls as young as 7th grade re-invent from scratch the resampling substitutes for the conventional tests that drive college students into confusion and despair. Within six or nine hours of instruction, students are generally able to handle problems usually dealt with only in advanced university courses.

The computer-intensive resampling method also provides a painless and attractive introduction to the use of computers. And it can increase teacher productivity in the school and university systems while giving students real hands-on practice.

Monte Carlo methods have long been used to teach conventional methods. But resampling has nothing in common with this teaching of conventional "parametric" statistics. Rather, resampling is an entirely different method, and one of its strengths is that it does not depend upon the assumption that the data resemble the "normal" distribution. Resampling should be the *method of choice* for dealing with a wide variety of everyday statistical problems—perhaps most of them.

To repeat, the purpose of resampling is *not* to teach conventional statistics. Rather, resampling breaks with the conventional thinking that dominated the field until the past decade, rather than being a supplement to it or an aid to teaching it.

For those in academia and business who use statistics in their work but who will never study conventional analytic methods to the point of practical mastery—that is, almost everyone—resampling is a functional and easily-learned alternative. But resampling is not intended to eliminate analytic methods for those who would be mathematical statisticians. For them, resampling can help to understand analytic methods better. And resampling may be especially useful for the introduction to statistics of mathematically disadvantaged students.

Though we and the mathematical statisticians who have focused on the bootstrap aspect of resampling (following Efron's developmental work in the 1970s) share an identical intellectual foundation, our efforts point in different directions. They see their work as intended mainly for complex statistical inference problems; we view resampling as a tool for all (or almost all) tasks in prob-stats. Our interest is in providing a tool that researchers and decision-makers, rather than statisticians, can use with lesser opportunity of error and with sound understanding of the process.

Like all innovations, resampling has encountered massive resistance. The resistance has largely been conquered with respect to mathematical statistics and advanced applications. But instruction in the use of resampling at an introductory level, intended for simple as well as complex problems, still faces a mix of apathy and hostility.

Conclusion

Estimating probabilities with conventional mathematical methods is often so complex that the process scares many people. And properly so, because the difficulties lead to frequent errors. The statistical profession has long expressed grave concern about the widespread use of conventional tests whose foundations are poorly understood. The recent ready availability of statistical computer packages that can easily perform conventional tests with a single command, irrespective of whether

The Pro's and Con's of Resampling

Does Resampling Produce Correct Estimates?

If one does not make enough experimental trials with the resampling method, of course, the answer arrived at may not be sufficiently exact. For example, only ten experimental bridge hands might well produce far too high or too low an estimate of the probability of five or more spades. But a reasonably large number of experimental bridge hands should arrive at an answer that is close enough for any purpose. There are also some statistical situations in which resampling yields poorer estimates about the population than does the conventional parametric method—usually "bootstrpp" confidence-inter-valeestimates made from small samples. But on the whole, resampling methods yield "unbiased" estimates, and not less often than do conventional methods. Perhaps most important, the user is more likely to arrive at sound answers with resampling through understanding the method, instead of grabbing the wrong formula in error.

Do Students Learn to Reach Sound Answers?

In the 1970s, Kenneth Travers (who was responsible for secondary mathematics at the College of Education at the University of Illinois) and Julian Simon organized systematic controlled experimental tests of the method. Carolyn Shevokas's thesis studied junior college students who had little aptitude for mathematics. Shevokas taught the resampling approach to two groups of students (one with and one without computer), and taught the conventional approach to a control group. Then the groups were tested on problems that could be done either analytically or by resampling. Students taught with the resampling method were able to solve more than twice as many problems correctly as students who were taught the conventional approach.

David Atkinson taught the resampling approach and the conventional approach to matched classes in general mathematics at a small college. The students who learned the resampling method did better on the final exam with questions about general statistical understanding. They also did much better solving actual problems, producing 73% more correct answers than the conventionally taught control group.

These experiments are strong evidence that students who learn the resampling method are able to solve problems better than conventionally taught students.

Can Resampling Be Learned Rapidly?

Junior high school students have in six hours learned how to handle problems that students taught conventionally do not learn until advanced university courses. In Simon's first university class, only a small fraction of total class time—perhaps an eighth—was devoted to the resampling method as compared to seven-eighths spent on the conventional method. Yet, the students learned to solve problems more correctly, and chose to solve more problems, with the resampling method than with the conventional method. This suggests that resampling is learned much faster than the conventional method.

In the Shevokas and Atkinson experiments the same amount of time was devoted to both methods yet the resampling method achieved better results. In those experiments, learning with the resampling method is at least as fast as the conventional method, and probably considerably faster.

Is the Resampling Method Interesting and Enjoyable?

Shevokas asked her groups of students for their opinions and attitudes about the section of the course devoted to statistics and probability. The attitudes of the students who learned the resampling method were far more positive toward the subject than were the attitudes of the students taught with the standard method. And the attitudes of the resampling students toward mathematics in general improved during the weeks of instruction, whereas the attitudes of the students taught conventionally changed for the worse.

Shevokas summed up the students' reactions as follows: "Students in the experimental (resampling) classes were much more enthusiastic during class hours than those in the control group; they responded more, made more suggestions, and seemed to be much more involved."

Gideon Keren taught the resampling approach for just 6 hours to 14- and 15-year old high school students in Jerusalem. The students knew that they would not be tested on this material. Yet Keren reported that the students were very interested. Between the second and third classes, two students asked to join the group even though it was their free period! Keren enjoyed teaching this material all the more because the students were enjoying themselves.

Atkinson's resampling students had "more favorable opinions, and more favorable changes in opinions" about mathematics generally than the conventionally taught students, according to an attitude questionnaire. The resampling students had much more positive attitudes about statistics in general than the conventionally taught students.

The experiments comparing the resampling method to conventional methods show that students enjoy learning statistics and probability this way. And they don't show the usual panic about the subject. This contrasts sharply with the less positive reactions of students learning by conventional methods, even when the same teachers teach both methods in the experiment.

the user understands what is going on or whether the test is appropriate, has exacerbated this problem. This had led teachers to emphasize descriptive statistics and even ignore inferential statistics.

Probabilistic analysis is crucial, however. Judgments about whether to allow a new medicine on the market, or whether to readjust a screw machine, require more than eyeballing the data to assess chance variability. But until now, the practice and teaching of probabilistic statistics, with its abstruse structure of mathematical formulas cum tables of values based on restrictive assumptions concerning data distributions—all of which separate the user from the actual data or physical process under consideration—have not kept pace with recent developments in the practice and teaching of descriptive statistics.

Beneath every formal statistical procedure there lies a physical process. Resampling methods allow one to work directly with the underlying physical model by simulating it. The term "resampling" refers to the use of the given data, or a data generating mechanism such as a die, to produce new samples, the results of which can then be examined.

The resampling method enables people to obtain the benefits of statistics and probability theory without the shortcomings of conventional methods because it is free of mathematical formulas and restrictive assumptions and is easy to understand and use.

Additional Reading

Edgington, E.S. (1980), *Randomization Tests, New York: Marcel Dekker.*

Efron, B. and Diaconis, P. (1983), "Computer intensive methods in statistics," *Scientific American*, May, pp. 116–130.

Noreen, E.W. (1989), *Computer Intensive Methods for Testing Hypotheses*, New York: John Wiley & Sons.

Simon, J.L. (1969), *Basic Research Methods in Social Science*, New York: Random House. (3rd Edition in 1985 with P. Burstein), Chapters 30–35.

Simon, J.L., Atkinson, D.T., and Shevokas, C. (1976), "Probability and statistics: Experimental results of a radically different teaching method," *American Mathematical Monthly*, 83(9), Nov. 1976.

Simon, J.L., *Resampling: Probability and Statistics a Radically Different Way*, (self-published text available from the author.)

[2]

Foreword

The innovation here is in how to *do* statistics rather than in how to *teach* conventional statistics. Unfortunately, the editor removed "and Do" from the title in publication.

An approach you may wish to experiment with

A NEW WAY to TEACH PROBABILITY STATISTICS*

By JULIAN L. SIMON
with the assistance of
ALLEN HOLMES
University of Illinois
Urbana, Illinois

THE purpose of studying probability and statistics is to learn how to solve the problems these tools can help solve. Such problems are found in the practice of science, of course. But many of the problems of *daily living* can also be better understood with the aid of probability and statistics. It is particularly for the latter reason that one may consider teaching these ideas to high school or even pre-high-school students.

This paper claims to offer a new (though really very old) way of teaching students to solve simple (and complex) problems in probability and statistics. The instructional method simply skips backwards over three hundred years of mathematical history; *all* problems are solved with experimental Monte Carlo methods rather than by analysis, just as gambling odds were estimated before the invention of probability theory. This method not only allows students to solve problems immediately—and probably with a better chance of a correct solution than after considerable conventional instruction—but, best of all, it forces explicit consideration of the process of constructing an appropriate model and of conversion of scientific questions into statistical questions. We hope that the reader comes to agree that these claims are justified as we illustrate the teaching method below.

It should be noted that the Monte Carlo method has long been used in teaching statistics. But it has been used *to illustrate analytic concepts rather than to solve the problems themselves*, as, for example, in using a quincunx to show how a binomial process approaches the normal distribution [4, pp. 260–64].[1] And, when Monte Carlo methods *have* been taught for problem solving, the rationale has been of this sort: "The Monte Carlo Method is experimental mathematics. If a problem is too difficult for computational solution, then it must be simulated" [2, p. 778]. In *this* course of instruction, however, Monte Carlo methods are taught for actual use in *simple* problems, rather than just for those too difficult for analytic solution.

Our class consisted of eighteen seniors in the handpicked University High student body. We began with a pretest that included these two questions:

Question A.1.—What is the chance of your having three daughters in your first three children?

Question A.2.—What are the odds that two cards of the same denomination will appear in a five-card poker hand from a well-shuffled deck?

Though in their attempts to answer question A.1 many of the students seemed to be aware of the multiplication-of-probabilities rule and of basic ideas of permutation, there were only six correct answers to this question. There were no correct answers to A.2.

---

* Max Beberman made the arrangements for the teaching experiment described here, and his sympathetic assistance is gratefully acknowledged.

[1] Numerals in brackets refer to the Bibliography.

The course of instruction over six class hours consisted of—

1. Instructing students that when they are faced with problems in probability and statistics they should *think first* of running a Monte Carlo experiment. The absolutely crucial element in the teaching is to instill the *habit* of turning to Monte Carlo experimentation in response to problems.

2. Practicing Monte Carlo experimentation on a variety of problems. In every case an actual quantitative estimate was developed.

3. Discussing the notions of *universe* and *sample* in the context of the problems worked in class.

The actual procedure in both the teaching and the problem solving itself may best be described by samples of the answers the students gave to examination questions at the end of six hours of instruction (plus homework reading of the material in Chapters 23 and 24 in [3]). Answers are verbatim except for changes in spelling, abbreviations, etc.

Question B.1.—What are the odds that three or more cards of any one suit (e.g., spades) will appear in a five-card poker hand from a well-shuffled deck? Give a numerical answer as well as show the steps by which you got the answer.

Student C. C.:

a) Get a regular poker deck.

b) Shuffle and deal out five cards.

c) Record the results, then put the cards back in the deck.

d) Shuffle and repeat until the sample is large enough.

x x x o o x o o x x o x x o x
(Circles denote success.)

Out of 15 trials 6 had three or more cards of one suit, so the probability is 6 in 15.

Student A. R.:

Use random number table.

a) 1–13→spades
14–26→diamonds
27–39→hearts
40–52→clubs
53–00→throw out

b) Count hands of five numbers in which three or more of some suit appears.

(09, 18, 32, 27, 04) (22, 08, 04, 38, 27)
(19, 07, 50, 47, 46) (18, 02, 07, 47, 29)
(18, 41, 36, 18, 27) (20, 18, 17, 49, 42)
(01, 40, 28, 13, 10) (03, 22, 20, 45, 32)
(44, 04, 51, 15, 06)
(06, 44, 27, 12, 46)
(22, 37, 50, 34, 31)
(07, 13, 08, 35, 10)

3 or More	No
/////	///// //

Five out of 12 trials—approximately 43 percent.

Almost every student got the procedure correct and obtained point estimates. The estimates among the correct answers varied considerably—from 17 percent to 60 percent—but the reader must remember that the number of trials the students could run was severely limited by the time limit of a 50-minute examination that included six questions (of which this first question was one of the easiest).

Question B.2.—If a coin is loaded so that the chance of a head's coming up is .4, what are the odds that one would get two heads in two flips? Give numerical answer and steps.

Student T. S.:

a) Take ten cards, four red and six black. Red = heads, black = tails.

b) Draw out two cards, one at a time, *replacing* the first card before drawing the second.

c) Record the result: two red = success; one red and one black or two black = failure.

d) Repeat.

Success	Failure
/////	///// ///// /////

Result, 5 in 20 = 25 percent.

Student M. G.:

To answer this question I would use the random number table, letting 0, 1, 2, and 3 be heads, and 4, 5, 6, 7, 8, and 9 be tails. I would then start on any row in the table, look at every successive pair of numbers and determine how many times I got two heads (represented by numbers) in two flips.

Trials	2 for 2
///// ///// ///// /////	/////

With limited trials, probability is 1/4.

Almost every student got the procedure right and worked up a point estimate.

Question B.3.—John tells you that with his old method of shooting foul shots in basketball his average (over a long period of time) was .6. Then he tried a new method of shooting and scored successes with nine of his first ten shots. Should he conclude that the new method is really better than the old method? Give odds and steps.

Student P. H.:

What are the chances of shooting nine out of ten if you normally shoot .6? This is the real question (the statistical question).

a) Numbers 0, 1, 2, 3, 4, and 5 are baskets.

b) Numbers 6, 7, 8, and 9 are misses.

c) Take ten numbers in table; if *nine or more* are "baskets" count as a success. Repeat and find percentage.

Trials
///// ///// ///// ///// /////
///// ///// ///// ///// /////
Successes / / /

Results, 3 in 50. This would happen 6 percent of the time using his old shot.

(Notice the first sentence in this answer. It is what we call the *translation from a scientific question*—that is, from the question as phrased in the examination—*into a statistical question.* Practice in such translation is an important part of the classroom drill.)

Student A. S.:

a) Take twelve hearts to represent hits in shooting and eight spades to be misses; this is John's old probability in scoring.

b) Shuffle, draw a card and record "hit" or "miss," replace it and shuffle. Repeat ten times altogether for one trial. See how many times nine hits or more come up in ten tries.

1. Hit, hit, miss, miss, h, h, h, h, m, 7/10 hits
2. 7/10
3. 8/10
4. 4/10
5. 6/10
6. 7/10
7. 7/10
8. 7/10
9. 6/10
10. 9/10 (boxed)
11. 5/10
12. 7/10
13. 8/10
14. 6/10
15. 8/10

Only 1 time in 15 will 9/10 shots be made by the old .6 chance, so it seems probable here that John's new method helped.

More than half of the students answered with correct procedures and reasonable quantitative estimates.

Question B.4.—If six fair coins are tossed, what is the probability that exactly three of them turn up heads [1, p. 92]? Give odds and steps.

Student J. B.:

a) Take random number table.

b) Use groups of six numbers.

c) If three are even, count as success; if not, count as failure.

Answer: 6/16.

Student B. M.:

Using random number tables—

a) Designate even numbers to be heads.

b) Designate odd numbers to be tails.

c) Take trials of six numbers and record it as a success if *exactly* three of them are even. Repeat many times.

d) Proportion of successes to trials is the probability.

Trials	Success
///// ///// /////	///// ///// /
///// ///// /////	

Probability $= 11/30 \approx 1/3$.

Question B.5.—A football team played nine games during last season. It won the first, lost the next three, and then won the last five. A sportswriter concluded that the team improved during the season. Is that a good conclusion, or is there a good chance that the team had the same six-in-nine chance of winning each game throughout the season? Give odds and steps.

This is a very difficult question to make sense of, even for an experienced statistician. The difficulty is not in mathematical manipulation, of course, but in reading the problem imaginatively and then setting it up correctly. The following answers are interesting attempts, and it is left to the reader to decide how correct the answers are.

Student A. B.:

This is a somewhat more complicated problem. It could be treated two basic ways. First, we could ignore the fact that five of the wins were in a row and at the end, but this seems to be the reason the sportswriter thought the team had improved. Five in a row seems impressive. Therefore, we will assume that the odds for each game were six in nine, and see how often five wins in a row at the end will occur. (This assumes that *if* the team improved, they did it after the last game they lost.)

a) Using random numbers, let numbers 1–6 be a "win," 7–9 a "loss," and disregard all 0's.

b) Look at sets of five numbers and record how often all are "wins." Repeat twenty or more times.

Success	Failure
//	///// ///// ///// ///// ///// ///

Odds, 2/30 or 1/15. Thus the chance of getting five wins in a row with 6-in-9 odds is only 1 in 15. The team most likely improved.

Student L. L.:

a) Take out nine cards, six reds and three blacks (reds = wins).

b) Deal out one card, record, and *replace*.

c) Shuffle and deal one card, record, and replace.

d) Deal out nine in all, replacing each time.

e) If last five cards are red, then success.

f) Repeat these steps twenty times.

g) Count total number of successes.

The number of successes/20 are odds team improved by winning last five games.

My answer: Time ran out.

Only a handful of the students did well on this question.

Question B.6.—If three accidents occur at random on a highway during one week, what is the probability that no two occur on the same day of the week? [In the manner of 1, p. 92.]

A variant of this question, using seven accidents instead of three, had been used in class drill, so the following answers might reflect the previous practice.

Student J. M.:

Pick groups of three numbers from the random number tables. Using the numbers 0–6, count the numbers of groups that have no repetition of numbers.

Yes	No
///// /	////

Answer, 4/10 = 2/5.

Student S. L.:

a) Call number 1 "Monday," 2 "Tuesday," . . . , 7 "Sunday"; ignore 8, 9, and 0.

b) Consider three numbers; if all three are different call the trial a "success."

c) Repeat twenty times, count successes.

Odds—75 percent success. Three quarters of the two accidents will not happen on the same day.

[Note.—This solution considers "no two . . . " to imply that if three occur on one day, then because two have occurred that day is counted as "failure."]

More than half the students did well on this question, even though it was at the end of a long examination and time was very limited.

It should be noted that each answer above is from a different student; five other students took the exam and each gave good answers to at least one question.

TWO other problems that were worked in the course of class drill should further illuminate the nature of the instruction. Unlike the problems described above, neither of these has a simple analytic solution. (1) The famous birthday problem: What is the chance that two people in a room of, say, eighteen people, have the same birthday? This problem is easily solved by examining a series of 18 random numbers between 1 and 365, recording whether or not there is duplication, and repeating this experiment enough times to constitute a fair test—perhaps 30 repetitions. (2) What is the probability of obtaining an "opening" hand in bridge, using the Goren point system? An estimate for this second problem is easily obtained by dealing a number of hands, though the problem is said to be quite difficult to solve analytically.

It should not be inferred that the tactics described here are limited in application to simple problems or to the types of problems described. Such problems as correlation and analysis of variance are easily handled with this method, as well as complex system simulations, of course [3, Chapters 23 and 24]. Only regression analysis is not easily done this way.

Now we must consider some criticisms of the use of Monte Carlo methods to solve simple problems. The first objection is the easiest to handle—that the estimates are inaccurate. First of all, one would usually take considerably larger samples than the students took; the students were faced with examination-time limits. And *some* sample size *must* be large enough for any desired level of accuracy.[2] Further and more importantly, it is easy to program any of these procedures onto any computer using general-purpose programs and hence to get samples of huge size in seconds. With the computer, even probabilities close to 0 or 1 can be estimated accurately in short compass of time. And students can do these problems on line without difficulty. (Our next project is to set this up for high school classes.) And lastly, students who use this method quickly grasp the importance of inaccuracy due to sampling error as they observe the variation in their Monte Carlo samples. This causes them to *worry* about it—the most important step of all. Then they increase their Monte Carlo samples until they reach acceptable levels of accuracy.

A more weighty objection is that this sort of teaching is obscurantist, anti-intellectual, and likely to limit the student's advance into formal mathematical analysis. There are several responses to this objection. First, there are many students who will never go forward with the study of statistics and mathematics, even if they are never exposed to this instruction. For these students this powerful engine of problem solving is an important educational bonus.

Second, this instruction actually interests many students. We would wager that it pushes more students forward into further study than it stops.

Third, and perhaps most importantly, this instruction is of extreme value to those who *will* study statistics and probability. The way the student must explicitly structure problems in this method is *also* necessary when problems are solved analytically—but the structuring process is too often done implicitly or without awareness, which often leads to the wrong model or unsound choice of a cookbook formula. This instruction is therefore of great value in teaching students what analytic methods are good for, and teaching how to use them correctly.

The level of success achieved in this

[2] The appropriate sample size can also be decided by simple Monte Carlo methods, as described in Simon [1969, Chapter 25]. One relevant method is to compare the results of two half-samples to see how closely they agree.

educational experiment may be too much to expect with a less exceptional group of children, or with younger children. But even if twelve or eighteen hours of instruction, instead of six, are needed to attain similar (or lower) levels of skill in the solution of statistical problems, the instruction will certainly be very worthwhile.

REFERENCES

1. Adler, Irving. *Probability and Statistics for Everyman.* New York: Signet Books. New American Library, 1966.
2. Engel, A. "Mathematical Research and Instruction in Probability Theory," The Mathematics Teacher, LIX (December 1966), 771–82.
3. Simon, Julian L. *Basic Research Methods in Social Science: The Art of Scientific Investigation.* New York: Random House, 1969.
4. Weaver, Warren. *Lady Luck: The Theory of Probability.* New York: Doubleday-Anchor, 1963.

[3]

Foreword

The experiments described in this paper were carried out in the first half of the 1970s, and hence were largely conducted without recourse to computers; this makes their outcomes all the more notable. I had earlier developed the resampling stats language and program, but on the mainframe computer the program was not interactive, and therefore not suitable for student use. The emergence of the personal computer, and the development of interactive versions of the program, have made the resampling approach to the practice of statistics more feasible and even more effective and enjoyable.

Reprinted from the AMERICAN MATHEMATICAL MONTHLY
Vol. 83, No. 9, November 1976
pp. 733–739

PROBABILITY AND STATISTICS: EXPERIMENTAL RESULTS OF A RADICALLY DIFFERENT TEACHING METHOD

JULIAN L. SIMON, DAVID T. ATKINSON AND CAROLYN SHEVOKAS

Introduction. With the Monte Carlo method, students from high school to graduate school can quickly acquire the ability to handle probabilistic problems of daily living or scientific research. And the students understand what they are doing, with little danger of the formula-grabbing which too often afflicts conventional analytic methods.

The Illinois procedure for teaching the Monte Carlo method has been used since 1965 with success: (a) for teaching research methods to graduate students in several fields at the University of Illinois who have already had one or several conventional statistics courses, but who nevertheless find themselves insufficiently equipped to handle the statistical problems in research projects; (b) with undergraduates in research methods courses; (c) with undergraduates as part of conventional statistics courses; and (d) with high school students down to age 13 or 14, in the U. S. (Simon and Holmes, 1969), in Israel and in Puerto Rico.

The results seem successful to the teachers and to the students, as evidenced by the teachers' judgments and the students' answers to informal questionnaires. But such "soft" evidence is insufficient to convince skeptics — which is perhaps as it ought to be. Harder evidence is therefore needed. To supply that evidence is the task of this paper.

We first recapitulate the method and its logic. Then we describe three experiments that test the value of the method in a variety of class settings.

The Monte Carlo method is not offered as a successor to analytic methods. Rather, it can be an underpinning for analytic teaching to help students understand analytic methods better. But it is also a workable and easily-taught alternative for students who will never study conventional analytic methods to the point of practical mastery — and this includes most students at all educational levels. It may be especially useful for the introduction to statistics of mathematically-disadvantaged students. (But please do not infer from this that the method is intellectually inferior; the method is logically acceptable and intuitively instructive for all students.)

It must be emphasized that the Monte Carlo method as described here really is intended as an alternative to conventional analytic methods in actual problem-solving practice. This method is *not* a pedagogical device for improving the teaching of conventional methods. This is quite different than the past use of the Monte Carlo method to help teach sampling theory, the binomial theorem and the central limit theorem. The point that is usually hardest to convey to teachers of statistics is that the method suggested here really is a complete break with conventional thinking, rather than a supplement to it or an aid in teaching it. That is, the simple Monte Carlo method described here is complete in itself for handling most — perhaps all — problems in probability and statistics.

The Monte Carlo method always provides a logically acceptable solution. But more specifically with respect to statistical hypothesis testing, the Monte Carlo tests based on a randomization logic have properties that statisticians are now finding attractive because they are more robust than traditional parametric tests. (For the test of differences in means between two groups based on Fisher's randomization test, see Dwass 1957, and Chung and Fraser, 1958; for a variety of other tests see Simon, 1969, Chapters 23 and 24.) Hence the Monte Carlo test is often a better scientific choice than the conventional test — in addition to its pedagogical advantages.

To illustrate the method, here is a sample question and examination answer by a high school student (one who qualified for an experimental course) after just six hours of classroom instruction:

> John tells you that with his old method of shooting foul shots in basketball his average (over a long period of time) was .6. Then he tried a new method of shooting and scored successes with nine of his first ten shots. Should he conclude that the new method is really better than the old method?
>
> *Student A.S.*:
> (a) Take twelve hearts to represents hits in shooting and eight spades to be misses; this is John's old probability in scoring.
> (b) Shuffle, draw a card and record "hit" or "miss", replace it and shuffle.
> (c) Repeat ten times altogether for one trial.
> (d) See how many times nine hits or more come up on ten tries.

1. Hit, hit, miss, miss, h, h, h, h, h, m, 7/10 hits	9. 6/10
2. 7/10	10. 9/10
3. 8/10	11. 5/10
4. 4/10	12. 7/10
5. 6/10	13. 8/10
6. 7/10	14. 6/10
7. 7/10	15. 8/10
8. 7/10	

> Only 1 time in 15 times will 9/10 shots be made by the old .6 chance, so it seems probable here that John's new method helped.

The Monte Carlo method is not explained by the instructor. Rather it is discovered by the students. With a bit of guidance the students invent, from scratch, the procedures for solution. For example, at the beginning of the first class the instructor may ask, "What are the chances that if you have four children three of them will be girls?" A few students do some calculations without success (in a naive class); the rest fidget. Then the students say that they don't know how to get the answer. The instructor presses the class to think of *some* way to come up with an answer. Someone suggests in jest that everyone in the class should go out and have four children. The instructor chooses to take this seriously. He says that this is a very good suggestion, though it has some obvious drawbacks. Someone suggests substituting a coin for a birth. This raises the issue of whether it is reasonable to approximate a 106:100 event with a 50–50 coin, and what is reasonable under various conditions. The instructor points out that the class still has no answer. Someone suggests that each student throw four coins. Someone else amends this by saying that four flips of one coin are just as good. The instructor questions whether the two methods are equivalent, and the class eventually agrees that they are. Finally, each student performs a trial, the data are collected, and an estimate is made. Someone wonders how good the estimate is. Someone else suggests that the experiment be conducted several more times to see how much variation there is.

The meaning of the concept "chances" comes up in the discussion, and "probability" is defined pragmatically. By this process of self-discovery, students develop useful operating definitions of other necessary concepts such as "universe," "trial," "estimate," and so on. And together they invent — after false starts and class corrections — sound approaches to easy and not-so-easy problems in probability and statistics. For example, with a bit of guidance, an average university class can be brought to re-invent such devices as a Monte Carlo version of Fisher's randomization test. In an earlier report (Simon, 1969, Chapters 23 and 24) the flexibility and range of the Monte Carlo method is shown in problems ranging from permutations to correlation to randomization tests.

In this manner the students learn more than how to do problems. They gain the excitement of true intellectual discovery. And they come to understand something of the nature of mathematics and its creation.

Though the experience of shuffling cards and counting tabled random numbers is educational at first, it tends to be a nuisance after awhile, and a deterrent to the use of the method. Furthermore, in some problems, the sample size required for the desired accuracy makes such hand methods onerous if not impossible. Therefore, a computer program, SIMPLE, has been developed that will perform the necessary operations rapidly and yet can be used immediately by a person with absolutely no computer experience. The SIMPLE program is also designed to be used as the method of choice for sophisticated statisticians in many sorts of applications. This program is described in Simon and Weidenfeld (1974), and materials are available upon request.

A *systematic* Monte Carlo method is taught at the University of Illinois; this is an important difference from some examples in the literature of *ad hoc* Monte Carlo problem solution, e.g. Zelinka, 1973. The student is taught to work in a series of discrete steps. The first step is the construction of the universe whose behavior one is interested in. The second step (or set of steps) is the drawing of a sample from that universe. The third step is the computation of the statistic of interest, and, in inferential statistics, comparison of the experimental statistic to the "observed" or "bench-mark" statistic. The fourth step is the repetition of the sampling procedure a large number of times. And then the fifth step is the calculation of the proportion of "successes" to experimental trials, which estimates the probability of the event in which one is interested.

The experiments. Three controlled experimental tests of the pedagogical efficiency of the Monte Carlo method have now been completed.

The University of Illinois Experiment: The experimental situation was a one-semester elementary statistics class of 25 mostly economics and business undergraduate majors in 1973 at the University of Illinois. The course, taught by Simon, was primarily a conventional statistics course, using a conventional text (Spurr and Bonini, rev. ed., 1973); the Monte Carlo method was taught only as a supplement, with no reading on it other than the simulation chapter in Spurr and Bonini and the Zelinka article (1973) and suggested reading in Simon (1969, Chapters 23–25). All problems that were treated by the Monte Carlo method in class were also demonstrated by analytic methods, whereas many problems were solved by analytic methods that were *not* treated in class by the Monte Carlo method. Therefore, analytic methods had a very large advantage over the Monte Carlo method in student time and attention, both in reading and in class.

Among the ten questions on the final exam (of which the student had to answer 8), there were four that the student could *choose* whether to answer by analytic methods or by Monte Carlo; the question given earlier is an example of these four questions. The choices of method by the students on the optional-method question give an indication of the usefulness of the Monte Carlo method.

Some additional conditions relevant to the experiment: The students could bring books and notes. (A closed-book exam, where formulae had to be remembered, would disadvantage analytic methods relative to Monte Carlo methods.) And the four optional-method problems were extremely simple ones for the use of analytic methods. (Complex problems would tend to improve the relative performance of the Monte Carlo method, because complexity is its comparative advantage.)

The results were as follows:

1. Almost every student used the Monte Carlo method for some question. This is the most exciting result of the experiment, because it suggests that the method has *some* usefulness to *almost everyone.* In total, more than half of the answers used the Monte Carlo method (44 of 86).

2. Almost every student did *some* questions by analytic methods. This implies that teaching the Monte Carlo method does not prevent the learning and use of analytic methods; that is, Monte Carlo does not drive out analytic methods. This is also a gratifying result.

3. There is a slightly-greater propensity for students who did better on the examination as a whole to do a larger proportion of problems by the Monte Carlo method. But the relationship is certainly not strong, which suggests that the Monte Carlo method is useful both to the good and to the less-good students. (And the lack of strong relationship also implies that we need not worry that the students who got better scores on the exam did so *because* they used the Monte Carlo more extensively and were therefore graded more easily.)

4. On *each question* some students used analytic methods and others used Monte Carlo methods. This shows that the Monte Carlo method is not specialized to some sorts of problems in the minds and practices of the students.

5. The average grades that the students received were higher on the questions answered with the Monte Carlo method than on those questions answered with analytic methods — 9.1 versus 7.5 on a scale of 10.

Polk Community College Experiment: At Polk Community College, Winter Haven, Florida in 1974, Shevokas taught separate classes of General Mathematics, a $6\frac{1}{2}$ week 17 class-hours unit in probability and statistics, in three ways: conventional analytic method, Monte Carlo method with computer, Monte Carlo method without computer. The enrollments were 19, 39, and 13, respectively. Beforehand, the groups were given a cooperative Arithmetic Achievement Test (Educational Testing Service, 1962) and two attitude-toward-mathematics tests (Aiken and Dreger, 1961; McCallon and Brown, 1971; sample item: "The feeling I have toward math is a good feeling"). The differences in results among groups were not statistically significant, so we can safely consider that the groups were similar to start with.

Only a mini-computer was available, and hence the types of programs that could be offered were not satisfactory. And the computer group had less time to learn probability because of the time devoted to learning about the computer programs. For these and other reasons we would have liked to confine our attention to the non-computer aspects of the experiment, but we include the with-computer group to increase Monte Carlo sample size.

The conventional analytic group was assigned two conventional chapters on probability and statistics in a basic text (Meserve and Sobel, 1973); the Monte Carlo group was given duplicated reading materials prepared by Shevokas.

1. All students were given the same seven-question exam on completion of the probability unit; a typical question was: "Suppose a machine produces bolts, 10% of which are defective. Find the probability that a box of three bolts contains as least one defective bolt." The mean scores were: conventional, 35.8; Monte Carlo no-computer, 58.5; Monte Carlo with-computer, 50.8, on a basis of 100. While one could wish for higher scores altogether, the Monte Carlo groups did better. The difference between Monte Carlo and conventional groups is statistically significant, but even more important, it is of an educationally significant magnitude; the Monte Carlo no-computer group got 62% higher scores than the conventional group.

2. The two attitude-toward-mathematics scales were again administered afterwards. The Monte Carlo groups showed more favorable attitudes than the conventional group, with the non-computer Monte Carlo group being most favorable; considering the two scales together, the post-scores differ significantly among the groups. Perhaps most interesting, the mean changes from "before" to "after" for the Aiken-Dreger and McCallon-Brown scales were: conventional, −5% and −9%; Monte Carlo with-computer, 0% and −8%; Monte Carlo no-computer, +22% and +8%. To put it more concretely, five of 19 conventional-group students had an improved attitude, 13 a worsened attitude (one tie); among the Monte Carlo no-computer group, 8 students had improved attitudes, 5 worsened. (The attitudes of the Monte Carlo with-computer group were apparently harmed by their need to spend extra hours on campus to use the computer.)

3. It is an important result that despite an initially-cool attitude toward the no-computer Monte Carlo method by the teacher, she came to enjoy teaching the Monte Carlo method much more than the conventional method, because the students reacted to the Monte Carlo work in an interested and enthusiastic manner.

Olivet Nazarene College Experiment: At Olivet Nazarene (four year) College, Kankakee, Illinois, during the second half of each semester in 1974–1975 one class in Mathematics for General Education was taught probability and statistics by Atkinson in a conventional analytic fashion, while a second class was taught the Monte Carlo method. Class size was 21 students in each section the first semester; in the second semester there were 37 and 34 students, respectively, in the Monte Carlo and conventional sections. As in the case of the Polk Junior College experiment, students in this course generally have low skills and little interest in mathematics. Comparable duplicated reading materials prepared by Atkinson on the conventional and Monte Carlo methods were distributed to the respective classes.

1. In the first semester two pre-exam quizzes were given to each group, whereas three quizzes were given in the second semester. These quizzes each contained 1, 2 or 3 probability or statistical problems. On each quiz the Monte Carlo section did better than the conventional group, achieving class mean scores as much as twice as high as the conventional group.

2. The first part of the final exam the first semester was "conceptual." It asked the student to analyze problem data and describe the population, the hypotheses, and so on. The conventional group did better, getting a mean score of 47.9 compared to 40.8 for the Monte Carlo group ($t = 1.35$). The analogous first part of the second semester's final exam was a 20-question multiple-choice test on the concepts of hypothesis testing. This time the Monte Carlo group did better, 60.3 to 51.8 ($t = 2.06$).

3. The most important measure of performance was the second part of the final exam containing, respectively, three and four problems in the first and second semesters. Mean scores were: Semester 1: Monte Carlo, 69.5; conventional, 59.4 ($t = 1.7$). Semester 2: Monte Carlo, 67.6; conventional, 56.6 ($t = 2.06$). Inspection of second-semester tests showed that the Monte Carlo group did better on each and every question.

4. If one considers questions and answers only as "right" or "wrong," in the second semester 45.9% of the Monte Carlo students answered at least two questions correctly, whereas among the conventional group only 26.5% got two or more questions right. And the Monte Carlo group got 34.4% of the total questions right whereas the conventional group got 19.8% of the questions right. Comparative scoring of Monte Carlo and analytic answers requires some judgment. But the fact that

the teachers in the Polk and Olivet Nazarene experiments (though not in the Illinois experiment) were not initially in favor of the non-computer Monte Carlo method provides some protection.

5. The Monte Carlo section had less mathematical ability than the conventional section in both semesters; the Monte Carlo groups had lower mean scores on the ACT math test, two quizzes and the midterm exam on the algebra material taught in the first half of the semesters, some of the differences being statistically significant. Hence the better performance shown by the Monte Carlo groups on the probability and statistics material was despite a lower endowment of mathematics ability.

6. A twenty-question attitude-toward-mathematics scale similar to the Aiken-Dreger scale was given before and after the probability-statistics unit. In both semesters the Monte Carlo groups began with less favorable attitudes. But by the end of the experiment the Monte Carlo groups' attitudes toward math were more favorable than those of the conventional groups.

7. An attitude-toward-probability-and-statistics scale was given after the probability-statistics instruction. In the first semester, eight of ten questions were answered more favorably among the Monte Carlo group by substantively large and statistically significant differences; the other two differences were tiny, and the questions referred to future plans rather than attitudes. In the second semester, 15 of 17 attitudes were more favorable in the Monte Carlo group, most of the differences being large and all with $t \geqq 1$; two other questions were very slightly more favorable in the conventional group, with $t \leqq .23$.

8. The teacher's subjective evaluation, as in other classes where the Monte Carlo has been taught, is that the students seem relatively interested in and enthusiastic about the material, with a great deal of class discussion. This made for an enjoyable experience for the teacher, despite initial doubts about the value of the Monte Carlo method.

Conclusions. Taken as a whole, the evidence shows that the Monte Carlo method is a tool that students can and will use to arrive at correct answers to probabilistic-statistical problems. Therefore, it would seem to make sense to teach students to do standard probabilistic questions with the Monte Carlo method. In a conventional university probability or statistics course, this implies teaching the Monte Carlo method along with the analytic methods. In high school or college situations in which the student will not get a course or even a long section on probability and statistics, this implies teaching a block of 6–10 hours of the Monte Carlo method in the basic mathematics course so that the student will have at least some tools at his disposal.

If one has to make a pedagogical choice between analytic and Monte Carlo methods, it would seem that Monte Carlo is the method of choice on a "cost/benefit" basis — that is, it yields more usable output per unit of learning input. But luckily one does not usually have to make such a choice, because there can be plenty of time in the conventional elementary course for the Monte Carlo method to be treated along with the analytic method. And in a situation where the Monte Carlo method and *only* the Monte Carlo method might be taught — say a high school and junior college — the conventional method usually has no real opportunity at present to receive the attention that it must for students to acquire a usable tool, and hence the conventional approach is not a real alternative to the Monte Carlo method.

Lest this be unclear or seem to equivocate: Where there is limited time, or where students will not be able to grasp conventional methods firmly, we advocate teaching the Monte Carlo approach, and perhaps that only. Where there is more time, and where students will be able to well learn conventional methods, we advocate (a) teaching Monte Carlo methods at the very beginning as an introduction to statistical thinking and practice; and (b) afterwards teaching the Monte Carlo method with the conventional method as alternatives to the same problems, to help students learn analytic methods and to give them an alternative tool for their use.

Teaching the Monte Carlo method also has additional pedagogical advantages. It produces (in fact, demands) a high level of class participation and teacher-student interaction. This makes the class time lively and enjoyable. The method also leads students to discover for themselves the intuitive meaning of fundamental concepts such as independence. And it increases their readiness to challenge the validity of the underlying data, which they must receive in raw form for the Monte Carlo method rather than in the defect-hiding summary form as, for example, "a population with $\mu = 100$ and $\sigma = 10$," the sort of language in which conventional problems are usually stated.

The advantage of the Monte Carlo Method seems to stem from its greater simplicity in a fundamental intuitive sense due to having fewer "working parts," and because the student never needs to take anything on faith, especially the sort of faith that is necessary with analytic methods that work by way of the central limit theorem ("It is shown in advanced texts that . . .).

Do we not owe it to our students and ourselves to at least give the Monte Carlo a hearing and a try?

Acknowledgment. Kenneth Travers supervised Atkinson's and Shevokas's theses at the College of Education of the University of Illinois, from which their results are drawn; we are grateful for Travers's important contribution to this work. We also appreciate helpful comments in an earlier draft from Bob Bohrer.

References

D. T. Atkinson, A Comparison of the Teaching of Statistical Inference by Monte Carlo and Analytical Methods, Ph.D. thesis, University of Illinois, 1975.

J. H. Chung and D. A. S. Fraser, Randomization tests for a two-sample problem, J. Amer. Statist. Assoc., 53 (September 1958) 729–35.

Meyer Dwass, Modified randomization tests for nonparametric hypothesis, Ann. Math. Statist., 28 (March 1957) 181–187.

Educational Testing Service, Cooperative Mathematics Tests, Arithmetic, Form A, Princeton, N. J. 1962.

A. L. Edwards, Techniques of Attitude Scale Construction, Appleton-Century-Crofts, New York, 1957.

E. L. McCallon and J. D. Brown, A semantic differential instrument for measuring attitude toward mathematics, J. Experimental Education, 39 (Summer 1971) 69–79.

B. E. Meserve and M. A. Sobel, Introduction to Mathematics, 3rd ed., Prentice-Hall, Englewood Cliffs, N. J., 1973.

Carolyn Shevokas, Using a Computer-Oriented Monte Carlo Approach to Teach Probability and Statistics in a Community College General Mathematics Course, Ph.D. thesis, University of Illinois, 1974.

J. L. Simon, Basic Research Methods in Social Science, Random House, New York, 1969.

———, with the assistance of Allen Holmes, A really new way to teach (and do) probability and statistics, The Mathematics Teacher, 62 (April 1969) 283–288.

———, and Dan Weidenfeld, SIMPLE: Computer Program for Monte Carlo Statistics Teaching, mimeo, 1974.

W. A. Spurr, and C. P. Bonini, Statistical Analysis for Business Decisions, rev. ed., Irwin, Homewood, 1973.

Martha Zelinka, How Many Games to Complete a World Series? in F. Mosteller, et al. (eds.), *Statistics by Example*, Addison-Wesley, Reading, Mass., 1973.

Department of Economics, University of Illinois at Urbana-Champaign, Urbana, IL 61801.

Department of Mathematics and Computer Science, Olivet Nazarene College, Kankakee, IL 60901.

Department of Mathematics and Physical Science, Thornton Community College, South Holland, IL 60473.

[4]

Foreword

These chapters are taken from the 1969 first edition rather than from the 1985 third edition (with Paul Burstein) because the treatment is more complete in the earlier edition. Though I knew that few readers would use these methods, this was the only possibility I could find to get them into print and at least to show what was possible. I also wanted to stake out the area for the future moment when statistics would move in this direction – as I believed that eventually it surely must, and as it finally did with Efron's development of the "bootstrap" (the method described here in Example 21, and in 1969 correspondence with William Kruskal and elsewhere).

CHAPTER 23

Statistics of Probability: Part I

Types of Statistics

A statistic is a *number*.[1] There are two kinds of statistics, summarization (descriptive) statistics and probability statistics. Chapter 4 discussed the most important summarization statistics: the total, average, range, distribution, and so forth. Those statistics are nothing new to you; you have been using them all your life.

The second kind of statistics, probability statistics, is the subject of this chapter and of statistics courses. Probability statistics can be used for two purposes: to aid scientific *understanding,* by estimating the probability that a statement is true or not, and to aid in making *sound decisions* by estimating which alternative among a range of possibilities is most desirable. The latter type of statistical theory—"decision theory"—is a recent arrival (really a revival) on the intellectual scene but is beyond the scope of this book; it is well-treated by R. Schlaifer (1961) and by I. Bross (1953) among others. This chapter will stick mostly to "hypothesis-testing theory," though there

1. A more conventional definition: "[S]tatistic: a summary value calculated from a sample of observations, usually but not necessarily as an estimator of some population parameter; a function of sample values" (Kendall & Buckland, 1957, p. 279).

will be comfortably little mathematical theory in our discussion. In the previous chapter, I discussed the types of analysis in which hypothesis-testing statistics are useful. Now we get down to the brass tacks of how to use probability statistics.

The Nature and Meaning of Probability

The idea of probability arises *when you are not sure* about something, that is, when you do not have enough information and therefore can only *guess*. For example, if someone asks you what your name is, you do not use the concept of probability to answer. To be sure, there is some chance that you do not know your own name, but for all practical purposes you can be quite sure of the answer. If someone asks you who will win tomorrow's ball game, however, there is a chance that you will be wrong, no matter what you say. Whenever the situation is such that there is a chance that you could be wrong, the concept of probability can help you.

The concept of probability helps you to answer the question, "What are the odds that . . . ?"[2] The purpose of this discussion of probability statistics is to help you to become a *good bettor*, to help you make sound appraisals of true and untrue conclusions (or, in terms of decision theory, to help you to decide which alternatives you should bet on). The concept of probability is especially useful when one has a sample from a universe and wants to know the probability of various degrees of likeness between the sample and the universe. In other words, one wants to know the probability that the universe's average I.Q., for example, will not differ from the sample's average I.Q. by more than some arbitrarily chosen number of I.Q. points, say ten points. A related question is, What is the probability that a sample was taken from a given universe rather than from another universe, so that one can safely draw conclusions about the universe from the sample evidence?

What *is* probability? Various definitions of the term are useful in particular contexts (see Ayer, 1965; Schlaifer, 1961, Chap. 1). The rest of this chapter contains many examples of the use of probability, and, as you work with them, you will develop a sound feeling for the concept. The following two definitions (which are not always compatible) may be helpful to start you off:

2. A given probability may be expressed in terms of probability, odds, or chances, and I shall use all three terms to help familiarize you with them. If the chances are 1 in 10, the odds are 9 to 1, and the probability is .1. If the odds are 2 to 5, the chances are 5 in 7, and the probability is 5/7. If the odds are 99 to 1, the chances are 1 in 100, and the probability is .01. If the odds are 100 to 1, the chances are 1 in 101, and the probability is 1/101. "Likelihood" is a synonym for "probability."

1. The probability that an event will take place or that a statement is true can be said to correspond to the odds at which you would bet that the event will take place. (Notice a shortcoming of this definition: You might be willing to accept a 5 dollar bet at 2–1 odds that your team will win the game, but you might be unwilling to bet 100 dollars at the same odds.)
2. The probability of an event can be said to be the proportion of times that the event has taken place in the past, usually based on a long series of trials. Insurance companies use this type of definition when they estimate the probability that a thirty-five-year-old postman will die during a period for which he wants to buy an insurance policy. (Notice this shortcoming: Sometimes you must bet upon events that have never or only infrequently taken place before, and so you cannot reasonably reckon the proportion of times they occurred one way or the other in the past.)

You have been using the concept of probability all your life, in practically every decision you have ever made and in every conclusion you have ever drawn. You place your blanket on the beach where there is a *low probability* of someone's kicking sand on you; you bet heavily on a poker hand when there is a *high probability* that you have the best hand; a hospital decides not to buy another ambulance when the administrator figures that there is a *low probability* that all the other ambulances will ever be in use at once.

How does one estimate a probability? First, let us consider how one can estimate an ordinary garden variety of probability, which is called an "unconditional" probability. Several ways to estimate an unconditional probability can be illustrated with an example from poker:[3] What is the probability of drawing an even-numbered spade from a deck of poker cards?

The first possible source for an estimate of the probability of drawing an even-numbered spade is *experience*. If you have watched card games casually from time to time, you might guess at the proportion of times you have seen even-numbered spades appear, and you might guess "about 1 in 15" or "about 1 in 6" or something like that. (The actual probability is 6 to 52, of course.) You might make an estimate based on your experience if someone asked you the probability that two cards of the same denomination will turn up in the same hand of five cards dealt from a poker deck. General information and experience are also the source for estimating the probability that

3. I hope you are not offended by the references to gambling games in the discussion of statistics in this and other chapters. Historically, however, the theory of probability was invented to answer questions about gambling games, and gambling games still provide the best examples.

your team will win tomorrow, that war will break out next year, or that a United States astronaut will reach the moon before a Soviet astronaut. (Is this example already out of date?) You simply put together all your relevant prior experience and knowledge and make a guess.

The second possible source of probability estimates is empirical scientific investigation with repeated trials of the phenomenon—called a "frequency series." In the case of the even-numbered spade, the empirical scientific procedure is to shuffle the cards, deal one, record whether or not the card is an even-numbered spade, replace the card, and repeat the steps a good many times. The proportion of times you observe an even-numbered spade come up is a probability estimate based on a frequency series.[4] Observation of frequency series might help you to estimate the probability that a machine will turn out a defective part or that a child can memorize four nonsense syllables correctly in one attempt. You watch and record the results of repeated trials of exactly the same event.[5]

A third source of probability estimates is *counting the possibilities*. For example, by examination of a common die one can determine that there are six different possible numbers that can come up. And one can then determine that the probability of getting a one or a two, say, is $2/6 = 1/3$, because two of six possibilities are one and two. One can similarly determine that there are two possibilities of getting a one *plus* a six out of thirty-six possibilities when rolling two dice, a probability of $2/36 = 1/18$.

Determining probabilities by counting has two requirements: that the *possibilities* all be known (and therefore limited) and few enough to be studied easily; and that the *probability* of each particular possibility be known, for example, that the probabilities of all sides of the die's coming up are equal, that is, equal to $1/6$.

A fourth source of probability estimates is *mathematical calculation*. If one knows by other means that the probability of a spade is $1/4$ and the probability of an even-numbered card is $6/13$, one can then calculate that the probability of turning up an even-numbered spade is $6/52$ (that is, $1/4 \times 6/13$). If one knows that the probability of a spade is $1/4$ and the probability of a heart is $1/4$, then one can calculate that the probability of getting a heart *or* a spade is $1/2$ (that is, $1/4 + 1/4$). The point here is not the particular calculation procedures but rather that one can often calculate the desired probability on the basis of already-known probabilities.

4. You might reasonably ask why we do not just *count* the number of even-numbered blacks in the deck of fifty-two cards. No reason at all. But that procedure would not work if you wanted to estimate the probability of a batter's getting a hit or a cigarette lighter's lighting.

5. Of course, no two events are exactly the same. But under many circumstances they are *practically* the same, and science is only interested in such "practical" considerations.

It is possible to estimate probabilities with mathematical calculation *only* if one knows *by other means* the probabilities of some related events. For example, there is no possible way of mathematically calculating that a child will memorize four nonsense syllables correctly in one attempt; empirical knowledge is necessary.

The mathematical theory of probability—with which we shall not deal here—concerns itself with developing ways to reckon complicated probabilities, for example, the probability that an even-numbered spade will come up three out of the next seven cards followed by a red queen followed by an odd heart at least twice in the next five cards, and so forth. These complex calculations are of great importance—for example, no rocket would be put in orbit without many such calculations—but in the social sciences one can usually avoid them, at least while one is a beginner.

The *conditional* probability is a second type of probability statement. Most of the use of probability in the social sciences is of this type. All hypothesis-testing statistics are conditional probabilities. A conditional probability is a statement that the probability of an event is such-and-such *if* something else is so-and-so; it is the "if" that makes a probability statement conditional. Now it is true that in *some* sense all probability statements are conditional; for example, the probability of an even-numbered spade is 6/52 *if* the deck is a poker deck and not necessarily if it is a pinochle deck or Tarot deck. But we ignore such conditions for most purposes.

The typical conditional-probability question used in social-science statistics is, What is the probability of obtaining this sample S (by chance) *if* the sample were taken from universe A? For example, what is the probability of getting a sample of five children with I.Q.s over 100 *by chance* in a sample randomly chosen from the universe of children whose average I.Q. is 100?

The first source of such conditional-probability statements is examination of the frequency series generated by universes like the conditional universe. For example, assume that we are considering a universe of children that average an I.Q. of 100. Write down "over 100" and "under 100" respectively on a big bunch of slips of paper, and put them into a hat, draw five slips several times, and see how often the first five slips drawn are all over 100. This system is called the "Monte Carlo method" of estimating probabilities.

The second source of such conditional-probability statements is by mathematical calculation. For example, if half the slips in the hat have numbers under 100 and half over 100, the probability of getting five in a row above 100 is 2^5, that is $2 \times 2 \times 2 \times 2 \times 2$. But, if you do not know the proper mathematical formula, you can come very close with the Monte Carlo method, which is what you will learn in this chapter.

The Concept of Independent Events

A key concept in the use of probability statistics is that of *independence* of two events. Two events are said to be "independent" when one of them does not seem to have any relation to the other. If I flip a coin that I know from other evidence is a fair coin and get a head, the chances of then getting *another* head are still 50-50 (one *in* two, or one *to* one). And, if I flip a coin ten times and get heads the first nine times, the probability of getting a head on the tenth flip is *still* 50-50.[6] This is why the concept of independence is characterized by the phrase "The coin has no memory."

Nevertheless, people commonly make the mistake of treating independent events as nonindependent, perhaps from superstitious belief. Roulette gamblers say that the wheel is "due" to come up red. And sportswriters make livings out of interpreting various sequences of athletic events that occur by chance and talk of teams that are "due" to win because of "the Law of Averages." For example, if Mickey Mantle goes to bat four times without a hit, all of us (including trained statisticians who really know better) feel that Mickey is "due" to get a hit and that the probability of his doing so is very high—higher, that is, than his season's average. The so-called "Law of Averages" implies no such thing, of course.

Not all events are independent, of course; far from it. A boy may call one of several girls chosen at random. But, if he calls the same girl *again* (or if he does *not* call her again), the second event is not likely to be independent of the first, and the probability of his calling her is *different* after he has gone out with her once.

This fact suggests another way to look at the concept of independence. If the occurrence of the first event *does not change the probability* that the second event will occur, then the events are independent.

Samples and Universes

The terms "sample" and "universe" (or "population")[7] have been used frequently throughout the book, and you have probably

6. Actually the matter is a bit more complicated. If you had previously flipped the coin many times and knew it to be a fair coin, then the odds would still be 50-50, even after nine heads. But, if you had never seen the coin before, the run of nine heads might reasonably make you doubt that the coin was a fair one.

7. "Universe" and "population" are perfect synonyms in scientific research. I choose to use "universe" because it seems to have fewer confusing associations.

understood what they meant. But now these terms must be defined in greater detail.

It is reasonably easy to define ''sample'' for our purposes here. A sample is the collection of observations for which you have data with which you are going to work. Almost any set of observations for which you have data constitutes a sample.

For every sample there must also be a universe ''behind'' it. But ''universe'' is harder to define, partly because it is often an *imaginary* concept. A universe is the collection of things or people *that you want to say that your sample was taken from.* A universe can be finite and well defined—''all live holders of the Congressional Medal of Honor,'' ''all presidents of major universities,'' ''all billion-dollar corporations in the United States.'' Of course, these finite universes may not be easy to pin down; for instance, what is a ''major university''? And these universes may contain some elements that are difficult to find; for instance, some Congressional Medal winners may have left the country, and there may not be any public records on some billion-dollar corporations.

Infinite universes are harder to understand, and it is often difficult to decide which universe is appropriate for a given purpose. For example, if you are studying a sample of schizophrenics, what is the universe from which the sample comes? Depending on your purposes, the appropriate universe might be all schizophrenics now alive, or it might be all schizophrenics who might *ever* live. The latter concept of the universe of schizophrenics is *imaginary* because some of the universe does not exist. And it is *infinite* because it goes on forever.

Not everyone likes this definition of ''universe.'' Others prefer to think of a universe, not as the collection of people or things that you *want* to say your sample was taken from, but as the collection that the sample was *actually* taken from. This latter view equates the universe to the sampling frame (discussed earlier on p. 000), which is always finite and existent. There is an analogy here to hypothetical and empirical variables; in my view one actually deals with an empirical variable that stands for a hypothetical variable that may itself be difficult to pin down; the other view ignores the hypothetical variable completely when it refuses to deal with imaginary universes. The definition of ''universe'' offered here is the most practical, in my opinion.

Translating Scientific Questions Into Probability (Statistical) Questions

Science does not begin and end with statistics. Professional statisticians are quite humble about the importance of statistics. But having taken a course or two has a way of going to a student's head, making him think that nothing can be proved without statistics and that anything can be proved if sophisticated statistics are used. This is the fallacy of "statistics is everything."

The fallacy of "statistics is nothing" is also dangerous, however. As M. D. Dunnette (1966) points out, researchers often disregard statistics because their *intuition* tells them that some conclusions *must* be so ". . . on the grounds that they are intrinsically good for humanity and that they need not, therefore, meet the usual standards demanded by scientific verification. . . . [Psychotherapy, for example] continues to survive in spite of a lack of evidence about its effectiveness" (Dunnette, 1966, p. 346).

A social-scientific study begins with a general question about the nature of the social world. The scientist then transforms this question into a form that he can study scientifically. The translation of general questions into scientific questions has been discussed earlier (Chapters 2, 14).

Let us suppose that, by this time, the researcher has not only translated his general question into a scientific question but has also *carried out* his scientific investigation as an experiment or survey. Suppose further that the data that he has collected are not entirely clear-cut in support of firm conclusions. At this juncture, if he does not want to or cannot collect more data, the researcher may turn to probability statistics to help him.

The first step in using probability statistics is to *translate the scientific question into a statistical question.* Once you know exactly what kind of probability-statistical question you want to ask, that is, exactly what probability you want to determine, the rest is relatively easy. The stage at which you are most likely to make mistakes is in stating the question you want to answer in probability terms. Though this step is hard, *it involves no mathematics.* This step requires only *hard, clear thinking;* you cannot beg off by saying "I have no brain for math!" To flub this step is to admit that you have no brain for *clear thinking,* rather than no brain for mathematics.

I repeat, the hardest job in using probability statistics, and the most important, is to *translate* the scientific question into the form to which statistics can give a sensible answer. This translation is in the spirit of the discussion in Chapter 2 of the language of science and operational definitions; you must translate scientific questions into the appropriate form for *statistical operations,* so that you know which statistical operations to perform. This is the part of the job that requires hard, clear thinking—though nonmathematical thinking—and it is the part that someone else cannot easily do for you.

The best way to explain how to translate a scientific question into a statistical question is to illustrate the process.

ILLUSTRATION 1

Are doctors' beliefs about the harmfulness of cigarette smoking (and doctors' own smoking behavior) affected by the *social* groups among whom they live (J. L. Simon, 1967–1968)? We decide to define the doctors' *reference groups* as the *states* in which they live, because data about doctors are available state by state (*Modern Medicine*, 1964). We can then translate this question into an operational and testable scientific hypothesis by asking this question: Do doctors in tobacco-economy states differ from doctors in other states in their smoking and beliefs about smoking?

But what numbers help us to answer this question, and how do we interpret them? We can now ask the *statistical* question: Do doctors in tobacco-economy states belong to the same universe (with respect to smoking) as do other doctors? That is, do doctors in tobacco-economy states have the same characteristics (at least of those we are interested in, smoking in this case) as do other doctors? Later we shall see that the way to proceed is to consider the statistical hypothesis that these doctors do indeed belong to that same universe; that hypothesis and the universe will be called "benchmark hypothesis" and "benchmark universe" respectively, though more conventional usage is "null hypothesis."

If the tobacco-economy doctors do indeed belong to the benchmark universe, that is, if the benchmark hypothesis is correct, then there is a 49/50 chance that doctors in some states *other* than the state in which tobacco is most important will have the highest rate of cigarette smoking. But in fact we observe that the state in which tobacco accounts for the largest proportion of the state's income—North Carolina—has a higher proportion of doctors who smoke than does any other state. (Furthermore, a lower proportion of doctors in North Carolina than in any other state say that they *believe* that smoking is a health hazard.)

Of course, it is possible that it is just *chance* that North Carolina doctors smoke most, but the chance is only 1 in 50 if the benchmark hypothesis is correct. Obviously, *some* state had to have the highest rate, and the chance for any other state was *also* 1 in 50. But, because our original *scientific* hypothesis was that North Carolina doctors' smoking rate would be highest and we then observed that it was highest, even though the chance was only 1 in 50, the observation is interesting and means something to us. It means that the chances are strong—49 in 50—that there is a connection between the importance of tobacco in the economy of a state and the rate of cigarette smoking among doctors living there.

To attack this problem from another direction, it would be rare for North Carolina to have the highest smoking rate for doctors if there were no special reason for it; in fact, it would occur only once in fifty times. But, if there *is* a special reason—and we hypothesize that the tobacco economy provides the reason—then it is *not* rare for North Carolina to have the highest rate; therefore we choose to believe in the not-so-rare phenomenon, that the tobacco economy causes doctors to smoke cigarettes.

ILLUSTRATION 2

Does medicine M cure cancer? You begin with this scientific question and give the medicine to six patients who have cancer; you do not give it to six similar patients who have cancer. Your sample is only twelve people because it is simply not feasible for you to obtain a larger one. Five of six "medicine" patients get well, two of six "no medicine" patients get well. Does the medicine cure cancer?

One way to translate the scientific question into a statistical question is to ask: Do the "medicine" patients belong to the same universe as the "no medicine" patients? That is, we ask whether "medicine" patients still have the *same* chances of getting well from the cancer as do the "no medicine" patients or whether the medicine has bettered the chances of those who took it and thus removed them from the original universe, with its original chances of getting well. The original universe, to which the "no medicine" patients must still belong, is the benchmark universe, and later we shall see that we proceed by making the benchmark hypothesis that they still belong to the benchmark universe (that is, still have the same chance of getting well as the "no medicine" patients).

We want to know whether or not the medicine does any good, which is the same thing as asking whether patients who take medicine are still in the same universe as "no medicine" patients or belong to a different universe, one which now has different chances of getting well. To recapitulate our translations, we go from Does the medicine cure cancer? to Do "medicine" patients have the same chance of getting well as "no medicine" patients? and finally to Do "medicine" patients belong to the same universe (population) as "no medicine" patients? Remember that "population" in this sense does *not* refer to the population at large but to a group of cancer sufferers (perhaps an infinitely large group) who have given chances of getting well, on the average. Groups with different average chances of getting well are called "different populations" ("universes"). Later we shall see how to *answer* this statistical question.

ILLUSTRATION 3

Is method A a better method of teaching reading than method B? Twenty children taught to read with method A have an average reading score of 79, whereas children taught with method B have an average score of 84. To translate this quite-satisfactory *scientific* question into a statistical question we ask: Do children taught with method A come from the same universe (population) as children taught with method B? Again, "universe" ("population") does *not* mean the town or social group the children come from, and indeed the experiment will make sense only if the children *do* come from the same population, in that sense. What we want to know is whether or not the children belong to the same population (universe), defined according to their *reading ability, after* they have studied with method A or method B.

Translating from a scientific question into a statistical question is mostly a matter of asking the probability that one or more samples come from some given benchmark universe. Notice that we must (at least for general scientific testing purposes) ask about a *given* universe whose composition we assume to be *known,* rather than about a *range* of universes or a universe whose properties are unknown. In fact, there is really only one question that probability statistics can answer: Given some particular benchmark universe of some stated composition, what is the probability that an observed sample comes from it? A variation of this question is: Given two (or more) samples, what is the probability that they come from the *same* universe? In this latter case, the relevant universe is implicitly the universe whose composition is of the two samples combined.

The necessity for stating the characteristics of the universe in question becomes obvious when you think about it for a moment. Probability-statistical testing adds up to comparison of a sample with a particular benchmark universe and asking whether or not there is probably a difference between the sample and the universe. To carry out this comparison, we ask *how likely* it is that the benchmark universe would produce a sample like the observed sample. But, in order to find out whether or not a universe could produce a given sample, we must ask whether or not some *particular* universe—with stated characteristics—could produce the sample. There is no doubt that *some* universe could produce the sample by a random process; in fact, some universe did. The only sensible question, then, is whether or not a *particular* universe, with stated (or known) characteristics, is *likely* to produce such a sample. In the case of the medicine, the universe with which we compare the sample who took the medicine is the benchmark universe to which that sample would belong if the medicine had had no effect. This comparison leads to the benchmark (null) hypothesis that the sample comes from a population in which the medicine (or other experimental treatment) seems to have *no effect.* It is to avoid confusion inherent in the term "null hypothesis" that I replace it with "benchmark hypothesis."

The concept of the benchmark (null) hypothesis is hard to grasp.[8] The best way to learn its meaning is to see how it is used in practice. For example, we say we are willing to believe that the medicine has an effect if it seems very unlikely from the number who get well that the patients given the medicine still belong to the same benchmark universe as the patients given no medicine at all—that is, if the benchmark hypothesis is unlikely.

ILLUSTRATION 4

If one plot of ground is treated with fertilizer and another similar plot is not treated, the benchmark (null) hypothesis is that the corn raised on the treated plot is no different from the corn raised on the untreated plot, that is, that the corn from the treated plot comes from the same universe as the corn from the untreated plot. If our statistical test makes it seem very unlikely that a universe like that from which the untreated-plot corn comes would *also* produce corn such as came from the treated plot, then we are willing to believe that the fertilizer has an effect. For a psychological example, substitute the words "groups of children" for "plot," "special training" for "fertilizer," and "I.Q. score" for "corn."

There is nothing sacred about the benchmark (null) hypothesis of "no difference." You could just as well test the benchmark hypothesis that the corn comes from a universe that averages 110 bushels per acre, if you have reason to be especially interested in knowing whether or not the fertilizer produces more than 110 bushels per acre. But in many cases it is reasonable to test the likelihood that a sample comes from the population that does not receive the special treatment of medicine, fertilizer, or training.

So far we have discussed the scientific question and the statistical question. Remember that there is always a generalization question too: Do the statistical results from this particular sample of, say, rats apply to a universe of humans? This question can be answered only

8. The classic discussion of the null hypothesis is by R. A. Fisher in his *The Design of Experiments* (1935, pp. 18–9), but even that discussion is not at all satisfactory. Another useful treatment is by J. Neyman (1950, Chap. 5), who substitutes the term "test hypothesis" for "null hypothesis," however. The fact is that this concept is among the slipperiest in all scientific research and the hardest to learn. Don't despair if the notion eludes you at first. It will come clear as you work with it in the later parts of the chapter and elsewhere.

with wisdom, common sense, and general knowledge, as was discussed in the previous chapter.

Estimating Probabilities for Statistical Testing

I have said that probability-statistical theory tells us the chance that something will (or will not) happen, expressed in the *odds* that it will (or will not) happen. Now let us see how we can *estimate* the odds of several concrete situations.

EXAMPLE 1

Let us begin, not with a scientific research problem, but with a pure problem in odds: What is the chance (what are the odds) that the first five cards chosen from a complete deck of fifty-two bridge (poker) cards will contain two cards of the same denomination?

We shall estimate these odds the way that gamblers have estimated gambling odds for thousands of years. First, check that the deck is not a pinochle deck and is not missing any cards. (Overlooking such small but crucial matters often leads to errors in science.) Shuffle thoroughly until you are satisfied that the cards are randomly distributed. (It is surprisingly hard to shuffle well.) Then deal five cards, and mark down whether the hand does or does not contain a pair of the same denomination. At this point, we must decide whether three of a kind, four of a kind, or two pairs meet our criterion for a pair; we decide *not* to count them.

Then replace the five cards in the deck, shuffle, and deal again. Again mark whether or not the hand contains one pair of the same denomination. Do this many times. (Table 23.1. shows 100 hands, which my good assistant has just dealt.) Then count the number of hands with pairs, and figure the proportion (as a percentage) of all hands. In Table 23.1., 44 per cent of the hands contained pairs, and that is our estimate of the probability that one pair will turn up in a poker hand.

This experimental estimation (called "Monte Carlo estimation" for obvious reasons)[9] does not require a deck of cards. For example, one might create a fifty-two-sided die, one side for each card in the deck, and spin it five times to get a "hand." But note one important part of the procedure: No single "card" is allowed to come up twice in the same set of five spins, just as no card can possibly appear twice in the same hand. If the same "card" did turn up twice or more in a

9. Monte Carlo methods have previously been used to help teach the *analytic* methods of statistics, but I do not know of other attempts to teach Monte Carlo methods as a device for answering statistical questions, except those too complex for ordinary analytic methods.

Table 23.1.

Trial	**1**	**2**	**3**	**4**	**5**	**6**	**7**	**8**	**9**	**10**	**11**	**12**	**13**
Results	Y	Y	N	N	Y	Y	N	N	Y	N	N	Y	N
Trial	**14**	**15**	**16**	**17**	**18**	**19**	**20**	**21**	**22**	**23**	**24**	**25**	**26**
Results	N	Y	Y	Y	Y	Y	N	N	Y	N	Y	N	Y
Trial	**27**	**28**	**29**	**30**	**31**	**32**	**33**	**34**	**35**	**36**	**37**	**38**	**39**
Results	N	Y	N	Y	Y	N	Y	N	N	N	N	Y	N
Trial	**40**	**41**	**42**	**43**	**44**	**45**	**46**	**47**	**48**	**49**	**50**		
Results	N	N	N	N	Y	Y	Y	N	N	Y	N		

Subtotal: 23 Yes, 27 No = 46%

Trial	**51**	**52**	**53**	**54**	**55**	**56**	**57**	**58**	**59**	**60**	**61**	**62**	**63**
Results	N	Y	N	N	Y	N	Y	Y	N	N	N	Y	Y
Trial	**64**	**65**	**66**	**67**	**68**	**69**	**70**	**71**	**72**	**73**	**74**	**75**	**76**
Results	Y	N	N	Y	N	N	N	N	Y	N	Y	N	N
Trial	**77**	**78**	**79**	**80**	**81**	**82**	**83**	**84**	**85**	**86**	**87**	**88**	**89**
Results	N	N	N	N	Y	N	N	N	Y	Y	N	Y	N
Trial	**90**	**91**	**92**	**93**	**94**	**95**	**96**	**97**	**98**	**99**	**100**		
Results	Y	Y	N	N	Y	Y	Y	Y	N	Y	N		

Subtotal: 21 Yes, 29 No = 42%

Total: 44 Yes, 56 No = 44%

die experiment, one could pretend that the spin had never taken place; this procedure is necessary to make the die experiment analogous to the actual card-dealing situation under investigation. Otherwise, the results will be slightly in error. This type of sampling is known as "sampling without replacement," because each card is *not replaced* in the deck each time it is dealt (until the end of the hand, that is).

Still another Monte Carlo method uses a *random number table,* a sample of which is shown in Table 23.2. (and which was introduced on p. 42). Arbitrarily designate the spades as numbers 01-13, the diamonds as 14-26, the hearts as 27-39, and the clubs as 40-52. Then proceed across a row (or down a column), writing down each successive two-digit number, except for numbers outside 01-52 and omitting duplication within sets of five numbers. Then translate them back into cards, and see how many "hands" of five "cards" contain one pair each. Table 23.3. shows six such hands, of which 2, 3, and 6 contain pairs.

Table 23.2. TABLE OF RANDOM DIGITS

14900	77763	66045	91851	02199	34221	58116	06648	55779	50353	16401
14901	93968	57080	56566	05093	12677	02035	34393	28765	83709	60080
14902	96185	55327	46929	21087	08191	54583	17963	18599	57717	26689
14903	50956	13999	05475	02687	20207	28492	18203	53613	64035	69836
14904	42925	13489	61425	07510	92172	78063	78247	34647	37710	71779
14905	74102	76512	99800	27498	08257	71444	29192	73165	85985	58584
14906	25963	77276	01566	26830	83288	89183	03636	91176	04673	48271
14907	00336	28332	95442	45548	92764	69320	67663	74935	45673	89406
14908	97190	07021	54689	76464	07125	60376	96263	81957	98097	89311
14909	42508	33579	74511	37271	66533	14980	87997	46543	20445	29364
14910	15095	69719	62380	00947	13581	49929	23187	04410	11076	50274
14911	46426	40638	80584	14926	70877	76023	31838	32280	61814	43410
14912	18432	53552	44904	13591	53696	28658	09538	77232	23728	49210
14913	98828	28017	51152	39704	04560	20423	63072	94843	02544	70033
14914	81052	43812	38934	31109	94872	40069	70062	53044	24375	70147
14915	74325	73599	05533	99548	74035	63714	07222	08337	76768	32818
14916	90928	47761	02291	80702	83239	25189	89692	19820	22468	05036
14917	07510	62086	73335	06373	14326	08408	25356	55568	57104	01080
14918	91192	26484	00867	88759	10759	33681	65027	20204	86513	09961
14919	67338	60292	26494	65254	72875	19913	77183	67772	63750	00160
14920	85269	97756	56322	57967	67739	07247	43739	71253	20167	27559
14921	53369	93055	91402	49671	04836	76592	94506	36169	53691	29980
14922	41545	08255	77112	08226	59377	64281	78805	43935	89642	28246
14923	25149	61362	56824	03083	87188	24545	92615	02467	24037	30907
14924	07811	48013	21451	00027	24292	19821	61891	50220	58751	50149
14925	59136	72788	65822	92765	11578	41707	67454	53971	22142	42152
14926	39413	48108	16818	63717	28962	08592	14709	06238	05846	00185
14927	71779	00051	96502	23391	64072	62357	28655	24549	11676	47937
14928	41939	06052	07881	75888	74477	40449	59968	83495	62878	49038
14929	16852	18740	41590	28762	40054	10564	35447	68877	44619	61061
14930	04631	58241	41013	05634	63332	39191	97358	71011	11686	52933
14931	95217	80882	38875	03353	78129	48089	28134	99469	34177	72409
14932	80365	85981	85997	77118	04077	83723	50303	98313	01146	18326
14933	58855	05833	18794	52072	59851	01483	88374	36319	36368	26524
14934	22006	45586	23893	41542	62646	33970	54241	92550	88540	53154

Source: *A Million Random Digits*, p. 299, 1955; reprinted by permission of The RAND Corporation.

14935	76337	68760	41026	08782	31730	07065	78387	09131	95071	42449
14936	51704	65196	41265	90097	94115	64082	07303	09377	66079	53441
14937	11956	30019	65444	09584	63013	05910	35455	06835	07600	47760
14938	00988	13313	60845	73629	86538	28154	40720	23743	74080	61846
14939	82782	41206	91879	63068	73995	33450	42509	41835	02510	68150
14940	62815	88785	71549	53948	45568	91775	64445	69381	54504	20164
14941	02789	77565	53885	46625	94662	68508	10054	72150	04929	75740
14942	33205	20135	52866	79816	34428	93968	20188	89365	06999	72626
14943	70754	59048	10608	60977	43019	40992	64986	44046	57345	81369
14944	67257	49810	80441	48662	80202	88476	92832	59513	49576	70442
14945	19528	97104	07494	33837	56317	50726	22873	10055	65019	49219
14946	83200	05043	58631	60432	19459	84344	86413	16919	12366	07169
14947	07620	18983	68990	07355	04329	00768	57835	81052	51801	73425
14948	19985	85275	69386	83316	67868	14206	93915	67465	51070	93820
14949	34214	29590	56826	01032	69498	81380	03108	37400	51142	14002

How accurate are these Monte Carlo methods? The accuracy depends on the *number of hands* we deal—the more hands, the greater the accuracy. Mathematical calculation tells us that, if we were to deal millions of hands, 42 per cent would contain a pair each; that is, the chance of getting a pair in the long run is 42 per cent. The estimate of 44 per cent based on 100 hands in Table 23.1. is close, though whether or not it is close enough depends on one's needs, of course. If one needs great accuracy, he should deal more hands.

Table 23.3.

	Ace	*Deuce*	*3*	*4*	*5*	*6*	*7*	*8*	*9*	*10*	*Jack*	*Queen*	*King*
Spades	01	02	03	04	05	06	07	08	09	10	11	12	13
Diamonds	14	15	16	17	18	19	20	21	22	23	24	25	26
Hearts	27	28	29	30	31	32	33	34	35	36	37	38	39
Clubs	40	41	42	43	44	45	46	47	48	49	50	51	52

1	10	09	25	33	52
2	01	35	34	36	48
3	17	39	29	27	49
4	45	20	48	05	47
5	42	24	52	40	37
6	20	04	02	29	16

How many trials (hands) should be made for the estimate? There is no easy answer. The best approach is to run several (perhaps ten) equal-sized sets of trials and then to examine whether or not the proportion of pairs found in the entire group of trials is very different from the proportion found in the various subgroup sets. If the proportions of pairs in the various subgroups differ greatly from one another or from the over-all proportion, then keep *quadrupling*[10] the number of trials until the over-all average is not much changed by the additional trials. In this case, Table 23.1. shows that the average of the total of 100 hands is not much different from the average of the first fifty hands, and so we could reasonably quit dealing after 100 hands.

EXAMPLE 2

What is the probability that the first four children in a four-child family will all be daughters? The first step is to state the approximate probability that a single birth will produce a daughter as 50-50 (1 in 2). This estimate is not strictly correct because there are 106 male children born to each 100 female children, but the approximation is not too far off for most purposes, and the 50-50 split simplifies the job considerably. (Such "false" approximations are part of the everyday work of the scientist. The question is not whether or not a statement is "only" an approximation but whether or not it is a *good* approximation for your purposes.)

The chance of a fair coin's coming up heads is 50-50, as are the odds in favor of the birth of a single daughter. Therefore flip a coin in groups of four flips, and count how often all four flips produce *heads*. (You must decide *in advance* whether four heads mean four girls or four boys.) It is as simple as that. I shall not bother to flip the coin myself, because it is easier to use the mathematical method known as the "multiplication formula." (If the probability of getting a head once is 1/2, then the probability of getting two heads in a row is $1/2 \times 1/2$, and the probability of getting four heads in a row is $1/2 \times 1/2 \times 1/2 \times 1/2 = 1/16$, if the events are independent. But, if you do not understand why this is so, stick to coin flipping, and you will be safe.)

The probability of getting four daughters in four births could also be found with a deck of cards, a random-number table, or a die. For example, half the cards in a deck are black, so the probability of dealing a black card ("daughter") from a full deck is 1 in 2. Therefore, deal a card, record "daughter" or "son," *replace* the card, deal again, and so forth for sets of four cards. Then count the proportion of groups of four cards in which you got four daughters.

10. The reason for *quadrupling* is that *four* times as big a sample give *twice* as much accuracy (as measured by the standard deviation, the most frequent measurement of accuracy). That is, the error decreases with the square root of the sample size. And a step that doubles accuracy is a comfortable arbitrary step in many cases. But, if you see that you need *much* more accuracy, then *immediately* increase the sample size even more than four times.

It is important that in this case, in contrast to what occurred in Example 1, the card be replaced *each time,* so that each card is dealt from a full deck. This method is known as *sampling with replacement.* One samples with replacement whenever the successive events are *independent;* in this case, we assume that the chance of having a daughter remains the same (1 in 2), no matter how many sons or daughters the family has previously had.[11] But, if the first card dealt is black and is *not* replaced, the chance of the second card's being black is no longer 26 in 52 (1 in 2) but is only 25 in 51 (less than 1 in 2). If the first *three* cards are black and are not replaced, then the chance of the fourth card's being black sinks to 23 in 49.

To push the illustration further, consider what would happen if we used a deck of only *six* cards, half (three) black and half (three) red, instead of a deck of fifty-two cards. If the card were replaced each time, the six-card deck would produce the same results as a fifty-two-card deck; in fact, a two-card deck would do as well. But, if the sampling were done *without* replacement, it would be *impossible* to obtain four "daughters" with the six-card deck because there would be only three "daughters" in the deck. To repeat, then, whenever you want to estimate the probability of some series of events of which each is independent of the other, you must sample *with replacement.*

One more point before leaving these four sweet daughters. We have estimated the likelihood of a *particular* family's having four daughters as 1 in 16—that is, odds of 15 to 1. But note: This is very different from stating that the odds are 15 to 1 against *some* family's having four daughters in a row. In fact, as many families will have four girls in a row as will have boy-girl-boy-girl in that order or girl-boy-girl-boy or *any* other series of four children. The odds against any particular series are the same—15 to 1—and one-sixteenth of all four-children families will have each of these series. This means that, if your next-door neighbor has four daughters, you cannot say "how out of the ordinary" that is. It is easy to slip into unsound thinking about this matter.

EXAMPLE 3

To see how powerful *and* simple Monte Carlo methods are, consider this famous examination question used in courses on probability: What is the probability that two or more people among a roomful of, say, twenty-five people will have the same birthday? To answer, simply examine the first twenty-five numbers from the random-number table that fall between 001 and 365 (days in the year) and record whether

11. This assumption is slightly contrary to scientific fact. A better example would be the probability that four mothers delivering in a row in a hospital will all have daughters. But that example has other nuisances.

or not there is a duplication among the twenty-five. Repeat the process enough times to get a reasonably stable probability estimate. Then pose the question to a mathematical friend of yours, watch him sweat for awhile, and compare your answer to his. (I think you will find the correct answer very surprising.)

EXAMPLE 4

Which is more likely, poker hands of two pairs or of three of a kind? This is a *comparison* problem, as are many social-science testing problems.

In a series of 100 hands (using random numbers), four hands contained two pairs, and two hands contained three of a kind. Is it safe to say, on the basis of these 100 hands, that hands with two pairs are more frequent than hands with three of a kind? I do not think so. To check, we deal another 300 hands. In this 300, we see fifteen hands with two pairs (3.75 per cent) and eight hands with three of a kind (2 per cent), for a total of nineteen to ten. Although the difference is not enormous, it is reasonably clear-cut. Another 400 hands might be advisable, but we shall not bother.

Earlier we obtained forty-four hands with *one* pair each out of 100 hands, which makes it quite plain that *one* pair is more frequent than *either* two pairs or three of a kind. Obviously, we need *more* hands to compare the odds in favor of two pairs with the odds in favor of three of a kind than to compare those for one pair with those for either two pairs or three of a kind. Why? Because the difference in odds between one pair and either two pairs or three of a kind is much greater than the difference in odds between two pairs and three of a kind. This observation leads to a general rule: The closer the odds between two events, the *more trials* are needed to determine which has the higher odds.

Again it is interesting to compare the odds with the mathematical computations, which are 1 in 21 (4.75 per cent) for a hand containing two pairs and 1 in 47 (2.1 per cent) for a hand containing three of a kind—not too far from the estimate of 3.75 per cent and 2.0 per cent based on 100 random hands.

EXAMPLE 5

You think you have developed a technique for irradiating the genes of fruit flies so that the sex ratio of the offspring will *not* be half males and half females. In the first twenty cases you treat, there are fourteen males and six females. Does this result confirm that the irradiation does work?

First convert the scientific question—whether or not the treatment affects the sex distribution—into a probability-statistical question: Is the observed sample likely to have come from a universe in which the sex ratio is one male to one female? The benchmark (null) hypothesis, then, is that the treatment makes no difference and that the sample comes from the one-to-one universe. Therefore, we investigate how likely a one-to-one universe is to produce a distribution of fourteen males to six females.

A coin has a one-to-one (one out of two) chance of coming up tails. Therefore, flip a coin in groups of twenty flips, and count the number of heads in each twenty flips. Or use a random-number table, calling even numbers or numbers 1-5 "males," odd numbers or numbers 6-0 "females." Table 23.4. shows the results obtained in twenty-five trials of twenty flips each.

Table 23.4.

Trial of 20 Coin Flips	*Number of Heads*	*Trial of 20 Coin Flips*	*Number of Heads*	*Trial of 20 Coin Flips*	*Number of Heads*
1	11	10	10	18	12
2	12	11	10	19	13
3	8	12	10	20	10
4	12	13	9	21	11
5	12	14	9	22	14
6	7	15	12	23	9
7	9	16	7	24	7
8	8	17	14	25	10
9	6				

In two of the twenty-five trials (8 per cent) there were fourteen or more heads, which we shall call "males," and in one of the twenty-five (4 per cent) trials there were fourteen or more tails ("females"). We can therefore estimate that, even if the treatment does *not* affect the sex and even if the births over a long period are really one to one, we would get fourteen or more of one sex or the other three out of twenty-five times (12 per cent). Therefore, finding fourteen males out of twenty births is not overwhelming evidence that the treatment has any effect, though it is suggestive.

How accurate is the estimate? Seventy-five more trials were made, and of the 100 trials ten contained fourteen or more "males" (10 per cent), and seven trials contained fourteen or more "females" (7 per cent), a total of 17 per cent. So the first twenty-five trials gave a fairly reliable indication. As a matter of fact, a mathematical computation (not explained here) shows that the probability of getting fourteen or more females out of twenty births is .057 and, of course, the same for fourteen or more males from a one-to-one universe, a total probability of .114 of getting fourteen or more males *or* females.

Notice that the strength of the evidence for the effectiveness of the radiation treatment depends upon the original question, whether or not the treatment had *any* effect on sex. But, if there were reason to believe at the start that the treatment could increase only the number of *males*, then we would focus our attention on the fact that in only two of our first twenty-five trials were there fourteen or more males. There would be only a 2/25 probability of getting the observed results by chance if the treatment really has no effect, rather than the weaker odds against obtaining fourteen or more of *either* males or females.

Therefore, whether you decide to figure the odds for just fourteen or more males (what is called a "one-tail test") or for fourteen or more males *plus* fourteen or more females (a "two-tail test"), depends upon your advance knowledge of the treatment. If you have no reason to believe that the treatment will have an effect *only* in the direction of creating more males and if you figure the odds for the one-tail test anyway, then you will be kidding yourself. Theory comes to bear here. If you have a strong hypothesis, deduced from a strong theory, that there will be more males, then you should figure one-tail odds, but if you have no such theory you should figure the weaker two-tail odds.[12]

"Significance level" is a common term in probability statistics. It corresponds roughly to the probability that the observed sample does not come from a particular universe by chance. The results of Example 5 can be phrased as follows: The hypothesis that the radiation treatment affects the sex of fruit-fly offspring is accepted as true at the 19 per cent level of significance. (A more common way of expressing this idea would be to say that the hypothesis is *not rejected* at the 19 per cent level of significance. But "not rejected" and "accepted" really do mean much the same thing, despite some arguments to the contrary.) This kind of statistical work is called *statistical testing*.

The question of *which* significance level should be said to be significant is difficult. How great must a coincidence be before you refuse to believe that it is only a coincidence? It has been conventional

12. If you are very knowledgeable, you may do some in-between figuring (with what is known as "Bayesian analysis"), but leave this alone unless you know exactly what you are doing.

in social science to say that, if the probability that something happens by chance is less than 5 per cent, it is significant. But sometimes the stiffer standard of 1 per cent is used. Actually, *any* fixed cut-off significance level is an arbitrary construction. (And even the whole notion of saying that a hypothesis "is true" or "is not true" is sometimes not very useful.)

EXAMPLE 6

Suppose that, instead of trying just one type of radiation treatment on the flies, as in Example 5, you try *four* different treatments, which we shall label A, B, C, and D. In treatment A you get fourteen males and six females, but in treatments B, C, and D you get ten, eleven, and ten males, respectively. It is immediately obvious that there is no reason to think that treatment B, C, or D affects the sex ratio. But what about treatment A?

Chapter 22 pointed out that it is fallacious to dig around in the data for the most extreme observation and then to treat it as if it were the only one made. In terms of this example, it would be fallacious to think that the probability of the fourteen males-six females split of treatment A is the probability that we figured for a single experiment in Example 5. Instead, we must consider that our benchmark universe is *four sets* of twenty trials, each trial having a 50-50 probability of coming out male. We can consider that old trials 1-4 in Example 5 constitute a single new trial, and each subsequent set of four old trials is another new trial. We then ask how likely a new trial of four sets of twenty flips is to produce *one* set with fourteen or more of one or the other sex. Three of the six trials do so, which indicates that it would be very common indeed to have one of four treatments show fourteen or more of one sex just by chance. This discovery clearly indicates that a result that would be fairly unusual (three in twenty-five) for the only sample is commonplace in one of four observed samples.

EXAMPLE 7

Example 5 used an observed sample of male and female fruit flies to test the benchmark (null) hypothesis that the flies came from a universe with a one-to-one sex ratio. Now we want to compare *two samples with each other,* rather than one sample with a hypothesized universe.

The scientific question is whether pill P cures cancer. A researcher gave the pill to six patients selected randomly from a group of twelve cancer patients, of whom five got well. He gave an inactive placebo to the other six patients, and two of them got well. Does the evidence justify a conclusion that the pill has a curative effect?

(An identical statistical example could be constructed with an experiment on methods of teaching reading to children. But in such a case the researcher would respond to inconclusive results by running the experiment on more subjects, though in cases like the cancer-pill example the researcher often cannot obtain more subjects.)

The scientific question can then be translated into the statistical question: How probable is it that the pill group and the placebo group come from the same universe? But of *what* universe do we ask whether or not it could have generated both these samples?

The answer is to *combine* the two samples and test both samples against the resulting combined universe. In this case, the universe is twelve subjects, seven $(5 + 2)$ of whom got well. Given such a universe, then, how likely would it be to produce two samples as far apart as five of six and two of six patients who get well? In other words, how often will two samples of six subjects each, drawn from a universe in which 7/12 of the patients get well, be as far apart as $5 - 2 = 3$ patients in favor of the sample designated "pill"? This is obviously a one-tail test, for there is no reason to believe that the pill group might do less well than the placebo group.

Construct a twelve-sided die, seven of whose sides are marked "get well." Or use pairs of numbers from the random-number table, with numbers 01-07 corresponding to get well, numbers 08-12 corresponding to "not get well," and all other numbers omitted. (If you wish to save time, you can work out a system that uses more and skips fewer of the numbers, but that is up to you.) Designate the first six subjects "pill" and the next six subjects "placebo," and record the results as in Table 23.5.

In three of twenty-five cases (12 per cent) the difference between the randomly drawn groups is three or greater. Apparently it is somewhat unusual for this universe to generate "pill" samples in which the number of recoveries exceeds the number in the "placebo" samples by three or more. Therefore the answer to the scientific question, based on these samples, is that there is some reason to think that the medicine does have a favorable effect. But the investigator might sensibly await more data before reaching a firm conclusion about the pill's efficacy, given the 7 to 1 (12 per cent) odds.

This method is not the standard way of handling the problem; it is not even analogous to the standard analytic difference-of-proportions method. Though the method shown is quite direct and satisfactory, there are *many other* Monte Carlo methods that we might develop to solve the same problem. You should by all means invent your own statistics, rather than simply aping the methods described here; the

Table 23.5.

Trial	*Pill*	*Placebo*	*Difference*
1	4	4	0
2	3	5	−2
3	4	3	1
4*	5	2	3
5	4	3	1
6	2	5	−3
7	4	4	0
8	4	5	−1
9	4	4	0
10*	5	2	3
11	4	5	−1
12	5	3	2
13	3	5	−2
14	3	2	1
15	3	4	−1
16	5	4	1
17*	6	3	3
18	4	5	−1
19	3	4	−1
20	2	3	−1
21	4	4	0
22	4	4	0
23	3	5	−2
24	3	3	0
25	3	3	0

*The total is 3 differences as great as 3 in favor of pill.

latter only illustrate the process of inventing statistics rather than offering solutions for all classes of problems.

EXAMPLE 8

A municipal official wanted to determine whether the *majority* of a town's residents were for or against the awarding of a cable-television franchise, and he asked you to take a poll. You assumed that the telephone book was a fair representation of the universe in which the politician was interested, and you decided to interview by telephone. Of a sample of fifty people who expressed opinions, thirty were for the plan and twenty were against it. How conclusively do the results show that the people in town want cable television?

The benchmark (null) hypothesis is that 50 per cent of the town does not want the plan. (This statement really means that "50 per cent or *more* do not want the plan.") Designate 1-5 as "no" in the random-number table, 6-10 as "yes." Count the number of "yes"es and "no"s in the first fifty numbers. Repeat for perhaps twenty trials, as shown in Table 23.6. Then count the proportion of the trials in which a 50-50 universe would produce thirty or more "yes" answers, four of twenty in Table 23.6. (20 per cent); this is the probability that as many as thirty of fifty people would say "yes" by chance if the population were "really" split evenly. (If the population were split so that *more* than 50 per cent were against the plan, the probability would be even *less* that the observed result would occur by chance. In this sense, the benchmark hypothesis is conservative.)

Table 23.6.

Trial	*Number of "No"s*	*Number of "Yes"es*
1	23	27
2	25	25
3	26	24
4	22	28
5	22	28
6	20	30
7	25	25
8	21	29
9	28	22
10	19	31
11	28	22
12	19	31
13	18	32
14	23	27
15	34	16
16	27	23
17	22	28
18	26	24
19	28	22
20	27	23

EXAMPLE 9[13]

Each of two new types of ration is fed to twelve pigs. A farmer wants to know whether ration A or ration B is better. The weight gains for pigs fed on ration A are 31.0, 34.0, 29.0, 26.0, 32.0, 35.0, 38.0, 34.0, 30.0, 29.1, 32.0, 31.0, and the weight gains for pigs fed on ration B are 26.0, 24.0, 28.0, 29.0, 30.0, 29.0, 32.0, 26.0, 31.0, 29.0, 32.1, 28.0.

The *statistical* question is whether or not the pigs fed on the different rations come from the same universe with respect to weight gains. One way to tackle this problem is to assume that the order of the pig scores listed *within* each ration group is random—perhaps the order of the stalls the pigs were kept in, their alphabetical-name order, or any other random order *not related to their weights*. Then match the first pig on ration A with the first pig on ration B, the second pigs, the third pigs, and so forth, and count the number of matched pairs on which ration A does better. On nine of twelve pairings ration A does better, that is, 31.0 > 26.0, 34.0 > 24.0, and so forth. (Actually, the tenth and eleventh pairs were ties in the original data, and I arbitrarily broke one tie in favor of ration A and the other in favor of ration B, respectively.)

Now we can ask, *if* the two rations are equally good, how often will one exceed the other nine or more times out of twelve. This is the same as asking how often either heads *or* tails will come up nine or more times of twelve tosses (because, as far as we know, either ration may be as good as or better than the other, this is a "two-tailed" test). Run perhaps fifty trials as in Table 23.7.

In eight of fifty trials one or the other ration had nine or more tosses in its favor. Therefore, the probability is eight of fifty (16 per cent) that samples this different would be generated by chance if the samples came from the same universe.

EXAMPLE 10

Another way to handle the data given in Example 9 is to order the twenty-four pigs from high to low this way: 38 (ration A), 35 (A), 34(A), 34(A), 32(A), 32(A), 32(B), 32(B), 31(A), 31(B), 31(A), 30(A), 30(B), 29(A), 29(A), 29(B), 29(B), 29(B), 28(B), 28(B), 26(A), 26(B), 26(B), 24(B).

Take twelve red and twelve black cards, shuffle them, and deal out thirteen cards. (It is neater to deal out twelve, half the total, but the tie for twelfth and thirteenth places makes the situation a bit messy.) Count the proportion of the hands in which one ration comes up nine or more times in the first *thirteen* cards, to reflect ration A's appearance nine times among the highest thirteen weight gains. Table 23.8. shows the results of fifty hands. In eight (marked by asterisks)

13. The data for this example are drawn from W. J. Dixon and F. J. Massey (1957, p. 122), which offers an orthodox method of handling the problem with a t test.

Table 23.7.

Trial	*Heads (Ration A)*	*Tails (Ration B)*	*Trial*	*Heads (Ration A)*	*Tails (Ration B)*
1	6	6	26	6	6
2	4	8	27	5	7
3	6	6	28	7	5
4	7	5	29	4	8
5	3	9	30	6	6
6	5	7	31	9	3
7	8	4	32	2	10
8	6	6	33	7	5
9	7	5	34	5	7
10	9	3	35	6	6
11	7	5	36	8	4
12	3	9	37	6	6
13	5	7	38	4	8
14	6	6	39	5	7
15	6	6	40	8	4
16	8	4	41	5	7
17	5	7	42	6	6
18	9	3	43	5	7
19	6	6	44	7	5
20	7	5	45	6	6
21	4	8	46	4	8
22	10	2	47	5	7
23	6	6	48	5	7
24	5	7	49	8	4
25	3	9	50	7	5

of the fifty (16 per cent) there were nine or more either red or black cards in the first thirteen cards. Again the results suggest that it would be slightly unusual for the results to favor one ration or the other so strongly just by chance if the universe is really the same, but this test is much less conclusive than the previous one because of the problem of the ties between the twelfth- and thirteenth-highest weight gains.

The decisions that are warranted on the basis of the estimates depend upon one's purpose. If a scientific paper on the merits of ration A is the ultimate purpose, it would be sensible to test another batch of pigs to get further evidence. (Or you could take these data to a trained statistician for a slightly more precise evaluation.) But, if the goal is a decision on which type of ration to buy for a small farm, just go ahead and buy ration A, because, even if it is no better than ration B, you have strong evidence that it is no *worse*.

Table 23.8.

Trial	*Black*	*Red*	*Trial*	*Black*	*Red*	*Trial*	*Black*	*Red*
*1	4	9	19	8	5	37	6	7
2	8	5	20	5	8	38	8	5
3	5	8	21	8	5	39	7	6
4	6	7	*22	9	4	40	6	7
5	6	7	23	7	6	41	6	7
*6	4	9	24	7	6	42	7	6
7	5	8	25	8	5	43	5	8
*8	4	9	26	5	8	44	8	5
9	8	5	27	7	6	45	7	6
*10	3	10	28	6	7	46	7	6
11	6	7	29	5	8	47	8	5
12	7	6	30	7	6	48	5	8
13	7	6	31	6	7	49	7	6
14	6	7	*32	9	4	50	7	6
15	7	6	*33	3	10			
*16	9	4	34	6	7			
17	5	8	35	6	7			
18	7	6	36	6	7			

Notice how we proceeded in Examples 9 and 10. The data were originally quantitative, that is, we had weight gains in *pounds* for each pig. But for simplicity we classified the data into simpler forms. The first form was simply *higher-lower,* obtained by randomly pairing the observations (assuming alphabetical letter or stall number or whatever was the cause of the order in which the data were presented to be random). The second form was a *rank order,* from highest to lowest. Classifying the data in either of these ways *loses some information* and makes the subsequent tests somewhat cruder than mathematical analysis could provide, but the loss of efficiency is not crucial in many such cases.

EXAMPLE 11

Another way to approach the pig-ration problem does not require converting the quantitative data into qualitative data and therefore loses no information. Begin by observing that, *if* the two rations are the same, then each of the observed weight gains came from the same universe. Therefore, write down each of the twenty-four weight gains on a blank index card. We then have one card each for 31, 34, 29, 26, and so on. (Drop the decimal points that were arbitrarily added in Example 9 to break ties.) Shuffle the twenty-four cards thoroughly, and deal two hands of twelve cards each. Call the first ''ration A'' and the second "ration B." Reckon the average weight gain for the two hands, and record it as in Table 23.9. Reshuffle, and repeat several times.

In none of the first ten trials did the difference in the means of the random hands exceed the observed difference between rations A and B. (The difference between group *totals* tells the same story and is faster, requiring no division calculations.) Ordinarily I would quit dealing at such a point, confident that a difference in means that great is not likely to happen by chance. For pedagogical purposes, however, Table 23.9. shows fifty trials of which only one (the thirty-ninth) is as "far out" as the observed samples. These data give us an estimate of the probability that the two rations do not come from the same universe—approximately 49/50, or 98 per cent. (Compare this estimate

Table 23.9.

	Mean of First Twelve Observations (First Hand)	*Mean of Second Twelve Observations (Second Hand)*	*Difference*
Actually Observed	381 ÷ 12 = 31.75	344 ÷ 12 = 28.67	3.08
Trial			
1	368 ÷ 12 = 30.67	357 ÷ 12 = 29.75	.87
2	364 ÷ 12 = 30.33	361 ÷ 12 = 30.08	.25
3	352 ÷ 12 = 29.33	373 ÷ 12 = 31.08	(1.75)
4	378 ÷ 12 = 31.50	347 ÷ 12 = 28.92	2.58
5	365 ÷ 12 = 30.42	360 ÷ 12 = 30.00	.42
6	352 ÷ 12 = 29.33	373 ÷ 12 = 31.08	(1.75)
7	355 ÷ 12 = 29.58	370 ÷ 12 = 30.83	(1.25)
8	366 ÷ 12 = 30.50	359 ÷ 12 = 29.92	.58
9	360 ÷ 12 = 30.00	365 ÷ 12 = 30.42	(.42)
10	355 ÷ 12 = 29.58	370 ÷ 12 = 30.83	(1.25)
11	359 ÷ 12 = 29.92	366 ÷ 12 = 30.50	(.58)
12	369 ÷ 12 = 30.75	356 ÷ 12 = 29.67	1.08
13	360 ÷ 12 = 30.00	365 ÷ 12 = 30.42	(.42)
14	377 ÷ 12 = 31.42	348 ÷ 12 = 29.00	2.42
15	365 ÷ 12 = 30.42	360 ÷ 12 = 30.00	.42
16	364 ÷ 12 = 30.33	361 ÷ 12 = 30.08	.25
17	363 ÷ 12 = 30.25	362 ÷ 12 = 30.17	.08
18	365 ÷ 12 = 30.42	360 ÷ 12 = 30.00	.42
19	369 ÷ 12 = 30.75	356 ÷ 12 = 29.67	1.08
20	369 ÷ 12 = 30.75	356 ÷ 12 = 29.67	1.08
21	369 ÷ 12 = 30.75	356 ÷ 12 = 29.67	1.08
22	364 ÷ 12 = 30.33	361 ÷ 12 = 30.08	.25
23	363 ÷ 12 = 30.25	362 ÷ 12 = 30.17	.08

	Mean of Frist Twelve Observations (First Hand)	*Mean of Second Twelve Observations (Second Hand)*	*Difference*
24	363 ÷ 12 = 30.25	362 ÷ 12 = 30.17	.08
25	364 ÷ 12 = 30.33	361 ÷ 12 = 30.08	.25
26	359 ÷ 12 = 29.92	366 ÷ 12 = 30.50	(.58)
27	362 ÷ 12 = 30.17	363 ÷ 12 = 30.25	(.08)
28	362 ÷ 12 = 30.17	363 ÷ 12 = 30.25	(.08)
29	373 ÷ 12 = 31.08	352 ÷ 12 = 29.33	1.75
30	367 ÷ 12 = 30.58	358 ÷ 12 = 29.83	.75
31	376 ÷ 12 = 31.33	349 ÷ 12 = 29.08	2.25
32	365 ÷ 12 = 30.42	360 ÷ 12 = 30.00	.42
33	357 ÷ 12 = 29.75	368 ÷ 12 = 30.67	(1.42)
34	349 ÷ 12 = 29.08	376 ÷ 12 = 31.33	2.25
35	356 ÷ 12 = 29.67	369 ÷ 12 = 30.75	(1.08)
36	359 ÷ 12 = 29.92	366 ÷ 12 = 30.50	(.58)
37	372 ÷ 12 = 31.00	353 ÷ 12 = 29.42	1.58
38	368 ÷ 12 = 30.67	357 ÷ 12 = 29.75	.92
39	344 ÷ 12 = 28.67	381 ÷ 12 = 31.75	(3.08)
40	365 ÷ 12 = 30.42	360 ÷ 12 = 30.00	.42
41	375 ÷ 12 = 31.25	350 ÷ 12 = 29.17	2.08
42	353 ÷ 12 = 29.42	372 ÷ 12 = 31.00	(1.58)
43	357 ÷ 12 = 29.75	368 ÷ 12 = 30.67	(.92)
44	363 ÷ 12 = 30.25	362 ÷ 12 = 30.17	.08
45	353 ÷ 12 = 29.42	372 ÷ 12 = 31.00	(1.58)
46	354 ÷ 12 = 29.50	371 ÷ 12 = 30.92	(1.42)
47	353 ÷ 12 = 29.42	372 ÷ 12 = 31.00	(1.58)
48	366 ÷ 12 = 30.50	359 ÷ 12 = 29.92	.58
49	364 ÷ 12 = 30.33	361 ÷ 12 = 30.08	.25
50	370 ÷ 12 = 30.83	355 ÷ 12 = 29.58	1.25

with the probability of roughly 99 per cent estimated with the standard *t* test, that is, a significance level of 1 per cent.) On the average, the test described in this section yields a significance level as high as such mathematical-probability tests as the *t* test, that is, it is just as efficient, though the tests described in Examples 10 and 11 are likely to be less efficient.[14]

14. Note to statisticians: The test described in this section is nonparametric and therefore makes no assumptions about the shapes of the distributions, which is well because we would be on soft ground if we assumed normality in the pig-ration case, given the sample sizes. This test does not, however, throw away information as do the rank and median tests illustrated earlier. And indeed, this test proves to be more powerful than the other nonparametric tests. After developing this test, I discovered that its general logic follows the tradition of the "randomization" tests based on an idea by R. A. Fisher (1935) and worked out for the two-sample cases by E. J. G. Pitman (1937). But the only mentions of *sampling* from the universe of possibilities are in M. Dwass (1957) and J. H. Chung and D. Fraser (1958). I am grateful to J. Pratt for bringing the later literature to my attention.

This example illustrates how the ***dispersion within samples*** affects the difficulty of finding out whether or not the samples differ from each other. For example, the average weight gain for ration A was 32 pounds, versus 29 pounds for ration B. If *all* the ration A-fed pigs had gained weight within a range of 29.9 and 31.1 pounds, say, and if all the ration B-fed pigs had gained weight within a range of 28.9 and 29.1 pounds—that is, if the highest weight gain in ration B had been lower than the lowest weight gain in ration B—then there would be no question that ration A is better, and even fewer observations would have made this point clear. Variation (dispersion) is thus of great importance in statistics and in the social sciences. The larger the dispersion among the observations *within* the samples—as measured by the standard deviation, the range, or some other device—the larger the *sample size* necessary to make a conclusive comparison between two groups or reliable estimates of summarization statistics.

Are you performing your tests by hand rather than using a computer? In a few years everyone will be using computers right at his desk for such tasks. But in the meantime you might prefer to work with the median instead of the mean, for the median requires less computation. Simply compare the difference in medians of the Monte Carlo twelve-pig samples to the difference in medians of the actual samples, just as was done with the means. You may need a somewhat larger number of Monte Carlo trials when working with medians, however, for they tend to be less precise than means.

EXAMPLE 12

The pig-ration example dealt with equal numbers of pigs in each litter. The general technique demonstrated in Example 11 is quite flexible, however, and can be used with unequal-sized samples. Consider the 1961 data for the price of a fifth of Seagram 7 Crown whisky in the various states. (Some states are omitted for technical reasons.) The question is whether the price is systematically different in the sixteen "monopoly" states in which the state government owns the retail liquor stores, compared to the twenty-seven states in which retail liquor stores are privately owned, or whether the observed differences might have occurred by chance. The prices for the sixteen monopoly states are $4.65, $4.55, $4.11, $4.15, $4.20, $4.55, $3.80, $4.00, $4.19, $4.75, $4.74, $4.50, $4.10, $4.00, $5.05, and $4.20.

The prices for the private-enterprise states are $4.82, $5.29, $4.89, $4.95, $4.55, $4.90, $5.25, $5.30, $4.29, $4.85, $4.54, $4.75, $4.85, $4.85, $4.50, $4.75, $4.79, $4.85, $4.79, $4.95, $4.95, $4.75, $5.20, $5.10, $4.80, and $4.29.[15] Now write each of the *forty-three* prices on

15. The data are from *The Liquor Handbook* (1962, p. 68). Seven states are omitted for various reasons.

a playing card, shuffle the cards, and deal out sixteen. Do this repeatedly. The probability that monopoly states' prices are "really" lower than those of the private-enterprise states is estimated by the proportion of times that the sum (or average) of the sixteen prices dealt is less than (or equal to) the sum (or average) of the actual sixteen prices.[16]

EXAMPLE 13

In Examples 2, 5, and 7 we investigated whether or not the results shown by a *single* sample are sufficiently different from a null hypothesis so that the sample really seems to have come from the hypothesized universe. In Examples 9, 10, and 11 we then investigated whether or not the results shown by *two* samples suggest that the *two* samples had come from the *same* universe, a universe that was assumed to be the sum (average) of the two samples. Now we investigate whether or not *several* samples come from the same universe.

If one tries each of 100 different pig rations on twelve pigs, *some* of the rations will show much better results than will others *just by chance,* just as one family in sixteen will have a "high" number of daughters in its first four children. Therefore, it is *wrong* to try out the 100 pig rations, to pick out the ration that shows the best results, and to compare it statistically with the average (sum) of all the other rations or, worse, with the poorest ration (Chapter 22 discusses why). Rather, we need a test that prevents our falling into such traps. Such a test usually operates by taking into account the differences among *all* the rations that were tried.

The method of Example 11 can be extended to handle this problem. Assume that *four* rations were each tested on twelve pigs. The weight gains in pounds for the pigs fed on ration C were 30, 30, 32, 31, 29, 27, 25, 30, 31, 32, 34, 33. For ration D the weight gains were 32, 25, 31, 26, 32, 27, 28, 29, 29, 28, 23, 25. Make a set of *forty-eight* index cards, one for each weight gain, and shuffle them. Then deal out sets of four hands randomly. Count the trials in which the differences between the highest and lowest groups are not as large as the differences between the highest and lowest observed samples. The proportion of such trials to the total number of trials is the probability that all four samples do not come from the same universe.

Another method of reckoning is to compute the absolute difference between each *pair* of rations, six differences in all, converting all minus (−) signs to plus (+) differences. Then *total* the six differences, and compare the total with the sum of the six differences in the *observed* sample. The proportion of times that the observed-sample sum

16. Various tests indicate that the difference between the groups of states is highly significant. See J. L. Simon (1966b).

is not exceeded by the sum of the differences in the trials is the probability that the observed samples do not come from the same universe —in this case.[17]

EXAMPLE 14

Some multisample problems lack quantitative data. Consider, for example, four different psychological treatments designed to rehabilitate juvenile delinquents. Instead of a score, there is only a "yes" or a "no" answer as to whether the juvenile has been rehabilitated or has gotten into trouble again. Label the treatments P, R, S, and T, each of which is administered to a separate group of twenty juvenile delinquents. The number of rehabilitations per group is P, seventeen; R, ten; S, ten; T, seven. Is it improbable that all four groups come from the same universe?

If all four groups come from the same universe, that universe has an estimated rehabilitation rate of

$$\frac{17 + 10 + 10 + 7}{20 + 20 + 20 + 20} = \frac{11}{20} = \frac{55}{100}$$

Therefore, select twenty two-digit numbers for each group from the random-number table, marking "yes" for each number 1–55 and "no" for each number 56–100. Conduct a number of such trials. Then count the proportion of times that the difference between the highest and lowest groups is larger than the widest observed difference, that between P and T $(17 - 7 = 10)$. Table 23.10. shows that none of the first

Table 23.10.

Trial	*P*	*R*	*S*	*T*	*Largest Minus Smallest*
1	11	9	8	12	4
2	10	10	12	12	2
3	9	12	8	12	4
4	9	11	12	10	3
5	10	10	11	12	1
6	11	11	9	11	2

17. Note to statisticians: Computing the sum of *squared* differences renders this test superficially more similar to the analysis of variance but will not alter the results. This test has not been discussed in the statistical literature, to my knowledge, except perhaps for a faint suggestion at the end of Chung and Fraser (1958). This and the two-sample test can easily be performed with canned computer programs. Beside their advantages of nonparametricity, they are equally efficient and vastly easier to teach and to understand than the t test and the analysis of variance. Therefore, I believe that these tests should be "treatments of choice," as the doctors say.

six trials shows anywhere near as large a difference, suggesting that it would be rare for four treatments that are ''really'' similar to show so great a difference. There is thus reason to believe that P and T differ in their effects.

This chapter has introduced the basic ideas of probability statistics, and it began the demonstrations of how problems in probability statistics may be solved with Monte Carlo methods. The next chapter continues the demonstrations and considers some pitfalls in the application of probability statistics. Exercises covering both chapters are found there.

CHAPTER 24

Statistics of Probability: Part II

Independence and Strength of Relationships

In this chapter we continue the demonstrations of Monte Carlo solutions to probability-statistical problems, beginning with such matters as tests of independence and strength of relationship. Then we shall discuss various situations that cannot be treated straightforwardly with probability techniques and how to avoid the dangers of such situations.

EXAMPLE 15

The important concept of independent events was introduced earlier; various scientific and statistical decisions depend upon whether or not a series of events is independent. But how does one know whether or not the events are independent? Let us consider a baseball example.

Baseball players and their coaches believe that on some days and during some weeks a player will bat better than on other days and during other weeks. But, even if his hits come randomly, a player will have runs of good luck and runs of bad luck just by chance, as does a card player. The problem, then, is to determine whether the runs of good and bad batting are merely runs of chance—which would imply that the batter's ability is the same at all times—or whether a batter really does have a tendency to do better at some times than at others.

Let's analyze the batting of a player we shall call "Slug." Here are the results of Slug's first 100 times at bat during the 1967 season (H = hit, O = out) :

OOOOOO H OO H O HH OOOOOOOO H
OOOOO H OOOO HH OOOOO H OO H O
H OOO HH OOOOO H O H OOOO HH
O HH OOOOOOOOOO H OOO H OO H
OO H O H OO H OOO H OOO.

Now, do Slug's hits tend to come in bunches? That would be the case if he really did have a tendency to do better at some times than at others. What we can do is to compare Slug's results with those of a deck of cards or a set of random numbers that we know has no such tendency to do better at some times than at others.

During this period of 100 times at bat, Slug has averaged .250—one hit in every four times at bat. This average is the same as the chance for one card suit's coming up. We choose hearts and prepare a deck of 100 cards, twenty-five H (hearts, or hit) and seventy-five O (other suit, or out). Here is the sequence in which the 100 randomly shuffled cards fell:

OO H OOOO HH OOO HHH OOOOO H OOO
H OO H OOOO H O HH OOOOOOOOO H
OOOOOO HH OOOOO HHH OOOOOO H
O H O H OO H O H OOOOOOOOO
H OOOOOOO HHH OO.

Then compare whether or not Slug's hits are bunched up more than they would be by random chance; you can do so by *counting the clusters* (also called "runs") of consecutive hits and outs for Slug and for the cards. Slug had forty-three clusters, which is more than the thirty-seven clusters in the cards; it therefore does not seem that there is a tendency for Slug's hits to cluster together. (A larger number of clusters indicates a lower tendency to cluster.)

Of course, the single trial of 100 cards shown might have an unusually high or low number of clusters. To be safer, lay out, say, ten trials of 100 cards each, and compare Slug's number of clusters with the various trials. The proportion of trials with more clusters than Slug has indicates whether or not Slug's hits have a tendency to bunch up. (But caution: This proportion cannot be interpreted directly as a probability.)

The coach insists, however, that there are some periods of time when a player is in a "slump," and he says this belief is proved by the fact that the player sometimes does not get a hit for an abnormally long period of time. We can test whether or not the coach is right by comparing an average player's longest slump in a season with the longest run of outs in the first card trial. Assume that Slug is a player picked *at random*. Then compare Slug's longest slump, ten outs in a row, with the longest cluster of the first trial with the cards, nine outs. This result suggests that Slug's apparent slump might well have resulted by chance, even though the chances of his getting a hit remained .250 during the entire season, that is, even if he really suffered no slump. The estimate can be made more accurate by taking the *average* longest slump (cluster of outs) in all ten trials. But notice that we do *not* compare Slug's slump against the longest slump found in the ten trials. We want to know the longest cluster of outs that would be found under *average* conditions, and the hand with the longest slump is *not* average or typical. Determining whether to compare Slug's slump with the *average* longest slump or with the *longest* of the ten longest slumps is a decision of crucial importance. There are no mathematical or logical rules to help you. What is required is hard, clear thinking. Experience can help you think clearly, of course, but these decisions are not easy or obvious even to the most experienced statisticians.

The coach may then refer to the protracted slump of one of the twenty-five players on his club to prove that slumps really occur. But, of twenty-five random trials, one will contain a slump longer than any of the other twenty-four, and that slump will be considerably longer than average. A fair comparison, then, would be between the longest slump of his longest-slumping player and the longest run of outs found among twenty-five random trials. In fact, the longest run among twenty-five hands of 100 cards was fifteen outs in a row. And, if we had set some of the hands for lower (and higher) batting averages than .250, the longest slump in the cards would have been even longer.

This study of batting illustrates how one can test for independence among various trials. The trials are independent if each observation is randomly chosen with replacement from the universe, in which case there is no reason to believe that one observation will be related to the observations directly before and after; "the coin has no memory." The year-to-year level of Lake Michigan is an example in which observations are *not* independent. If Lake Michigan is very high in one year, it is likely to be higher than average the following year because some of the high level carries over from one year into the next.[1] We could test this hypothesis by writing down whether the level in each year from, say, 1860 to 1955 was higher or lower than the median

1. Example from W. A. Wallis (1957).

level for those years and then comparing the number of runs with a deck of that many cards; we would find fewer runs in the lake level than in an average hand of ninety-six (1956 — 1860) cards, though this test is hardly necessary. (But are the *changes* in Lake Michigan from year to year independent? If the level went up last year, is there a better than 50-50 chance that the level will also go up this year? The answer to this question is not so obvious. One could compare the numbers of runs of ups and downs against an average hand of cards, just as with the hits and outs in baseball.)

EXAMPLE 16

A scientist often wants to know whether or not two characteristics go together, that is, whether or not they are correlated (associated). For example, is athletic ability correlated with high I.Q.? That is, do youths with high athletic ability tend to also have high I.Q.s?

Physical-education scores of a group of ten high-school boys are shown, ordered from high to low, in Table 24.1., along with the I.Q. score for each boy. The ranks for each student's athletic and I.Q. score are then shown in columns 3 and 4.

Table 24.1. HYPOTHETICAL ATHLETIC AND I.Q. SCORES FOR HIGH SCHOOL BOYS

Athletic Score (1)	*I.Q. Score* (2)	*Athletic Rank* (3)	*I.Q. Rank* (4)
97	114	1	3
94	120	2	1
93	107	3	7
90	113	4	4
87	118	5	2
86	101	6	8
86	109	7	6
85	110	8	5
81	100	9	9
76	99	10	10

Now take ten cards, one of each denomination from ace to ten, shuffle, and deal five cards to correspond to the first five athletic ranks. The face values then correspond to the I.Q. ranks. Under the null hypothesis the athletic ranks will not be associated with the I.Q. ranks. Add the face values in the first five cards in each trial; the first hand includes 2, 4, 5, 6, and 9, so the sum is 26. Record, shuffle, and repeat perhaps ten times, as in Table 24.2.

Table 24.2.

Trial	*Sum of I.Q. Ranks*	*Trial*	*Sum of I.Q. Ranks*	*Trial*	*Sum of I.Q. Ranks*	*Trial*	*Sum of I.Q. Ranks*
1	26	11	35	21	30	31	30
2	23	12	36	22	31	32	21
3	22	13	31	23	35	33	25
4	37	14	29	24	25	34	19
*5	16	15	32	25	33	35	29
6	22	16	25	26	30	36	23
7	22	17	25	27	24	37	23
8	28	18	29	28	29	38	34
9	38	19	25	29	30	39	23
10	22	20	22	30	31	40	26

Now compare the random results to the sum of the observed ranks of the five top athletes, which equals 17 (Table 24.1., column 4). The observed sum is lower than that in all but one (shown by an asterisk) of the ten random trials (trial 5), which suggests that there is a good chance (9 to 1) that the five best athletes will not have I.Q. scores that high by chance. But it might be well to deal some more to get a more reliable average. We add thirty hands, and thirty-nine of the total forty hands exceed the observed rank value, so the likelihood that the observed correlation of athletic and I.Q. scores would occur by chance is about 2.5 per cent. In other words, the odds are 39 to 1 against there being no association between athletic ability and I.Q. score, and it therefore seems reasonable to believe that high athletic ability tends to accompany a high I.Q.

Some explanation is required of the procedure for adding ranks for the first *five* athletes and comparing them with the second five, rather than comparing the top three, say, with the bottom seven. We could indeed have compared the top three, two, four, or one with the rest. The first reason for splitting the group in half is that an even split provides fuller information and therefore greater efficiency. (I cannot prove this to you, but perhaps it makes intuitive sense.) A second reason is that getting into the habit of looking at an even split reduces the chances that you will pick and choose in such a manner as to fool yourself. For example, if the I.Q. ranks of the top five athletes were 3, 2, 1, 10, and 9, we would be kidding ourselves if, after looking the data over, we drew the line between athletes 3 and 4.

A simpler but less efficient approach to this same problem is to classify the top-half athletes by whether or not they were also in the top half of the I.Q. scores. Of the first five athletes, four were in the top five I.Q. scores. Then shuffle five black and five red cards and see how often four or more (that is, four or five) blacks come up within the first five cards. The proportion of times that four or more blacks occurs in the trial is the likelihood that the observed scores come from the same universe, that is, that there is no association. Table 24.3. shows a proportion of five trials out of twenty, yielding a much weaker result than did the previous method.

Table 24.3.

Trial	*Score*	*Trial*	*Score*	*Trial*	*Score*	*Trial*	*Score*
1	4	6	2	11	3	16	3
2	2	7	4	12	1	17	2
3	2	8	3	13	3	18	2
4	2	9	3	14	3	19	2
5	3	10	4	15	4	20	4

We have proceeded on the theory that, if there is *any* relationship between athletics and I.Q., then the better athletes have higher rather than lower I.Q. scores. The justification for this assumption is that past research suggests that it is probably true. But, if we had *not* had the benefit of that past research, we would then have had to proceed somewhat differently; we would have had to consider the possibility that the top five athletes could have I.Q. scores either higher *or* lower than those of the other students. The results of the "two-tail" test would have yielded odds weaker than those we observed.

EXAMPLE 17

In Example 16 we considered how to determine *whether or not* there is a relationship between two variables—in that particular case, whether the characteristics of I.Q. and athletic ability are associated or not. But a scientist frequently wants to know *how strong* a relationship is too, and that is not the same thing as whether or not there *is* a relationship. One important point of difference is that whether or not a relationship is shown to exist with a high probability depends upon how big a sample you have. If only a very faint relationship existed between I.Q. and athletic ability, the relationship would appear significant in a sample of perhaps 100,000 boys, but the same faint relationship would not show up clearly in a sample of ten, because the chance variation in a small sample masks the effect. This is why the *probability of a relationship's appearing* depends upon the sample size. (This is also an important way in which tests of significance can be deceiving; with a big enough sample, *every* relationship seems significant.) But the *strength* of a relationship is the *same,* no matter how large the sample (though the small sample will yield a less accurate estimate of the strength than will a larger sample).

One way to measure the strength of a relationship is by estimating how good a prediction of one variable can be made on the basis of the other variable. Consider, for example, predicting a boy's I.Q. score. Without any other information, your chance of predicting correctly that a boy will have an I.Q. in the top half of his class is 1 in 2, a probability of .5. Now we ask, How much better a prediction can be made if we know his athletic score? Column 4 in Table 24.1. shows that four of five top athletes are in the top half in I.Q. If we predict that a top athlete will be in the top I.Q. half, the chance of being right is four in five, or .8, a measure of the strength of the relationship showing that a prediction based on the relationship will be considerably better than chance. (Or, one might compute a statistic like

$$\frac{.80 - .50}{.50}$$

to indicate *how much* better than chance the prediction will be.)

There are many measures of the strength of an association other than the simple one just shown. The most conventional is the *correlation coefficient,* which has the advantage that it is used so frequently that one soon gets an intuitive idea of what is a strong coefficient and what is a weak one, though this intuition varies from field to field. (Educational psychologists are often delighted with correlation coefficients that an economist or experimental psychologist would throw down in disgust.) On the other hand, the concept of the correlation coefficient is sufficiently complex so that it remains a black-box mystery to students for quite a while. (But see the following example for some clues to what correlation is.)

Our simple example can illustrate that the strength of the relationship does not depend upon the sample size. If the sample were larger and there were two boys or ten boys instead of only one boy for each score shown in Table 24.1., 80 per cent of the top athletes would still be in the top half on I.Q., and a prediction based on the relationship would still have a probability of .8 of being right. But, if you go back and rework Example 16 using two (or ten) observations instead of just one (that is, a sample of twenty or 100 boys) for each line of data, you will find that the probability that the relationship is caused by chance is smaller than the .025 (2½ per cent) found with the sample of ten boys. This comparison shows that one's judgment of *whether or not* there is a relationship is affected by sample size, whereas the *strength* of a relationship is not.

EXAMPLE 18

The previous examples investigated the relationship between I.Q. and athletic score by ranking the two sets of scores. But ranking scores loses some efficiency because it uses only an ordinal, rather than a cardinal, scale (see Chapter 20) ; the numerical shadings are lost when we convert to ranks. Therefore it is worth considering a test of correlation that uses the original cardinal scores.

First a little background: Figures 24.1. through 24.3. show two hypothetical cases of very high association among the I.Q. and athletic scores used in previous examples.

Figure 24.1. indicates that, the higher the I.Q. score, the higher the athletic score. With a boy's athletic score you can thus predict quite well his I.Q. score by means of the hand-drawn line—or vice versa. The same is true of Figure 24.2., but in the opposite way. (Notice that, even though athletic score is on the x axis [horizontal]

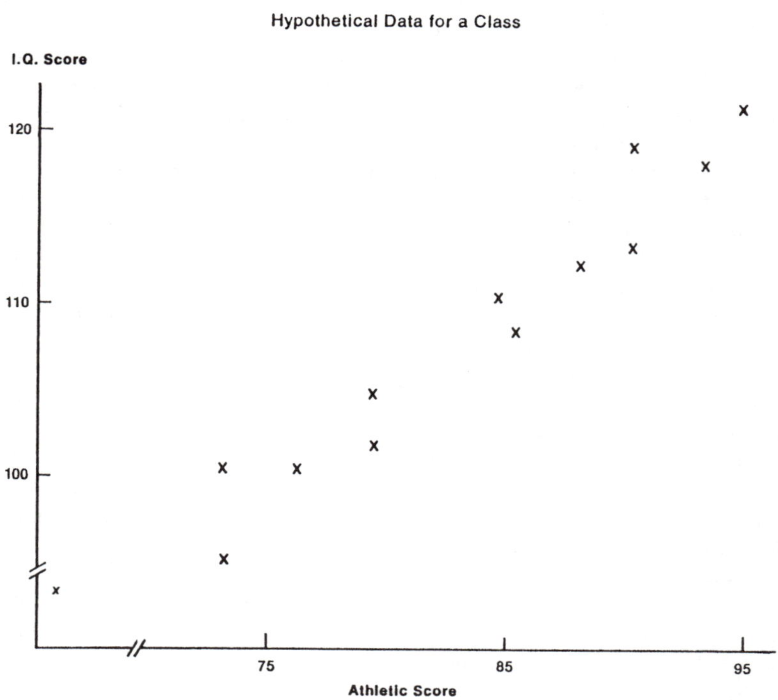

Figure 24.1.

Hypothetical Data for a Class

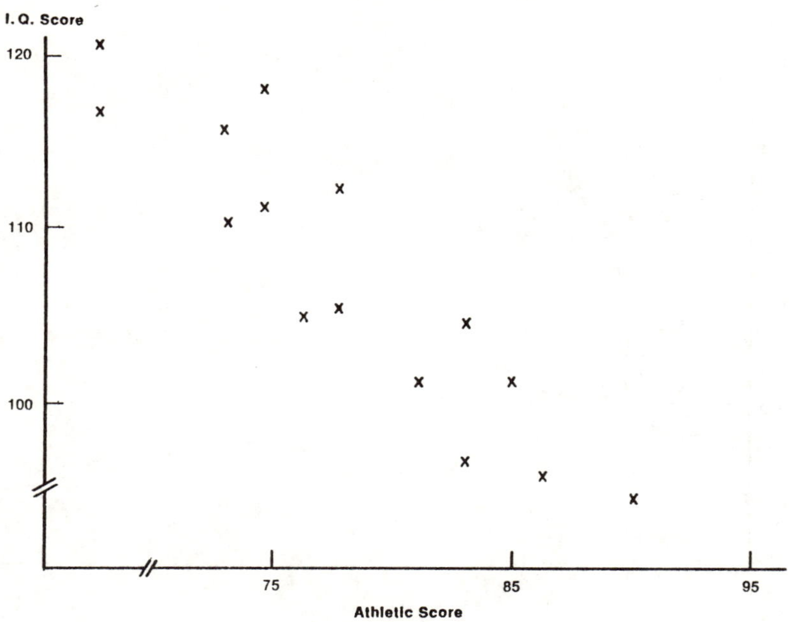

Figure 24.2.

and I.Q. score is on the y axis [vertical], the athletic score does not cause I.Q. score. It is an unfortunate deficiency of such diagrams that *some* variable must arbitrarily be placed on the x axis, whether you intend to suggest causation or not.)

In Figure 24.3., which plots the scores as given on page 399, the prediction of athletic score given I.Q. score, or vice versa, is not so clear-cut. On the basis of the figure alone, one can say only that there *might* be some association between the two variables.

Now we can use a handy property of numbers. Consider the cases in which there is a perfect (linear) association between x and y_1 and x and y_2; the numbers shown in Table 24.4. are those that would be consistent with perfect associations. Notice the sum of the multiples of the x and y values. It is higher (xy_1) and lower (xy_2) than for any other possible way of arranging the y's. Any other arrangement of the y's (y_3, for example, chosen at random), when multiplied by the x's (for example, xy_3), produces a sum that falls somewhere between the sums of xy_1 and xy_2, as is the case when y_3 is also less correlated with the x's. (Table 24.4. shows how the sum of the products of the ob-

Hypothetical Data for a Class

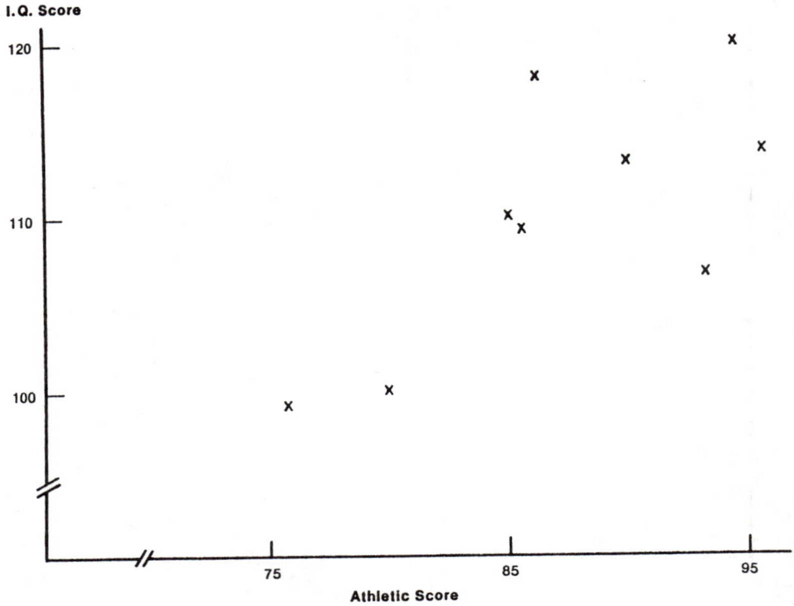

Figure 24.3.

served I.Q. scores multiplied by athletic scores [column 7] is *between* the sums that would occur if the I.Q. scores were ranked from best to worst [column 3] and worst to best [column 5].) The extent of correlation (association) can thus be measured by whether the sum of the multiples of the observed x and y values is relatively high or low compared to random sums.

Table 24.4.

1	2	3	4	5	6	7
x	y_1	xy_1	y_2	xy_2	y_3	xy_3
2	2	4	10	20	4	8
4	4	16	8	32	8	32
6	6	36	6	36	6	36
8	8	64	4	32	2	16
10	10	100	2	20	10	100
		220		140		192

Table 24.5.

1 *Athletic Score*	2 *I.Q. Score*	3 *Column 1 × Column 2*	4 *I.Q. Score*	5 *Column 1 × Column 4*	6 *Actual I.Q.*	7 *Column 1 × Column 6*
97	120	11640	99	9603	114	11058
94	118	11092	100	9400	120	11280
93	114	10602	101	9393	107	9951
90	113	10170	107	9630	113	10170
87	110	9570	109	9483	118	10266
86	109	9374	110	8460	101	8686
86	107	9202	113	9718	109	9374
85	101	8585	114	9690	110	9350
81	100	8100	118	9558	100	8100
76	99	7524	120	9120	99	7524
		95859		95055		95759

Table 24.6.

Athletic Score	1	2	3	4	5	6	7	8	9	10
97	114	109	110	118	107	114	107	120	100	114
94	101	113	113	101	118	100	110	109	120	107
93	107	118	100	99	120	101	114	99	110	113
90	113	101	118	114	101	113	100	118	99	99
87	120	100	101	100	110	107	113	114	101	118
86	100	110	120	107	113	110	118	101	118	101
86	110	107	99	109	100	120	120	113	114	120
85	99	99	104	120	99	109	101	107	109	109
81	118	120	114	110	114	99	99	100	107	100
76	109	114	109	113	109	118	109	110	113	110

Athletic Score	11	12	13	14	15	16	17	18	19	20
97	109	113	101	109	107	100	99	113	99	110
94	101	110	114	118	101	107	114	101	109	113
93	120	120	100	120	114	113	100	100	120	109
90	110	118	109	110	99	109	107	109	110	99
87	100	100	120	99	118	114	110	110	107	101
86	118	99	107	100	109	118	113	118	100	118
86	99	101	99	101	100	99	101	107	114	120
85	107	114	110	114	120	110	120	120	118	100
81	114	107	113	113	110	101	109	114	101	114
76	113	109	118	107	113	120	118	99	113	107

Now we attack the I.Q.-athletic score problem in this fashion. First multiply the x and y values of the observations, and sum them (95,759) as in Table 24.5. Then write the ten I.Q. scores on cards, shuffle well, and assign the cards in random order to the ten athletes, as shown in column 1 in Table 24.6. Multiply by the x's, and sum. Do this for a number of trials. If the I.Q. scores and athletic scores are *positively* associated, that is, if high I.Q.s and high athletic scores go together, then the sum of the multiplications for the observed sample will be higher than for most of the random trials. (If high I.Q.s go with low athletic scores, the sum of the multiplications for the observed sample will be *lower* than most of the random trials.)

The sums of the multiplications for 20 trials are shown in Table 24.7. No random-trial sum was as high as the observed sum, which suggests that the probability of an association this strong happening by chance is very low, approaching zero (an empirically observed probability is never actually zero).

Table 24.7.

Trial	*Sum of Multiplications*	*Trial*	*Sum of Multiplications*
1	95430	11	95406
2	95426	12	95622
3	95446	13	95250
4	95381	14	95599
5	95542	15	95323
6	95362	16	95308
7	95508	17	95220
8	95590	18	95443
9	95379	19	95421
10	95532	20	95528

EXAMPLE 19

The scores for athletic ability and I.Q. in the previous example were *quantitative* data. Therefore, we could use them in their cardinal form and also split them up into "high" and "low" groups, as in Example 16.

Often, however, the individual observations are recorded only as "yes" or "no," which makes it more difficult to ascertain the existence of a relationship. Consider these answers to two public-opinion survey questions: "Do you drink beer?" and "Are you in favor of local option on the sale of beer?"[2]

Table 24.8.

ARE YOU IN FAVOR OF LOCAL OPTION ON THE SALE OF BEER?	DO YOU DRINK BEER?		
	Yes	*No*	*Total*
Approve	37	20	57
Disapprove	15	6	21
Total	52	26	78

Here is the question: Is a person's opinion on local option related to whether or not he drinks beer? There are seventy-eight respondents, fifty-seven of whom approve local option and twenty-one of whom do not. Therefore write "approve" on fifty-seven index cards and "not approve" on twenty-one index cards. Now take *another* set of seventy-eight index cards, preferably of a different color, and write "yes" on fifty-two of them and "no" on twenty-six of them, corresponding to the numbers of people who do and do not drink beer in the sample. Now shuffle the two piles *separately*, and lay them down in random *pairs*, one from each pile. Write down the results of each pair in a table like Table 24.8. Repeat for perhaps ten trials.

If there is a high association between the variables, the observations will bunch up in the two diagonal cells on either diagonal. Therefore, subtract one sum of two diagonal cells from the other sum for the observed case: $(37 + 6) - (20 + 15) = 8$. Compare this difference to those found in random trials. The proportion of times that the trial differences do not exceed the observed difference is the probability that the observed association is not caused by chance. (Notice that, in this case, we are working on the assumption that beer drinking is *positively* associated with approval of local option and not the inverse. We are interested only in differences that are equal to or exceed $+8$ when the northeast-southwest diagonal is subtracted from the northwest-southeast diagonal.)

A series of ten trials in this case (see Table 24.9.) indicates that the observed difference is very often exceeded, which suggests no relationship between beer drinking and opinion.

In a way this test of whether or not there is a relationship in the data in Table 24.9. between beer drinking and option approval is

2. These data are from an example in W. J. Dixon and F. J. Massey (1957, p. 226), in which the problem is tackled with a conventional test (the chi-square).

Table 24.9.

Trial	APPROVE-Yes	APPROVE-No	DISAPPROVE-Yes	DISAPPROVE-No	(Column 1 + Column 4) − (Column 2 + Column 3)*
1	33	24	18	3	36 − 42 = − 6
2	38	19	14	7	45 − 33 = 12
3	39	18	13	8	47 − 31 = 16
4	38	19	14	7	45 − 33 = 12
5	35	22	17	4	39 − 39 = 0
6	35	22	16	5	40 − 38 = 2
7	38	19	14	7	45 − 33 = 12
8	40	19	12	9	49 − 31 = 18
9	40	17	12	9	49 − 31 = 18
10	37	20	15	6	43 − 35 = 8

* In absolute figures.

really a red herring, for such a test is not really sensible. If we compute the proportions of drinkers and nondrinkers who approve local option, we get the results in Table 24.10.

First of all, the *size* of the difference between the groups—only 6 per cent—is too small to mean anything to anyone. But, more important, it simply would not make sense to assume that *not* drinking beer should cause *higher* approval of local option. On both grounds it makes sense simply to act as if there were no difference between the two groups and to run no test.

This example also illustrates another important point. The particular method I used to test for association is decidedly off-beat, but it is still quite correct in the sense that it gives the right answer. But it is not a good test to imitate; instead you should invent your *own* test. The purpose of the forgoing examples is *not* to teach you how to solve problems of these exact types—though you may use any one of them as a model if it closely matches your research situation. Rather, the primary purpose of all these examples is to illustrate how you can set up a set of cards or dice or random numbers that will represent the benchmark universe in which you are interested, in order to see how it behaves when you sample randomly from it, so that you can compare your observed sample with the random trials.

Table 24.10.

	Percentage Approve	*Percentage Disapprove*	*Total*
Beer drinkers	71%	29%	100%
Nonbeer drinkers	77%	23%	100%

Advantages and Disadvantages of Monte Carlo Methods

With card and dice experiments one can make many statistical tests without the mathematical theory of probability. But figuring the answer mathematically is often *quicker,* especially for problems with many observations. For example, imagine that you want to know how often you will get two aces if you deal out hands of only two cards. A random experiment would take a while, but one can figure the answer in a hurry by multiplying $1/13 \times 1/13 = 1/269$, which tells us that, on the average, we shall get two aces in a hand of two cards once in 269 hands.

Mathematical methods can also be useful in more complex problems, though there are many problems that are *so* complex that mathematicians resort to random experiments for estimating the probabilities, using computers rather than cards or dice, to run the experiments in a hurry.

Mathematical methods make handling cardinal quantitative data easy. But, as we demonstrated in the pig-ration example, sometimes card and dice experiments can also be run with quantitative data, without assuming as much as is necessary for the use of mathematical methods.

Though mathematical methods can be quicker, a person who does not expect to use probability statistics very often might find that, in the long run, it is more efficient to spend extra time on slow Monte Carlo trials than on studying the mathematical methods. On the other hand, anyone who plans to work in scientific research should study probability statistics thoroughly, especially because the study deepens one's *intuition* about scientific and mathematical relationships.

A last advantage of Monte Carlo methods is that everything that you do is very explicit and you must think through each step. Such discipline reduces the probability of erroneous calculations from blindly plugging in the wrong method and formula.

It is an apparent disadvantage of Monte Carlo methods executed by hand that large sample sizes are clumsy to work with, as are very small probabilities; for example, it is difficult to work with data on the viewership of educational television stations because the probability of a given person watching may be only 1 in 1,000. But testing problems arise only when the samples are small; with large masses of data the conclusions are obvious without probability statistics. Furthermore, computers can easily be programmed to handle Monte Carlo methods.

One can avoid the tedious work of Monte Carlo experiments by getting the help of a statistician who will use mathematical methods. But—and it is a huge "but"—to be sure that the answer the statistician gives you is the answer you want, you must describe the Monte Carlo trial you would otherwise run to test your results. Then and only then can you be sure that the mathematical test the statistician performs is the right one. If you simply go to him and say, "I want to test whether or not these two samples are different," you are much more likely to get a misleading answer than if you describe to him a Monte Carlo experiment and then ask him merely to perform the same task with mathematical analysis.

If you can say exactly what kind of Monte Carlo trial will give the test you want, you have performed 90 per cent of the work—and the hardest 90 per cent. It takes very hard, very clear thinking. Again, the job is *not* mathematical; if you tell yourself that you cannot do these and similar probability-statistical tests because you do not understand mathematics, you are fooling yourself. If you cannot do correct tests of the type described in this chapter, it is because you are not willing to think hard and clearly. And you cannot shift the burden to a statistician, because then *he* will have to do the hard, clear thinking for you, and he does not know what your study needs as well as you do. Furthermore, mathematical statisticians develop formulas to imitate the Monte Carlo trials you want to run, but they have no special training in deciding which Monte Carlo trials to perform. To repeat, that is the hard, clear thinking that you must do for yourself.

Postscript on Probability Statistics

You should be familiar with two basic calculations in mathematical statistics, and you should know when they are applicable. The first calculation is the *rule of addition.* It states that, when two events are mutually exclusive, the probability of one event *or* the other event (*or* both) is the *sum* of the probabilities of each event happening alone. For example, the probability of drawing a spade is 1/4, and the probability of a heart is 1/4, and both cannot occur in the draw of one card. The probability of drawing *either* a spade *or* a heart is $1/4 + 1/4 = 1/2$. Remember that the rule of addition should be used whenever you use the words "either . . . or (or both)" in the question.

The *multiplication rule* is the most important handy calculation in everyday statistical work. It is used whenever the question is, What is the probability that A *and* B will happen? For example, the probability of having a daughter the first time *and* a daughter the second time is $1/2 \times 1/2 = 1/4$ (on the assumption that the sex of each newborn child is independent of that of the preceding ones). The probability of having four daughters in a row is $1/2 \times 1/2 \times 1/2 \times$

$1/2 = 1/16$, as we approximated earlier with card shuffling. If you want a more precise estimate using the data that 106 males are born for each 100 females, the appropriate calculation would be $(100/206) \times (100/206) \times (100/206) \times (100/206)$. The multiplication rule is very handy for quick estimates of whether or not data result from chance. For example, if you compare the advertising effectiveness of large versus small firms in five separate years and if the small firms do better in each of the five years, the probability that this performance results from chance is $(1/2)^5 = 1/2 \times 1/2 \times 1/2 \times 1/2 \times 1/2 = 1/32$ (if you hypothesized that small firms do better). If the data show that the smaller firms do better in seven years out of eight, you will need a more complicated calculation than the multiplication rule, and you had best use a Monte Carlo method.

Evaluating the Significance of "Dredged-Up" Relationships

In all the previous examples of hypothesis-testing statistics, we have assumed that the researcher had a specific hypothesis before examining the raw data and making the test. But there are other types of analysis, like secondary analysis (described in the previous chapter), in which the researcher searches through the raw data in hopes of "dredging up" some relationships. Dredged-up relationships must *not* be tested with the probability apparatus described earlier in this chapter.

There are two ways to go astray in searching through raw data. The first is to seize upon the extreme observation of a *large* randomly generated sample distribution and to consider it unusual when in reality it is to be expected sometime. An example is the birth of ten daughters in a row. The second way to go astray results from the *smallness* of the sample rather than from its largeness: finding specious patterns that exist simply because *some* patterns must apparently occur. An example is bettors' finding patterns in a series of horse races. We shall take up these two fallacies in order.

"UNUSUAL" OCCURRENCES IN LARGE SAMPLES

If you are the dealer in a game of bridge and you deal yourself the ace, two, and three of spades; the four, five, and six of diamonds; the seven, eight, and nine of hearts; and the ten, jack, queen, and king of clubs, you probably will not think much of it. Now, will you think that there is a *pattern* (that is, a nonrandom deal) if you get thirteen spades? You will not think so if you yourself are dealing, because you will know that you did not cheat. But if *someone else* deals thirteen spades to himself, you may be suspicious and think the deal is a nonrandom (that is, cheating) deal. The point is that whether or not you think there is a pattern depends on more than the observed data; it also depends on what else you know—in this case, that you dealt and did not rig the cards.

To push the example further, remember that the first bridge hand we described did not surprise you much. But, if one of the players had *predicted* that you would get exactly that hand, you would be very surprised indeed. You would think that the hand was nonrandom and that the other person had either fixed the cards or was possessed of extrasensory perception. Again, your surprise depends on what you knew in advance—in this case, that your friend had predicted the exact hand.

Here is another example of the same sort:

> . . . On 16 May 1965, reading the San Francisco *Sunday Chronicle* I noticed an article on page 22 entitled "Ancient Men on the Nile." In scanning this story, I saw the phrase ". . . the expert appraisal of Philadelphia anthropologist Dr. Carleton S. Coon." To anyone who had been an undergraduate student at the University of Chicago in the early 1930s, this unusual name would call up nostalgic memories of another Carleton Coon and his partner, Joe Sanders, whose popular Coon-Sanders dance band was then playing at the Blackhawk. So I found myself thinking about Joe Sanders, very probably for the first time in 30 years.
>
> Less than five minutes later, having turned the pages of the paper to page 33, I saw an obituary notice headed "Joe Sanders." It read, ". . . died Friday. . . . [W]ith the late Carleton Coon . . . organized the Coon-Sanders band." These two closely spaced recollections of a person forgotten for 30 years, with the second event involving a death notice, is in the classical pattern; but it is obvious that no causal relationship could have existed between the two events.
>
> The probability of a coincidental recollection of a known person in a 5-minute period just before learning of that person's death can easily be calculated, to within a factor of 10. Let us take a 30-year period, and assume that an average person would recognize the names of 3000 different people who might die in that period of time. . . . We assume that our subject will learn of the death of each of these persons at some time in the 30 years. If we restrict our attention to the time when our subject learns of the death of a particular person, we can then ask how probable it is, that in the 5 minutes just preceding that exact time of learning of the death, an unrelated recollection that is unique to the 30-year period will occur. This probability, to within a factor of 2, is the ratio of a 5-minute interval to a 30-year interval, or 3×10^{-7} [1/10 million]. (It is clear that if one thinks of the particular person once a year rather than

once every 30 years, the probability will rise by a factor of 30, to about 10^{-5} [1/100,000].) The probability that one will have such an experience when learning of the death of any one of the 3000 recognizable persons is clearly 10^{-3} [1/1000] in a 30-year period, or approximately 3×10^{-5} per year. If we take the sample of 10^8 [100 million] adults in the United States, 3×10^3 experiences of the sort related above should occur per year, or about 10 per day. . . . With such a large sample to draw from, it is not surprising that some exceedingly astonishing coincidences are reported in the parapsychological literature as proof of extrasensory perception in one form or another. (L. Alvarez, 1965, p. 1541)

Still another example of the attribution of meaning to far-out observations occurs on the stock market from time to time. *Someone* must be lucky in a series of consecutive stock-market transactions, just by chance. When it happens, the fellow who hits it right by chance a large number of times assumes that the good results result from his *knowledge* and his method of stock analysis. Thereupon, he writes a book called *How I Made My Fortune in Stocks* and makes *another* small fortune in book royalties.

The data in Table 24.11. illustrate this problem as it often ap-

Table 24.11.

	PSYCHOLOGICAL CHARACTERISTIC I		PSYCHOLOGICAL CHARACTERISTIC II		PSYCHOLOGICAL CHARACTERISTIC III	
	%		%		%	
Brand of Men's Suit Purchased	*High*	*Low*	*High*	*Low*	*High*	*Low*
A (26 buyers)	38(10)	62(16)	35(9)	65(17)	50(13)	50(13)
B (21 buyers)	38(8)	62(13)	71(15)	29(6)	57(13)	43(9)
C (7 buyers)	43(3)	57(4)	43(3)	57(4)	43(3)	57(4)
D (14 buyers)	43(6)	57(8)	43(6)	57(8)	28(4)	72(10)
E (19 buyers)	37(7)	63(12)	47(7)	53(10)	47(9)	53(10)
F (27 buyers)	48(13)	52(14)	52(14)	48(13)	41(11)	59(16)
Don't know (15 buyers)	27(4)	73(11)	20(3)	80(12)	47(7)	53(8)

pears in social-science research. The investigator collected data on three psychological characteristics of seven groups of people who exhibited different purchasing behavior, hoping to find characteristics that would distinguish the various groups. None of the three characteristics is *consistently* different for all seven groups of people.[3] But the investigator noticed a split of 71 per cent to 29 per cent in favor of the

3. Statistical tests conducted by the investigator indicate that none of the three characteristics in the seven groups is significant at the .05 level.

buyers of brand B on characteristic 2. *If* one treats this comparison as if it were the *only* comparison under examination, it appears to be very significant statistically and unlikely to occur by chance. The investigator offered the split as a valid finding from the data.

But there are twenty-one possible comparisons in the table (seven purchasing groups by three characteristics), which means that the likelihood of *one* comparison appearing to be significant is *much* higher than if only one comparison were examined (refer to Example 6 in the previous chapter). The investigator argued that, for *a priori* theoretical reasons, this was the only one of the twenty-one comparisons that he *expected* to be significant, and a confirmation of his expectation would strengthen his case for the finding's significance. But the reader is entitled to be skeptical of such *post facto* discussion, and skepticism is reinforced by the small number of subjects in the comparison—only twenty-one.

To determine whether or not any meaning should be attached to the apparently unusual event is not easy. At the very least, one should remain alert to such events and explore them, rather than ignoring them; it would be foolish to shrug off a bridge dealer who twice deals himself a perfect hand. "An erroneous rejection of extreme observations profoundly affected the course of history when, shortly after seven o'clock on the morning of December 7, 1941, the officer in charge of a Hawaiian radar station ignored data solely because they seemed so incredible" (Wallis & Roberts, 1962, p. 170).

The examination of such "unusual" observations is known as "analysis of deviant cases" (Kendall & Lazarsfeld, 1950, p. 167), and it is an important source of scientific knowledge. For two examples, if a country has an unusually low rate of lung cancer or if an individual lives through a plague in which everyone else dies, an investigation of the causes of such an unusual occurrence may be instructive, *or* it may reveal only that the apparent exception is the result of random chance. One should consider the unusual event as a clue that *may* lead to an explanation. And certainly keep your eyes open for a repetition of the event, just as you watch a card dealer whom you suspect.

But pay attention only to those events that have some importance; there is no sense in doing more than exclaiming about a card hand that has a peculiar combination of numbers but no special significance in the game.

A second way of dealing with an unusual event is to calculate just *how* unusual it really is. That is what L. Alvarez did with his memory of Joe Sanders, and he found that the event was not very unusual, considering all possible opportunities for it to happen in the United States. But, if the same thing had happened to Alvarez three times on successive days, the probability of the sequence's happening to anyone anywhere would be astronomically small, and he would not be likely to reason it away as he did. One could also calculate the probability of the observance of a split as wide as 15 to 6 for a single comparison among the twenty-one comparisons in Table 24.11. That calculation is rendered muddy, however, by the argument about the theoretical basis for that observation, as well as by the presentation of still other tables and data in the same study.

A third—and most important—way to evaluate unusual dredged-up events is to see if the same thing happens elsewhere. In Illustration 1 in the previous chapter, North Carolina was seen to have both the biggest stake in tobacco growing *and* the highest rate of doctors' smoking. Assume that one had merely *noticed* this fact, rather than having sought these data to test a hypothesis. This observation *could* be a coincidence. But we can look to see if the same relationship holds elsewhere—as indeed it does for the other major tobacco-economy states—confirming our belief that the observed association for North Carolina is not just a fluke (J. L. Simon, 1967–1968). And in the study of psychological characteristics and purchasing behavior, the investigator should repeat the test on another sample from the group in question, to see if the same sort of finding appears again, before he places much confidence in the finding.

PATTERNS IN SMALL SAMPLES

A second error in data dredging is reading a pattern into too small a sample. This is the error horse-racing fans frequently fall into. They look over the back records of races and find what they think is a pattern—say, that jockey A has been winning *every other race.* They then bet him to win after he loses his next race, and they are surprised when the "pattern" does not continue. Their error lies in not understanding how easy it is to think there is a pattern when there really is none, just as patterns apparently appear with randomly thrown dice or cards or random numbers. (Look at all the apparent patterns in Slug's batting record on page 397.)

Statistics offer little help in deciding whether or not a newly discovered pattern really means anything. If there were some way to calculate how many possible patterns might appear, then one might estimate the likelihood that *some* pattern of a particular strength would appear. But the possibilities of the human imagination in generating possible patterns are almost limitless, so even this statistical hope goes aglimmering.

The only safe test is to find the pattern *first* and then to see if it repeats itself in *different data*—data that you had not seen when you found the original pattern. If the pattern does repeat, you can use probability statistics to determine how likely the data would have been to repeat the pattern *had you predicted it in advance on the basis of finding your first pattern.*

Such a procedure points up the importance of theory once again. If you have a general theory about some subject matter, you can deduce specific hypotheses from it and then ask whether or not the data show the expected pattern. Without the theory your hypothesis will not be very strong, and therefore it will be more difficult to ask and answer a clear-cut question about whether or not the pattern of the data means anything.

NUMERICAL ARTIFACTS

Still another way to go astray in examining data is to discover artifacts—apparently interesting findings *that could not be otherwise.* An example is the children's teaser: "Did you know that exactly the same number of men got married last year as did women?" Sometimes this sort of artifact is not so obvious. Consider the observation that "Even though in the United States there are many fewer women than men with Ph.D. degrees, the data show that there were almost as many women with Ph.D. degrees who married men with Ph.D. degrees as men with such degrees who married women with such degrees." (Think about it!)

The famous "regression fallacy" is an artifact that occasionally slips into the work of even the wisest scientists. The regression fallacy takes its name from F. Galton's observation that the height of the population was "regressing to the mean." That is, Galton thought that the heights of people were becoming more uniform because the sons of the tallest fathers and of the shortest fathers were closer to the average than their fathers had been. What Galton overlooked was that in each generation sons of *other* fathers are by chance much taller or shorter than are their fathers, so that each generation has equal numbers of very tall and very short people. One can avoid the regression fallacy by considering *all* the members of the universe (or sample) and not simply looking at selected members, for example, the sons of the tallest or shortest fathers.

Economics is often afflicted with the regression fallacy. Consider this conclusion based on the data that follow it:

> . . . [S]ome pretty big variations in advertising-sales ratios between different industries seem to be narrowing. For example, a spread of 0.49% in 1948 between metalworking machinery and equipment, and fabricated structural metal products, had been reduced to 0.32% by 1962. (The metal-working ad-sales ratio declined from 1.03% to 0.91% during the period, while fabricated structural gained from 0.54% to 0.59%.)

Similarly, the advertising-sales ratios of other industries, such as pulp, paper and paperboard, have moved closer to the levels of other groups . . . the ratios [are] "quickly approaching the level of stability."

Industry	*Advertising Expenditures-Sales Ratio* 1948	*Advertising Expenditures-Sales Ratio* 1962
Primary metals	0.21%	0.39%
Fabricated structural metal products	0.54	0.59
Cutlery, hand tools and general hardware	1.91	3.28
Heating apparatus & plumbers' supplies	1.14	1.06
Miscellaneous fabricated metal products	0.54	0.92
Stone, clay & glass products	0.63	0.78
Construction, mining & material handling machinery and equipment	0.71	0.85
Metalworking machinery & equipment	1.03	0.91
Electrical generating, transmission, distribution & industrial apparatus	1.27	1.51
General industry machinery & equipment	1.02	1.09
Special industry machinery	0.77	0.94
Office, computing & accounting machines	1.25	0.72
Professional, scientific & controlling instruments, photographic & optical goods	1.93	2.15
Industrial organic & inorganic chemicals	0.72	1.24
Pulp, paper & paperboard	0.33	0.87
Converted paper & paperboard boxes	0.87	1.07
Motor freight transportation and warehousing	0.30	0.32

(Reprinted from *Industrial Marketing*, June 1966, pp. 64 ff. Copyright 1966 Advertising Publications, Inc., 740 Rush Street, Chicago, Ill. 60611.)

But, viewed in their entirety, the data do *not* show that the advertising ratios are moving together. One measure is the ratio of the range to the median:

$$\frac{1.93 - 0.21}{0.77} = 2.2$$

for 1948 and

$$\frac{3.28 - 0.32}{0.94} = 3.2$$

for 1962. (Another measure of dispersion, the ratio of the standard deviation to the mean, is also higher in 1962 than in 1948.) To conclude that the ratios are "approaching stability" is therefore not reasonable.

I suspect that the regression fallacy is at the root of many doubtful observations about changes in society over time. Consider, for example, the common observation that people are becoming more conformist with sucessive generations. (Put aside for now the difficulty of defining and measuring conformity.) Perhaps the writers who make this statement have themselves been nonconformists in their lives. It is likely that their own children are more conformist than they are, as the laws of chance would predict. Therefore, the writers observe a "trend toward conformity." But they are ignoring the nonconformist children that come out of conformist homes, children whom the writers do not see but yet who probably make up a generation that contains as many nonconformists as other generations do.

EXERCISES

1. What would be the probability of having three daughters in a row, if the probability of a girl child were 0.4?
2. You employ ten interviewers to ask people whether they prefer candy bar A to candy bar B. Each interviewer interviews twenty people and the preferences for candy bar A were 10, 14, 4, 16, 7, 3, 2, 15, 14, 5. Are the differences among interviewers those that might be expected by chance, or is there reason to believe that the interviewers differed in what they did?
3. Pick a problem randomly from a set of randomly chosen exercises in any basic statistics book, and solve the problem with Monte Carlo methods.
4. Three merchandising plans were tried out on a random sample of stores. Plan A raised sales by 2, 1, 0, 2, and 1 units in the five stores, respectively. Plan B raised sales by 1, 0, 0, 1, and 0 units in five stores. Plan C raised sales by 2, 0, 0, 0, and 1 units in five stores. What is the probability that plan A is "really" better than plans B and C?
5. What is the probability that four of your first five children will be daughters, assuming that you will have five children? What is the probability that you will have either four boys or five girls among your first five children?
6. What are the odds that three or more cards of any one suit (for instance, spades) will appear in a five-card poker hand from a well-shuffled deck? Give a numerical answer, as well as showing the steps by which you got the answer.
7. John tells you that with his old method of shooting foul shots in basketball his average (over a long period of time) was .6. Then he tried a new

method of shooting and scored successes with nine of his first ten shots. Should he conclude that the new method is really better than the old method?

8. "If six fair coins are tossed, what is the probability that exactly three of them turn up heads?" (Adler, 1963, p. 92)

9. A football team played nine games during last season. It won the first, lost the next three, and then won the last five. A sportswriter concluded that the team had improved during the season. Is that a good conclusion? Or is there a good chance that the team had the same six in nine chance of winning each game throughout the season? (This is a very tricky problem to set up.)

10. "If seven accidents occur at random on a highway during one week, what is the probability that one occurs each day of the week?" (Adler, 1963, p. 92)

11. Two different diets were tested on a randomly selected group of overweight people. The weight losses in pounds were:

Diet A	0	5	10	9	6	4	1	3	8	7	3	4
Diet B	4	6	4	1	1	3	2	8	5	9	1	2

Judge whether or not diet A is better for losing weight than diet B is. Outline a procedure, discuss the logic of your procedure, and estimate.

12. Each of ten people secretly chooses a number between 1 and 100. What is the probability that at least two of them will choose the same number? State a procedure and an estimate.

13. What are the odds that two cards of the same denomination will appear in a five-card poker hand from a well-shuffled deck?

14. On the average, how many times must a die be thrown before it comes up 6? (Mosteller, 1965, p. 1)

15. There are ten boys in a grammar-school class, three Negro and seven white. In a foot race the order of finishing is, from first to last (N = Negro, W = white), NWNWNWWWWW. Should one say that Negro boys are faster afoot than white boys are?

16. If I sent the manuscript of this book to five publishers chosen more or less randomly and if all five rejected it for publication, what would be a sensible probability that a sixth publisher (chosen in the same way) would accept it? (Hint: A sensible solution requires that you assume some additional information. This is what Mosteller calls a "problem without structure.")

17. You show me a jar that only you know has 4,322 stones in it, and you ask me to guess the number of stones. Estimate the probability that I shall guess correctly. (This is another problem without structure.)

CHAPTER 25

How Big a Sample?[1]

Sometime in the course of almost every study —preferably early in the planning stage—the researcher must decide how big a sample to take. The first examples taken up here are from the descriptive type of study, and the latter deal with sample sizes in relationship research.

Samples in Descriptive Research

EXAMPLE 20

What proportion of the homes in Countryville are tuned in to television station WCNT's ten o'clock news program? That is the question your telephone survey aims to answer, and you want to know how many randomly selected homes you must telephone to obtain a sufficiently large sample.

1. R. Schlaifer (1961) attacks the sample-size problem in the wider context of decision making, costs, and benefits. The statistically knowledgeable reader can find an excellent discussion of sample size in M. Hansen, *et al.* (1953). A. E. Mace (1965) gives many examples of the appropriate calculation in an engineering framework.

Begin by guessing the likeliest answer, say 30 per cent in this case. Do not worry if you are off by 5 per cent or even 10 per cent, and you will probably not be further off than that. Select a first-approximation sample size of perhaps 400; this number is selected from my general experience, but it is just a starting point. Then proceed through the first 400 numbers in the random-number table, marking down a "yes" for numbers 1-3 and "no" for numbers 4-10 (because 3/10 was your estimate of the proportion listening). Then add the "yes"es and "no"s. Carry out perhaps ten sets of such trials, the results of which are in Table 25.1.

Based on these ten trials, you can estimate that if you take a sample of 400 and if the "real" viewing level is 30 per cent, your average percentage error will be 1.375 per cent on either side of 30 per cent. That is, with a sample of 400, half the time your error will be greater than 1.375 per cent if 3/10 of the universe is listening.

Table 25.1.

Trial	*Number "Yes"*	*Number "No"*	*% Difference From Expected Mean of 30% (120 "Yes")*
1	115	285	1.25
2	119	281	0.25
3	116	284	1.00
4	114	286	1.50
5	107	293	3.25
6	116	284	1.00
7	132	268	3.00
8	123	277	.75
9	121	279	.25
10	114	286	1.50
Mean			1.375

Now you must decide whether or not the estimated error is small enough for your needs. If you want greater accuracy than a sample of 400 will give you, increase the sample size, using this important rule of thumb: To cut the error in half, you must *quadruple* the sample size. In other words, if you want a sample that will give you an error of only 0.55 per cent on the average, you must increase the sample size to 1,600 interviews. Similarly, if you cut the sample size to 100, the average error will be only 2.75 per cent (double 1.375 per cent) on either side of 30 per cent. If you are distrustful of this rule of thumb, run ten or so trials on sample sizes of 100 or 1,600, and see what error you can expect to obtain on the average.

If the "real" viewership is 20 per cent or 40 per cent, instead of 30 per cent, the accuracy you will obtain from a sample size of 400 will not be very different from an "actual" viewership of 30 per cent, so do not worry about that too much, as long as you are in the right general vicinity.

Accuracy is *slightly* greater in smaller universes but *only* slightly. For example, a sample of 400 would give *perfect* accuracy if Countryville had only 400 residents. And a sample of 400 will give *slightly* greater accuracy for a town of 800 residents than for a city of 80,000 residents. But, beyond the point at which the sample is a *large fraction* of the total universe, there is no difference in accuracy with increases in the size of universe. This point is very important. For any given level of accuracy, *identical* sample sizes give the same level of accuracy for Podunk (population 8,000) or New York City (population 8 million). The *ratio* of the sample size to the population of Podunk or New York City means nothing at all, even though it intuitively seems to be important.

The size of the sample must depend upon which population or subpopulations you wish to describe. For example, A. Kinsey's sample size would have seemed large, by customary practice, for generalizations about the United States population as a whole. But, as Kinsey explains: "The chief concern of the present study is an understanding of the sexual behavior of *each segment of the population,* and it is only secondarily concerned with generalization for the population as a whole" (Kinsey, *et al.,* 1948, p. 82, italics added). Therefore Kinsey's sample had to include subsamples large enough to obtain the desired accuracy in *each* of these subuniverses. The U.S. Census offers a similar illustration. When the U.S. Bureau of the Census aims to estimate only a total or an average for the United States as a whole—as, for example, in the Current Population Survey estimate of unemployment—a sample of perhaps 50,000 is big enough. But the decennial census aims to make estimates for all the various communities in the country, estimates that require adequate subsamples in each of these subuniverses; such is the justification for the decennial census' sample size of so many millions.

Television ratings illustrate both types of purpose. Nielsen ratings, for example, are sold primarily to national network advertisers. These advertisers on national television networks usually sell their goods all across the country and are therefore interested primarily in the total United States viewership for a program, rather than in the viewership in various demographic subgroups. The appropriate calculations for Nielsen sample size will therefore refer to the total United States sample. But other organizations sell rating services to *local* television and radio stations for use in soliciting advertising over the local stations rather than over the network as a whole. Each local sample must then be large enough to provide reasonable accuracy, and, considered as a whole, the samples for the local stations therefore add up to a much larger sample than the Nielsen and other nationwide samples.

EXAMPLE 21

This example, like Example 20, illustrates the choice of sample size for estimating a *summarization* statistic. Later examples deal with sample sizes for *probability* statistics.

Hark back to the pig-ration data in Chapter 23 (Example 8). Assume that our purpose now is to estimate the average weight gain for ration A, so that the feed company can advertise to farmers how much weight gain to expect from ration A. If the universe is made up of pig weight gains like those we observed, we can simulate the universe with, say, 1 million weight gains of thirty-one pounds, 1 million of thirty-four pounds, and so on for the twelve observed weight gains.[2] Or, more conveniently, as accuracy will not be affected much, we can make up a universe of say, thirty cards for each thirty-one-pound gain, thirty cards for each thirty-four-pound gain, and so forth, yielding a deck of $30 \times 12 = 360$ cards. Then shuffle, and, just for a starting point, try sample sizes of twelve pigs. The means of the samples for twenty such trails are as in Table 25.2.

Table 25.2.

Trial	*Mean*	*Absolute Deviation of Trial Mean from Actual Mean*	*Trial*	*Mean*	*Absolute Deviation of Trial Mean From Actual Mean*
1	31.77	.01	11	32.10	.34
2	33.27	1.51	12	30.67	1.09
3	31.75	.02	13	32.42	.66
4	30.83	.93*	14	30.67	1.09
5	30.52	1.24	15	32.25	.51
6	31.60	.16	16	31.60	.16
7	32.46	1.00	17	32.33	.57
8	31.10	.66*	18	33.08	1.32
9	32.42	.34	19	33.01	1.25
10	30.60	1.16	20	30.60	1.16

Actual Mean = 31.76

* Indicates medians of trials.

2. Only twelve weight gains are involved, because we are now estimating the variation for ration A only.

Now ask yourself whether or not a sample size of twelve pigs gives you enough accuracy; there is a 50-50 chance that the mean for the sample will be more than .66 or .93 pounds (the two median deviations) from the "real" mean of the universe, which is 31.76 pounds. Is this close enough? That is up to you to decide in light of the purposes for which you are running the experiment.

To see how accuracy is affected by larger samples, try a sample size of forty-eight pigs dealt from the same deck. (But, if the sample size were to be much larger than forty-eight, you might need a "universe" greater than 360 cards.) The results of twenty trials are in Table 25.3.

Table 25.3.

Trial	*Mean*	*Absolute Deviation of Trial Mean from Actual Mean*	*Trial*	*Mean*	*Absolute Deviation of Trial Mean From Actual Mean*
1	31.80	.04	11	31.93	.17
2	32.27	.51	12	32.40	.36*
3	31.82	.14	13	31.32	.44
4	31.39	.37*	14	32.07	.69
5	31.22	.54	15	32.03	.73
6	31.88	.12	16	31.95	.19
7	31.37	.39	17	31.75	.01
8	31.48	.28	18	31.11	.65
9	31.20	.56	19	31.96	.20
10	32.01	.25	20	31.32	.44

Actual Mean = 31.76

* Indicates medians of trials.

In half the trials with a sample size of forty-eight the difference between the sample mean and the "real" mean of 31.76 will be .36 or .37 pounds (the median deviations) or more. Again, is this too little accuracy for you? If so, increase the sample size further.

The attentive reader of this example may have been troubled by this question: How do you know what kind of a distribution of values is contained in the universe *before* the sample is taken? The answer is that you guess, just as in Example 20 you guessed at the mean of the universe. If you guess wrong, you will get either more accuracy or less accuracy than you expected from a given sample size, but the results will not be fatal; if you obtain more accuracy than you wanted, you have wasted some money, and, if you obtain less accuracy, your sample dispersion will tell you so, and you can then augment the sample to boost the accuracy. But an error in guessing will *not* introduce *error* into your final results.

The guess should be based on *something,* however. One source for guessing is your general knowledge of the likely dispersion; for example, if you were estimating male heights in Rhode Island, you would be able to guess what proportion of observations would fall with 2 inches, 4 inches, 6 inches, and 8 inches, perhaps, of the real value. Or, much better yet, a very small pretest will yield quite satisfactory estimates of the dispersion.

EXAMPLE 22

This is the first example of sample-size estimation for *probability* (testing) statistics, rather than the summarization statistics dealt with in Examples 20 and 21. Recall the problem of the sex of fruit-fly offspring discussed in Chapter 23 (Example 5). The question now is, How big a sample is needed to determine whether or not the radiation treatment results in a sex ratio other than a 50-50 male-female split?

The first step is, as usual, difficult but necessary. As the researcher, you must *guess* what the sex ratio will be if the treatment *does* have an effect. Let's say that you use all your general knowledge of genetics and of this treatment and that you guess the sex ratio at 75 per cent males and 25 per cent females *if* the treatment alters the ratio from 50-50.

Look at the random-number table, and let 1-25 stand for females and 26-00 for males (0 stands for 10, 00 for 100 and so forth, when all 10, all 100 and so forth, numbers are being used). Take twenty successive pairs of numbers for each trial, and run perhaps fifty trials, as in Table 25.4.

In Example 5 we found that, if a sample of twenty flies contained fourteen or more males, we could estimate the odds at 23 to 2 (92 per cent) that the ratio is not "really" 50-50. Now Table 25.4. tells us that, if the ratio is really 75-25, then a sample of twenty will show fourteen or more males forty-two of fifty times (84 per cent of the time). If we take a sample of twenty flies and if the ratio is *really* 75-25, we will make the correct decision by deciding that the split is not 50-50 84 per cent of the time.

Perhaps you are not satisfied with reaching the right conclusion only 84 per cent of the time. In that case, still assuming that the ratio will really be 75-25 if it is not 50-50, you need to take a sample larger than twenty flies. How much larger? That depends on how much surer you want to be. Follow the same procedure for a sample size of perhaps eighty flies. First work out for a sample of eighty, as was done in the previous chapter for a sample of twenty, the number of males (or

Table 25.4.

Trial	*Females*	*Males*	*Trial*	*Females*	*Males*	*Trial*	*Females*	*Males*
1	4	16	18	7	13	34	4	16
2	6	14	19	3	17	35	6	14
3	6	14	20	7	13	36	3	17
4	5	15	21	4	16	37	8	12
5	5	15	22	4	16	38	4	16
6	3	17	23	5	15	39	3	17
7	7	13	24	8	12	40	6	14
8	6	14	25	4	16	41	5	15
9	3	17	26	1	19	42	2	18
10	2	18	27	5	15	43	8	12
11	6	14	28	3	17	44	4	16
12	1	19	29	8	12	45	6	14
13	6	14	30	8	12	46	5	15
14	3	17	31	5	15	47	3	17
15	1	19	32	3	17	48	5	15
16	5	15	33	4	16	49	3	17
17	5	15				50	5	15

more) out of eighty that you would need to find for the odds to be, say, 9 to 1 that the universe is not 50-50; your estimate turns out to be forty-eight males, say. Then run fifty trials of eighty flies each on the basis of 75-25 probability, and see how often you would not get as many as forty-eight males in the sample. Table 25.5. shows the results I got. No trial was anywhere near as low as forty-eight, which suggests that a sample of eighty is bigger than necessary if the split is really 75-25.

It is obvious that, if the split you guess at is 60-40 rather than 75-25, you will need a bigger sample to obtain the ''correct'' result with the same probability. For example, run some eighty-fly random-number trials with 1-40 representing males and 51-100 representing females. Table 25.6. shows that only twenty-four of fifty (48 per cent) of the trials reach the necessary cut-off at which one would judge that a sample of eighty really does not come from a universe that is split 50-50; therefore, a sample of eighty is not big enough if the split is 60-40.

Reviewing the main principles of this example: First, the closer together the two possible universes from which you think the sample might have come (50-50 and 60-40 are closer together than are 50-50 and 75-25), the bigger the sample needed to distinguish between them. Second, the surer you want to be that you reach the right decision based upon the sample evidence, the bigger the sample you need.

Table 25.5.

Trial	*Females*	*Males*	*Trial*	*Females*	*Males*	*Trial*	*Females*	*Males*
1	21	59	18	13	67	34	21	59
2	22	58	19	19	61	35	17	63
3	13	67	20	17	63	36	22	58
4	15	65	21	17	63	37	19	61
5	22	58	22	18	62	38	21	59
6	21	59	23	26	54	39	21	59
7	13	67	24	20	60	40	21	59
8	24	56	25	16	64	41	21	59
9	16	64	26	22	58	42	18	62
10	21	59	27	16	64	43	19	61
11	20	60	28	21	59	44	17	63
12	19	61	29	22	58	45	13	67
13	21	59	30	21	59	46	16	64
14	17	63	31	22	58	47	21	59
15	22	58	32	19	61	48	16	64
16	22	58	33	10	70	49	17	63
17	17	63				50	21	59

Table 25.6.

Trial	*Females*	*Males*	*Trial*	*Females*	*Males*	*Trial*	*Females*	*Males*
1	35	45	18	32	48	34	35	45
2	36	44	19	28	52	35	36	44
3	35	45	20	32	48	36	29	51
4	35	45	21	33	47	37	36	44
5	36	44	22	37	43	38	36	44
6	36	44	23	36	44	39	31	49
7	36	44	24	31	49	40	29	51
8	34	46	25	27	53	41	30	50
9	34	46	26	30	50	42	35	45
10	29	51	27	31	49	43	32	48
11	29	51	28	33	47	44	30	50
12	32	48	29	37	43	45	37	43
13	29	51	30	30	50	46	31	49
14	31	49	31	31	49	47	36	44
15	28	52	32	32	48	48	34	46
16	33	47	33	34	46	49	29	51
17	36	44				50	37	43

EXAMPLE 23

Referring back to Example 8, on the cable-television poll, in Chapter 23, how large a sample *should* you have taken? Pretend that the data have not yet been collected. You need *some* estimate of how the results will turn out before you can select a sample size. But you have not the foggiest idea of how the results will turn out. Therefore, go out and take a very small sample, maybe ten people, to give you some idea of whether people will split quite evenly or quite unevenly. Seven of your ten initial interviews say they are for CATV. How big a sample do you now need to provide an answer of which you can be fairly sure?

Using the techniques of the previous chapter, we estimate roughly that from a sample of fifty people at least thirty-two would have to vote the same way for you to believe that the odds are at least 19 to 1 that the sample does not misrepresent the universe, that is, that the sample does not show a majority different from that of the whole universe if you polled everyone. That estimate comes from the Monte Carlo experiment whose results are in Table 23.6., p. 386. That table shows that, if half the people (or more) are against cable television, only one in twenty times will thirty-two (or more) people of a sample of fifty say that they are for cable television; that is, only one of twenty trials with a 50-50 universe will produce as many as thirty-two "yes"es if a majority of the population is against it. Therefore, designate numbers 1-30 as "no" and 31-00 as "yes" in the random-number table (that is, 70 per cent, as in your estimate based on your presample of ten), work through a trial sample size of fifty, and count the number of "yes"es. Run through perhaps ten or fifteen trials, and reckon how often the observed number of "yes"es exceeds thirty-two, the number you must get for a result you can rely on. In Table 25.7. we

Table 25.7.

Trial	*No*	*Yes*	*Trial*	*No*	*Yes*
1	13	37	9	15	35
2	14	36	10	9	41
3	18	32	11	15	35
4	10	40	12	15	35
5	13	37	13	12	37
6	11	39	14	14	36
7	13	37	15	17	33
8	7	43			

see that a sample of fifty respondents, from a universe split 70-30, will show that many "yes"es a preponderant proportion of the time—in fact, in fifteen of fifteen experiments; therefore, the sample size of fifty is large enough if the split is "really" 70-30.

EXAMPLE 24

How large a sample is needed to determine whether or not there is any difference between the two pig rations in Examples 9, 10, and 11 in Chapter 23? The first step is to guess the results of the tests. You estimate that the average for ration A will be a weight gain of thirty-two pounds. You further guess that twelve pigs on ration A might gain thirty-six, thirty-five, thirty-four, thirty-three, thirty-three, thirty-two, thirty-two, thirty-one, thirty-one, thirty, twenty-nine, and twenty-eight pounds. This set of guesses has an equal number of pigs above and below the average and more pigs close to the average than farther away. That is, there are more pigs at thirty-three and thirty-one pounds than at thirty-six and twenty-eight pounds. This would seem to be a reasonable distribution of pigs around an average of thirty-two pounds. In similar fashion, you guess an average weight gain of twenty-eight pounds for ration B and a distribution of thirty-two, thirty-one, thirty, twenty-nine, twenty-nine, twenty-eight, twenty-eight, twenty-seven, twenty-seven, twenty-six, twenty-five, and twenty-four pounds.

Let us review the basic strategy. We want to find a sample size large enough so that a large proportion of the time it will reveal a difference between groups big enough to be accepted as not attributable to chance. First, then, we need to find out how big a difference must be to be accepted as evidence that the difference is not attributable to chance. We do so from trials with samples that size from the benchmark universe. We state that a difference larger than the benchmark universe will usually show is not attributable to chance.

In this case, let us try samples of twelve pigs on each ration. First we draw two samples from a combined benchmark universe made up of the results that we have guessed will come from ration A and ration B. (The procedure is the same as was followed in Example 11 on page 389.) We find that in nineteen out of twenty trials the difference between the two drawn groups of twelve was three pounds or less. Now we investigate how often samples of twelve pigs each, drawn from the *separate* universes, will show a mean difference as large as three pounds. We do so by making up a 25- or 50-card deck for *each* of the twelve hypothesized As and each of the twelve Bs, with the ration name and the weight gain written on it, that is, a deck of, say 300 cards for each ration. Then from each deck we draw two sets of twelve cards at random, record the group averages, and find the difference.

The differences in the fifteen trials turn out invariably to be four pounds or larger. Therefore, two samples of twelve pigs each are clearly large enough, and, in fact, even smaller samples might be sufficient if the universes are really like those we guessed at. If, on the other hand, the differences in the guessed universes had been smaller, then twelve-pig groups would have seemed too small, and we would then have had to try out bigger sample sizes, say forty-eight pigs in each group and perhaps 200 pigs in each group if forty-eight were not enough. And so on until the sample size is large enough to promise the accuracy we want. (In that case, the decks would also have to be much larger, of course.)

If we had guessed different universes for the two rations, then the sample sizes required would have been larger or smaller. If we had guessed the averages for the two samples to be closer together, then we would have needed bigger samples. Also, if we had guessed the weight gains *within* each universe to be less spread out, the samples could have been smaller and vice versa.

I hope that the examples in this chapter have not seemed unpleasantly complex or tedious. One cannot estimate necessary sample size without going through procedures like those we have illustrated, though mathematical methods can speed up the tedious shuffling-and-dealing phase. There is just no easy answer to the question of how large a sample to take.

Step-Wise Sample-Size Determination

Often it is wisest to determine the sample size as you go along, rather than fixing it firmly in advance. In sequential sampling, which was discussed briefly in Chapter 17, you *continue* sampling until the split is sufficiently even to make you believe you have a reliable answer. Related techniques work in a series of *jumps* from sample size to sample size. Step-wise sampling makes it less likely that you will take a sample that is much larger than necessary. For example, in the cable-television case, if you took a sample of perhaps fifty you could see whether or not the split was as wide as 32-18, which you figure you need for 9 to 1 odds that your answer is right. If the split were not that wide, you would sample another fifty, another 100, or however large a sample you needed until you reached a split wide enough to satisfy you that your answer was reliable and that you really knew which way the entire universe would vote.

Step-wise sampling is not always practical, however, and the cable-television telephone-survey example is unusually favorable for its use. One major pitfall is that the *early* responses to a mail survey, for example, do *not* provide a random sample of the whole, and therefore it is a mistake simply to look at the early returns when the split is not wide enough to justify a verdict. If you have listened to early radio or television reports of election returns, you know how misleading the reports from the first precincts can be if we regard them as a fair sample of the whole.[3]

Stratified sampling is another device that helps reduce the sample size required, by balancing the amounts of information you obtain in the various strata. Chapter 17 discussed the general idea of stratified sampling. (Cluster sampling does not reduce the sample size. Rather, it aims to reduce the cost of obtaining a sample that will produce a given level of accuracy.)

3. See J. Lorie and H. Roberts (1951, pp. 155–7) for more discussion of the limitations of sequential sampling. And M. Hansen, *et al.*, warn against the danger of increasing the sample size in this fashion:

> The investigator examines the returns from an initial sample to determine whether they appear acceptable to the investigator; if they do, he uses the results as they are; if they do not, he discards the sample results [or keeps the old sample] and draws a new sample, perhaps by a different method, in the hope that he will obtain a result more nearly like the one he expected. Such an approach can be utilized to obtain almost any results desired, or can "prove" any point even when unbiased or consistent methods of selecting the sample and making the individual estimates are used if the initial results are subject to relatively large sampling errors. (Hansen, *et al.*, 1953, p. 78)

References

Alvarez, Luis W. "A Pseudo Experience in Parapsychology." *Science*, XVIII (June 18, 1965), 1541.

Ayer, A. J. "Chance." *Scientific American* (October 1965), 44–54.

Bross, Irwin. *Design for Decision.* New York: Macmillan, 1953.

Chung, J. H., and D. A. S. Fraser. "Randomization Tests for a Two-Sample Problem." *Journal of the American Statistical Association*, 53 (September 1958), 729–35.

Dixon, Wilfred J., and Frank J. Massey, Jr. *Introduction to Statistical Analysis*, 2nd ed. New York: McGraw-Hill, 1957.

Dunnette, Marvin D. "Fads, Fashions, and Folderol in Psychology." *American Psychologist*, XXI (April 1, 1966), 343–52.

Dwass, Meyer. "Modified Randomization Tests for Nonparametric Hypothesis." *The Annals of Mathematical Statistics*, 28 (March 1957), 181–87.

Fisher, R. A. *The Design of Experiments*, Edinburgh: Oliver & Boyd, 1935.

Hansen, Morris H., W. N. Hurwitz, and W. G. Madow. *Sample Survey Methods and Theory*, Vol. I. New York: Wiley, 1953.

Kendall, Maurice, and William R. Buckland. *A Dictionary of Statistical Terms.* London: Oliver & Boyd, 1957.

Kendall, Patricia L., and Paul F. Lazarsfeld. "Problems of Survey Analysis," in Robert K. Merton and Paul F. Lazarsfeld (eds.). *Continuities in Social Research.* New York: Free Press, 1950, pp. 133–96.

Kinsey, Alfred C., Wardell B. Pomeroy, and Clyde E. Martin. *Sexual Behavior in the Human Male.* Philadelphia: Saunders, 1948.

Lorie, James H., and Harry V. Roberts. *Basic Methods of Marketing Research.* New York: McGraw-Hill, 1951.

Mace, Arthur E. *Sample Size Determination.* New York: Reinhold, 1965.

Modern Medicine, March 2, 1964, and *Modern Medicine* press release of February 24, 1964.

Neyman, Jerzy. *First Course in Probability and Statistics.* New York: Holt, 1950.

Pitman, E. J. G. "Significance Tests Which May Be Applied to Samples from Any Population." *Journal of the Royal Statistical Society*, Supplement 4 (1937), 119–30.

Rand Corporation, The. *A Million Random Digits.* New York: Free Press, 1955.

Schlaifer, Robert. *Introduction to Statistics for Business Decisions.* New York: McGraw-Hill, 1961.

Simon, Julian L. "The Effect of Income Upon Utility." Urbana (mimeographed): 1967. (b)

Simon, Julian L. "Doctors, Smoking, and Reference Groups." *Public Opinion Quarterly*, 3 (Winter 1967–1968), 646–7.

Wallis, W. Allen. "Some Useful Nonparametric Methods." Chicago: University of Chicago (mimeographed), October 1957.

Wallis, W. Allen, and Harry V. Roberts. *The Nature of Statistics.* New York: Free Press, 1962.

[5]

Foreword

I'm not sure how I came to the idea in this paper. I think I got to wondering: Why should nature be like a Normal Curve? I clearly remember having read that the results of IQ tests resemble the Gaussian distribution only because the test-makers include and exclude questions to produce such a distribution.

Having in mind the idea expressed in this paper made it easier for me to suggest that non-parametric resampling statistics be preferred to Normal-based conventional tests, as discussed in earlier articles in this section.

What does the Normal Curve "mean"?

Abstract

Early in the history of the Normal Distribution, several writers, notably E.G. Boring (1920) (1), pointed out that the Normal Distribution does not inhere in nature, and that there is nothing "normal" about distributions that follow the function $(1/\sqrt{2\pi})e^{(-x^2/)2}$. Unfortunately, many have not understood this.

The point of this article goes further. The Normal Distribution is actually *created by the researcher*. It is common scientific practice to successively isolate and control for all important explanatory variables, each of which causes the original distribution *not* to resemble the Normal. The appearance of the Normal Distribution only indicates that most of the major explanatory variables have been allowed for, and the rest of the many relevant variables each have small influence – the point at which the scientist ends his labors. This is what the Normal Curve "means."

One can simply define the Normal Curve as the function traced by the expression $(1/\sqrt{2\pi})e^{(-x^2/)2}$. Or, one can speak of the Normal Curve as the distribution function generated by a process of the following sort. Put 16 coins in a dice cup, shake the coins, and throw them on a table; count +1 for each head, –1 for each tail; write down the score; then repeat the process many times. The scores will resemble Figure 1. If the number of coins is increased to a greater number – a thousand, say, or a million – and if the coins are thrown many times, the resulting bar chart resembles the bell shape of the Normal Curve.

But students want to know what is "normal" about this particular curve. Why is it found so often in nature, and especially, why was it given as justification by their former high school teachers for the number of A's, B's, and so on distributed to their classes?

Statements such as the following are found in many of the leading textbooks in various fields: "... the great majority of the distributions [the psychologist] will meet approach the normal type" (3:107); and "... there are many biological variables whose distributions are approximately normal, such as heights of men, for example, or lengths of ears of corn, or dressing percentages of swine" (6:36).

One of the unfortunate aspects of such explanations is that the word "normal" is written without a capital N, so that the statements suggest that the writer is referring to *normal experience* rather than the Normal Curve. It is no wonder that the average student who has completed a half year of statistics believes that the Normal Curve stands for a basic law of nature, a law which takes on a mystic quality because of the name and because of the student's imperfect understanding of the concept. Nor is the student without precedent in such a belief. The discoverer of the Normal Curve, De Moivre himself, thought it "was a theological problem; he was determining the frequency of irregularities from the Original Design of the Deity ..." (4:403).

Some writers (e.g., 7) point out that there is nothing *ab*normal about distributions that do not resemble the Normal, and eschew the title "Normal" for "Gaussian Distribution." But this does not dispel the notion that there is something deep in the nature of nature that corresponds to this special type of curve.

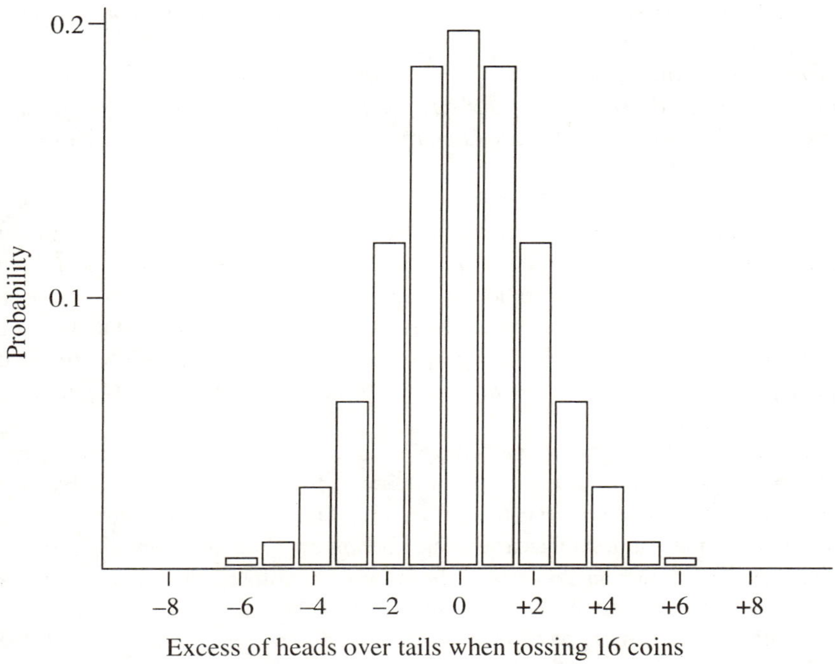

Figure 1 *Distribution of probabilities for 16 coins expressed in terms of excess of heads (7:246)*

Serious explanations of the Normal Curve are in terms of *errors*, and indeed the Normal Curve is sometimes called the "Error Law." In any measurement there are a great many minor sources of error, just as there are a great many small, complicated forces operating to make a given coin come up a head or a tail – the wind, the exact pressure of the coins near it, its initial position, and so on. Therefore, we expect that the pattern followed by the coins will also be the pattern followed by scientific measurements that contain many small and unidentifiable errors. This explains why the Normal Curve is so frequently used in the course of scientific study; there is *always* error, and the errors most frequently are "Normally distributed." Ebbinghaus was very clear on this restricted meaning of the concept long ago (2:18).

Forty years ago Boring (1:18) summed up the situation brilliantly:

> Here we may leave the question of *a priori* nature of the normal law. There is, after all, no magic in it. It gives us back always what we put into it. If we know from experience what nature is up to, as we do with the coin, then we can proceed upon cogent reasons to apply the law and we get results. If we do not know, we must appeal to nature and see. We have then no reason to expect that we are going to find the law before the appeal is made, whereas we have considerable reason to expect not to find it, since the form of distribution depends on the unit of measurement and we have an arbitrarily chosen one of a possible infinite number of units. When we do go to nature we find all degrees of resemblance to the law and divergence from it, and we many even find that the degree of divergence from the normal becomes the significant fact of our observation.

But I think that such an explanation still misses the fullest and most important meaning of the function in question.

The most important characteristic of the Normal Distribution is that its occurrence is entirely caused by the researcher, and its appearance "means" that the researcher may consider that his research work is complete.[1] I shall justify the two halves of this claim in that order.

When you decide to count a given phenomenon, it is a decision *not* to count all the other phenomena in this world, both those that are similar and those that are dissimilar to what you do count. The choice is made for a particular scientific purpose (taken in the widest sense), and the more homogeneous[2] is the set of events that is chosen to be counted, the more likely it is that the Normal Curve[3] will be a good fit to the data.

It is because the Normal Curve results from his *choices* and *scientific tactics* that I argue that the Normal Curve is *made* by the researcher, rather than *met* by him, as Guilford (3) suggests.

There is also another sense in which the Normal Curve is made by the researcher. If a "far-out" datum (known as a "sport" in some fields of research, for reasons unknown to me) is observed, the researcher may take one of two courses. After investigation, he may (a) treat it as a separate phenomenon, or (b) assure himself that its cause was extraneous; an example of the latter is that of an earthquake occurring at the same time as a far-out observation in some branches of physics, in which case the experiment would simply be repeated or the observation ignored. (Sometimes the researcher simply throws out the observation in the belief that there *must* have been an extraneous cause even if he cannot find what it is; this course of conduct is obviously dangerous, but is often followed anyway.) But either of these courses of action (a) or (b) results in the empirical distribution more closely resembling the Normal.

Height is the most frequent example of a Normally-distributed variable, so we shall analyse it. Imagine that we are mad enough to want to survey the heights of all organisms on earth, to do a census of all living things. I can hardly guess at the sort of distribution we would observe, partly because the distribution would depend so heavily on what we decided to count and on the fineness with which we measured height. More specifically, would we count viruses as independent organisms? And would we be able to distinguish among the heights of the individual viruses? Also, in which direction do you measure a whale's height? Our distribution might look like

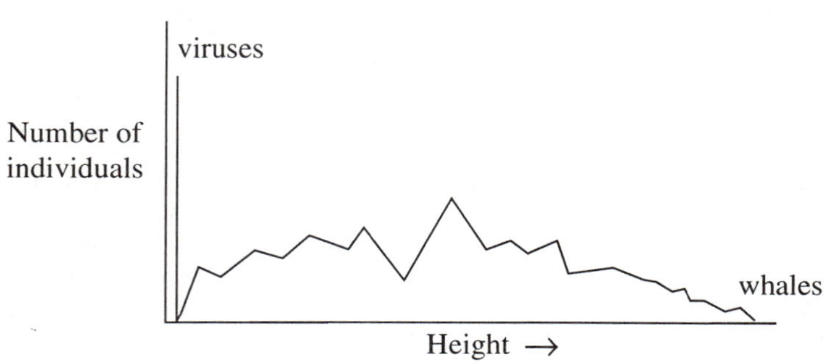

Figure 2

Figure 2, in part. In any case there is no reason to think that the distribution would resemble the Normal.

No scientist would start such a project. He might, though I doubt it greatly, want to survey the heights of *all mammals*. Again, I have trouble guessing what the distribution would look like. But notice that the distribution would depend on whether city authorities had been exterminating rats, whether the number of humans has increased relative to the number of whales, etc. Again there is no reason to think that the distribution of heights would closely resemble the Normal.

It would not be so unlikely for a scientist to survey the heights of the entire species *Homo sapiens*, though apparently it has never been done. Still I doubt that the results would resemble the Normal. The pigmies of Africa and the aborigines of Australia, plus the large and increasing number of children in the world, might make the curve look like Figure 3.

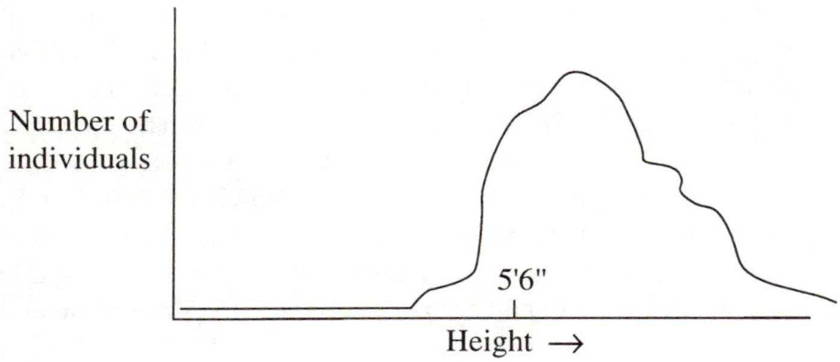

Figure 3

Almost any scientist would react to data on heights of all humans by sub-classifying them by race. Just how he would do this is not obvious, because of racial mixtures in many countries. But he would certainly try to isolate such groups as the pigmies. Frequently the scientist will confine his inquiry to one country or locality, especially if his inquiry is motivated by such practical considerations as theater owners wanting to know how far apart rows of theater seats must be. But even the distribution of heights of people in the United States will not necessarily be a close fit to the Normal Curve. In 1967 there probably is a higher proportion of children not yet full grown than there was in the population in 1945, so *either* in 1967 or in 1945, the distribution certainly would not resemble the Normal – and perhaps in neither year.

Well, you say, how about if we exclude children from the distribution? Yes, the resulting distribution will probably come closer to the Normal. But the curve may still look like Figure 4.

Even a layman will guess that the two peaks are caused by the inclusion of men and women. And indeed, studies usually sub-classify the data and present distributions of heights for men and women separately. And by *this* stage in the investigation of height the data may well bear a close resemblance to the Normal.

Still the data will diverge somewhat from the Normal. But if we successively narrow down the data by sub-classifying by age, country of ancestral origin, education,

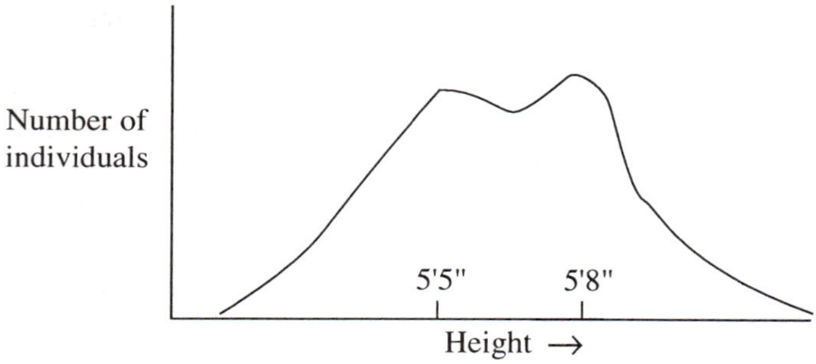

Figure 4

and other variables, *each* of the resulting curves will come closer and closer to the Normal. Why? Because the variation in heights of each of the sub-classified groups is the result of a great many forces, each of which has a relatively small effect, but *none* of which has a very large effect or about which we cannot gather information: specific diet elements, amounts of exercise, genetic and psychological factors of many kinds, and so on. In other words, the situation is now much like that of a bunch of coins, each of which is affected by numerous small factors.

The important point is that by this process of continually narrowing the population towards homogeneity, the scientist *causes* the distribution to resemble the Normal. A similar explanation holds for each piece of scientific work which shows this marvelous but artificial curve. To say it another way, Normal Curves are made and not born.

Now for the second idea, that the occurrences of a Normal Curve in a set of results may be taken as a *sign* that the scientific investigation is complete.

For our purposes here we can say that a scientist attempts to find relationships between classes of phenomena, i.e., he attempts to find independent variables that help him explain or predict variation in phenomena he designates as the dependent variable. But the scientist is not after just *any* relationships. He seeks *important* relationships, i.e., relationships that tell him a lot about the variation of the dependent variable. To paraphrase the words of a mail-order businessman (5:33), the good scientist looks for "relationships that scream, not relationships that whisper."

The Normal Curve arises from a linear combination of many variables, independent of each other and none of which is large relative to the others. To put it another way, a class of phenomena that resembles a Normal Curve does *not* contain any relationships that "scream," but *only* those whose effect is not great compared to the other variables.

Consider how our imaginary scientist proceeded when presented with the data on the heights of the various objects in the world. He immediately excluded the large group of inanimate objects from the investigation. Then he began to sub-classify the remainder, probably by species, race, age, size, and many other variables. If, within any sub-group, the distribution looked like Figure 5, he attempted to sub-classify even further. He stopped trying to further classify a given sub-group when its distribution resembled a Normal Curve. He stopped because he believed that he could find no more important independent variables that would explain much of the variation in the dependent variables. This is the same as saying that the remaining variation is a result of many small and unrelated independent variables. And this is why we say that, when the distribution resembles the Normal Distribution, the scientist can then assume that his job is done. The existence of a distribution that differs from the Normal is a sign that there is still work to be done, that there are still important variables operating that have not been identified and whose influence has not been allowed for.

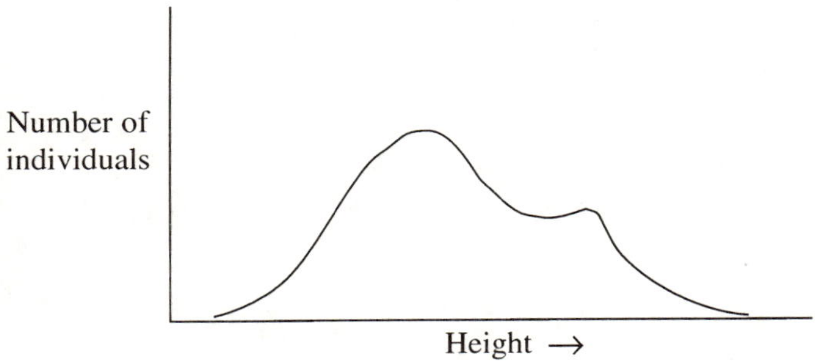

Figure 5

Intelligence tests are an interesting example. Tests could be designed which would produce almost any type of distribution of scores. It would be easy to design tests in which everyone scores either 0 or 100; any one-question test will do that. This result could be achieved, however, almost as well with multi-question tests. We should note also that the shape of the distribution will depend on the particular population. In a neighborhood with only poor and rich children, it requires a different type of test to obtain a Normal Curve.

Why then do test-makers rest satisfied only when the test scores are distributed "Normally"?[4] Perhaps because of the great statistical convenience offered by Normal Distributions – but perhaps also because they still believe that the Normal Distribution is "normal."

Notes

1. The same argument applies to the Poisson and the logarithmic-Normal distributions.
2. By "homogeneous," I mean events that fall within a very narrow common definition, with respect to the dimension under study.
3. The Poisson or the Logarithmic-Normal may fit the data.
4. Of course, the test must pass tests of prediction of other phenomena also – usually school success.

References

1. Boring, Edwin G. (1920), "The Normal Law in Mental Measurement," *American Journal of Psychology*.
2. Ebbinghaus, Herman (1913), *Memory: A Contribution to Experimental Psychology*, translated by H.A. Ruger and C.E. Bussenius (New York: Teachers College).
3. Guilford, J.P. (1936), *Psychometric Methods* (New York: McGraw-Hill).

PART II

THEORETICAL AND APPLIED ECONOMETRICS

[6]

Foreword

While I was still in the mail-order business on my own, I did some consulting for a liquor-trade association. The elasticity of demand – the extent to which liquor sales are affected by a change in price – is a key issue in industry lobbying against tax increases. In advance of a legislative hearing they asked me to prepare a statement. In the past the association had offered some carefully chosen examples that seem to show that the elasticity is high. When I went to the literature to find scientifically produced estimates, I found lots of fancy econometric studies, but none that seemed reliable. None of the many methods tried, many of them extremely complex, seemed very persuasive to me. So I went back to first principles.

After much meditation, it occurred to me that with a simple set of adjustments, comparison of the sales before and after state changes in liquor-tax laws should yield a reliable answer. But before I had an opportunity to do the research, I was fired, for reasons I never understood; the likeliest explanation is that my poking around in the files for data of various kinds that would support basic research in the economics and marketing of liquor was interpreted as suspicious activity.

The next year I began teaching advertising at the University of Illinois. I soon did the calculations for the liquor study, and after writing them up I sent the study to *Econometrica*, then the most high-powered mathematical-statistical journal. To my great surprise and delight, after a good many months the article was accepted for publication. This was amazing because the article contained not a single equation in algebra (though it did contain an equation in plain English), probably the first time in the history of the journal that such a "mathematically unsophisticated" article had been published.

The explanation for the happy accident of the article being accepted is that the referee was the world-class statistician Herman Wold, far too capable a man to be put off by the lack of mathematical dazzle in the piece. And he requested the editor to put me in touch with him because he wanted to tell me about a similar piece of work he had done in Sweden with postal rates, though he had never analysed the method or written it up.

Badi Baltaggi and Rajeev K. Goel have recently brought this work up to date, and ingeniously allowed for interstate movement of sales. Their results are much the same as mine here.

Econometrica, Vol. 34, No. 1 (January, 1966)

THE PRICE ELASTICITY OF LIQUOR IN THE U.S. AND A SIMPLE METHOD OF DETERMINATION

BY JULIAN L. SIMON[1]

Arc elasticity is estimated for liquor by simply comparing state sales before and after price increases, standardized by states in which price did not change. The technique can be used wherever there are several economic units independent with respect to price changes; it allows causal interpretation and it permits comparison of various length-of-run elasticities.

1. INTRODUCTION AND LITERATURE SURVEY

THE PRICE elasticity of demand for liquor is of considerable practical importance to the American community because it is the basis for calculations of the effect of liquor taxes upon total tax revenue and upon liquor industry sales and profits. Estimates of liquor elasticity affect the judgments of legislators when they consider tax bills and, hence, the estimates affect the levels of taxes.

At this time we do not have a satisfactory elasticity estimate for the United States. These are the studies that bear on the matter.

(1) Richard Stone [7] developed estimates from time series in England covering the period 1920–1938. His best estimates were −0.57 for price and 0.60 for income. Stone's work is sufficiently well known so that we need not evaluate it here. The major drawback for our purposes is that the elasticity in the U.S. may differ from that in England for a host of cultural and economic reasons.

(2) A. R. Prest [6] developed price elasticity estimates from time series in England, 1870–1938, using a method similar to Stone's. He obtained −0.57 using a logarithmic function and −0.031 using a linear function.

(3) Using a time-series technique for the years 1923–1939 in Sweden, S.Malmquist [2] estimated a price elasticity of −0.2 to −0.4. Liqor was rationed in Sweden during that period, which introduced great complexities into Malmquist's analysis, and thus reduces the comparability to the U.S. Also, the price of liquor was extremely stable over the measured period.

(4) As part of an exhaustive institutional study of the liquor industry, Harold Wattell [8] regressed sales linearly on price and income in Pennsylvania from 1935 to 1951. His estimate was that price was decidedly inelastic.

(5) William A. Niskanen developed a structural equation system of linear demand and supply functions for the U.S. beer, wine, and liquor markets. His endogenous variables were total consumption of each beverage type and price indices for each beverage type. His exogenous variables were demand deposits, time

[1] Professor James M. Ferguson was kind enough to read this manuscript and offered helpful comments.

trend (last two digits of year), and average tax revenues for beverage types. Prices and taxes were deflated to 1947. He estimated the structural parameters indirectly by least squares from the reduced form equations.

For the period 1934–1954, Niskanen estimated the price elasticity of liquor to be −1.74 [**4**]. In a longer and later work [**5**, p. 61] ,he estimates that for 1934–1941 and 1947–1960 the "price elasticity is around −2.0 . . .," and this was the estimate on which he relied. Before further adjustment, however, the elasticity estimate of his most-relied-on regression is −1.420 [**5**, Table 44].

2. RELEVANT PROBLEMS OF CONVENTIONAL METHODS

Basic sources [**1, 9**] mention two methods of evaluating elasticities: time-series and cross-sectional analysis. The two methods are sometimes used in combination, cross section for income and time series for price.

The difficulties in *time-series* analysis pertinent to liquor-elasticity determination are:

(1) Over time, changes in taste occur with a vengeance in liquor consumption. Per capita consumption[2] in the U.S. has been as high as 3.25 gallons in 1860, compared to 1.14 gallons in 1949. And there is considerable fluctuation from year to year even when income and price are held constant. The year-to-year changes are more than large enough to obscure the effect of even a very large price change, as is the case with the Federal excise increase in 1951.

It should not surprise us that liquor consumption is more variable and more subject to general cultural influences in the short run than is food, say. Liquor's major psychological function is to reduce fear and inhibition, and the tension level of our society varies with various external stimuli. And in the long run, shifts in religious beliefs and general style of life also affect drinking behavior.

(2) Changes in relative income, relative price, price levels, and other variables also cause trouble.

(3) Price indices are hard to create.

(4) Typically, the current price of liquor changes very infrequently, and it changes only slightly when it changes at all, because of government regulation and the nature of the commodity. This means that the time series has few observations to work with, scattered over long periods of time during which other variables can change radically. None of the studies mentioned above had data meeting L. R. Klein's requirement that ". . . we want a time-series sample that has a wide representation of experiences" [**1**, p. 4].

These difficulties with time-series analysis are sufficiently great that investigators of liquor price elasticity have indicated little confidence in their estimates.

[2] Throughout this paper we shall work with data standardized by the total population, rather than the adult population or particular age-group populations. The latter type of analysis can be very illuminating, but the necessary data are scarcer and less reliable than total population data.

The main difficulty with *cross-sectional* analysis is that the population of the various states—which would be the appropriate price-change units for a U.S. study—have very different tastes for liquor. Nor are the differences explained by income. Compare the four states in which the price of Seagrams 7 Crown was $4.85 in January, 1962 as shown in Table I.

TABLE I

State	January 1962 Price of Seagrams 7 Crown	Per capita Liquor Consumption in 1961	Gallons of Liquor Consumed per $1 Million of Income
Indiana	4.85	1.26	350
Massachusetts	4.85	2.76	681
Minnesota	4.85	2.22	613
New Mexico	4.85	1.75	506

Source: *Liquor Handbook*, 1962.

These variations in taste render useless a simple cross-sectional correlation of consumption and price in the various states. Furthermore, even if states were far more numerous than they are, we probably could not expect random differences in state tastes to wash out because of the likely association between state price and state taste.[3]

3. DESCRIPTION OF METHOD

This investigation uses a method that has features of both the cross section and the time series. Though it has not been used by economists, to my knowledge,[4] it is very similar to designs used for experiments in psychology and the natural sciences and to sociological paradigms. Because this method is not an experiment, though similar to one, I call it the "quasi-experimental" method.

Klein [**1**, p. 62] mentions a method similar to the quasi-experiment: "A sequence of cross-section samples may over time perhaps be used to estimate price parameters; but such procedures have not been widely used, if at all."

[3] The price level is set arbitrarily by each state legistature in "license" states when it fixes excise taxes. In the case of "monopoly" states, in which there are no free-enterprise liquor stores, the state fixes price levels directly. The effects of the two governmental systems on prices, revenues, and consumption are studied in my unpublished "The Economic Effects of State Monopoly of Liquor Retailing."

[4] Subsequent to writing this, Professor Herman Wold has advised that a similar method has been used for some time by Swedish economists under the name "impulse elasticity." The only reports, however, are in Swedish and mimeographed. Professor Wold also provided several clarifying comments.

The essence of the method is to examine the "before" and "after" sales of a given state, sandwiched around a price change and standardized with the sales figures of states that did not have a price change. The standardizing removes year-to-year fluctuations and the trend. We then pool the results of as many quasi-experimental "trial" events as are available.

When it can be used, this method avoids the important difficulties of time series and cross section and introduces no major new difficulties. Moreover, it has some special advantages which we shall discuss later.

This is the procedure:

1. Select as quasi-experimental events each state price increase of 2 per cent or more from 1950 to 1961. Exclude states where moonshine is an important part of liquor consumption. Exclude price change events that occur within 18 months before or after a Federal tax change.

2. Notation: "-1" is the month preceding a state price change, "$+1$" is the month following a price change.

3. Compute the per capita consumption for the twelve-month periods, -14 to -3 and $+5$ to $+16$. Find the per cent of change in consumption between "before" and "after." The periods before and after the tax change are timed to avoid the stock-up that occurs before a price change and the liquidation of stock-up.[5]

4. Compare each monopoly-state trial with other monopoly states, private license states with other private license states.[6] (The two groups differ in consumption measurements and in the structure of liquor retailing.) Compare each trial state against other states in its group, excluding (a) states that themselves had price changes between -18 and $+18$, (b) states that had sales tax changes, (c) moonshine states, (d) the District of Columbia and two anomalous states. Data for the comparison states were combined (i) by simple averaging of the per capita consumption figures of the individual states, (ii) by totaling the consumption and population figures and computing per capita estimates from the totals, and (iii) where applicable, computing total estimates with and without Pennsylvania. Elasticity estimates were generated for all three sets of data.

The index used for comparison is:

[5] The proximate sources of the publicly issued monthly state consumption data are publications of the Distilled Spirits Institute.

[6] In 16 "monopoly" states the state owns and operates the retail liquor stores. In "private-license" states the stores are owned and operated by private enterprisers under state licenses. In Montana the state runs liquor wholesaling, but retail stores are privately owned. In those comparisons in which Wyoming was used as a comparison state, it was incorrectly classed as a monopoly state rather than a license state, but this error is not sufficiently important to warrant recomputation.

$$\frac{\text{Trial state, per capita consumption “after”} - \text{trial state, per capita consumption “before”}}{\text{Trial states, per capita consumption “before”}}$$

minus

$$\frac{\text{Comparison states, p.c. consumption “after”} - \text{comparison states, p.c. consumption “before”}}{\text{Comparison states, per capita consumption “before”}}$$

5. Estimate the per cent price change in the test state. In most monopoly state tax changes in our sample, the price increase actually is a change in the markup percentage, perfectly appropriate for our purposes. In a few monopoly state cases, there was the complication that part of the state's pricing formula included flat per gallon taxes. In those cases the writer made *ad hoc* adjustments somewhat similar to the license state situation below, in order to arrive at a point estimate.

The usual form of a tax change in license states is a change in the flat gallonage excise tax. This causes the same *absolute* change in the wholesale, and subsequently the retail, prices of all brands of liquor. The per cent price change for low priced liquors is therefore greater than for high priced liquors. A percentage estimate of price change for the state as a whole therefore depends implicitly upon the distribution of liquor in each price range sold in the state, data which are not available.

The license state estimate was made in this fashion. Assuming customary retail markups, the increase in the retail price of a fifth was calculated. This price change was then expressed as a per cent of the retail price of a fifth of a medium priced liquor before the tax change. The calculated change was then compared against the actual change in Seagrams 7 Crown and other large selling brands, to the extent that these data were available.[7]

6. Divide the index in paragraph 4 by the per cent price change in paragraph 5 to get an estimate of price elasticity.

7. As in all statistical investigations, there were exceptions that required special handling. For example, one state changed its price structure in two steps spaced three months apart. The "before" and "after" periods therefore required special adjustment.

4. PROBLEMS WITH THIS METHOD

Most of the difficulties that arise in this investigation also plague other techniques. They include:

[7] Seagrams 7 Crown was used as an index of a medium priced brand, based on *Liquor Handbook* estimates of quantities sold at various prices in the U.S. Seagrams 7 Crown is by far the largest selling brand in the U.S., selling 2.5 times as much as the next biggest seller, and accounting for more than 7 per cent of total U.S. liquor consumption. Its price is commonly used as a standard in the liquor industry and its price to the retailer practically never changes except in response to tax level changes.

We may gain some reassurance from the fact, inherent in the relative sizes of the quantities with which we are working, that the per cent estimate of price change is quite insensitive to errors in the choice of index of the central tendency of the distribution.

1. Consumption figures in private license states refer to wholesale rather than retail purchases. The wholesale purchases lead retail purchases by weeks or months. Wholesale purchases are also subject to greater fluctuation from period to period than are retail sales, one cause of which is changes in brand prices not associated with general price changes and business anticipations.[8] Monopoly state consumption, on the other hand, is measured by actual retail sales.
2. The accuracy of population figures is unexpectedly crucial. We used interpolated yearly adjusted census figures, but they are far from perfect. This is a major source of variability in the elasticity estimates.
3. As discussed above, there are flaws in the estimates of price changes. Individual brand price changes during the before and after periods will also affect consumption. But the remarkable stability of most liquor prices, in large part a result of fair trade and state control, renders this source of error very minor.
4. Bar and carry-out sales are differentially affected by price changes. Carry-out sales account for 70–75 per cent of the total and we used carry-out prices as an index of all prices. Different states have different laws controlling or limiting bar sales.
5. Price changes can affect interstate purchase traffic.

5. RESULTS: AN ESTIMATE OF PRICE ELASTICITY

The median of the elasticity estimates for the non-moonshine trial states shown in Column 6 of Table II is -0.79. This median, adjusted upwards somewhat to take account of the moonshine states but still closer to -0.79 than to -1.0, is perhaps our best estimate of elasticity for the United States as a whole, subject to the following considerations:

1. The median was chosen as an estimate of the central tendency of the data because (a) it is not affected by the extremity of the extreme observations, and (b) it has no conceptual difficulty with positive elasticity estimates. If we were to compute a mean it would be reasonable, but theoretically uncomfortable, to include the positive estimates as being positive.
2. We may say with .965 probability that the mean of the population from which this sample of elasticity estimates was drawn is between -0.03 and -0.97 [3].
3. The variation among elasticity estimates for the various states in the sample may be due to true variation among the states as well as to random error. Variation among the states may result from different states' elasticities, or from different trends in consumption, or both.

If there is true variation among the states, the accuracy of our over-all elasticity estimate depends upon how fair a sample of the states (with respect to the char-

[8] For the periods May, 1960—April, 1961 and November, 1961—October, 1962, per capita consumption in Illinois was respectively, 2.13 and 1.71, while for the calendar years 1960, 1961, and 1962, consumption was respectively, 1.60, 1.63, and 1.72.

acteristic under consideration) that we actually obtained. We can only hope that the states that fell into our sample were not self-selected in some biased fashion.

It might be sensible to weight estimates by size of state to arrive at an all-U.S. estimate. But then we would have to add in the moonshine states (see paragraph 7 below), while excluding all those states for which we have no estimate at all. I prefer not to attempt this exercise.

In light of the extremely small price changes with which we worked, the amount of variation in the elasticity estimates is not surprising.

4. Inclusion of two observations for some states is a questionable practice. It is done because of the fewness of observations. The paired observations are in the center of the distribution, however, which suggests that they do not cause a serious bias.

5. The extreme states are small states, which increases our confidence in the median estimate. Nevada might well be eliminated from the sample on the same ground that the District of Columbia was, namely, that its liquor clientele is heavily transient, which would induce an artificially high elasticity estimate. And Idaho's price change was only 2 per cent which makes the elasticity estimate unduly sensitive to random error.

6. Some liquor traffic among states is possible. The estimate for the U.S. as a whole therefore must be less elastic than for the individual states, just as an industry elasticity must be lower than the mean elasticity for the firms in the industry.

7. The states in Table II do not include those states in which important quantities of moonshine are made. Table III shows estimates for price changes in moonshine states. We had hypothesized that estimates of elasticity would be higher in moonshine states. There is an indication in the skimpy data of a somewhat higher elasticity. However, more than 90 per cent of moonshine production takes place in states that consume less than 9 per cent of legal U.S. consumption.

8. This method ignores substitution effects of beer and wine. In some cases, wine prices are changed along with liquor prices; in other cases they are not. The amount of wine sold (measured in alcohol) is small compared to liquor consumption. Therefore, the shift to wine will not be very important in affecting liquor consumption even if, as Malmquist suggests, wine is very elastic with respect to liquor prices. Niskanen found that beer is a very weak (!) substitute for liquor, while the liquor-wine relationship is highly variable [**5**, p. 2].

9. This method estimates price elasticity by way of estimating the change in quantity sold, and assuming the mean price-paid-per-bottle changes as the price index changes. This estimate must be more elastic than an estimate based upon the total revenue before and after the price change, because the price change will shift some purchases to relatively cheaper brands. Investigation shows, however, that the switch to cheaper brands as a result of product price changes is slight, even when the trend to higher priced brands is taken into account.

10. It is not immediately clear what the length-of-run nature of these elasticities

TABLE II

State	Date of price change	Price of Seagram 7 Crown fifth before price change	Relative price change (Price "after" minus price "before" divided by price "before")	For the trial state: per capita consumption "after" minus per capita consumption "before" divided by per capita consumption "before"	For the comparison states totaled: per capita consumption "after" minus per capita consumption "before" divided by per capita "before"
	(1)	(2)	(3)	(4)	(5)
Rhode Island	6/1/58	4.60	.033	+.073	+.041
Idaho	5/1/61	4.45	.020	+.035	+.018
Ohio	6/6/55	3.46	.061	+.083	+.033
Washington	4/15/61	4.80	.052	+.031	+.018
Oregon	5/11/59	4.35	.035	+.053	+.051
Washington	4/1/59	4.58	.048	+.059	+.058
Oregon	7/1/61	4.60	.033	+.017	+.018
Maine	7/1/61	4.15	.024	+.015	+.018
Montana	12/1/58	4.25	.071	+.036	+.047
Nevada	5/1/61	4.55	.039	+.041	+.047
Vermont	8/1/57	(3.60) est.	.143	−.046	+.034
Missouri	5/1/61	(4.70) est.	.028	+.025	+.047
Idaho	3/16/55	4.05	.086	−.047	+.025
Maine	1/2/59	4.05	.025	+.040	+.061
California	7/1/55	4.38	.048	+.039	+.085
Oregon	5/2/55	4.10	.061	−.025	+.036
Iowa	7/1/61 & 4/1/59	4.03	.030	−.013	+.018
Connecticut	7/1/61	(4.50) est.	.066	−.031	+.054
Ohio	7/1/59	3.67	.100	−.081	+.051
Iowa	4/2/55	(3.78) est.	.050	−.070	+.025
Illinois	8/1/59	4.19	.036	−.018	+.053
Montana	7/1/57	(4.09) est.	.040	−.182	−.033
Alaska	7/1/61	5.85	.026	−.059	+.054

is. Because the "after" time period begins four months after the price change, the estimate is certainly not a very-short-run elasticity of the type that Wold alludes to: ". . . the consumer's first reactions to price changes are often capricious, sometimes being exaggerated, in other cases absent. Such irregularities are, as everybody knows, partly due to the advertising and propaganda that usually accompany even minor price changes" [9].

After an initial unsettled period, theory would lead us to expect that demand would become progressively less elastic as liquor drinkers re-tool their tastes and stomachs and switch to beer, wine, and other liquor substitutes. To test for this effect, I broke the "after" period into two six-months segments and developed elasticity estimates for the second six-month segments, as shown in Column 11.

The signs of the differences between the six-month period and the twelve-month

TABLE II (continued)

Price elasticity (comparison states totaled): (Col. 4 − Col. 5) / Col. 3	For the comparison states totaled without Pennsylvania 1959 tax change: per capita consumption "after" minus per capita consumption "before" divided by per capita "before"	Price elasticity (comparison states totaled without Pennsylvania): (Col. 4 − Col. 7) / Col. 3	For the means of the comparison states: per capita consumption "after" minus per capita consumption "before" divided by per capita "before"	Price elasticity (means of comparison states): (Col. 4 − Col. 9) / Col. 3	Price elasticity using total comparison states, and as the "after" period the six months from +11 to +16
(6)	(7)	(8)	(9)	(10)	(11)
+0.97		+0.97	+.051	+0.67	−0.24
+0.85	+.009	+1.30	+.020	+0.75	+1.65
+0.82		+0.82	+.029	+0.88	+0.28
+0.25	+.009	+0.42	+.020	+0.21	+1.02
+0.06	+.063	−0.29	+.060	−0.20	−0.20
+0.02		+0.02	+.061	−0.04	+0.04
−0.03	+.009	+0.24	+.036	−0.58	+0.51
−0.12	+.009	+0.25	+.036	−0.88	+4.63
−0.15		+0.15	+.049	−0.18	−0.48
−0.15		−0.15	+.038	+0.08	+2.95
−0.56		−0.56	+.014	−0.42	−5.38
−0.79 [median]		−0.72 [median]	+.038	−0.46	−2.07
−0.84		−0.84	+.023	−0.81	−0.98
−0.84	+.071	−1.24	+.065	−1.00	−5.72
−0.96		−0.96	+.077	−0.79 [median]	−2.00
−1.00		−1.00	+.029	−0.88	−0.92
−1.03	+.009	−0.73	+.036	−1.63	−1.30
−1.29		−1.29	+.046	−1.17	−1.02
−1.32	+.063	−1.44	+.059	−1.40	−1.39
−1.90		−1.90	+.024	−1.88	−1.94
−1.97		−1.97	+.039	−1.58	−2.39
−3.73		−3.73	−.025	−3.93	−3.23
−4.35		−4.35	+.046	−4.04	−0.08

period are thoroughly mixed. In 13 cases the late-period estimate is higher, and in 10 cases it is lower. There is no reason to think that the elasticity was falling during the "after" period, or that the longer-run estimate should be less elastic.

It is worth noting, however, that if there *had* been differences between long- and short-run elasticities, this method could have detected the differences. The time-series method alone cannot compare long- and short-run elasticities. Indeed, the interpretation of the length-of-run nature of elasticities derived from cross-section methods, and from time series, including the various transformations of time series, is far from clear-cut. Nor can we claim a perfectly straightforward interpretation for quasi-experimental elasticities either, because the world in which the price changes play out their effect is not an otherwise static world, even after we standardize with the comparison states. Nevertheless, the interpretation

TABLE III

State	Date of price change	Price of Seagram 7 Crown fifth before price change	Relative price change (Price "after" minus price "before" divided by price before)	For the trial state: per capita consumption "after" minus per capita consumption "before" divided by per capita consumption "before"	For the comparison states totaled: per capita consumption "after" minus per capita consumption "before" divided by per capita "before"
	(1)	(2)	(3)	(4)	(5)
Georgia	6/6/55	(4.80) est.	.069	+.127	+.085
Alabama	12/1/59	4.20	.101	−.075	+.019
Virginia	7/1/60	3.65	.100	−.140	0
West Virginia	7/1/57	3.85	.065	−.086	+.021
Virginia	7/1/58	3.55	.028	−.013	+.050

would seem to be less difficult than for other methods, the biggest advantage being that the periods during which we examine the effect of particular price changes are exactly defined in length and are the same in each case, which is not true of the time-series method.

Elasticities may not be the same for a price decrease as for a price increase. Though we have not done so here, the quasi-experimental method would make possible the comparison of down-side and up-side elasticities, as time series and cross-sectional methods will not.

11. Informal inspection suggests no relationship between elasticity estimates and (a) amount of price change, (b) absolute price of liquor, or (c) secular date of price change. But if such relationships did exist, this method could reveal them. This is an important advantage over time series, which can estimate only *an* elasticity, whether or not it is constant over the range of prices.

6. COMPARISON OF RESULTS WITH OTHER STUDIES

Our elasticity estimate jibes with all studies except Niskanen's in that our estimate is substantially below −1.0. Our estimate, however, is higher than the other estimates.

Because Niskanen worked on the U.S. and because his technique was the most sophisticated, we must consider the differences between his results and ours.

1. Niskanen suggests that the presence of a thriving moonshine industry in this country explains the difference between his estimate for the U.S. and Stone's estimate for England. Moonshine can indeed be a strong substitute for legal liquor.

TABLE III (continued)

Price elasticity (comparison states totaled) Col. 4 − Col. 5 / Col. 3	For the comparison states totaled without Pennsylvania 1959 tax change: per capita consumption "after" minus per capita consumption "before" divided by per capita "before"	Price elasticity (comparison states totaled without Pennsylvania): Col. 4 − Col. 7 / Col. 3	For the means of the comparison states: per capita consumption "after" minus per capita consumption "before" divided by per capita "before"	Price elasticity (means of comparison states): Col. 4 − Col. 9 / Col. 3	Price elasticity using total comparison states, and as "after" period the six months from 11 to 16
(6)	(7)	(8)	(9)	(10)	(11)
+0.61		+0.61	+.077	+0.72	+1.17
−0.93	+.049	−1.23	+.042	−1.16	−0.77
−1.40	−.023	−1.17	+.012	−1.52	−1.36
−1.65	+.032	−1.82	+.020	−1.63	−1.66
−2.25	+.061	−1.71	+.053	−2.36	−2.14

But moonshining is mostly confined to a few states and little is exported to other states. Compared to a total of 4,835 illegal stills seized in Alabama in 1961, there were only 11 other states in which more than 100 stills were seized in that year, and only 4 other states with more than 1,000 seizures. In most states moonshine is not an available substitute, and hence, is not likely to affect national estimates very much.

Furthermore, most liquor sold is not sold at the lowest brand prices in any category of distilled spirits. Lower priced brands would seem, intuitively, to be closer substitutes for legal liquor than is moonshine. But price increases do not induce marked shifts to the cheaper brands. This lends further credence to the belief that moonshine is not an important substitute for legal liquor.

2. It is difficult to find a reasonable method of comparing the variability in Niskanen's results with the variability in this investigation. If we consider the estimates that result from Niskanen's various techniques as independent observations (which they obviously are not), the dispersion among them suggests considerably greater variability than is found in this study.

Niskanen, however, included elasticity estimates derived from techniques other than the method he finally chose to rely upon, and most of those other estimates were considerably less elastic than his basic estimate. Among them were [5; Appendix, Tables 37–44]:

(a) Alternate model including price of beer and wine as well as the price of liquor: −0.935.

(b) Wet states total population: −0.824.

(c) Wet states adults: −0.673.

(d) Dropping independent variables generally gave less elastic estimates.
(e) Using implicit retail prices instead of Niskanen's distillery index: −0.761.
(f) Using a quarterly index: −1.006.
(g) The entire time period 1934–1960: −0.397 (to be compared with the three-price estimate of −0.925).

We might also note that Niskanen used the R^2 as his test of the value of a regression, and therefore as the basis of choice for the estimates he relied upon, rather than a test of prediction of fresh data.

7. EVALUATION OF METHOD

1. All the cited time-series studies take explicit account of income changes, and some take account of taste trends and changes in general price level, as devices to reduce the variability in the universe and to isolate the effect of price changes. By comparison, the method used in this study not only takes out the long-term trends, but also the period-to-period variability, to the extent that income and taste changes affect the various states in the same way. Furthermore, the use of a sample of trial states must help wash out the idiosyncratic movements of given states with reference to all other states. On balance, I think this method has vast advantages over the time series in accounting for variations and trends in income, price level, and taste.

2. The method of this study is limited by the paucity of data. There are only 25 price changes to be considered. But no other method can develop *more* information than is provided by this number of price changes. And, in fact, the regression method tends to *lose* information where there are changes in consumption when prices do not change, if the consumption changes are not completely explained by the other variables—as, of course, they cannot be. It is true that a regression approach using a composite price index gains some information from brand price changes that take place in addition to tax-induced price changes. But liquor prices are remarkably sticky, so this is not a great advantage.

Furthermore, composite indices of liquor prices must be extremely crude, because of the multiplicity of brands and the lack of knowledge about individual brand sales, especially if the regression is for the U.S. as a whole.

3. The quasi-experiment method has in common with true experimental methods that causation is clearly established, because we can be reasonably sure which is the exogenous variable. This is a great advantage over time series.

4. A major advantage of this method is that it permits the critical reader to test it with his intuition at every step of the way to see if the method and results are reasonable. Complex econometric techniques are too often black boxes even to adepts; their complexity makes it impossible to *understand* the relationships, and consequently they leave one with a sense of unease. Such is not the case with the quasi-experiment. It does not demand faith for one to have belief in its results.

5. The method used in this study would seem to be useful in investigations where there are several divisible and independent economic units *within* which prices (or other sales-influencing variables) move together, but *among* which prices change independently. As an example, this author is presently using the same method in an investigation of the elasticities of retail and local advertisers with respect to newspaper advertising rates.

University of Illinois

REFERENCES

[1] KLEIN, LAWRENCE R.: *An Introduction to Econometrics* (Prentice Hall Inc., Englewood Cliffs, 1962).

[2] MALMQUIST, S.: *A Statistical Analysis of the Demand for Liquor in Sweden* (University of Uppsala, 1948), pp. 9 and 25.

[3] NAIR, K. R.: "Table of Confidence Interval for the Median in Samples From Any Continuous Population," *Sankhya*, Vol. 4 (1940), reproduced in Wilfred J. Dixon and Frank J. Massy, Jr., *Introduction to Statistical Analysis* (McGraw-Hill, 1957), p. 462.

[4] NISKANEN, WILLIAM A.: "Taxation and the Demand for Alcoholic Beverages," P-1872 (Santa Monica: The Rand Corp., Jan., 1960), pp. 5 and 6.

[5] ———: "The Demand for Alcoholic Beverages," Ph. D. thesis, (University of Chicago, 1962).

[6] PREST, A. R.: "Some Experiments in Demand Analysis," *Review of Economics and Statistics*, Vol. xxi, No. 1 (Feb., 1949), pp. 33–49.

[7] STONE, RICHARD: *The Role of Measurement in Economics* (Cambridge, University Press, 1951), p. 72.

[8] WATTELL, HAROLD: "The Whiskey Industry: An Economic Analysis," Ph. D. thesis, (New School of Social Research, 1954), Chapter 4.

[9] WOLD, HERMAN, AND LARS JUREEN: *Demand Analysis* (John Wiley & Sons Inc.: New York, 1951).

[7]

Foreword

Given that the quasi-experimental method worked so well for liquor, why not for cigarettes? And this study provided an opportunity to develop additional ways to exploit the method.

It was happenstance that I chose the same title – quasi-experimental method – as did Donald Campbell working in psychology and sociology. He means something a bit different than I do, however – all interrupted time-series are included in his set, whereas I include only those situations where there are non-changing "control" situations against which to compare the "experimental" situation.

Price Elasticity of the Demand for Cigarettes in the United States

HERBERT L. LYON AND JULIAN L. SIMON

The retail price elasticity of demand for cigarettes is a particularly important parameter for social decisions at this time. Results from prior cigarette elasticity studies vary widely, ranging from —0.10 to —1.48. Temporal changes may explain some of this variation, but differences in research methods are more important. The quasi-experimental approach used in this article yields an elasticity estimate (—0.511) free of many of the extraneous and irrelevant systematic influences that afflict time-series and cross-section methods. In addition, the length of run of the elasticity is known and explicit. The method provides built-in protections against bias from trends in collinear variables and produces sensible estimates with reasonably small and measurable dispersion.

THE retail price elasticity of demand for cigarettes is a particularly important parameter for social decisions at this time. It is the overwhelming consensus among scientists that cigarette smoking increases mortality.[1] And price increases are a possible sanction that the government might use to decrease cigarette use.

Several studies of this elasticity have been done previously [1, 2, 4, 5, 9, 12]. Our main reason for delving again into the matter is that the previous estimates differ rather widely, ranging from −0.10 to −1.48. Change over the course of time may explain some of the variation, but differences in method are more important, especially the difference between time series and cross sections.[2]

Study of the demand for cigarettes also provides another opportunity for trying out the "quasi-experimental" method in economics, and this study has led to further development of the method. Under this procedure, we estimated the arc elasticity of demand from the sales before and after a tax change in a state. These sales were standardized for secular changes in cigarette consumption in other states where price was unchanged. The method is therefore free of many of the extraneous and irrelevant systematic influences that afflict time series and cross sections. The method was used earlier to estimate the price elasticity of liquor [6], and cigarette consumption offers a particularly good chance to test further the usefulness and accuracy of the method.

---

[1] The Surgeon General's Committee *unanimously* agreed to use the term "causal" for the smoking–mortality relationship [11].

[2] The most elastic estimate was from the cross-section study [2]. This is what one would expect, assuming that the year-to-year correlation in cigarette prices among states is extremely high and that the price of cigarettes has at least some lagged effect

HERBERT L. LYON *is assistant professor of business administration at the University of Kentucky, and* JULIAN L. SIMON *is associate professor of economics and marketing at the University of Illinois.*

As with liquor, the quasi-experimental method is especially appropriate for cigarettes because retail price changes are very infrequent. Infrequency of change is helpful for this quasi-experimental method and damaging to time-series analysis. Also, the length of run of the computed elasticity is known and explicit, unlike time-series and cross-section estimates, for which the lengths of run are "short" and "long," respectively, but unspecifiable in either case. This property is useful to policy makers who contemplate price alterations. Still another relevant property of the method is that it controls for forces such as culture, religion, international tension, and other influences which might bias time-series estimates. One possible drawback of the method is that there might be "leakage" across state borders in response to price differentials, but this effect was observed not to be important in the case of liquor, and hence we think it safe to disregard it here.

For each tax-change "trial" or "experiment," we computed an arc elasticity,

$$e_p = \frac{\dfrac{Q_2 - Q_1}{Q_1} - \sum_{i=1}^{N}\left(\dfrac{Q_4 - Q_3}{Q_3}\right) \Big/ N}{\dfrac{P_2 - P_1}{P_1}},$$

where

e_p is the price elasticity,

Q_1 is the consumption for the year (January to December) ended before price change in the trial state,

Q_2 is the consumption for the year (January to December) beginning after price change in the trial state,

Q_3 is the consumption for the year (January to December) before price change in the comparison states, for example, all states in which price was unchanged during the relevant period,

Q_4 is the consumption for the year (January to December) after price change in the comparison states,

P_1 is the price for the year before change,

P_2 is the price for the year after change, and

N is the number of comparison states.

The resulting estimates of price elasticity refer to the response in a defined period of time, in this case the year from 6 to 18 months after the

---

on consumption; the rationale is that a simple cross-section estimate sums up much of the effect of past as well as present price influence. Short time series, such as those used in some of the studies [1, 4, 5, 9, 12], are less likely to cumulate lagged influence into the estimate because of the relatively low serial correlation; hence, they produce smaller elasticities. The logic underlying the remarks in this footnote is worked out in Simon and Aigner [8].

price change. It is implicitly assumed that no other price changes occur in the state between the price change being studied and the measurement period. If the observed elasticity is, say, −0.50, and a price change of 10 percent occurs, consumption will be 5 percent less than it would otherwise be during the 12-month period beginning six months after the price change. Estimates of state retail prices and per capita consumption in the years before and after the tax changes were taken from data published by the Tobacco Tax Council [10, pp. 61–111]. These data are obtained annually by means of a sample survey conducted in all states which impose cigarette taxes. These price terms are a weighted average retail price per pack, with both the form of sale (over the counter, single pack price, carton lot price, and vending machine price) and the types of cigarettes sold (regular size, king size, and filter tip) being taken into consideration. It seems fair to conclude that this survey produces reasonable state price estimates, since the price of cigarettes is much the same throughout a state. Substantial price differentials are normally found only by comparing states and are due primarily to the variation in state tax schedules.

The denominators in each ratio on the right-hand side of the equation are "before" quantities, despite the fact that some writers advise using the midpoint of the before and after values. Our reasoning is that when in policy discussions people ask, "What percentage change in consumption will a price change of x percent cause?" they mean, "What proportion *of the existing level* of consumption will the future level be?" Such a question calls for an answer derived from an elasticity formula with the existing level in the denominator, such as is used here. But this discussion may be moot, because the differences between estimates derived from the two formulas are quite small.

The individual estimates for each "trial" are shown in Table 1. The median estimate is −0.511. We think that the median is a more sensible central-value estimate than the mean in this case, because it is less sensitive to the kind of sampling variation that is present here. This is illustrated by the fact that the overall mean is −0.571 but the omission of only a single observation—the −7.100 observation for Maine's 1961 price change—shifts the mean to −0.477. No single observation affects the median anywhere near so much. In any case, the difference between the two estimates of central value is sufficiently small that we need not argue about which one to pitch upon as the more appropriate. Almost any policy decision would be the same no matter which estimate was used.[3]

[3] An interesting methodological sidelight comes out of an earlier time-series attempt by Lyon. Regressions were computed for each of 37 states for the years 1950–1965, using price and per capita income as independent variables, with per capita sales as the dependent variable. The estimates of price elasticity ranged from +1.497 to —1.614. This gives some idea of the accuracy of any single time-series

Table 1. Arc elasticities for changes in the price of cigarettes in individual states

State	Year of price change	Price in preceding year	Price increase (new price minus old price, divided by old price)	Computed elasticity
		cents	*percent*	
Illinois	1960	26.4	−1.8	1.725
Iowa	1959	24.8	4.8	1.139
Illinois	1961	25.9	0.3	0.957
Alabama	1955	24.0	2.9	0.863
Connecticut	1956	22.5	8.4	0.802
North Dakota	1963	27.1	5.2	0.517
Delaware	1961	24.6	10.6	0.407
Ohio	1956	20.7	8.2	0.304
Minnesota	1963	28.7	4.9	0.204
New Hampshire	1951	20.2	0.5	0.125
Mississippi	1964	30.4	3.2	0.122
Kentucky	1960	23.9	0.4	0.106
Kansas	1957	22.8	9.6	0.031
Rhode Island	1960	26.0	2.3	−0.032
Nevada	1961	25.9	11.6	−0.100
Tennessee	1963	26.1	11.1	−0.142
Michigan	1962	27.1	6.2	−0.174
Idaho	1955	22.2	7.2	−0.234
Pennsylvania	1955	23.3	5.6	−0.240
Michigan	1960	26.5	4.5	−0.251
South Dakota	1959	24.8	9.7	−0.277
Georgia	1964	29.4	1.0	−0.301
Tennessee	1951	19.4	20.1	−0.302
New Mexico	1955	22.9	7.4	−0.302
Kansas	1964	25.6	9.7	−0.307
Iowa	1963	26.4	5.7	−0.328
Maine	1955	23.0	4.8	−0.329
Pennsylvania	1963	26.8	10.8	−0.346
Arkansas	1951	20.5	18.5	−0.357
New Jersey	1956	23.1	10.3	−0.376
Georgia	1955	23.0	12.2	−0.377
Mississippi	1958	26.1	3.8	−0.383
Mississippi	1962	27.4	11.3	−0.385
South Dakota	1955	22.1	3.7	−0.393
Texas	1955	24.5	0.8	−0.444
New Jersey	1963	28.8	4.2	−0.482
Nebraska	1957	22.4	11.2	−0.511
Mississippi	1955	23.3	5.6	−0.538
Utah	1954	20.8	11.1	−0.541
Michigan	1957	22.9	13.1	−0.549
Minnesota	1959	24.8	7.7	−0.554
Utah	1963	24.9	18.1	−0.600
Kentucky	1954	20.0	16.5	−0.613
Connecticut	1961	26.6	0.8	−0.644
Rhode Island	1964	27.3	9.2	−0.692
Illinois	1959	24.5	7.8	−0.713
Iowa	1953	22.0	0.5	−0.724
Florida	1963	26.3	12.9	−0.734
New York	1959	24.0	6.7	−0.749
Alabama	1959	25.8	10.1	−0.752
New Jersey	1961	26.3	8.7	−0.753
Oklahoma	1961	26.1	9.6	−0.766
Massachusetts	1958	26.7	4.1	−0.805

Table 1. (*Continued*)

State	Year of price change	Price in preceding year	Price increase (new price minus old price, divided by old price)	Computed elasticity
Montana	1957	23.7	27.0	−0.886
South Carolina	1951	21.9	0.5	−0.926
South Carolina	1959	24.4	8.2	−0.971
Connecticut	1963	26.8	3.7	−0.972
Ohio	1959	23.8	8.9	−0.975
Texas	1959	25.6	12.1	−1.018
Minnesota	1961	26.6	7.9	−1.024
Michigan	1961	27.7	−2.1	−1.066
Pennsylvania	1959	26.2	2.3	−1.118
Idaho	1961	26.3	4.1	−1.145
Rhode Island	1958	23.6	9.3	−1.146
North Dakota	1951	22.8	0.4	−1.157
Delaware	1953	21.0	0.5	−1.282
New Mexico	1961	26.9	11.5	−1.339
Nebraska	1963	25.8	6.6	−1.420
South Dakota	1963	26.6	7.1	−1.443
Idaho	1959	25.9	1.5	−1.478
Idaho	1963	28.0	5.0	−2.041
Georgia	1951	24.8	−16.9	−2.092
Maine	1961	26.4	1.1	−7.100

One of the characteristics of this method is that it lends itself to meaningful measurement of the accuracy of the estimate. A 95-percent confidence interval around the median spans −0.346 and −0.713, the twenty-eighth and forty-sixth observations [3, p. 551], suggesting a high reliability for the estimate. The chosen central-value estimate seems quite reasonable in light of previous estimates; it is of the same general order as the time-series estimates and much lower than the cross-section estimate. This estimate can be said to be the elasticity of demand for the 12-month period centered on 6 to 18 months after the price change.[4]

Table 1 shows that in many cases there are considerable differences between the computed arc elasticities for different years for the same state; for example, the observed elasticities for Illinois were +1.725 in 1960, +0.957 in 1961, and —0.713 in 1959. Similarly for Iowa they were +1.139 in 1959, —0.328 in 1963, and —0.724 in 1953; but there are only small differences between successive observations in other states. This leads us to ask how much of a given observation's deviation from the mean

estimate for cigarettes. There is no reason to believe that an aggregate U. S. time series should be more accurate than the estimate for any single state, except that aggregate U. S. population figures are more accurate in intercensal years than are estimates for states.

[4] If monthly data had been available by states, the analysis could have been sharpened by starting the 12-month observation periods at more sensible intervals around the price changes.

is accounted for by the particular elasticity that inheres in the state and how much by chance variation. Therefore, we examined the pairs of estimates for states that appear twice or more in our list. (For states that appeared more than twice, two of the estimates were selected randomly to make a pair.) If the estimates reflect properties of the state, the members of pairs of observations should be relatively close together. We therefore counted the numbers of pairs both of whose members are on the same side of the group median. Only seven are found to be on the same side, as compared to 17 pairs that straddle the median, a result which is "more random" than the random expectation of half being straddles. We may therefore conclude that deviation of a state observation from the median is not a property of the state. This supports our procedure of lumping together all the individual observations and considering them as a sample from which to estimate the elasticity of the United States as a whole.

A useful property of this method is that one may easily examine whether price elasticities differ from place to place, among subgroups within the population, or over the course of time. We shall begin with the last.

Many changes occurred in the cigarette market over the period of this study: for example, the shift to filters, and the growing awareness of the threat to health from cigarette smoking. Therefore, it is interesting to see if there were any systematic changes in elasticity during the period, which this method allows us to examine. The estimates were grouped by years in Table 2.

Table 2. Elasticity estimates grouped by years in which change in the prices of cigarettes occurred

Year	Median elasticity	Number of observations
1951	−0.691	6
1953	−1.003	2
1954	−0.577	2
1955	−0.329	9
1956	+0.304	3
1957	−0.530	4
1958	−0.805	3
1959	−0.971	11
1960	+0.037	4
1961	−0.766	1
1962	−0.279	2
1963	−0.541	12
1964	−0.304	4

No apparent time trend in elasticity observations is found. Besides the light this throws on actual elasticities, it also suggests an absence of secular trends that might bias our central-value summary estimate. The ability to inspect for such trends seems to be an inherent advantage of the quasi-experimental method; by comparison the time-series method throws together observations from different dates, and the cross-section method yields an estimate that applies to only a single date.

Another interesting question is whether elasticity depends importantly upon income. Theory suggests that the higher per capita income is, the less elastic should demand be. We therefore examined the two median elasticity estimates for the trial states above and below the median per capita disposable income. The median for the lower-income states was −0.419 and for the higher-income states was −0.549. This does not accord with the theoretical expectation. Furthermore, a significance test[5] suggests that such a spread or an even wider one would occur frequently by chance. We may therefore conclude that there is no important relationship between income and elasticity over the range of state incomes.

Another question is whether the size of the price change influences the sharpness of response to it. The medians of the observations from price changes less than and greater than 6.7 percent (the median price change) were, respectively, —0.419 and —0.549. This enables us to conclude that elasticity is not strongly a function of size or price change (see the Nair test earlier), although the difference suggests that a bigger change tends to be associated with a higher elasticity.

A last inquiry was into regional differences in elasticity. The observed medians were —0.743 for the West, —0.360 for the North Central, —0.563 for the North East, and —0.415 for the South. A spread this great or greater would happen quite frequently just by chance even if there were no systematic difference among regions.

At the outset it was noted that price changes might be considered as a device to reduce smoking. And an elasticity of −0.50 or slightly more suggests that price is a not insignificant control variable. It is simply not true that "people will go on smoking no matter what it costs them." If the elasticity estimates can be extrapolated far beyond the range of observation, doubling price would halve sales in the first year, a very large effect by any standard. However, if there are any alternatives which would reduce consumption, and there are [7], tax increases probably should not be used for such purposes, because there may well be a vicious boomerang effect. The higher the price, the further toward the butt-end cigarettes are smoked, and the toxicity per puff increases rapidly as the cigarette grows shorter

[5] This was a randomization test using Monte Carlo drawings. We asked how often the median of a randomly drawn sample of 36 of the 73 observed values would be outside the observed bracket, —0.419 to —0.549. Of 20 trials run, only 5 were outside it.

and collects tars. The extent of this effect should be studied carefully before prices are increased to reduce consumption.

References

[1] Federal Reserve Bank of Richmond, Research Department, *Flue-Cured Tobacco, An Economic Survey,* Richmond, Va., Federal Reserve Board of Richmond, 1952.

[2] MAIER, FRANK H., "Consumer Demand for Cigarettes Estimated from State Data," *J. Farm Econ.* 37:690–704, Nov. 1955.

[3] NAIR, K. R., "Table of Confidence Intervals for the Median in Samples from Any Continuous Population," *Sankhya* 4:551–558, Part 4, 1940.

[4] SACKRIN, S. M., "Factors Affecting the Demand for Cigarettes," *Agr. Econ. Res.* 14:81–88, Aug. 1962.

[5] SCHOENBERG, E. H., "The Demand Curve for Cigarettes," *J. Bus.* 6:15–35, Jan. 1933.

[6] SIMON, JULIAN L., "The Price Elasticity of Liquor in the U. S., and a Simple Method of Determination," *Econometrica* 11:193–205, Jan. 1966.

[7] ———, "The Health Economics of Cigarette Consumption," *J. Human Resources* 3:111–117, Winter 1968.

[8] SIMON, JULIAN L., AND DENNIS AIGNER, "The Nature of Cross-Section and Time-Series Parameter Estimates," Systems Formulation, Methodology, and Policy Workshop Paper 6801, Social Systems Research Institute, Madison, University of Wisconsin, Jan. 1968.

[9] STONE, RICHARD, *The Measurement of Consumers' Expenditures and Behavior in the United Kingdom, 1920–1938,* Cambridge, England, Cambridge University Press, 1954.

[10] Tobacco Tax Council, Inc., *The Tax Burden on Tobacco: Historical Compilation,* Richmond, Va., 1966.

[11] U. S. Surgeon General's Advisory Committee, *Smoking and Health,* Washington, Government Printing Office, 1964.

[12] U. S. Treasury Department, Division of Tax Research, *Federal Excise Taxes on Tobacco,* 1948, mimeo.

[8]

Foreword

This paper was born when a colleague of ours seemed to draw some illegitimate conclusions about the relationships of cross-section and time-series elasticities in a study he showed me. I tried to sort out what was going on econometrically, but could only arrive at a vague intuition. When I explained to Denny Aigner as best I could what I thought was happening, he was able to bring the power of formal reasoning to bear in the most fruitful sort of way – and within a day or two. This is mathematics performing at its best, in my view – to truly clarify rather than to impress and hence to obscure.

Our method is applied in Chapter 30.

A SPECIFICATION BIAS INTERPRETATION OF CROSS-SECTION VS. TIME SERIES PARAMETER ESTIMATES

DENNIS J. AIGNER and JULIAN L. SIMON*
University of Wisconsin and University of Illinois

This paper is addressed to two related problems. First, within the context of a given model what are the proper interpretations of coefficient estimates generated by cross-section and time-series estimation procedures? Second, how may a cross-section or time-series estimate be adjusted so as to yield an unambiguous interpretation, for its own interest or for subsequent combination with another estimation procedure?[1] Our development of answers to these questions extends a suggestion of Malinvaud [23, pp. 126-9] and builds on an earlier contribution of Grunfeld [11].

The paper's core idea refers to structures in which the dependent variable is a function of lagged independent variables. If the estimating equations were fully specified as to these lagged variables, the problem we attack would not exist. But such is seldom the case because, on the one hand, multicollinearity prevents an adequate time-series evaluation of coefficients, and on the other, only single-period data are usually available for cross-section analysis. The problem therefore is how to make sense of estimates generated by cross-sections and time-series that are underspecified with respect to lagged independent variables. The problem is most frequent and most acute in cross-sections, so we shall concentrate upon them.

A standard misspecification bias analysis of the incorrectly specified cross-section equation provides a clear answer. As is well known, the extent of the bias depends on the (unknown) structural coefficients of the lagged independent variables and the correlations of excluded with included variables [9]. After working out the specification bias analysis in Section I, we proceed in Section II to show how many conflicting yet apparently comparable cross-section and time-series coefficients can be reconciled on the grounds of left-out variables.

One wishes not only to understand the nature of estimated coefficients, but also to adjust for the bias in them. Such adjustment requires imputing values to the omitted coefficients and to the independent variable correlation pattern, based on other empirical studies or on a priori beliefs about the structure. This problem is attacked in Section III. Time-series

*The authors are grateful to Daniel Laughhunn for bringing the problem to their attention and for thoughtful discussion at the formative stage of the work.

1. We concentrate here on the problem of the direct interpretation of estimates, though most of the literature is in the context of combined estimation techniques.

estimates of the structural coefficients of left-out variables are often available for adjusting or interpreting the bias content of a given cross-section estimate (although their statistical significance may be dubious). And if one is willing to use a geometrically declining lag structure for these coefficients, bounds on the bias in the given cross-section coefficient are readily computed. Two examples from the permanent-income-hypothesis literature illustrate the quantitative analysis of bias in Section IV. Finally, in the context of Durbin's [4] method for combined estimation of coefficients from time-series and available cross-section data, we show how the bias analysis may be incorporated directly, eliminating the need to know or willingness to assume the values of coefficients of left-out variables.

I. THE INTERPRETATION OF CROSS-SECTION AND TIME-SERIES ELASTICITIES

It has been usual in demand studies to characterize cross-section estimates of price and income elasticities[2] as "long run" in nature, and the corresponding time-series estimates as "short run" [15, p. 54] [19, p. 390] [38]. Taylor's explanation of the distinction is particularly succinct:[3]

> Time series variation is dominated by dynamic, intertemporal factors that are absent from cross section data. As a consequence ... time series estimates will largely reflect short-run adjustment to changes in income and prices, while cross section estimates will tend to reflect long-run adjustment .... not all households will be affected equally by cyclical and other time-varying factors, in which case cross section estimates will also reflect some short-run phenomena .... however ... the impact of time-varying factors on cross-section variation is small relative to the impact of factors peculiar to individual households. Factors such as family size, age of head of household, race, education of head, etc., all vary from household to household, but very little from year to year. As a result, they will be reflected only to a small extent in time series variation .... These facts go a long way toward explaining why cross section estimates [of income elasticities] are usually substantially higher than time series estimates, since in terms of flows, long-run coefficients are always at least as large as short-run coefficients [33, pp. 12-13].

The "short-run" versus "long-run" distinction made by Taylor is a very special one, and in the cross-section refers to a set of distributed lag relationships, as follows

$$(1) \qquad q_{it} = a_0 x_{i,t} + a_1 x_{i,t-1} + a_2 x_{i,t-2} \cdots + a_k x_{i,t-k}$$

$$q_{i,t+1} = a_0 x_{i,t+1} + a_1 x_{i,t} + a_2 x_{i,t-2} \cdots + a_k x_{i,t-k+1}$$

$$\vdots$$

$$q_{i,t+n} = a_0 x_{i,t+n} + a_1 x_{i,t+n-1} + a_2 x_{i,t+n-2} \cdots + a_k x_{i,t-k+n}$$

2. We shall hereafter use the terms "elasticity" and "coefficient" interchangeably.

3. We are grateful to Professor Taylor for permission to quote from this unpublished work.

where the $\{x_{t-j}\}$ form a series of stimuli such as prices or incomes or profits or advertising in the current and past periods, q_t is a response such as consumption or investment, and the model is understood to apply to some decision unit *i*. Any particular coefficient a_j gives $\partial q_t/\partial x_{t-j}$ for a given period.

The coefficients for any period may be estimated unambiguously in two ways. First, in some opportune circumstances, price changes occur *infrequently* and fortuitously. In such cases, the change in q between the "before" base-line period and any particular subsequent time period may be studied. Such "quasi-experimental" income elasticities of consumption have been estimated for single periods (e.g., the year after the price change) for liquor [29] and cigarettes [21]. A similar attempt was made to measure the "impulse elasticities" of postal rate changes in Sweden [1].

Second, the coefficient a_j for any period $(t - j)$ may be estimated by a time-series regression analysis of data for the "average" decision unit using a traditional distributed-lags model, say

$$q_t' = a_0 x_t' + a_1 x_{t-1}' \ldots + a_k x_{t-k}' + \epsilon_t \qquad t = 1, \ldots, T \tag{2}$$

where primes denote average or aggregate quantities, ϵ_t is a random term, and the aggregation is a straightforward arithmetic one on the linear (or geometric for the log-linear) equation. All variables are assumed to be measured from their respective sample means. For simplicity, the coefficients $a_0, a_1, \ldots, a_k$ in (2) are assumed identical to those in (1) to allow our discussion to cover cross-comparisons of the cross-section and time-series cases. Without this simplifying assumption our analysis is still useful, but we must limit ourselves to speaking of the cross-section case relative to *its* set of coefficients, and the time-series case relative to *its* coefficients, with the linkage between the coefficient sets unspecified. In any event, there is no question of the length-of-run nature of an a_j; it applies to the labeled period, $t - j$. This ends the interpretation problem for any properly specified time-series analysis. Later we shall discuss the interpretation of coefficients generated by time-series regressions that are misspecified.

The problem of interpretation for cross-section elasticities is not so easily disposed of. Let us first assume that a regression framework with least-squares estimation is appropriate: the model is of the equation (2) variety but specified over the decision units with only independent variables and their lags on the right-hand side. The question is, when one estimates a_0 from a cross-section regression $q_{it} = a_0 x_{it} + e_i$ what does a_0— the least-squares estimate—estimate? Two obvious limit cases provide intuitive ground:

(a) If $x_t = x_{t-1} = x_{t-2} \ldots = x_{t-k}$ then the expected value of a_0 equals $a_0 + a_1 + a_2 + \ldots + a_k$.

(b) If x_t is independent of x_{t-j} in all periods ($j = 1, \ldots, k$), then the expected value of a_0 equals a_0 because the collinear effects of the various $x_{i,t-j}$ upon q_{it} wash out (the x's are orthogonal).

Now for a more formal analysis of the meaning of the observed coefficient a_0 obtained from a cross-section analysis. Assume that only one independent variable is a priori relevant and that its lagged effect extends for only two periods, from $t-1$ to t, all more distant lags having zero effect. The analysis easily generalizes to an arbitrary number of independent variables and time periods, and is a conventional evaluation of specification bias.

The specified model (measuring all variables from their respective means) is

$$q_{it} = a_0 x_{it} + \epsilon_i^* \qquad i = 1, \ldots, N \tag{3}$$

whereas the true behavioral equation is assumed to be

$$q_{it} = a_0 x_{it} + a_1 x_{i,t-1} + \epsilon_i \qquad i = 1, \ldots, N \tag{4}$$

with ϵ_i a classical disturbance, having zero mean and constant variance.

A least-squares estimate from (3) is calculated by

$$a_0 = [\Sigma q_{it} x_{it}] [\Sigma x_{it}^2]^{-1} \tag{5}$$

the summation running over $i = 1, \ldots, N$, unless otherwise indicated.

Substituting for q_{it} from (4):

$$\begin{aligned} a_0 &= [\Sigma(a_0 x_{it} + a_1 x_{i,t-1} + \epsilon_i) x_{it}] [\Sigma x_{it}^2]^{-1} \\ &= [a_0 \Sigma x_{it}^2 + a_1 \Sigma x_{it} x_{i,t-1} + \Sigma \epsilon_i x_{it}] [\Sigma x_{it}^2]^{-1} \end{aligned} \tag{6}$$

By specification, ϵ and x_t are uncorrelated, so that upon taking the expectation of (6)

$$E(a_0) = a_0 + a_1 [\Sigma x_{it} x_{i,t-1} / \Sigma x_{it}^2] = a_0 + a_1 b_{t,t-1} \tag{7}$$

where $b_{t,t-1}$ is the (cross-section) regression slope from running x_{t-1} on x_t. In terms of correlation coefficients

$$E(a_0) = a_0 + a_1 r_{t,t-1} [\Sigma x_{i,t-1}^2]^{1/2} [\Sigma x_{it}^2]^{1/2} \tag{8}$$

Over two of the usual periods of analysis—years, say—the variance of price, income, or other such economic variables is not likely to change greatly, so that $[\Sigma x_{i,t-1}^2]$ will approximate $[\Sigma x_{it}^2]$, and (8) may be reduced to

$$E(a_0) \doteq a_0 + a_1 r_{t,t-1} \tag{9}$$

This stripped-bare equation is the key to understanding the nature of cross-section estimates. (And later essentially the same formula will help us understand time-series estimates as well.) The extent to which the expected cross-sectional elasticity a_0 differs from the "actual" current-period elasticity α_0 (the specification bias[4]) is a function only of the correlation between the independent variables from period $t-1$ to period t and of the relative size of the lagged effect, α_1/α_0.

Generalizing equation (4) to include many prior periods, we write

$$q_{it} = \alpha_0 x_{it} + \alpha_1 x_{i,t-1} + \ldots + \alpha_k x_{i,t-k} + \epsilon_i \qquad i = 1, \ldots, N \tag{4a}$$

Following the same logic as in equations (5) and (6), we get

$$E(a_0) = \alpha_0 + \alpha_1 b_{t,t-1} + \alpha_2 b_{t,t-2} \ldots + \alpha_k b_{t,t-k} \tag{7a}$$

and

$$E(a_0) \doteq \alpha_0 + \alpha_1 r_{t,t-1} + \alpha_2 r_{t,t-2} + \ldots + \alpha_k r_{t,t-k} \tag{9a}$$

As will be seen in what follows, (9a) is the main working relationship of the paper.[5]

Almost inevitably, the longer the span between time periods, the lower the correlation between independent variables in the cross-section. That is, we can expect $|r_{t,t-1}| > |r_{t,t-2}| > \ldots > |r_{t,t-k}|$, and in most cases of the sort under consideration the structural effect of more distant periods may be expected to be smaller than that of less distant periods; that is, $|\alpha_1| > |\alpha_2| > \ldots > |\alpha_k|$. Therefore, the sum of the effects of past periods, as given by the products $|\alpha_j r_{t,t-j}|$, tends to zero as the lag is extended, the bias being thereby dominated by the most recent terms, which is reasonable.

Now let us consider the interpretation of *time-series* estimates that are biased because the incorrectly specified model is

$$q_t' = a_0 x_t' + \epsilon_t^* \qquad t = 1, \ldots, T \tag{10}$$

Reasons why this might be the specified model are multicollinearity or extreme shortage of observations. The analysis is exactly the same as above. Using the aggregate analogue of (4) as the true equation,

$$E(a_0) = \alpha_0 + \alpha_1 r'_{t,t-1} [\Sigma_t x_{t-1}'^2]^{1/2} [\Sigma_t x_t'^2]^{-1/2} \tag{11}$$

The x_{t-1}' and x_t' series differ by only one term at each end, and so

$$E(a_0) \doteq \alpha_0 + \alpha_1 r'_{t,t-1} \tag{12}$$

4. Sometimes a_0 may be a quantity of legitimate interest rather than just an imperfect approximation to another quantity, and in such case the term "bias" may be inappropriate. But we shall refer to the difference between a_0 and α_0 as "bias" because of the statistical use of the term.

5. While specified only in terms of a_0, it should be clear that (9a) can be formulated so as to yield the specification bias for any estimated (included) coefficient a_j in terms of the left-out variables. And, pursuant to the previous footnote, if in (9a) the α_j's are replaced by their counterpart *estimated* multiple regression coefficients, the equation expresses an approximate algebraic relation for a_0 (rather than $E(a_0)$). Equation (7a) with a like substitution gives the exact relationship.

$r'_{t,t-1}$ representing a one-period autocorrelation. In the extended form (9a), the r's would encompass second- and higher-order autocorrelation influences.

If the time-series has no trend, $r'_{t,t-1} = 0$ and $E(a_0) = a_0$. If the trend of the time-series is upward or downward, in general $r'_{t,t-1} > 0$ and hence a_0 is biased upwards, assuming a_0, $a_1 > 0$. If it is generally true that the set of autocorrelations is pairwise closer to zero than the analogous set in the cross-section case, this implies that the bias in time-series estimates from time-period misspecification will often be small relative to cross-section estimates no matter what the specified model.[6]

II. QUALITATIVE USES OF THE BIAS ANALYSIS

A few examples of how the specification bias analysis can be used to make sense of conflicting empirical results are now discussed.

Income elasticities. Observers of income elasticities (e.g., the earlier Taylor quote) note that cross-section estimates are commonly higher than time-series estimates. In light of the bias analysis, this makes sense if the elasticity is positive and the correlation of current income on its lags is higher in cross-sections than in most time-series of "short" length, which seems the case.

Price elasticities. The one-year lag price elasticity of cigarettes has been estimated to be -.511 (standard deviation = .18), using a quasi-experimental technique that has no time-specification error [21]. Maier [22] arrived at estimates of -1.08 and -1.48 from a cross-section analysis of the states. The difference between the two results is explainable if the cross-section lagged price correlations are very high—as they are—and if the lagged influence embodied in coefficient relationships is not very small.

The effect of income on fertility.[7] The difference between household cross-sections and business-cycle time-series of the relationship of income to birth rate has long been a conundrum, because the former is commonly negative[8] and the latter is quite positive. This led Wold to think that

6. It is apparent that lags in some time-series rapidly approach low correlations, especially over short periods with high cyclical variation. To illustrate, the period-to-period income correlations of cross-sections of Wisconsin taxpayers (between the years 1929-55) are as follows [7, pp. 187-88]; $r_{t,t-1} = .83$, $r_{t,t-2} = .78$, $r_{t,t-3} = .76$, $r_{t,t-4} = .70$, to be compared to serial correlations of U.S. per capita income over a short and long period:

	1923-40	*1897-1949*
$r'_{t,t-1}$	.78	.97
$r'_{t,t-2}$	.40	.91
$r'_{t,t-3}$	.04	.85
$r'_{t,t-4}$	-.36	.79

7. This issue is discussed in [31].

8. Except in Sweden and perhaps recently in the U.S., cases which we shall ignore.

"... the factor catalogue behind fertility variations over time seems to be different from the catalogue behind the cross-section variations of the fertility" [36, p. 10]. Furthermore, there is what Easterlin calls "... the oft-raised question of how one reconciles the apparent contradiction between the secular inverse (gross) association between income and fertility, on the one hand, the shorter-term positive association on the other ..." [3, p. 142]. Application of our analysis reconciles the contradiction and uses only a single "factor catalogue."

For the representative individual, we write

$$(13)\quad B_{it} = a_0 y_{it} + a_1 y_{i,t-1} \dots + a_{45} y_{i,t-45} \pm \beta_2 E_{i,t-2} \pm \beta_3 E_{i,t-3} \dots \pm \beta_{45} E_{i,t-45} + \epsilon_i$$

where B_{it} is the number of births in year t in the person's family; y_{it} is the person's family income in t; and E_{it} is a dummy variable indicating whether or not the person was in school in year t. This latter variable can be considered a proxy for all taste changes systematically associated with income.

Equation (13) states that the partial effect of income on births in any year t is positive and that education in any year may have a negative or positive partial effect. Income and education terms run back only to $t - 45$ on the assumption that children are born to people under the age of 50. Education terms begin with $t - 2$ to suggest that generally there is a time gap between the end of one's formal education and the fertility period.

Also, it is posited that whether a person is in school or not at any point in time is a positive function of income (up to a random term u_i):

$$(14)\quad E_{i,t-j} = \gamma_j y_{i,t-j} + u_i \qquad j = 2, \dots, t-1$$

Substituting, we get

$$(15)\quad B_{it} = a_0 y_{it} + a_1 y_{1,t-1} \dots + a_{45} y_{i,t-45} \pm \beta_2 \gamma_2 y_{i,t-2} \pm \beta_3 \gamma_3 y_{i,t-3} \dots \pm \beta_{45} \gamma_{45} y_{i,t-45} + (\epsilon_i \pm \beta_2 u_i \pm \dots \pm \beta_{45} u_i)$$

We now see that in this model the total effect of income can be positive or negative, depending upon the relative weights of the various coefficients.

By the arguments above, a cross-section fit of B_{it} on only y_{it} might well produce a negative a_0 if the $(\beta\gamma)$ coefficient products are negatively large relative to the corresponding a's and if the lag is great. It is also reasonable that a long historical series that is dominated by secular trend (and hence has high positive lag correlations) should also generate a negative a_0. But $r'_{t,t-2}$ and the higher order serial correlations seem sufficiently close to zero over the business cycle (cf. footnote 7) so that a_0 may not differ much from $\mathbf{a}_0$ in the time-series, and hence be positive, so the contradictions disappear.

The effect of income on the suicide rate. Over the business cycle the suicide rate is negatively correlated with income and employment, whereas cross-sections reveal a positive relationship between family income and suicide rate [12]. An analysis analogous to that used in the birth rate example, simply substituting the probability of suicide for the number of births, resolves the apparent paradox [30].

The consumption function and the permanent income hypothesis.[9] The device described in this paper is related to the explication of the relationship of the consumption function to cross-section studies by Friedman [7] and by Modigliani and Brumberg [26]. Those writers did not, however, arrive at a quantitative means to express the relationship, except by using more-or-less arbitrary estimates of the length of the permanent-income horizon. Our device invites both a more compact statement of the operational version of the permanent-income hypothesis, and permits further quantitative explorations of its role in explaining observed budget (and time-series) study results.

First let us consider the problem of a qualitative reconciliation of budget data with the permanent-income hypothesis. Why is the slope coefficient in budget studies (the marginal propensity to consume) less than the average propensity to consume as estimated from the budget study or from time-series (say, .88)? The answer may be put succinctly in terms of the bias analysis.

A three-period version of the operational model Friedman used frequently is

$$c_{it} = K(w_0 y_{it} + w_1 y_{i,t-1} + w_2 y_{i,t-2}) + \epsilon_i \qquad i = 1, \ldots, N \tag{16}$$

where y_t is measured income in t, $w_0 + w_1 + w_2 = 1$, and c_{it} is measured consumption in t.

The budget study estimates a slope a_0 from

$$c_{it} = a_0 y_{it} + e_i \tag{17}$$

Substituting into the basic equation (9a), we get

$$E(a_0) \doteq Kw_0 + r_{t,t-1} Kw_1 + r_{t,t-2} Kw_2 \tag{18}$$

We see that a_0 must on the average be less than K because the r's are less than one. The explanation of this difference that Friedman and Modigliani-Brumberg worked so hard to put forth in terms of "transitory"

9. This problem is discussed at length in [32].

and "permanent" income was laborious, then, because it was intrinsically tied to the empirical specification of permanent income.[10]

Now we are in a position to press further and ask *quantitatively* to what extent the magnitudes of observed budget coefficients are explained by specification error. Two examples are given later of the quantitative usefulness of this bias analysis.

III. "ESTIMATION" OF CROSS-SECTION SPECIFICATION BIAS

Nirvana is having sufficient data to run a fully specified time-series regression in which the variables exhibit low multicollinearity. Because this ideal is not attained in earthly work on income and price elasticities, recourse is often had to cross-section data. The purpose of this Section is to discuss methods by which cross-section estimates may be adjusted so that their interpretation is clear, either as estimates of period elasticities for use in policy decisions or for subsequent combination with a time-series regression.

Kuh argues for a starkly empirical approach to the problem: "*.... cross-sections cannot be used successfully to make time series predictions unless a systematic relationship between the cross-section and time series estimates has been firmly established.... It is most important that the numerical value of differences between estimates be ascertained. If the time series estimate is some function of the typical cross-section estimate, one estimate can be translated into the other irrespective of the causal factors that determined the discrepancy*" [18, pp. 210-11]. But this suggestion presupposes the availability of both sorts of estimates. And when both are available, we can do better than such brute empiricism. The important task is to consider the predicament when comparable estimates are just not available.

Two kinds of information are needed for cross-section estimate adjustment; the set of $\{r_{t,t-j}\}$, and at least the *relative* structure of the coefficients. Given this information, the adjustment is straightforward. For example, let us say that a_0 is found to be 1.5 in a cross-section study; the relative weights of a_0, a_1, a_2, and a_3 are assumed (perhaps on the basis of a time-series study) to be 1 (the numeraire), .5, .25, .125, with observed correlation coefficients of $r_{t,t-1} = .80$, $r_{t,t-2} = .70$, $r_{t,t-3} = .60$. Then, from (9a)

$$(19) \qquad 1.5 \doteq \sum_{j=0}^{3} a_j r_{t,t-j} = a_0 + (.80)(.5a_0) + (.70)(.25a_0) + (.60)(.125a_0) \doteq 1.65a_0$$

10. We owe the distinction between the measurement of permanent income and the permanent income hypothesis to a comment by Professor Friedman on a previous draft.

and thus $a_0 = .9$.

The only possible objective source of both necessary ingredients is multi-period data. This requirement seems to put us right back where we started, because the usual reason for turning to cross-section data is that multi-period time-series estimation is unsatisfactory in the particular situation. And, of course, if one possesses cross-section data over time, our whole exercise is irrelevant; one simply fits a random coefficients model or a regression model with a random effect (intercept) à la Kuh [18] or Balestra-Nerlove [2].

But the impasse may not be so absolute as it seems. Extraneous estimates of interperiod cross-section correlations are often available. (For the example of income, see Friedman's collection of interperiod correlations [7, pp. 187-88].) And various devices can help us get a foothold on the relative coefficient structure. These devices are necessarily combinations of extraneous information and simplifying assumptions.

An obvious convenient a priori construction of the lag structure is as a geometric series. For example, let the model be written in terms of one independent variable and its time lags, as

$$q_{it} = a \sum_{j=0}^{k} \lambda^j x_{i,t-j} + \epsilon_{it} \qquad i = 1, \ldots, N \tag{20}$$

with the usual assumptions about ϵ_{it} and $0 < |\lambda| < 1$. Also suppose the model we actually fit is merely the regression of q_{it} on x_{it}. The specification bias on the resulting least-squares estimate (a) of a is [from (7a)]:

$$\left[E(a) - a\right] = a(\lambda b_{t,t-1} + \lambda^2 b_{t,t-2} + \ldots \lambda^k b_{t,t-k}) \tag{21}$$

To evaluate (21), we require an assumption about or knowledge of the cross-section interperiod regression slopes of $x_{t-1}, \ldots, x_{t-k}$ on x_t. Alternatively, we may apply the approximate bias form (9a). In this instance the maximum (absolute) bias is given when the set of interperiod correlations is the unit vector. Under this assumption we have

$$\left[E(a) - a\right] = a \sum_{j=1}^{k} \lambda^j \tag{22}$$

Since $\sum_{j=0}^{k} \lambda^j = 1/(1 - \lambda)$ for $0 < |\lambda| < 1$ as $k \to \infty$, we have

$$\lim_{k \to \infty} \left[E(a) - a\right] = a[(1 - \lambda)^{-1} - 1] = a\lambda(1 - \lambda)^{-1} \tag{23}$$

The bias cannot be larger than the absolute value of $a\lambda(1 - \lambda)^{-1}$. If the lag effect is a lengthy one (λ close to one), obviously the bias will be substantially larger in absolute value than a itself. If the lag effect dissipates quickly (λ close to zero), the bias will be small. Clearly if one is willing to assess λ, he can produce a representation of the exact bias or a general approximate bound for it in terms of the coefficient to be estimated, a. If for instance, $\lambda = 1/3$ in (23), the estimated bias amounts to $|a/2|$ and the required adjustment is to either use $(2/3)a$ or $2a$ depending on whether the signs of interperiod correlation coefficients are positive or negative, respectively.

Other formulations of the interdependence relationship of the x's may be interesting and empirically reasonable, allowing a more precise estimate of the bias than the approximate bound (23) provides. For instance, an autoregressive interperiod correlation structure, $\rho, \rho^2, \ldots, \rho^{k-1}$, many times corresponds to empirical observation. Under this specification in conjunction with (21) we get a bias in the limit of

$$\text{(24)} \qquad \lim_{k \to \infty} \left[E(a) - a \right] = a\rho\lambda(1 - \rho\lambda)^{-1}$$

The distributed lag model in (20) is alternatively expressable in such a way that the indicated misspecification is much simpler. By writing out $q_{i,t-1}$, multiplying the resulting equation (both sides) by $-\lambda$ and adding to q_{it}, we get

$$\text{(25)} \qquad q_{it} = ax_{it} + \lambda q_{i,t-1} + w_{it}$$

where $w_{it} = \epsilon_{it} - \lambda\epsilon_{i,t-1}$. This is the formulation studied by Koyck [17] and Liviatan [20] and is important for us here since it suggests that one need not possess a continuum of observations $x_t, x_{t-1}, \ldots$ for the cross-section in order to estimate relevant coefficients. What is required are adjacent sets of observations on the dependent variable. The misspecification form (21) still applies to (25) as the true equation, although were we to attempt to *estimate* the true form (25) outright, least-squares would produce biased estimates due to the dependence of q_{t-1} on w_t. We obtain as an alternative to (21) the form

$$\text{(26)} \qquad \left[E(a) - a \right] = b_{q_{t-1}x_t}\lambda$$

Again for a quantitative evaluation, λ must be given some value, and we must be able to say something about $b_{q_{t-1}x_t}$. One would expect that the approximate formula would not be adequate in this case, since $\Sigma q_{i,t-1}{}^2/$

Σx_{it}^2 (with the variables expressed as deviations from their respective means) may be very different from one.

The above exercises should make clear the crucial requirement of an estimate of the lag structure, an estimate that must somehow be produced from some evidence or a priori reasoning. If no expedient for producing the estimate seems satisfactory, then one must recognize that he is in the position of trying to make bricks without straw. One-period cross-sections simply cannot be interpreted without extraneous estimates of the lag structure (and of the interperiod correlation coefficients). Some time-series evidence is absolutely necessary to estimate lags; this is why it is so important that panel data be collected in household budget surveys.

While we have directed our attention above to bias evaluation with a_0 the goal of estimation, it is an easy matter to consider $\sum_{j=0}^{k} a_j$ (or any partial sum) in the same light. And clearly, conditions that make the bias in a_0 small when attempting to estimate a_0 act in exactly the opposite way if the attempt is to estimate $\sum_{j=0}^{k} a_j$ by a_0. For example, high interperiod correlations make a_0 a poor estimator of a_0 but a good estimator of $\sum_{j=0}^{k} a_j$. This is the essential difference between the concepts of cross-section bias in the discussion of permanent income by Friedman and by Modigliani-Brumberg, and in the discussion of combining cross-sections and time-series by Kuh-Meyer.

With an eye toward bias control rather than evaluation, it may sometimes be possible to subdivide the total sample into strata that have lower interperiod correlation coefficients than that of the total sample, and thereby to effectively compensate for inherent misspecification bias. If the correlations in the strata approach zero, the current period coefficient, a_0, will be closely estimated with the cross-section no matter what the structure of the lags. Or it may be possible to evaluate the bias by comparing the cross-section estimates yielded by two groups of known but different interperiod correlations, e.g., comparing a stratum against the entire sample.

There is ample precedent for such stratification. Houthakker used a similar device in testing Friedman's permanent-income theory. He assumed that "there is less variation in permanent income amongst steelworkers than there is amongst people from all occupations combined" [13, p. 400] (also see Friedman [7, p. 216]). Houthakker then (incorrectly) deduced from Friedman's theory that the cross-section slope would be lower for the individual stratum, and this provided his test (see also [5]).

The necessary stratification vehicle to reduce specification bias in estimating a_0 is some instrumental device or demographic variable that will bring together persons in such a way as to produce low interperiod income correlation. For consumption models the most effective stratification scheme would seem to be stratifying directly on income. Friedman and Kuznets [8, pp. 327-438], for example, used a similar device in attempting to explain the incomes of professionals. However, if one actually had such lagged income data he would presumably use it directly to estimate the implied additional coefficient(s). One might group persons with very high and very low *current* incomes under the assumption that their dependence on past income is much different and likely to generate a correlation coefficient close to zero. It would not do simply to segregate the sample into groups with first lag correlations of zero and non-zero, because there is likely to be a relationship between a unit's income coefficient a_0 and its income stability from period to period.

IV. SOME EXAMPLES OF THE QUANTITATIVE ANALYSIS OF BIAS

We now move to demonstrate the quantitative usefulness of the bias analysis via two illustrations from the permanent income literature.

The first task will be to determine how much of the difference between K and $a_0 = Kw_0$, the average and short-run marginal propensities to consume of equation (16), may be explained by the lagged effect of income (i.e., by the "permanent-income" effect), on the evidence of budget studies.

Thomas Mayer [25][11] recently performed an ingenious test on the same point we shall attack. He reasoned that for large occupational groups transitory income averages out to zero in any given year, and that the mean measured income of a group is its mean permanent income. A plot of the ratios of mean measured-consumption to mean measured-income for occupational groups with different mean incomes would, if the "strict" permanent-income hypothesis is correct, pass through the origin. Furthermore, the actual location of the plot allows one to say *how much* of the difference between the average propensity to consume (for the society as a whole) and the marginal propensity is explained by the *statistical illusion* due to the (measured) permanent-income effect. Mayer found that ".... the results ... strongly reject the modified permanent income theory ... if one uses permanent income in place of measured income, only about one-third of the difference between the average propensity and marginal propensity to consume disappears" [25, pp. 1167 and 1170]. We shall now attack the problem differently, providing another estimate to compare with Mayer's.

11. See also his [24] and Eisner [5].

On the theoretical assumption that the lag structure is exponentially declining, Friedman estimated the geometric rate of decline from aggregate data. If the permanent income hypothesis is strictly correct, the coefficients in a regression of consumption on income and its lags must sum to .88, Friedman's estimate of K. From Friedman's Table 15 [7, p. 147n] the lag coefficients are roughly (assuming a cut-off at seven years): $a_0 = .31$, $a_1 = .21$, $a_2 = .14$, $a_3 = .09$, $a_4 = .06$, $a_5 = .04$, $a_6 = .03$.

In order to implement equation (9a) we next require the period-to-period correlation coefficients of income; one set is available from a study of Wisconsin taxpayers as cited by Friedman [7, p. 187]: $r_{t,t-1} = .83$, $r_{t,t-2} = .78$, $r_{t,t-3} = .78$, $r_{t,t-4} = .71$, $r_{t,t-5} = .70$, $r_{t,t-6} = .69$. Now substituting directly into equation (9a) we get $E(a_0) = .31 + (.83)(.21) + (.78)(.14) + (.78)(.09) + (.71)(.06) + (.70)(.04) + (.69)(.03) = .75$. This expected value of .75 for a_0 is the marginal propensity to consume that we would expect to observe in a cross-section budget study if the permanent-income hypothesis is strictly correct (and if the a_j and $r_{t,t-j}$ values used are reliable).

We may compare the .75 estimate to actually-observed budget slopes. Empirical estimates of a_0 range from .75 for the 1950 United States sample (Friedman, [7, p. 41])—which would suggest that the permanent-income hypothesis explains all of the effect—downward to estimates that *average* perhaps .70. In any case, this approach suggests that the permanent-income hypothesis explains considerably more than the one-third of the effect as estimated by Mayer; upwards of two-thirds may be more correct.[12]

As a second illustration, still within the general context of the permanent income literature, Klein [15, p. 221] found that the savings-income ratio of twenty-four months was less sensitive to income classifications than that of annual data, a result that is in the direction predicted by Friedman's hypothesis. Now let us see what equation (9a) suggests about a_0 if the period of analysis is two years instead of one. Writing out an extended version of (16) for c_{t+1} and adding to c_t gives the structure

$$c_{i,t} + c_{i,t+1} = Kw_0(y_{i,t+1} + y_{i,t}) + Kw_1(y_{i,t} + y_{i,t-1}) + Kw_2(y_{i,t-1} + y_{i,t-2}) + \dots \tag{27}$$

Assuming that we run $(c_{i,t} + c_{i,t+1})$ on $(y_{i,t+1} + y_{i,t})$, the bias form is

$$E(a_0, \text{two-year periods}) \doteq Kw_0 + Kw_1 r_{[t+(t+1)],[t+(t-1)]} + Kw_2 r_{[t+(t+1)],[(t-1)+(t-2)]} + \dots \tag{28}$$

12. Estimates using the Houthakker-Taylor [14] parameter estimates are more in Mayer's direction.

Now supposing that $\sigma_{y_t}{}^2 = \sigma_{y_{t-1}}{}^2$, etc., and $\text{cov}(y_t, y_{t-1}) = \text{cov}(y_{t-1}, y_{t-2})$, etc., the required correlation coefficients may be written in terms of available constituent parts, viz.,

(29) $$r_{[t+(t+1)],[(t-j)+(t-j-1)]} = [r_{t,t-j} + 2r_{t,t-j-1} + r_{t,t-j-2}]/2(1 + r_{t,t-1})$$

Carrying out the computations suggested by (28) and (29) with the data at hand gives an expected value of .76 for a_0 from two-year data under the permanent income hypothesis, as compared to the .75 expected value calculated previously for annual information. As one would expect also, further aggregation of time periods under a declining correlation structure will produce even higher expected marginal propensities to a limit of K.

V. COMBINED ESTIMATION UNDER CROSS-SECTION MISSPECIFICATION

In matrix notation, the specification bias form develops from considering the misspecified model

(30) $$q = X_1 A_1 + \epsilon^*$$

with the true model being

(31) $$q = X_1 A_1 + X_2 A_2 + \epsilon$$

in which q is a vector of N cross-section observations on the dependent variable; X_1 is the set of observation vectors on included independent variables with coefficient vector A_1; X_2 is the set of observation vectors on misspecified (left-out) variables with coefficient vector A_2; and ϵ is the disturbance vector in the true form with $E(\epsilon) = 0$, $E(\epsilon\epsilon') = \sigma^2 I$.

Misspecification bias in regression coefficients $A_1{}^*$ based on (30) is given by the second term in

(32) $$E(A_1{}^*) = A_1 + (X_1'X_1)^{-1} X_1'X_2 A_2$$

in which $B = (X_1'X_1)^{-1} X_1'X_2$ is a matrix of regression coefficients of the excluded variables on the included ones. (For us X_1 and X_2 are not entirely arbitrary. They contain sequential lags of independent variables, so that we speak of the bias in some a_j, for instance, in terms of left-out variables $x_{j-1}, \ldots$, but *not* in terms of $x_{j+1}, \ldots$, etc.)

Durbin's [4] technique for incorporating extraneous (cross-section) information into a time-series estimation problem may be utilized to alleviate the requirement of knowledge about A_2 for assessing the misspecification bias and simultaneously to produce estimates that incorporate cross-section and time-series information in "ideal" proportions. The procedure is a generalized least squares approach.

We state the *time-series* estimation problem in terms of the equation

(33) $$q = XA + u$$

with the usual assumptions on u. Here the dimensions of q are $T \times 1$; of X, $T \times k$; of A, $k \times 1$; and of u, $T \times 1$. From equation (32), we have

(34) $$A_1{}^* = A_1 + BA_2 + v$$

with $E(v) = 0$, which simply states that the expected value of $A_1{}^*$ from the cross-section is $A_1 + BA_2$. A is partitioned into $A = (A_1 A_2)'$ referring to the $(h \times 1)$ vector of included coefficients A_1 and the $[(k-h) \times 1]$ vector of left-out coefficients A_2, respectively. Now (34) becomes

(35) $$A_1{}^* = [I\ B]A + v$$

with I an $(h \times h)$ identity matrix. The estimation problem is written in the form

(36) $$\begin{bmatrix} q \\ A_1{}^* \end{bmatrix} = \begin{bmatrix} X \\ \hline I\ B \end{bmatrix} A + \begin{bmatrix} u \\ v \end{bmatrix}$$

with $E(u) = 0$, $E(v) = 0$, $E(uu') = \sigma_u{}^2 I$, and $E(vv') = \sigma^2 (X_1{}'X_1)^{-1} = W$. If we let $\Phi = 1/\sigma_u{}^2$ and $R = [I\ B]$, the generalized least squares estimates of A are given by

(37) $$A_D{}^* = \left[(X'R') \begin{bmatrix} \sigma_u{}^2 I & 0 \\ 0 & W \end{bmatrix}^{-1} \begin{bmatrix} X \\ R \end{bmatrix} \right]^{-1} (X'R') \begin{bmatrix} \sigma_u{}^2 I & 0 \\ 0 & W \end{bmatrix}^{-1} \begin{bmatrix} q \\ A_1{}^* \end{bmatrix}$$

$$= A + (\Phi X'X + R'W^{-1}R)^{-1}(\Phi X'u + R'W^{-1}v)$$

Since $E(u) = E(v) = 0$, $E(A_D{}^*) = A$, and we have as the variance-covariance matrix of $A_D{}^*$

(38) $$\Sigma_{A_D}{}^* = [\Phi X'X + R'W^{-1}R]^{-1}$$

We do not usually have $\sigma_u{}^2$ and W at our disposal, but estimates of them are available from the two samples.[13] The entire analysis hinges on availability of the matrix of cross-section sample regression coefficients B of the excluded independent variables, X_2, on the included ones, X_1. Presumably, if we could *actually* obtain this information we would have estimated the fully specified equation for the cross-section, and the bias analysis would not be of interest. The relevant and interesting question is: to what extent is the above technique useful when B is unknown?

The answer seemingly is not available analytically, but only in terms of

13. We can easily obtain an estimate for W from the cross-section. Theil [34] has shown that using the usual time-series estimate for σ_u^2 in (37) will make the resulting estimate consistent.

the sensitivity of generalized least-squares estimates to variations in B. Some a priori information on B may be available, e.g., when the left-out variables are time-lags of the included variables. Then we might expect the correlation (and hence the regression slope) between any x_t and x_{t-j} to fall off for j increasing. If we are dealing in terms of time-lags alone, we may approximate the required regression coefficients by their respective correlation coefficients, and likewise generate conditional estimates by assigning them all values of one, etc. It would seem that a sensitivity check is easy to implement for any actual problem.

Finally, if the precision of the cross-section estimates is poor, we would expect the final results to be insensitive to alternative specifications of the matrix B since (37) shows that the final estimates $A_D{}^*$ are derived (figuratively speaking) as weighted averages of the cross-section and time-series estimates (were they to be computed alone), the weights being the inverses of their respective precision measures, so that the more precise estimate receives commensurately higher weight in the final computation.

VI. SUMMARY

We have presented a device with which one may quantitatively interpret the estimates produced by cross-section regressions and time-series regressions that omit lagged variables. The development is an analysis of specification bias. Proper interpretation of observed estimates requires knowledge of interperiod correlations of the lagged independent variables and the relative lag (coefficient) structure, but no correct interpretation could ever be possible without that information, which may be developed in various empirical and a priori ways. The specification bias analysis has wide application, including a quantitative analysis of consumption-function phenomena to clarify notions about the effect of measured permanent-income and other examples given in the text.

REFERENCES

1. G. Andersson and E. Johansson, *et al.*, "Analysis of Demand for Postal Services," *First International Congress of Econometric Society*, Rome 1965, cited in H. O. A. Wold, "Time is the Realm of Forecasting," *Annals of the New York Academy of Sciences*, 1967, *138*, 525-60.
2. P. Balestra and M. Nerlove, "Pooling Cross-Section and Time-Series Data in the Estimation of a Dynamic Model: The Demand for Natural Gas," *Econometrica*, July 1966, *34*, 585-612.
3. R. A. Easterlin, "On the Relation of Economic Factors to Recent and Projected Fertility Changes," *Demography*, 1966, *3*, 131-53.
4. J. Durbin, "A Note on Regression When There Is Extraneous Information About One of the Coefficients," *Jour. Am. Stat. Assoc.*, Dec. 1953, *48*, 799-808.
5. R. Eisner, "The Permanent Income Hypothesis," *Amer. Econ. Rev.*, Dec. 1958, *48*, 972-90.
6. ———, "A Permanent Income Theory for Investment: Some Empirical Explorations," *Amer. Econ. Rev.*, June 1967, *57*, 363-90.
7. M. Friedman, *A Theory of the Consumption Function*. Princeton 1957.
8. ——— and S. Kuznets, *Income from Independent Professional Practice*. New York 1945.
9. Z. Griliches, "Specification Bias in Estimates of Production Functions," *Jour. of Farm Econ.* Feb. 1957, *39*, 8-20.

10. ———, "Distributed Lags: A Survey," *Econometrica*, Jan. 1967, *35*, 16-49.

11. Y. Grunfeld, "The Interpretation of Cross-Section Estimates in a Dynamic Model," *Econometrica*, July 1961, *29*, 397-404.

12. A. F. Henry and J. F. Short, Jr., *Suicide and Homicide*. Glencoe 1954.

13. H. S. Houthakker, "The Permanent Income Hypothesis," *Amer. Econ. Rev.*, June 1958, *48*, 396-404.

14. ——— and L. D. Taylor, *Consumer Demand in the United States*, 1929-1960. Cambridge 1966.

15. L. R. Klein, "Statistical Estimation of Economic Relations from Survey Data," in *Contributions of Survey Methods in Economics*, G. Katona *et al.*, eds., New York 1954.

16. ———, *An Introduction to Econometrics*. Englewood Cliffs 1962.

17. L. M. Koyck, *Distributed Lags and Investment Analysis*. Amsterdam 1954.

18. E. Kuh, "The Validity of Cross-Sectionally Estimated Behavior Equations in Time-Series Applications," *Econometrica*, April 1959, *27*, 197-214.

19. ——— and J. Meyer, "How Extraneous are Extraneous Estimates?" *Rev. Econ. Stat.*, Nov. 1957, *39*, 380-93.

20. N. Liviatan, "Estimates of Distributed Lag Consumption Functions from Cross-Section Data," *Rev. Econ. Stat.*, Feb. 1965, *47*, 44-53.

21. H. L. Lyon and J. L. Simon, "Price Elasticity of the Demand for Cigarettes in the United States," *Amer. Jour. Agric. Econ.*, Nov. 1968, *50*, 888-95.

22. F. H. Maier, "Consumer Demand for Cigarettes Estimates from State Data," *Jour. Farm Econ.*, Nov. 1955, *37*, 690-704.

23. E. Malinvaud, *Statistical Methods of Econometrics*. New York 1966.

24. T. Mayer, "The Permanent Income Theory and Occupational Groups," *Rev. Econ. Stat.*, Feb. 1963, *45*, 16-22.

25. ———, "The Propensity to Consume Permanent Income," *Amer. Econ. Rev.*, Dec. 1966, *56*, 1158-77.

26. F. Modigliani and R. Brumberg, "Utility Analysis and the Consumption Function," in *Post-Keynesian Economics*, K. Kurihara, ed., New Brunswick 1954.

27. Y. Mundlak, "Long-Run Coefficients and Distributed Lag Analysis: A Reformulation," *Econometrica*, April 1967, *35*, 278-93.

28. M. Nerlove, *Distributed Lags and Demand Analysis for Agricultural and Other Commodities*, Agriculture Handbook 141, U.S. Department of Agriculture, 1958.

29. J. L. Simon, "The Demand for Liquor in the U.S. and a Simple Method of Determination," *Econometrica*, Jan. 1966, *11*, 193-205.

30. ———, "The Effect of Income on Suicide," *Amer. Jour. Soc.*, Nov. 1968, *74*, 302-3.

31. ———, "The Effect of Income Upon Fertility," *Population Studies*, Nov. 1969, *23*, 327-41.

32. ——— and D. J. Aigner, "Cross-Sectional Budget Studies, Aggregate Time-Series Studies, and the Permanent Income Hypothesis," *Amer. Econ. Rev.*, June 1970, *60* (forthcoming).

33. L. D. Taylor, "Combining Budget and Time-Series Information in Projecting Personal Consumption Expenditures," mimeo., 1967.

34. H. Theil, "On the Use of Incomplete Prior Information in Regression Analysis," *Jour. Amer. Stat. Assoc.*, June 1963, *58*, 401-14.

35. ——— and A. Goldberger, "On Pure and Mixed Statistical Estimation in Econometrics," *Int. Econ. Rev.*, Jan. 1961, *2*, 65-78.

36. H. O. A. Wold, "The Approach of Model Building," in *Model Building in the Human Sciences*, H. O. A. Wold, ed., Monaco, 1966.

37. ———, "Unbiased Predictions," in *Proc. of the Fourth Berkeley Symposium on Mathematical Statistics and Probability*. Berkeley 1961.

38. ——— and L. Jureen, *Demand Analysis*, New York, Jan. 1953.

[9]

Foreword

This is still another application of the method described in Chapter 8. In this case it resolves puzzling apparent contradictions between cross-section and time-series evidence.

Reprinted from
POPULATION STUDIES Vol. XXIII No. 3 p. 327, *November*. 1969

The Effect of Income on Fertility*

JULIAN L. SIMON

I. INTRODUCTION

The effect of income upon people's propensity to have children has been a persistently open question in the 1960's. Over the course of the business cycle the relationship is positive, whereas most cross-sectional studies show a negative relationship.[1] This puzzle suggests to Wold that '. . . the factor catalogue behind fertility variations over time seem to be essentially different from the catalogue behind the cross-section variations of the fertility'.[2] Furthermore, there is what Easterlin called '. . . the oft-raised question of how one reconciles the apparent contradiction between the secular inverse (gross) association between income and fertility, on the one hand, the shorter-term positive association, on the other . . .'[3]

Becker[4] offered an austere analysis in the classical mode to reconcile the conflicting evidence. He suggested that having children is not dissimilar to purchasing consumer durables, and *ceteris paribus* one therefore expects more income to lead to more children. The key condition in Becker's *ceteris paribus* clause is that as income changes there be no systematic downward change in the taste for children. That is, higher income must not shift people's indifference curves at the same time that their budget lines are moved upwards.

To reconcile his point of view with the observed negative long-term secular relationships and negative cross-section relationships Becker argued that lack of contraceptive knowledge might cause *realized* (and observed) fertility behaviour to be different from *desired* fertility behaviour. And he adduced some cross-section studies of people with high knowledge of birth control, and other cross-sections where the dependent variable was 'desired' rather than actual number of children,

* I am grateful to Professors Ansley J. Coale and Richard A. Easterlin for reading this manuscript carefully and for making useful suggestions. I also appreciate the opportunity of reading in mimeo a valuable paper of Professor Easterlin's on a closely related topic, after the first draft of this piece was completed. R. A. Easterlin, 'Towards a socio-economic theory of fertility', in *Fertility and Family Planning. A World View* (edited by S. J. Behrman, L. Corsa and R. Freedman) (Ann Arbor, 1969).

[1] Specific citations will be given later for general references made in this introductory section.

[2] H. A. Wold, 'The approach of model building', in *Model Building in the Human Sciences* (Monaco, 1966), p. 10.

[3] R. A. Easterlin, 'On the relation of economic factors to recent and projected fertility changes', *Demography*, 3, 1, 1966. Freedman neatly sums up the issues: 'Certainly factors related to individual variations in a cross-section sample may also be the causes of major historical changes. But this may not necessarily be the case. We very well may find that factors which are related to differences in fertility and family planning as between societies do not explain differences within the society. This may be true for income variations, for example. We still need to learn how cross-section data can best be related to historical series.' R. Freedman, 'American studies of family planning and fertility: A review of major trends and issues', in C. V. Kiser (Ed.), *Research in Family Planning* (Princeton, 1962).

[4] G. S. Becker, 'An economic analysis of fertility', in National Bureau of Economic Research, *Demographic and Economic Change in Developed Countries* (Princeton, 1960).

showing that the relationship was indeed positive. But since Becker's article appeared, much new evidence (discussed later) has accumulated showing that 'desired number of children' cross-sectional studies – especially cross-national studies – do not show a positive relationship to income. This suggests that the negative cross-sectional evidence cannot be explained away as Becker attempts, and one therefore cannot reasonably assume a lack of systematic relationship between income and taste. Therefore we must go deeper.

This paper will show that there is no real statistical contradiction between the various types of evidence. Rather, the various estimation techniques yield different images of fertility behaviour because they take pictures in different ways. All of the images are seen to be consonant as soon as we look beyond some statistical artifacts. However, this analysis also shows that the *unconditional* effect of an income change cannot be deduced *a priori*. Therefore, we then turn to several classes of situations in which the income–fertility relationship is important and consider in which direction the relationship is likely to go in each class of situations.

II. THE INTERPRETATION OF CROSS-SECTION AND TIME-SERIES STUDIES OF THE INCOME–FERTILITY RELATIONSHIP

Let us begin by writing a generalized function relating fertility to various influential variables whose values differ from large group to large group. (This excludes personality variables, which are not likely to explain fertility differences between demographic groups.)

Births in family $= f$ (absolute income, relative income, education, child mortality, rural–urban residence, religion, knowledge of contraception, investment value of children, cost of raising children . . .). (1)

Because our purpose here is to understand the effect of *aggregate income* on fertility we can simplify by henceforth ignoring all variables that are not themselves influenced by income at the aggregate level, as in Equation (2):

Births in family $= f$ (income, education, rural–urban residence, child mortality, contraceptive knowledge, cost of raising children, investment value of children). (2)

Now let us write these variables as a linear function (Equation (3)) that has these features:

(*a*) The direct effect of income (Y_t) in any period is assumed to be positive.

(*b*) Investment value (I_t) and child-raising cost (C_t) have the unarguable signs as shown. I_t and C_t will be ignored in this technical analysis (though included later in the substantive discussion) because they are not germane to the main point.

(*c*) Education, rural–urban residence, child mortality, and contraceptive knowledge are included in the composite variable 'modernization' (M_t), with a plus-or-minus sign to indicate that the effect of this variable is not subject to hypothesis yet. The reason for creating this composite variable is mostly to simplify the *technical* analysis, though one could argue plausibly that the constituents of this variable move together relative to income (which is what is important for our purposes) and that any one of them is quite a good substitute for the others. In the later substantive analyses, however, I will jettison the modernization portmanteau and discuss the constituent variables by themselves.

(As a substitute for modernization, I considered a taste variable to represent all those changes in preferences systematically related to income. But in the end such a variable would have to be represented by one or more empirical proxies such as literacy. Furthermore, the taste concept immediately raises economists' hackles. So modernization seems the better choice here.)

(*d*) Lagged values of variables other than cost and investment are included. It is this that unravels the paradoxes.

$$B_{i,t}=b_{i,0}Y_{i,t}+b_{i,1}Y_{t-1}\ldots b_{i,45}Y_{t-45}\pm c_{i,5}M_{i,t-5}$$
$$\pm c_{i,6}M_{i,t-6}\ldots \pm c_{i,45}M_{i,t-45}+d_iC_t+e_iI_t, \qquad (3)$$

where

$B_{i,t}$ = Births (one or zero) in family i in year t;
$Y_{i,t}$ = Income of family i in year t;
$M_{i,t}$ = Modernization state of family i in year t.

Individual subscripts are shown in Equation (3) for each coefficient. As is customary in such work, however, we shall henceforth drop them and work with coefficients that are some pooled community analogies to the individual coefficients. The aggregation problem need not detain us here.

The modernization terms run from t–5 back, to suggest that the effect of modernization variables is primarily during the pre-adult taste-formative years.

Now, modernization is surely a positive function of income:

$$M_{i,t-K}=mY_{i,t-K}. \qquad (4)$$

Substituting we get

$$B_{i,t}=b_0Y_{i,t}+b_1Y_{i,t-1}\ldots b_{45}Y_{t-45}$$
$$\pm c_t m_{t-5}Y_{i,t-5}\ldots \pm c_{45}m_{45}Y_{i,t-45}. \qquad (5)$$

We now see that in Equation (5) *the total effect of income can be positive or negative*, depending upon the relative weights of the various coefficients.

The key point is that, given the same model above and a given set of coefficients, a cross-section and a time series may well show different relationships between $B_{i,t}$ and $Y_{i,t}$. This breaks open the apparent paradox, as we shall see.

Take the cross-section first. Assume that the specified cross-section model is, as is conventional, $B_{i,t}=bY_{i,t}$. Elsewhere[5] it is shown rigorously that

$$\hat{b}\doteq b_0+r_{Y_tY_{t-1}}b_1+r_{Y_tY_{t-2}}b_2\ldots r_{Y_tY_{t-45}}b_{45}$$
$$\pm r_{Y_tY_{t-5}}C_{t-5}M_{t-5}\pm r_{Y_tY_{t-6}}C_{t-6}M_{t-6}\ldots r_{Y_tY_{t-45}}C_{t-45}M_{t-45} \qquad (6)$$

[5] Y. Grunfeld, 'The interpretation of cross-section estimates in a dynamic model', *Econometrica*, July, 1961; E. Malinvaud, *Statistical Methods of Econometrics* (Chicago), 1966.

where $\hat{b}$ is the observed coefficient in the contemporaneous cross-section, the b_{t-K}, c_{t-K} and m_{t-K} are the 'true' coefficients, and the $r_{Y_tY_{t-K}}$ are the correlation coefficients between the incomes of individuals in one period and their incomes in another period. This means that the extent to which $\hat{b}$, the estimated mean coefficient, differs from b_0, the 'true' mean coefficient for the current period, is a function only of the relative sizes of the coefficients, and of the correlations between the sets of independent variables in each pair of two periods. If the correlations are high, as they always are in income from period to period, and if the lagged effect is substantial, then $\hat{b}$ can differ greatly from b_0. It can be seen intuitively that if $r=1$, $\hat{b}$ equals the sum of all the b_K and b_Km_K. And that sum might well be negative if the b_Km_K are large relative to the b_K, and if the lags are strong. Hence a cross-section of this model can yield a negative $\hat{b}$.

This analysis certainly does not *require* cross-section relationships to be negative; in fact, it may cast further light on some reported positive cross-section results. Becker offers some positive-relationship cases – a Consumers' Union sample, and an urban Swedish sample among them – as evidence that the 'real' relationship is positive and shows up *when contraception is well known.* But a positive relationship was also observed among Polish peasants[6] among whom there is no particularly strong reason to think that modern contraception is well known or much practised. (The Polish peasants are surely mostly Catholic. And a clear positive relationship between children per wife and the size of the farm was found in China by Buck.[7]) Spengler, among others, has explained such results with an argument to the internal similarity of the samples: '. . . family size often tends to be positively associated within groups that are otherwise homogeneous'.[8] But homogeneous samples necessarily have relatively low period-to-period income correlations, and hence the positive relationship is *forced,* in the sense that the omitted past variables are washed out by the way the sample is constituted. Hence these homogeneous sample results are not at all inconsistent with the model put forward above.

Now consider a time-series regression analysis over the course of the business cycle. By definition, the fluctuations in income over the cycle are large relative to the secular change. While $r'_{Y_tY_{t-1}}$ might be fairly high (letting the prime stand for the time series case) the $r'_{Y_tY_{t-K}}$ for periods further back – which are the periods of taste formation by the modernization variables – will be low and there will be both negative and positive cases, effectively cancelling the effect of those lagged variables. Therefore, there will be little specification bias if a time-series regression is run on the usual specification:

$$B_t = b'Y_t. \tag{7}$$

That is, $\hat{b}'$ will not differ much from the true b_0. Given that the effect of modernization is largely in the past, the effect of modernization cancels out in such an analysis, and the observed relationship is the positive one between $B_{i,t}$ and $b_{i,t}$ in the micro-model.

[6] W. Stys, 'The influence of economic conditions on the fertility of peasant women', *Population Studies,* 11, 2 (November 1957), pp. 136ff.

[7] J. L. Buck, *Land Utilization in China* (Nanking, 1937), p. 385.

[8] J. Spengler, 'Population Theory' in B. Haley (Ed.), *A Survey of Contemporary Economics* Vol. 2 (Homewood, 1952) p. 10, Fig.1.

The last aspect of the reconciliation refers to long-run secular time series, which are observed to be negative over the course of development. In such long series, unlike short series over business cycles, the $r'_{Y_t Y_{t-K}}$ will be positive and quite high, because the year-to-year fluctuations are small relative to the long secular trend.[9] Therefore if the graph is simply plotted as in Equation (7), the specification error can cause the relationship to be negative just as in the cross-section, if the $c_K m_K$ are relatively large and if the time-lag is considerable.

The above section shows that with the *same* factor catalogue (to use Wold's term) one can understand why cross-section and time-series analyses of the relationship of birth rate to income can lead to different results if some or all of the analyses are carried out with insufficient time specification.[10] In closing this section, it must be emphasized that the basic model, Equation (3), should *not* be interpreted as an hypothesis about fertility behaviour or as a useful explanation of fertility, but only as a simple possibility to show how paradoxes can arise. Explanation and forecast require assumptions about coefficient values; such assumptions must depend on substantive knowledge and differ among types of situations, as we shall explore in the next section.

III. PREDICTION OF THE EFFECT OF INCOME CHANGE ON FERTILITY IN VARIOUS SITUATIONS

The outcome of the argument given above is that one cannot make unambiguous predictions about the effect of income on fertility without specifying the time structure of the weights for income, education, child mortality, urban–rural residence, cost of raising children, and others. And there is little or no theory about these weights. Therefore we must get our answers by inspection of evidence relevant to each type of situation for which we want to predict. Unfortunately the evidence is not clear because of the form in which it is aggregated as well as the technique and manner in which it was collected. But we shall do the best we can.

Case A. The effect of secularly increased income per head in less developed countries

Let us consider the fertility in a country with an average income of perhaps \$150 as it doubles to \$300. We focus on the number of *births*, and ignore changes in infant mortality. This is actually a fairly easy case because almost all the evidence we shall review points in the same direction.

The ideal evidence would be a fertility series from a non-Western underdeveloped country over the course of its development. Such evidence would be, as the lawyers say, 'on all fours' with the situation for which we want to predict. But there are few or no such cases, and no statistical series in any case. Therefore we must go a bit further afield for analogies.

[9] The truth of this proposition – that if there is trend in a time series, the longer the series the higher the serial correlation – may not seem obvious to the reader. This can, however, be shown both empirically and theoretically, though space precludes the demonstration here.

[10] Exactly the same sort of analysis is shown to explain the apparent paradox between cross-sectional and time-series analyses of suicide. J. L. Simon, 'The effect of income on suicide', *American J. of Sociology*, 74 (November 1968), pp. 302–303.

(1) The histories of the European countries all show declines in fertility as national income increased during the course of development. Becker wants to dismiss this evidence as not relevant because knowledge of birth control may be an important element in the mechanism. But it is reasonable to suppose that knowledge of birth control is a function of income, and the basic conclusion therefore is undisturbed even if Becker is correct about contraceptive knowledge.

(2) Weintraub and Adelman[11] ran cross-sections *across nations* with fertility as the dependent variable. Mrs. Adelman found that the partial effects of income and education were positive and negative respectively, which lends support to the model described in the previous section even though lagged variables were not included, because the presence of the education variable prevents the income variable from picking up the effect of income through education. Weintraub found that the proportion of population living on farms, and the infant mortality rate, both showed a negative effect on the birth rate, and the effect of income was positive. The partial effects of income and other variables are not of interest, however,[12] and computation of the partial correlations leads to statements such as the following, which I think can only be misleading:

> 'For economic development, the implications of this study are therefore rather encouraging. They indicate, for example, that the increase induced in the ratio of population growth by a 25 per cent. improvement in *per capita* income would not raise the population by more than 1 per cent. over a 5-year period. Furthermore, if the development program were accompanied by an effective educational effort, the rate of population expansion might actually decline.'[13]

If we have learned anything about development it is that there can be no question that any development programme will indeed be 'accompanied by an effective educational effort', as well as decreased infant mortality, increased urbanization, etc. What is directly relevant is that the *unconditional* effect of income is negative; that is, the $c_K m_K$ coefficients for education apparently outweigh the b_K coefficients. Indeed, a reconstruction by Weintraub of the effect of plausible variations in income, using his partial coefficients, yields a total negative effect of the income changes on the birth rate. In his example, doubling Venezuela's income per head from $392 to $784 would result in the crude birth rate dropping from 46·4 to 38·8. A similar exercise with Mrs. Adelman's coefficients would surely produce even a larger effect because of the relative salience of the education elasticity in her results.[14]

[11] R. Weintraub, 'The birth rate and economic development. An empirical study', *Econometrica* (October 1962); Irma Adelman, 'An econometric approach to population growth', *Amer. Econ. Rev.* (June 1963).

[12] It seems to me that we are *only* interested in the total result. Because income and education cannot be manipulated separately in underdeveloped countries, the partial coefficients have absolutely no value in themselves.

[13] Adelman, *loc. cit.*, p. 37.

[14] It is difficult to judge what to infer from the Weintraub and Adelman studies taken together. For example, on the one hand Mrs. Adelman found that 'since infant mortality is highly correlated with income per head, the partial regression coefficient of age-specific birth rates upon infant mortality was not statistically significant and fluctuated in direction. This variable was therefore eliminated . . .' (pp. 318–319). But both those variables were found to be significant in Weintraub's regression. Mrs. Adelman clearly probed more deeply into her data, especially in considering age–specific birth rates rather than crude birth rates. But a referee has suggested two possible problems with Mrs. Adelman's method: (1) Her findings in underdeveloped countries could be explained just as well by a correlation between income per head and completeness of birth registration, a difficulty that her weighting scheme does not handle; and (2) Among the developed countries, geographical clustering might explain much of the pattern that she attributes to income per head, e.g. Sweden, West Germany, England and Wales account for all the lowest gross reproduction rates. I have not yet had the opportunity of looking at Mrs. Adelman's tables or comparing the sample and data with Weintraub's, but I hope to do so.

(3) A third set of data relevant to predictions of fertility as income rises in underdeveloped countries are the recent surveys of the number of children people say they *want*, or the number people think make up an *ideal* family. Berelson[15] arrayed countries cross-nationally (Fig. 1) and found a strong negative relationship (except for an upturn at the U.S. end of the income scale, which is not relevant to this section). Not only does this buttress the Adelman–Weintraub evidence, but it also demonstrates empirically that knowledge of birth control methods alone does not explain the negative relationship; other systematic concomitants of income must also be exerting influence.[16]

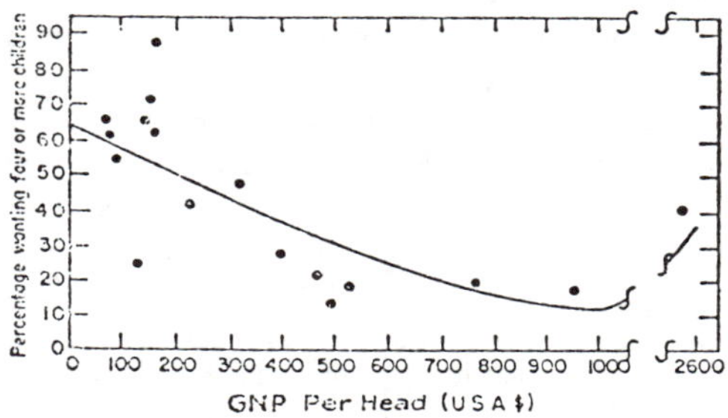

FIGURE 1. *Percentage wanting four or more children, by income.*

SOURCE: Berelson, 1966.

(4) Given that we are considering the effect of a change in average income from, say, $150 to $300, part (but not all) of the evidence from cross-sections *within* less developed countries is relevant. That is, the fertility of people with incomes that are common in less developed countries *is* relevant, but the fertility of the high-income classes is *not* relevant. Within the relevant range, most studies indicate a negative relationship.[17] This must mean that the lagged modernization coefficients $c_K m_K$ dominate the direct income coefficients b_K; there is little other explanation of a negative cross-sectional relationship, except perhaps a higher cost of children (despite Becker) or a lower investment value of children in higher-income families.

[15] B. Berelson, 'KAP studies on fertility', in B. Berelson *et al.* (Eds.), *Family Planning and Population Programs* (Chicago, 1966).

[16] But Hauser (1967) argues that the surveys may tell us nothing except the number of children people actually have, plus a desire to please the interviewer. P. M. Hauser, 'Family planning and population programs: A book review article', *Demography*, 4 (Summer 1967).

[17] L. Tabah and R. Samuel, 'Preliminary findings of a survey on fertility and attitudes toward family formation in Santiago, Chile', in C. V. Kiser (Ed.), *Research in Family Planning* (Princeton, 1962). It should be mentioned, however, that the average 'ideal number of children' does *not* vary much with income under the 40,000-peso-and-over class. And the highest income class, which is the only one showing an ideal number of children *under* 4, has a *higher actual birth rate* than the income class just below it (pp. 280 and 293). All these ideal figures for Chile might be discounted, however, on the basis of the fact that they are *higher* than *completed* family sizes (p. 278). But see the study by A. H. Hawley and V. Prachuabmoh, 'Family growth and family planning in a rural district of Thailand', in B. Berelson *et al.* (Eds.), *Family Planning and Population Programs* (Chicago, 1966), where no relationship occurred.

(5) There is, however, one qualification to the general statement that birth rates will fall during the course of the economic development of countries which are at present less developed. Kuznets suggests that a fertility increase is likely to occur in the *very earliest* stages of development:

> '. . . changes in pre-modern institutional practices, many of which accompany the beginning of modern economic growth, may have eased the restrictions on the birth rates, permitting them to rise for a while above the previous levels. . . . There may therefore be much validity in recent writings that stress the role of rising birth rates in the early acceleration of population growth in some older European countries. This finding bears upon under-developed countries today, for they also may have retained a number of institutional practices (e.g. prohibition of remarriage of widows) that keep the birth rates below their high potential level. Abandonment of such practices under the pressure of modernization as well as the possible reduction of diseases that cause involuntary sterility, may produce a significant rise in the birth rate that could continue for a long period before other effects of modernization and economic growth combine to bring it down.'[18]

The evidence that convinces me of this early rise in fertility is that of the anthropologists who conclude that tribes invariably control the birth rate with a variety of personal and social devices, and achieve birth rates that are not very high.[19] If this is so, and if fertility in many post-tribal underdeveloped countries is now close to the biological limit, then one must conclude that fertility rises in the earliest stages of the modernization process. But the relationship of this change to income and to modernization is too uncertain to analyse, because it does not make much sense to talk about changes in family income as tribal life breaks up. The most one can say is that this fertility rise probably will accompany the beginning of the process we call economic development

Taken together, the evidence cited in paragraphs (1)–(5) above forces the conclusion that in underdeveloped countries fertility will drop as average income increases, with the possible exception of the very earliest stage of development as long-existing institutions begin to break up. That is, in underdeveloped countries the unconditional effect of income on fertility is negative, even though its partial effect (after abstracting from other operative variables) may well be positive.

Case B. The effect of cyclical economic fluctuations on fertility

The birth rate may affect aggregate demand in industrial countries,[20] and therefore the cyclical determinants of birth rates are relevant to economic planning.

The income–fertility relationship is strongly positive over the business cycle. Study after study has brought in the same conclusion, starting with Yule and Mrs. Thomas, and including several countries – the United States, Great Britain and Germany.[21] The data are quite good because

[18] S. Kuznets, *Modern Economic Growth* (New York, 1966), pp. 48–49.

[19] The evidence is collected in A. M. Carr-Saunders, *Population* (London, 1925), and L. Krzywicki, *Primitive Society and its Vital Statistics* (London, 1934).

[20] A. J. Coale, 'Population change and demand, prices and the level of employment', in National Bureau of Economic Research, *Demographic and Economic Change in Developed Countries* (Princeton, 1962). But compare Losch, who emphasizes the effect of population changes on business activity by way of the labour supply. A. Losch, 'Population cycles as a cause of business cycles', *Qtly. J. Econs.* (August 1937).

[21] For a summary of the evidence see Virginia Galbraith and Dorothy S. Thomas, 'Birth rates and the inter-war business cycles', *J. Am. Stat. Ass.* (December 1941), and D. Kirk, 'The influence of business cycles on marriage and birth rates', N.B.E.R., *Demographic and Economic Change in Developed Countries* (Princeton, 1960).

they relate to relatively short time spans and because business cycles appear only in relatively well developed countries. And the findings are not likely to be flawed with specification errors due to omitted lagged variables, because the period-to-period income correlation is low over the business cycle. That is, the effect of the omitted lagged variables cancels out.

The positive relationship is bolstered by the analogous and related findings of positive relationships between income and marriage, and income and migration.[22]

Easterlin[23] has provided strong additional support for the positive cyclical relationship, though he has concerned himself largely with wider swings (the long Kuznets cycles) than have previous investigators. By the expedients of disaggregating the population into constituent sub-groups[24] (e.g. foreign-born, urban native-born white, rural native white, non-white), and measuring employment conditions delicately, Easterlin has caused many anomalies to disappear. In particular, the sharp birth rate decrease in the 1930's, the baby boom, and the recent decline can all be seen as sensible continuations of past history, modified by contemporary economic conditions.

All in all, there is every reason to believe that fertility will exhibit a positive relationship to income and employment over business cycles.

Case C. The effect of a secular increase in income per head in developed countries such as the United States

This case is the tough one. On the one hand, unlike the business-cycle case the period under consideration is long enough for the effect of income on lagged taste-affecting variables, and thereby indirectly on the birth rate, to 'catch up' and not to cancel. On the other hand, as we shall see, unlike the developing-nation case, the role of the most important taste-affecting variables (education, infant mortality, rural–urban shifts, contraceptive knowledge) is complicated. It is the unravelling of the effect of these taste-affecting variables that is the nub of the problem.

First let us check that no clear answer to our question is immediately available from empirical studies. Easterlin's work is closest to the point. He notes that the most important group (quantitatively) in American fertility is increasingly the urban native-born (white) population. And Easterlin found surprisingly 'substantial stability' in the fertility ratio for this group from 1895–99 to 1925–29.[25] But income was rising throughout this period, so there was apparently a

[22] Cf. D. Kirk, *loc. cit.*, and Dorothy S. Thomas, *Social and Economic Aspects of Swedish Population Movements* (New York, 1941); S. Kuznets, 'Long swings in the growth of population and in related economic variables', *Proc. Amer. Phil. Soc.* (February 1958); R. A. Easterlin, 'Long-term swings in U.S. demographic and economic growth: Some findings on the historical pattern', *Demography*, 2 (1965), pp. 497ff.

[23] R. F. Easterlin in article cited above. See also the same author's 'The American baby boom in historical perspective', *Amer. Econ. Rev.* (December 1961), and 'On the relation of economic factors to recent and projected fertility changes', *Demography*, 3, 1 (1966).

[24] As people migrate from farm to city, they take on urban fertility behaviour. Therefore, even if the fertility of rural and urban people remains the same, the aggregate birth rate changes. It is *distributional* changes such as this that Easterlin's disaggregation reveals so well.

[25] R. F. Easterlin, 'The American baby boom in historical perspective', *Amer. Econ. Rev.* (December 1961), p. 880.

tradeoff between the direct effect of income and its indirect effect through taste-affecting variables.[26] This means that we cannot simply extrapolate the stability observed in the past. Though we can reasonably assume that in the longer run income and employment opportunities will improve for the young age groups who are so important in fertility, we cannot immediately say what will be the effect of the taste-affecting variables (that are in turn affected by income). Therefore it is not clear whether the net secular effect of future income growth will be positive or negative. (Easterlin's own projections are only for the shorter run during which cyclical variations in the economic condition of the young parents dominate the picture.)

Let us separately consider the partial effects of income and modernization, the former first. (1) The business cycle data in the previous section clearly show the positive partial relationship. (2) There is a remarkably consistent negative relationship between income and the proportion of couples childless in an income group[27]; childlessness is not a perfect substitute variable for fertility, by any means, but it is an important component of fertility. (3) When the homogeneity of the subgroups is increased sufficiently by the expedient of finely cross-classifying, the partial effect of income is clearly seen to be positive. Consider Table 1 which displays a crude index of the effect of income on fertility for women married at ages 22 or over – the ratio of the numbers of children born to women in the $7,000–9,999 and the $2,000–3,999 husband's-income classes. Of the ninety cells for which there are data, only ten do not show higher fertility for the higher income group. And there is only one instance in which both age cells within the same occupation-education-residence categories fail to show higher fertility with higher income, suggesting that sampling error may account for some or all of the reversals.[28]

When we consider countries that are relatively well developed by 1969 standards, we can no longer lump together all the variables that were earlier considered under the rubric 'modernization'. Rather, education is quite different from farm or urban residence, knowledge of contraception, and infant mortality, in two important respects. First, the latter three variables may attain saturation plateaus in well developed countries; infant mortality may approach 10 per thousand, knowledge of contraception may reach 100%, and farm residence may approach some level so low that even a large proportional change in the remaining farm population would be small relative to the rest of the society. This means that the education variable may be crucial in the fully-developed country case, which brings us to the second distinction between education and the other three variables. The

[26] R. Tomasson, 'Why has American fertility been so high?' in B. Farber (Ed.) *Kinship and Family Organization*, (New York, 1966), and in conversation points to another interesting tradeoff underlying the apparently stable relationship. The proportion of Catholics in the urban native white population must have increased over time, both from the higher Catholic birth rate and from the relatively large number of first-generation Catholics in the city whose parents were classified as foreign-born. *Ceteris paribus* Catholic fertility should be higher, so a constant aggregate birth rate for urban native whites should indicate a decrease in the non-Catholic white native birth rate.

[27] U.S. Department of Commerce, Bureau of the Census: *Women by Number of Children Ever Born*, Final Report, PC (2)–(3A), Washington, 1964. These data have been analysed by the present author in J. L. Simon, 'Income, Childlessness and Fertility in America in the Census of 1960' (mimeographed, 1968).

[28] It might be objected that if a positive income–fertility relationship means anything for the women married at age 22 or over, the same relationship should appear among women married at 21 and under – which it does not. But a major difference between the age groups surely is the knowledge and practice of birth control in early years of marriage – a matter which seems to be part of education and modernization. I confess to some uneasiness over this explanation, however.

TABLE 1. *Ratio of children ever born per thousand wives in families where husbands earned $7,000–9,999 to $2,000–3,999 families. (1959, women married at age 22 or over, white, husband present.)*

	Urban		Other urban		Rural non-farm		Rural farm	
	35–44	45–54	35–44	45–54	35–44	45–54	35–44	45–54
Professional								
No high school								
High school	2,232/1,763 =1·266	1,633/1,299 =1·257		1,658/1,692 =0·980				
College	2,239/1,925 =1·163	1,658/1,594 =1·040	2,412/1,986 =1·215	1,902/1,576 =1·207	2,391/2,164 =1·105	1,891/1,649 =1·147		
Managers								
No high school	2,066/2,116 =0·976	1,853/1,602 =1·157	2,182/2,159 =1·011	2,203/1,827 =1·206	2,381/2,309 =1·031	1,767/1,918 =0·921		
High school	2,232/1,734 =1·287	1,729/1,528 =1·132	2,283/1,922 =1·188	1,789/1,578 =1·134	2,262/2,043 =1·107	1,816/1,601 =1·134		
College	2,269/1,962 =1·156	1,769/1,561 =1·133	2,397/1,820 =1·317	1,862/1,859 =1·002	2,464/2,390 =1·031	1,883/1,641 =1·147		
Clerical								
No high school	2,043/1,853 =1·103	1,644/1,478 =1·112		1,825/1,494 =1·222				
High school	2,269/1,660 =1·367	1,679/1,397 =1·202	2,318/1,887 =1·228	1,705/1,533 =1·112	2,449/1,904 =1·286	1,747/1,705 =1·025		
College	2,304/1,740 =1·324	1,683/1,245 =1·352	2,416/1,983 =1·218	1,902/1,705 =1·116	2,281/1,986 =1·149	2,006/1,802 =1·113		
Craftsmen								
No high school	2,223/2,061 =1·079	1,865/1,809 =1·031	2,555/2,121 =1·205	1,756/2,095 =0·838	2,095/2,492 =0·841	2,099/2,216 =0·947		
High school	2,324/1,841 =1·262	1,820/1,615 =1·127	2,384/1,786 =1·335	1,831/1,859 =0·985	2,421/2,142 =1·130	2,000/1,863 =1·074	2,685/2,744 =0·978	2,624/2,264 =1·159
College	2,298/1,843 =1·247	1,812/1,309 =1·384		1,888/1,765 =1·070				
Operatives								
No high school	2,273/2,058 =1·104	1,929/1,812 =1·065	2,553/2,173 =1·175	2,112/1,980 =1·067	2,749/2,403 =1·144	2,493/2,476 =1·007		
High school	2,286/1,823 =1·254	1,900/1,553 =1·223	2,507/2,054 =1·221	2,215/1,871 =1·184	2,292/2,196 =1·044	2,190/2,030 =1·079		
College	2,307/1,351 =1·707	1,838/1,388 =1·324						
Service worker								
No high school	2,219/1,931 =1·149	1,792/1,570 =1·141						
High school	2,446/1,716 =1·425	2,092/1,560 =1·341	2,352/1,973 =1·192					
College	2,474/1,839 =1·345	1,889/1,080 =1·749						
Labourers								
No high school	2,551/2,315 =1·102	2,209/2,277 =0·970						
High school	2,418/1,995 =1·212	1,619/1,794 =0·902						
College								
Farmers								
No high school							3,364/2,968 =1·133	3,140/2,712 =1·158
High school							2,799/2,700 =1·037	2,623/2,329 =1·126
College							3,043/2,711 =1·122	1,911/2,412 =0·792

SOURCE: Table 39, U.S. Department of Commerce, 1964.

other variables almost surely bear a monotonic relationship to fertility, but the effect of education *might* reverse at high education levels, producing higher rather than lower fertility. Therefore we would like to know the likely effect of more education in already highly educated societies.

At least two studies suggest that the partial effect of education is indeed a U-shaped function,[29] declining with income rises at low income levels, and *increasing with income at relatively high income levels*. The first data are from urban whites in North Central U.S. in 1940. Whereas at lower income levels higher education was associated with lower fertility, the $5,000-and-over group showed *substantially* higher fertility for the women who had a year or more of college than for women who only completed high school[30] (Ruggles and Ruggles 1962, Table A-6 and page 161). And Moberg (cited in Johnson[31]) showed that in a sample of Swedish employers and town officials in 1935–36, within the two income groups below 5,000 kroner per year there was a negative relationship between education and fertility, whereas within the two higher income classes better-educated families had more children.

If both education and income have positive partial effects at high levels of both, and if child mortality, farm leaving and contraceptive knowledge are stable, then it is reasonable to expect *higher* fertility as developed nations raise their income per head even higher. And indeed, this is what intra-country cross-sections in the high-income countries suggest. Miss Johnson surveyed the data as of 1962 and summarized her findings this way:[32]

> 'The often-observed inverse association of fertility with socio-economic status is still present in some, and possibly in the majority of the industrialized countries in Europe. But where it does exist, it has, with few exceptions, been significantly modified. In general, the higher professionals and the wealthier classes no longer have the smallest families; this position is now occupied by intermediate occupational groups and by married couples of average means.
>
> 'Little is known directly of the relation of family size to the level of educational attainment in these countries, but according to such information as is now available, the fertility of individuals with higher education exceeds that of the general population. This pattern has existed for some years in England and Wales and in Sweden, and has recently become evidence in the Netherlands.'

Particularly clear data show the upturn in the U.S. In the higher-status occupational groupings (professional–technical, managers–officials–proprietors, clerical–sales), in the higher husband's-income groups ($7,000–9,999 and $4,000–6,999), more children were born per thousand women aged 35–44 and 45–54, in families where the husband had one or more years of high school than where the husband had some high school education. (The upper-income open interval is biased toward college education, and the lower income groups are less relevant in this context; hence they are not included here.) This effect holds both for women married before and after 22 years of age.[33]

[29] This is one of those cases in which linear correlations can mislead. Near-zero correlation coefficients of education and fertility have been reported but these are thoroughly consistent with a decline in fertility as people get a *little* education, and then an increase in fertility as they get a *lot* of education.

[30] R. and Nancy Ruggles, 'Differential fertility in United States census data', in N.B.E.R., *Demographic and Economic Change in Developed Countries* (Princeton, 1962).

[31] Gwendolyn Z. Johnson, 'Differential fertility in European countries', *ibid.*, p. 53.

[32] *Ibid.*, p. 72.

[33] C. V. Kiser and Myrna E. Frank, 'Fertility of non-white women of college attainment', *Milbank Memorial Fund Qtly.*, 41, No. 4 (October 1963), pp. 427–450. Also U.S. Department of Commerce, *op. cit.*, Table 39.

It is the present upper ends of the education and income scales in which the direction of the relationship is of most interest here, because more people will fall into those categories as the secular income trend continues. It is also not irrelevant that the fertility rate turns upwards with the highest economic-educational group even in some poorer countries at present, and in some European countries in earlier, less prosperous years, e.g. Santiago Chile, France in 1906; and Oslo in 1930.[34] Income and education are highly collinear in such studies, of course. But this is not a flaw in the method for our purposes, because we are interested in the total unconditional effect rather than the partial effects. Nor are these cross-sections rendered invalid for our purposes by specification error; the neglected variables are those that might make the observed coefficient negative speciously, but not positive.

There is a minor cautionary note about these cross-sectional data, however, due to Mrs. Freedman's finding that *within* narrow occupation categories, there is a *relative* income effect on fertility.[35] That is, the higher-income families among an occupation of given prestige-level will have more children than the lower-income families in the same occupational group (though the mean-income family in that occupation will have more children than the mean-income members of higher income occupations). One might then view the entire population as a single reference group and all (positive) differences within the population as due to relative income differences. In that case one might infer that the entire income distribution might shift upwards with no effect on fertility since relative income positions would remain the same. But this seems a strained and unlikely extension of Mrs. Freedman's findings.

The upturn at the U.S. end of the income scale in Berelson's *cross-national* plot of size of *desired* family (Fig. 1) also suggests larger families as developed countries develop even further. It is the concurrence of actual and desired fertility that is particularly impressive here.

It would seem, then, that the big problem in making a fertility prediction for a relatively well developed nation is knowing whether it has reached the trough-point at which the combined effect of income and education begins to be positive. It is probably not sufficient to determine that decreases in child mortality, farm leaving, and increases in contraceptive knowledge have become small, because the effect of education may not yet have become positive at that stage. And there is no reason to believe that education alone is an insignificant variable; just the opposite.[36] On the other hand, unless variables not mentioned in the analysis in this section suddenly become dominant at higher income levels – notably cost of raising children to one's own standard of living – then one may forecast that if a developed country's fertility has reached a point of stability, an upturn in fertility will follow. Given Easterlin's finding of stability for urban white natives in the U.S. over the early twentieth century, it is reasonable to expect a secular upturn in fertility here. The baby

[34] Cf. Tabah and Samuel, *loc. cit.*; also U.N. Department of Social Affairs, *The Determinants and Consequences of Population Trends* (1953), p. 87.

[35] Deborah Freedman, 'The relation of economic status to fertility' *American Econ. Review*, June, 1963.

[36] O. D. Duncan, 'Farm background and differential fertility', *Demography*, 2 (1965).

boom of the 1950's may have been a herald of this, albeit exaggerated by the upturn in cyclical conditions described by Easterlin.[37]

Case D. The effect of incentive payments for higher and lower fertility

Consider first a programme to *raise* fertility through bonuses for children, or child payments, or income tax deductions for children. We shall proceed as if such a programme had no effect on gross national product, but only upon the distribution of the product among families by numbers of children. Fertility incentives *must* have *some* effect on fertility, because *some* people must be at the margin of indifference about more or fewer children than they have, and there is no negative trade-off effect flowing from an incentive programme to offset the main effect. The sole question is *how much* of an effect an incentive programme will have.

The effect of the incentive will depend upon its average size, and upon its size relative to income for particular income classes.[38] The only source of a response estimate must be studies of actual programmes. And useful data are practically non-existent. Kirk[39] found that the effect of the Nazi experiment is blurred: '... a major part of the Nazi successes on the demographic front must have been the result of re-employment, as opposed to the more spectacular appeals of race and "folk" on the one hand, and specific inducement to child-bearing on the other'. And Petersen said of the Dutch experience: 'Whether the cumulative effect of these [pro-natality] measures is to keep Dutch fertility high cannot be shown one way or another – first because the determinants of fertility are very imperfectly understood; secondly because in any case it would probably be impossible to isolate the effect of these measures. Actually, however, no one doubts their effect ...'[40] Clearly we have here no solid ground for quantitative estimates. However, a preliminary study I have done has shown a substantial relationship between the average amount paid by U.S. States to foster parents, and the proportion of state-aided children in foster homes. And it seems reasonable to suppose that fertility and foster-parenthood are not unrelated motivationally. (Social workers are unanimous on this point; foster parents do not take in children just for the money.)

One must take care not to base estimates of the effect of *incentives* on the results of studies of the effect of *income* changes on fertility over the business cycle, say. A change in income shifts the budget line proportionally, which is the same as lowering the price of *all* goods, whereas an incentive scheme lowers the price only of children, which is exactly the logic of incentive plans.

Our uncertainty about the effect of *anti*-natal incentives is equally great. Anecdotal evidence suggests that small pay-offs such as time off from work can boost the sterilization rate in India. But what is clearly needed is social experimentation (on a small scale) with varying levels of

[37] In passing, Easterlin's interesting (but tentative) finding of a relative income effect *between generations* does not affect the basic conclusion given above. Such an effect would only *exaggerate* the actual income effect. R. Easterlin, 'Long swings...', *Demography*, 2 (1965).

[38] The present incentive in the U.S. increases slightly with income, because a $600 tax deduction reduces taxes by more dollars to a rich man than to a poor man. On the other hand, if the demand for children is iso-elastic, the effect on the rich man's fertility will be less because the deduction is a decreasing *percentage* of income as income rises.

[39] D. Kirk, 'The relation of employment levels to births in Germany', *Milbank Mem. Fd. Qtly.* (April 1942), p. 206.

[40] W. Petersen, 'Family subsidies in the Netherlands', *Marriage and Family Living* (August 1955).

substantial bonuses. The rationale for such payments has been given by Enke and discussed further by Simon.[41]

SUMMARY AND CONCLUSIONS

The first part of the paper showed how specification error could account for the apparent contradiction between time-series and cross-section evidence about the direction of the effect of income on fertility. A model which specifies the lagged effects of income, as well as systematic changes in taste for children caused by income changes (summed up for convenience as a modernization effect), is compatible with all the observed data. However, this model provides no *a priori* predictions about the total effect of income on fertility. That must depend on the taste (modernization variable) changes caused indirectly by income, as well as the direct effects, and those taste effects may be in either direction.

Several particular cases were then examined, and predictions made about the effect of income changes based on relevant available evidence. The prediction for underdeveloped countries is the standard forecast of a drop in fertility as development takes place, though an initial rise from pre-modern levels may well occur. The prediction for the effect of cyclical changes in industrial countries is a direct relationship between income and fertility. And the prediction for the secular trend in high-income countries is for higher fertility, based largely on the apparent increase in fertility with more education at the highest socio-economic levels, toward which such societies are moving. But this last prediction is chancy, indeed.

[41] S. Enke, 'The gains to India from population control: Some money measures and incentive schemes', *Rev. of Econs. and Stats.* (May 1960); 'The economics of government payments to limit population', *Econ. Dev. and Cult. Change* (July 1960); 'A rejoinder to comments on the superior effectiveness of vasectomy–bonus schemes', *ibid.* (July 1961); 'Some misconceptions of Krueger and Sjaastad regarding the vasectomy bonus plan to reduce births in overpopulated and poor countries', *ibid.* (July 1962); *Economics of Development* (New York, 1963), Ch. 20; 'The economic aspects of slowing population growth', *Econ. J.* (March 1966); J. L. Simon, 'The role of bonuses and persuasive propaganda in the reduction of birth rates', *Econ. Dev. and Cultural Change*, **16**, 3 (1968), pp. 404–411.

[10]

Foreword

This piece was an offshoot from studies of immigrants. It occurred to me that the immigrants' labor-market experiences in various states could throw light upon differences among native-born Americans in those states.

Economics of Education Review, Vol. 12, No. 2, pp. 105–115, 1993.
Printed in Great Britain.

0272–7757/93 $6.00 + 0.00

Why Don't State Incomes Converge? Effective Worker Pay Does Not Differ Among States

JULIAN L. SIMON

College of Business and Management, University of Maryland, College Park, MD 20742, U.S.A.

Abstract — Differing education levels affect mean income differences among states. But mean earnings also differ holding constant the amounts of education and experience; persons in higher income states earn more. The causes could operate either during the process of growing up, or currently. To distinguish between these two possibilities, the paper compares natives' and immigrants' earnings. Immigrants show a smaller state income effect than do natives, or no effect. This suggests that the differences among states are mainly due to influences during development (when immigrants were not present) rather than during adulthood. That is, the observed state differentials represent not different pay for the same work but (in addition to differences in occupational composition) different pay for different qualities of work, and most likely stem from differences in the quality of schooling.

1. INTRODUCTION

INCOME DIFFERENTIALS among the states in the United States have long been troubling. Policy makers are distressed by the inequality. And economists are affronted by the continued disequilibrium.[1]

This paper finds that the observed differentials do not represent different pay for the same work, but instead (in addition to differences in occupational composition) represent different pay for different qualities of work. Workers tend to receive the same pay for the same amount of production in high-income and low-income states. Apparent pay differentials in given jobs most likely stem from differences in the quality of schooling.

The argument runs as follows: natives of the United States with given amounts of education earn lower incomes in states with lower mean incomes; this result is shown with a conventional earnings equation with state average income as a variable. However, this effect does *not* hold for persons who were not raised in the states in which they are now working — immigrants from abroad — among whom the observed state income effect is much smaller than for natives, and perhaps non-existent. There seems to be no plausible reason why immigrants would select states in such a fashion as to produce this result if there actually are real wage differences among the states. Therefore, it would seem reasonable that if immigrants receive the same wage for the same work in all places, natives also receive the same wage for the same work in all places.

Corroborating evidence of other sorts is offered in the Discussion section. Other possible explanations of the apparent differential are also examined there.

Absence of a complementarity effect between workers of different skill levels is also found. The state effect is positive for native workers with both more and less education, whereas complementarity suggests that the effect should be positive for workers with less education but negative for workers with more education.

An implication of the analysis is that external effects of human capital in the market place are not large. If such an effect were to operate, the incomes of immigrants in the various states would be seen to be affected by the average stock of human capital in those states, as represented by the mean incomes of those states. But this is not observed.

[Manuscript received 6 February 1992; revision accepted for publication 10 June 1992.]

2. CONCEPTUAL FRAMEWORK: THE VARIABLES TO BE STUDIED

The money earnings of a worker are in theory determined by two elements, the marginal physical product of the worker, and the price of the product in the place where the worker sells his/her wares. The possible difference in prices is too important not to be mentioned here. But auxiliary evidence, as well as some findings in this paper (referred to in the Discussion section), suggest an absence of a relevant pattern of price differences within the United States, and hence the matter can be left aside. It is not unreasonable to assume that a given marginal physical product receives the same return in all states, and, therefore, that earnings may be assumed to be proportional to the individual's output.

An individual worker's output may be viewed as a function of many factors: genetic elements which possibly affect intelligence and drive, parental nurturing, quantity of schooling, quality of schooling, quantity of experience on the job, physical capital complement, human capital complement, human capital in the environment from whom one may learn on and off the job, health, environmental factors such as temperature that may affect performance, and still others. Because of this paper's interest in the quality of the educational inputs to a person's productive capacity, this study tries to compare individuals with the same amounts of formal education, and hence the purpose of the variables for schooling and experience is to hold these factors constant rather than to throw light on the magnitudes of the effects. A proxy for physical environment — temperature — is used to adjust for differential effects upon people in different locations. Many other factors such as genetics are not considered, hopefully without harm to the analysis.

The effects of quality of schooling, quality of the surrounding human capital at home and school, and the amount and quality of parental nurturing, are theoretically obvious. Data are lacking to infer the separate effects of these elements, and hence they will be considered together here as a single factor called "developmental quality".

For completeness, the topic of externalities in learning is discussed in an appendix available upon request from the author.

3. ESTIMATION

The Size of the Effect for Persons Born in the U.S.A.

The first task is to establish that the apparent differentials which we are investigating actually exist. Therefore, the first regression estimates the effect of a state's average income upon the earnings of individual workers, holding their quantities of education constant in a standard earning function. Such a model is

$$LME = f(PPE, SCHL, EXP, EXP^2, TEMP)$$

where LME = log male earnings for an individual worker

PPE = mean per-person earnings for the state population as a whole, as a proxy for the mean "effective" educational level, which in turn is a proxy for human capital per person. Assuming away other factors of production (as is probably reasonable, even physical capital), this is a good economic measure of the average quality of schooling for the labor force.

$SCHL$ = number of years of school for the individual

EXP = length of work experience for the individual

$TEMP$ = average temperature in the state, included to ensure that state income does not pick up variance due to temperature because of correlation between them; it is possible that the correlation between temperature and income (or economic development) is partly due to temperature affecting income, as many writers have speculated.

The earnings function used is conventional except for the inclusion of the state's temperature and mean income.

Demographic characteristics are not included in the income function, partly because the numbers of cases for each language and country of origin would be small in each state, and because the sex ratio could be expected to be the same in each state. The absence of such demographic characteristics would only cause difficulty if they are systematically related to location in a way that is linked to income, and I have no reason to believe that this is likely.

The 1976 Survey of Income and Education conducted by the U.S. Bureau of the Census on about 150,000 households provides data on the earnings of individuals in various states, along with

Table 1. Regressions with the logarithm of wages and salaries as the dependent variable

	Natives and Puerto Ricans				
Variable	Weighted (1)	Weighted (2)	Unweighted (3)	≤12 years schooling Weighted (4)	≥13 years schooling Weighted (5)
State average earnings (*PPE*)		0.00007	0.00012	0.0001	0.0001
		(0.000)	(0.000)	(0.012)	(0.000)
		[0.07]	[0.12]	[0.05]	[0.11]
Schooling (*SCHL*)	0.0851	0.0843	0.0781	0.0851	0.0867
	(0.000)	(0.000)	(0.000)	(0.000)	(0.000)
	[0.35]	[0.34]	[0.31]	[0.24]	[0.20]
Experience (*EXP*)	0.0546	0.0538	0.0502	0.0406	0.0870
	(0.000)	(0.000)	(0.000)	(0.000)	(0.000)
	[0.86]	[0.84]	[0.78]	[0.59]	[1.32]
Experience²	−0.0009	−0.0009	−0.0009	−0.0006	−0.0017
	(0.000)	(0.000)	(0.000)	(0.000)	(0.000)
	[−0.76]	[−0.74]	[−0.71]	[−0.55]	[−1.14]
SMSA residence	0.1544	0.1360	0.1076	0.1249	0.1712
	(0.000)	(0.000)	(0.008)	(0.005)	(0.003)
	[0.05]	[0.05]	[0.03]	[0.05]	[0.06]
Not married (*NOTMSP*)	−0.2443	−0.2527	−0.2784	−0.1961	−0.3106
	(0.000)	(0.000)	(0.000)	(0.000)	(0.000)
	[−0.10]	[−0.10]	[−0.11]	[−0.07]	[−0.14]
State temperature (*STTEMP*)		−0.0046	−0.0012	−0.0059	−0.0021
		(0.006)	(0.412)	(0.011)	(0.357)
		[−0.04]	[−0.01]	[−0.05]	[−0.02]
Years in state					
Immigrant cohort 70–74	n.a.	n.a.	n.a.		
Immigrant cohort 65–69	n.a.	n.a.	n.a.		
Immigrant cohort 60–64	n.a.	n.a.	n.a.		
Immigrant cohort 50–59	n.a.	n.a.	n.a.		
Immigrant cohort 20–49	n.a.	n.a.	n.a.		
Constant	7.45	7.31	6.99	7.65	6.61
	(0)	(0.000)	(0.000)	(0.000)	(0.000)
	n.a.	n.a.	n.a.		
N	5428	5428	5428	3252	2176
$\bar{R}^2$	0.142	0.149	0.136	0.088	0.190
Standard error	0.745	0.741	0.750	0.777	0.668
Elasticity of dependent variable with respect to state average earnings (computed from log–log run)	n.a.	0.43	0.71		

Code for statistics: estimated regression coefficient, (probability of occurrence by chance −*t* value), [beta coefficient]. n.a.: Not applicable.

Notes: 1. The *t* values for the weighted regressions were computed by adjusting the total weights to be approximately equal to the actual sample size, as advised by standard texts.

2. There were a considerable number of no answers to the question about time living in the state, which puts that variable into considerable doubt. Regressions using that variable omitted observations with no answer.

Table 1 — *Continued*

Immigrants '20–'74 Entry Weighted (6)	Immigrants '20–'74 Entry Unweighted (7)	Immigrants '65–'74 Entry Weighted (6)	Immigrants '65–'74 Entry Unweighted (9)	'20–'74 Entry ≤12 years schooling Weighted (10)	'20–'74 Entry ≥13 years schooling Weighted (11)	'20–'74 Entry Immigrants Weighted (12)	Natives Weighted (13)
0.00002	0.00009	−0.00002	0.00003	−0.00001	0.0001	0.00003	0.0001
(0.376)	(0.000)	(0.631)	(0.290)	(0.715)	(0.042)	(0.268)	(0.000)
[0.01]	[0.09]	[−0.01]	[0.03]	[−0.01]	[0.05]	[0.02]	[0.07]
0.0706	0.0613	0.0654	0.0583	0.0500	0.1015	0.07	0.08
(0.000)	(0.000)	(0.000)	(0.000)	(0.000)	(0.000)	(0.000)	(0.000)
[0.38]	[0.35]	[0.39]	[0.36]	[0.22]	[0.23]	[0.38]	[0.34]
0.0370	0.0386	0.0199	0.0356	0.0191	0.0534	0.04	0.05
(0.000)	(0.000)	(0.027)	(0.000)	(0.016)	(0.000)	(0.000)	(0.000)
[0.35]	[0.64]	[0.26]	[0.50]	[0.27]	[0.77]	[0.55]	[0.83]
−0.0006	−0.0006	−0.0003	−0.0006	−0.0004	−0.0010	−0.001	−0.001
(0.000)	(0.000)	(0.049)	(0.000)	(0.005)	(0.000)	(0.000)	(0.000)
[0.32]	[−0.60]	[−0.22]	[−0.42]	[−0.31]	[−0.63]	[−0.32]	[−0.75]
0.0045	0.0414	−0.0233	0.0354	−0.0111	0.0642	0.004	0.14
(0.953)	(0.561)	(0.894)	(0.826)	(0.917)	(0.558)	(0.961)	(0.000)
[0.00]	[0.01]	[−0.00]	[0.01]	[0.00]	[0.01]	[0.00]	[0.05]
−0.2176	−0.3046	−0.2303	−0.1892	−0.0178	−0.3013	−0.23	−0.25
(0.000)	(0.000)	(0.001)	(0.003)	(0.017)	(0.000)	(0.000)	(0.000)
[−0.09]	[−0.13]	[−0.09]	[−0.07]	[−0.14]	[−0.14]	[−0.09]	[−0.10]
−0.0119	−0.0038	−0.0185	−0.0134	−0.0178	−0.0058	−0.01	−0.004
(0.000)	(0.010)	(0.001)	(0.003)	(0.017)	(0.034)	(0.000)	(0.012)
[−0.09]	[−0.04]	[−0.14]	[−0.13]	[−0.14]	[−0.05]	[−0.10]	[−0.03]
						−0.003	0.002
						(0.055)	(0.019)
						[−0.05]	[0.04]
BASE	BASE	BASE	BASE	BASE	BASE	BASE	
0.1154	0.1727	0.1292	0.1630	0.0614	0.1923	0.12	
(0.006)	(0.000)	(0.006)	(0.000)	(0.278)	(0.002)	(0.006)	
[0.05]	[0.08]	[0.08]	[0.10]	[0.03]	[0.10]	[0.06]	
0.2668	0.2713	n.a.	n.a.	0.2520	0.3322	0.28	
(0.000)	(0.000)			(0.000)	(0.000)	(0.000)	
[0.11]	[0.12]			[0.10]	[0.16]	[0.12]	
0.2531	0.2551	n.a.	n.a.	0.2171	0.3501	0.29	
(0.000)	(0.000)			(0.000)	(0.000)	(0.000)	
[0.14]	[0.15]			[0.12]	[0.21]	[0.15]	
0.3316	0.3169	n.a.	n.a.	0.2700	0.4838	0.41	
(0.000)	(0.000)			(0.000)	(0.000)	(0.000)	
[0.17]	[0.18]			[0.14]	[0.27]	[0.21]	
8.29	7.47	9.21	8.42	8.27	6.92	8.32	7.25
(0)	(0)	(0.000)	(0.000)	(0.000)	(0.000)	(0.000)	(0.000)
n.a.	n.a.	n.a.	n.a.				
3375	3375	1137	1137	1989	1386	0.206	0.150
0.205	0.178	0.172	0.136	0.120	0.189	3375	5428
0.732	0.702	0.766	0.745	0.769	0.669	0.736	0.742
0.14	0.58	−0.14	0.20				

other necessary information such as the immigrant's date of entry into the United States.

Consider the regression results (extracted, as are other results, from Table 1, except as noted) for *native* employed males age 24–64, in Table 2.

State *PPE* clearly has a substantial effect, statistically and economically.[2] The elasticity of 0.39 (taken from a regression like 2 but using the log of *PPE*) seems very large. To put this effect in perspective, the beta coefficient for the state effect (0.07) is almost a fifth of the beta for the native individual's own years of schooling (0.34). That is, the state effect apparently explains almost a fifth as much of the variance in natives' earnings as does the individual effect.[3,4]

Does the Effect Arise During Development or While Working?

There are two main possible causes of lower productivity per worker with given amounts of education and experience — poorer education in the past, or lesser quality of cooperating human capital in the present. (Physical capital may safely be disregarded for reasons given below.) This section discriminates between these possibilities by examining the pattern of earnings data for a group for which differences in education are not a factor — immigrants from abroad, who did not grow up in the area.[5]

Regression 6 in Table 3 shows a much smaller effect for *PPE* in a sample of immigrants, when controlling for their time in the United States, than for natives (see regression 2), and the coefficient is not statistically significant.

Given that the current environment is the same for natives and for immigrants, this finding suggests that the difference in productivity among natives in various states arises during the educational period in the past, rather than being due to differences in the human capital with which workers cooperate on the job. *This is the major finding of the paper.*

To put the matter in different words, the data suggest that the observed lower income for natives of given education levels in low-income states, compared to natives in high-income states, is due to their lower skills as a result of their having been educated in a state where the effective education per year of formal schooling is less. Less effective education is due to lower average human capital (including lower income of teachers). This force does not apply to immigrants, and hence it accounts for the difference in pattern between immigrants and natives.

The result that apparent unexplained differences in income are due not to current market conditions in different places but rather to differences in learning during development (holding quantity of income constant), is similar to the finding by

Table 2. Effect of residence state on earnings of natives

Regression no.	Group	State earnings	Education	Other variables in regression
2	Natives, weighted	$b = 0.00007$ beta = 0.07 $t = 0.000$ elasticity = 0.39	$t = 0.000$ $b = 0.084$ Beta = 0.34	Experience, residence, marital status, temperature

Source: Table 1, column 2, except elasticity from log–log regression.

Table 3. Effect of residence state on earnings of immigrants and natives

Regression no.	Group	State earnings	Education	Other variables in regression
6	Immigrants, weighted	$b = 0.00002$ beta = 0.01 $t = 0.38$	$b = 0.07$ beta = 0.38	Experience, residence, marital status, temperature, (and for immigrants, date of immigration)
2	Natives, weighted	$b = 0.00007$ beta = 0.07 $t = 0.000$	$b = 0.08$ beta = 0.34	Experience, residence, marital status, temperature, (and for immigrants, date of immigration)

Source: Table 1, columns 6 and 2.

Behrman and Birdsall (1984) that apparent differences between geographic regions in Brazil, and between urban and rural areas, are largely explained by the quality of education.

Though the data indicate a learning effect during the developmental period, they also contain some suggestion of an on-the-job effect as well. This may be seen in the strongly significant *PPE* coefficient for the unweighted regression for immigrants (a beta of 0.09 in regression 7, Table 1), though the weighted regression coefficient (regression 6) is weaker. This is also consistent with the clear absence of effect among the most recent immigrants (regressions 8 and 9), who have had the least exposure to the human capital environment surrounding them and whose less-than-perfect English may have slowed their assimilation to the people around them.[6]

The reader may wish to view the results for natives alone in the perspective of international comparisons. Consider a given person working in a country with 1/20 the per-person money income of the U.S., say India. If the elasticity is 0.20, then one would expect the person's earnings in India to be ¼ of what they are in the U.S.A.[7] This does not seem to be out of joint with casual observation, and with the fact that the difference in mean education is very different in the U.S.A. and India and, therefore, must account for most of the difference in average incomes — a ratio of 1 to 20, not holding education constant.

The fact that the state income coefficient is positive for U.S. natives but less so for immigrants suggests that some mechanism operates during the developmental period to affect later productivity. But at least two mechanisms could be responsible: the quality of schooling, and the quality and quantity of nurturing. This suggests an attempt to distinguish between them.

Expenditures on schooling were, therefore, substituted for per-person income, on the assumption that the former would be a better proxy than the latter for educational quality, and 1950s data were used because workers in 1976 were in school in earlier years.[8] Expenditures on education do indeed show an influence. However, the effect, as measured by the sizes of the *t* ratios and of the betas, is not as large as the effect of per-person income; and the effect of expenditures disappears when both variables are included in the regression. The same is true of expenditures on education in 1976, median state education in 1950 and 1976, and state per person income in 1950. The explanation of these results is the high collinearity between state per person incomes in 1976 and the other variables, as may be seen in the correlation matrix in the appendix. The attempt to discriminate between schooling and nurturing, therefore, must be considered unsuccessful (results are available upon request).[9]

Distinguishing Between Learning and Complementarity

The next step is to distinguish between a learning effect and complementarity in production. If there is complementarity, individual high-skill persons should have *lower* earnings in states where there are relatively many persons in that high-skill group, and the opposite for low-skill groups. A learning effect suggests the *same* outcome as does the complementarity model for the low-skill groups, but suggests a *different* outcome for the high-skill groups (i.e. learning implies higher earnings for high-skill persons in states where there is a high average income and human capital, because high-skill immigrants would learn more from their colleagues there than they would if they lived in states where colleagues have less skill on average). Hence, an examination of the effects of state income on high-education and low-education groups separately is needed.

Regressions 4 and 5 (Table 4) show the results for native males with education of 12 years or less, and 13 years or more, respectively, and the basic regression specification.

The coefficient for state income for the lower-education natives is positive as expected, due either to complementarity or to learning. The coefficient for the higher-education natives is *also* positive, which suggests a learning effect rather than complementarity. Furthermore, because there must be *some* complementarity effect, the PPE coefficient for the high-skill group should be biased downward. Therefore, since that coefficient is positive, it would seem to provide a lower bound to the effect, and vice versa for the low-skill group.

Results for immigrants split into high and low education groups (regressions 10 and 11 above) with respect to state income effect (*PPE*) do not accord with expectations if a complementarity effect were to be operating. The state income coefficient for the higher education group is considerably stronger than

Table 4. Complementarity versus learning

Regression no.	Group	State earnings	Education	Other variables in regression
4	Natives, <12 years schooling, weighted	$b = 0.0001$ $t = 0.01$	$b = 0.09$	Experience, residence, marital status, temperature, (and for immigrants, date of immigration)
5	Natives, ≧13 years schooling, weighted	$b = 0.0001$ $t = 0.000$	$b = 0.09$	Experience, residence, marital status, temperature, (and for immigrants, date of immigration)
10	Immigrants, <12 years schooling, weighted	$b = -0.00001$ $t = 0.72$	$b = 0.05$	Experience, residence, marital status, temperature, (and for immigrants, date of immigration)
11	Immigrants, <13 years schooling, weighted	$b = 0.0001$ $t = 0.04$	$b = 0.10$	Experience, residence, marital status, temperature, (and for immigrants, date of immigration)

Source: Table 1.

that for the lower education group, both among natives and among immigrants. This is consistent with education increasing a person's capacity to learn from his or her environment (as it certainly ought to). The difference in the education coefficient between the education groups is interesting, but will not be pursued here.

4. DISCUSSION

Differences in Schooling Quality Versus Informal Learning

The source of the learning during development may be in or out of school. Behrman and Birdsall (1984) emphasize the effect of in-school education quality in Brazil. Consistent with that idea is the stronger coefficient for *PPE* with more schooling compared to less schooling (regression 5 versus regression 4). But going in the other direction is the fact that the schooling coefficient is much the same in regressions that do and do not contain an argument for state income (results not shown here).

Supporting evidence for the main conclusion of this paper is that the size of gross migrations back and forth between various pairs of states are not very different from each other, but both are large relative to the difference between them (i.e. net migration). If there were real wage differentials, one would expect migration to reduce the differentials. But the mean difference between the outcome distributions in pairs of states must be small relative to the variances of the distributions, because the net migration is small relative to the gross migration, though it is in the expected direction (Sjaastad, 1960, 1962).

Additional evidence that supports the conclusion is that the total labor costs that enter into retailing of goods must be the same, because the prices of standardized goods are not systematically different in states with different incomes (Love, 1979). That is, efficiency labor must be the same across states.

Other Possible Explanations of the Observed Phenomenon

The next issue is whether there are plausible explanations for the observed state income coefficient other than differences in marginal output (holding constant the years of education).

Differences in the Cost of Living. Certainly there are always temporary disequilibria in earnings. But there seems no obvious reason why there should be long-standing disequilibria associated with long-standing differences in living costs from place to place, and therefore the neo-classical model would not seem to be inappropriate. That is, even if workers are attracted to an area because of living costs as well as because of wages, in the long run the labor market should be no tighter in one place than in another. Employers might be able to take advantage of temporary differences in labor market tightness in the short run. But unless there is some geographical difference in bargaining power or other structural conditions that allows employers in some places to permanently hold wages below marginal output, the cost of living should not matter.

Data that jibe with this theoretical analysis with respect to the cost of living will be adduced in the next section.

Differences in Prices Among States for Identical Goods and Services. Surprising to many, data suggest that the cost of living is not related to income. Consider those classes of goods that, in comparison shopping by the Bureau of Labor Statistics for the Consumer Price Index, can reasonably be considered identical when sold in various markets — for example, pipe tobacco, bath towels, floor wax, clothes dryers.

Love (1982) and Simon and Love (1990) studied the elasticities of prices of various types of goods with respect to the mean wages (as a measure of income) in various cities. Excluding those services for which it is almost impossible to hold constant the quality of those products in a cross-city comparison, the average elasticity of the other categories is not even positive. Excluding women's apparel and men's clothing on the grounds of difficulty of holding style and quality constant even pushes the comparison strongly negative, suggesting that there is *not* a positive relationship between mean income of the city (and state) and the amount paid for quality-adjusted labor in retailing, at least. So even if one does not accept the theoretical argument given in the section above, these data suggest that the cost of living is not higher in higher income places. Therefore, both the empirical evidence and the theoretical argument concur in suggesting that the cost of living is not an important explanatory factor.

Differences in Capital Used by Workers. Lower worker skill may lead to lower quality physical capital being used in a given place. This might at first seem to constitute two-way causation. But an investment decision to use relatively low technology equipment could have only two relevant causes: (a) relatively low worker skill because of relatively low formal education, which does not affect the analysis here; or (b) low worker skill because of low quality education or a low amount of human capital in the surrounding work environment, both of which constitute the phenomenon which the analysis here focuses upon. That is, the type of capital is endogenous, an intermediate variable rather than an independent variable which is a separate competing cause of lower wages for equal worker skill, and hence lower capital per worker in low-pay states does not call into question the conclusion arrived at here.

Selective Migration. General migration toward high-income states is not inconsistent with the conclusion arrived at here, but in any case is not observed according to the low ratio of net to gross migration. Selective migration of higher skill workers within homogeneous education groups also is not inconsistent with the conclusion arrived at here that pay is in accordance with skill and productivity.[10]

Persisting Disequilibrium. Perhaps the argument offered in this paper will seem more plausible if it is turned around. Is it not likely, if quality-adjusted wages really are (and have been for a long time) lower in low-income states, that producers would exploit this advantage by moving their operations to the areas of lower labor cost? The only reasonable explanation for business *not* moving to exploit such a potential advantage is fixity of capital, together with other frictions that resist immediate response. But interstate income differences have existed from the most distant relevant economic past, with plenty of time for all appropriate adjustments to take place if these differences really indicate adjusted wage differences. Therefore, the fact that differences in per-person income have not disappeared, though they have narrowed somewhat in proportional terms, suggests that differences in adjusted wages are not associated with differences in per-person income.

Length of Time in Job. Mincer (in conversation) suggested that the length of time working on the current job, if not allowed for explicitly, might account for some of the results observed here. Number of years residing in the current state of residence, which should be at least a partial proxy for that variable, is included in the regressions shown in regressions 12 and 13. Some positive effect is seen for natives, but the coefficient for immigrants has the wrong sign, which throws doubt upon the meaningfulness of the result for natives. More important, however, is that the other results discussed in the paper are not affected by the inclusion of this variable.[11]

5. SUMMARY

Though much of the mean income differences among states is due to different compositions of persons with various amounts of education, earnings also differ among people with the same amount of education and experience; persons in higher income states earn more. The causes could operate during the process of growing up, or in the current environment. The results of comparing natives' and immigrants' earnings suggest that this effect is mainly due to influences during development rather than during adulthood, because immigrants show a smaller state-income effect (or none).

Differences in the quality of education, and in parental nurturing, are possible explanations. Children may receive lower quality education in poorer states. Children with poorer parents may receive less income-increasing education at home, or both may be operative.

Other possible explanations for the observed positive regression coefficient for state income were examined and found not to be persuasive; these include the costs of living, prices of output, selective migration and capital endowment. The main result is also empirically distinguished from complementarity of different skill levels in production.

The result for immigrants also implies that the average quality of human capital of the state within which a person works does not have an observable effect upon the person's earnings, at least within the first 10 years in the state, suggesting that informal learning externalities are not a major influence.

This paper may be viewed as following in the footsteps of the human-capital studies of Schultz (1960), Mincer (1963) and Becker (1967), in attempting to throw light on the determinants of a person's earning capacity.

Acknowledgements — I appreciate valuable comments by Jere Behrman and Jacob Mincer, and excellent typing by Becky Smith and Helen Demarest.

NOTES

1. Sjaastad may serve as a classic example:
   Economists and others are generally dissatisfied with the past performance of migration in narrowing geographic income differentials . . . How can these large income differences persist in the face of such massive movements? (1962, p. 80).
   The labor market, with respect to migration, has often been declared ineffective, and the evidence produced by this study to date indicates that the market is probably not up to the task that has been imposed upon it. That is, it seems a spatial misallocation of labor is not eliminated within a tolerable length of time (1960, p. 5).
2. A regression including state temperature but not state income shows much the same coefficients for all other variables as does regression 1, and much the same coefficient for temperature as does regression 2; therefore, the results are not shown.
3. A relatively small number of specifications are shown here. This is because much experience has been acquired with variations of the model in regression 1 in the course of work by Mincer (1974), Chiswick (1978), and others.
4. These arise from regressions which weight each observation to allow for its probability of inclusion into the Bureau of the Census sample. (The purpose of the weighting was to ensure that in each state a sufficiently large number of poor persons were included.) There is some controversy as to whether it is more appropriate to use weighted or unweighted observations in the regression, and to my knowledge, the matter has not been settled by formal analysis. The reasons for putting more emphasis on the weighted regressions (while also presenting results for the unweighted regressions) are as follows:
   (1) The state effects shown by the weighted regressions are smaller than those of the unweighted regressions (an elasticity of 0.39 and a beta of 0.065, compared to 0.65 and 0.12, respectively, for the unweighted regressions; see column 3). This makes the presentation of the weighted estimate less dramatic and, therefore, a more modest scientific claim. However, for completeness it seems important to present the larger unweighted estimates, too.
   (2) More importantly, on the basis of this reasoning the weighted regression seems more appropriate to the writer. If the data really are not completely linear — and no set of data ever will be completely linear — then the relative number of observations at either end of the distribution will affect the coefficient. If the sampling scheme affects the distribution in that fashion, it therefore affects the coefficient, and the very purpose of a stratified sample is just that: to affect the distribution of

observations with respect to the variable of stratification, which in this case is the key variable — income. Therefore, it seems reasonable to attempt to reproduce the population distribution by applying the weighting scheme in the version of the sample that is used in our statistical manipulations.

Replicating the work with the 1980 and 1990 U.S. Census samples would be useful in answering remaining questions about the weighting scheme, and replicating with data for other countries would test the generality of the findings.

5. This matter could be pursued further by separating those who migrated domestically into the state from those who were born there, but this will require a better body of data than is now available. The fact that domestic migrants are lumped with natives operates to bias downwards the observed state income effect, of course.
6. Domestic migration might conceivably account for some part of a positive coefficient for all immigrants. And migration must be less for more recent immigrants, which would be consistent with the absence of a *PPE* effect among them. However, in general, selective migration would seem an unlikely force to be operating in this context. And a years-in-state variable does not have a significant coefficient (column 12), and a comparable regression for natives even has the wrong sign (column 13).
7. This is a rough calculation for illustrative purposes only. It assumes that human capital is all-important and ignores physical capital. However, because the amount of physical capital is a function of the amount of human capital in the intermediate and long run — the experiences of Germany and Japan after World War II are dramatic evidence of this — the absence of physical capital from the calculation does not make it wildly wrong.
8. Some sort of weighted average would be more appropriate, but there is high correlation in the state expenditure pattern from year to year.
9. The variable for state expenditures on education in 1950 considered by itself has a significant effect on earnings, whereas state expenditures on education in 1976 does not, which makes sense and suggests that the effect is not just being exerted through the collinearity with per-person income.
10. If a lower cost of living is associated with the lower wages, it would work *against* this migration taking place. Hence, the presence of a low cost of living would tend to work against seeing what is actually observed here, rather than causing it.
11. The code "O" was used both for no answer and for persons who were born in the state. The number of persons coded "O" was sufficiently small for immigrants, however, (less than half of one percent) so that it was deemed safe to substitute age for number of years in the state for all natives coded "O".

REFERENCES

BECKER, G. (1964) *Human Capital*. New York: National Bureau of Economic Research–Columbia.

BEHRMAN, J.R. and BIRDSALL, N. (1983) The quality of schooling: quantity alone is misleading. *Am. Econ. Rev.* **73**, 928–947.

BIRDSALL, N. and BEHRMAN, J.R. (1984) Does geographical aggregation cause overestimates of the returns to schooling? *Oxford Bull. Econ. Stat.* **46**.

CHISWICK, B.R. (1978) The effects of Americanization on the earnings of foreign-born men. *J. Political Econ.* **86**, 897–921.

LOVE, D. (1982) City population size and item prices. In *Research in Population Economics* (Edited by SIMON, J.L. and LINDERT, P.H.), pp. 83–92. Greenwich, CT: JAI Press.

MINCER, J. (1963) Market prices, opportunity costs, and income effects. In *Measurement in Economics* (Edited by CHRIST, C.). Stanford: Palo Alto.

MINCER, J. (1974) *Schooling, Experience, and Earnings*. (Edited by CHRIST, C.). New York: National Bureau of Economic Research.

SCHULTZ, T.W. (1960) The formation of human capital by education. *J. Political Econ.* **68**.

SIMON, J.L. and LOVE, D.O. (1990) City size, prices, and efficiency for individual goods and services. *Annals Regional Sci.* **24**, 163–175.

SJAASTAD, L.A. (1962) The costs and returns of human migration. *J. Political Econ.* 80–93.

SJAASTAD, L.A. (1960) *The Relationship Between Migration and Income in the United States*. Papers and Proceedings of the Regional Science Association, **6**, 37–64.

WEISBROD, B.A. (1962) Education and investment in human capital. *J. Political Econ.* **LXX**, 106–123.

APPENDIX

Variables, statistics, and correlations (for natives including Puerto Ricans; data for immigrants available upon request)

Variable	Mean	Standard deviation	Cases
Log male earnings (*LME*)	9.2	0.8	5428
Experience (*EXP*)	24.9	12.5	5428
EXP^2	783.0	669.9	5428
State temperature (*TEMP*)	55.9	6.6	5428
SMSA	0.9	0.2	5428
Age	42.2	11.3	5428
Schooling (*SCHL*)	12.1	3.2	5428
Not married (*NOTMSP*)	0.1	0.3	5428
State per-person earnings 1976 (*PPE*)	5865.0	714.3	5428
State per-person earnings 1950 (*PPE*)	1457.0	305.3	5428
State education expenditures 1950 (*STEDX*50)	178.0	51.7	5428
*STEDX*76	1364.9	247.3	5428
State mean education 1976 (*STAED*76)	12.4	0.1	5428
*STAED*50	9.5	1.0	5428

Note: Demographic characteristics are shown only for natives, and not for immigrants, because immigrants taken altogether do not figure in the analysis; an aggregate display would be heavily affected by the size of the cohorts over the decades. The appropriate comparable displays would require data for each of the cohorts, which is impossible from the point of view of space.

Correlation coefficients

	LME	EXP2	EXP	TEMP	STEDX50	SMSA	IIDAGE	SCHL	NTMSP	PPE76	PPE50	STAEDX76	STAED50
EXP2	−0.08722												
EXP	−0.04563	0.97413											
TEMP	−0.07275	0.01198	0.00812										
STEDX50	0.07786	−0.03640	−0.03409	−0.16740									
SMSA	0.07145	−0.02513	−0.02469	−0.00706	0.11910								
AGE	0.03287	−0.94178	−0.96813	0.00515	−0.00998	−0.00928							
SCHL	0.29033	−0.48343	−0.49162	−0.01341	0.09683	0.06298	−0.25785						
NOTMSP	−0.11178	−0.03246	−0.06080	0.01175	0.05485	0.03120	−0.05872	0.03038					
PPE50	0.09684	−0.00667	−0.00122	−0.40975	0.75334	0.10017	0.00954	0.03787	0.05600				
PPE76	0.09663	−0.00681	0.00061	−0.46633	0.78254	0.12703	0.01201	0.03940	0.05782	0.93544			
STEDX76	0.05012	−0.00038	0.00503	−0.34958	0.52716	0.14144	0.00809	0.00873	0.05936	0.71042	0.71824		
STAED50	0.06710	−0.05563	−0.05563	−0.21580	0.79545	0.13203	−0.02108	0.14132	0.07010	0.57761	0.63269	0.37987	
STAED76	0.08636	−0.05620	−0.05721	−0.31418	0.78422	0.13263	−0.02279	0.14148	0.05866	0.67276	0.68092	0.50211	0.84678

Foreword

Sitting in the social-science teachers' lounge at Hebrew University in Jerusalem in 1968, I heard economist-statistician Yoel Haitovsky say, "God wrote a set of equations, and it is our task to find out what the equations are" – that is, what the "true model" is, as statisticians often put it. He was expressing a view of science which became dominant in the 19th century. As Kant (1781/1965) put it, the "Author of the world" caused there to be "the glorious order, beauty, and providential care everywhere displayed in nature" (p. 31). This surely is still the common view today.

I replied to Haitovsky roughly as follows, "God wrote no equations. Rather, God (though let's not get hung up on that word) gave the formless mass a kick and deformed it so that it is no longer totally random and without order. We try out various equations to see which ones come closest to fitting our needs."

This view – that it is scientists who invent neat models to imitate some aspects of messy reality – has come into vogue because of Einstein and Bohr. Einstein was fond of saying that physical theories are the products of human imagination. On this matter, the almost-unreadable Kant may have pointed in the right direction, though it is quite unclear whether he had any influence on the likes of Einstein and Bohr or whether they developed this point of view on their own. Kant wrote that "reason" – by which he meant something like what we call theory or logic or both – must "show the way with principles of judgment based upon fixed laws, constraining nature to give answer to questions of reason's own determining" (p. 20). He said that the scientist should not approach nature "in the character of a pupil who listens to everything that the teacher chooses to say, but of an appointed judge who compels the witness to answer questions which he has himself formulated" (p. 20). And he went on to say that we can know of phenomena "only what we ourselves put into them" (p. 23). Admittedly it is unclear whether Kant was talking of experience-based theories as we know them, or purely tautological mathematical propositions. (He claims to be talking of the latter, but he understood the former quite well, and alluded to such theory though excluding it from his "a priori" category.) In any case, Kant surely did emphasize that our scientific vision of a phenomenon is, and should be, a product of our ideas about how best to think about the phenomenon, as well as the data that we collect about the phenomenon, just as Einstein and Bohr later insisted was the heart of their scientific approaches.

This subject was on my mind when I overheard Haitovsky's remark because I had recently been working on the relationship of income to family size, and I had once more seen how it made no sense to talk about a "true" or "underlying" relationship, and how it is impossible to ever "purify" a relationship of extraneous forces in such fashion as to reach a "true" model. Rather, one must always make a choice of which model to work with, and the choice must be made with reference to the purposes of the investigation; different purposes should lead to different views of a scientific relationship, unattractive as this seems because of its apparent lack of "objectivity." It also lacks attractive power, I think, because its appeal is not to a particular theory being out-and-out correct but rather to its being *approximately* correct, or being "convenient," in Bertrand Russell's term (1945, p. 832). This is not palatable to people who view themselves as searching for eternal truth rather than searching for workable ideas that will help us get on with additional learning about the world and with dealing with our human problems more successfully. But perhaps the imprimatur of Einstein and Bohr will have some persuasive power; they are tough names to be contemptuous of, even if they are not names that I can actually conjure with.

The article shows how analysis of the data on income and fertility is hampered rather than aided by the concept of the "true" relationship.

References

Kant, Immanuel (1781/1965) *Critique of Pure Reason*, New York: St Martin's.
Russell, Bertrand (1945) *A History of Western Philosophy*, New York: Simon and Schuster.

On the concept of the 'true model': the case of income and fertility

Appendix B
Difficulties in the Inference of Income Effects from Cross-Sectional Data[68]

The ultimate aim of cross-section analysis is to throw light on what is likely to happen to fertility *in a country as a whole* if income rises, for purposes of prediction. If one could find a very similar place at a similar point in its history, or if one could find a similar period in the history of the *same* place, one might predict that the same observed unconditional (i.e., total) income-fertility relationship will occur in the place for which one is predicting. This total relationship might be either direct or inverse, and it might be of any magnitude. An example of the same-place different-time case is a prediction of the effect of

[68]I have benefited from discussion of the material in this section with Yoram Ben-Porath, though he disagrees with much of it.

a business cycle on the percentage rate of change in births over the business cycle. An example of the different-place case might be a prediction that Macao will follow the same pattern of fertility as Hong Kong if its income rises as fast.

But it is seldom possible to find places or periods "on all fours" with the case for which you wish to predict. For example, the effect of a secular change in Indian income from a given starting point cannot be predicted with confidence on the basis of the experience of any other country, for India is very different than other countries in many relevant ways. Even more is this true of a prediction about the effect on India of large incentive payments to reduce births; there is no experience with this anywhere in the world.

Within-country cross-section data on fertility and income in MDCs are plentiful and good, being the product of censuses and modern sample surveys. Therefore these data seem like a good ground on which to test hypothesis and estimate parameters. But these cross-section data may glitter more than they yield. It is the purpose of this appendix to indicate some of the limitations and snares in these data, and some of the confusions that they can lead to.

Before proceeding to the more fundamental and subtle problems of cross-sections, one must mention the confusion that has arisen from *various measures of the income variables.* The most important such confusion in past studies has been between husband's income and family income. If there were no systematic effects within the chain of intermediates that links husband's income and fertility, the relationship between family income and fertility should be the same as between husband's income and fertility. But this is not so. Let us consider some data on income and childlessness. In column 2 of Table 61, which is similar to column 1 except that the former shows *family* income and the latter *husband's* income, the pattern is rather mixed, both within and between age groups. It is important to note, however, that the data in column 2 do not argue against the possibility that a change in *husband's* income has a *direct* effect on fertility (as suggested by column 1), and if a reasonable causal link can be shown, it will be reasonable to accept that such a relationship holds. And the explanation of the difference in patterns is surely that the likelihood of women working is a negative function of income; poorer women are more likely to take jobs to increase family income.[69] The lowest-family-income families in column 2 are

[69]There is also a slight difference in *coverage,* column 1 having slightly fewer cases due to not including women whose husbands are not family heads.

those in which the wife does not work. But the higher-family-income brackets contain women who were in lower brackets in column 1. Therefore, it would seem that in column 2 we see the compound of *at least two* important influences on fertility (or more specifically here, childlessness) which have mixed effects. Ceteris paribus, lower income produces lower fertility. But lower income also leads to more women working, an effect which has a ceteris paribus negative effect on fertility at the same time that it raises family income. But too often in the past, husband's income and family income have been used indiscriminately in income-fertility studies, with consequent confusion.

Two other income-variable problems that occur in cross-section data — the "permanent income effect" and the "relative income effect" — were discussed in the text earlier. Another major problem with the cross-section studies as they have commonly been done is that the effect of income is quite different on different birth orders, as was also discussed earlier.

The choice of definition of fertility as the dependent variable also poses some problems in cross-sectional data. If one is interested in the total number of births, completed family size is the likely choice in cross-sectional work. But for some purposes — for example, governmental decisions about fertility incentives — one may be particularly interested in the second, third, or fourth parities. The relationships of income to these various measures of fertility are not the same. Other things being equal, the relationship between income and the decision to have *no* children is stronger than is the relationship between income and total number of children. Many explanations are possible, e.g., that the marginal cost of children drops very low after three or four, or that after a certain number of children the mother is committed to being out of the labor force. But whatever the explanation, the fact exists and must be considered when choosing a dependent variable in a cross-sectional study.

Now to proceed to the more subtle problems of cross-sections. The underlying idea in cross-sectional analysis is that as the mean income of a group changes from one level to another, the same differences in fertility can be expected as are seen between *subgroups* with those two income levels. But it is immediately clear that the cross-sectional relationship between income and fertility is affected by other variables. That is, holding other variables constant changes the observed coefficient of income. This was noted in the text as the cross-sectional groups were made progressively more homogeneous, and the income coefficient became progressively more positive. The question is, then, which specification is most appropriate?

Table 61. Proportion of Women Childless in Various Income Classes, United States, 1959

Age of woman and husband's or family income	Working and non-working wives: Husband's income (1)	Working and non-working wives: Family income (2)
Women 15 to 19 years old		
No income	54.2	
$1 — $1,999 or loss	56.6	52.9
$2,000 — $2,999	50.2	44.7
$3,000 — $3,999	45.7	42.8
$4,000 — $4,999	44.1	44.3
$5,000 — $6,999	41.1	55.4
$7,000 — $9,999	39.1	61.9
$10,000— $14,999	32.7	49.6
$15,000 and over	—	—
Regression coefficient	-.19E-02	.53E-03
Women 20 to 24 years old		
No income	40.7	
$1 — $1,999 or loss	46.7	26.4
$2,000 — $2,999	34.9	22.4
$3,000 — $3,999	30.2	20.6
$4,000 — $4,999	26.6	19.7
$5,000 — $6,999	22.3	26.3
$7,000 — $9,999	20.8	41.5
$10,000— $14,999	26.6	49.5
$15,000 and over	31.9	39.8
Regression coefficient	-.55E-03	.13E-02
Women 25 to 29 years old		
No income	24.1	
$1 — $1,999 or loss	27.2	13.0
$2,000 — $2,999	20.4	10.0
$3,000 — $3,999	17.5	8.2
$4,000 — $4,999	15.9	7.8
$5,000 — $6,999	12.2	9.3
$7,000 — $9,999	10.5	18.1
$10,000— $14,999	11.6	19.3
$15,000 and over	11.2	19.3
Regression coefficient	-.73E-03	.79E-03
Women 30 to 34 years old		
No income	19.3	
$1 — $1,999 or loss	18.3	11.9
$2,000 — $2,999	16.3	9.2
$3,000 — $3,999	13.1	7.0
$4,000 — $4,999	12.5	6.6
$5,000 — $6,999	10.0	7.1
$7,000 — $9,999	8.1	11.0
$10,000— $14,999	7.5	16.4
$15,000 and over	8.1	12.7
Regression coefficient	-.59E-03	.30E-03

Table 61. Proportion of Women Childless in Various Income Classes, United States, 1959 (continued)

Age of woman and husband's or family income	Working and non-working wives	
	Husband's income	Family income
Women 35 to 39 years old		
No income	17.3	
$1 — $1,999 or loss	18.6	13.1
$2,000 — $2,999	17.3	12.3
$3,000 — $3,999	14.5	10.1
$4,000 — $4,999	13.0	8.3
$5,000 — $6,999	10.4	8.1
$7,000 — $9,999	8.9	10.6
$10,000 — $14,999	8.3	13.7
$15,000 and over	7.3	10.6
Regression coefficient	-.59E-03	-.68E-06
Women 40 to 44 years old		
No income	20.2	
$1 — $1,999 or loss	21.0	18.8
$2,000 — $2,999	17.9	17.7
$3,000 — $3,999	17.1	14.9
$4,000 — $4,999	15.8	13.0
$5,000 — $6,999	13.9	12.6
$7,000 — $9,999	11.8	13.1
$10,000 — $14,999	10.9	13.8
$15,000 and over	10.1	11.7
Regression coefficient	-.56E-03	-.30E-03
Women 45 to 49 years old		
No income	25.2	
$1 — $1,999 or loss	25.9	26.1
$2,000 — $2,999	23.5	24.5
$3,000 — $3,999	20.7	20.8
$4,000 — $4,999	19.3	19.7
$5,000 — $6,999	17.6	18.9
$7,000 — $9,999	16.5	17.4
$10,000 — $14,999	16.1	16.4
$15,000 and over	14.6	14.6
Regression coefficient	-.56E-03	-.57E-03
Women 50 years old and over		
No income	24.3	
$1 — $1,999	21.4	24.6
$2,000 — $2,999	22.4	24.3
$3,000 — $3,999	22.6	24.4
$4,000 — $4,999	21.9	23.0
$5,000 — $6,999	21.6	22.4
$7,000 — $9,999	22.2	21.1
$10,000 — $14,999	22.0	18.9
$15,000 and over	20.1	18.3
Regression coefficient	-.13E-03	-.39E-03

SOURCE: United States Department of Commerce, 1964, pp. 182 and 189.

Some writers have suggested that, ideally, *all* other variables would be held constant and the "true" coefficient of income estimated. Conceptually this would represent an "instantaneous" relationship, the effect of an increment of income on fertility in such a short run that nothing else would have a chance to change. But such an instantaneous coefficient would not seem to be very meaningful, because any significant increase in income will in fact lead to changes in other variables, such as children's education, in the not-so-long run.

Another difficulty with the conception of the "true" coefficient is that in practice one cannot ever hope to get rid of what would here be specification bias. That is, the partial estimate will continue to be affected by the addition of more variables as one continues to add more variables, certainly to the limit of presently available data. The reason is that income affects a multitude of factors that themselves affect fertility. And since this set of factors must be larger than the set of variables we can control for in regression or classification analysis, the most comprehensive such investigation will still yield an estimate different from what would be obtained in a still more detailed investigation.

One might think, as I earlier did, that one might extrapolate from a series of progressively finer subclassification estimates by fitting a curve to the observed series of estimates. But this would make no sense, because there is no way to establish a cardinal distance between the degrees of fineness on the abscissa. That is, there is no reason to believe that the difference between the estimate with rural-urban and men's education held constant and the estimate with women's education also added is the same size as the difference between the latter and the estimate with men's occupation also added to the latter.

The nature of the difficulty is brought out clearly when the problem is considered in the context of an experiment. When non-experimental methods lead to results that are difficult to interpret, it is often helpful to ask which experiment one *would* run *if* such an experiment were feasible. In this case, there is *no* experiment that would produce an estimate that would resemble what is meant by the "pure" effect of income on fertility. Consider giving an increment of income to a randomly selected half of the members of any given subpopulation, the other half being given no income increment — for example, incentive payments not to have more children. Such an experiment is itself quite valid and unexceptionable. But the outcome would not be an estimate of the partial effect of income on fertility of the sort that is sought in multivariate studies, because as a result of the additional income people will buy different educational and living patterns that will then affect their fertility. So the factors of education and rural-urban residence, etc., are not being held constant as they are sought to be held constant in multivariate studies that seek to estimate the "pure" effect. Nor *can* they be held constant in an experiment. It will not help to take explicit account of the lagged effects, for while it might be interesting to see the effects in various future periods of the one-time income increment, no period's estimate will hold all the other variables constant, not even the first period estimate, because people will immediately take into account in their fertility decisions the future effect of the education they will later buy. And even if one could hope that the "instantaneous" estimate would be relatively free of the other variables, of what possible use could it be? Any possible policy decision must take into account the longer run effects of an income change, and there is no way to parley a short-run "sanitized" estimate into a longer run sanitized estimate. (It is also relevant that the long-run elasticities as estimated by experiment might well be negative.)

The point of the discussion of the experiment is *not* to argue that experiments on fertility and income may not be extremely useful ad hoc estimators, but rather that the notion of a "pure" effect of income on fertility is rendered suspect by the inability to estimate it by experimentation.

Even if one could estimate the "true instantaneous coefficient" for any subgroup, there is every reason to believe that the coefficient would differ among cells. This is clearly so for whites and blacks in the U.S.; for example, childlessness is much higher among blacks than among whites at the same level of income. And there is some evidence (Sanderson and Willis, 1971) that among higher socioeconomic groups the ceteris paribus fertility response to an increment of income is more positive than among lower socioeconomic groups.[70] If so, what can be the standing of the estimates with respect to the "true" effect of income on fertility? One might hedge by saying that there is a different "true" estimate for each subgroup. But not only does this line of argument lead to a useless result for practical purposes, but it is reasonable to suppose that if the cells were partitioned once more by another relevant variable — and there will *always* be one more such variable — different estimates will result among the resulting sub-sub-groups. One might argue that the "pure" effect is some weighted average of the coefficients in all the groups, but this makes very clear that the result will depend upon which groups are included in

[70]Sanderson and Willis (1971) argue, however, that the addition of their interaction team removes much of the difference among cells.

the overall sample. This suggests that if a different basic population had been chosen, the estimate of the "true" effect would be different. And if the "true" estimate varies from population to population, and from period to period, there is no reason to believe that a true effect can be estimated on one population and then used to "build up" a "total" estimate for another population. And certainly there is never a need to build up an estimate for the population that is itself observed, because the total relationship can be observed directly.

If Sanderson and Willis' recent work (1971; discussed above on pages 59-61) stands up, however, these comments may be too pessimistic. Their results suggest that in a non-linear regression of husband's income, wife's market wage, and the *interaction* between them, the combined effect of husband's income and the interaction term (wife's wage, too) is quite stable across cohorts — though the husband's-income term is negative! If the relationship is indeed stable in this fashion, the prospect for prediction would be satisfactory.

Having said all the above, how might cross-sectional data be used? Let us consider several possible ways.

Gross Differential Fertility

The goal is to predict the change that will occur in aggregate fertility as average income will change in the future. One might simply examine the mean fertility of the group with present income equal to the present mean of the country, and the mean fertility of the income group whose mean income is presently that which society's as a whole will be in the future, in, say, twenty years. Then one might guess that the difference in fertility between the groups is an estimate of the aggregate change that will take place.

An important shortcoming of this method is that other relevant variables such as education and urbanization may very well not take a course that will resemble the difference between the income groups, thereby rendering the method suspect.

A related method would be to work with each income class separately, estimating the number of people who will be in each income class in the forecast period, attributing to each one the present fertility of that income class, and aggregating. But this more disaggregated method also seems subject to the objection given just above.

Refined Differential Fertility

One might examine subgroups defined by social variables (e.g., education) as well as by income, then estimate the number of people who will be in each of these groups in future years and attribute to them the present fertility of people in these groups. One shortcoming of this method is that it would be very hard work. Another shortcoming, more serious, is that when one looks *across* nations, fertility is different in similar socioeconomic groups. Or to put it another way, fertility is similar in countries with different socioeconomic make-ups. For example, aggregate fertilities in England and the U.S. are certainly much more similar than their socioeconomic compositions. This suggests that the differentials among socioeconomic groups *within* a society may be at least *partly relative,* which renders less valid this method of differential-fertility projections.

Synthetic Estimates with the "Pure" Income Effect

Earlier in this appendix was mentioned the notion of a "pure" or "true" income effect. The motivation in seeking such a magnitude is to combine it with estimates of the effects on fertility of the other social variables, so as to "build up" a synthetic estimate of the overall effect of an income change. But even if it could be estimated satisfactorily, the "pure" effect would surely be found to be quite different in different groups, even to the extent of being negative in some subgroups and positive in others. This implies that this synthetic method has no advantages because of its lack of generality. It would have to be done separately for each subgroup. The behavior of the group could more easily be estimated directly, without going by way of extracting the individual effects and then combining them.

For Understanding the Fertility Mechanism

Cross-sectional data may indeed be useful for unraveling the secrets of the fertility-decision mechanism for basic scientific understanding.

It is illuminating to compare the use of cross-section data for estimating income elasticities for children and for other "purchases." Consider the classic case of food and the Engel curve. In a poor country, an income elasticity computed from an Engel curve is likely to yield a good estimate of what will happen if income rises, even without allowing for other variables. This is surely because, unlike the fertility case, income by itself is the decisive factor in determining how much grain and meat a poor family will eat. The income-food purchase decision almost surely is not mediated in as uncertain a fashion as is the fertility decision, by all the factors shown in Figure

1 (at least in a poor country. In a rich country the case of food may, however, be more complex and more akin to the income-fertility situation.) Hence, if one knows the income elasticity of food in one or a few places, one can directly apply it to another country or era, with some confidence that its sign and general magnitude will be correct. But this is not so for children.

In the case of automobiles in MDCs, cross-section income elasticities may be less useful, even though the auto-purchase decision is still much less complex than is the fertility decision — though more complex than the poor-country food decision. Hence for autos, reliance is usually put upon time-series estimates.

PART III

INDIVIDUAL BEHAVIOR

[12]

Foreword

This article summarizes a book on the same subject which unfortunately fell "deadborn from the press," in Hume's immortal words about such an event. In a massive administrative failure, review copies were not even sent out by the publisher. Such are the hazards of the book writer.

The concept of incentive is used very frequently by economists. But heretofore, it has not been specified rigorously. This paper does that.

The paper shows the influence of my having studied experimental psychology as an undergraduate.

Under the tutelage of Stephen T. Gould (the independent scholar, not the biologist), I have come to see that the power function – which I had only mentioned in passing – might well be a better model than a logarithmic function, in principle. Comparison of the two possibilities would be interesting.

A Theory of Effort as an Economic Variable

JULIAN L. SIMON*
University of Maryland

ABSTRACT: This article postulates that the amount of effort a person exerts is influenced by two factors: (a) the opportunity to earn additional income, and (b) the "need" for additional income as measured by the person's wealth. Specifically, the amount of effort (drive) is a function of the arithmetic difference between wealth with and wealth without the opportunity in question, considered relative to the person's current wealth. Formally

Drive-Effort Measure = expected likelihood of a positive response to a given opportunity by an individual or nation

$$= a \left[\frac{W_{n+1} - W_n}{W_n} \right]$$

Effort here includes both the amount of time expended at work, and the intensity of given work periods.

This formulation is a precise definition of the concept of incentive. And it provides the basis for analysis of a wide variety of phenomena that are not well understood without a systematic concept of effort, such as: differences in amount of time worked by people differing in such characteristics as number of children, amount of assets, and minority vs. majority group status; the propensity for economic development in benign, moderate, and harsh climates; the decline of empires; and the rate of productivity of individual workers in piecework vs. flat-rate industrial payment plans.

* Direct all correspondence to: Julian L. Simon, College of Business and Management, University of Maryland, College Park, MD 20742.

The Journal of Socio-Economics, Volume 20, Number 2, pages 105-123

ISSN: 1053-5357

INTRODUCTION

All of us act as if the concept of effort has meaning and is useful. We believe that the amount of effort exerted differs among people and depends on circumstances. In common speech and in popular writing, we use effort to help explain the outcome in many activities such as sports, school, and work. We feel our own exertions of effort in our minds and in our bodies, both while exerting the effort and afterward. Yet variations in effort have heretofore not been taken account of by economists in analyses of economic phenomena.

This article postulates that the amount of effort a person will exert is influenced by two factors: (a) the opportunity that the person perceives to earn additional income, and (b) the person's "need" for additional income as measured by the person's wealth. Of course, effort depends on a host of other factors, too, but those other factors are considered extraneous here. The argument focuses on only wealth, opportunity, and the relationship between them.

More particularly, it is postulated that the amount of effort (drive) is a function of the arithmetic difference between wealth with and wealth without the opportunity in question, considered relative to the person's current wealth. The concept of wealth refers to what one can purchase with one's present assets. The concept of opportunity refers to the additional assets one can obtain conditional on accepting the alternative under discussion. This Drive-Effort formulation, therefore, can serve as a precise definition of the concept of incentive.

Effort is manifested in the *amount of time* that a person works, and in the *intensity* with which a person exerts himself or herself during the time devoted to work. The two aspects of effort are linked in being substitute methods of achieving the same end; one may work harder, or longer, or both, to finish the job. Intensity is the more interesting and perhaps the more important aspect of effort. Regrettably, however, work time is easier to discuss because there are more extant relevant data, and also because economic theory has given it more attention.

The general question addressed here is as follows: Will an individual, or a group[1] such as a nation, undertake a particular economic opportunity which involves increased work effort? There are two types of subquestions: (a) Will an alternative that would increase total money income—such as working more intensively, spending extra time weeding the family farm plot, reopening the store door to serve a customer after customary closing time, pushing back the closing time itself, or undertaking risk with one's assets or person—be undertaken or rejected? Will an independent mason accept a small contract to fix a driveway, or a mathematics tutor take on another student, or a factory worker accept proffered overtime work this evening? (b) Will an alternative that seems not to be "profitable" in money terms—such as building the world's highest cathedral in the Middle Ages, or contributing one's time to distribute food to the starving—be undertaken anyway? Questions of both types may be considered as inquiries into the extent to which people act like *homo economicus* in the popular caricature. The aim here is not to throw light on that ideal type, but rather to understand the output of economic goods by various individuals and nations at various times.

To make as clear as possible the subject of the article, the theoretical formulation will immediately be stated formally. Discussion of the role and justification of this formulation follows. But first I discuss an example that I hope will demonstrate the usefulness of this study.

Assume that an increase in police pressure on drug merchants immediately pushes up the street price of drugs, and that this leads to an increase in crime. How can we explain the phenomenon? A casual explanation is ready at hand: When the price goes up, addicts need more money to get a fix, and they steal to get the money. But this explanation is outside the conventional logic of economics, because need is not a concept found in economic theory. There is no substitute mode of formal analysis, to my knowledge.

The hypothesis offered here provides an explanation within the domain of economic analysis. A rise in price implies a fall in wealth to the addict. A fall in wealth increases the propensity to exert effort, *ceteris paribus,* according to the Drive-Effort hypothesis. The commission of a crime is one of the avenues into which an increased propensity to exert effort may drive the addict. Hence, we have a systematic explanation of the phenomenon that does not require the term *need* and which introduces only economic variables as right-hand-side variables.

THE FORMAL STATEMENT

The Drive-Effort Concept

There are many influences other than time and money cost that may cause a person not to undertake a job or project. These examples are representative: (a) the fatigue and/or pain which accompanies physical and mental effort; (b) the loss of reputation and the incurring of social disapproval for doing work which is against social customs (e.g., breaking a strike or working with a lower caste); and (c) the fear of loss which accompanies accepting the risk of an uncertain enterprise. Not all of the factors opposing work operate in any given situation, of course. But it is reasonable to think that all of them are monotonic, and to the extent that they operate, all increase in force with the amount of time spent working at a task. If so, we can treat them all as a single negative factor—a "cost"—incurred when a person works.

Let us label *Drive* (denoted *Dr*) the tendency to respond with work to a particular set of conditions, and *Effort* (denoted *Ef*) the force which a person exerts to overcome the congeries of work-resisting forces.[2] Drive is equivalent in magnitude to the amount of effort a person *would be willing* to expend in response to a given set of conditions. When discussing the motivation of an individual or group, *Dr* and *Ef* may be thought of as the joint concept Drive-Effort (*DrEf*), the objective work effort that one is willing to expend in a given situation in response to the subjective driving impulse. In some contexts it may be appropriate to speak of *Dr* and *Ef* separately, while in other contexts it is appropriate to talk of *DrEf* as a single concept.

The Formulation

The payoff to an alternative may be defined as

$$\overset{\text{yes}}{(W_{n+1} - W_n)} - \overset{\text{no}}{(W_{n+1} - W_n)}$$

where *yes* and *no* mean respectively that the opportunity will or will not be undertaken, $n - 1$ and n indicate the states before and after the alternative would be carried out, and W stands for wealth (including all otherwise-expected lifetime income) divided by expected years of life. This may be shortened to $(W_{n+1} - W_n)$ for convenience on the assumption of no change otherwise.

It is reasonable that Drive-Effort—or the expected strength of response to an opportunity, if one prefers to view the matter that way—depends on (a) the payoff per unit of work time, and (b) the individual's or group's wealth. The effect of the expected payoff is obvious without examples. The effect of wealth becomes equally obvious with a few simple examples such as the following: (a) In a subsistence agriculture economy, you do not build a house for yourself if you already have a house. (b) You do not prepare a meal if you have one prepared already. (c) Campers only work at setting up camp until it is set up. In these primitive examples, wealth in the widest sense obviously affects the supply of work. Hopefully, this observation is enough to establish the point, although the desire for money to buy goods seems less specific than the desire for specific goods, and the marginal utility of money does not so obviously decrease the marginal utility of additional goods.

It does not seem reasonable, however, that the simple difference between W_{n+1} and W_n, written $(W_{n+1} - W_n)$, indicates the strength of the desire for money, or of Drive-Effort; a millionaire will not perform the same acts to get an additional dollar as will a pauper, on average; rather, it is reasonable to think that the difference is seen relative to the individual's wealth, assuming that the net money flow is positive and that the opportunity offers a payoff higher than the value of time in Becker's (1965) reckoning (see section below). Therefore, I propose the formulation

Drive-Effort Measure = expected likelihood of a positive response to a given opportunity by an individual or nation

$$= a \left[\frac{W_{n+1} - W_n}{W_n} \right]$$

which takes the exponential form shown in Figure 1. The function has the property that a doubling of wealth leads to a halving of Drive-Effort, where wealth refers to the person's situation with and without the opportunity in question. Therefore, the function's value changes as a person does more and more work. That is, Drive-Effort is proportional to $(W_{n+1} - W_n)$ at any given level of initial wealth, and it is inversely proportional to W_n, as may be seen in Figure 1, and at subsequent wealth positions.

The Drive-Effort measure might be better represented with some other concave-downward function. The power function is one such candidate (as has been suggested in some psychophysical experiments), and there may be others. But the particular function is not of crucial importance; only its downward concavity matters, or even just its downward slope.

The effort that one *would* expend must be distinguished from the effort that one *must* expend to undertake a given opportunity. The *DrEf* measure refers to the amount of effort a person *would* expend for a given payoff. If the effort actually *required* for a given alternative is below the Drive-Effort measure for that alternative at a given level of wealth, the opportunity will be accepted; if not, not. For example, assume that the level of effort required for a particular opportunity Z with $W_{n+1} - W_n = 1$ is shown by the horizontal line Z in Figure 1. At all wealth positions producing *at least* the effort required for Z, the alternative Z will be undertaken.

The types of decisions discussed here could conceivably be crammed within the framework of the pure logic of choice. But if that were to be done, there would be no gain in understanding the particular forces that affect the choices, an understanding which is vital for many economic analyses.

SPECIFICATION AND MEASUREMENT OF KEY CONCEPTS

If this theory is to be useful, one must be able to measure its key variables. The measurement of wealth is straightforward though it may not be easy. The individual's (or family's or group's) assets, as valued in market prices, constitute an appropriate measure in most cases. In some other cases, the person's expected stream of earnings may be the appropriate concept, and the stream may often be estimated with characteristics such as education that are related to income, as human capital theory teaches. In some cases, an appropriate measure of

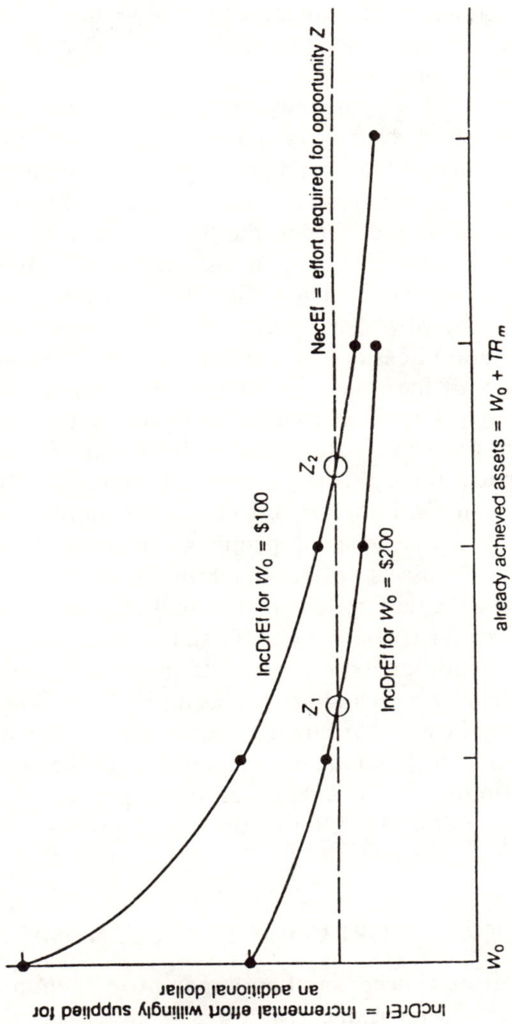

Principle of construction: IncDrEf $= \dfrac{(TR_{m+1} + W_0) - (TR_m + W_0)}{(TR_m + W_0)}$

where TR_m = total revenue obtained from efforts until now
TR_{m+1} = total revenue from efforts until now plus another unit of effort
W_0 = initial endowment
IncDrEf = effort willingly supplied for another dollar

Figure 1: Graphic Illustration of Drive-Effort Hypothesis

wealth may not be obvious, and will require hard thought and serious justification. But in principle, the measurement of wealth presents no problem. (The measurement of *relative* wealth and the role of that factor is beyond the limits of the present discussion.)

The measurement of opportunity may be difficult. Some cases are straightforward, however, such as (a) increasing the payment offered for an evening's overtime work; (b) increasing the reward to a commercial diver who hesitates to descend to a dangerous depth; and (c) offering a reward to a Delhi pedicab driver for getting the rider to the destination before a specific hour.

The income effect causes difficulty in measuring a change in opportunity and its effects. A physicians' move from the Philippines to the United States assuredly increases the physician's opportunity, but the income effect may reduce the amount and intensity of work that the physician exerts.

A price reduction, or the equivalent of a price reduction in the guise of the onset of availability of a product to a group or individual, raises perhaps the most complex issues of specification and measurement. Such a phenomenon has offsetting impacts through the channels of changes in both wealth and opportunity. For example, if the tax on automobiles in the Soviet Union were to be removed and the price lowered, people would suddenly be more wealthy because their financial assets would enable them to own a good that was previously unobtainable, thereby leading to a reduction in Drive-Effort. On the other hand, the lower price would represent an increase in opportunity because any given amount of additional earnings would constitute increased opportunity to own an auto, thereby inducing an increasing in *DrEf*. Another example is the increased availability of consumer goods in the early stage of economic development. The net effect, and hence the outcome of the two impacts, would seem to be indeterminate in these cases, although perhaps further analysis of lifetime income (including present wealth) would produce an unambiguous predicted effect.

THE ROLE OF AN EFFORT CONCEPT IN ECONOMIC ANALYSIS

The need for an effort concept is often apparent in economic analysis. The example of drug enforcement and crime was given earlier. Foreign aid is an illuminating example of how the absence of the effort concept affects analysis. According to the fundamental definition of economic welfare, a gift to a person increases that person's welfare because the gift increases the person's *endowment*, that is, the person's purchasing power. But even the best of economists may be heard to say that giving food as foreign aid is usually bad. So we have an apparent logical contradiction: If the weather gives us more wheat, we are better off, but if we give the wheat to Mexico, they may be made worse off. In the case of market agriculture and a government-to-government gift, a satisfactory explanation can be framed in standard terms, although the explanation lacks the logical precision usually demanded of economics: Reduction of the market price caused by the gift leads farmers to reduce agricultural activity, which causes reduction in physical and human investment, which will have bad effects after the aid has ended. If the aid will go to a subsistence farmer, however, the need for an effort concept is plain: The gift causes reduction in effort by the farmer, which leaves the farmer less prepared to exert effort later when there is no aid.

Another example: In a discussion of economic policies—as distinct from a discussion of economic theory—economists typically suggest privatizing economic activities and resources and internalizing costs, to provide incentive for hard and diligent work. But the term *incentive* invariably goes undefined, and is usually just a synonym for money, on the assumption that people prefer more to less purchasing power. No distinction is made among persons as to the motivating incentive power of a given sum of money; no method of measurement of incentive is offered. With respect to incentive, as in most other respects, economic analysis usually assumes that all the decision units are identical. Among the few exceptions to this rule are differences in natural resource endowment, differences in consumer tastes that lead to exchange, differences in risk preference, and Engel-curve-type consumption systems. This assumption of homogeneity of economic agents is convenient theoretically. By discussing the behavior of the representative firm or consumer as it interacts with similar firms or consumers, the standard analysis can arrive at an equilibrium without the complications which would arise if the interacting units were assumed to differ on such dimensions as size, assets, knowledge, and market share.

For some purposes, however, the assumption of homogeneity does not serve us well. The external disequilibria that induce profit-seeking economic activity, and the internal conditions that lead firms and individuals to respond to these disequilibria, often depend on differences in abilities of the competing firms and individuals caused by prior experiences, as well as by differences in such characteristics as size. Austrian economists, especially Hayek, have emphasized that these differences have an important effect on the nature of competition. Arrow's analysis of organizations and their behavior takes a similar point of view (1974). Industrial-organization theorizing about such phenomena as price leadership and price umbrellas also exemplifies analysis that necessarily deals head-on with such differences among firms. Recently, such concepts as implicit contract, specific human capital, and firm-specific effects have arisen to deal with differences among business units. These concepts point in the same general direction as does this article. But such departures from the assumption of uniformity are still only a small part of economic thinking.

The differences among firms and individuals are not analyzed here because they are interesting in their own right. Rather, these differences in internal conditions are employed to explain differences in economic behavior and economic outcomes as, for example, why one nation waxes richer while another wanes poorer, and why firms exert different amounts of effort when there is competition and when there is monopoly.

Better understanding of the influence of one's economic circumstances on one's economic behavior may help us understand a variety of interesting and important questions, such as the following:

1. Why do some nations and groups of people work longer hours than others? Answers such as "Because they are poorer" and "Because they have a value for hard work" are inadequate; although such statements may be suggestive, they are not easily rendered precise in terms of economic theory.
2. Why have the once-richest nations been surpassed in wealth by other nations that were formerly less rich? Answers citing wars and political personalities may be strengthened by consideration of economic conditions and consequence changes in effort.
3. Why has economic development tended to take place in temperate climes? The answer "Because there is enough challenge, but not too much," may have much truth in it but cannot easily be coordinated with other economic propositions.
4. How does one sensibly think about a situation such as that of the Crow Indians, who own "huge coal reserves" and also have "an unemployment rate approaching 70%" (*Wall Street Journal,* Jan. 31, 1984)? Talk about "lack of jobs" is obviously an incomplete explanation at best; before the whites arrived, there were no "jobs" at all in the modern sense, and no one worried about a high unemployment rate or idleness. In another guise, this is the omnipresent question about the trade-off between giving welfare and providing incentive to work.

WHAT IS NEEDED FROM THE THEORY

The theory necessary to understand the behavior of individuals must be more complex than the theory necessary to understand the behavior of firms. For example, when discussing the firm, it is usually reasonable to assume that the firm maximizes the real present value of the stream of future money incomes and expenditures. For some analytic purposes it may be necessary to consider the risk of various alternatives, or the effect on stock prices. But it will seldom be necessary to consider ethical and social constraints such as the desire for community goodwill. When such a constraint must be considered, it may sensibly be thought of with respect to the present value of the firm rather than as an end in itself; this enables the objective function to be simple. Furthermore, one does not need to consider the number of hours the firm works in total or on average. Nor does one need to consider the effort the firm makes in one activity or another, apart from consideration of all the real resources expended, unless some employees' efforts affect them or their fellows negatively or positively in such manner as to affect the future smooth working of the organization.

If one wishes to understand the economic behavior of individuals or of nonprofit groups, however, the objective function often cannot be assumed to be so simple. Here a distinction is necessary: When economists discuss a firm, their interest invariably is in the firm's economic behavior. But some economists' interest in individuals and groups—for example, Becker's interest in household behavior, and Schelling's (1960) and Boulding's (1977) interest in conflict—is in understanding behavior for reasons that go beyond its economic effects, that is, for more general scientific reasons. In contrast, as noted earlier, the interest of this article is only in the acts of individuals and groups that affect the economic (or purchasing power) status of themselves and of others. This makes it possible to omit some elements that are necessary in the more general inquiry into human behavior that interest theorists of household and conflict behavior. On the other hand, the subject of this article may require bringing into the analysis such elements as creativity and self-discipline that may reasonably be omitted from economic approaches to the study of human behavior for its own sake.

A firm's decision problem may be characterized as choosing those among the available set of alternatives which will produce maximum profit from its given stock of resources (including its line of credit); this stock of resources can be specified in advance of the decision. There is no benefit to the firm from leaving some resources unused, except perhaps the opportunity to perform maintenance work on its capital equipment, which can be reckoned objectively along with everything else in the calculation. The firm's decision process can be seen as first constructing a ladder of alternatives, and then selecting that subset of the best alternatives which together will yield maximum profit, using whichever technical criterion of profit may be appropriate.

Not all of the resources available to an individual can be specified in the same fashion as for a firm, however. Therefore, the individual's decision about a work opportunity is not perfectly analogous to that of the firm.

The individual's opportunity-accepting decision may be modeled as a business-like decision subject to additional constraints—first, the constraint of the reservation price for additional work time, as determined systematically by the sort of time-allocation process among production and consumption activities that Becker analyzed (1965); and second, the set of constraints related to the individual's own physical and mental attributes. The latter constraints may be thought of as analogous to the variety of needs and tastes that influence purchasing decisions for consumption. All of these latter constraints can be fruitfully dealt with as the single variable which is here called the Drive-Effort factor (*DrEf*).

This formulation has advantages in addition to its plausibility and simplicity. First, it corresponds to the classic Weber-Fechner law in psychophysics, according to which the likelihood of response to a given difference in stimuli (the just-noticeable difference, or JND) is proportional to the lower level of the stimuli. Second, it may be seen as an operationalization of the standard logarithmic conception (when viewed cumulatively) of (Benthamite) diminishing marginal utility of money.[3] (The two functions are one and the same, but viewed in different ways.) Of course, this shape of function is consistent with the conventional assumption of concave-indifference curves between pairs of goods. There is some empirical support for a semilogarithmic utility function (e.g., in Galanter's study[4] that asked questions about the respondent's speculations about his or her own happiness in connection with various levels of wealth).

The similarity of the Drive-Effort concept to the concept of diminishing marginal utility of money suggests that we look into the meaning of the latter for our purposes here. That concept suggests that a given increment of money is "worth" less when one is richer. But how does one measure an increment's "worth" except by evaluating what a person will trade for it? The only exchange that might provide grounds for analysis would be a nonmarket good, because money has no economic meaning except as power to purchase goods. (Conceivably, one might measure the amounts that rich and poor persons would pay for food or water on a lifeboat, but this would be neither an easy test nor a very meaningful one, for a variety of reasons.) It seems reasonable, however, to measure the utility of money according to the time and effort that people will give up to get it, and the goods that it will purchase.[5] If so, the utility and the effort become operationally indistinguishable, although some people may wish to continue thinking of them as separate concepts.

One may also measure the utility of money (really, the utility of goods) with such questions as how happy an additional sum would make one, or with the probability of suicide connected with various wealth (income) levels.[6] But such measurements seem more relevant for making income redistributions than for predicting how people will behave in the face of various opportunities, which is our subject here (Simon, 1974).

The relationship between wealth and effort implies a cyclical effect: Lack of wealth leads to effort, effort leads to wealth, wealth leads to lack of effort, and lack of effort leads to lack of wealth. This is similar to the cycle described in the saying, "shirtsleeves to shirtsleeves in three generations." But this cycle need not suggest a trap of economic stagnation, for at least two reasons. First, the advance of technology (itself a result of effort) enables successive generations to live better at a given level of effort. Second, it may be that there is a relative wealth effect (see Brenner, 1983) which causes people at a given level of absolute wealth to exert more effort if the wealth of others is higher, *ceteris paribus,* and makes them feel poorer. This could be explained in absolute wealth terms, however, if higher observed wealth of others increases perceived opportunities and hence induces more effort.

The viewpoint offered here may be contrasted with (a) Schultz's view of the related topic of entrepreneurship (1980) wherein the key element is a dimension of human capital of the same order as education and physical strength; and (b) Kirzner's view of entrepreneurship (1985) wherein the activity with which he is concerned is "costless." My viewpoint contrasts sharply with Becker's view of effort wherein the hours-worked aspect of effort is an allocation decision at the expense of leisure, taken from a total fixed quantity of available time, and wherein the intensity aspect of effort is considered in a similar fashion. Further discussion of the relationship to Becker's view follows.

Although the feeling aspect of effort is at the heart of the mechanism, the subject matter is completely academic. Both of the determinants of effort, and the consequences of it that are discussed here, are wholly material and objective; that is, they are economic in magnitude. This is in contrast with Becker's approach, a main objective of which is an improvement in our understanding of the individual, that is, an advance in psychology.

The form in the which Drive-Effort hypothesis is currently stated will lack esthetic appeal for economists because it is not framed in terms of utility maximization. But there is no reason to doubt that, if desired, further work can forge that connection with microeconomic theory, as has occurred with ideas such as mean-variance analysis that were originally stated in a form uncorrelated with other theories.

Some other writers may be mentioned here in case the reader is interested in connections between the Drive-Effort hypothesis and other work. Lenin (Possony, 1966, p. 208) and Schumpeter (1942/1950) have opined that with the advance of economic civilization, there is a decrease in the variability of the behavior of economic actors, and that economic activity can be routinized. Marshall (1920) argued in the other direction, as did Toynbee, in agreement with the Drive-Effort hypothesis. Chayanov (1923/1966), Hicks (1932/1963), and Becker (1965) wealth with the theory of leisure and labor in various fashions. Fisher (1930), von Neumann, Morgenstern (1947), Feldstein (1974), and others analyzed wealth effects. Leibenstein contributed a book on effort, but its viewpoint is more psychological than the viewpoint offered here. James (1890/1963) was the great explorer of effort as a psychological entity, and Dewey (McDermott, 1973, p. 154) also worked on the subject. Their tool was introspection, which continues to teach us much about effort.

RELATIONSHIP TO BECKER'S EFFORT CONCEPT

For convenience in comparing with Becker's effort concept, let us deal with simple decisions in which all consequences, except for the carrying over of profit from period to period, occur within a single short period. That is, no long-lived capital equipment needs to be purchased, and no long-run contracts or customer relationships are involved, in the examples discussed. In such cases, the individual begins by comparing expected income (money revenue) with outgo (expenditures on purchased inputs). If the income does not exceed the outgo, the opportunity need not be considered further unless there are other benefits to be considered (e.g., charitable benefits, the consideration of which may be deferred until later). That is, if total revenue (R) exceeds total expenditure (C), excluding the value of the decision maker's time, the alternative is considered further. This calculation of the lower boundary of "gross profit" is the first step in the sequential decision-making process (one which is not mentioned by Becker, perhaps because it seems too obvious).

Clearly, however, many work alternatives where $R > C$ in money are not undertaken; the individual is limited by, if nothing else, having only 24 hours in the day. Economists have long used the notion of a "reservation price" (Davenport, 1913/1968, p. 128) to explain why some alternatives with $R > C$ are not accepted. But the matter was not understood systematically until Becker's 1965 work, where he showed how to compute the reservation price as a function of the individual's income, wealth, time intensity of consumption possibilities, and time budget.

Becker's system, however, was not framed to comprehend the sort of economic opportunity[7] of main interest here. His formal analysis deals with a situation in which the wage is constant; that is, where the marginal earnings per hour equal the average earnings. Becker (1976, p. 93) also mentioned the situation in which "marginal wage-rates were below average ones," but he noted that in such a case the key "resource constraint in [his relevant] equation would not have any particularly useful interpretation"; the situation of a farmer for whom there are diminishing returns to weeding illustrates this case.

The most interesting economic opportunities, however, are those that have expected payoffs per hour *higher* than average payoffs to presently-undertaken opportunities. They are particularly interesting because they are unusually valuable (by their very definition) from a private as well as social point of view. They also are likely to be particularly valuable socially in the long run because they represent change, that is, a break with preceding activity.

There are two ways an individual or a nation can respond to a new high-payoff opportunity. One way is to rearrange one's entire set of work opportunities so that the high-payoff opportunity would have priority ahead of some existing opportunities which are presently accepted; in that case, some presently-marginal opportunities would probably be bumped out of the presently-accepted set. This process would be roughly equivalent to a wage increase, and the overall amount of work might go up or down, as discussed by the traditional theory as well as by Becker. This response could be analyzed formally, but the complicated nature of the rise in "wage" would make the analysis complex, and in any case, such analysis is not necessary here.

The new opportunity also could be responded to as an *additional* opportunity, while continuing to fulfill the work schedule previously decided on. In this case, if the new opportunity can be accepted in greater or smaller amounts, rather than just with a yes or no answer, Becker's analysis implies that at least some amount of the additional opportunity would be accepted. This can be seen directly from the following reasoning: Assume that the present set of work decisions implies that the value of the marginal unit of time spent in consumption equals the value of the marginal unit of time spent in production. If the latter value increases, the work-time decision must change (work must increase) as a new point of equality of the marginal quantities is determined.

These two ways of looking at the matter correspond to different responses over the life cycle of an opportunity. When the opportunity first appears, and before there is time to rearrange commitments, the opportunity must be dealt with as if all else is fixed and the new opportunity must be an addition to the set of opportunities. But with the passage of time, commitments loosen and the new opportunity can be dealt with as its priority would suggest. Without further analysis, it can be seen that a rich new opportunity would eventually lead to less work, *ceteris paribus,* by making the person wealthier (by way of increasing the income from the better opportunities now fixed into the schedule, which can now be seen as an "endowment" or "wealth" in Becker's analysis).

Even if it were expanded, Becker's framework would not complete the story. This is evident when we notice that some alternatives which pass the Becker time test are not undertaken. Examples include (a) work which is unethical or unpleasant or dangerous to the reputation; and (b) work which requires leaving one's family and friends. These examples undoubtedly could be squeezed into the Becker framework by supplying some shadow prices, but this would be so tortuous that it would do serious violence to the time-allocation analysis.

A more recent article by Becker (1983) expands his framework and includes a concept of effort that helps to delineate the difference between the context of his interest and the context of this article. Becker equates effort with the expenditure of energy, whereas I equate it with a much wider range of personal goods, such as reputation, and with accepting pain, as well as with the use of human energy. Becker's definition enables him to assume plausibly that the total supply of effort by a person is fixed over the period of analysis, which may be a reasonable assumption for some applications of his theory. But the essence of the analysis offered here is that it applies to contexts in which the total effort is variable rather than fixed.

The difference between Becker's approach and mine does not hinge on different biological assumptions. It may be that the supply of effort over an entire lifetime is indeed fixed, either at birth or later, in which case more effort exerted this year implies less capacity for effort next year, or else it implies a shorter lifespan within which to exert effort; such may or may not be the case, but either way it has no implication for the analysis given here (although if it is grossly not the case, it might complicate Becker's analysis).[8] Rather, the analysis offered here is intended to fit a case in which the focus is on a particular period within which a person may or may not change *total* effort—a given month or year or decade—whereas Becker mainly focuses on *allocation* of some total within an energy conservation framework.

In the present framework there may also be an increase in effort expended in work at the expense of effort expended in consuming, as in Becker's analysis, but that case brings out the difference between Becker's analysis and mine even more sharply. An increase in economic opportunity in Becker's framework—typically an increase in the wage rate—may lead to greater or less expenditure of total effort in work, because capacity to enjoy nonworking time by buying more commodities is increased by the wage increase; this is exactly analogous to the possibility of a backward-bending supply curve of work time. But such a possibility does not exist within the framework offered here because the new opportunity is considered to be separate from the old opportunity set, and in the "temporary" period under analysis the new opportunity does not replace the old opportunity set. For example, imagine that to induce you to work at shoveling manure instead of sitting at your desk for the next hour, a person offers you a sum three times as great as you have ever earned for an hour's work. There is no way that the offer can decrease your effort during the next hour (apart from unusual psychological twists not under consideration here), and it may increase it; such is the subject of the analysis offered here. Becker's analysis suggests that the manure-shoveling offer may decrease the total effort for the day or lifetime beginning with this hour, and that might well be the case. In the framework offered here, however, the decision for the subsequent hours is assumed to be made separately of the decision for this labor and will use different data, to wit, the increased wealth (or "property income," in Becker's framework) at the start of the next period (compared to the wealth if the manure-shoveling opportunity is not offered or accepted), which may reduce effort later on. This subsequent reduction in effort is also an important part of the analysis offered here, and is part and parcel of many of the applications. That subsequent reduction is not part of an allocation process but rather is the result of an allocation made separately.

The point of contact between Becker's and this analysis—the point at which they are consistent—is the effect of property income or wealth; an increase leads to a reduction in work effort. This point of contact helps highlight the difference in the approaches: Becker implicitly envisions an increase in wage opportunity as extending over a lifetime, within which long period it has an effect like an increase in property income, along with its main effect, leaving the overall impact ambiguous. My analysis envisions the new opportunity as applying to the present short period apart from latter periods (even if it will extend to a lifetime), and the resulting increase in wealth at the end of this present period is analyzed separately as such; hence both effects—within this period and within the next—are determinate.

RELEVANT EMPIRICAL EVIDENCE

In the book from which this article is drawn (Simon, 1987) various types of evidence are offered in support of this postulation which can only be mentioned here. None of the evidence by itself is strong enough, or sufficiently direct, to constitute full confirmation of the hypotheses. But the totality of the evidence may make a persuasive case in support of the Drive-Effort formulation.

The following are just a few examples of the relevant evidence:

1. the negative correlation between countries' income levels and the length of the average work week;
2. studies of industrial payment systems which show lower levels of output for hourly pay than for systems in which output is tied directly to output;
3. the positive relationship between hours of work, and the propensity to moonlight on a second job, with the number of children in a family (per-person income is lower by definition where the number of children is higher, *ceteris paribus*);
4. the negative relationship between students' family incomes and the number of hours per week that they study in college;
5. the greater propensity of immigrants than of natives (who have greater wealth on average than do immigrants) to participate in the labor force, start new businesses, and to work at demanding, unpleasant jobs; and
6. the observed negative relationship between length of time unemployed and the individual's reservation price.

There are also a variety of phenomena which are candidates for explanation by the Drive-Effort hypothesis but which also supply casual evidence for it, such as (a) the relationship of "need" to the willingness to innovate; (b) the rise and fall of empires; (c) the backward-bending supply curve of labor, which this hypothesis seems to explain neatly; (d) the causes of international migration; (e) the relationship of professorial tenure to output; and (f) the relationship of economic development to climate.

CONCLUSION

This article offers a formulation for analysis of a wide variety of phenomena that are not well understood without a systematic concept of effort. Effort here includes both the amount of time expended at work and the intensity of given work periods; the latter is the more interesting and perhaps the more important, but more data are available on the former. Examples of phenomena which a theory of effort may illuminate include differences in amount of time worked by people differing in such characteristics as number of children, amount of assets, and minority versus majority group status; the propensity for economic development in benign, moderate, and harsh climes; the decline of empires; and the rate of productivity of individual workers in piecework versus flat-rate industrial payment plans.

This article hypothesizes that the amount of effort which may be exerted depends on the payoff from the opportunity in question, the size of the individual's (or group's) endowment prior to accepting the opportunity, and the ratio of the former to the latter. Formally, the hypothesis is stated as

Drive-Effort Measure = expected likelihood of a positive response to a given opportunity by an individual or nation

$$= a \left[\frac{W_{n+1} - W_n}{W_n} \right]$$

NOTES

1. Hereafter the term *nation* is used instead of *group* unless the subject is a group other than a nation, such as a town or an ethnic or religious community.
2. A few notes on the relationship between the Drive-Effort concept as used here, and the common terminology of psychologists: (a) The work activity under discussion here is instrumental rather than consummatory (i.e., people were assumed to want money for what it will purchase rather than for the sort of gratification misers might get). (b) Historical determinants of behavior such as habit, learning, and genetic and other structure are assumed the same for the comparisons made. The only "internal" condition that varies is wealth, which may be thought of as corresponding to the psychologists' concept of need. (c) The opportunities under discussion are assumed known to the individual or group in question and have the same probability in all comparisons unless otherwise stated.

   A brief outsider's review of the psychological literature on motivation and drive (aside from the physiological level) suggests that there is no consensus on the use of these and related terms, and there is disagreement about whether there might be any meaning in the concepts for which the terms could stand; some theorists suggest that these intervening variables might be eliminated. But psychologists' disagreements about these concepts in general should not call into question our use of them as intervening variables in this context for two reasons: First, the measures of input (wealth, opportunities) and output (work, innovations, etc.) can be well specified in most of the applications we are interested in. Second, it is possible to get independent measures of the intervening drive variable, and this has been done as in such studies as Galanter's, when he asked people the effect on their psyches of various sums of money (described by Stevens, 1959, p. 55). It may be that the relatively clear-cut status of the concept of drive in the context of this article might offer opportunities for psychologists to exploit in clarifying the theoretical status of the concept in that field.
3. The concept of utility referred to in this article harks back to the original Benthamite concept. In the writing of Bentham and his followers, *utility* referred to *ex post* happiness and pleasure and was frankly psychological. Economists gradually purged the term of its pleasure-pain psychological content, culminating in the work of Slutsky (1951) and von Neumann-Morgenstern (1947) in which utility became an unobservable *ex ante* magnitude that was theoretically useful to postulate as a foundation for a consistent, positive choice theory. This article returns to the original Benthamic meaning of the term.

   Much confusion also has arisen because of the shift over the years in the use of the concept of utility, from the theory of public policy to the theory of choice. When the utility concept was introduced by Bentham, the subject of discussion was legislation and governance. The "moral arithmetic" of utility was intended to promote wise laws and human social structure. But economists have come to use "utility theory to *explain* economic behavior (particularly demand theory) and only secondarily (when at all) to amend or justify economic policy" (Stigler, 1965, p. 67). The distinction between the two uses has frequently been blurred or overlooked, which has led to great confusion. Nothing said here, however, implies that I advocate a utilitarian framework for evaluating social policies.

4. Described by Stevens (1959, pp. 54-55).
5. As Marshall put it,

> If the desires to secure either of two pleasures will induce people in similar circumstances each to do just an hour's extra work, or will induce men in the same rank of life and with the same means each to pay a shilling for it; we then may say that those pleasures are equal for our purposes, because the desires for them are equally strong incentives to action for persons under similar conditions. (1920, p. 16)

This suggests that the payoffs which two people in different circumstances will each sacrifice a given amount of time to attain have the same value for both of them.

6. For a review of such material, see Simon (1974).
7. The concept of opportunity should be understood as the opportunity *perceived* by the individual or nation, just as for Hicks and Becker wages are assumed to be those the individual knows to be available.
8. There certainly is some relationship between the capacity to exert effort during short, contiguous periods (e.g., a day or even a week or month). And there is widespread belief in even longer carryover, as expressed in such expressions as "She is worn out by a hard life." But I do not know of any scientific evidence on the quantitative nature of such a relationship, if it exists, and therefore a rational person would lack data for a lifetime allocation. In addition, all the uncertainties of life bedevil a lifetime allocation of wealth with respect to saving and consumption, as well as the issue of discounting. So even if lifetime allocation were an appropriate context for the line of analysis presented here—which it is not—the process would be fraught with grave difficulties.

REFERENCES

Arrow, K. J. (1974). *The limits of organization.* New York: Norton.

Becker, G. S. (1965). A theory of the allocation of time, *Economic Journal* 75: 493-517.

Becker, G. S. (1976). *The economic approach to human behavior.* Chicago: University of Chicago Press.

Becker, G. S. (1983). *Specialized human capital, the allocation of effort, and differences in earnings and time allocation of married men and women.* Mimeo.

Boulding, K. E. (1977). *Economics as a science.* New York: McGraw-Hill.

Brenner, R. (1983). *History–the human gamble.* Chicago: University of Chicago Press.

Chayanov, A. V. (1923/1966). In *The theory of peasant economy,* edited by D. Thorner, et al. Homewood: Irwin.

Davenport, H. J. (1913/1968). *The economics of enterprise.* New York: Augustus M. Kelley.

Feldstein, M. Social security, induced retirement, and aggregate capital accumulation, *Journal of Political Economy,* 82:5.

Fisher, I. (1930). *The theory of interest.* New York: Macmillan.

Hicks, J. R. (1932/1963). *the theory of wages.* London: Macmillan.

James, W. (1890/1963). *Psychology.* New York: Fawcett Publications.

Kirzner, I. M. (1985). *Discovery and the capitalist process.* Chicago: University of Chicago Press.

Marshall, A. (1920). *Principles of economies.* London: Macmillan.

McDermott, J. J. (1973). *The philosophy of John Dewey: The structure of experience.* New York: Putnam.

Possony, S. T., ed. (1966). *The Lenin reader.* Chicago: Regnery.

Schelling, T. C. (1960). *The strategy of conflict.* Cambridge: Harvard University Press.

Schultz, T. W. (1980). Investment in entrepreneurial ability, *Scandinavian Journal of Economics* (December).

Schumpeter, J. A. (1942/1950). *Capitalism, socialism and democray.* New York: Harper Torchbooks.

Simon, J. L. (1987). *Effort, opportunity, and wealth: Some economics of the human spirit.* New York: Basil Blackwell.

Simon, J. L. (1974). Interpersonal comparisons can be made—and used for distribution decisions, *Kyklos* 27(1): 63-98.

Slutzky, E. E. (1951). On the theory of the budget of the consumer. Pp. 27-56 in *Readings in price theory,* edited by K. E. Boulding and G. J. Stigler. Homewood, IL: Irwin.

Stevens, S. S. (1959). Measurement, psychophysics, and utility. Pp. 18-63 in *Measurement: definitions and theories,* edited by C. W. Churchman and P. Ratoosh. New York: Wiley.

Stigler, G. (1964). *Essays in the history of economics.* Chicago: University of Chicago Press.

Toynbee, A. J. (1962). *A study of history: The genesis of civilizations, part two.* New York: Oxford University Press.

Von Neumann, J., and O. Morgenstern. (1947). *Theory of games and economic behavior,* 2nd edition. Princeton: Princeton University Press.

[13]

Foreword

Another application of the technique shown in Chapter 8 for reconciliation of cross-section and time-series evidence.

Reprinted from The American Journal of Sociology
Vol. 74, No. 3, November 1968

The Effect of Income on the Suicide Rate: A Paradox Resolved

Two sorts of research techniques produce quite conflicting evidence about the direction of the effect of income on the suicide rate. Time-series regression analysis over the period of the business cycle suggests that suicide falls as income (employment) rises.[1] Cross-sections, on the other hand, suggest that more people with higher incomes commit suicide than people with lower incomes.[2] The purpose of this paper is to reconcile the two sorts of evidence. The answer arrived at is that the paradox arises because the empirical analyses have been guilty of "specification error." More specifically, the various studies have omitted lagged variables from the analyses. A model that contains lagged variables is then shown to be compatible with all the existing evidence.[3]

Assume that suicide is a function of income and education:[4]

$$\begin{aligned} S_{i,t} &= a_{i.0}Y_{i,t} + a_{i.1}Y_{i,t-1} \\ &+ a_{i.2}Y_{i,t-2} \ldots a_{i.k}Y_{i,t-k} \\ &\pm b_{i.0}E_{i,t} \pm b_{i.1}E_{i,t-1} \\ &\pm b_{i.2}E_{i,t-2} \ldots \pm b_{i.k}E_{i,t-k} + u_{i,t}, \end{aligned} \tag{1}$$

where

$S_{i,t}$ = probability of suicide of person i in year t,
$Y_{i,t}$ = income of person i in year t,
$E_{i,t}$ = whether or not person i was in school in year t,
$u_{i,t}$ = disturbance term whose specification we shall ignore.

Equation (1) is written to indicate that the a and b coefficients pertain to the individual i. But as is common in work of this sort, from here on we shall work only with somewhat vague pooled community analogies to the individual coefficients, and hence i subscripts will not be given for the coefficients.

Consider further that education is a function of income—perhaps income in the prior year. (A better statement would make education a function of income in all previous years, and/or a function of prior education, but let that go.) That is,

$$E_{i,t} = c_1 Y_{i,t-1} + v_{i,t}. \tag{2}$$

Now if one substitutes equation (2) into equation (1) one gets:

$$\begin{aligned} S_{i,t} &= a_0 Y_{i,t} + a_1 Y_{i,t-1} \\ &+ a_2 Y_{i,t-2} \ldots a_k Y_{i,t-k} \\ &\pm b_0 c_1 Y_{i,t-1} \pm b_1 c_2 Y_{i,t-2} \ldots \\ &\pm b_k c_{k+1} Y_{i,t-k} + u_{i,t}. \end{aligned} \tag{3}$$

Equation (3) represents what we postulate as the "true" model. But the *specified* model for a cross-section analysis is:

$$S_{i,t} = a'_0 Y_{i,t} + w_{i,t}. \tag{4}$$

The observed coefficient $\hat{a}'_0$ is the outcome of the usual least-squares regression of the cross-section model (4). It is the empirical estimate of a', and it is an undefined composite of the individual coefficients that we are now assuming are equal, or at least independent of income. This $\hat{a}'$ differs from

[1] Andrew F. Henry and James F. Short, Jr., *Suicide and Homicide* (Glencoe, Ill.: Free Press, 1954), Appendix IV.

[2] *Ibid.*, p. 137.

[3] Elsewhere a completely analogous analysis is given for the paradoxical income-fertility relationship, with the same clarifying results (see Julian L. Simon, "The Effect of Income on Fertility" [1968] [mimeographed]).

[4] Please note that I am *not* asserting that other factors do not also influence the suicide rate. And, indeed, the addition of such variables as religion would certainly increase the amount of variance explained by this or any other model, perhaps greatly. The following models are not offered as a best explanation but only to show how the paradox of the discrepant evidence disappears when even a simple model is more fully specified as to time.

the *real* mean coefficient, a_0, in important ways, which is the nub of the problem. Specifically, it is shown elsewhere[5] that:

$$\begin{aligned} a'_0 \simeq a_0 &+ r_{Y_tY_{t-1}}a_1 \\ &+ r_{Y_tY_{t-2}}a_2 \ldots r_{Y_tY_{t-k}}a_k \\ &\pm r_{Y_tY_{t-1}}b_0c_1 \pm r_{Y_tY_{t-2}}b_1c_2 \ldots \\ &\pm r_{Y_tY_{t-k}}b_kc_k\,. \end{aligned} \tag{5}$$

Therefore, in a cross-sectional study of the effect of current income, Y_t, upon suicide, the observed coefficient, $\hat{a}'_0$, differs from the "real" coefficient, a_0, by the entire right-hand side of (5) less a_0. This difference is the specification bias resulting from the fact that the cross-section does not include lagged income variables in the analysis.

If the "real" coefficients of income through education, b_kc_{k+1}, are positive and the coefficients of direct income, a_k, are negative, then whether the observed coefficients in the cross-section, $\hat{a}'_0$, show up as positive or negative depends upon the relative weights of the education and income variables as well as upon the correlation coefficients $r_{Y_tY_{t-k}}$.

The $r_{Y_tY_{t-k}}$ will be very high for almost any cross-section, however, so the relative weights of the coefficients are all-important. And it is not implausible that the education weights are relatively high, which would be compatible with an observed negative relationship.

Now assume that the underlying model is the same, but a time-series analysis is conducted of the nature

$$S_t = a''_0\, Y_t + z_{i\,t}\,. \tag{6}$$

This is the simplest regression plot of suicide on income in the same year, as exemplified by the correlations reported in Henry and Short, and others. Over the business cycle (the period over which these time-series regressions are usually done) $r_{Y_tY_{t-k}}$ is quite *low;* that is, the year-to-year income fluctuations are large relative to the secular change. This means that specification bias (following the same analysis as above) must be relatively small, and the effect of the lagged education variables (as well as the lagged direct income variables) washes out. Therefore, if the true coefficient a_0 is negative, the observed time-series coefficient $\hat{a}''_0$ will also be negative, which is indeed what is observed.

It should be noted that the resolution of the contradiction between cross-section and time-series evidence on the suicide-income relationship is *not* that different factors operate over time as compared to across observations at the same point in time. Rather, *statistical illusion* is responsible for the contradiction, because some lagged factors that wash out in the time series make their presence felt in the cross-section. The reality is the same; it is just the ways the pictures are taken that produce different images.

It seems reasonable, then, to conclude that the evidence confirms a model like (1) in which the partial effect of direct income on suicide is negative and the partial effect of education and other variables for which it is a proxy (which indirectly reflects the effect of income) is positive.

JULIAN L. SIMON

Hebrew University
and
University of Illinois

[5] Julian L. Simon and Dennis J. Aigner, "The Length-of-Run Nature of Cross-sectional and Time-Series Parameter Estimate" (Social Science Research Institute, University of Wisconsin, 1968).

[14]

Foreword

Regression analysis is only appropriate when there are insufficient data in individual cells for separate analysis of them. This study illustrates what can be done when there are sufficient data to work with. Each cell is treated separately, rather than pooling them and holding constant their differences statistically. (Within each cell, regression analysis is used, of course – actually, discriminant analysis.) The results of the individual cell analyses are then pooled.

The Mixed Effects of Income upon Successive Births May Explain the Convergence Phenomenon

JULIAN L. SIMON*

INTRODUCTION

The lower the order of the birth, the stronger is the positive relationship between husband's income[1] and the probability of the additional birth taking place, *ceteris paribus*. That is, this study finds that a given increment of income has a more positive (or less negative, as the case may be) effect on the probability that a family with n children will go on to have $(n+1)$ or more children, than on the analogous probability for a family with $(n+1)$ children. In absolute terms, the relationship between income and the probability of another birth is positive at low birth orders but negative at high birth orders, other things being equal.

This finding is interesting for at least two reasons:

(1) It offers an explanation of why the cross-sectional relationship of income to mean fertility in the United States and other more developed countries has been so difficult to characterize and has spawned so many contradictory results, even with homogeneous groups. Since income has both positive and negative effects on different orders of births, the net effect on mean fertility may go either way, depending upon the composition of the sample.

(2) Another implication, stemming from another way of interpreting these data, is that the variance in size of family is smaller among the group of higher-income families than among the group of lower-income families, *ceteris paribus*. This interpretation suggests an explanation for the 'convergence' phenomenon (the trend toward families with at least two and not more than four children in the United States): higher income reduces the propensity to stop at zero or one child, and *also* reduces the propensity to add children after the third or fourth, according to the results presented here.

The main finding, obtained from a cross-sectional multivariate study of the 1960 U.S. Census, is consistent with the discovery by Galbraith and Thomas[2] that the business cycle is strongly associated with probabilities of marriage, and successively less strongly with parity progressions. But the relationship they found is probably largely due to timing, as is shown by the particularly strong effect on marriages. In contrast, the cross-sectional census data on women aged 35–54 reported here reflect mainly completed fertility and hence do not indicate timing shifts, except in so far as temporary timing and spacing decisions become unintentionally permanent. Another difference between the findings presented here and those of Galbraith and Thomas is that they did not find a *negative* relationship between income and the probability of any order

* The work reported in this paper was conducted in part under H.E.W. Contract NIH-NICHD-71-2034; I am grateful for that support. And I appreciate thoughtful and helpful comments on an earlier draft by Yoram Ben-Porath, Bonnie Birnbaum, Dennis N. DeTray, Bruce Gardner, Karen O. Mason, Robert T. Michael, T. Paul Schultz, and Robert J. Willis. I also appreciate skilled computer programming by Anne Morehart Credicott, Israel Luski, Jay McElligott, and Dan Weidenfeld.

[1] 'Income' means husband's income throughout this paper unless otherwise noted. Family income is a much more complex concept in fertility analysis than husband's income, because of the effect of husband's income upon the wife's decision whether to take up gainful employment and consequently upon her fertility, and because of the interdependence between the decision to take a job and the decision to have more children.

[2] Virginia Galbraith and Dorothy S. Thomas, 'Birth Rates and the Interwar Business Cycles,' *Journal of the American Statistical Association*, December 1941. Reprinted in J. J. Spengler and O. D. Duncan (eds.), *Demographic Analysis* (Glencoe: Free Press, 1956).

of birth. The finding presented here is also consistent with Bernhardt's recently published results on Sweden.[3]

The paper also suggests some new ways of analysing the influences upon successive orders of births, as well as results on several matters of current interest relating to income, education, and fertility.

THE THEORY

There are two fundamental ways to explain a difference in the shapes of distributions of the dependent variable (in this case fertility) between two groups that differ with respect to the independent variable (in this case income). One is deterministic, finding economic grounds for a change in one or more of the *particular* transition probabilities. Economic theory is the obvious source of deterministic explanations. But the relevant propositions that I could find in economic theory are not helpful, and will not be pursued here. The interested reader will find a brief discussion in the Appendix.

One may also analyse a change in pattern in a purely statistical manner, focussing on the distribution as a whole rather than on particular transitions. This quite different approach suggests that the variance itself is the subject of interest. That is, instead of variation among families within the same income class being seen as bothersome 'error' around a deterministic value, the variance parameter itself moves to the centre of the stage.

There are at least two ways in which the variance in family sizes might be influenced by income:

(1) Contraceptive practice and control of family size are plausibly associated with income, either because of greater contraceptive knowledge among higher income groups,[4] or because of greater cost of error in higher income groups, or both. But in an earlier report, I adduced evidence that fertility control is not likely to account for the *entire* difference in variance among income groups.[5]

(2) Another explanation assumes only that within the population at any time there is variation among people in their response to two linked variables that work in opposite directions—as income and women's education might well act.[6] Consider this two-variable model of fertility behaviour:

$$F = a+b_1 Y+b_2 E,$$

where F stands for fertility, Y for current income and E for education. Imagine two groups of women with the *same average fertility* but with different incomes. If we assume that income has a positive effect and education a negative effect on fertility (over the ranges being considered), then for the same mean fertility to occur the higher income groups must also have higher average education. (And, of course, it is in fact the case that higher income groups have more education on the average because of the correlation between incomes of this generation and those of their parents' generation, and between parents' income and amount of education for this generation.)

The important point here is that there must be *different amounts of dispersion in fertility* in

[3] Eva M. Bernhardt, 'Fertility and Economic Status—Some Recent Findings on Differentials in Sweden', *Population Studies*, **26**, July 1972, pp. 175–184. cf also K. Namboodiri, 'Which Couples at given Parities expect to have additional births?' *Demography*, **11**, February 1974, pp. 45–56; D. A. Seiven, Ph.D. Thesis, Yale University, 1974.

[4] Robert T. Michael and Robert J. Willis, 'Contraception and Fertility: Household Production Under Uncertainty,' National Bureau of Economic Research Working Paper No. 21, 1974.

[5] Julian L. Simon, 'Income, Childlessness, and Fertility in the 1960 U.S. Census,' Paper given at Population Association of America meeting, 1969.

[6] The following explanation is drawn from Simon, *loc. cit.* in footnote 5. A related explanation was independently suggested by Robert Willis (letter of 9 October 1972).

the two groups, i.e. the variances around the mean numbers of children will be different in the two income groups, though one cannot know *a priori* which group will have the higher dispersion. This must be true if some of the people in the groups are more affected by one of the two variables than by the other. To see why this is true, consider the idealized diagram in Figure 1. On the horizontal axis are income and education, which are assumed to be related in a manner such that a person with a higher income has more education; the vertical axis is fertility. The relationships of fertility with income and education, other things being equal, are shown as linear functions (linear for simplicity: more plausible logarithmic or other functions would yield the same result.) Now consider the situation of three families who have incomes of $2500 and educations of 2500 education units. Assume that one family is influenced equally by income and education; its fertility will be x_1. Assume the second family is totally influenced by education and the third family is totally influenced by income; their fertilities will be Y_1 and Z_1 respectively. The variation in the fertility of this group of three families may be measured by the range of Y_1 to Z_1.

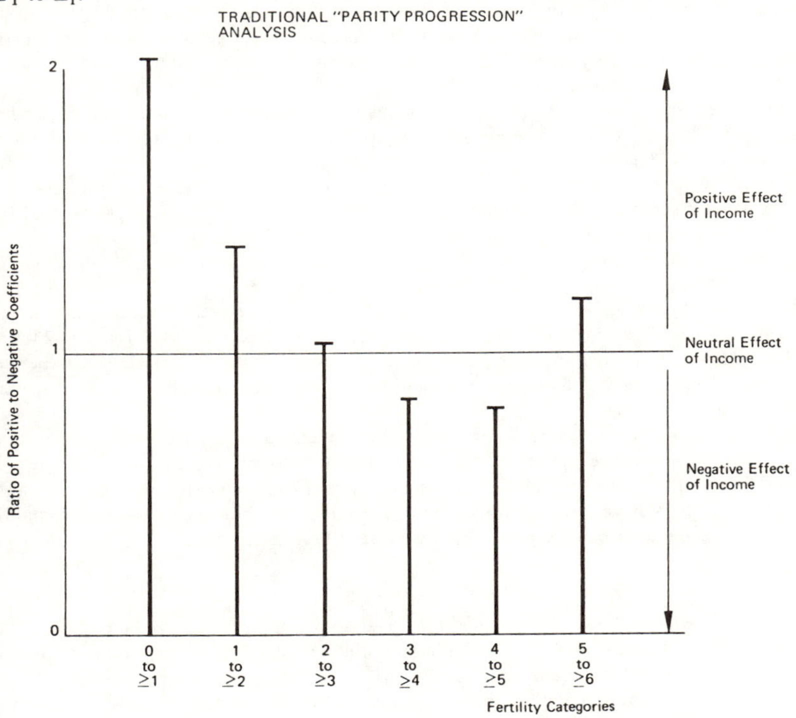

Figure 1

Now assume that the three families instead have incomes of $5000 and 5000 units of education. All three families will have fertility of X_2, though their tastes differ and they are subject to the influence of income and education to different degrees. Therefore, a shift from $2500 income to $5000 income *reduces* the variation in these fertilities.

But now assume the families have incomes of $7500 and 7500 education units. The families that are totally influenced by education and income will have fertilities of Y_3 and Z_3 respectively, and the family that is equally influenced by income and education will have fertility of X_3. So we see that the move from $5000 to $7500 *increases* the variation in fertility.

At all incomes in our example the mean fertility is the same (though the basic conclusion holds at least as strongly, for situations where the mean fertility changes, too). And tastes – the weights of the influences of income and education – may change with shifts in income and education, whereas tastes are assumed to be constant in this example; a shift in tastes would also influence the dispersion. But this example is designed to show that dispersion must change with a change in income *even if* mean fertility remains the same and if tastes remain unchanged.

We do not know *a priori* whether an increase in income will lead to greater or smaller dispersion. But we do know that *any* such change in income and education must result in *some* change in dispersion, even if the trade-off effect leaves mean fertility unchanged. This example has been worked here for only a single income and education sub-group before and after a change in income (or, this may be thought of as the comparison between two sub-groups at a point in time). And in the example, the mean fertility is the same for both the 'before' and 'after' states (or for the two sub-groups if one thinks about the example that way). But the same principle holds (with some further complexity) where the fertility means also change. And, of course, the point holds equally for the collection of such sub-groups that constitute the population as a whole.

In the context of the observed data, this explains why two or more income groups can have the same mean fertility (or the lower income group can have higher fertility) and the lower income group can also have a higher proportion of childlessness.

Earlier it was noted that offsetting linked changes in the two variables might produce either greater *or* smaller dispersion. In fact, at most income levels the combination of higher income and higher education leads to a *smaller* rather than a greater dispersion, as may be seen by comparing the amount of childlessness in groups with equal overall fertility in the U.S. in 1960. For example, consider the 40–44-year-old women not in gainful employment with incomes of $4,000–4,999, $5,000–6,999, $7,000–9,999, and $10,000–14,999 respectively. These groups all have much the same overall fertility (total children ever born: 2,788, 2,686, 2,678, 2,716, 2,782 respectively), but the higher the income group the smaller the proportion of childlessness (per cent childless: 10·8, 10·2, 9·4, 8·2, 7·8 respectively), and less childlessness indicates smaller dispersion in the fertility distribution.

A by-product of this line of reasoning is that it provides a reasonable explanation of the frequently noted convergence of Americans to families of between two and four children, i.e. fewer very large and fewer very small families as time goes on. The two opposing variables, income and education, have been moving in opposite directions, but both toward 'the middle', as it were. Hence, the distribution of families by size has been narrowing.

THE METHOD

The general method is a fine sub-classification by various demographic characteristics of the 1-in-1,000 1960 U.S. Census sample. Discriminant analysis is then applied to the parity progression ratios within each cell. Where the dependent variable is limited to two groups – as is the case here where the two groups (depending on the mode of analysis) in each birth-order variation are (i) families with n (or in some analyses $\leq n$) children, and (ii) families with $>n$ (or in some analyses $n+1$) children – discriminant analysis is equivalent to regression analysis, and the two terms will therefore be used interchangeably throughout the paper. The independent variable of central interest here is husband's income, and wife's education is of secondary interest; other factors are included in the discriminant function and classification scheme in order to hold them constant.

Now to be more specific about the method: the units of observation are women, aged 35–54, with husband present. In the central analyses the observations are then sub-classified by race (white-non-white), degree of urbanization of place of residence (urban with more than 50,000, urban with less than 50,000, rural non-farm, rural farm), husband's occupation (eight standard categories), wife's education (≤ 8, 9–12, ≥ 13 years), husband's education (≤ 8, 9–12, ≥ 13 years) and wife's age (35–44, 45–54). None of these variables is itself a function of husband's income. (If a fertility-related variable of classification or regression were to depend heavily upon husband's income, it would distort the relationship between husband's income and fertility, the relationship of primary interest here.) Nor do any of these variables depend heavily upon wife's education, a variable of secondary interest in this paper.

The aim of the sub-classification is twofold: (a) to create a large enough number of cells so that the regression coefficients for the classification cells could be used as sample of meta-observations; and (b) to hold constant the variables of classification so as to render the observations within cells more homogeneous.

Fine sub-classification[7] is intrinsically the best possible way to hold factors constant and render homogeneous the observations upon which a regression is run. It is superior in this regard to holding others constant by entering them as independent variables in the regression, because the latter device linearizes the effects of those other factors though they may well not be linear.[8] The reason why one may nevertheless choose the latter device in some situations is to insure that the number of observations within cells is large enough for the desired analysis. In the situation at hand, the price in reduction in observations seems acceptable because of the relatively large number of observations in the original 1-in-1,000 census sample.

The dependent variable in each regression is a dichotomous yes-no variable. In the central mode of analysis the two categories in each birth-order variation are whether the wife has n children, or more than n children. This is the traditional demographic parity-progression[9] analysis. In this analysis, in the first of the six birth-order variations the two categories contain wives with no children, and those with one or more children respectively; this variation is designated as the $n = 0$ run. In the second ($n = 1$) variation the categories are one child, and two or more children. There are six variations, the $n = 5$ variation having wives with five children in one category, six or more children in the other. The discriminant function finds those values of the independent variables that most effectively separate the observations into the two dependent-variable categories.

This 'parity-progression' mode of analysis refers to the act of proceeding from n children to *more than n* children. The regression coefficient of income in that model refers to the effect of income on the probability of being in the class of n-child or $\geq(n+1)$-child families.

In the secondary mode of analysis, called 'birth-order transition' analysis here, the categories are n and *exactly* $(n+1)$ children, e.g. in the $n = 0$ birth-order variation the categories are no children and one child, and in the $n = 5$ variation the categories are five children and six children. To repeat, this secondary birth-order-transition model of analysis discriminates between people ending up with exactly n and exactly $(n+1)$ children. The interpretation of this birth-order-transition mode of analysis seems closer to economic theory than does the traditional parity-progression method because it refers to families who are near their 'equilibrium' or 'optimizing' stopping point. But this mode excludes from each analysis many of the people who actually make a decision about that particular birth, and hence this analysis is less interesting to demographers. In any case, these two modes of analysis (and also discriminant analyses run with $<n$ versus

[7] Hanoch used much the same device in his Ph.D. thesis, University of Chicago, 1965.

[8] Using dummy variables for the parameters has the related though milder effect of applying the *same constant* to all observations.

[9] In strict usage 'parity' refers to the act of giving birth, while 'birth order' refers to the child. The terms, however, tend to be used by demographers as synonyms. In this paper they will be used separately for different methods of analysis, as discussed below.

$\geq n$ children)[10] yield essentially the same main results, so it is not necessary to argue their merits.

The difference between the two modes of analysis may be dramatized as follows: In parity-progression analysis we can imagine a couple debating: 'Should we stop at (say) two (or n) children, or should we not stop?' In birth-order analysis we may imagine that the decision being modelled is 'Should we have a family of (say) two (or n) children, or should we have three (or $n+1$)?'

The independent variables of regression were: husband's income, years of education of wife, years of education of husband, and wife's age. The latter three variables were variables of classification *and* variables within the regression, to aid in holding constant the variables to be treated as parameters in the analysis of the effect of husband's income and wife's education.

Discriminant functions were run in each cell that contained more than ten observations. The sub-classification scheme produces many such regressions, ranging from just under 100 to over 500 in the various sets of runs and variations. The numbers of cells with more than ten non-whites were relatively small, and hence few enter the analysis. Each regression was treated as a meta-observation, and the conclusions drawn here are based on the central values of the aggregates of the regressions conducted in each fertility variation. That is, instead of running a single regression and calculating a single set of estimating coefficients for each variation, as would be done if all variables were included in the regression rather than used as variables of classification, many regressions were run for each variation – one for each cell with enough observations – and the central values of the coefficients for each variable were used as the estimates of the effects of the variables.

The most reliable estimation for the effect of a given variable in the group of runs in a given variation is the ratio of the coefficients that are positive to those that are negative. For example, in the $n = 0$ variation of the parity-progression analysis reported in Row 1 of Table 1, the income coefficients in 199 cells were positive, while 96 were negative. (Zero coefficients were not counted.) The ratio (199/96) = 2·07 is an index of the direction of income's effect in that variation, to be compared with 160/118 = 1·36 for the $n = 1$ variation in that set of runs, and so on, as seen in Table 1. A coefficient greater than unity implies a positive effect, and a coefficient smaller than unity implies a negative effect.

This comparison is not biased by the proportions of families in the two dependent-variable categories, as a comparison of the mean or median coefficients would be. Bias in mean or median coefficients would be due to the split in the numbers of observations between the dependent-variable categories being different in different variations; it is far from a 50-50 split for the $n = 0$ and $n = 5$ runs, but closer to 50-50 for the $n = 2$ and $n = 3$ variations. That is, few families have as few as zero or as many as six children. And the sizes of the coefficients of individual regressions are affected by the proportions of cases in the two categories, thereby biassing a comparison of the sizes of coefficients.[11] But the proportion of numbers of coefficients does not suffer from this defect.

[10] The implicit meaning of the coefficient of an independent variable in the analyses of $\leq n$ versus $>n$ children is that it is a measure of the influence of that variable on the likelihood of the family proceeding from the category with n children or less to the category with ($n+1$) children or more. Earlier regressions (*not* discriminant functions) were run on the dependent variable truncated to different extents. The variations had the following fertility scales: 0, 1+; 0, 1, 2+; . . . 0, 1, 2, 3, 4, 5, 6+, where all the highest-birth-order groups were assigned the number shown for the '+' group in each variable. The sizes of the coefficients showed the same trend patterns as the discriminant function with dichotomous variables given here, though in absolute terms at higher parities the signs for income were less likely to be negative than in the discriminant analyses. This is to be expected because of the greater weight given to lower birth orders in the high-n truncated regressions than in the high-n discriminant functions.

[11] If one were to use the method of running a single regression for each variation, handling all variables within the regression, the coefficients of the various birth-order variations would similarly be biased relative to one another. This is another reason for preferring the method used here.

An intuitive explanation of the bias is that the farther is the split from 50-50 in the number of observations in the dependent-variable categories, the less *information* is contained in the observations. A distribution of observations approaching 0-100 would necessarily yield a coefficient of 0.

RESULTS

The Effect of Husband's Income on Various Orders of Birth

The effect of husband's income on various birth orders may be seen by looking across the rows in

TABLE 1. *Effect of husband's income on various birth orders*

The ratio of positive income coefficients to negative income coefficients among discriminant functions of the form: dichotomous fertility category = f (*husband's income, education of wife, education of husband, wife's age*). *The variables of cell sub-classification are: race, urbanism, wife's education, husband's education, husband's occupation wife's age.*

	Fertility categories in dependent variable					
	0, ⩾1	1, ⩾2	2, ⩾3	3, ⩾4	4, ⩾5	5, ⩾6
Traditional 'parity progression' analysis	2·07 (n = 295)	1·36 (n = 278)	1·03 (n = 246)	0·82 (n = 189)	0·78 (n = 107)	1·16 (n = 67)
	0, 1	1, 2	2, 3	3, 4	4, 5	5, 6
Birth-order transition analysis	1·7 (n = 153)	1·5 (n = 176)	0·92 (n = 173)	0·78 (n = 130)	0·89 (n = 70)	1·3 (n = 35)

Interpretation: Compare across the rows. Numbers greater than unity indicate a *positive* relationship between husband's income and fertility, on the average; numbers less than unity show a negative association. The sample size, *N*, shows the number of sub-groups with more than ten observations in which the regression coefficients were son-zero.

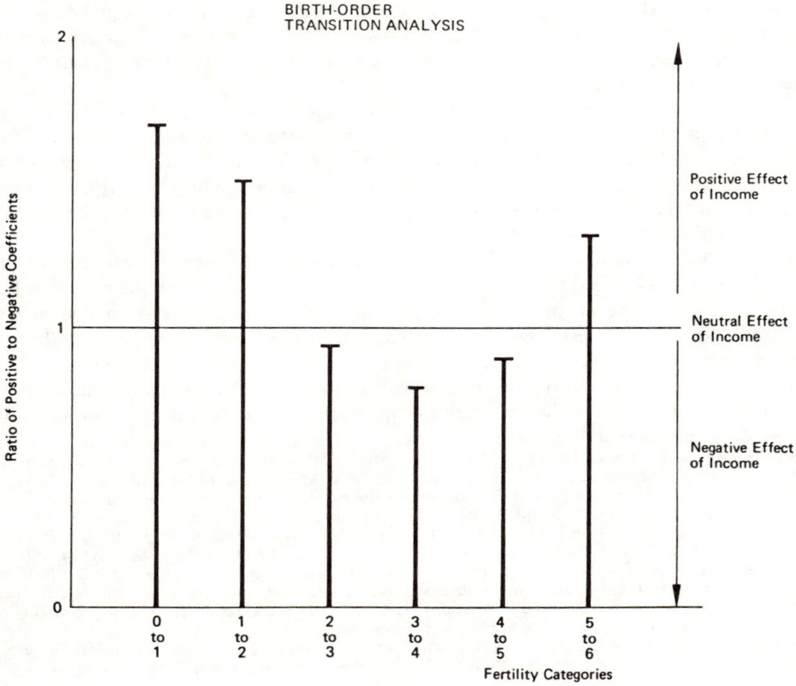

Figure 2

Table 1 and in Figure 2. Higher husband's income is *positively* associated with the family having at least one child rather than none. The relationship then moves smoothly from positive to negative as one looks to the higher birth orders up to the sixth birth in Row 1 and the fifth birth in Row 2. The association between the husband's income and the probability of having additional children becomes negative in the neighbourhood of the third or fourth child. That is, though a larger income *increases* the probability that the family will have more children when they have no children or one, it *decreases* the probability that they will have additional children when they already have as many as three, four or more.[12] No meaning can be attached to the *absolute* sizes of the ratios because they depend on the numbers of observations; if the sub-group cells contained more observations and hence had smaller sampling errors, and if there were no bias from the permanent-income effect in the cross-section, the ratios on both sides of unity could be expected to be much farther from unity.

The pattern breaks down at the highest parity progression, from five to six children or more. And in runs using other sets of variables there also appeared a reversal at the high birth-order end. It is quite possible that this is due to sampling error as the numbers in the cells become smaller, which would tend to drive the ratio toward unity. For example, in the run reported in Row 1 of Table 1, only 67 cells have ten or more observations at $n = 5$ whereas 295 cells have ten or more observations at $n = 0$. And the largest cell in the $n = 0$ run (in Row 1) has 448 observations, whereas the largest cell in the $n = 5$ run has 64 observations. Hence, perhaps the reversal should not be considered as a real phenomenon without further investigation.

Analyses were also made (a) by weighting the observations by the square root of the cell size; (b) using the t-values as the observations; (c) using weighted t-values; (d) using only values of $t > 1$ or $t < -1$. All these tend to confirm the analyses made with unweighted regression coefficients, except that the ratios of the t values for which $|t| > 1$ 'reverse' sooner, which (in view of the small number) goes hand-in-hand with a sampling-error explanation of the reversal of direction in the unweighted coefficients.

Results similar to those reported in Table 1 also emerge with various other variables of classification and regression added or subtracted. In particular, the results are invariant to deletion of husband's education (which is closely related to husband's income) and to addition of women's labour-force participation (the results being similar within both participation groups). These additional findings, together with those discussed in the paragraph above, suggest that the finding reported in Table 1 is quite robust.

Row 2 in Table 1 shows the results of the analysis with the dependent-variable categories being n and exactly $(n+1)$ children. The results are generally in accord with the results in Row 1 except that the reversal occurs at a lower order of birth. This may be due to small sample sizes (which could most easily be tested by running the data from the 1/100 tape rather than the 1/1000 tape for the 1970 Census). But if the phenomenon is real, the explanation is not obvious.[13]

The finding in Table 1 also is in accord with the fact that husband's income is strongly related to childlessness (i.e. to the first parity progression) but mixedly related to total children

[12] There can be little doubt of the statistical significance of this trend among the set of observations in Table 1. The most obvious proof is the very low probability of a perfect or almost-perfect monotonic relationship among even one set of six observations, let alone two or three such sets. And the *size* of the differences – the ratio for $n = 5$ being less than half the ratio for $n = 0$ – only makes the statistical significance more conclusive. For those who like formal significance tests, the simplest device is to lump and compare the three left-hand cells and the three right-hand cells in one set such as in Table 1. We ask the probability that a sample of 484 positive signs out of 819 observations and a sample of 168 positive signs of 363 (proportions of 0·59 and 0·46 respectively) came from the same universe. By a binomial test of proportions $Z = 4{\cdot}1$ and the probability is extremely small. But further, this is a very inefficient test of the difference among results in even a single set, and it takes account of only the runs reported in Table 1. And a great many other variations yield the same general result. Hence, the probability of the observed set of results in Table 1 occurring by chance is even smaller.

[13] Several of the other differences between Rows 1 and 2 are not behavioural, but purely statistical. For example, the higher ratio for $n = 0$ in Row 1 merely reflects the fact that the effect of income in higher birth-order transitions is lower than in $n = 0$ and $n = 1$.

ever born[14]. The finding is also generally confirmed by the findings for Sweden recently reported by Bernhardt[15]. And this finding is also supported by the consistency noted earlier with the results of runs with the dependent variable being the classes $\leq n$ and $\geq(n+1)$, and with regressions successively on 0, 1+; 0, 1, 2+; 0, 1, 2, 3+ . . . , 0, 1, 2, 3, 4, 5, 6+.

Quite another way of looking at the raw data is by examining the transitions between each pair of income groups within each demographic cell to see which transitions are positively related to income and which are not, rather than running discriminant functions. I call this the 'income progression' method. More specifically, the families were divided by race, urbanism and so on into demographic cells as described earlier. Then, *within* each demographic group they were sub-divided by the census income groups. For each income group the proportion reaching the birth order in question (in each run) was then computed. Then, each income group was compared with the next lower income group to see whether the proportion reaching birth-order $n+1$ was greater or smaller than in the preceding income group. Depending upon whether the higher income group had a higher or lower proportion reaching the order of birth $n+1$, a 'positive' or a 'negative' or an 'equality' was recorded.[16] Then, the sum of the positives (increases in parity-progression probability with income increase) was compared with the sum of the negatives for each order of birth. A greater number of positives than negatives (a ratio >1) indicates that higher income is positively related to additional births at that order of birth.

This income-progression method has the advantage that it does not linearize the income variable. It also enables each income increment's effect to be examined separately.

For clarity's sake, let us illustrate the income-progression method on the parity progression from zero to one child within the very first demographic cell. These are families with husband's education: high school; wife's education: college; rural farm residence; white; husband's occupation: farmer; wife's age: 35–44. The illustrative data are as follow:

Income group	*Number of families*	*Number with ≥1 child*	*Proportion with ≥1 child*	*Comparison between groups*	*Indication*
1	2	1	0·5		
2	1	1	1·0	1–2	+
3	4	4	1·0	2–3	=
4	2	2	1·0	3–4	=
5	2	2	1·0	4–5	=
6	2	2	1·0	5–6	=
7	7	6	0·857	6–7	−
8	2	2	1·0	7–8	+
9	3	2	0·667	8–9	−
10	1	1	1·0	9–10	+
11	0				none
12	0				none

The summary for this one demographic cell is three positives and two negatives. The results for the various demographic groups are then summed to yield the statistic of interest for the particular birth-order variation.

[14] See U.S. Bureau of the Census, *1960 Census Population. Women by Number of Children ever born.* PC(2)-3A. Washington. Government Printing Office, 1964. It was this observation, analysed in Simon, *loc. cit.* in footnote 5, that was the genesis of the work reported here.

[15] *Loc. cit.* in footnote 2.

[16] If the next-lower income sub-group contained no observations, the income sub-group was compared with the nearest lower income group, that did contain such observations.

TABLE 2. *Association of parity progression to income-class progression (the income-progression method)*

	Fertility categories in the dependent variable					
	0, ≥1	1, ≥2	2, ≥3	3, ≥4	4, ≥5	5, ≥6
Number of 'positives'	829	786	709	504	264	151
Number of 'negatives'	741	746	709	521	271	155
Positives/negatives	1·119	1·054	1·000	0·967	0·974	0·974

Note: 'Positive' indicates a case in which the higher of a successive pair of income groups within a demographic group has a higher proportion of people reaching the higher-order birth.

Using the parity progression model for the dependent variable (i.e., comparing families with n with those with $\geq (n+1)$ children), the income-progression data in Table 2 show that income is less positively related to the probability of additional births at higher orders of birth.[17] These results agree with the quite different discriminant-function approach. This increases confidence in the validity of the finding.[18]

Interactive Effects of Income and Education Levels

The basic discriminant-function technique described in this paper readily permits analysis of the interactive effect of various variables upon parity progressions and birth-order transitions. For example, the interactive effect of husband's income and wife's education suggested by Sanderson and Willis[19] may be analysed by examining the discriminant-function coefficients for income separately among various women's-education and men's-education sub-groups (where education may be thought of as a proxy for income). Some results of this sort are shown in Table 3. Income

TABLE 3. *The effects of husband's income within various wife's education groups: The interaction of income and education effects on parity progression.* (*For explanation of numbers in cells, see Table 1.*)

	Fertility categories in the dependent variable					
	0, ≥1	1, ≥2	2, ≥3	3, ≥4	4, ≥5	5, ≥6
Classified by:						
Wife's Education						
0–8 years	1·75	0·979	0·766	0·566	0·667	0·800
	(n = 99)	(n = 93)	(n = 80)	(n = 70)	(n = 45)	(n = 36)
9–12 years	2·233	1·491	1·034	0·917	0·926	2·000
	(n = 139)	(n = 132)	(n = 120)	(n = 92)	(n = 52)	(n = 30)
13+ years	2·353	1·944	1·867	1·455		
	(n = 57)	(n = 53)	(n = 43)	(n = 27)		

Note: The reader is cautioned about the small sample sizes in the cells in the right hand columns. Cells with ten or fewer demographic-group observations have been omitted.
Interpretation: See Table 1, Note.

[17] All the ratios are so close to zero because there were so few observations in each demographic-income cell, many of the cells containing just *one family*. (More than half the observations for each parity progression are 'equals'.) Therefore, sampling error is very great. This blurs the phenomenon and pushes the result toward unity. It is noteworthy that a trend can emerge nevertheless.

[18] Each demographic group has an equal weight in the estimate for each income-group transition in this method; if the groups were weighted by absolute size, the results would reproduce the unconditional aggregated results for the population as a whole.

[19] Warren Sanderson and Robert J. Willis, 'Economic Models of Fertility: Some Examples and Duplications', *National Bureau of Economic Research Annual Report*, 1971, pp. 32–42.

TABLE 4. *Differences by income category in the association of parity progressions to income progressions*

	Fertility categories in dependent variable					
	0, ≥1	1, ≥2	2, ≥3	3, ≥4	4, ≥5	5, ≥6
Higher income groups						
Number of 'positives'	358	326	284	199	119	73
Number of 'negatives'	377	365	324	221	130	89
Positives/negatives	0·950	0·893	0·877	0·900	0·915*	0·820*
Lower income groups						
Number of 'positives'	344	347	332	226	104	59
Number of 'negatives'	276	295	285	234	106	45
Positives/negatives	1·246	1·176	1·165	0·966	0·981*	1·311*

* Note sharp drop in sample sizes.

is seen to have more positive effects in higher-education groups. And the effect of additional income is negative as early as the transition to the third or perhaps the second child in the lowest education group, which is consistent with their hypothesis.

The interaction of income and education was originally examined by Sanderson and Willis as a means of investigating whether the effect of income on fertility is different at different *income* levels. The income-progression method described above allows this matter to be investigated directly, for each of the various parity progressions. That is, the results shown in Table 2 are now disaggregated, divided into the top five and bottom five income groups (omitting the middle income group). The same ratios as in Table 2 are computed for the high and low income groups, and these are shown in Table 4. It is seen in Table 4 that income has a greater positive effect on the fertility of the high income groups than of the low income groups, at all parity progressions. And the effect of income *differs much more* from birth order to birth order in the high income groups than in the low income groups; for the latter, the effect of income on parity progression may be much the same at all orders of birth. This suggests that the main finding of this paper stems largely from the impact of the higher income group within the total composition.

The discriminant-function results may be used to examine Ben-Porath's hypothesis[20] that

TABLE 5. *The effects of women's education within various education groups: The effects on parity progression. (For explanation of numbers in cells see Table 1, except that the ratios here are of education coefficients.)*

	Fertility categories in the dependent variable					
	0, ≥1	1, ≥2	2, ≥3	3, ≥4	4, ≥5	5, ≥6
Classified by:						
Wife's education						
0–8 years	0·870	0·508	0·680	0·556	0·406	0·440
	(n = 101)	(n = 92)	(n = 84)	(n = 70)	(n = 45)	(n = 36)
9–12 years	0·533	1·030	0·681	0·586	1·038	0·824
	(n = 141)	(n = 136)	(n = 121)	(n = 92)	(n = 53)	(n = 31)
13+ years	0·639	1·409	1·200	0·933		
	(n = 59)	(n = 53)	(n = 44)	(n = 29)		

Note: The reader is cautioned about the small sample sizes in the cells in the right hand columns. Cells with ten or less demographic-group observations have been omitted.

Interpretation: See Table 1, except that the ratios here are of education coefficients.

[20] Yoram Ben-Porath, 'Fertility in Israel: An Economist's Interpretation,' Mimeographed, Rand, 1970.

an additional increment of women's education has a sharper effect at women's low education than at high education. Some results are shown in Table 5. Among women with 0–8 years education, at all parity progressions the effect of additional education is strongly negative. And it is stronger than for women with 9–12 years education or 13+ years of education. There is even some doubt whether the effect of additional education is negative at all among the highest-education group, which, as Ben-Porath has speculated, calls into question the opportunity-cost effect of women's education on fertility.

Other interactive effects on various orders of birth, such as that between race and income, should be investigated. It is clear from the crude data, for example, that childlessness is perhaps twice as high among non-whites as among whites, within income or occupational groups,[21] though in many of the same groups there are more *large* families among non-whites than among whites.

Some Other Results

Experiments were run with various other sub-classification schemes and sets of regression variables. Some of the more interesting results were these:

1. When the data are not subclassified by wife's education, the income coefficient is successively less positive from the $n = 0$ run until the $n = 3$ run, and then becomes more positive between the $n = 3$ and $n = 4$ run and between the $n = 4$ and $n = 5$ run. It seems reasonable that this is due to the association between husband's income and wife's education when the latter is not used as a variable of sub-classification. (If wife's education were also deleted from the regression this effect should appear even more strongly.)

2. Referring to the regression coefficients for *wife's education* now: The wife's education coefficients are negative throughout, but show little or no trend. But if age of marriage is added to the regression, these coefficients trend strongly downwards in higher-numbered runs. This indicates that when one is interested in the overall effect of wife's education, it is better not to include age at marriage as a variable, as has been done in some studies.[22]

3. When wife's education is held constant by classification and regression, the coefficients for husband's education are somewhat less positive (more negative), with higher-order transitions.[23] This may be partly an effect of income as related to husband's education, or it may be an independent effect of education. But the important fact is the absence of strong trend or large difference from unity. To the extent that the strong influence of women's education among women with little education is *not* an opportunity cost effect, it is puzzling why the effects of men's and women's education should be so different when both are handled in the same way at the same time in the analysis.

IMPLICATIONS OF THE FINDINGS

Ceteris paribus, a rise in income contributes to an explanation of the 'convergence' of Americans to two- to four-child families, and away from families with fewer or more than two to four children, as income has risen with time in the United States during the 1900s and before.[24] The mechanism can be seen as follows: Assume a group of people distributed among tendencies to have completed families of 0, 1, 2, 3, 4, 5 . . . An increase in income for each of the families in-

[21] U.S. Bureau of the Census, *op. cit.* in footnote 14.

[22] T. Paul Schultz brought this issue to my attention.

[23] The effect is also seen much more sharply when wife's education is not a variable of classification, of course, but that tells us that men with more education marry women with more education, rather than anything about the direct effect of husband's education on fertility.

[24] Norman B. Ryder, 'The Emergence of a Modern Fertility Pattern: United States, 1917–66', in S. J. Behrman *et al.* (eds.) *Fertility and Family Planning: A World View* (Ann Arbor: University of Michigan, 1969).

creases the likelihood that those who would have no children will have one child instead, or two instead of one. At the other end of the distribution, the data observed here suggest that those who would have, say, four children *ex ante* will have three instead. That is the increase in income changes some 'no's' to 'yes's' for the small families and some 'yes's' to 'no's' for the large families. The overall effect is a narrowed distribution of families by total number of children. The final distribution is determined by the original proportions of people in the various sub-groups. And whether the increase in income will have a positive or a negative effect on the central value (median or mean) of the distribution is also determined by the original distribution as well as by the effects of income on the various sub-groups. This is also consistent with the observed fact that poor people are disproportionately represented at *both* ends of the total-completed-family size distribution.[25] Simply increasing the income of some of the poorer people will cause some to leave both ends of the distribution and to obtain a family size nearer the centre of the distribution.

Ryder[26] suggested that economic research should focus on what he regards as the key transition from the second to the third child. The data presented here suggest that the effect of an increase in income produces effects that net out at about zero effect on that transition.

APPENDIX

Some Deterministic Economic Theory

This Appendix searches economic theory for deterministic propositions that could account for differences in the effect of income on *particular* parity progressions (and birth-order transitions) *over and above* the variation (among families with the same incomes) due to the variety of other determinants of fertility.

The family's economic situation affects each birth-order probability both through the benefit and the cost of that particular child, i.e. through demand and supply. The different birth-order probabilities may be affected differently by income on the cost side, the benefit side, or both.

As to benefits, diminishing marginal utility of successive 'units' that are 'purchased' suggests that higher-order birth probabilities will be *more* affected by increments in income than will those of lower order. This can be shown loosely by inspection of an indifference curve that shows trade-offs between children and other goods. A trade for a low-order birth would require more of other goods to leave the family indifferent than would a trade at a higher-order birth. This is equivalent to a higher price for a given amount of 'child utility' at higher birth orders. This implies that a given shift in the budget constraint will have *more* effect at a lower-order birth than at a higher order. To repeat, the concept of diminishing marginal utility implies that, *ceteris paribus*, the probability of moving from, say, no children to one child will be less elastic with respect to an income shift than will the probability of moving, say, from the third to the fourth child. This conclusion runs counter to the main effect observed here, and therefore cannot be very important in this context.

On the cost side, there are economies of scale in raising children of a given 'quality'. Marginal cost decreases with additional children, and hence the elasticity of successive 'purchases' with respect to income should decrease; it is an established proposition that the smaller the unit of sale, the less elastic is demand with respect to income. This may be seen intuitively by thinking about the case where the cost approaches zero: where there is no cost, the income constraint does not matter. The concept of economies of scale is consistent with the direction of the effect observed here. But there is nothing in the notion of economies of scale that would predict a *negative* effect of income at any birth-order.

Also possibly relevant are the 'quantity' and the 'quality' elasticities of births of various

[25] *Loc. cit.* in footnote 17.

[26] Norman B. Ryder, 'Comment', *Journal of Political Economy*, **81**, March/April 1973, Supplement, S65–S69.

orders, and the interaction of these elasticities. This line of argument, first suggested by Becker[27] and recently elaborated by Becker and Lewis[28] is complex and hence will not be elaborated here. Briefly, Becker and Lewis show that when both the monetary and non-monetary expenditures (especially time) on children are taken into account, the larger the number of children in the family, the smaller are both the 'true' and the observed elasticities of the quantity of children with respect to family income.[29] This implies that the effect of income should be *less* positive on successive parity progression ratios. Becker and Lewis further show that on the assumption that the 'true' elasticity of 'quality' with respect to income is greater than that of 'quantity', the *observed* elasticity of quantity *may* be *negative* – even if the true elasticity of quantity is positive (as it may be assumed to be). That is, an observed negative effect of income on (higher) orders of birth is at least consistent with economic theory, though not predicted by it.

Deterministic economic theory, then, is not very helpful here. Diminishing marginal utility suggests that income will have a *more positive* effect at higher orders of birth, which is not observed. Economies of scale in child-raising, and the interaction of quality and quantity considerations, imply that income should have a *less positive* effect at higher orders of birth. So at best, comparative statics yields an indeterminate result. And worse, it provides no strong argument for believing that the effect of income should be negative at higher parity progressions. In brief, deterministic economic theory is little help in understanding the results obtained in this paper.

[27] Gary S. Becker, 'An Economic Analysis of Fertility', in National Bureau of Economic Research *Demographic and Economic Change in Developed Countries* (Princeton: Princeton University Press, 1960).

[28] Gary S. Becker and H. Gregg Lewis, 'On the Interaction Between the Quantity and Quality of Children', *Journal of Political Economy*, **81**, March/April, 1973, Supplement, S279/S288.

[29] *Loc. cit.* in footnote 27, equations 5 and 6.

ERRATUM

In the article "The Mixed Effects of Income Upon Successive Births may Explain the Convergence Phenomenon" by Julian L. Simon, in *Population Studies*, Vol. 29, No. 1, (1975), the diagram for Figure 1 was omitted. What should have been Figure 2a was labelled Figure 1, and what should have been labelled Figure 2b was labelled Figure 2.

The correct diagram for Figure 1 is shown below.

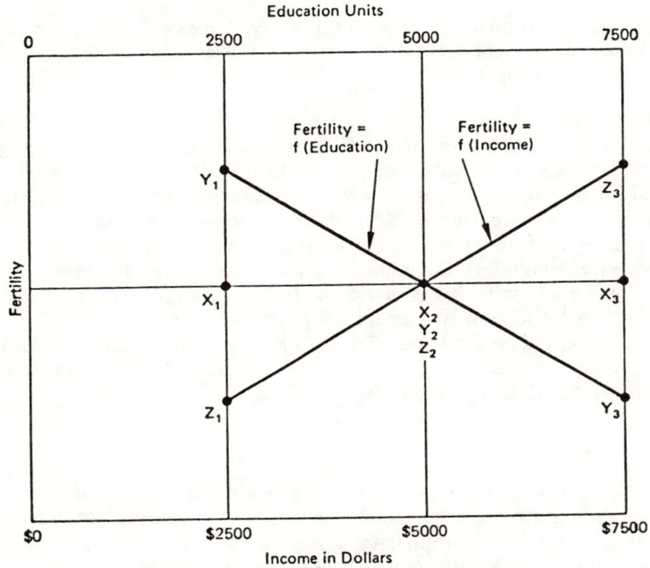

It is suggested that this correction be placed with the original.

DEMOGRAPHY© Volume 12, Number 2 May 1975

PUZZLES AND FURTHER EXPLORATIONS IN THE INTERRELATIONSHIPS OF SUCCESSIVE BIRTHS WITH HUSBAND'S INCOME, SPOUSES' EDUCATION AND RACE

Julian L. Simon
The Jerusalem School of Business, Hebrew University, Jerusalem, Israel, and Departments of Economics and Business Administration, University of Illinois at Urbana-Champaign, Urbana, Illinois 61801

Abstract—When fertility is examined in the detail of individual parity progressions and birth-order transitions, important interactions between the effects of income and education are seen. Among the findings are: the negative effect of education on fertility is stronger at all parities for less educated compared to more highly educated women. Additional income has a more positive effect for more highly educated than for less educated women. For women with 0–8 years of education the effect of more income is positive when the family has no children but negative thereafter, but for college-educated women the effect of more income is positive. And additional income has a less positive (more negative) effect on fertility among nonwhites than among whites.

A companion article reports that higher income has a quite different effect upon the average family's propensity to have more children when the family has few children than when it has many children. That is, if a family has one child, additional income is associated with a higher propensity to have another child. But if the family already has several (say four or five) children, additional income *reduces* the likelihood that the family will have an additional child (see Simon, 1975).

This provocative result, which is consistent with Bernhardt's (1972) recent findings for Sweden (see also Namboodiri, 1974; Snyder, n.d.; Seiver, n.d.), may also be interpreted as a relationship between income and the variance in the family-size distribution, due to the effect of income on family-planning practice and/or through other more complex mechanisms. It casts light on the "convergence" in more developed countries to the 2–4 child family and also calls into question the findings of fertility studies that work with mean family size as the dependent variable.

This finding, obtained from a cross-sectional multivariate study of the 1960 U.S. Census, is consistent and strong, making it particularly welcome in an area in which many of the results about economic variables—especially about the effect of income—are mixed and controversial (for a summary of this literature, see Simon, 1974).

The present paper delves deeper into these data to learn about the interactions of income with education, and of income and education with race and women's labor-force participation at various parities.

Some of the main findings are as follows: the negative effect of education on fertility is found to be stronger at all parities for less educated compared to more highly educated women. Additional income has a more positive effect on fertility for more highly educated women than for less educated women. For women with 0–8 years of education, the effect of more income is positive when the family has no children but negative thereafter, but for college-educated women (with four or less children) the effect of more income is positive. And additional income has a less positive (more negative) effect on fertility among nonwhites than among whites. But both whites and nonwhites show the same pattern of a less positive (more negative) effect of income on fertility with successive births.

The paper also offers some new ways of delving into the effects of income and other variables upon transitions from one birth order to the next.

The Method

The general method is fine subclassification by various demographic characteristics of the 1/1000 1960 U.S. Census Public Use Sample. Discriminant analysis is then applied to the parity progressions or birth-order transitions within each subgroup cell. (Where the dependent variable is limited to two groups, discriminant analysis is equivalent to regression analysis, and the two terms will therefore be used interchangeably.)

The main method is described in detail in Simon (1975), but a few specifics are needed here. The units of observation are women aged 35–54, with husband present. In the central analyses the observations are then subclassified by race (white-nonwhite), degree of urbanization of residence place (urban with more than 50,000, urban with less than 50,000, rural nonfarm, rural farm), husband's occupation (eight standard categories), wife's education (8 or less, 9–12, 13 or more years), husband's education (8 or less, 9–12, 13 or more years) and wife's age (35–44, 45–54). None of these variables is itself a function of husband's income. (If a fertility-related variable of classification or regression were to depend heavily upon husband's income, it would distort the relationship between husband's income and fertility, the relationship of primary interest here.) Nor do any of these variables depend heavily upon wife's education—a variable of secondary interest in this paper—except for a few exploratory runs with women's labor-force participation.

The dependent variable in each regression is a dichotomous yes-no variable. In the central mode of analysis the two categories in each birth-order variation are whether the wife has n children or more than n children. This is the traditional demographic parity-progression analysis. In this mode of analysis, in the first of the six birth-order variations the two categories contain wives with zero children and those with one or more children, respectively; this variation is designated as the $n = 0$ run. In the second ($n = 1$) variation the categories are one child and two or more children. There are six variations, the $n = 5$ variation having wives with five children in one category and those with six or more children in the other. The discriminant function finds those values of the independent variables that most effectively separate the observations into the two dependent-variable categories.

This "parity-progression" mode of analysis refers to the act of proceeding from n children to *more than* n children. The regression coefficient of income in that model refers to the effect of income on the probability of being in the class of n-child or $\geq (n + 1)$-child families.

In the secondary mode of analysis, called "birth-order transition" analysis here, the categories are n and *exactly* $(n + 1)$ children, e.g. in the $n = 0$ birth-order variation the categories are zero children and one child and in the $n = 5$ variation the categories are five children and six children. To repeat, this secondary birth-order-transition mode of analysis discriminates between people ending up with exactly n and exactly $(n + 1)$ children.

The independent variables of regression are husband's income, years of education of wife, years of education of husband, and wife's age. The latter three variables are variables of classification *and* variables within the regression to aid in holding constant the variables to be treated as parameters in the analysis of the effect of husband's income and wife's education.

Discriminant functions were run in each cell that contained more than ten observations. The subclassification scheme produces many such regressions, ranging from just under 100 to over 500 in the various sets of runs and variations. The numbers of cells with more than ten nonwhites were relatively small, and hence few enter the analysis. Each regression is treated as a meta-observation, and the conclusions drawn here are based on the central values of the aggregates of the regressions conducted in each fertility variation.

The most reliable estimator for the effect of a given variable in the group of runs in a given variation is the ratio of the coefficients that are positive to those that are negative. For example, in the $n = 0$ variation of the parity-progression analysis for 0–8 years of education (wife's) reported in row 1 of panel 1 in Table 1, the education coefficients in 47 cells were positive, while 54 were negative. (Zero coefficients were not counted.) The ratio $(47/54) = .870$ is an index of the direction of education's effect in that variation. A coefficient greater than unity implies a positive effect, and a coefficient less than unity implies a negative effect.

This comparison is not biased by the proportions of families in the two dependent-variable categories, as a comparison of the mean or median coefficients would be.

The Effect of Wife's Additional Education on Fertility at Different Education Levels

Ben-Porath (1973) found that in Israel the major fertility differential by education is at low education levels; at higher education levels the differential is less sharp. In an effort to throw more light upon this matter, I broke the data into groups by wife's (and later, by husband's) education. The effect of more education on fertility is then assessed *within* each broad educational group.

Table 1 confirms Ben-Porath's finding that at all birth orders the effect of additional education is more negative (that is, ratios farther below unity) in the 0–8-years-of-education group than in the 9–12- or 13-or-more-years-of-education groups, *except* for the transition from zero to one child and a mixed result for the 2–3-child transition. With respect to the transition from zero to one child, additional education acts more strongly against fertility in the *higher* education groups. Why this should be so, in contrast to the other parity progressions, is open to speculation. One possibility is that more highly educated families are strongly against a one-child family because they believe that a single child is disadvantaged psychologically, and hence they make a decision about zero children versus two (or more) children (rather than zero versus one). With respect to the pattern exception in the 2–3-child transition in the birth-order analysis, no explanation at all comes to this writer's mind. Despite these exceptions, however, there does seem to be a pattern that the negative effect of education is greater among families of less educated women than among those of more highly educated women.

Some of the results in Table 1 are due to the effect of additional education on *mean* fertility. The larger part, however, is due either to the effect of education on the variances of the distributions or on the *particular* parity progressions. Un-

TABLE 1.—The Effect of Wife's Education on Fertility at Various Birth Orders within Various Education Levels

Fertility Categories in Dependent Variables	Wife's Education (in Years)		
	0-8	9-12	13 or More
		Traditional Parity Progression Analysis	
0, ≥1	.870 (N=101)	.533 (N=141)	.639 (N=59)
1, ≥2	.508 (N= 92)	1.030 (N=136)	1.409 (N=53)
2, ≥3	.680 (N= 84)	.681 (N=121)	1.200 (N=44)
3, ≥4	.556 (N= 70)	.586 (N= 92)	.933 (N=29)
4, ≥5	.406 (N= 45)	1.038 (N= 53)	
5, ≥6	.440 (N= 36)	.824 (N= 31)	
		Birth-Order Transition Analysis	
0, 1	1.042 (N= 49)	.580 (N= 79)	.421 (N=27)
1, 2	.559 (N= 53)	1.163 (N= 73)	1.750 (N=33)
2, 3	1.217 (N= 51)	1.000 (N= 88)	.800 (N=36)
3, 4	.538 (N= 40)	.795 (N= 70)	1.100 (N=21)
4, 5	.833 (N= 22)	.909 (N= 44)	

Note: The table shows the ratio of positive education coefficients to negative education coefficients among discriminant functions of the form: dichotomous fertility category = f (husband's income, education of wife, education of husband, wife's age). The variables of cell subclassification are race, urbanity, wife's education, husband's education, husband's occupation, wife's age.

Compare across the rows. Numbers greater than unity indicate a positive relationship between wife's education and fertility, on the average; numbers less than unity show a negative association. The sample size, N, shows the number of cells with more than ten observations in which the regression coefficients were non-zero.

raveling the relative importance of these effects is an additional major statistical project.

The results for husband's education (Table 2) show much the same effect as those for wife's education except for additional reversals in the pattern at the 4–5 birth order and the 2–3 parity progression. The explanation for the effect of men's education may be the residual association between husband's and wife's education even after subclassification and regression. Husband's education also may work through contraceptive practice and the changed value of his time.

When one looks *across* parity progressions, the pattern for wives with 13 or more years of education is opposite that for wives with 0–8 years (Table 1). Additional education for high-education wives has a very negative effect on the 0–1 transition but a neutral or positive effect on all subsequent transitions. But additional education for the low-education wives has a small negative or even positive effect on the 0–1 transition and a strong negative effect on all other transitions. That is, it seems as if additional education for a low-education woman makes a one-child family *more* attractive, whereas additional education for a high-education woman makes a one-child family less attractive. (This may again be because of a middle-class belief that an only child is disadvantaged psychologically, together with a lower-class belief that an only child is advantaged materially.) Again, one may interpret these results in terms of the effects on particular birth orders or on the variance as a whole.

Another possible explanation is that for high-education women the decision to take a job is seen as interrelated in an all-or-nothing way with the decision to have some or no children. This may be contrasted with a more graded decision-making process of the low-income women; low-education women probably can go into and out of the labor force more easily than can women with professional jobs. This is pure speculation, however.

To review briefly the findings in Tables 1 and 2, if a woman has a grade-school education, additional education has a relatively slight negative effect upon the decision to have children rather than be childless. Furthermore, the additional education has a positive effect on the decision to have one child rather than none. But after she has the first child, additional education has a relatively strong negative effect on the fertility of the grade-school-educated woman. In contrast, additional education strongly influences a college-educated woman to choose no children rather than one. But if she does choose to have at least one child, additional education for

TABLE 2.—The Effect of Husband's Education on Fertility at Various Birth Orders within Various Education Levels

Fertility Categories in Dependent Variables	Husband's Education (in Years)		
	0-8	9-12	13 or More
		Traditional Parity Progression Analysis	
0, ≥1	.747 (N=131)	.606 (n=114)	.556 (N=56)
1, ≥2	.725 (N=119)	.836 (N=112)	1.500 (N=50)
2, ≥3	.710 (N=106)	.702 (N= 97)	1.000 (N=46)
3, ≥4	.371 (N= 85)	.842 (N= 70)	1.000 (N=36)
4, ≥5	.606 (N= 53)	.727 (N= 38)	
5, ≥6	.452 (N= 45)	.909 (N= 21)	
		Birth-Order Transition Analysis	
0, 1	.765 (N= 60)	.561 (N= 64)	.722 (N=31)
1, 2	.811 (N= 67)	1.000 (N= 78)	1.615 (N=34)
2, 3	1.308 (N= 60)	.902 (N= 78)	.850 (N=37)
3, 4	.353 (N= 46)	.828 (N= 53)	1.667 (N=32)
4, 5	1.067 (N= 31)	.647 (N= 28)	
5, 6	.571 (N= 22)		

Note: See Table 1 note for an explanation of numbers in cells and an interpretation of this table with the difference that husband's education rather than wife's education is the variable whose effect is shown in the cells here.

the college-educated women has a generally positive influence on the decision to have additional children and a relatively strong positive effect on the influence to have at least a second child. The effects of men's education are mostly in accord with the effects of women's education, but there are a few more exceptions to the pattern.

Concerning the statistical significance of the findings presented here, no formal statistical tests are presented for two reasons. Firstly, there is the well-known difficulty of judging the significance of any particular finding when it appears within a set of findings but without being sought on the basis of strong a priori theory, e.g., in Table 1 the finding of a less negative effect of more education (wife's) on the 1–2 child transition for the two higher-education groups. The difficulty is even greater when one is analyzing *patterns*, for example the pattern in Table 1 that the effect of more education for wives is less negative for the 13-or-more years-of-education group than for the 9–12-year group. One may simply observe that in four of four cases the finding holds, which would happen one in eight times $[(\frac{1}{2}^4) \times 2]$ by chance (on a two-tailed test). But *some* patterns must appear by chance if one runs enough tables. Even more difficult is the comparison of the 0–8-year group to the other education groups because it contains a reversal.

It seems to me that results like these are best approached by a reader who does not seek formal significance tests but who constantly uses his significance-test orientation to inquire whether a particular finding is likely to be caused by chance, given the entire set of data presented here. And, of course, the reader should attach somewhat less significance to any result reported here than might be appropriate for these data if they were all that exist and if a formal significance test had been constructed, because of the fact that various other analyses were made and not reported here because they turned out not to be interesting (a downward adjustment that must be made for practically every piece of work reported in the literature but which is seldom taken account of in significance testing—another fundamental problem of the formal statistical testing framework).

With respect to the significance of the underlying regressions themselves, the ratios of *statistically significant* positive coefficients to negative coefficients have been examined for many of the runs, and the results are much the same as when *all* coefficients are included.

The Effects of Income on Fertility within Various Education Groups

It is clear from Table 3 that additional income has a more positive (less negative) effect on fertility at low parity progressions than at high parity progressions for all education groups. It is also clear that the positive effect at low parities is more marked among higher-education groups. Both of these findings may be taken as confirmation at the more detailed birth-order level of the hypothesis of interaction between the effects of education and income on fertility suggested by Sanderson and Willis (1971). But neither they nor I have a satisfying behavioral explanation of the phenomenon. One might suggest that the child-*quality* elasticity is different at low income levels than at high income levels, and income and education are highly correlated. That is, at a low-education (low-income) level additional education for children gets first call on additional income, whereas at higher-education (higher-income) levels the education for additional children has already been allowed for, and additional income goes to other uses. This speculation is without substantiation. But the fact remains that these data provide considerable support for belief in the interaction in

TABLE 3.—The Effect of Income on Fertility at Various Birth Orders within Various Education Levels

Fertility Categories in Dependent Variables	Wife's Education (in Years) 0-8	9-12	13 or More
	Traditional Parity Progression Analysis		
0, ≥1	1.750 (N=99)	2 333 (N=139)	2.353 (N=57)
1, ≥2	.979 (N=93)	1.491 (N=132)	1.944 (N=53)
2, ≥3	.766 (N=83)	1.034 (N=120)	1.867 (N=43)
3, ≥4	.556 (N=70)	.917 (N= 92)	1.455 (N=27)
4, ≥5	.667 (N=45)	.926 (N= 52)	
5, ≥6	.800 (N=36)	2.000 (N= 30)	
	Birth-Order Transition Analysis		
0, 1	1.130 (N=49)	2.208 (N= 57)	1.700 (N=27)
1, 2	1.167 (N=52)	1.528 (N= 91)	2.091 (N=34)
2, 3	.793 (N=52)	.870 (N= 86)	1.333 (N=35)
3, 4	.379 (N=40)	1.059 (N= 70)	
4, 5	.692 (N=22)	1.000 (N= 40)	

Note: For explanation of numbers in cells and an interpretation of this table, see Table 1 note, with the difference that income rather than education is the variable whose effect is shown in the cells here.

the effects of income and education upon fertility.

THE EFFECTS OF INCOME AND EDUCATION FOR WORKING AND NONWORKING WOMEN

A woman's education is likely to influence her decision about taking a wage job. Hence subclassifying families by women's labor-force participation introduces complexity at best and confounding at worst and is the sort of analysis I earlier foreswore. Nevertheless, I could not resist examining the data in such a manner and, once having run the analysis and obtained various results, present them here for whatever meaning the reader may extract from them.

Table 4 shows that the effect of additional income is much the same for wives who are and for those who are not in the labor force at all parity progressions. But Table 5 shows that the effect of wife's additional *education* is very *different* for wives who are and those who are not in the labor force. For those who are in the labor force, additional education has a negative effect at all parity progressions, while for those who are not in the labor force additional education has a positive or neutral effect at low parity progressions.

One might explain why income and education show such different results with respect to labor-force participation with the fact that an increase in husband's income lowers the utility of the income per hour that a woman can obtain by working an additional hour, but higher education for the wife *raises* the utility to her of any given amount of work time. (The former effect is from the assumed diminishing marginal utility of money, the latter from the higher wage the woman can earn.) Hence it

TABLE 4.—The Interactive Effect of Husband's Income and Wife's Labor Force Status on Fertility

Fertility Categories in Dependent Variables	Labor Force Status: Wife Out of Labor Force	Labor Force Status: Wife in Labor Force
	Parity Progression Analysis	
0, ≥1	1.847 (N=205)	1.582 (N=173)
1, ≥2	1.538 (N=198)	1.742 (N=140)
2, ≥3	.810 (N=181)	1.111 (N=114)
3, ≥4	.667 (N=125)	.688 (N= 54)
4, ≥5	.771 (N= 85)	
5, ≥6	1.263 (N= 43)	

Note: Explanation of numbers in cells and interpretation of this table is the same as in Table 3.

makes sense that increases in husband's income and in wife's education should not have the same sort of influence.

Another result seen in Table 5 is that, for women not in the labor force, additional education has a positive effect at low parity progressions but a negative effect at high parity progressions. No such trend is seen for women in the labor force. This suggests that education's economic opportunity-cost effect better explains fertility for women in the labor force than for women out of the labor force.

It is also clear that additional education has a much more negative effect on fertility for women in the labor force than for those not in the labor force, at all parities. This suggests that the decision to work is a function not only of education (and earning capacity) but also is affected by other forces among which may be a taste for children.

To repeat, in view of the fact that

TABLE 5.—The Interactive Effect of Wife's Education and Labor Force Status on Fertility

Fertility Categories in Dependent Variables	Labor Force Status: Wife Out of Labor Force	Labor Force Status: Wife in Labor Force
0, ≥1	1.019 (N=216)	.589 (N=178)
1, ≥2	1.000 (N=200)	.778 (N=144)
2, ≥3	.896 (N=182)	.727 (N=114)
3, ≥4	.685 (N=123)	.500 (N= 54)
4, ≥5	.700 (N= 85)	
5, ≥6	1.000 (N= 42)	

Note: See Table 1 note for an explanation of numbers in cells and an interpretation of this table.

TABLE 6.—The Effects of Income within Racial Groups

Fertility Categories in Dependent Variables	White	Nonwhite
	Parity Progression Analysis	
0, ≥1	2.282 (N=256)	1.167 (N=39)
1, ≥2	1.470 (N=247)	.722 (N=31)
2, ≥3	1.084 (N=223)	.643 (N=23)
3, ≥4	.784 (N=173)	
4, ≥5	.849 (N= 98)	
5, ≥6	1.071 (N= 58)	

Note: Explanation of numbers in cells and interpretation of the table is the same as in Table 3.

education influences labor-force participation, an appropriate analysis would consider the effects of education on fertility and labor-force participation jointly (as some authors have attempted to do for completed fertility, e.g. Mason, 1973). These provocative results, then, should be taken only as an indication that such a more complex analysis is well worth doing with respect to parity progressions and birth-order transitions.

DIFFERENTIAL EFFECTS OF INCOME AND EDUCATION BY RACE

Table 6 shows that income has a less positive effect for nonwhites than for whites (at least at the low parity progressions for which sufficient data is available). Table 7 suggests that education has a more negative effect for nonwhites than for whites at the first two parity progressions (the sample size for nonwhites at the third progression is just

TABLE 7.—The Effects of Wife's Education within Racial Groups

Fertility Categories in Dependent Variables	White	Nonwhite
	Parity Progression Analysis	
0, ≥1	.658 (N=262)	.625 (N=39)
1, ≥2	.908 (N=250)	.632 (N=31)
2, ≥3	.725 (N=226)	1.091 (N=23)
3, ≥4	.620 (N=175)	
4, ≥5	.782 (N= 98)	
5, ≥6	.639 (N =59)	

Note: See Table 1 note for an explanation of numbers in cells and an interpretation of this table.

big enough to be included). A simple explanation might be that beyond the first birth the patterns for nonwhites relative to whites are the same as for the low-education, low-income group relative to the high-education, high-income group, as seen in Tables 1 and 3. And nonwhites have less income and education on average than do whites. So perhaps the phenomenon has nothing to do with race but only with the income and education levels of the groups. Unfortunately the nonwhite samples are too small to test this proposition.

Another possible explanation (or contributing explanation) is statistical rather than substantive: a family's "permanent" income is likely to be the relevant income variable for fertility. However, the variability from year to year in the income of nonwhites is likely to be greater than that for whites, and hence current income is likely to be a poorer proxy for permanent income for nonwhites than for whites. If so, one would expect a weaker relationship between income and any fertility indicator for nonwhites than for whites because of the greater measurement error with nonwhites. (But this explanation would not be very consistent with the negative effect of income for nonwhites at the 2–3 + parity progression compared to the neutral effect for whites.)

If the effect of education really is more negative for nonwhites (which assumes the data on the 2–3+ transition are not convincing), it might be due to inferior schooling for nonwhites. Inferior schooling might be seen as equivalent to *less* schooling, and this might then diffuse the negative effect of education over more grades rather than having most of its effect at the lowest grades. The distribution of whites and nonwhites by education and by family size then might help explain a more negative effect of education among nonwhites (if it really exists). But much further analysis would be necessary before any conclusion could be drawn.

The main difference between racial groups offered here is the less positive (more negative) effect of income on the various birth orders for nonwhites than for whites.

Detailed Analysis of the Relationship of Income Group to Exact Size of Family

Studies of the *mean* size of family in the United States generally indicate that the *partial* effect of income on mean family size is positive (see citations in Simon, 1974, Chapter 2). But delving into the individual birth orders with linear regression reveals that the effect of income is positive at low parity progressions but negative at high birth progressions, as seen earlier. A linear regression may, however, obscure nonlinear effects across income groups. One could try to investigate with nonlinear regressions, but the results would be hard to understand intuitively. Therefore a different method is adopted here.

Table 8 shows the proportions of families in each separate income group (a) having exactly *n* children and (b) having *n* or less children, for the age groups 35–44 and 45–54. The cumulative data are also plotted in Figures 1 and 2. This display shows that having less income does result in a relatively greater propensity to have zero children, a tendency which is, however, more pronounced in the 35–44 than the 45–54 age group (and the younger cohort has much less childlessness than the older cohort). But the data show that having less income *also* is associated with having *many* children, say, four or more. This is the pattern of "convergence" to 2–3 children with increasing income.

This analysis might be improved by allowing for other influences upon fertility, but that must await further work.

TABLE 8.—Distributions of Families by Number of Children within the Various Income Groups

Number of Children in Family	Income Group												Total
	≤$0	$1-999	$1,000-1,999	$2,000-2,999	$3,000-3,999	$4,000-4,999	$5,000-5,999	$6,000-6,999	$7,000-9,999	$10,000-14,999	$15,000-24,999	≥$25,000	
							Wife Aged 35-44						
0-child family, N	15	59	82	103	140	215	199	135	192	64	26	9	1,239
Percent	11.0	16.0	17.3	15.2	14.5	14.7	11.8	10.0	10.2	08.9	08.3	05.8	12.2
Cum. percent	11.0	16.0	17.3	15.2	14.5	14.7	11.8	10.0	10.2	08.9	08.3	05.8	12.2
1-child family, N	25	57	60	103	142	274	285	211	286	104	43	17	1,607
Percent	18.4	15.4	12.7	15.2	14.7	18.7	16.9	15.7	15.2	14.4	13.8	11.0	15.8
Cum. percent	29.4	31.4	30.0	30.4	29.3	33.4	28.6	25.7	25.5	23.2	22.1	16.8	27.9
2-child family, N	32	59	95	112	233	360	494	389	608	226	107	52	2,767
Percent	23.5	16.0	20.1	16.5	24.2	24.6	29.2	28.9	32.4	31.3	34.3	33.5	27.2
Cum. percent	52.9	47.4	50.1	47.0	53.5	58.0	57.9	54.6	57.9	54.5	56.4	50.3	55.1
3-child family, N	14	42	82	106	165	256	316	291	396	167	85	49	1,969
Percent	10.3	11.4	17.3	15.7	17.1	17.5	18.7	21.6	21.1	23.1	27.2	31.6	19.3
Cum. percent	63.2	58.8	67.4	62.6	70.6	75.5	76.6	76.3	79.0	77.6	83.7	81.9	74.5
4-child family, N	18	34	45	89	124	161	202	154	211	98	28	18	1,182
Percent	13.2	09.2	09.5	13.1	12.9	11.0	12.0	11.4	11.2	13.6	09.0	11.6	11.6
Cum. percent	76.5	68.0	77.0	75.8	83.5	86.5	88.5	87.7	90.2	91.1	92.6	93.5	86.1
5-child family, N	12	32	34	44	65	77	101	94	84	27	13	3	586
Percent	08.8	08.7	07.2	06.5	06.7	05.3	06.0	07.0	04.5	03.7	04.2	01.9	05.8
Cum. percent	85.3	76.7	84.1	82.3	90.2	91.8	94.5	94.7	94.7	94.9	96.8	95.5	91.8
6-child family, N	3	16	27	40	38	54	43	39	46	19	6	4	335
Percent	02.2	04.3	05.7	05.9	03.9	03.7	02.5	02.9	02.5	02.6	01.9	02.6	03.3
Cum. percent	87.5	81.0	89.9	88.2	94.2	95.5	97.0	97.6	97.1	97.5	98.7	98.1	95.1
7-child family, N	4	13	9	17	19	26	20	14	24	9	1	1	157
Percent	02.9	03.5	01.9	02.5	02.0	01.8	01.2	01.0	01.3	01.2	00.3	00.6	01.5
Cum. percent	90.4	84.6	91.8	90.7	96.2	97.3	98.2	98.7	98.4	98.8	99.0	98.7	96.7
8-child family, N	4	18	14	32	15	15	17	9	13	5	2	2	146
Percent	02.9	4.9	03.0	04.7	01.6	01.0	01.0	00.7	00.7	00.7	00.6	01.3	01.4
Cum. percent	93.4	89.4	94.7	95.4	97.7	98.3	99.2	99.3	99.1	99.4	99.7	100.0	98.1
9-child family, N	5	13	5	11	8	9	7	4	9	1	0	0	72
Percent	03.7	03.5	01.1	01.6	00.8	00.6	00.4	00.3	00.5	00.1	00.0	00.0	00.7
Cum. percent	97.1	93.0	95.8	97.0	98.5	98.9	99.6	99.6	99.6	99.6	99.7	100.0	98.8
10-child family, N	1	7	4	9	5	4	0	2	5	1	0	0	38
Percent	00.7	01.9	00.8	01.3	00.5	00.3	00.0	00.1	00.3	00.1	00.0	00.0	00.4
Cum. percent	97.8	94.9	96.6	98.4	99.1	99.2	99.6	99.8	99.8	99.7	99.7	100.0	99.2
11-child family, N	3	19	16	11	9	12	6	3	3	2	1	0	85
Percent	02.2	05.1	03.4	01.6	00.9	00.8	00.4	00.2	00.2	00.3	00.3	00.0	00.8
Cum. percent	100.0	100.0	100.0	100.0	100.0	100.0	100.0	100.0	100.0	100.0	100.0	100.0	100.0
Total number of families	136	369	473	677	963	1,463	1,690	1,345	1,877	723	312	155	10,183

Table 8.--Continued

Number of Children in Family	≤$0	$1-999	$1,000-1,999	$2,000-2,999	$3,000-3,999	$4,000-4,999	$5,000-5,999	$6,000-6,999	$7,000-9,999	$10,000-14,999	$15,000 24,999	≥$25,000	Total
	Income Group												
Wife Aged 45-54													
0-child family, N	36	72	94	122	182	182	171	123	187	72	40	14	1,295
Percent	22.0	15.9	17.6	18.6	23.1	18.7	17.1	17.0	18.7	16.6	20.2	10.8	18.4
Cum. percent	22.0	15.9	17.6	18.6	23.1	18.7	17.1	17.0	18.7	16.6	20.2	10.8	18.4
1-child family, N	28	71	112	114	138	205	200	147	196	102	32	28	1,373
Percent	17.1	15.7	21.0	17.4	17.5	21.1	20.0	20.3	19.6	23.5	16.2	21.5	19.5
Cum. percent	39.0	31.6	38.6	35.9	40.7	39.8	37.2	37.3	38.3	40.1	36.4	32.3	37.8
2-child family, N	25	77	90	135	157	242	282	211	297	129	65	45	1,755
Percent	15.2	17.0	16.9	20.5	19.9	24.9	28.3	29.2	29.7	29.7	32.8	34.6	24.9
Cum. percent	54.3	48.6	55.5	56.5	60.6	64.6	65.4	66.5	67.9	69.8	69.2	66.9	62.7
3-child family, N	20	62	63	87	103	160	154	109	175	79	44	23	1,079
Percent	12.2	13.7	11.8	13.2	13.1	16.4	15.4	15.1	17.5	18.2	22.2	17.7	15.3
Cum. percent	66.5	62.3	67.4	69.7	73.7	81.1	80.9	81.6	85.4	88.0	91.4	84.6	78.0
4-child family, N	15	45	49	55	78	74	86	67	82	30	8	13	602
Percent	09.1	09.9	09.2	08.4	09.9	07.6	08.6	09.3	08.2	06.9	04.0	10.0	08.5
Cum. percent	75.6	72.2	76.5	78.1	83.6	88.7	89.5	90.9	93.6	94.9	95.5	94.6	86.6
5-child family, N	21	30	42	45	46	47	44	35	31	10	7	0	358
Percent	12.8	06.6	07.9	06.8	05.8	04.8	04.4	04.8	03.1	02.3	03.5	00.0	05.1
Cum. percent	88.4	78.8	84.4	84.9	89.5	93.5	93.9	95.7	96.7	97.2	99.0	94.6	91.6
6-child family, N	4	19	29	31	32	21	25	10	14	5	2	2	194
Percent	02.4	04.2	05.4	04.7	04.1	02.2	02.5	01.4	01.4	01.2	01.0	01.5	02.8
Cum. percent	90.9	83.0	89.9	89.6	93.5	95.7	96.4	97.1	98.1	98.4	100.0	96.2	94.4
7-child family, N	3	16	14	20	19	13	21	8	11	2	0	3	130
Percent	01.8	03.5	02.6	03.0	02.4	01.3	02.1	01.1	01.1	00.5	00.0	02.3	01.8
Cum. percent	92.7	86.5	92.5	92.7	95.9	97.0	98.5	98.2	99.2	98.8	100.0	98.5	96.2
8-child family, N	2	20	7	13	11	10	8	7	3	3	0	1	85
Percent	01.2	04.4	01.3	02.0	01.4	01.0	00.8	01.0	00.3	00.7	00.0	00.8	01.2
Cum. percent	93.9	90.9	93.8	94.7	97.3	98.0	99.3	99.2	99.5	99.5	100.0	99.2	97.4
9-child family, N	4	18	8	21	9	8	4	2	0	0	0	1	75
Percent	02.4	04.0	01.5	03.2	01.1	00.8	00.4	00.3	00.0	00.0	00.0	00.8	01.1
Cum. percent	96.3	94.9	95.3	97.9	98.5	98.9	99.7	99.4	99.5	99.5	100.0	100.0	98.5
10-child family, N	3	5	9	2	4	5	3	2	2	0	0	0	35
Percent	01.8	01.1	01.7	00.3	00.5	00.5	00.3	00.3	00.2	00.0	00.0	00.0	00.5
Cum. percent	98.2	96.0	97.0	98.2	99.0	99.4	100.0	99.7	99.7	99.5	100.0	100.0	99.0
11-child family, N	3	18	16	12	8	6	0	2	3	2	0	0	70
Percent	01.8	04.0	03.0	01.8	01.0	00.6	00.0	00.3	00.3	00.5	00.0	00.0	01.0
Cum. percent	100.0	100.0	100.0	100.0	100.0	100.0	100.0	100.0	100.0	100.0	100.0	100.0	100.0
Total number of families	164	453	533	657	787	973	998	723	1,001	434	198	130	7,051

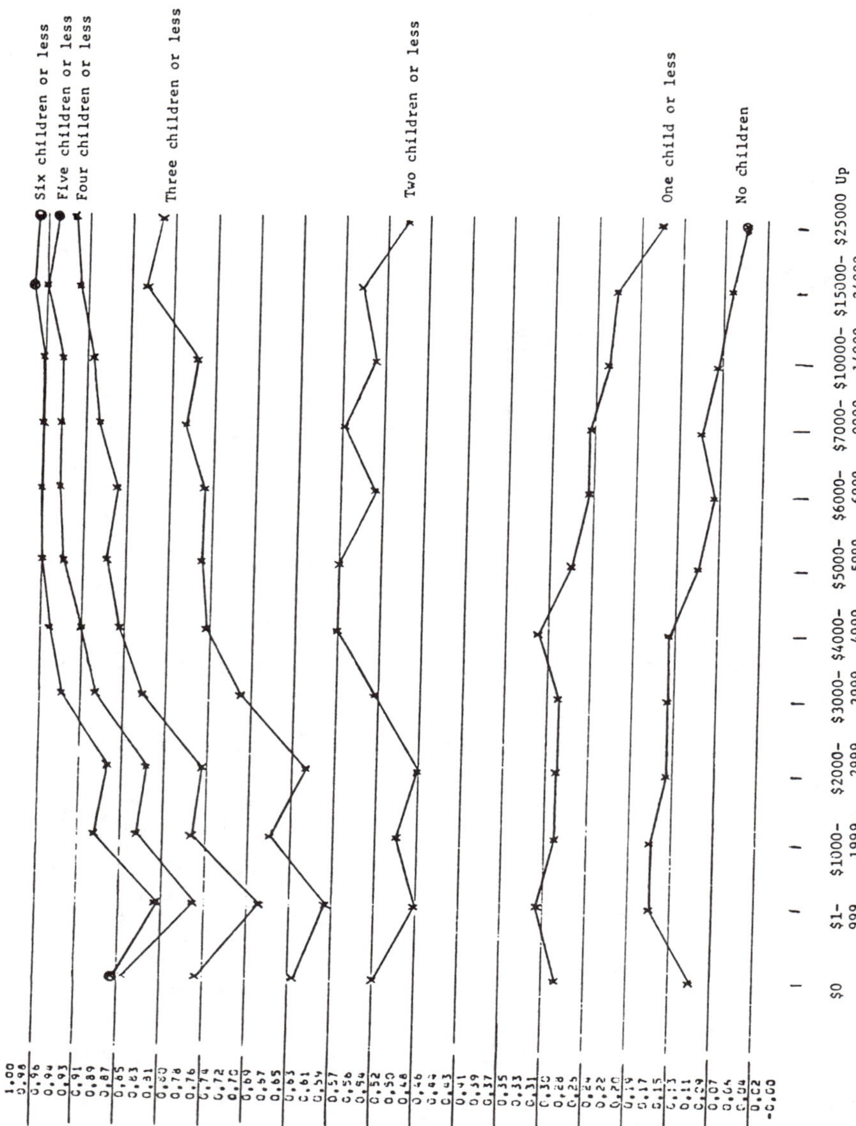

FIGURE 1.—Cumulative Distribution of Families by Number of Children (First Seven Parities) within Various Income Groups (Age of Wife 35–44) (Cells with ten or less observations are circled)

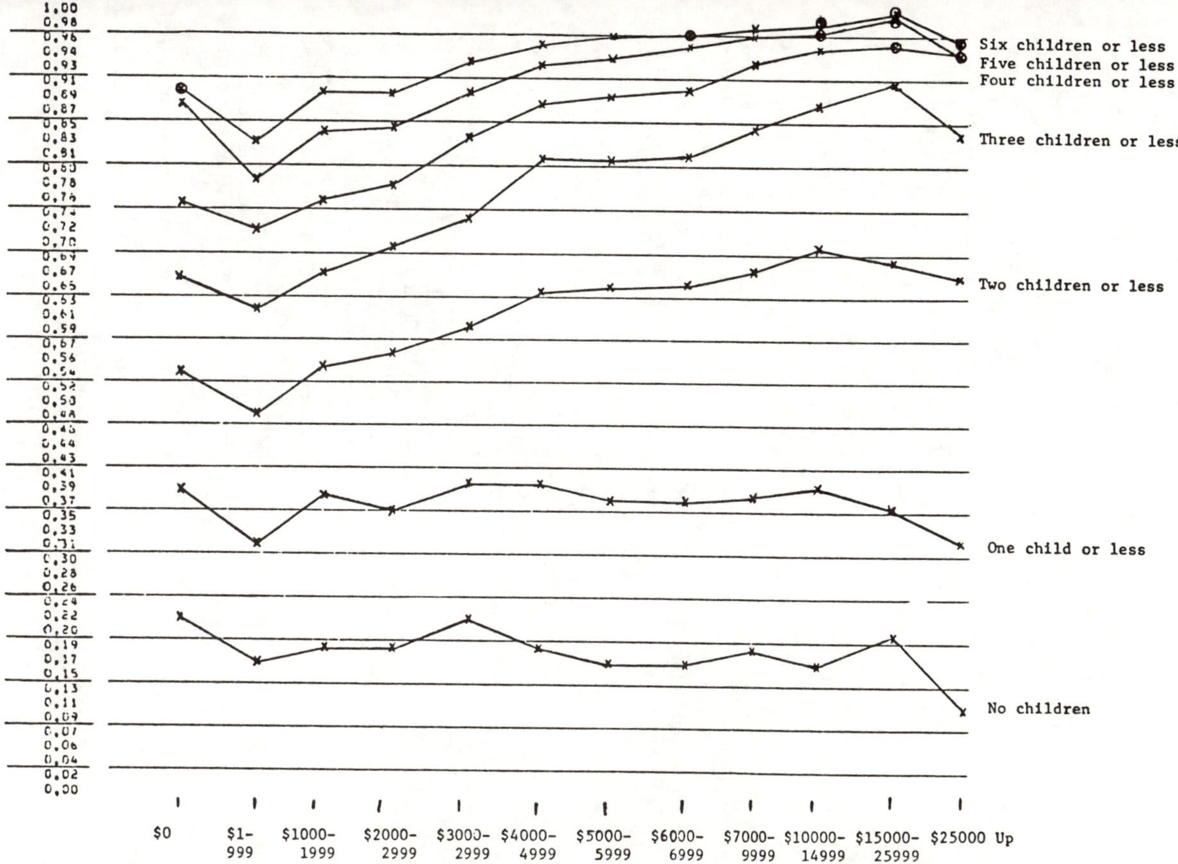

FIGURE 2.—Cumulative Distribution of Families by Number of Children (First Seven Parities) within Various Income Groups (Age of Wife 45–54) (Cells with ten or less observations are circled)

Summary

When fertility is examined in the detail of individual parity progressions and birth-order transitions, important interactions between the effects on fertility of income and education, and of additional education and educational level, are seen. The evidence is less clear for an interaction between income or education and race. This emphasizes the importance of using birth-order data rather than mean family size in studies of the determinants of fertility.

More specifically, the main findings are: the negative effect of education on fertility is found to be stronger at all parities for less educated women compared to more highly educated women. Additional income has a more positive effect on fertility for more highly educated women than for less educated women. For women with 0–8 years of education the effect of more income is positive when the family has no child but negative thereafter, but for college-educated women the effect of more income is positive. Additional income has a less positive (more negative) effect on fertility among nonwhites than among whites. But both whites and nonwhites show the same pattern of a less positive (more negative) effect of income on fertility with successive births.

Acknowledgments

The work reported in this paper was conducted in part under H.E.W. Contract NIH-NICHD-71-2034; I am grateful for that support. Referees have been very helpful with this draft. And I appreciate thoughtful and helpful comments by Yoram Ben-Porath, Dennis N. DeTray, Bruce Gardner, Karen O. Mason, Robert T. Michael, T. Paul Schultz, and Robert J. Willis on a related earlier work. I also appreciate skilled computer programming by Anne Morehart Credicott, Israel Luski, Jay McElligott, and Dan Weidenfeld.

References

Becker, Gary S. 1960. An Economic Analysis of Fertility. Pp. 209–231 in National Bureau of Economic Research (ed.), Demographic and Economic Change in Developed Countries. Princeton: Princeton University Press.

———. 1965. A Theory of the Allocation of Time. Economic Journal 75:493–517.

———, and H. Gregg Lewis. 1973. On the Interaction between the Quantity and Quality of Children. Journal of Political Economy 81: S279–S288.

Ben-Porath, Yoram. 1972. Fertility in Israel. An Economist's Interpretation: Differentials and Trends, 1950–70. In Charles Cooper and S. Alexander (eds.), Economic Development and Population Growth in the Middle East. New York: Elsevier.

———. 1973. Economic Analysis of Fertility in Israel: Point and Counterpoint. Journal of Political Economy 81:S202–S233.

Bernhardt, Eva M. 1972. Fertility and Economic Status—Some Recent Findings on Differentials in Sweden. Population Studies 26: 175–184.

Cain, Glen G., and Adriana Weininger. 1972. Economic Determinants of Fertility. Mimeo.

Cho, Lee-Jay, Wilson H. Grabill, and Donald J. Bogue. 1970. Differential Current Fertility in the United States. Chicago: Community and Family Study Center.

DeTray, Dennis N. 1970. An Economic Analysis of Quantity-Quality Substitution in Household Fertility Decisions. Mimeo.

———. 1973. Child Quality and the Demand for Children. Journal of Political Economy 81:S70–S93.

Galbraith, Virginia L., and Dorothy S. Thomas. 1941. Birth Rates and the Interwar Business Cycles. Journal of the American Statistical Association 36:465–476.

Hanoch, Giora. 1965. Unpublished Ph.D. dissertation. Chicago: University of Chicago.

Harman, Alvin H. 1970. Fertility and Economic Behavior of Families in the Philippines. Mimeo.

Mason, Karen O. 1973. The Relationship of Women's Labor Force Activity to Their Fertility Behavior: Findings from U. S. Data. Mimeo.

Michael, Robert T. 1973. Education and the Derived Demand for Children. Journal of Political Economy 81:S128–S164.

Mincer, Jacob. 1963. Market Prices, Opportunity Costs, and Income Effects. Pp. 67–82 in Carl F. Christ, Milton Friedman, Leo A.

Goodman, Zvi Griliches, Arnold C. Harberger, Nissan Liviatan, Jacob Mincer, Yair Mundlak, Marc Nerlove, Don Patinkin, Lester G. Telser, and Henri Theil (eds.), Measurement in Economic Studies in Mathematical Economics and Econometrics in Memory of Yehuda Grunfeld. Stanford: Stanford University Press.

Namboodiri, Krishnan. 1974. Which Couples at Given Parities Expect to Have Additional Births? An Exercise in Discriminant Analysis. Demography 11:45–56.

Nerlove, Marc, and T. Paul Schultz. 1970. Love and Life between the Censuses: A Model of Family Decision-Making in Puerto Rico, 1950–60. Mimeo. Rand Corporation.

Preston, Samuel H. 1972. Marital Fertility and Female Employment Opportunity: United States, 1960. Mimeo.

Ryder, Norman B. 1969. The Emergence of a Modern Fertility Pattern: United States, 1917–66. Pp. 99–123 in S. J. Behrman, Leslie Corsa, Jr., and Ronald Freedman (eds.), Fertility and Family Planning: A World View. Ann Arbor: University of Michigan.

——— 1973. Comment. Journal of Political Economy 81:S65–S69.

Sanderson, Warren, and Robert J. Willis. 1971. Economic Models of Fertility: Some Examples and Duplications. Pp. 32–42 in National Bureau of Economic Research (ed.), Annual Report. New York: National Bureau of Economic Research.

Seiver, Daniel A. 1974. Unpublished Ph.D dissertation. New Haven: Yale University.

Shultz, T. Paul. 1969. An Economic Model of Family Planning and Fertility. Journal of Political Economy 77:153–180.

Simon, Julian L. 1970. Income, Childlessness, and Fertility in the United States in the Census of 1960. Unpublished paper presented at the annual meeting of the Population Association of America, Atlanta.

———. 1974. The Effects of Income on Fertility. Chapel Hill: Carolina Population Center.

———. 1975. The Effect of Income and Education upon Successive Births. Population Studies 29:23–46.

Snyder, Donald W. n.d. Economic Determinants of Fertility. Mimeo. Norfolk: Old Dominion University.

U. S. Bureau of the Census. 1964. U. S. Census of Population: 1960. Subject Reports. Women by Number of Children Ever Born. Final Report PC(2)-3A. Washington, D. C.: U. S. Government Printing Office.

Willis, Robert J. 1973. A New Approach to the Economic Theory of Fertility Behavior. Journal of Political Economy 81:S14–S64.

[15]

Foreword

There seems nothing very special about this paper to have it included here – and yet I feel a strong urge to do so. Age has its privileges (I hope).

The Effect of Foster-Care Payment Levels on the Number of Foster Children Given Homes

Julian L. Simon
University of Illinois, Urbana, and Hebrew University of Jerusalem

One possible way to increase the number of available foster homes is to raise the level of payments to foster parents. This article estimates the effect of the payment level on the supply of potential homes. The relationship is estimated on data from the various states. One method is a simple cross-sectional comparison of the states. Another, and more satisfactory, method is an examination of the changes over time in the various states. There is rough agreement in the results of the two methods, suggesting that a given percentage change in payment level would result in a percentage change in the supply of homes somewhere between half as large and fully as large—for example, a 5–10 percent change in available homes in response to a 10 percent change in payment level.

Foster homes are crucial to American society's program of care for children without good parental homes. But there are not always as many good foster homes available as there are children who need them.

Money influences people's behavior in many areas of life. Therefore, it is natural and reasonable for welfare administrators to wonder whether the supply of foster homes also depends to an important degree on the level of payments to foster parents. If so, administrators can obtain more foster homes for needy children by arranging for higher payments.

The aim of this paper is to estimate the effect of the payment level on the number of people who are willing to take foster children into their homes. The method of research is statistical analysis of the numbers of foster homes in the various states as related to the level of payments in the states. The data suggest that the effect of the pay-

Social Service Review (September 1975).

ment level is indeed substantial. In technical economic terms, the "elasticity"[1] of the number of foster homes with respect to the payment level is between 0.5 and 1.0. That is, an increase of, say, 10 percent or 100 percent in the payment level should produce an increase of somewhere between 5 and 10 percent, or 50–100 percent, respectively, in the number of homes offered to foster children.

The relationship between the payment level for foster homes and the number of foster homes offered may also throw some interesting light on the relationship between the cost of raising children (that is, the "price" of having children) and people's desire to have *natural and adoptive* children in their homes. Most welfare workers agree that people do not take in foster children just to make money, and that, in fact, people cannot make money doing so. Therefore, foster parents must wish to have more children in their homes, a motive similar to that which motivates natural parents to have more children. (In fact, the link between foster parentship and regular parentship is the foundation of the recent movement to make payments to needy parents who adopt children.)[2] Hence it is reasonable to think that the supply of foster homes in response to various levels of payments offers a clue to the effect of the cost of raising children on the demand for natural children. This may also offer a clue about the likely effect of incentive payments offered to people to have more (or fewer) children.[3]

The Theory

When considering the short-run relationship *over time* of foster-child payments to foster-child placements within a given state, the theory can be classically simple. When comparing yearly observations within a decade or even two, all the characteristics of the potential foster-parent population may be assumed to be much the same for all the time-series observations. Some part of the observed response to a price change may be thought of as due to the *demand* for children in the home; when the foster payments go up, the "price" of a child—for any given "quality" of child—goes down, and the quantity of children demanded may be expected to rise. Some part of the response of foster parents to a price change may also be interpreted as a *supply-of-labor* decision; the labor-supply effect goes in the same direction as does the demand-for-children effect; the higher "wage" for taking care of children induces a higher supply of foster-parent care.

When making a comparison among states at a given time, however, the relationship of foster-care payment levels to the number of children in foster homes might be more complex, because the payment level might be systematically related to state per-capita income and other characteristics of the states. The relationships in such a cross-section analysis are long run rather than short run in nature, and an analysis that does not take into account the lagged long-run effects might therefore introduce biases.[4] A great many variables might enter such a system, including men's education, women's education and opportunity cost, natural fertility levels, and many other possible differences among the states.

Simple cross-sectional regressions are run here, nevertheless, on the assumption that these other variables do *not* work systematically to invalidate the simple cross-sectional relationship. But this assumption need not be taken on faith, because an additional method is also used—a sample of changes over time—which is free of these problems. Happily, it turns out that the results of the two methods jibe rather well, which increases confidence that the simple cross-sectional results are meaningful.

The Data

The basic data are the payment levels and the number of foster children per capita in the various states in the United States, collected by the Children's Bureau of the Department of Health, Education, and Welfare.

Data collection was complicated by the fact that some foster children are in publicly run foster homes while others are in homes run by voluntary organizations. And the public welfare funds that are given to voluntary organizations to help support child care programs cannot be separated into those given for foster care and those for other programs. This led to a decision to deal only with children in "foster family homes supervised by public welfare agencies." The *sums* paid for children in this category are well defined and are without major definitional change over the period of study.[5] Unfortunately, however, they include some payments for group homes and other non-foster-child categories. But these latter sums are not likely to be important, because all sums paid to *personnel* of the public welfare agencies are separately accounted for.

Data for the *numbers* of children in foster homes also present statistical problems. In the years prior to 1963, the reporting did not distinguish between children in foster homes, children in group homes, and children receiving care while in the process of being adopted. Therefore, for regressions involving the year 1959, the adoptive and group-home categories were added to the foster-home categories for the other years involved.

All the necessary data were available for 1959, 1963, and 1968 for thirty-two states plus the District of Columbia; data for the other states were not reported in one or more years. There were also a few cases (notably Pennsylvania and South Dakota in 1959, Kentucky and Oklahoma in 1968) in which some sums could not be allocated to public or private care, or in which there was a change in the method of reporting. But these flaws did not seem sufficient to delete the states from the sample. There surely are other problems with these data which have escaped notice here. I hope they are minor.

The Analysis and Results

The data were first regressed cross-sectionally across the states in the observation years 1959, 1963, and 1968. This model is as follows: foster children per capita in state i in year t is a function of the average payment per foster child in state i in year t. More specifically, the regressions were run log linearly, where the b_1 coefficients may be read as elasticities:

$$\log \frac{C_{i,t}}{N_{i,t}} = a_1 + b_1 \log \frac{P_{i,t}}{C_{i,t}}, \tag{1}$$

where $C_{i,t}$ = the number of children in foster care in state i in year t, $N_{i,t}$ = the population of state i, and $P_{i,t}$ = total payments to foster parents in state i in year t.

The coefficients for 1959, 1963, and 1968, which can be interpreted as elasticities, were 0.13 (t = 0.5), 0.63 (t = 1.4), and 0.41 (t = 1.3), respectively. The 1968 and 1963 runs do not include the adoptive category, but that category could not be eliminated from the 1959 data. When the District of Columbia is dropped from the sample on the grounds that it is not much like the states in political or geographic configuration, and Kentucky and Oklahoma are dropped because the 1968 data reported were "not comparable with that of the previous year because of a change in reporting," the corresponding results were as follows for 1968, 1963, and 1959, respectively: 0.07 (t = 0.20), 0.68 (t = 1.5), 0.45 (t = 1.1).

It is gratifying that the signs are in the expected direction, and that the magnitudes are meaningful in size and not insignificant by statistical definition in two of three years. It should be noted, however, that these three sets of observations are far from independent of each other and should *not* be viewed as three separate observations that corroborate each other. However, the 1959 regression does differ from the 1963 and 1968 regressions in that it includes the "adoptive" category.

As noted above, these simple cross sections may suffer from the defect that there are many social and economic differences among the states, and some of these differences may be systematically related either to the independent variable or to the dependent variable, or to both. In a second set of analyses, these differences are mostly eliminated by making each state its own control in a cross-sectional sample of changes over time. This second set of regressions constitutes the basic material of the study. The model underlying these regressions is as follows:

$$\left(\frac{C_{i,t+k} - C_{i,t}}{C_{i,t}}\right) = a_2 + b_2\left(\frac{P_{i,t+k} - P_{i,t}}{P_{i,t}}\right), \tag{2}$$

where b_2 may be interpreted directly as an elasticity.

The main regression uses the percentage changes for each state over the entire period from 1959 to 1968. The regression coefficient estimating the elasticity is 1.1 ($t = 3.9$). The elasticity for the subperiod 1963–68 is 1.6 ($t = 2.6$).[6] But the estimate for subperiod 1959–63 is −0.42 ($t = -3.4$), which has the "wrong" sign.[7] The corresponding results without the District of Columbia, Oklahoma, and Kentucky are 1.2 ($t = 4.3$), 1.9 ($t = 2.9$), and −0.26 ($t = -3.7$).

As in all econometric analyses of this sort, the nature of the statistical model is open to question. In this case, the main question would seem to be the direction of causality. Though our interest is in the effect of payments on foster-child placements, the payment for foster children *might* be influenced by the number of foster children in homes; if the number of children whom administrators believe need placement in foster homes rises above the available foster-home openings, the administrators might well press for higher payments for children. If so, the observed relationship between payments and numbers of foster children might reflect such a line of influence wholly or in part.

To test for this effect, change-over-time regressions were run with payment level as the dependent variable but with the independent variable (number of children) lagged. The idea is that if a shortage of homes occurs in period t, then a higher payment can be expected to appear in period $t + 1$; and a lag of several years is appropriate here because the payment-changing mechanism is likely to be bureaucratically slow. The model is

$$\left(\frac{P_{i,1968} - P_{i,1963}}{P_{i,1963}}\right) = a_3 + b_3\left(\frac{C_{i,1963} - C_{i,1958}}{C_{i,1958}}\right). \tag{3}$$

On the other hand, if higher payments induce more people to accept foster children, then a lagged, change-over-time analysis might also indicate that fact, though the lag might be expected to be shorter than in (3) above. The model to test for this relationship is

$$\left(\frac{C_{i,1968} - C_{i,1963}}{C_{i,1963}}\right) = a_1 + b_4\left(\frac{P_{i,1963} - P_{i,1958}}{P_{i,1958}}\right). \qquad (4)$$

The results of these experiments are as follows: (1) The lagged influence of the number of foster children on the payment level is insignificantly small: $t = 0.52$ for all states and $t = 0.17$ without the District of Columbia, Oklahoma, and Kentucky. This suggests that the relationship in the concurrent cross sections described above may be interpreted as the causal effect of payment level on the number of foster children, rather than the opposite. (2) The lagged effect of payment level on the number of foster children is smaller than the concurrent effect (the regression coefficient b_4, which is an elasticity, = 0.63), but it is statistically meaningful ($t = 1.7$). The corresponding results without the District of Columbia, Oklahoma, and Kentucky are an elasticity (b_4) of 0.28 and $t = 1.6$.

Concordance of Results

Viewed together, and remembering that the various runs within the simple cross-section and cross-section-of-time-series sets are not independent of each other (which means that a low or negative sign is less worrisome by itself than if the observations are independent), the regression results suggest that there is indeed a positive relationship between the level of foster-child payments and the number of foster homes offered, and that the size of the relationship is fairly substantial—an elasticity of perhaps 0.50–1.0. This suggests that doubling the foster-child payment level would increase the number of foster homes offered by 50 to 100 percent. But the regressions reported here, using the available data, certainly do not offer a conclusive estimate of the sign and size of the relationship.

Notes

I appreciate the research assistance of Mr. Carl Barnes. I am also grateful for a letter from Mr. Robert H. Mugge that helps to clarify the nature of the child-welfare statistics.

1. An elasticity is a measure of the responsiveness of one variable with respect to another. It is defined as the percentage change produced in the dependent variable by a 1 percent change in the independent variable.
2. *New York Times* (March 4, 1969), pp. 1, 46.
3. A different sort of approach to the likely effects of incentive payments on fertility in the United States is described in Rita J. Simon and Julian L. Simon, "The Effect of Money Incentives on Family Size," *Public Opinion Quarterly* (Spring 1975).
4. Dennis J. Aigner and Julian L. Simon, "A Specification Bias Interpretation of Cross-Section v. Time Series Parameter Estimates," *Western Economic Journal* 8 (June 1970): 144–61; Y. Grunfeld, "The Interpretation of Cross-Section Estimates in a Dynamic Model," *Econometrica* 29 (July 1961): 1, 46; Edmond Malinvaud, *Statistical Methods of Econometrica* (Chicago: Rand-McNally & Co., 1966).
5. U.S. Children's Bureau, Department of Health, Education, and Welfare, *Child Welfare Statistics* (Washington, D.C.: Children's Bureau, 1959), p. 21; (1964), p. 36; (1968), p. 41.
6. The regression for this period *without* the "adoptive" category yields an elasticity of 1.5 (t = 3.1), or 2.3 (t = 4.4) without the District of Columbia, Oklahoma, and Kentucky.
7. A regression for the years 1946–57 also yielded a negative sign, −.28 (t = −.72). But there were only twenty-six observations, and the data for the earlier period were very rough, indeed.

[16]

Foreword

The connection between the physician's self-interest and smoking seems so tenuous as to be non-existent. And yet the results of the paper strongly imply that such a force is influential. Curious.

Offprint from THE PUBLIC OPINION QUARTERLY
Volume 31, Winter 1967-1968

DOCTORS, SMOKING, AND REFERENCE GROUPS

BY JULIAN L. SIMON*

North Carolina's economy is heavily dependent on tobacco, far more so even than runners-up Kentucky, Virginia, and South Carolina. It is therefore of interest that only 90.3 per cent of North Carolina doctors, lowest percentage of any state and far below the states' mean of 94.8 per cent, answer affirmatively the question "Do you believe cigarette smoking is a health hazard?" And Virginia, South Carolina, and Kentucky have the next lowest percentages of affirmative answers, in that order.[1]

This finding is unusually neat, for two reasons. First, it is statistically unequivocal; the chance that North Carolina alone would head the list is 1 in 50, and the chance of the other tobacco producers following close on North Carolina is far less, taken together. Second, unlike almost any other data collected by survey rather than by laboratory experiment with randomized subjects, the cause-and-effect mechanism is very clear, and there is very little danger of confounding. It stretches the imagination to propose any possible cause of this result except that North Carolina is a state of tobacco farmers. Other Southern but non-tobacco-producing states such as Arkansas, Georgia, and Mississippi show results very close to the national mean.

This finding cannot be interpreted as a result of nonresponse bias, because the existence of such differential nonresponse itself would lead to the same conclusion as if the data are considered to have come from random samples of the state universes.

It is clear that the beliefs of doctors in North Carolina are affected by the people among whom they live. This might simply be taken as an illustration of a reference (membership) group phenomenon, and a further proof of the theory. But I think we should scrape deeper to try to lay more of the mechanism bare.

In this case, unlike many group-anchored belief phenomena, it is

* Julian L. Simon is an Associate Professor in the Department of Marketing at the University of Illinois.

[1] The source of the smoking data is the March 2, 1964, issue of *Modern Medicine,* and a press release from the magazine issued on February 24, 1964. *Modern Medicine* is a controlled-circulation (free) magazine sent to 192,000 physicians, effectively all the physicians in private practice. A questionnaire card was attached to the cover of the issue of February 3, 1964. 68,212 questionnaires were returned, but the tabulations were based on only the first 56,004. (Analysis of prior surveys conducted by *Modern Medicine* showed that late returns do not differ significantly from early returns.)

not sensible to think that doctors share the beliefs of (various groups of) people around them simply because they allow themselves to be persuaded by the beliefs of others. The others in the community are laymen, and this issue is a matter of technical knowledge for physicians, so the doctors are not likely to credit the authority of laymen. Rather, it is as if the doctor shares the *goals* and *wishes* of those around him for tobacco prosperity. It is those common *wishes* that then affect his propensity to credit the reports he receives from elsewhere. The wish is father to the belief. This makes more sense than thinking of beliefs as being transmitted from the group to the doctor.

It is important to notice that these beliefs of the doctors are expressed *privately* in this anonymous survey. If they were expressed publicly, we could argue that the responses were the result of face-to-face group pressure rather than real belief, but the anonymous questionnaire form suggests that the answers are honest ones.

Further credence is lent to the statements of belief by the finding that 29.9 per cent of North Carolina physicians report presently smoking cigarettes, the highest figure among the states and far above the states' mean of 22.5 per cent; Kentucky is next highest. To maul an old poker metaphor, the doctors of North Carolina are willing to put their lives where their mouths are.

It seems most likely that the causal mechanism runs from beliefs to actions, i.e. that the lesser belief in health danger leads to more cigarette smoking. This hypothesis is more plausible than a causal chain that runs from smoking to beliefs, because it does not seem so likely that a doctor will smoke cigarettes because he believes it is good for the group's prosperity. (He could smoke safer cigars.)

Apparently, it is not merely a matter of the congruence of doctors' *beliefs* with the beliefs of laymen. Fewer laymen in the South as a whole believe that the medical reports are factual (63 per cent) than in the East (68 per cent), Midwest (69 per cent) or Far West (74 per cent).[2] But in Southern states *other* than the four biggest tobacco states, doctors' beliefs are *not* noticeably below the national average. And it is not likely that laymen's beliefs in only the tobacco states could account for the aggregate low figure for the South.

Therefore, it seems as if doctors' beliefs are affected by the beliefs of their communities, when those beliefs are *important* and where the beliefs indicate strong wishes, rather than merely being affected by the state of community belief.[3] That doctors in tobacco-economy states smoke more and believe less in the dangers of smoking than do doctors elsewhere is evidence for this assertion.

[2] Lloyd C. Jamieson, "Cigarettes and Health," New York, MacFadden-Bartel, May 1964, p. 17, mimeographed.

[3] However, there is considerable agreement between doctors' and laymen's beliefs in the Far West, namely, California, Washington, Oregon.

[17]

Foreword

The situations that Schelling described fascinated me, but his mode of explanation did not sit comfortably with me. This paper presents what I believe to be a simpler and more general explanation, which turned out to be the kernel within the complex analysis that Strotz had proposed decades ago.

Self-control theories of struggle among several coexisting "selves" have recently been offered to explain such behaviors as foregoing anesthesia, quitting smoking, and ordinary saving. Strotz formally modeled such situations without the concept of coexisting selves, however. This article (a) boils down the Strotz formalism to three simple present-value equations, (b) argues that the framework applies to many ordinary commercial transactions rather than only to exceptional personal decisions, (c) does not require the concept of simultaneous selves, (d) places the subject within conventional economics with the concept of externalities, and (e) suggests that intra-individual allocation is similar to allocation between the given individual and other individuals. The key assumption is that the discount between the individual's present "person" and the individual's future "persons" is great compared to discounts among the future persons. This assumption is central to the analysis of Strotz and to Ainslie's behavioral analysis of self-control mechanisms.

The Theory of Binding Commitments Simplified and Extended, with Generalization to Interpersonal Allocation

JULIAN L. SIMON
University of Maryland

In his 1983 Ely lecture, Schelling (1984a; see also Schelling 1984b) offered a theory of struggle among several coexisting "selves" to explain a variety of interesting behaviors, such as foregoing anesthesia and quitting smoking. Other writers, including Thaler and Shefrin (1981), Elster (1979), and Parfit (1984), also suggested self-control explanations for such activities as ordinary saving and "Christmas Club" saving.

Author's Note: *I appreciate useful bibliographical suggestions by Robert Pollak. George Ainslie and two anonymous referees offered valuable comments, and Editor James Coleman provided important encouragement as well as a searching set of fundamental questions and suggestions. The sympathetic and understanding editorial treatment of this manuscript is the most constructive that it has been my pleasure ever to experience, the kind of treatment that fulfills one's youthful romantic vision of the collegial process.*

RATIONALITY AND SOCIETY, Vol. 2 No. 3, July 1990 287-309

Strotz (1955) provided a formal framework that models such situations without the concept of coexisting selves. Following in the formal line of Strotz, this article:

1. Boils down the formalism to a system of three simple and transparent present-value equations which highlight the key element: the structure of discount factors, which Strotz discovered.
2. Argues that the decisions to which this framework is relevant include many ordinary commercial transactions rather than only exceptional decisions as Schelling suggests.
3. Does not require the concept of simultaneous selves as used by Schelling and others, but instead employs the concept of a sequential set of person-states which make up the individual's life.
4. Places the subject squarely in the context of conventional economics by showing that the analysis hinges on the concept of externalities, using conventional theory of how externalities are best managed. The contemporary views of property rights and of rules are all that is necessary to complete the analysis. This seems more conformable to the conventional economic point of view than does the concept of self-control.
5. Shows how the explanation of intra-individual allocations is continuous with allocations between the given individual and other individuals.

The key assumption is that the discount between the individual's present "person" and the individual's future "persons" is great compared to discounts among the future persons. This assumption — which Pollak (1968) refers to as a "non-exponential discount function"—is central to the analysis of Strotz (1955). The assumption also is the pivot of Ainslie's (1975) extensive behavioral analysis of self-control mechanisms.

ELEMENTS OF THE ANALYSIS

Several elements are used in the analysis.

1. The mental states of a single legal individual at a given moment or during a given period comprise the basic entity, here called the "temporal person." The "I" or "me" that one is conscious of at any moment is part of the "current person," or "present person," which is one particular time-dated or "temporal" person in the individual's lifetime. By contrast, in James's ([1890] 1950, chap. XII) system, as also in the systems of Schelling, Elster, Parfit, and Thaler and Shefrin, there are *several* "selves" at a given moment operating within (in Schelling's terminology) a single, legally-unique and physically-distinct "identity."

Schelling writes that he had difficulty in getting two selves to sit down and negotiate with each other. Assuming that only one self is present at a time eliminates that difficulty by definition, and enables me to dispense with the concept of self in this analysis. Where it will help to avoid confusion, however, I will refer to a current or future "self-person" to distinguish from other individuals.

An individual has a repertoire of personalities available to serve the current self-person. The repertoire may be thought of as a set of cassettes, or the files on a disk, any one of which may be popped into operation at any moment. The personalities are to be distinguished from temporal persons in that a personality is a set of *capacities*; it does not have desires or feel pleasure or pain and is more superficial than the "me" that one feels oneself to be at any moment. Except in rare individuals, only one personality is on stage at any given moment. Personalities do not enter into the present analysis, and the distinction is made here only for clarity.

2. The sequential temporal persons may be thought of as distinct from each other just as individuals are ordinarily thought of as distinct from each other, although the temporal persons are much more closely related to each other than are individuals. A key aspect of the suggested point of view is the analogy between (on one hand) the feelings of kinship between "oneself" and other legally distinct individuals and (on the other hand) the feelings of kinship between different temporal persons within a given individual's lifetime. Many expressions in our language suggest this, such as "I'm not the same person I was then."

3. The feeling of sympathy between one and another of the temporal self-persons—and especially between the current person in operation and any future temporal self-person—may be measured by a discount factor of the ordinary kind. No explanation for the phenomenon of discounting will be offered here. Rather, time discounting will simply be assumed to take place as an almost universal characteristic of human behavior.

4. The feeling of sympathy between the current person and another individual may also be measured by a discount factor. The sympathy discount weight for another individual is likely to be small relative to the discount weights among an individual's temporal persons, except perhaps the weights for close beloved persons, but may be of the order of the weights for the individual's temporal persons many years in the future. Operationally, one is likely to divide one's assets less evenly between another individual and one's current person (in the form of one's legal identity) than, say, between one's current person and one's person next year.

5. The discount from the current person to any future self-person is considerably greater than the discount between a pair of future self-persons that is separated by the same length of time. This is the key assumption that makes "self-control" appear "rational," as will be seen in the examples; without this assumption, self-control behavior does not make sense in conventional terms. This assumption may be viewed as a behavioral hypothesis which may be tested by either questionnaires or experiments; in support of this assumption, Ainslie (1975) adduced evidence from animal experiments showing that reward potency declines with delay at a rate greater than exponential. This phenomenon need not be considered an anomaly, for reasons given in the Discussion section.

The strength of kinship feeling to other individuals is likely to be affected systematically by relationships of blood, geography, common views, caste, ethnicity, and religion, among others. The interindividual discount factor could be estimated for some scientific purposes by examining such phenomena as the relationship of charitable giving to geographic distance (or number of people living in between the donor and the donee), the closeness of blood relationship, and the number of newspaper stories about countries at different geographic distances and having different degrees of ethnic and religious kinship from the reference point.

Sidgwick ([1907] 1962) noted the similarity between the interpersonal and the intertemporal sympathies as, more recently, did Sen (1977). Adam Smith ([1759] 1976) masterfully explored this idea and mapped the typical relative strengths of sympathy toward individuals at different distances from us:

> Every man . . . is first and principally recommended to his own care; and every man is certainly, in every respect, fitter and abler to take care of himself than of any other person. Every man feels his own pleasures and his own pains more sensibly than those of other people. The former are the original sensations—the latter the reflected or sympathetic images of those sensations. . . .
>
> After himself, the members of his own family, those who usually live in the same house with him, his parents his children, his brothers and sisters, are naturally the objects of his warmest affections. They are naturally and usually the persons upon whose happiness or misery his conduct must have the greatest influence. He is more habituated to sympathize with them: he knows better how every thing is likely to affect them, and his sympathy with them is more precise and determinate than it can be with the greater part of other people. It approaches nearer, in short, to what he feels for himself.
>
> This sympathy, too, and the affections which are founded on it, are by nature more strongly directed towards his children than towards his parents. . . .

The earliest friendships, the friendships which are naturally contracted when the heart is most susceptible of that feeling, are those among brothers and sisters. Their good agreement, while they remain in the same family, is necessary for its tranquillity and happiness. They are capable of giving more pleasure or pain to one another than to the greater part of other people. . . .

The children of brothers and sisters are naturally connected by the friendship which, after separating into different families, continues to take place between their parents. Their good agreement improves the enjoyment of that friendship—their discord would disturb it. As they seldom live in the same family, however, though of more importance to one another than to the greater part of other people, they are of much less than brothers and sisters. As their mutual sympathy is less necessary, so it is less habitual, and, therefore, proportionably weaker.

The children of cousins, being still less connected, are of still less importance to one another; and the affection gradually diminishes as the relation grows more and more remote. . . .

. . . A father is apt to be less attached to a child who, by some accident, has been separated from him in its infancy, and who does not return to him till it is grown up to manhood.

Among well-disposed people the necessity or conveniency of mutual accommodation very frequently produces a friendship not unlike that which takes place among those who are born to live in the same family. Colleagues in office, partners in trade, call one another brothers, and frequently feel towards one another as if they really were so. . . .

Even the trifling circumstance of living in the same neighbourhood has some effect of the same kind. We respect the face of a man whom we see every day, provided he has never offended us. . . .

The same principles that direct the order in which individuals are recommended to our beneficence, direct that likewise in which societies are recommended to it. . . .

The state of sovereignty in which we have been born and educated, and under the protection of which we continue to live, is, in ordinary cases, the greatest society upon whose happiness or misery our good or bad conduct can have much influence. It is accordingly by nature most strongly recommended to us. . . .

Every independent state is divided into many different orders and societies, each of which has its own particular powers, privileges, and immunities. Every individual is naturally more attached to his own particular order or society than to any other. His own interest, his own vanity, the interest and vanity of many of his friends and companions, are commonly a good deal connected with it: he is ambitious to extend its privileges and immunities—he is zealous to defend them against the encroachments of every other order or society. (Pp. 359, 360, 361, 362, 366, 371, 372, 376)

THEORETICAL APPARATUS

The individual is assumed to plan a course of behavior so as to maximize the present value of the expected positive pleasures and negative pains experienced by the present and future persons and by other individuals with whom one feels sympathy, discounted and summed. This is the definition of "rationality" employed here. (Allocation between the reference individual and other individuals will mostly be ignored here despite the fact that its inclusion in the same conceptual apparatus could be a large step toward greater generality.)

Symbolically, find the maximum

$$\begin{aligned} V_{t,\, i=0} = {} & G_{t,\, i=0} - B_{t,\, 0} + d'G_{t+1,\, 0} - d'B_{t+1,\, 0} + d''G_{t+2,\, 0} - d''B_{t+2,\, 0} \cdots \\ & + e_{j=1}G_{t,\, j=1} - e_1 B_{t,\, 1} + d'e_1 G_{t+1,\, 1} - d'e_1 B_{t+1,\, 1} \cdots \\ & + e_{j=2}G_{t,\, j=2} - e_2 B_{t,\, 2} + d'e_2 G_{t+1,\, 2} - d'e_2 B_{t+1,\, 2} \cdots \\ = {} & \sum_{i=0}^{j=n} e_{i,j} \sum_{h=0}^{m} d^k_{t+h} \left(G_{t+h;\, i,j} - B_{t+h;\, i,j}\right) \end{aligned} \tag{1}$$

subject to $F_1 \leq$ alpha, $F_2 \leq$ beta . . .

where

$V_{t,\, i=0}$	=	present value of the relevant experiences—perhaps better called "expected utility"—for the reference individual $i = 0$ evaluated at time t
i, j	=	index of an individual, the decision-maker ($i = 0$) or another individual ($j = 1, 2 \ldots$)
G	=	a positive event, a "good" or "pleasurable" experience
B	=	a negative event, a "bad" or "painful" experience
d	=	a time-discount weight, for convenience taken to be the same for the decision-making individual's future persons and for other individuals (it need not be so assumed), where $d < 1$.
$e_{i,\, j}$	=	sympathy weight for the self-person i or for another individual j where $e_i = 1$ and $e_j < 1$.
F_1, F_2, and so on	=	lifetime endowments of time, strength, and other elements affecting the quantities of pleasure and pain; alpha, beta, and so on are constants.

Consider that an individual will make either one or two choices among three alternative courses of action: The first choice consists of the option (a_1) of binding oneself at time $t = -T$ to accept a future negative event (or series of events) at $t = 0$ in order that a positive event (or series of events) will occur at $t < 0$, $t = 0$, or $t > 0$; the alternative option (a_2), not making a binding commitment, leads to a second choice, made at time 0, between options (b) and (c). The valuation of option (a_1) is made as follows:

$$V(a_1)_{t=-1} = -B_{t=0}d^k + G_{t=1}d^{k+1} + G_{t=2}d^{k+2} + G_{t=3}d^{k+3} \ldots \quad (2)$$

where k = a constant > 1, and where all other goods and bads, those unconnected with this option, are considered to net out to an arbitrary reference point of zero for notational convenience.

Option (b), which becomes open at $t = 0$ if option (a_1) is not chosen earlier, consists of choosing the negative event at hand in order to obtain the positive event(s); at the moment it might be chosen it is valued as follows:

$$V(b)_{t=0} = -B_{t=0} + G_{t=1}d^k + G_{t=2}d^{k+1} + G_{t=3}d^{k+2} \ldots \quad (3)$$

Option (c), which also becomes open at time $t = 0$ if option (a_1) is not chosen earlier, consists of choosing against the negative event; the option is valued as of $t = 0$

$$V(c)_{t=0} = 0 \quad (4)$$

The choice of interest here is between (a_1) and (a_2), whether or not to make a binding commitment. The value of (a_2) is the greater of the values of (b) and (c), that is, the alternative which will be chosen if (a_1) is previously not chosen; the conditional choice between (b) and (c) will depend on the values of the right-hand sides of equations 3 and 4 as of $t = 0$. If (c) would be chosen, its value as of $t = -T$ would be zero because its value as of $t = 0$ is zero.

If (b) would be chosen over (c), conditional on (a_1) not being chosen, then there is no need for a binding commitment; the same course of action would be arrived at anyway. It is only if (c) would be chosen over (b) that there is a role for a binding commitment.

In order that the choice of (a_1) be "rational," then, two conditions must hold: (c) must be seen as preferable to (b) as of $t = 0$, and (a_1) must be seen as preferable to (c) as of time $t = -T$ (at which time c has a value of zero, as explained earlier). That is, the ordering (of the right-hand sides) of equation

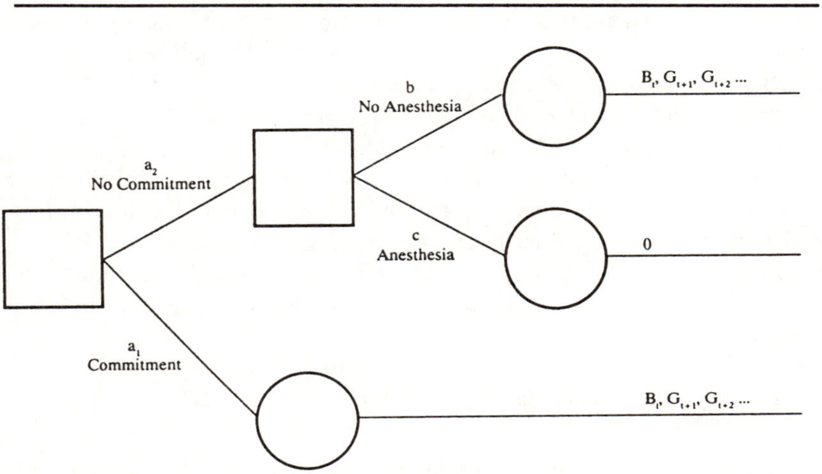

Figure 1: Decision tree for expectant woman.

2 > equation 4 (valued as of $t = -T$), and equation 4 > equation 3, is necessary if a binding commitment is to make sense.

Please note that equations 2 and 3 contain exactly the same "goods" and "bads" on their right-hand sides. They therefore can only differ in sign if the discount factor for the first period has an exponent k greater than unity, that is, if the discount from the present to the next period is greater than forward discount factors. This is the idea at the heart of Strotz's analysis, expressed here in a simple and transparent fashion which points to a wide variety of applications.

The structure of the decision making is portrayed as a dynamic program in Figure 1, labeled for specificity according to application 1 in the following section, where two lines across a path indicate that that option would not be chosen if the decision maker would be at that choice point.

ILLUSTRATIVE APPLICATIONS

1. THE CHOICE OF REFUSING BIRTH ANESTHESIA

For comparison, let us begin with Schelling's (1984b) vivid example of a woman about to give birth who arranges beforehand for attendants not to give her anesthetic while in labor even if she requests it. At any moment of evaluation, there will be (a) a pain (negative) that will be felt by the person in labor, weighted by the length of time she will be in labor;[2] and (b) the unanesthetized knowledge and memories that her temporal self-persons will enjoy during the periods after labor, weighted by their durations. The negative intensity of the hours during labor surely will be much greater than the positive intensity of the memories later on, but the length of the time during which the positive mental material will persist will be much greater.

If we let the discount periods equal a month, *at one month before the birth* the woman will evaluate as *positive* the present value of choosing not to have the anesthesia.

$$V_{t=-1,\ \text{no anesthesia}} = -B_{t=0}d^{k} + G_{t=1}d^{k+1} + G_{t=2}d^{k+2} + G_{t=3}d^{k+3} \ldots > 0, \qquad (2a)$$

In contrast, the present value of giving birth without anesthesia evaluated *at the time of giving birth* will be seen as *negative*, that is

$$V_{t=0,\ \text{no anesthesia}} = -B_{t=0} + G_{t=1}d^{k} + G_{t=2}d^{k+1} + G_{t=3}d^{k+2} \ldots < 0 \qquad (3a)$$

The alternative of having the anesthesia has neither "goods" nor "bads" attached to it (the zero reference point by assumption), so

$$V_{t=0,\ \text{anesthesia}} = 0$$

and therefore the right-hand side will then be seen as preferable to the right-hand side of equation 3a.

To repeat, the alternative of irrevocably choosing no anesthesia at time $t = -1$, which has a positive present value (equation 2a), is preferable to the alternative of not choosing it irrevocably at time $t = -1$. If commitment is not chosen and the binding does not take place, there will ensue a less desirable course of events—the choice of anesthesia at birth and a $V = 0$ (equation 4a)—because that alternative would then be chosen in preference to no anesthesia (equation 3a).

Again, please note that the right-hand sides of equations 2a and 3a differ in sign only because the discount factor for the first period has an exponent greater than unity; that is, the discount from the present to the next month is greater than forward one-month discount factors.

The decision making expressed by equations 2a through 4a may also be viewed as follows: From the vantage point *prior* to the birth, the woman foresees the benefits that will accrue *after* the birth if she refrains from anesthesia *during* the birth; that is, by not taking anesthesia, the "person" who gives birth bestows positive externalities on later "self-persons." And as of the reference point "prior" to being in labor, the later benefits are calculated to have greater (discounted) value than the cost. The decision-making prebirth "person" then arranges the situation to compel the birth "person" to produce the positive externalities for later self-persons.

The quasi-ethic embodied in this sort of decision making is quite dissimilar from ordinary interpersonal ethics in a free society. That is, one "person" is being *forced* to suffer for the benefit of another "person." Aside from taxation and some other special situations, such "coercion" is not ideologically acceptable in free societies. But it is analogous to the ideology of philosophies that glorify the state. And this quasi-ethic may be in keeping with original utilitarianism. Of course, the issue of coercion does not arise publicly in this case because all events occur privately. But this aspect of such situations may account for the reluctance of other individuals—such as medical personnel who are involved in the birth—to cooperate in imposing suffering on the birth person.

Please note that the "cost of self-control" which is a key part of the analyses of Thaler and Shefrin, Elster, and Schelling is not found in the aforegoing explanation and is unnecessary here, though it could be embodied in the present analysis.

The externality in this case could in logic be viewed as either positive or negative. The birth person's *nonuse* of anesthesia could be seen as *sacrifice* on behalf of later persons. Or, the *use* of anesthesia could be seen as an *indulgence* for which later persons must pay. This symmetry is added rationale for using the same framework for all the sorts of situations discussed here, rather than thinking of them differently. At the same time, the symmetry makes the apparently special situations seem less special and less different from ordinary economic behavior. This does not deny that one could logically and usefully distinguish between the positive and negative view in such cases, but there seems no need to do so.

2. CHRISTMAS CLUB SAVING

The explanation of self-forced saving such as a Christmas Club plan is only trivially different from the explanation of the binding commitment to forswear anesthesia in giving birth. In this case, an entire stream of events —the forced saving in each pay period—is committed to in advance rather than the one-time event of withholding anesthesia.

3. SAVING

Let us begin the topic of saving with three stylized facts:

1. Consumption in any period is less than an individual's assets and borrowing capacity could make possible. That is, saving occurs, or at least dissaving is less than maximum.
2. Saving is less than the perfect lifetime smoothing implied by Modigliani's life-cycle hypothesis. The empirical evidence—summarized in great detail by Mayer (1972), and more recently in this connection by Shefrin and Thaler (1983)—makes this argument conclusively.
3. The proportion of saving out of windfalls is less than out of ordinary income.

The self-control theory of Shefrin and Thaler (1983) explains these facts reasonably well. However, the mode of analysis offered here seems to be simpler and more consistent with standard economic concepts, as follows: Saving occurs because—given diminishing marginal utility of money—the present value of utility over the lifetime (equation 1) is higher when consumption is distributed among the various temporal persons making up the individual's lifetime, rather than all consumption taking place by one temporal person. But because of the discounting of future temporal-persons' utilities (actually, the expected positive and negative experiences), the distribution of consumption is tilted toward the current and near-future persons, as per stylized fact 2. (So far in the argument, the discount-factor structure need not be nonexponential.) Saving is proportionally smaller out of windfalls than out of normal income (stylized fact 3) because the large discount from the current person to future self-persons operates on windfalls but not on normal income. That is, the large first-period discount does not affect saving which is routinized and preplanned. Hence previously arranged saving out of each period's normal income is higher than it would be if the decision were made separately during that current period; its logic, using the future-to-farther-future discount factor, is similar to the logic of Christmas Club saving, although the commitment is less binding; the formal analysis for each segment of it is the same as for the birth-anesthesia case in equations 2 and 3. In contrast, saving out of a windfall is subject to decision in the current period during which the current-to-future discount factor—higher than the future-to-farther-future discounts—is in operation.

Please note that while some elements of this analysis of saving are similar to Schelling's and Thaler and Shefrin's self-control theory, the mechanism described here does not employ the idea of two or more selves battling each other. Rather, it depends on the different evaluation of the same event held by the different temporal persons at different moments within the individual's history, all of the temporal persons using the same logic. And that logic is a conventional, purely economic logic.

Self-control theories attribute a cost to controlling oneself. "Willpower control is costly" (Shefrin and Thaler 1983). The analysis offered here does not require this analytic element; indeed, the concept of self-control need never be employed explicitly. And, of course, such further assumptions made by Shefrin and Thaler as "the increasing marginal costs of exercising self-control" are ipso facto unnecessary. Also unnecessary are such concepts as "temptation" which Shefrin and Thaler use.

Schelling asks (1984b, 57): "Why is it so hard . . . to do the things we already decided to do?" It is *not* harder than doing things that *others* compel us to do—in the service, parachuting out of a plane or getting up at 3:45 a.m. for a four-hour watch on a dark ship; or in one's job, showing up for work after a night's binge. It is only the absence of *another's* compulsion in, say, quitting smoking that allows us to be indecisive.

Putting future persons and other individuals on the same footing in the current person's framework of assessment immediately renders understandable the phenomenon of bequests, which have been a problem for the life-cycle theory. In contrast, there is no provision for bequests in self-control theories.

4. ORDINARY PURCHASES ON CREDIT

Schelling considers the class of phenomena which he discusses to be different from ordinary commercial transactions. But purchases on credit are like self-commitment arrangements in there being an interval between the occurrences of benefit and cost and in the need for a binding commitment. Credit purchases differ, however, in that the commitment is enforced by the purchaser and the legal system; one need only sign the contract and need not bind oneself to the mast in the fashion of Ulysses. This being so, a business firm will simply buy on credit (rather than pay in full) whenever its discount factor is lower than the implied discount factor in the cost of credit. The appropriate first-period discount factor for the firm is the same as later discount factors, because proper business decision making (and business survival) requires that the structure of discount factors have that character.

Curiously, though, there is widespread evidence of a kinked discount factor even among business firms: the famous formula "two ten net zero"—that is, 2% off for cash within ten days, with another twenty days to pay the full price if the 2% discount is not taken. This implies an annual discount factor or at least 36%, far in excess of the normal cost of business borrowing, suggesting that it takes much effort on the part of both seller and buyer to get the buyer to part with the purchase price. (The discount is fully 8% per month in the textile industry, but only .5% in electronics, I am told.)

The nonkinked analysis for firms also applies to consumer purchases on credit, but in some cases, the nonexponential discount factor may also operate in the decision to purchase on credit rather than pay in full. Consider as an example the purchase of a new car on credit by a person who has liquid assets that will cover the purchase price or has fixed assets against which a loan could be taken to pay for the car. In that case, it is likely that the credit will cost more than the foregone earnings on assets if the purchaser pays in full. Purchasing on credit in such a situation so as not to pay immediately for the car in a lump sum might then be seen as the current person (legally) binding future persons to perform negative acts.

The matter may be illuminated from a different direction by noticing that for a large proportion of buyers, the timing of auto purchases could easily be arranged so that sums equal to the loan repayments would be saved each month *in advance* of purchase, the car then being bought free-and-clear. The prevalence of buying on credit suggests that in many cases, the present person sharply discounts the pain suffered by future persons who will pay the bill.

Also common is the device of deferring *all* payment so as to avoid the undiscounted pain to the present person who makes the buying decision, as in the case of magazines that offer the potential subscriber the option of being billed later. "Fly now, pay later" is fundamentally sound marketing psychology, not to be explained by the objective facts of individuals' asset and credit situations. There is no material difference in effort or money of writing a check thirty days hence rather than now. The deferred-payment option fits with the analytic scheme offered here.

Empirical investigation of the extent to which people purchase on credit when it would be cheaper for them to draw down savings might throw light on the extent to which people have a kinked discount factor in situations like this one (or more generally).

5. SELF-BINDING RELIGIOUS VOWS AND COMMITMENTS

Many Christians go to church every Sunday whether they "want" to or not. ("Want" is in quotes to indicate that the term is ambiguous in this context as in so many others.) And some Jews take upon themselves a commitment not to ride or write or flip a light switch on their Sabbath, even though they recognize that any of these acts might be enjoyable or useful at a given moment. How may we explain these commitments other than with theological reasons?

Consider the Jew's choice between forswearing ever riding on the Sabbath, and allowing him- or herself to choose whether or not to ride on any given Sabbath. The cost of not riding on particular occasions is obvious.[3] The benefits of not riding include the serenity of the Sabbath as well as gratifications after the Sabbath from keeping the vow. Choosing on each individual occasion would reduce the positive balance by imposing a decision-making cost on those days when the choice would be made against riding. A binding commitment not to ride, which avoids these costs of deciding, may be preferable. Furthermore, the choice must be irrevocable, because on an occasion when the individual might want to ride, he or she might not choose to do so by *breaking* the rule on a one-time basis but instead might choose to *permanently change* the rule.

This case is sufficiently similar to the anesthesia case so that formal proof would be repetitive. It should be noted, however, that the assumption of a large discount from the present person to future persons is again crucial for making sense of this case.

Ainslie (1975, 1986) provides a rich analysis of a variety of cognitive-behavioral devices that people may and do use for imposing their current "values on future motivational states" (letter of 4 October, 1989).

6. "POWER CORRUPTS . . . "

Many office-seekers say that they can judge fairly what should be allocated to themselves and to others from the common pool. This might well be a false promise made in order to get elected. But it is possible that this claim is honest but flawed. Benefits to a future self-person may at present be discounted enough to put the person on a fair basis with other individuals. But when the time is at hand, the actual allocation is likely to be affected by the changed discounting structure which then favors the present person.[4]

This situation may be analyzed as the allocation "power" "corrupting" the decision maker. But the explanation implicit in the system of equations offered here seems simpler (though more complex than the explanation of false promise) and has the advantage in only calling on the broad interrelated logical system that we call "economic theory" rather than on less well-defined, free-standing concepts, such as "power."

This case probably could be linked with public-choice theory. Indeed, Elster (1979, and others he refers to) explicitly relates this body of thought to social decisions through the use of a constitution, different sorts of voting systems, and modes of succession. The link is analogous to the link between two-person contracts and binding self-commitments.

7. "SELFISHNESS" VERSUS "ALTRUISM"

The conceptual framework employed here obviates the age-old question about whether an act of giving by one individual to another should properly be labeled "altruism" or whether, instead, one is "really" being "selfish" by making oneself feel good. An individual's discount weights vis-à-vis other individuals may be considered a full description of the individual in this connection. In this scheme, there is no place for intentions, and hence there are no false intentions. Revealed preferences comprise the entire system.

The unit of consciousness can be viewed as composed of continuously extended rings of "interest" or "sympathy" or "empathy" around the core of the self-person, in close analogy to the notion of continuous successive temporal persons. In this way, a sharp distinction between oneself and others need not be assumed, and it becomes less surprising when an individual will, for example, sacrifice one's life to save the life of one's child. I have found this image of the extended interest and domain of the self-person, the extent of "identification," remarkably useful for casual understanding of daily life. It also mitigates the theoretical problem that "in the supply of public goods, far less free-riding actually occurs than traditional theory predicts" (Harrison and Hirshleifer 1989, 201). And such theories as Hirshleifer's "weakest link, best shot" discussed in Harrison and Hirshleifer 1989) may more reasonably be seen as having the sympathy-empathy discount structure as its subject rather than actual maximizing self-interested behavior because there is no likely real connection between, say, one's contribution to a disaster fund and one's own safety, any more than there is a connection between one's own nonvoting in a presidential election and others' voting; the idea that "if everyone does as I do" is contrary to fact because the individual's behavior is effectively independent in such matters.

8. "WHO AM I?"

Troubled young persons are often encouraged to ask themselves, "Who am I?" But this exercise frequently produces even more confusion. The framework offered here suggests why confusion occurs. If an individual's lifetime is comprised of different "persons," and if the current person is aware of the roles of various future persons, attempting to focus on a single "identity" means forcing unnecessary choices between the wants of different persons that need not be made—indeed, choices that cannot satisfactorily be made.

9. "PLEASE CATCH ME . . . "

Criminals sometimes send such messages to the police as "Catch me before I kill again." This behavior seems to be self-contradictory, assuming the message is not just a cruel tease; if the individual wishes to be caught by the police, that individual can immediately turn him- or herself in. But the felt pain to the present person of being caught is likely to be much greater than the felt pain to a future person of being caught. The present person may envision some benefits of being stopped from the criminal activity, and the balance may seem positive compared to the discounted pain of the future person, whereas the comparison to the pain of the present person may result in a negative balance.

DISCUSSION

Elster (1979) emphasized the lack of complete rationality in the mechanisms which are discussed here. He began his discussion with "Ulysses was not fully rational, for a rational creature would not have to resort to this device" (p. 36). The viewpoint of this article is different: As long as there is a lag between costs and benefits and "externalities" therefore exist, there cannot be any better solution than a binding commitment, in the same way that laws requiring the internalization of externalities are unavoidable in interpersonal relationships and are not considered irrational. That is, the binding commitment maximizes present value as viewed by the decision maker, which would seem a reasonable definition of rational behavior in these contexts. Hence we may forego calling the behavior in question "not fully rational."

The concept of will, which is frequently used by Elster (e.g., 1979, 43) and Schelling, but which is not easily defined or quantified, also is rendered unnecessary by the analysis here.

The nonexponential discount from the present person to future self-persons need not to be viewed as irrational or anomalous. The present self-person stands on a different basis with respect to stimuli and other information than do future persons. The difference between (a) having a thorn in your thumb at this moment and (b) the memory of the event tomorrow is not of the same sort as the difference between (c) tomorrow's memory and (d) the memory the day after tomorrow. Similarly, the difference between (e) your experience of having a thorn in your thumb now and (f) your thoughts about your next-door neighbor having a thorn in his or her thumb is not like the difference in your thoughts about (g) a thorn in the thumb of your next-door neighbor and (h) the neighbor two doors away. Elster (1979) mentions this: "The absolute priority of the present is somewhat like my absolute priority over all other persons: I am I—while they are all 'out there' . . . the far future is like a distant relative, while the near future is more like a close one" (p. 71). There is an analogy between these phenomena and the emphasis of Austrian economics (following Hume and Smith) on the importance of local knowledge in decision making. There is no reason to think of the clock-time differences among the present person and various future persons as being the appropriate metric for discounting, and hence departure from it should not be viewed as an anomaly.

To put it differently, it does not seem reasonable to assume that the current self-person "knows" how the then-present and then-future will feel and appear to future self-persons, or to other individuals current or future, in anything like the same way that the present feels and the future appears to the current self-person. The current self-person imputes feelings and thoughts to future self-persons and to other individuals on the basis of whatever information and imagination he or she can muster. Our belief that our knowledge about others is poorer than about our current self-persons surely is a partial explanation for the sharp discounts from the current self-person, just as our uncertainty about just how needy a beggar is and what a dollar given to the beggar will be used for influences the propensity to give money to the beggar. In the quotation earlier, Smith ([1759] 1976) made a similar argument.

There does seem to be some confusion, however, about whether there is discontinuity between the immediacy of the present and the closest instant which is felt to be future rather than present, or whether (as Ainslie suggests) the curve is simply more sharply bowed than an exponential function. Clearly, there is no discontinuity in objective commercial dealings. But the difference between having one's hand on or off a hot stove seems different in nature than a money loan. The fact that in experiments, people "reporting how long they would wait to get double a hypothetical prize, usually generate answers reflecting annual discount rates in the billions, trillions, or quadrillions of percent" (Ainslie, 1986, 138) is puzzling.

Schelling (1984a) said that "attempting to overrule one's own preferences is certainly exceptional, as consumer behavior goes" (p. 1). Schelling (1984b) distinguished the "normal case" and abnormal self-control cases by the presence of a "superself" in the former:

> The phenomenon that I want to deal with can be described as alternating preferences, or alternating values that are incompatible or uncompromisable. In the normal case there is a dynamic programming self that looks over wants and desires that continually change, anticipating preferences and attempting to satisfy them. It is as if there were a succession of momentary selves, each with its own wants and desires, all under the supervision of a timeless superself, an overall manager or referee who treats the transient selves evenhandedly.
>
> In the case I want to discuss, that superself, that dynamically programming referee, does not exist, Instead, there is a succession or alternation of impermanent selves, each in command part of the time, each with its own needs and desires during the time it is in command but having—at least some of them—strong preferences about what is done during the period that another one is in command. (p. 86)

But the approach suggested here does not need to postulate a superself for any of the cases dealt with, including "normal" consumer purchases on credit. From the vantage point of the scheme offered here, the phenomena analyzed by Schelling are seen not to be different in kind from much ordinary consumer behavior. If a contract signed by the current person is viewed as an overrule of the preferences of a future self-person, then all credit purchases have a character similar to those Schelling analyses.

As Ainslie puts it, both he and I impose the "discipline that a unitary choice-maker must maximize his expected utility at every moment." Yet "it is still possible to account for the committing power of resolutions . . . seemingly conflictual phenomena can arise from the operation over time of a single motivational clearinghouse" (letter of 4 October, 1989).

Seen most generally, the commonality in the cases under discussion is that the benefits and the costs of an activity do not occur simultaneously. But this is true of almost all economic activities. One seldom trades on-the-spot dishwashing for the meal being eaten, or forages and eats simultaneously in the manner of a hunter-gatherer. Because of the nonsimultaneity of the production of purchasing power and the consumption of goods, ordinary economic behavior involves "sacrifice," "temptation," and "regret," as well as the other psychological aspects of the phenomena that Schelling analyses. Most fundamentally, entering into an employment arrangement that one does not exit from lightly, in order to earn the means to purchase goods later, is like joining a lifetime Christmas Club. This should be proof-positive of the ubiquity of the kind of behavior that Schelling studies in more exceptional forms.

The lag may be in either direction. Negative experiences may precede positive experiences or vice versa. Saving for later consumption is an example of the former case. An example of the latter case is the remorse—similar to that of the sufferer from an alcoholic hangover—of the purchaser of an encyclopedia, the sale of which is often heightened by the offer of deferred payment. That offer uses the knowledge embedded in the analytic scheme of this article to manipulate the customer. The law now tries to protect people from such temptation by allowing for a "cooling off" period during which the purchaser may decide to renege on the agreement. Salespeople are well aware of the crucial role of the timing of consumer evaluation and commitment; this is why they try so hard to close a sale before the prospect leaves the auto or furniture showroom.

The existence of regret does not *necessarily* indicate a situation in which a binding commitment would have been advisable, however; failure to obtain proper information or apply sufficient skill could also account for postevent remorse. Nor can one prove by after-the-event analysis that having made a sensible binding commitment led to a higher state of welfare, unlike the situation with financial present-value analysis, because at present we lack intellectual machinery to assess the current value of past psychic costs and benefits.

The main conceptual difference between the analysis of cases involving sacrifice and temptation, on one hand, and environmental pollution and positive social externalities such as knowledge-creation, on the other hand, is the vantage point of the decision making. In the social case, the decision maker is assumed not to inject his or her preferences into the system but rather to maximize a "social welfare function" which takes into account the preferences of all the participants in the system. In the cases under discussion, however, the "person" making the decision is assumed to give special place to the individual's present preferences as well as the individual's future preferences, which are assumed to be known as of the present. But this difference between individual and social decision making requires only a slight expansion of the standard intellectual machinery. The key step is to ensure that the action is taken in consideration of the full costs and benefits, which requires that there be mechanisms available which enable responsibility for costs to be properly assigned and attached to the benefits.

Viewing individual decision-making in the fashion suggested here renders it similar to the situation of social governance in which rules, binding and enforceable contracts, and similar devices are appropriate. Elster and Schelling also note the intellectual connection between personal and social governance.

Within the same ambit of analysis lie the individual's decisions about allocation among that individual and other individuals. Again, such decisions are not the exception. Rather, every individual who lives in a family and belongs to a community is faced with such decisions as a matter of course.

Treating the interpersonal situation along with the intraindividual situation casts new light on the issue of individual "rationality." Elster and others (e.g., Ramsay 1928) regard discounting of future experiences as "irrational" or lacking in "imagination" and even Ainslie (1975, 464) refers to it as an "imperfection." But choosing to keep some larger or smaller share of one's legal possessions to oneself rather than to share equally with other individuals is not usually considered irrational; indeed, a person who goes into the street and gives away an inheritance to passers by may be arrested as "crazy." Therefore, why should it be considered foolish or myopic to sharply discount future self-persons' experiences, given the very different states of knowledge that the current person has about him- or herself and about future self-persons? None of the labels connected with rationality helps the analysis; therefore, it seems better to avoid them altogether.

The single "rational" element required is that the individual have and use the capacity to foresee positive and negative preferences for the future. This enables the individual to arrange future activities at a time when the current person is relatively "disinterested," that is, at a time when the passions experienced in moments of intense feeling may be taken into account but not when the time-discount structure gives them extra weight. The word "use" means here that the individual enters into binding commitments when foresight indicates that it is appropriate to do so. I find no reason to think that putting greater weight on near-term than on far-term consumption is dysfunctional.

Jevons says that "to secure a maximum of benefit in life, all future events, all future pleasures or pains, should act upon us with the same force as if they were present" (cited by Ainslie 1975, 464). I do not agree for reasons similar to those given in the previous paragraph. The institution of private property is seen to be functional rather than dysfunctional when one moves beyond the simplest static welfare assessment. Similarly, tilting toward present consumption may induce more effort, just as the institution of private property induces more effort than does the communist Chinese "common pot."

Sometimes, the concept called "changing tastes" is used to refer to some of the phenomena dealt with here (e.g., Hammond 1976). But it is not necessary to say here that preferences change. Rather, the present and future experiences are taken to be data by the decision-making person, though their weights in the decision depend on when the evaluation is made. Sound decision making requires that one decide and commit oneself at a moment that, from a much later vantage point, would be considered appropriate timing for the decision making. I think that the term "changing perspective" is more appropriate, leaving "changing tastes" to refer to such phenomena as one's inability to stomach peanut butter after having gorged on a whole jar of it or one's aversion to butter after learning of its cholesterol-producing effect.

It is not clear how much novelty should be claimed for the analytical approach presented here. All the elements may be found one place or another in the literature. Its main contribution may be seen as employing only standard tools to deal with problems that are considered not susceptible to conventional analysis because of their element of nonrationality. Again, the critical concept is the notion of externalities.

SUMMARY

The Christmas Club and other self-forced saving plans have seemed not to square with economic theory. Recently, Schelling (1984b), Elster (1986), and Thaler and Shefrin (1981), among others, have offered multiself theories of self-control to explain these and other phenomena involving temptation, regret, and sacrifice.

This article suggests viewing these phenomena as cases of externalities and using conventional theory to deal with them. A key element is the assumption (first made by Strotz and later exploited by Ainslie) that the allocational discount factor between the current conscious "person" and future "self-persons" within the same individual is greater than the discount factor between equal-length forward periods within the same individual. A related element is that the discount also is greater between the current conscious person and other individuals than among other individuals at different psychic distances from the current self-person. Applying a conventional present-value framework to evaluate utility, as seen at various decision-making moments, then makes sense of the phenomena under discussion.

In comparison to analyses which require additional assumptions about individual psychology, this mode of analysis has the advantage that it sticks strictly to the conventional concepts of economic analysis rather than requiring concepts which are not conformable with standard theory. Also, it does not need to distinguish between "self-forced" plans and much ordinary economic behavior, and it thereby points up that "self-control" situations are not abnormal.

NOTES

1. An argument could be made, on Austrian-school grounds, that a policy in which charity begins (but does not end) at home maximizes welfare.

2. If the woman believes that the anesthesia might have a bad effect on the unborn child—children born of women who have had general anesthesia are apparently born rather dazed, an "insult" to the small body which certainly would seem to be a negative symptom—then the positive benefits would weigh much larger. Damage from artificial intervention is likely to be part of the thinking of those who want wholly natural childbirth.

3. There is a charming story that by refusing to trade on a Jewish holiday, Bernard Baruch made a large gain. The story is not relevant, however, even if true.

4. The analysis does not require that the structure of interpersonal discount factors have a kink or any other special shape in this and other situations of allocation among individuals.

REFERENCES

Ainslie, George. 1975. Specious reward: A behavioral theory of impulsiveness and impulse control. *Psychological Bulletin* 82:463-96.

———. 1986. Beyond microeconomics: Conflict among interests in a multiple self as a determinant of value. In *The multiple self*, edited by Jon Elster, 133-75. Cambridge: Cambridge University Press.

Elster, Jon. 1979. *Ulysses and the sirens*. Cambridge: Cambridge University Press.

———, ed. 1986. *The multiple self*. Cambridge: Cambridge University Press.

Hammond, Peter. 1976. Changing tastes and coherent dynamic choice. *Review of Economic Studies* 43:159-73.

Harrison, Glenn W., and Jack Hirshleifer. 1989. An experimental evaluation of weakest link/best shot models of public goods. *Journal of Political Economy* 97:201-25.

James, William. [1890] 1950. *The principles of psychology*. 2 vols. New York: Dover.

Mayer, Thomas. 1972. *Permanent income, wealth, and consumption*. Berkeley: University of California Press.

Parfit, Derek. 1984. *Reasons and persons*. London: Oxford University Press.

Pollak, Robert A. 1968. Consistent planning. *Review of Economic Studies* 35:201-208.

Ramsey, Frank P. 1928. A mathematical theory of saving. *Economic Journal* 38:543-59. (Reprinted in *Readings in welfare economics*, edited by K. J. Arrow and T. Scitovsky. Homewood: Irwin, 1969.)

Schelling, Thomas C. 1984a. Self-command in practice, in policy, and in a theory of rational choice. Richard T. Ely Lecture. *American Economic Review* 74:1-11.

———. 1984b. The intimate contest for self-command. In *Choice and consequence*, by Thomas C. Schelling, 57-82. Cambridge, MA: Harvard University Press.

Sen, Amartya. 1977. Rational fools: A critique of the behavioral foundations of economic theory. *Philosophy and Public Affairs* (Summer): 317-44.

Shefrin, H. M., and Richard H. Thaler. 1983. Life cycle vs. self-control theories of saving: A look at the evidence. Paper presented at the Econometric Society meetings, San Francisco, December; later titled: The behavioral life-cycle hypothesis, forthcoming in *Economic Inquiry*.

Sidgwick, Henry. [1907] 1962. *The methods of ethics*. 7th ed. Reprint. Chicago: University of Chicago Press.

Smith, Adam. [1759] 1976. *The theory of moral sentiments*. Reprint. Indianapolis: Liberty.

Strotz, Robert. 1955. Myopia and inconsistency in dynamic utility maximization. *Review of Economic Studies* 23:165-80.

Thaler, Richard H., and H. M. Shefrin. 1981. An economic theory of self-control. *Journal of Political Economy* 89:392-406.

[18]

Foreword

This paper arose out of my desire to make sense of people's *loyalties* – that is, the connections to other individuals that affect their allocation of their resources. As I thought about this problem I was also working on Chapter 17, and it became clear that the two questions and answers are interlinked formally and in spirit.

Gifts and bequests trouble economic theory. A solution is to deal similarly with distributions for consumption among (a) the current person, (b) future self-persons who are legally and physically the same individual who is allocating, and (c) other individuals at present and in the future. Instead of a one-dimensional maximizing entity, or even the two-dimensional individual who allocates intertemporally, this model envisages a three-dimensional surface, with an interpersonal "distance" dimension replacing the concept of altruism. A key assumption, as in Strotzian intertemporal allocations, is that the discount between the current conscious "person" and future "self-persons" within the same individual is greater than the discount between other equal-length forward periods within the same individual. Applying a conventional present-value framework to evaluate utility, as seen at various decision-making moments, then makes sense of the phenomena under discussion.

Interpersonal Allocation Continuous With Intertemporal Allocation

BINDING COMMITMENTS, PLEDGES, AND BEQUESTS

JULIAN L. SIMON
University of Maryland

> The ultimate human mystery may not be anything more than the claims on us of clan and race.
>
> Arthur Miller (1987)

> Christmas came early for shoppers on a South Side street Thursday when an unidentified man handed out $1,200 worth of $10 bills.
>
> Police later took the man . . . into custody when he returned to a savings and loan institution to withdraw $2,000 more from his account. Authorities said

Author's Note: *The University of Chicago's famed "free discussion" of a much earlier version of this article at the Seminar on Rationality and Society forced much beneficial rethinking on me, for which I became wholly grateful after my wounds had healed. James Coleman and Gary Becker, coorganizers of the continuing seminar, were most helpful, and other participants also made many useful comments. I appreciate valuable criticisms, ideas, and citations from George Ainslie, Dennis Mueller, and two anonymous readers of this article.*

RATIONALITY AND SOCIETY, Vol. 7 No. 4, October 1995 367-392

the sidewalk philanthropist had a history of mental problems and would be placed under mental observation.

Chicago Daily News (December 25-26, 1971, 1)

In his survey of "The Expanding Domain of Economics," Hirshleifer (1985) wrote that gifts and bequests are a "scandal" for economic theory (p. 55), a "difficulty [which] can be resolved only in the light of bioeconomic considerations" (p. 55). Within the framework offered here, however, gifts and bequests present no greater difficulty than does intertemporal allocation of lifetime resources within a given individual's lifetime, which economists routinely deal with theoretically.

The core of the issue is to explain how "one," or the "self," allocates the available resources for consumption among (a) the current person, (b) future self-persons who are legally and physically the same individual who is allocating, and (c) other individuals at present and in the future. Quotation marks are around "one" as in "one should," and the equivalent "self" as in "self-interest," because the definition of the unit for which they stand is the very heart of the explanation.

The key intellectual obstacle is that economists consider the legal-physical individual throughout his or her lifetime, or just a disconnected single chunk of that life, to be the appropriate entity for analysis. The mechanism that overcomes this obstacle is to consider the future periods of the given individual's life— future "self-persons"—on the same footing as other individuals. That is, instead of a one-dimensional point for the maximizing unit, or even the two-dimensional individual who allocates intertemporally, this scheme envisages a three-dimensional space; the interpersonal "distance" dimension replaces the concept of altruism. This is the main point of the article: to argue that other individuals with whom we are close should not be considered as distinct from us but rather as part of our "identity" to greater or lesser degrees. The analytic apparatus and the particular examples analyzed are presented as devices to show the general value of this way of thinking as well as for their technical value.

The model suggested here aims not only to remove a theoretical difficulty but also to adjust the economist's thinking more closely to reality. The individualistic asset-maximizing model apparently leads some economists to assume that human nature is like the model's assumptions. For example, a panel of six "expert" economists on average made very poor predictions about outcomes to laboratory experiment on a Prisoner's Dilemma game; theory led them to expect no cooperation and their overall predictions ranged from 0% to 30% cooperation, whereas the outcomes averaged between 40% and 60%. It is also interesting that economics graduate students exhibited less cooperation (about 20%) than did noneconomists (Marwell and Ames 1981). The individualistic model also leads to puzzlement about such phenomena as gifts (Camerer 1988) and behavior in catastrophes (Hirshleifer 1987), which do not puzzle noneconomists.

My aim is to make gift giving or "altruism" as "rational" in the context of economic theory as is intertemporal intrapersonal allocative saving and spending.

The article does not deal with the consequences of various amounts of altruism, as do Becker (1981, chap. 8), Becker and Barro (1988), and Mulligan (1993), who seek to understand how nonselfish activities fit into the larger scheme of human behavior. Nor does the article discuss the causes of altruism; Mueller (1986), for example, attempts to explain such behavior in a backward-looking fashion in the context of behaviorist learning theory,1 and H. Simon (1990) offers a model of the genetic and social-learning causes of altruism. Rather, the article offers intellectual machinery intended to be a consistent framework to help make understandable otherwise puzzling choices, and especially their timing (such as timed transfers). For Becker's purpose, a one-period framework suffices, although he discusses dynamics in passing. In contrast, my point is that either intertemporal transfers and time discounting cannot be integrated and made understandable within economic theory or interpersonal transfers discounting can be so made, along with intrapersonal transfers over time.

ELEMENTS OF THE ANALYSIS[2]

These are the elements used in the analysis:

1. The mental states of a single legal individual *at a given moment or during a given period* compose the basic entity, here called the "temporal person." The "I" or "me," of which one is conscious at any moment is part of the "current person" or "present person"; it is one particular time-dated or "temporal" person in the individual's lifetime. By contrast, in William James's ([1890] 1950, chap. 12) system, as also in the systems of Schelling (1984a, 1984b), Elster (1986), and Thaler and Shefrin (1981), there are *several* "selves" at a given moment operating within (in Schelling's terminology) a single legally unique and physically distinct "identity."

2. The sequential temporal persons may be thought of as distinct from each other just as individuals are ordinarily thought of as distinct from each other. This analogy between (on the one hand) the feelings of kinship between "oneself" and other legally distinct individuals and (on the other hand) the

feelings of kinship between different temporal persons within a given individual's lifetime is central to the point of view of this article.

3. The feeling of sympathy between one and another of the individual's temporal self-persons—and especially between the current person in operation and any future temporal self-person—may be measured by a discount factor of the ordinary kind. Time discounting will be assumed to be a common characteristic of human behavior, although it might be absent or even negative in a given situation.

4. The discount from the current person to any future self-person typically is considerably greater than the discount between a pair of the individual's future self-persons who are separated by the same length of time. This is the key assumption that makes "self-control" appear "rational," as will be seen in examples to come; without this assumption, self-control behavior does not make sense in conventional terms. This assumption is supported by considerable evidence derived from questionnaires and laboratory experiments with animals and humans; in support of this assumption see, for example, Ainslie (1975) for evidence from animal experiments showing that reward potency declines with delay at a rate greater than exponential, and Ainslie and Haendel (1983) for a review of other evidence.

5. The feeling of sympathy between the current person and another individual may also be measured by a discount factor. The sympathy discount weight for another individual is likely to be small, relative to the discount weights among an individual's temporal persons, except perhaps the weights for close beloved persons, but they may be of the order of the weights for the individual's temporal persons many years in the future. Operationally, one is likely to divide one's assets less evenly between another individual and one's current person (in the form of one's legal identity) than, for example, between one's current person and one's person next year.

The strength of kinship feeling to other individuals is likely to be affected systematically by relationships of blood, geography, common views, caste, ethnicity, religion, and extent of interaction (emphasized by Hume; see Mulligan 1993, chap. 2) among others. The interindividual structure of discount factors could be estimated for some scientific purposes by examining such phenomena as the relationship of charitable giving to geographic distance (or number of people living in between the donor and the donee), the closeness of blood relationship (even identical twins as compared to fraternal twins), and the number of newspaper stories about countries at different geographic distances and having different degrees of ethnic and religious kinship from the reference point. One would also expect people to exhibit more sympathy—and even bequests in wills, for example—for animals such as gorillas that are relatively close to us biologically than for animals that are relatively further away, or are commonly pets compared to those species that are not commonly pets. A survey of the importance of preserving various species confirms this: "The 20 top-ranked animals are all mammals, relatively large birds, or relatively large turtles. . . . Almost all of the 20 bottom-ranked animals are obscure rodents, snakes, insects, or snails" (Coursey 1994, 10), and this ranking squares with government expenditures on preserving the various species (p. 11). A similar propensity is exhibited in such public policy as U.S. immigration laws that have favored persons who live in countries from which much of current native stock was originally drawn.

Adam Smith ([1759] 1976) masterfully explored this basic idea and mapped the typical relative strengths of sympathy toward individuals at different distances from us.

> Every man . . . is first and principally recommended to his own care; and every man is certainly, in every respect, fitter and abler to take care of himself than of any other person. Every man feels his own pleasures and his own pains more sensibly than those of other people. The former are the original sensations—the latter the reflected or sympathetic images of those sensations.
>
> After himself, the members of his own family, those who usually live in the same house with him, his parents, his children, his brothers and sisters, are naturally the objects of his warmest affections. They are naturally and usually the persons upon whose happiness or misery his conduct must have the greatest influence. He is more habituated to sympathize with them: he knows better how every thing is likely to affect them, and his sympathy with them is more precise and determinate than it can be with the greater part of other people. It approaches nearer, in short, to what he feels for himself.[3]

The proof of Smith's observation may be seen on the front pages of the newspaper. For example, on May 24, 1971, *The Jerusalem Post* had as its main and highest headline "Elrom Found Murdered in Istanbul Flat," a story about an Israeli Council-General. Lower and smaller was "1,000 Feared Dead in Quake," a story about a Turkish earthquake. And down toward the page in much smaller type was "70 Dead in Plane Crash," about a Yugoslav airliner.

Sidgwick ([1907] 1962) noted the similarity between the interpersonal and the intertemporal sympathies, as did Sen more recently (1977), and Elster (1979) who wrote: "The absolute priority of the present is somewhat like my absolute priority over all other persons" (p. 71). Derek Parfit makes the same point—that "our later selves are properly to be seen as rather like other people" (Williams 1984), although Parfit (1984, chap. 10) takes seriously the idea of psychological continuity.

The scheme presented here uses a weighted set of discount factors representing a preexisting set of attachments that "explain" the allocations and that one might even infer from external evidence. This scheme supports a quantitative formalization that can make sense of binding decisions as well as allocational behavior that involves both intertemporal and interpersonal dimensions.

The basic descriptive equation used here is formally the same as the literature on utility functions that include the utility of others (see, e.g., Becker 1981, chap. 8), and one may consider it as a development within that tradition. If so, the new technical contribution of this article is the analysis of pledges and bequests that hinges on the combination of the analysis of intertemporal binding commitments, as developed in J. Simon (1990), with the familiar-looking multi-individual utility function.

Underlying the approach given here, however, and also Smith's view, I believe, is a different vision of the phenomenon than the vision embodied in the literature on altruistic utility functions. That literature seems to envision decision making based on a cool assessment of costs and benefits, and well-thought-out maximizing intentions. In contrast, the vision here is more that of a mother bear instinctively defending her cubs, or a mother sparrow feeding her young. Some research in the laboratory describes such a state:

1. Krebs obtained subjects' opinions on various subjects and then showed the subjects supposed questionnaire responses by confederates, varying the extent of agreement between confederates and subjects. The subject then observed the confederate performing tasks with various degrees of success, or participating in roulette where the outcome was either money winnings or electric shock.

> When the confederate was perceived as similar, the observers demonstrated more physiological response (increased heart rate and the like) as a function of the outcome experienced by the confederate. Also, when the confederate was perceived as similar, subjects were more likely to sacrifice some of their own reward for the confederate, when given an opportunity to do so. (Krebs 1975, as described by Baron 1988, 409).

2. In Milgram's (1975, see table 2) experimental work on pain induction, subjects who were remote from their "victims" were willing to administer much more punishing electric shocks than were subjects in closer proximity to the "victims."

The approach presented here also differs from the Becker-type formulation in that it emphasizes the similarity of sentiment toward an individual's own future persons and the present and future persons of other individuals. Becker views them as formally symmetrical, but he uses such language as that "other selves" are included in his utility function (letter of February 1,

1990), and the notion of a discount factor is limited to the reference individual's intertemporal decisions. The term *altruism* suggests a distinction that I wish to do without. Placing interpersonal and intertemporal allocation on the same footing, which is the key element in this article, makes the term *altruism* as unnecessary when talking of allocation to other individuals as when talking of allocation to future periods of the same individual. Further discussion of the difference in viewpoints may be found below.

This framework also supports systematic understanding of such phenomena as pledges and bequests, which cannot be understood without the conjunction of the intertemporal and interpersonal dimensions plus the nonexponential discount-factor structure while remaining squarely within the received body of economic theory without invoking auxiliary psychological elements.

The issue addressed here is not whether a person is "really" different persons over time, but whether it is useful to *treat* the legal individual *as if* he or she is different over time in a fashion similar to the differences among legal individuals at a particular time, so as to better understand behavior toward other individuals.

THEORETICAL APPARATUS

The individual is assumed to maximize the present value of the expected (positive) pleasures and (negative) pains experienced by the present and future self-persons and by other individuals with whom he or she feels sympathy, discounted and summed.

$$
\begin{aligned}
\max V_{t,\, i=0} = {} & G_{t,\, i=0} - B_{t,\, 0} + d'G_{t+1,\, 0} - d'B_{t+1,\, 0} + d''T_{t+2,\, 0} - d''B_{t+2,\, 0} \ldots \\
& + e_{j=1}G_{t,\, j=1} - e_1 B_{t,\, 1} + d'e_1 G_{t+1,\, 1} - d'e_1 B_{t+1,\, 1} \ldots \\
& + e_{j=2}G_{t,\, j=2} - e_2 B_{t,\, 2} + d'e_2 G_{t+1,\, 2} - d'e_2 B_{t+1,\, 2} \ldots \\
& \text{etc.} \\
& = \sum_{i=0}^{j=n} e_{ij} \sum_{k=0}^{m} d^k (G_{(t+k;\, i,\, j} - B_{t+k;\, i,\, j}) \qquad [1]
\end{aligned}
$$

subject to $F_1 \leq \alpha$, $F_2 \leq \beta$,

where $V_{t,\, i=0}$ = present value of the expected relevant experiences for the reference individual $i = 0$ evaluated at time t

i, j	=	index of an individual, the decision maker ($i = 0$) or another individual ($j = 1, 2 \ldots$),
G	=	a positive event, a "good" or "pleasurable" experience,
B	=	a negative event, a "bad" or "painful" experience,

d	=	a time-discount weight, where $d < 1$ for the normal cases discussed here, and the superscript powers k are undefined for now.
$e_{i,j}$	=	sympathy weight for the self-person i or for another individual j where $e_i = 1$ and $e_j < 1$, and
F_1, F_2, and so on	=	lifetime endowments of time, strength, and other elements affecting the quantities of pleasure and pain, where α, β and so on are constants.

Let us first exercise this machinery for the case of an intraindividual choice that involves the idea of precommitment.

Consider that an individual will make either one or two choices among three alternative courses of action: the first choice consists of the option (a_1) of binding oneself at time $t = -T$ to accept a future negative event (or series of events) at $t = 0$ in order that a positive event (or series of events) will occur at $t < 0$, $t = 0$, or $t > 0$; the alternative option (a_2), not making a binding commitment, leads to a second choice between options (b) and (c).

The valuation of option (a_1) is made as follows:

$$V(a_1)_{t=-1} = -B_{t=0}d^k + G_{t=1}d^{k+1} + G_{t=2}d^{k+2} + G_{t=3}d^{k+3}, \quad [2]$$

where k = a constant > 1, and where all other goods and bads, those unconnected with this option, are considered to net out to an arbitrary reference point of zero for notational convenience.

Option (b), which becomes open at $t = 0$ if option (a_1) is not chosen earlier, consists of choosing the negative event at hand in order to obtain the positive event(s); it is valued at the moment it might be chosen as follows:

$$V(b)_{t=0} = -B_{t=0} + G_{t=1}d^k + G_{t=2}d^{k+1} + G_{t=3}d^{k+2} \ldots \quad [3]$$

Option (c), which also becomes open at time $t = 0$ if option (a_1) is not chosen earlier, consists of choosing against the negative event; the option is valued as of $t = 0$

$$V(c)_{t=0} = 0. \quad [4]$$

The choice of interest here is between (a_1) and (a_2), whether or not to make a binding commitment. The value of (a_2) is the greater of the values of (b) and (c), that is, the alternative that will be chosen if (a_1) is previously not chosen; the conditional choice between (b) and (c), will depend on the values of the right-hand sides of equations 3 and 4 as of $t = 0$. If (c) would be chosen, its value as of $t = -T$ would be zero because its value as of $t = 0$ is zero.

If (b) would be chosen over (c), conditional on (a_1) not being chosen, then there is no need for a binding commitment; the same course of action would be arrived at anyway. It is only if (c) would be chosen over (b) that there is a role for a binding commitment.

In order that the choice of (a_1) be "rational," then, two conditions must hold: (1) (c) must be seen as preferable to (b) as of $t = 0$, and (2) (a_1) must be seen as preferable to (c) as of time $t = -T$ (at which time c has a value of zero, as explained above). That is, the ordering (of the right-hand sides of) equation 2 > equation 4 (valued as of $t = -T$), and equation 4 > equation 3, is necessary if a binding commitment is to make sense.

Please note that equations 2 and 3 contain exactly the same goods and bads on their right-hand sides. They therefore can only differ in sign if the discount factor for the first period has an exponent k greater than unity, that is, if the discount from the present to the next period is greater than forward discount factors.4 This is the idea at the heart of Strotz's (1955- 56) analysis, expressed here in a simple and transparent fashion that points to a wide variety of applications.

My earlier article (J. Simon 1990) illustrates this machinery with Schelling's vivid example of a woman about to give birth who arranges beforehand for attendants not to give her anesthetic while in labor even if she requests it. Also discussed there are Christmas Club saving, which is very similar to the birth-anesthesia situation; life-cycle savings, which can be explained more neatly and more in consonance with standard theory with this system than with self-control theories;[5] ordinary purchases on credit, most of which (especially minor purchases) are better explained by a kinked (or faster than exponential) discount structure than by credit-market constraints; and a variety of assorted behavior such as binding religious vows and the pathological killer who sends messages to the police saying, "Please catch me."

INTERPERSONAL ALLOCATIONS

Now we move to the individual's decisions about allocation among that individual and other individuals. Again, such decisions are not the exception, just as intrapersonal self-binding decisions in the case of credit purchases are the rule rather than the exception. Rather, every individual who lives in a family and is part of a community makes such allocations as a matter of course.

The conceptual framework employed here obviates the age-old question about whether an act of giving by one individual to another should properly be labeled "altruism," or whether instead one is "really" being "selfish" by making oneself feel good. An individual's discount weights vis-à-vis other individuals may be considered a full description of the individual in this connection, assuming that the individual's behavior corresponds to his or her discounts in relation to other individuals. In this scheme, there is no place for intentions, and hence there are no false intentions. Revealed preferences constitute the entire system.

Because the reader is likely to wish to see the model in operation as soon as possible, reflections about the meaning of the model are deferred until the Discussion section of the article. The analysis concentrates on three illustrative issues: (a) the *charity pledge*, because it illustrates extension of the technical innovation offered here; (b) the *bequest* in the context of life-cycle savings, because it illustrates generalization of the basic idea, as well as itself being an important issue theoretically; and (c) predictions about the effects of *changes in a person's expected lifetime or the set of interpersonal connections*.

PLEDGES

Charities routinely suggest that donors pledge gifts for future payment if they do not wish to make an immediate donation. And many persons do just that. In 1992, 14,665 Harvard College alumni pledged and paid at a later date, whereas 18,864 paid immediately with check, credit card, or securities (Hokanson 1993).

What explains the pledges? Surely it is not mainly that the pledger is reducing cost through future discounting. The greatest number of the gifts to Harvard are sufficiently small that the difference between the current amount and the discounted amount is very small (perhaps even small relative to the time cost of two transactions—pledge and payment, rather than just immediate payment). And if the pledger wishes to reduce the value of the gift by the discount amount, he or she can simply do so by giving a bit less in the present (and the amount less will not much affect the amount of "honor" or satisfaction obtained from the gift).

The explanation that follows views the phenomenon as similar to buying on credit or "with no money down," which involves just one individual's persons in several periods, in that both phenomena work with contractual binding. A pledge is also similar to forswearing anesthesia and to the case of Ulysses, both of which also use the mechanism of self-binding.

Imagine a good of any one of these illustrative types: (a) the harvest from a designated plot in the owner's garden *either* this year *or* next year; (b) an opportunity to spend an afternoon viewing a lovely picture in the possession of its owner for an hour either now or tomorrow at the same time; and (c) a given nominal sum of money (the appropriate discounting is contained within the analysis) either this period or next period. Because the good in question is the same according to its *physical* description in each period, it is written without distinguishing period subscripts; rather, the enjoyment of it is attached to the period in which it occurs.

Now consider three alternative possibilities: (I) consumption of such a good by the *owner in both periods*, (II) a gift by the owner so that *another* individual consumes the good in the *present* period and the *owner* consumes it in the *next* period, and (III) consumption by the *owner* in the *present* period and by the *receiver* of a gift in the *next* period. That is,

$$V^{I}_{i,t=0} = U_{i,t=0}(G) + d^{k}U_{i,t=1}(G), \qquad [5]$$

where U(G) = utility of experience G.

$$V^{II}_{i,t=0} = e_{t=0}U_{j,t=0}(G) + d^{k}U_{i,t=1}(G). \qquad [6]$$

Please note that e has now been given a period subscript because in the current analysis it may differ between periods.

$$V^{III}_{i,t=0} = U_{i,t=0}(G) + e_{t=1}d^{?}U_{j,t=1}(G), \qquad [7]$$

where the question mark indicates that the relative size of the discount factor that the decision maker applies for the other person is not known to us—whether it is larger or smaller than d^k.

For analytic convenience, let us suppose that the present values to the contemporary self-person of the reference individual i are the same for alternatives I and II. But the contemporary self-person is willing to choose III over I, pledging him- or herself to make good on the gift in the next period. That is,

$$V^{I} = V^{II},\ V^{III} > V^{II}, \text{ and } V^{III} > V^{I}. \qquad [8]$$

The aim of the analysis is to make clear why this preference-and-choice system might exist— that is, why the present person might choose now to consume in the present period rather than to give in the present period, yet choose now to give in the next period rather than consume in the next period—and then to draw from the analysis conclusions that may illuminate other decisions.

In order for that alternative III to come about, the owner must bind him- or herself to carry it out; without a pledge, alternative III will seem, when the second period arrives, as II seems now, and the gift-transfer alternative will not come about; that is, without a commitment, III's higher present value than the present value of II or I will not be attained. This is analogous to self-binding decisions of the Strotz-Ainslie-Schelling nature analyzed in the previous section.

Comparison of III to either II or I shows that either the one-period time-discount factor on j's utility (written $d^?$ because it is unknown) is higher than d^k for i's utility, or the interpersonal discount $e_{t=0}$ is greater in the present period than $e_{t=1}$ in the next period (as seen in the present), or the differences are such that the multiplicand of the two discount factors d and e is greater in III than in II. That is, either $d^? > d^{1+k}$ or $e_{t=1} > e_{t=0}$ or both. I shall now show why this inequality is true.

Assume that

$$U_{i,t=1}(G) = U_{i,t=0}(G), \text{ and } U_{j,t=1}(G) = U_{j,t=0}(G)$$

(all as assessed when they would take place). [9]

Subtract II from I (equation 6 from equation 5) to get (as also by definition)

$$U_{i,t=0} = e_{t=0}U_{j,t=0}. \quad [10]$$

Now subtracting I from III (equation 5 from equation 7), substituting $U_{i,t=0}$ for Ui, t = 1, and substituting the left-hand side of equation 10 for the right-hand side, which (after the substitution) appears in the subtraction of III from I, we get

$$d^?e_{t=1} > d^ke_{t=0}. \quad [11]$$

If (11) is true, then either $d^? > d^{1+k}$ or $e_{t=1} > e_{t=0}$ or both. (Because of the confusing nature of the algebra with subscripts, the steps are presented in detail in the appendix.)

To put the matter differently, if we think of the two periods as points on an east-west horizontal time scale and the two persons on a vertical north-south "social" scale, we may think of the present value of a point on that surface as a height above the base. We do not know whether the other-person-next-period point in the height surface is higher than the other two points that enter into the equations because of the slope in the time dimension or because of the slope in the interpersonal dimension, or both. But such knowledge is not vital, at least for the present analysis.

If we were to assume—as may be reasonable—that e remains the same from period to period, then the driving element in the analysis is the difference in d functions that the decision maker holds for him- or herself and for the other person. Given the empirical evidence on the sharp immediate-period discount for animals and humans, it would not be surprising if the discount from the present to, say, the next period is less sharp for the other person's function than for one's own function, following which the function for oneself might be at the same rate (or at a slower rate) than for the other person. This can account for the greater willingness to (commit to) transfer goods to another person in future periods than in the present.

The solicitor of the pledge can read from this analysis a rationale for soliciting a pledge rather than an immediate gift. And the giver of the pledge can read in the analysis the rationale for binding him- or herself to the future gift. Hence they agree that a pledge should take place. The analysis is in this respect quite parallel to the self-binding activities described in the first part of the article. That is, the alternative of making the gift in the future has a higher present value than not making it, or than making it now. Please note the role of the formal pledge to increase the extent to which the commitment is binding.

Politicians' promises have quite the same rationale.

BEQUESTS AND LIFETIME SAVINGS

Assuming (a) diminishing returns, (b) a discount factor less than unity (i.e., a discount *rate* greater than zero), (c) no risk aversion, (d) no bequest motive, and (e) correct assessment of life expectancy on average, we would expect people to run out of money before death, rather than leaving bequests. But instead we do find bequests, on average. Various plausible explanations have been offered (see, e.g., Modigliani 1988; Kotlikoff 1988). Nevertheless, an explanation that is conformable with standing theory seems preferable to an ad hoc theory.

The basic present-value equation 1 suggests that bequests be seen as part of that function, in which case there is no longer reason to think that consumption in the early periods in the life-cycle consumption plan will be at a running-out level. However, first we should ask, Why do people not give the bequests as immediate gifts? Uncertainty about the length of one's life and the possible "need" for consumption funds, that is, a "precautionary motive," have been suggested. As others have pointed out, an individual can avoid this set of problems by purchasing an annuity. Yet the usage of annuities is rare.

The structure of discount factors offers a plausible explanation. The present person first makes an allocation plan that includes a gift to another individual. A planned gift can be of sufficient size to overcome the tilt of consumption toward the present and make the present period's consumption less than E/n, where E is the lifetime endowment and n the expected number of future periods of life—as is observed to be the case. The next step is that the present person observes that actually giving the gift now is less attractive than postponing the giving until at least next period, by exactly the same logic as was shown formally for pledges. The process then repeats each period until death, at which point the bequest is realized.

The fact that a person makes a will is not evidence that the person intends to hold onto the gift throughout his or her life; a will is a precaution against death before plans have been completed, among other possibilities.

The mode of thinking described here is not distinguishable in behavior from the desire to hold onto assets because of the power they bestow over the prospective recipient. But the explanation offered here is more parsimonious and is wholly consistent with standard economic theory, which should make it relatively attractive.

EFFECTS OF CHANGES IN CONDITIONS

The model can help understand, and make predictions about, the allocations that will be made when the claimant periods/persons or their weights are changed exogenously. Here are several examples:

1. If the individual's life expectancy is shortened (lengthened), the allocations to the present and future persons, and to other individuals, will be increased (decreased). If you learn that you may expect to die next month, you are likely to give away some of your books today and treat family and yourself to a fancy dinner.

2. If there is an increase or decrease in the set of individuals whom you feel a responsibility to assist, you will allocate less to each prior claimant. That is, if your prodigal brother-in-law, whom you despise but feel obligated to help, reappears in your life, he will get some of your endowment, and others and yourself will get less. This sort of change is a "move through social distance" (a phrase of Ainslie's) akin to the move through temporal distance that we experience in our lives.

3. A change in the expected lifetime or the number of interpersonal connections is likely to change work effort. For example, the model predicts increased work on the part of the parents when the number of children increases because the wealth of the present person is decreased thereby (because more is being allocated away from the present person). And indeed there is considerable evidence for this hypothesis in data on hours worked per year by both parents and on moonlighting (see review in J. Simon 1988). The mechanism is simply that an additional "claimant" in the utility function decreases the amount the earner spends on him- or herself. This diminished wealth implies greater work effort. (Becker's analysis does not imply such behavior, so far as I can see, because the earner's "social income" is increased by the additional child, and there would therefore seem to be no motive for

increased work. This model may be seen as focusing on the *production* of utility, whereas the Becker-type model focuses on the "consumption" of utility.)

DISCUSSION

1. Viewing the unit of consciousness as composed of continuously extended rings of "interest" or "sympathy" or "empathy" around the core of the self-person, in close analogy to the notion of continuous successive temporal persons, illuminates many phenomena in everyday life. For example, it is not surprising or irrational when an individual endangers or sacrifices his or her life to save the life of his or her child. This way of thinking also mitigates or eliminates the theoretical problem that "in the supply of public goods, far less free-riding actually occurs than traditional theory predicts" (Harrison and Hirshleifer 1989, 201).

Hirshleifer (1985) defines as follows: "[S]omeone is non-self-interested to the extent that he or she attaches utility to the impact of events upon the bodies or psyches of other parties" (p. 55). And he says that if the economist allows a person's "ends in life [to] include the well-being of others [so that] *their* interests become his 'self- interest,' " this becomes "an evasion that robs the concept of self-interest of any distinguishable content" (p. 55). Whether the concept is "robbed" or not I shall not try to say. I hope this article shows that such an inclusion does not get in the way of useful analysis, but rather is crucial for some analyses.

Perhaps I can best bring out this point by comparing the situation to the individual's various periods of life. The periods are treated separately in personal planning, as indicated by the different discount factors applied to them. And as I show at length in my previous paper (J. Simon 1990), much analysis is facilitated by assuming that the period-persons are different, each of them bearing much the same relationship to the current person as do other individuals. Nevertheless, including the "ends" of those future self-persons in one's current planning does not "rob the concept of self-interest of . . . content."

Again, the sharp line between oneself and others is replaced in this analysis by a continuum. In a related view, John Donne wisely says that each person's death *diminishes* "me"—not eliminates, or leaves untouched, but reduces me to some degree. And Adam Smith's earlier quote orders the degree of attachment in the typical case. In the extreme mystic vision a person is one with all humanity—present, future, and past (although one cannot allocate to the past). This might be the vision of the saint who keeps no worldly goods.

Floyd Allport (1965) came to much the same view in the study of social psychology.

> As with the concept of the "group," we . . . find that the very notion of a "thing," instead of being distinct and absolute, is shifting, ambiguous in denotation, misleading as to its singularity, overlapping, relativistic, and blurred. Our understanding of "group" realities depends, therefore, on our finding some suitable substitute for our present concept of an entity or thing. But since a "thing" and what it does, that is to say, the events in which it is involved, has long been one of the very pillars of our notion of causality, this realization leaves us baffled as to where to turn. (p. 30)

Even though, as Hirshleifer (1985) puts it, "in the domain of the family no-one can seriously deny that benevolence plays an overwhelming role" (p. 57), analysis using the concept of individual self-interest gets along just fine. This should demonstrate that self-interest need not be defined as narrowly as Hirshleifer demands it be. This is not to say that for some purposes economic analysis using narrow self-interest may not help us sort out what happens within a family, but rather that in most situations ordinary family caring can be acknowledged without causing difficulty.

Indeed, *most* of a main breadwinner's purchasing power is not spent on his or her own bodily and mental needs. Rather, it is spent on other members of the family, future self-persons and future family members' self-persons, other "gifts," and the government.

There is nothing particularly "natural" about an individualistic focus for analysis. Indeed, Hayek (1989) talks about "instincts of solidarity and altruism" (p.12) and asserts that one of the problems of development is to discipline such instincts. "[C]ontinued obedience to the command to treat all men as neighbours would have prevented the growth of an extended order" (p. 13).

> If we were to apply the unmodified, uncurbed, rules of the micro-cosmos (i.e., of the small band or troop, or of, say, our families) to the macro-cosmos (our wider civilization), as our instincts and sentimental yearnings often make us wish to do, *we would destroy it.* Yet if we were always to apply the rules of the extended order to our more intimate groups, *we would crush them.* So we must learn to live in two sorts of worlds at once. (p. 18, italics in original)

This implies that if economics wishes to apply its logic to both impersonal markets and personal relationships, it ought to adapt its mode of analysis to the context—either (a) markets or (b) the current person's allocation—rather than simply applying the machinery developed for analysing markets to kin-like situations.

2. An observation about the family conveys the flavor of the analysis offered here: Parents spend less on children's clothing than on their own, even

after children are old enough not to outgrow clothes. This suggests that the children's "utility" is discounted relative to the parental allocators', although of course a myriad of other explanations of this phenomenon are possible. (Why, in a traditional household, does the wife spend more for clothes than the husband? I think that many other issues, on which I dare not speculate, come into play here.)

3. A nice illustration of the close analogy between (a) other individuals and (b) the given individual's future persons is shown by the fact that what economists suppose to be altruistic behavior is often enforced by community norms or even the law, indicating that it is not exceptional. For example, the traditional male breadwinner is legally required to allocate assets to his wife and children even if divorced. And ethics require a variety of contributions of time, energy, and money to the welfare of neighbors and coworkers in need.

The commonality between the intertemporal and interpersonal situations also is illuminated by the interventions of the law in the dispositions of an individual's assets over time. Social Security is a leading example; one is required to make provision for one's future self-persons. (It would be interesting to compare what the law requires in private-scheme countries such as Chile.) Another example is unemployment insurance. Also relevant are laws regulating the wearing of seat belts and motorcycle helmets, underage drinking, enforcing housing codes with respect to, for example, wiring safety even in owner-occupied homes, and involuntary commitment to the hospital (paid for by the person being committed) if a person does not take care of oneself properly or even if—sin of sins—one is not prudent in guarding one's money.

4. Concerning the principle "Charity begins at home" as a precept: There are advantages to the public at large if individuals focus their charitable attention close to home rather than farther from home. This is analogous to a decentralized economic system, which takes advantage of people's extensive knowledge of both nearby resources and needs and people's ability to monitor the workings of businesses that they observe firsthand either as owners or as consumers. Similarly, charity close to home can be more efficient than charity farther away because of one's ability to know which individuals and organizations have the need for more resources—that is, which ones are suffering from lack of resources—as well as which individuals and organizations make effective use of the resources that they receive, rather than wasting them. You can know much more about a family that belongs to your lodge, whose main breadwinner has just died and whose talented child cannot afford violin lessons, than you can about a family a 1,000 or 10,000 miles away whom you have never met. And you can check that the local family is not spending what they receive on expensive mail solicitations to

obtain even more money, most of it going to the professional fund-raisers. You cannot easily obtain the same information about Greenpeace or the Hunger Project; even their annual reports are hard to interpret.[6]

Does a close-to-home policy mean that richer communities give "too little" aid to poorer communities? Yes, there is such a danger. Assets are not distributed evenly or at random, and the person "closest to the home" of a wealthy person is not likely to be the person in greatest need of charity. This is the rationale underlying Combined Charities, United Way, and their like. However, even these omnibus organizations concentrate on local charities. It is an interesting question how far afield such an umbrella charity collector *should* go, and in what proportions relative to distance.

Furthermore, the improvement of communications all over the world means that now it is easier to have firsthand or reliable secondhand knowledge of needs and capacities much farther away than in the past. The key issue is not geographic propinquity. Closeness on other dimensions such as religious or ethnic characteristics can fill the same role. And it is easier to obtain reliable information about people related to you in such ways than it is about complete strangers. In this fashion it is possible to avoid confining your loyalties and resources to well-off people geographically close to you.

Shoveling the next-door neighbor's snow is not efficient, so the pattern has evolved to doing your own sidewalk except in an emergency.

5. Differences in concern for animals that more or less closely resemble us—gorillas, for example, as compared with moles—suggest an instinctive basis for allocational weights.

6. Paragraph 1 above points to an important distinction between public and private allocation. Hayek's point that to develop a modern, extended society we must learn to deny our instinctive urges to favor those close to us pertains to public allocation. A moral government treats all individuals alike. But an individual putatively does best by *not* treating all persons alike, as in charity begins at home. (Bentham's utilitarianism often falls into confusion by failing to make this distinction.)

7. Individuals often recommend or implore other individuals (such as parents urging their children) to make gifts to third persons. This is consistent with the idea that there is a lesser discount in the reference person's mind between the second individual and the third than there is between the reference individual and the second individual, although the connection is not logically tight. (There also is an analogy here to politicians freely disposing of other people's tax moneys in welfare programs.)

8. The framework suggested here could give economics a better image with the public. The individualism model contrasts "greed" and selfishness

versus altruism. It invites glorification of the state, which supposedly acts nonselfishly, "idealistically." However, in the model described here, private economic maximization seems kindly and loving and cooperative because it takes full account of allocation beyond the legal individual. It does away with the idea of "contributing" to an abstract society in order to feel like a good person; instead, it includes such acts as part of the standard behavior.

9. It might be fruitful to study some cases in which convicted persons, such as spies, accept longer prison sentences for themselves in exchange for shorter or no prison sentences for spouses; the interpersonal discount factor may be surprisingly small. Such cases would be particularly illuminating because the currency of one's time is not subject to the complication, which exists with money, that one person has more of it than another and therefore has a lower marginal utility for it. And such cases may be quite analogous with a person allocating prison time (or other restriction on freedom such as a commitment to work) among present and future time periods, for example, "I'll work a month for you next year if you'll free me from a week's work now so I can be with my beloved, or finish my book."

10. It might be fruitful to systematically compare the probabilities of death of a person who might save the life of another, and of the savee, in various relationships—father and son, lifeguard and anonymous swimmer, passerby and anonymous swimmer, and so on.

11. One wonders: Are there normative extensions to this model? The answer is negative, I believe. It may be that explicit consideration of the structure of discount factors across individuals and through time may improve the consistency of allocation, the way in which explicit financial planning may help a person attain one's temporal allocation goals. But anything beyond that would require bringing additional constraints into the model, which have not yet been required by the discussion until now.

12. The interpretation of human behavior that is involved in the analysis here matters for both behavior and feeling. First note Hutcheson's ([1725/1738] 1991) analysis of the cause of giving:

> Whence the conjunction of interest between the parent and child? Do the child's sensations give pleasure or pain to the parent? Is the parent hungry, thirsty, sick, when his children are so? No; but his naturally implanted desire of their good, and aversion to their misery, makes him be affected with joy or sorrow from their pleasures or pains. This desire then is antecedent to the conjunction of interest, and the cause of it, not the effect: it then must be disinterested. (p. 279)

Then he analyses it philosophically:

> Is there then a natural disposition in every man to love his like, to wish well

not only to his individual self, but to any other like rational or sensitive being? and this disposition strongest, where there is the greatest likeness in the more noble qualities? If all this is called by the name self-love; be it so. (p. 279)

Nonetheless, the concept of altruism as self-interest is not just a matter of tautology, as Hutcheson suggests it is; it also affects the outlook of people who come to believe it, as this quotation from the autobiography of a Japanese young man shows:

I finally put my doubts to Matsue Yaichiro. I thought he was probably the most sincere of the students at the academy. I asked him this question: "I recognize your sincerity. When you speak of devoting your life to the country and to the service of our people, do you do this without any thought of self at all, without any idea of bringing honor to your own name? I wish you would reveal your true feelings to me." Matsue laughed aloud and said, "Doesn't everybody think about his own reputation? Isn't that why people do what they do? My reputation means everything to me." That was his reply. On hearing it I was startled: was it that way even with him? "Well," I asked, "what about Iichiro-san?" He was emphatic in his answer: "Why, Iichiro-san is even more concerned with fame than we are." When he saw how disappointed I was, he tried to reassure me. "It's best not to worry too much about unnecessary matters like this," he said. "A man is born in the world, achieves something, and builds a fine reputation; then he dies. That is enough. You shouldn't worry any further." But these reassurances didn't console me in the slightest. I thought to myself that it was elegant and splendid to die for one's country and for one's people. But if you did so just to build up your own fame, wasn't it only another form of egoism?

So-called "idealists" of this sort seemed to me no better than butchers who labeled dog meat as lamb. In fact, if this was really true of Iichiro-san, shouldn't he be exposed too? As a result of all this I became dogmatic and arrogant. I despised not only my fellow students, but even my teacher. And then, by extension, all the great heroes, the men of high purpose of former and present times: they too became objects of my contempt. After a while I began to examine myself as well. . . . If I were to despise my fellow students, I had no choice but to go on to despise myself. Right. I too was despicable. As a result I was without hope, deep in melancholy, and unable to sleep or eat. (Toten 1982, 14-15)

This idea can lead to people reducing the coefficients on the social relationships in the belief that there is no moral basis for having relatively high coefficients of giving to others; this might explain the attitudes of economists, so different than other groups in this respect (although philosophers were not studied), as reported by Marwell and Ames (1981).

SUMMARY

Gifts and bequests have seemed anomalous in economic theory. The article offers a framework within which such allocations cause no more difficulty than does intertemporal allocation of lifetime resources within a given individual's lifetime, which economists routinely deal with theoretically. The essence of the matter is to place on the same footing the allocation of the available resources for consumption among (a) the current person, (b) future self-persons who are legally and physically the same individual who is allocating, and (c) other individuals at present and in the future. That is, instead of a one-dimensional point for the maximizing unit, or even the two-dimensional individual who allocates intertemporally, this model envisages a three-dimensional surface, the interpersonal "distance" dimension replacing the concept of altruism.

The key intellectual obstacle is that economists conventionally take the legal-physical individual throughout his or her lifetime, or just a disconnected single chunk of that life, as the entity of analysis.

A key element in both purely intertemporal allocations and in (at least some) mixed intertemporal-interpersonal allocations is the assumption (first used by Strotz in this connection) that the allocational discount between the current conscious "person" and future "self-persons" within the same individual is greater than the discount between other equal-length forward periods within the same individual. A related element is that the discount also is greater between the current conscious person and other individuals than among other individuals at different psychic distances from the current self-person. Applying a conventional present-value framework to evaluate utility, as seen at various decision-making moments, then makes sense of the phenomena under discussion.

In comparison to analyses that require additional assumptions about individual psychology, this mode of analysis has the advantage that it sticks strictly to the conventional concepts of economic analysis rather than requiring concepts that are not conformable with standard theory. Also, it does not need to distinguish between "self-forced" plans and much ordinary economic behavior, and it thereby points up that "self-control" situations are not abnormal. The article views temptation, regret, sacrifice, and similar phenomena as cases of externalities, and it uses conventional theory to deal with them.

This conceptual framework obviates the age-old question about whether an act of giving by one individual to another should properly be labeled "altruism," or whether instead one is "really" being "selfish" by making oneself feel good. An individual's discount weights vis-à-vis other individuals may be considered a full description of the individual in this connection, assuming that the individual's behavior corresponds to his or her stated discounts vis-à-vis other individuals. In this scheme, there is no place for intentions, and hence there are no false intentions. Preferences, revealed and stated, constitute the entire system.

APPENDIX

Here are details of the derivation of the proposition that either $d^? > d^{1+k}$ or $e_{t=1} > e_{t=0}$ or both.

Subtracting option II from option I (whose values are equal by assumption)

$$V^{I}_{i,t=0} = U_{i,t=0}(G) + d^{k}U_{i,t=1}(G) \qquad [5]$$

$$V^{II}_{i,t=0} = e_{t=0}U_{j,t=0}(G) + d^{k}U_{i,t=1}(G). \qquad [6]$$

$$0 = U_{i,t=0} - e_{t=0}U_{j,t=0}, \text{ or}$$

$$U_{i,t=0} = e_{t=0}U_{j,t=0}.$$

The right side of the above equation is (10) used below.

Now subtracting I from III

$$V^{III}_{i,t=0} = U_{i,t=0}(G) + e_{t=1}d^{?}U_{j,t=1}(G) \qquad [7]$$

$$V^{I}_{i,t=0} = U_{i,t=0}(G) + d^{k}U_{i,t=1}(G) \qquad [5]$$

$$e_{t=1}d^{?}U_{j,t=1} > d^{k}U_{i,t=1}$$

because (by assumption in text) $V^{III}_{i,t=0} > V^{I}_{i,t=0}$.

Using the inequality just above

$$e_{t=1}d^{?}U_{j,t=1} > d^{k}U_{i,t=0} \text{ remembering that } U_{i,t} = U_{i,t=1}$$

and using

$$U_{i,t=0} = e_{t=0}U_{j,t=0}, \qquad [10]$$

we get

$$e_{t=1}d^{?}U_{j,\,t=1} > d^{k}e_{t=0}U_{j,\,t=0}.$$

Hence

$$e_{t=1}d^{?} > d^{k}e_{t=0},$$

which is the proposition of interest to us.

NOTES

1. I agree with Mueller that much such behavior can best be understood by seeing it as driven rather than as chosen, although I guess that much of it is hardwired genetically in humans as it is in animals rather than being entirely learned. I concur with the viewpoint expressed by Frances Hutcheson in point 12 in the Discussion section.

2. This section draws on J. Simon (1990). Anyone familiar with that piece should skip the next two sections to Interpersonal Allocations.

3. Smith continues:

> This sympathy, too, and the affections which are founded on it, are by nature more strongly directed towards his children than towards his parents. . .
>
> The earliest friendships, the friendships which are naturally contracted when the heart is most susceptible of that feeling, are those among brothers and sisters. Their good agreement, while they remain in the same family, is necessary for its tranquillity and happiness. They are capable of giving more pleasure or pain to one another than to the greater part of other people. . .
>
> The children of brothers and sisters are naturally connected by the friendship which, after separating into different families, continues to take place between their parents. Their good agreement improves the enjoyment of that friendship—their discord would disturb it. As they seldom live in the same family, however, though of more importance to one another than to the greater part of other people, they are of much less than brothers and sisters. As their mutual sympathy is less necessary, so it is less habitual, and, therefore, proportionably weaker.
>
> The children of cousins, being still less connected, are of still less importance to one another; and the affection gradually diminishes as the relation grows more and more remote. . .
>
> A father is apt to be less attached to a child who, by some accident, has been separated from him in its infancy, and who does not return to him till it is grown up to manhood.

> Among well-disposed people the necessity of conveniency of mutual accommodation very frequently produces a friendship not unlike that which takes place among those who are born to live in the same family. Colleagues in office, partners in trade, call one another brothers, and frequently feel towards one another as if they really were so. . .
>
> Even the trifling circumstance of living in the same neighbourhood has some effect of the same kind. We respect the face of a man whom we see every day, provided he has never offended us.
>
> The same principles that direct the order in which individuals are recommended to our beneficence, direct that likewise in which societies are recommended to it. . .

> The state of sovereignty in which we have been born and educated, and under the protection of which we continue to live, is, in ordinary cases, the greatest society upon whose happiness or misery our good or bad conduct can have much influence. It is accordingly by nature most strongly recommended to us. . .
>
> Every independent state is divided into many different orders and societies, each of which has its own particular powers, privileges, and immunities. Every individual is naturally more attached to his own particular order or society than to any other. His own interest, his own vanity, the interest and vanity of many of his friends and companions, are commonly a good deal connected with it: he is ambitious to extend its privileges and immunities—he is zealous to defend them against the encroachments of every other order or society. (Smith [1759] 1976, 359, 360, 361, 362, 366, 371, 372, 376)

4. I hold no brief for any particular shape of discount function— including the exponential— for any particular set of periods in the future. The kinked shape used here is purely for convenience in discrete analysis. I have been persuaded by the writings of Herrnstein (1981) and Ainslie and Haendel (1983) that the hyperbolic function makes the most sense for many animal and human experiments, and that the "matching law" . . . I am even willing to agree that negative time discounting fits some facts, for example, "Deliver it tomorrow instead of today, because I can't find a place to put it today" or "I'll enjoy it more after I finish the day's work," and even across persons, "You take it; I've gotten too old to use it" or "It's more fun to watch you do it than to try to do it myself." Securities markets give us some general ideas about time-discount factors of one sort, but we need not assume them to hold in all circumstances of life. (See Loewenstein and Elster 1992 for an authoritative collection of writings on the subject of the discount factor in relationship to individuals' decisions.)

Willingness to admit a wide variation of time discounts makes easier the analogy to relationship discounts. I (and Adam Smith, almost surely) do not assume a fixed relationship between kinship or geography and degree of sympathy, but assume instead that there are tendencies in those respects and that sympathy is not independent of kinship or other measures of social distance. And there may even be negative sympathies for some relationships, for example, a parent torturing a child, as there may be negative time discounts in some cases. But this need not fall into circularity by defining social distance by degree of exhibited sympathy as long as objective factors have *some* predictive power.

5. Deily and Reed (1993) offer an interesting theory that takes explicit account of the stock of willpower and the cost of using it. Nevertheless, that theory seems less applicable to the important everyday problems of saving, credit, charity pledges, and the like than to such behavior as eating and drinking.

6. However, you can be sure that many such charities transfer much less than half of what they receive to the supposed objects of charity; the occasional exposés of these frauds are sickening.

REFERENCES

Ainslie, George. 1975. Specious reward: A behavioral theory of impulsiveness and impulse control. *Psychological Bulletin* 82 (4): 463-96.

Ainslie, George, and Varda Haendel. 1983. The motives of the will. In *Etiological aspects of alcohol and drug abuse*, edited by Eward Gottheil, Keith A. Druley, Thomas E. Skoloda, and Howard M. Waxman, 119-39. Springfield, IL: Charles C Thomas.

Allport, Floyd H. 1965. Logical complexities of group activity. In *Philosophical problems of the social sciences*, edited by David Braybrooke, 27-30. New York: Macmillan.

Baron, Jonathan. 1988. *Thinking and deciding*. Cambridge: Cambridge University Press.

Becker, Gary S. 1981. *A treatise on the family*. Cambridge, MA: Harvard University Press.

Becker, Gary S., and Robert J. Barro. 1988. A reformulation of the economic theory of fertility. *Quarterly Journal of Economics* 103 (February): 1-25.

Camerer, Colin. 1988. Gifts as economic signals and social symbols. *American Journal of Sociology* 94:S180-214.

Chicago Daily News. 1971. 25-26 December.

Coursey, Don L. 1994. The revealed demand for a public good: Evidence from endangered and threatened species. Harris School Working Paper no. 84-2, University of Chicago.

Deily, Mary E., and W. Robert Reed. 1993. Temptation, willpower, and the problem of rational self-control. *Rationality and Society* 5 (October): 455-72.

Elster, Jon. 1979. *Ulysses and the sirens*. Cambridge: Cambridge University Press.

———, ed. 1986. *The multiple self*. Cambridge: Cambridge University Press.

Harrison, Glenn W., and Jack Hirshleifer. 1989. An experimental evaluation of weakest link/best shot models of public goods. *Journal of Political Economy* 97:201-25.

Hayek, Friedrich A. 1989. *The fatal conceit*. Chicago: University of Chicago Press.

Herrnstein, Richard J. 1981. Self control as response strength. In *Quantification of steady-state operant behavior*, edited by C. M. Bradshaw, E. Szabadi, and C. F. Lowe, 3-20. Amsterdam: Elsevier/North-Holland.

Hirshleifer, Jack. 1985. The expanding domain of economics. *American Economic Review* 75 (December): 53-68.

———. 1987. *Economic behaviour in adversity*. Chicago: University of Chicago Press.

Hokanson, Kimberly A. 1993. Letter to author, 9 September.

Hutcheson, Francis. 1991. An inquiry into the original of our ideas of beauty and virtue (1725/1738). Excerpted in *British moralists 1650-1800*, edited by D. D. Raphael, 261-99. Indianapolis, IN: Hackett.

James, William. [1890] 1950. *The principles of psychology*. 2 vols. Reprint, New York: Dover.

Kotlikoff, Laurence J. 1988. Intergenerational transfers and savings. *The Journal of Economic Perspectives* 2 (spring): 41-58.

Loewenstein, George, and Jon Elster. 1992. *Choice over time*. New York: Russell Sage.

Marwell, Gerald, and Ruth E. Ames. 1981. Economists free ride, does anyone else? *Journal of Public Economics* 15:295-310.

Milgram, Stanley. 1975. *Obedience to authority*. New York: Harper & Row.

Miller, Arthur. 1987. *Timebends: A life*. New York: Harper & Row.

Modigliani, Franco. 1988. The role of intergenerational transfers and life cycle saving in the accumulation of wealth. *The Journal of Economic Perspectives* 2 (spring): 15-40.

Mueller, Dennis C. 1986. Rational egoism versus adaptive egoism as fundamental postulate for a descriptive theory of human behavior. *Public Choice* 51:3-23.

Mulligan, Casey Bryant. 1993. On intergenerational altruism, fertility, and the persistence of economic status. Ph.D. diss., University of Chicago.

Parfit, Derek. 1984. *Reasons and persons*. London: Oxford University Press.

Schelling, Thomas C. 1984a. The intimate contest for self-command. In his *Choice and consequence*, 57-82. Cambridge, MA: Harvard University Press.

———. 1984b. Self-command in practice, in policy, and in a theory of rational choice (Richard T. Ely lecture). *American Economic Review* 74 (May): 1-11.

Sen, Amartya. 1977. Rational fools: A critique of the behavioral foundations of economic theory. *Philosophy and Public Affairs* summer:317-44.

Sidgwick, Henry. [1907] 1962. *The methods of ethics*. 7th ed. Reprint, Chicago: University of Chicago Press.

Simon, Herbert A. 1990. A mechanism for social selection and successful altruism. *Science*, 21 December, 1665-68.

Simon, Julian L. 1988. *Effort, opportunity, and wealth*. Cambridge: Basil Blackwell.

———. 1990. The theory of binding commitments simplified and extended, with generalization to interpersonal allocation. *Rationality and Society* 2 (3): 287-309.

Smith, Adam. [1759] 1976. *The theory of moral sentiments*. Reprint, Indianapolis, IN: Liberty.

Strotz, Robert. 1955-56. Myopia and inconsistency in dynamic utility maximization. *Review of Economic Studies* 23 (3): 165-80.

Thaler, Richard H., and H. M. Shefrin. 1981. An economic theory of self-control. *Journal of Political Economy* 89 (April): 392-406.

Toten, Miyazaki. 1982. *My thirty-three years' dream*. Autobiography. Translated, with an introduction, by Eto Shinkichi and Marius B. Jansen. Princeton: Princeton University Press.

Williams, Bernard. 1984. "Personal identity," a review of Parfit. *London Review of Books*, 7-20 June, 141.

[19]

Foreword

The decision tree (dynamic programming) is beautifully elegant mathematically. But when you come to implement it in a multi-period context, large difficulties arise.

When I sent this fragment to Robert Schlaifer, he replied (sometime in the early 1970s or late 1960s):

> Dear Mr Simon:
>
> I have great sympathy for your worries over the various problems you discuss in your letter of October 19 because I have worried over most of them myself and come to no answers that are at all satisfactory for practice. We even developed some special vocabulary to use in worrying publicly, e.g., the "value of immediate resolution" of a gamble.
>
> One of the only two things of which I feel sure is negative, viz. that it does *not* make sense to talk about a person's having more than one preference function. His one and only preference function must in one way or another assign a single value to every possible *complete* outcome of an act, even if this complete outcome consists of a great many elements such as cash flows at various points in time and also of what we have called (almost exactly like you) "joy and sorrow along the way."
>
> The other thing of which I feel certain is that the preference function must depend exclusively on decisions (real or hypothetical) which a person would make *now*. If a decision affects a person's future as well as his present state, he will of course want to consider how he may feel in the future before reaching a decision now; but that is quite different from basing the preference function on future choices.

Reflections on utility functions, time preference, and dynamic programming

The literature on decision-making under uncertainty with dynamic programming does not seem to provide a way to handle time preference. That is, no guidance has yet been offered for choosing the appropriate utility functions when time preference and the sequence of decision will affect the utility function (over and above the individual's tastes for risk at a point in time). This note contains some reflections on the problem.

First let us consider a situation in which there is *only one* payoff but *you will not know until a year after you make the investment* which payoff you will receive. The nub of the situation is that one cannot know for a year whether to plan on the funds, and (for a going business) how to plan for the employment of the labor force and plant.

There are two major reasons why the year's uncertainty makes the situation less attractive than if the payoff were known immediately. First, one is less able to make plans for one's long-run affairs. The point needs no expansion. Second, one cannot adjust one's consumption over one's lifetime as well as if one now knew what would happen. The explanation is as follows: Imagine a poor person who learns tomorrow that he has received an inheritance of $50,000. He may now decide to buy a new car this year. He may therefore spend $2,000 of it this year, and budget the rest of the inheritance for savings and expenditures in the rest of his life. But if he might or *might not* receive an inheritance of $50,000 a year from now, he does not have as much freedom of maneuver and he is likely not to buy the car this year. If he does receive the inheritance after a year, he will then budget the entire $50,000 for the years after that. But this year he will not have had the opportunity to take advantage of the inheritance, and hence the deferring of the information for a year makes the later inheritance less worthwhile now.[1]

A utility function is needed to construct a certainty equivalent here. But it is far from clear just what the utility function should represent in this situation. In my judgment, the appropriate utility function must reflect your feelings and tastes *at the point in time when the payoff would be known as well as at present*. In other words, for each possible payoff you must ask yourself, "In light of my situation now *and* in light of what I think my situation will be one year from now, and assuming I could have (say) a 0.95 chance to get $50,000, a 0.04 chance to get $10,000, and a 0.01 chance to get nothing, how much for sure would I be willing to pay *now* so that I could have the investment change *at that time*?" I reason that the decision is being made *now*, so your present tastes and financial situation certainly must be allowed to affect the decision. But the impact will be felt a year from now, so it makes sense that your tastes and financial situation *then* – including any other expected cash flows in the meantime – should *also* be reflected. Perhaps the most crucial part is that you should ask yourself how much you would pay *now* for the uncertain outcomes *then*, rather than asking how much you would pay *then* for the uncertain outcomes then. I argue for the former because you must *decide* now, and it seems to me that you can make a more realistic judgment when thinking about actions you are about to take right now. That is, to ask yourself how much you would pay *now* seems operationally closer to your real decision than asking how much you would pay then when you will not have any real decisions to make.

But one further adjustment must be made: The certain sum you decide you would pay now must be *compounded* (the inverse of discounting) to find the value of that sum *then* that is equal to the sum *now*. And of course the appropriate compounding rate is the riskless rate, because it is a sum without uncertainty. For example, if you would pay $1,000 now for the set of uncertain outcomes that someone offers you a year from now, you should compare the expected utility of that set of outcomes against $1,000 × 1.05 (if 1.05 is the riskless rate) to see which is larger.

It may be possible to make just as sensible judgments by thinking about how much you would pay *then* for the uncertain outcomes *then*. The certainty equivalent would then embody both the allowance for risk *and* the allowance for time preference. But I think this latter procedure is less close to the operational realities, and also will be more difficult to work with in more complex situations.

One thing *is* certain: Any system of allowing for risk with a certainty equivalent when time preference is involved is philosophically and psychologically complicated, and it is quite possible that the different ways of looking at the situation will arrive at different conclusions. For example, because of the complexity of the effects on one's life situation of not knowing for a year which payoff one would receive, there is not likely to be any simple relationship between the utility function now and the utility function a year from now.[2]

At the very least, even if the person's other wealth and life situation stays the same throughout the year, there is more uncertainty about his entire lifetime financial situation, and less ability to plan and insure, if the payoff will not be known for a year. So, the utility function for a payoff to be known a year from now would probably show more risk aversion than a utility function for a payoff now, all other things being equal. The uncertainty and risk are different, and hence the appropriate adjustments will be different.

Next, let us consider a situation in which there will be payoffs in *several* successive periods. The key issue is whether the use of utility functions for the end points in period k (at some time after $t = 0$) as constructed and figured with in period $k - 1, k - 2, \ldots k = 0$, is the appropriate way to account for all the future uncertainty when making a decision in period $k - 1, k - 2, \ldots k = 0$. One thing is clear: Such a calculation makes no allowance for the decision-maker's feelings *along the way*. Of course the decision-maker could try to appraise the amount of intermediate risk when constructing his utility functions for end points, but there is no systematic evaluation and incorporation of the intermediate risk in the calculation. It is as if one considered how well one would like being at one set of vacation spots or another set of vacation spots (when you're not sure which one you will reach *within* a given set if you choose it), without making allowance for the fact that the trip to some vacation spots may be much rougher than the trip to others. Now it might be that the variation among the final positions, taken into account with the end-point utility functions, might embody much or all of the uncertainty along the way – but I have no theoretical reason to assume that it does. I shall simply hope that not explicitly taking into account the intermediate uncertainty will not lead to decisions very different than if it were taken into account in some more proper way. But we should at least be clear on the fact that paths with different risk configurations could lead to the same final distribution of end points.

The shape of the utility function ought to depend upon the person's position in life, that is, upon his needs and the way he perceives his needs. But discussion of the utility function at just a *single point in time* usually asserts that the meaning of an additional dollar to a person depends upon how many dollars he already has, i.e., upon his wealth. So the utility of additional funds is seen to depend on these *two* factors, wealth and need. Now, the common way to simplify the analysis is to assume that the utility function depends only upon the individual's wealth, and *not* upon his needs and perception of them. If one makes this assumption, then one may proceed to use the same utility function in the analysis no matter at which date the payoff will be received, assuming his wealth will be the same at those times.

Obviously, it is not true to life, however, to assume that the utility of additional funds does not depend upon the person's life situation. One can imagine a male college student married two years with two children, $2,000 in the bank and a tiny income of $3,000 a year, saying: "Getting 20 dollars (or $1,000) would mean a lot more to me than when I was a bachelor, even though I did not then have a dime in the bank and had the same tiny income of $3,000." Similarly, you can imagine a man whose kids have finished college saying: "I don't have much in the bank now, not even the $2,000 I had when I got married, and far much less than I had before my kids started college. And my income is lower now than it has been in the past. But an additional 20 dollars (or $1,000) would mean a lot less to me now than it would have in either of those two earlier periods."

It seems to me that whether you choose to use a single utility function for all future periods, or whether you choose to construct separate ones for separate future periods, should probably depend on the following factors: (1) How much of a time span the analysis will cover. A shorter time span can more reasonably be viewed with a single utility function. (2) How much your life circumstances are expected to change over the period of analysis. More radical changes such as getting married, expanding the size of your family, or finishing up some obligations, may make big changes in your perceived needs. (3) How anxious you are to avoid the extra complication in the analysis of constructing separate utility functions.

Constructing separate utility functions would be very time-consuming because of the need for preparing a separate utility function for the set of end points for each choice point. But unless one wishes to make simplifying assumptions, one is simply stuck with this difficulty – if one wishes to make a thorough analysis. The apparently simplifying assumption (implicitly made by some writers) that the owner's utility function is the same at all times, no matter how his finances change or are expected to change in the course of the activity's progress is, in a very important way, unrealistic and inappropriate. If the decision-maker's utility function would be much the same no matter how his finances changed over the course of the business career, then he cannot be a person who is much affected by the risks of this venture. In that case, his personal utility function may be very close to a straight line for the sums involved on this project, i.e., he is then a person who needs no discount for his feelings about risk. On the other hand, it would not be sensible to assume that one should therefore make no allowance for risk. Even if the individual is not risk-averse here, he surely prefers to get as high a return as possible on his money, and therefore this project should be compared to investments available to the securities markets *with the same amount of risk*.

Much additional thought will be required before dynamic programming with utility functions and certainty equivalents is sufficiently understood.

Notes

1. This point stems from the lifetime consumption hypothesis of Modigliani *et al.* See Volume One, Chapter 32.
2. One may wonder whether such a relationship could be deduced from the life-cycle consumption hypothesis. Maybe. But I doubt the usefulness of the attempt.

PART IV

POPULATION ECONOMICS

[20]

Foreword

For two years or so around 1968, late each evening I would wander around the living room and kitchen and puzzle how to reconcile Malthus's view of innovation as a cause of increasing population growth, and Boserup's view of innovation as a result of population growth. Boserup's model of population-pushed adoption of techniques from an already existing reservoir of technology is not consistent with observed ups and downs in the standard of living – perhaps most notably in Ireland in the decades around the Famine, and in Europe in the centuries before and after the Black Death. Finally I realized that Malthus and Boserup had in mind different sorts of innovations. This paper shows how the analyses of both Malthus and Boserup are correct descriptions for particular types of innovations, and how together they convey a more general and sound (though more complex) picture of the overall process of demographic-economic growth than either alone.

This article originally contained (as presented here) both the theoretical analysis and an application of the analysis to a set of historical examples. A wide variety of journals rejected the article, and I therefore decided to include the material in a compressed form in my 1977 book. Then the opportunity to edit the series *Research in Population Economics* presented itself – which role I took on in considerable part to have a guaranteed outlet for one or more pieces of my work in each annual. I split this article into the historical material which went into the book, and the formal analysis which went into *RPE* I. (I also ran two other pieces of mine in *RPE* I, one with a co-author, but under a pen-name so that the volume would not look as if it were simply a vehicle for publishing my own stuff – which to some extent it actually was.)

3

An Integration of the Invention-Pull and Population-Push Theories of Economic-Demographic History

PREFACE

This essay integrates (a) the view of Malthus, that a new invention is immediately followed by a population increase that eventually ''eats up'' the benefits of the invention until the population returns to subsistence living, with (b) the view of Boserup, that inventions are only used when population pressure increases to the extent that it is worthwhile to adopt the new invention. The explanation hinges on the nature of inventions, which may be of various sorts; some inventions fit Malthus's view and some Boserup's. The argument is given geometrically and by numerical illustrations, and historical examples of both sorts of inventions are provided.

This essay was the result of two years of late-night wrestling (about 1970) with the puzzle of how Malthus and Boserup could both be right in their theoretical analyses—as they both are. As is so often in such debates, the contending parties focus on different phenomena. And when one distinguishes the separate phenomena and finds different explanations for them, one has a better and fuller picture of the overall situation.

There has been a recent spate of work on the general subject of reconciling Malthus and Boserup, including articles by Lee (1989), Darity (1980), and Pryor and Maurer (1982), but none of it directly articulates with this essay.

The present form of this essay recombines the formal theoretical framework and the historical support, originally part of a whole separated by the vagaries of publication requirements.

PROBABLY before, and certainly since Malthus, the established theory of the growth of human populations has been that which Baumol labeled ''the magnificent dynamics.'' The associated hypothesis about demographic-economic history, which will be called ''invention-pull'' in this chapter, suggests that

Reprinted from *Research in Population Economics* and *The Economics of Population Growth*.

I am grateful to Ester Boserup, Nathaniel Leff, and Harold F. Williamson for thoughtful and useful criticism. James Millar introduced me to Chayanov's writings, and Larry Neal referred me to White's account of plow history.

from time to time, independently of population growth, inventions appear which increase productive capacity and provide subsistence to more people. According to the Malthusian hypothesis, population then increases to use this new capacity until all the productive potential has been exhausted, and thus, the history of population growth is only the reflection of the history of autonomous inventions.

In 1965, Boserup published a lengthy statement of a diametrically opposite point of view, here called the ''population-push'' hypothesis. This hypothesis asserts that though production-increasing inventions may occur independently of the prior rate of population growth, the adoption of ''new'' knowledge depends upon population growth. Hence in the population-push hypothesis, population growth directly *causes* changes in productive techniques, and indirectly causes further population increase—a self-sustaining deterministic process. This hypothesis is found implicitly in von Thunen's classic economic analysis of the interrelationships of agricultural method and location [(1826) 1966]. The economic elements of the analysis, along with a wealth of supporting data for the peasant economy of Russia, are given very explicitly by Chayanov [(1925) 1966]. The hypothesis was used in geographic analysis of the tropics by Gourou (1966), in the explanation of European agricultural history by Slicher van Bath (1963), and probably by other writers of whom I am not aware. It was Boserup's contribution, however, to have developed the idea and thrust it forward for our attention at this time.

Whereas the Malthusian invention-pull hypothesis is a single-influence explanation of history, the population-push hypothesis sees two forces at work: (1) independent invention occurring sometime prior to its adoption; and (2) population growth leading to adoption of previously unused existing knowledge. The causes of the inventions are not central in either hypothesis.

The two hypotheses imply very different judgments about population growth. The invention-pull hypothesis sees nothing good or necessary about population growth, either in past history or (by implication) in the future. But the population-push hypothesis views population growth as necessary, though not sufficient, for economic growth.

The aim of this chapter is to formally explicate the invention-pull and population-push hypotheses and the economic mechanisms that presumably underlie them, to make more precise the examination of their claims to explain economic-demographic history. The main finding is that the apparent conflict between the hypotheses is illusory. The conflict results from failure to distinguish between the types of inventions to which each of the two hypotheses does and does not apply. Put crudely now, both hypotheses make microeconomic sense if (a) the invention-pull hypothesis is restricted to inventions that are purely labor-saving relative to established practice; and (b) the population-push hypothesis is restricted to inventions that have no labor-saving advantages at the time of invention but can produce *higher* levels of output with relatively less labor per unit of output (though absolutely more labor per person) than the existing technology; hence such inventions come to be used later on as population grows. Together the two hypotheses constitute *complementary* explanations of complementary elements, rather than being substitute hypotheses. And taken together in this way, they constitute a more general and more satisfying explanation of demographic-economic history in subsistence-agriculture situations than does either hypothesis alone.

The argument can also be phrased another way: Any invention increases the choices available to the farmer. But inventions can be of two sorts: (a) compared to the technology in use at present, the invention may produce the same output with the same amount of land and with less labor (a better calendar is an example); or (b) though *at present* the invention will not produce more output with the same labor and land than the presently used alternative technology, at the *higher* rates of output that would be necessary at a higher population density the invention *will* produce more output than the alternative method with given amounts of labor and land (an example is multiple cropping when shifting agriculture is being practiced and where output is still plentiful). An invention must do one *or* the other or it is not useful (putting capital requirements aside for now).

If an invention is of the sort that produces the same output with less labor and no additional capital right now, the invention enables the price of output to be lower in terms of labor, and a sensible farmer will adopt the invention immediately. That is, the lower cost of output in terms of labor input makes immediate adoption economically sensible. This also increases the total "capacity," and population is likely to grow in response to the invention and its adoption. But if the invention will only produce more output with the same amount of labor as the old technology *after population and the demand for food has grown* and made land and output more scarce relative to labor, then it does not make sense to adopt the invention *until* population has grown to that point at which the adoption is sensible. Whereas in the previous case the invention and its adoption "pulls" population growth, in this case population growth eventually "pushes" the adoption of the invention that was discovered earlier.

(Of course the capital requirements of various inventions, and the relative scarcities of capital, labor, and output also affect the situation, but I abstract from this problem just as do the two apparently conflicting theories being reconciled here.)

The last section of this chapter examines some historical and anthropological examples of economic-demographic growth in order to determine for each of the examples whether one or the other hypothesis seems to fit best. Enough examples are found in which each of the hypotheses fits to suggest that both processes are important in history and economic development. This confirms the theoretical analysis.

This chapter is concerned only with those possibilities that eventuate in economic change. Ignored here are all those possible sequences of events, beginning with population growth, that *do not* result in economic change. This is very different from the policy-oriented question which asks the *likelihood* that population growth will be followed by economic change in particular circumstances.

The chapter does not discuss the issue of induced innovation because the cause of original invention is not a part of either the invention-pull or population-push hypotheses; that is, invention is exogenous to both. Rather, both hypotheses concern the outcome of invention. And the chapter should be distinguished from the choice-of-techniques literature; the latter's point of view is normative whereas both the hypotheses under discussion here are descriptive.

Boserup (1965) considered the issue in the framework of subsistence agriculture, as did Malthus, and the focus of this paper is therefore limited to subsistence agriculture, though at least Clark (1967) extends the same argument to the full sweep of human history.

It is very important to notice that *neither* the invention-pull nor the population-push theories (nor their integration as suggested here) deals with the original discovery of invention. Rather, both implicitly assume that discovery is spontaneous and without reference to need or economic demand at the macro level. (This is not to say that they assert that the original discovery occurs as an exercise in ''pure science,'' without reference to an individual's or group's needs or desires at a given moment, but rather that the discovery occurs without reference to the society's needs and desires.) In this respect they differ from the issue addressed most sharply by Schmookler (1962) and discussed in chapters 15 and 16 about the extent to which invention is the outcome of current economic conditions at the level of the industry and the economy. And thus the theories discussed in this chapter also are not related to the connection between the supply of potential investors and the flow of invention.

Invention-Pull: The Malthusian Explanation of Population Growth

Although the invention-pull theory is labeled ''Malthusian,'' it is *not* explicit in Malthus's *Essay on Population*. It is, however, the explicit line of thought of most writers on the subject, of whom Childe (1937) and Cipolla (1962) may serve as representatives. Crudely stated now, the argument begins with a society that is somewhat above the subsistence level. Population expands until it reaches the subsistence limits of the technology in use. Then sometime thereafter population size becomes stationary, by mortality alone in the narrow Malthusian view which shall be discussed here, or by mortality and/or birth control in the wider Malthusian view which is closer to Malthus's later editions. Someone then makes a discovery that permits more food to be produced on the same land area, and a shift to the new technology then takes place. Population expands again until it reaches the subsistence limit of the newer technology, and so on. If a society is observed to be at a position above subsistence, it is assumed in this theory to be in a transitory state on the way to the stationary equilibrium at subsistence-level. The process is shown in figure 3.1: a direct causal line from an autonomous invention to a change in the food situation, to a decrease in mortality, to an increase in population, the process continuing until the new food constraint is reached. Technological change is assumed to have social and economic causes apart from the growth of population itself.

A particularly clear-cut contemporary version of the invention-pull Malthusian theory of progress and growth is that of Schultz (1964), who emphasizes (a) education that enables farmers to use existing technology, and (b) developmental research that adapts fundamental inventions to particular situations. According to Schultz, the cause of a shift in production technique is the arrival of knowledge that the farmer can clearly perceive as being profitable to him, including allowance for risk. (An important aspect of Schultz's argument—as will be seen later—is that individual and cultural preferences with respect to work and leisure are not invoked to explain farmers' choices of agricultural techniques; 1964, 27–28.)

Let us first analyze the basic Malthusian process from the standpoint of the individual, assumed to be a single head-of-household provider who has rights to the produce of a given piece of land.[1] The agriculturalist can choose between different amounts of product and leisure. If population increases so that he has less land to work with, he will have to work harder than before. That is, the price of his leisure in terms of output is higher than before, so he trades more leisure for output. But nevertheless he obtains less output than before. This will now be demonstrated geometrically. The nontechnical reader may wish to skip the next three paragraphs.

The analysis begins with the present production-possibility frontier Q_a in figure 3.2. The farmer also has a set of indifference curves I_0, I_1, I_2, and I_3, that show the loci of indifference between various amounts of leisure and output. The intersection, Z_o, of I_o and Q_a is the point of highest attainable satisfaction, so output will be Q_o and M_o hours will be worked, with the given land

FIGURE 3.1
Invention-Pull Malthusian Process for the Subsistence Agriculture Community

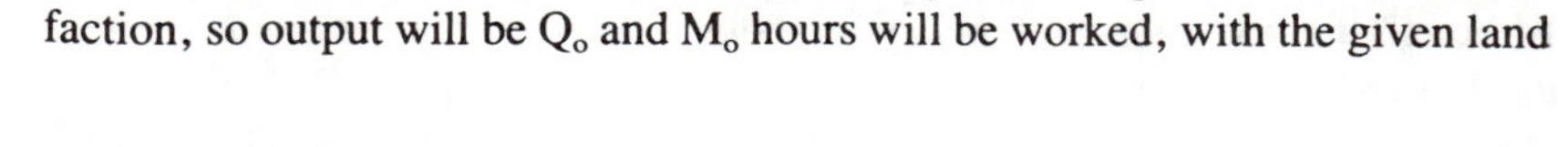

FIGURE 3.2
Production and Leisure Choices for a Representative Farmer

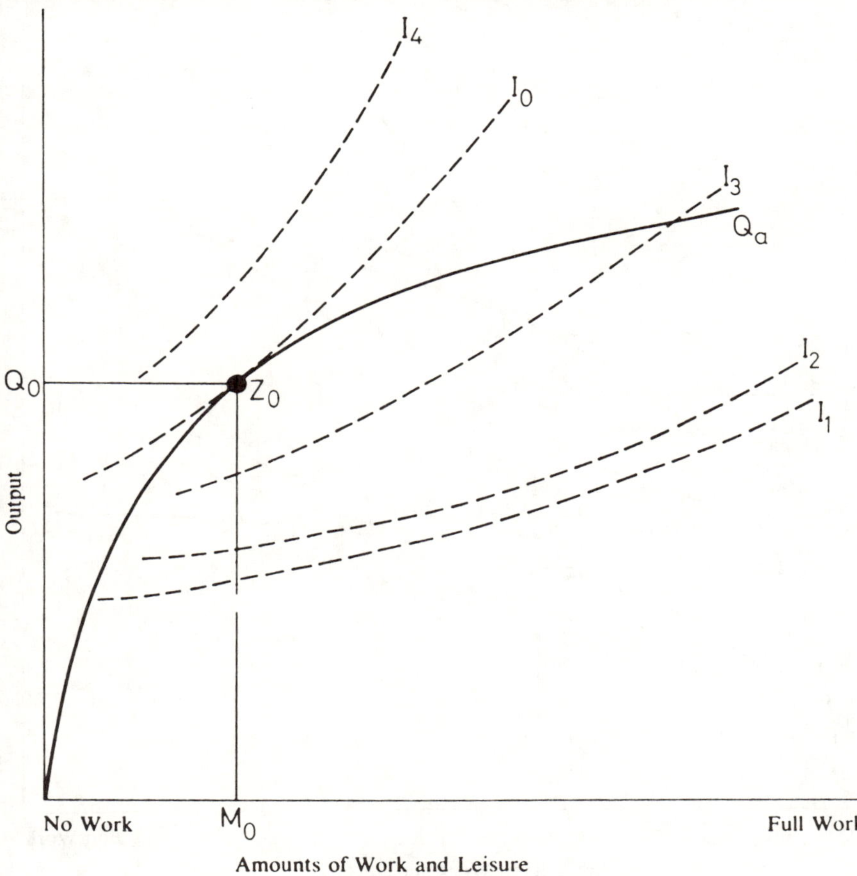

and accompanying production function Q_a. (This sort of micro-analysis, which has come to be called "subjective equilibrium analysis," was developed completely by Chayanov [(1925) 1966] more than half a century ago. It has also been independently re-invented in several other papers including this one. The technical method used here has much in common with Mellor's interesting paper [1963], though Mellor's analytic objective was different. Nakajima [1969] and Sen [1966] also used this sort of analysis to different ends.)

Now consider what happens if at some later time population increases by a factor of 4, and the average plot is now only a fourth of the previous size (figure 3.3). Assuming the same technological know-how but the smaller plot

FIGURE 3.3
Production and Leisure Choices for a Representative Farmer

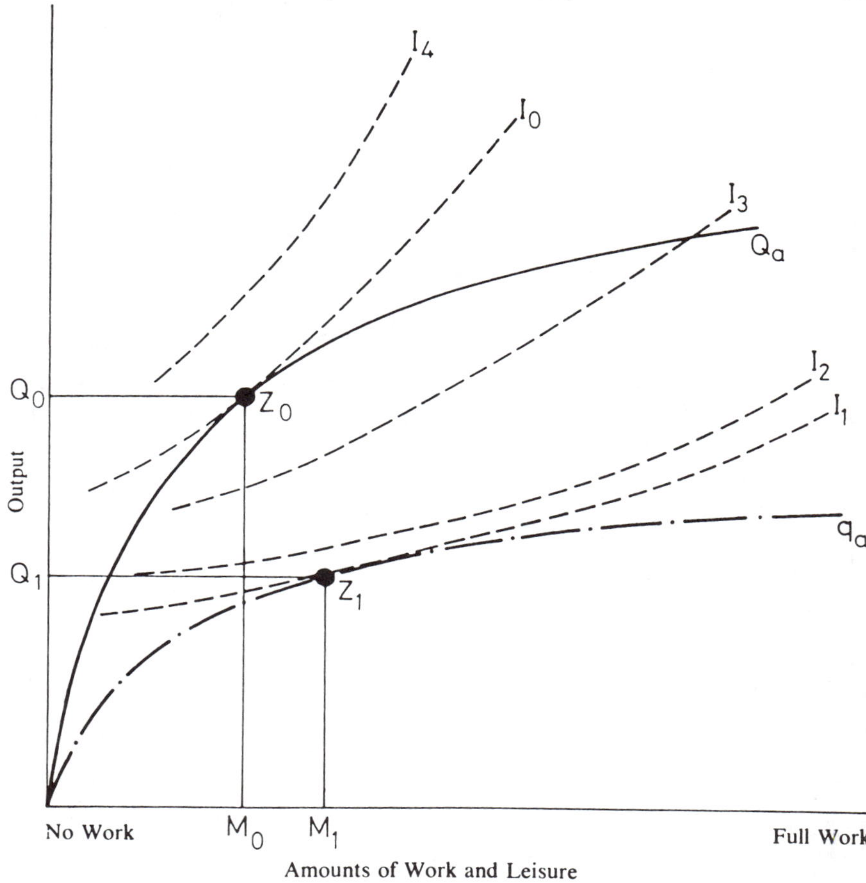

of land, the production-possibility function facing the representative farmer is now q_a, half the height of Q_a at each amount of labor.[2] If he has the same tastes as before, his highest indifference curve will be reached at Z_1 and he will now work harder—M_1 hours instead of M_0—but produce less—output Q_1 instead of Q_0 (though production per unit of land rises).

According to the Malthusian hypothesis, as population increases even more, the production-possibility frontier facing each farmer will continue to shift downward until each man is working as hard as he can with the same technology as before and producing only a subsistence output, at which point population growth ceases. Of course, this analysis depends on the way the indifference curves and production functions are drawn in the figure; it would be possible to draw curves that imply less work per person, rather than more, as population increases. But the curves in figure 3.3 seem reasonable in light of received theory and knowledge of production and consumption. Perhaps more to the point, the curves in figure 3.3 represent the functions that are implicit in the Malthusian invention-pull hypothesis. And the aim here is to explicate that hypothesis rather than to argue its validity. Hence the shapes of the functions will not be discussed further.

A key digression: The analysis assumes that there is *physical* capacity for harder work in some or most cases. And there is evidence to believe that this is so among "primitive" peoples. Among the Hadza in Tanzania "Over the year as a whole probably an average of less than two hours a day is spent obtaining food . . ." (Woodburn 1968, 54). The "Kung Bushmen of Dobe (Botswana), despite their harsh environment, devote from twelve to nineteen hours a week to getting food" (Lee 1968, 37). And the Australian aborigines of Arnhem Land average less than four hours a day getting food (Sahlins 1968, 86–87, quoting McCarthy and McArthur, 1960). Some observers (e.g., Thomsen 1969, 180) believe that the state of health in less-developed countries makes impossible any more work than is now done, especially in the tropics. But Gourou's examples from Congo-Leopoldville are convincing to me (1966, 84–85). There the Zande men work many fewer hours than do the Zande women, though both sexes are equally nourished.[3] And the Lélé men spend a great deal of energy in hunting, though they obtain very little food from it. Both groups are underfed and badly nourished. But both groups have plenty of land. Apparently the men just are not willing to do agricultural work, leaving it to the women (1966, 84–85). End of digression.

According to the invention-pull hypothesis, an invention suddenly appears at some time. This invention increases the output that can be attained at all or some labor inputs. Put technically, the invention expands upward the production-possibility frontier for the representative farmer (figure 3.4). The expansion may be at all points, which might be the result of a new production-function equivalent to the old Q_a but on the smaller plot of land ($q_c = Q_a$). Or if the farmer is in the higher labor-input region of q_a, the expansion might come from new production function q_b, in which case the new production-possibility frontier is q_b when it is above q_a, and q_a at lower amounts of work. (To be more accurate, if the use of both techniques together is feasible, then the production-possibility frontier combines the two, and will be discussed later.)

If we assume that the new invention corresponds to production-function q_b, then the "solution" is at Z_2, with output Q_2 and M_2 hours worked—more work than before, but less work for output Q_2 than could be gotten with the old technology q_a.

This technological change enables the farmer to obtain the same output with

FIGURE 3.4

Production and Leisure Choices for a Representative Farmer

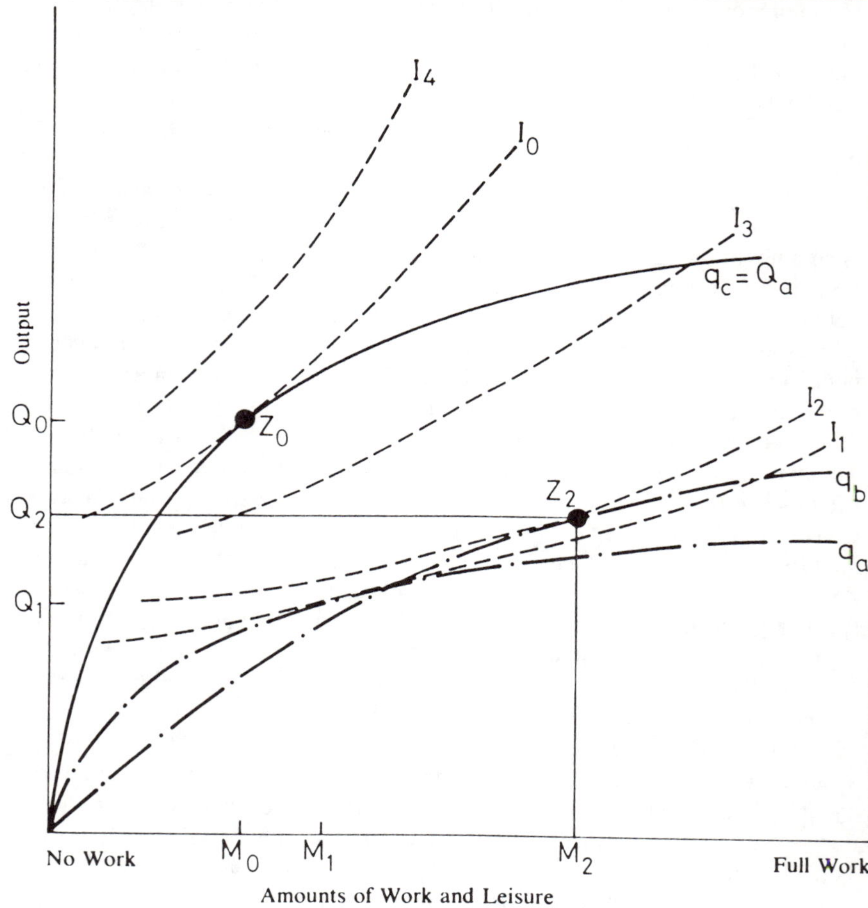

less labor than previously, or he can obtain more output with the same labor as before. Hence the invention makes possible further increase in population, and the growth process then proceeds in the fashion of the ''magnificent dynamics.''

Now let us consider the same process at a higher level of aggregation and from the point of view of a fixed unit of land, as in table 3.1. Assume a given self-contained, rather homogeneous area of 800 square kilometers. With a given agricultural technique and a population of ten people (or better, ten worker-equivalents), which is too few people to exploit all the area, the return

TABLE 3.1
Illustrative Food Production with Various Population Densities and Productive Systems

Row	*Worker equivalents in the society* (1)	*Hours worked per day per worker equivalent* (2)	*Total hours worked per year (assuming 250 days work) in units of 5 x 10³ hours* (3)	*Total calories produced yearly, in units of 1.3 x 10⁶* (4)	*Subsistence food units per consumer equivalent (assuming one consumer equivalent per worker equivalent) 10(Col 4 ÷ Col 1)* (5)
		PANEL A			
		Hunting and Gathering			
1	10	2	1	1.0	1.0
2	40	2	4	2.5	0.62
3	40	4	8	3.8	0.90
4	40	8	16	3.8	0.95
		Primitive Agriculture			
5	40	2	4	2.1	0.52
6	40	4	8	4.0	1.0
7	200	4	40	18	<1.0
8	200	5	50	21	1.0
9	800	4	160	56	0.7
10	800	8	320	72	0.9
		Slash-and-Burn Agriculture			
11	800	4	160	50	0.64
12	800	8	320	82	>1.0
13	6000	4	1200	540	0.9
14	6000	6	1800	605	>1.0
15	24000	6	7200	1920	0.8
16	24000	8	9600	2160	0.9
		Settled Three-Course Agriculture			
17	24000	4	4800	2160	0.9
18	24000	6	7200	2410	>1.0
19	48000	4	9600	3360	0.7
20	48000	6	14400	4320	0.9
21	48000	8	15200	4800	1.0
22	72000	6	21600	5040	0.7
23	72000	8	28800	6480	0.9
		PANEL B			
		Slash-and-Burn Agriculture			
		Before Invention			
101	6000	2	600	300	
102	6000	4	1200	540	
103	6000	6	1800	700	
104	6000	8	2400	800	

TABLE 3.1 (*cont.*)

Row	*Worker equivalents in the society (1)*	*Hours worked per day per worker equivalent (2)*	*Total hours worked per year (assuming 250 days work) in units of 5 x 10^3 hours (3)*	*Total calories produced yearly, in units of 1.3 x 10^6 (4)*	*Subsistence food units per consumer equivalent (assuming one consumer equivalent per worker equivalent) 10(Col 4 ÷ Col 1) (5)*
		After Labor-saving Invention			
105	6000	2	600	500	
106	6000	4	1200	650	
107	6000	6	1800	750	
108	6000	8	2400	820	
		After Production-increasing Invention			
109	6000	2	600	450	
110	6000	4	1200	810	
111	6000	6	1800	1050	
112	6000	8	2400	1200	

on an increased amount of work per year will be almost proportional to the increment of work. The only causes of diminishing marginal returns then are (a) the slightly poorer land being brought successively into cultivation; and (b) the diminished strength and energy output of a man when he works a longer day. (See row I in panel A.)

According to the invention-pull hypothesis, population expansion comes to a halt through increased mortality when the "carrying capacity" of the land is reached with the known method of farming. (One may think of the limit of carrying capacity roughly as the point at which the average level of output is at subsistence, and where not much additional output can be produced even if a large amount of additional work is done.) That is, this hypothesis assumes that the number of people that can be supported in a given area is rigidly limited at a given time by the available technological know-how and capital. For a forty-person society of hunters and collectors on 800 square kilometers, this would occur at something below eight hours of work a day. Or to put it another way, a group of forty hunters and collectors is at or near the "carrying capacity" of 800 square kilometers. The same would be true, by the invention-pull hypothesis, for a group of 200 that had learned to practice the most primitive agriculture, and for somewhere between 6,000 and 24,000 people who had learned slash-and-burn agriculture.[4] Then at some later time after the population becomes stationary, again someone discovers a "better" form of agriculture, the people begin to practice the new agriculture, and the population begins to expand once more. This process is traced out in panel A of table 3.1.

The invention-pull hypothesis assumes that an invention will begin to be adopted "immediately" after the invention is made,[5] no matter whether the population is close to or far from that level of subsistence at which further population growth must cease. Therefore, we must now consider the characteristics of an invention whose adoption would begin immediately. One class of examples includes inventions that will yield the *same amount of output for less labor* than does the established practice, assuming no change in the amount of land or other capital—for example, replacement of the wooden plow with the iron plow, the stone ax with the iron ax, and the substitution of one shape of digging stick, sickle, or scythe with another and faster-operating shape—inventions classified as "mechanical" by Heady (1949), all of whose effects are to reduce the amount of labor required to produce a given quantity of food. There would be no point in increasing the total amount of output in most circumstances, because total calorie consumption is reasonably inelastic.[6] There would not be any point in adopting an innovation that would increase the amount of output per unit of land unless one could reduce the amount of land in use and thereby get the same amount of output with less labor.

Another relevant class includes inventions that yield *greater* output with the *same* labor per acre. Such inventions make it possible *either* to enjoy greater output with the same labor *or* to cut back on capital and labor and have the same output as before. An example is a better calendar. This second class of inventions may be found among either the "biological" or the "mechanical-biological" classifications of Heady. (The difference between the two classes in this context is that an innovation that increases productivity with the same land and labor can produce more food per capita, and hence increases potential population. An innovation that only reduces labor and does not increase output cannot provide for more people, but only gives more leisure.)

Both classes of inventions mentioned above may be regarded as "labor saving" (or "laboresque" in Sen's [1959] scheme) because they produce the same or more output with less or the same amount of labor (assuming a fixed amount of the major capital element, land) than does the technology currently in use,[7] and therefore they will be adopted immediately after invention. And the second class of inventions in turn provides the basis for further population growth. The effect of such inventions in the context of slash-and-burn agriculture may be seen by comparison of rows 101–104 with rows 105–108 in panel B of table 3.1.

It is an important part of the intellectual history of the invention-pull hypothesis that the kind of inventions to which it refers has generally not been made clear.

In summary, then, the Malthusian invention-pull hypothesis accurately describes economic-demographic history in cases where an invention occurs that produces the same output with less labor compared to the technology in use.

The Population-Push Hypothesis

Next we consider the "population-push hypothesis." The key idea is that at a given moment an agricultural people know a method of obtaining higher yields from their lands than given by the methods they use. But the higher-yield method demands more work, and will *not* produce the *same* output with less labor. The new method therefore is not used. But a later increase of population then pushes people to adopt the new methods despite that they require more work. In other words, population growth makes labor less scarce relative to land, and output is more scarce relative to labor. Therefore there then occurs a shift to the more labor-intensive method. For comparison with figure 3.1, the population-push hypothesis may be schematized as in figure 3.5.

There are two population-push mechanisms that can bring about the shift to the new methods. In the first mechanism, there comes to be less land available to each family because of the *increased number of families*. This reduces the output that can be obtained by the average family with a given amount of labor, and this makes it sensible to shift to a method that yields relatively more output at a higher labor input. Put technically, it is assumed that two technological methods are known, represented in figure 3.6 by Q_a and Q_b for population-density state 0, or q_a and q_b in population-density state 1. Consider a representative head of household in population-density state 0. Method Q_a gives higher yields at lower labor levels, whereas Q_b gives higher yields at higher labor levels. In state 0, the family will choose to be at Z_0 with production method *a* because it hits a higher indifference curve, I_0, than can be achieved with production method *b*. But when population increases and the land available to each family shrinks to the point that it is in state 1, it chooses productive process *b* with which q_b touches indifference curve I_2 and Z_2. This requires the family to work M_2 rather than M_1 hours, but yields output Q_2 instead of output Q_1 which would be obtained at Z_1 with the old technique. (Once more, the outcome of population increase shown by the diagram de-

FIGURE 3.5

Population-Push Hypothesis for a Subsistence Agriculture Community in the Presence of Unused Technological Knowledge

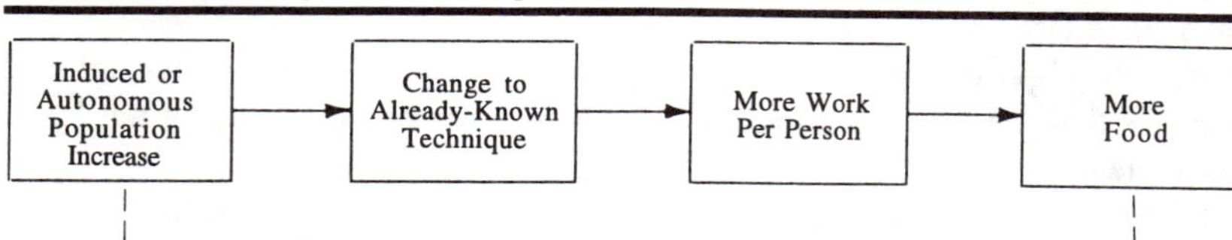

FIGURE 3.6
Production and Leisure Choices for a Representative Farmer

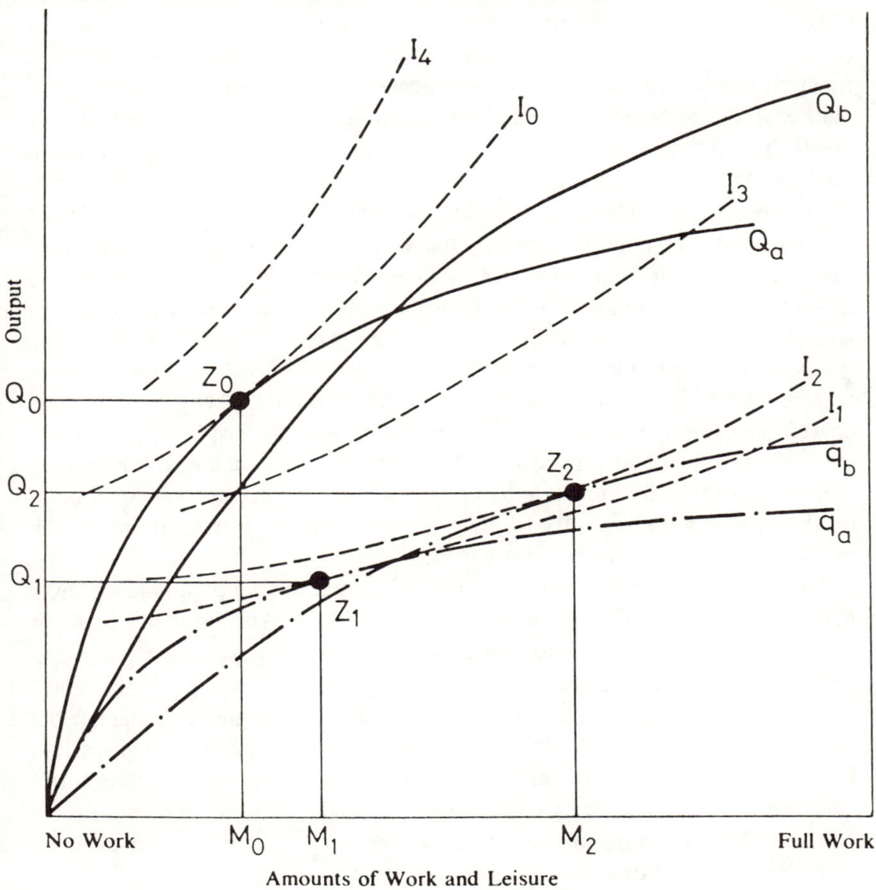

pends upon the shapes of the curves. And to repeat, no claims are made for the realism of these curves. Rather, they are a didactic device, shapes that make explicit the ideas implicit in the population-push hypothesis being explicated here, and that are consistent with a reasonable explanation of adaptations that occur following population increase.)

(All these diagrams and numerical examples contain an important inaccuracy. They imply that one technique *or* the other will be used. But theory would lead us to expect *both* techniques to be used in situations where one technique produces more than the other at some labor inputs but less at other labor inputs—as is the case of the production functions implied by Boserup's discussion (1965) and shown in the *a* and *b* production functions. The appropriate production function, then, is that *combination* of the two techniques that yields the greatest total output at each labor input. This will be at or above either separate technique's production function at every labor input. But showing how the invention of a new method leads to the new composite production function would add considerable complication to the paper. Furthermore, for one reason or another, many [perhaps most] agricultural groups do use only one technique rather than two, and hence the presentation here may not be too far from the institutional facts.)

The second population-push mechanism refers to an increase in the size of the representative family, assuming the same size plot of land. If there are, say, six rather than four consumer equivalents in the family, it is reasonable to assume that the subsistence level will be higher and the desired output will rise. Therefore, it is reasonable to shift to the method that will produce the *greater* amount of output with relatively less labor. In technical terms, there will be a shift in people's indifference curves,[8] from the I set of indifference curves in earlier figures to the $\bar{I}$ set in figure 3.7. With the original plot of land, the optimization point for the I indifference set is at Z_0 using technological method *a*. But the optimization point for the $\bar{I}$ indifference set is at Z_3, a point on the production-possibility frontier at which method *b* is used and which produces output Q_3, which is more than Q_0.

The population-push hypothesis implicitly suggests that population growth puts *both* of the above mechanisms into operation. And both mechanisms work in the same direction to induce a shift to previously known but previously unused production methods.

To discuss the population-push hypothesis in a more aggregated manner, let us start with a hunting and/or food-collecting group of ten people on 800 square kilometers of land. This is ample to support them with a minimum of labor, say two hours work by each person on 250 days a year, as shown in row 1 in table 3.1. (In arctic and desert regions food gathering is, of course, much more laborious. With a group as small as ten people the workings of chance necessarily make for some variation in population size over time, leading either to the disappearance of the small family group or to its increase. If population rises toward forty people, the group will find it harder to make a living because game does not increase with the population size—instead, it probably decreases as hunting is intensified. The workers now need to work four to eight hours a day, instead of only two hours a day, to kill or collect the same amount of food per person as before (rows 2–4). And if population then grows even more, it will be difficult or impossible to make a living by hunting and collecting, no matter how hard the people work.

According to the population-push hypothesis, what now happens is that the group begins to farm a bit. The data shown in rows 5–10 are intended to rep-

FIGURE 3.7
Production and Leisure Choices for a Representative Farmer

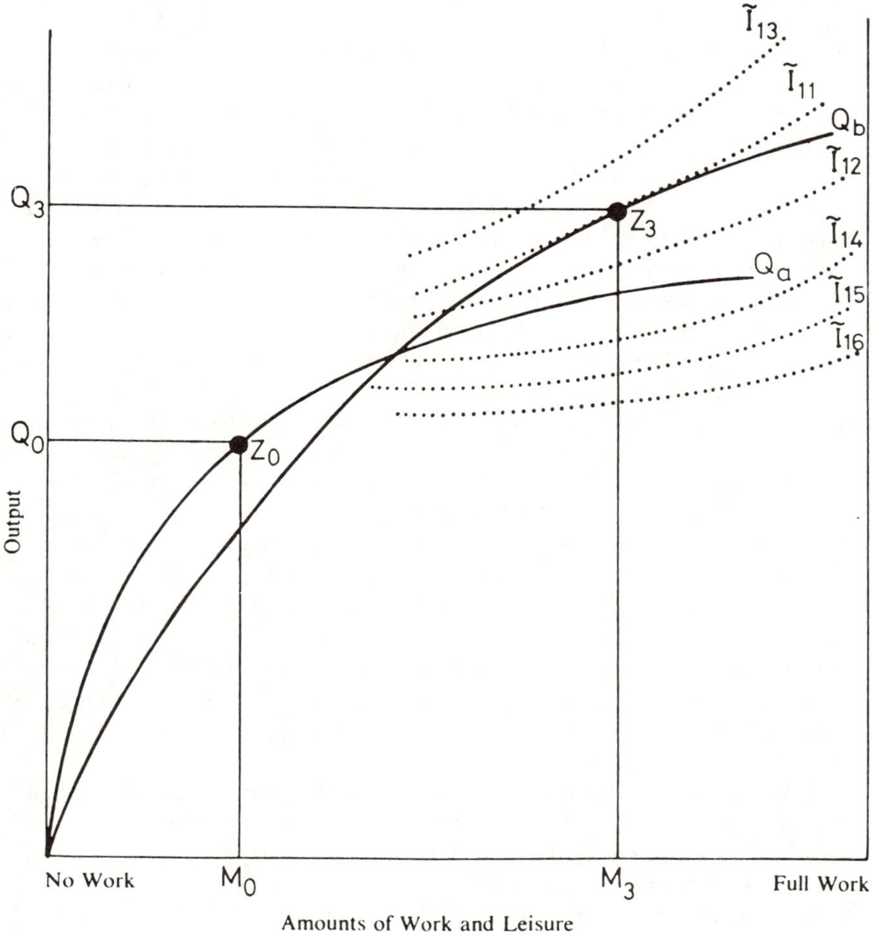

resent a very primitive kind of agriculture, perhaps that which was done at Jericho or Jarmo where little or no land clearing was needed. Because of the shapes of the idealized production functions shown in the table, the forty people could get more food from four hours farming per person than from four hours hunting and collecting. (Compare rows 3 and 6, but note that hunting and collecting would still provide more food for the forty people with a *two-hour* work day than would farming, rows 2 and 5.) Please remember that the population-push hypothesis assumes that the group already has the technological knowledge necessary for this primitive agriculture long before it shifts to the new technique. And the shift from one food-getting method to another need not be sudden or all at once, but rather is likely to be gradual as is consistent with the basic economic logic implicit in the production function. The forty people could minimize the time required to get the basic food ration by employing both methods at once—at least until population grows much larger. This is consistent with the observation that in many primitive communities, the women farm while the men hunt (Clark and Haswell 1967, 27).

The idealized scheme in table 3.1 traces the process as population on this 800 square kilometer tract expands to 200 people, according to the population-push hypothesis. At that point all work would be primitive agriculture and none would be hunting (rows 7 and 8). Then population expands to 800 people, which nears the limit for this type of simple farming (even if animals have been tamed and kept in pasture). The population-push analysis suggests that in the course of the expansion to 800 people agricultural technique shifts again, this time to slash-and-burn agriculture. With short work days, slash-and-burn agriculture produces less food than the more primitive agriculture (row 9 versus row 11). But if the 800 people work somewhat harder, they can get a *full* ration of food with less effort using slash-and-burn long-fallow agriculture than using a more primitive system (row 10 versus row 12). So—assuming, as the population-push writers do, that people already know about the method—people will now gradually shift to slash-and-burn agriculture. And the shift to slash-and-burn will be completed as population expands to, say, 6,000 people on the 800 kilometer tract. Then, as population grows even more, there will be a shift to three-course agriculture. These successive shifts from one type of agricultural system to the next, each system demanding more labor per worker and a shorter fallow period than the one before and each shift caused by growth in population, are the heart of the population-push hypothesis.

A variant hypothesis, closer to population-push than invention-pull, is that technological development in agriculture is *induced* by changes in demand elsewhere in the economy. For example, a rise in the degree of urbanization, *ceteris paribus*, increases the demand and hence the price for agricultural products. Changes in crops and methods of farming may be caused thereby (Dovring 1966). This hypothesis is clearly more applicable in stages later than subsistence agriculture, so the matter will not be pursued here. But the invention-pull and population-push hypotheses are not very useful once labor and product markets develop and people can trade labor and output with a non-agricultural sector.

Now let us restate the characteristics of the kinds of inventions that might not be adopted until some time after their discovery and as a result of a population-push. These inventions will not be labor-saving relative to the technology in use, because there is every reason for the adoption of labor-saving inventions to begin *immediately* after discovery. Instead they will be inventions that meet the need of producing *more output as population grows* and require *more labor*—the latter being the reason that their adoption did not begin immediately upon invention. All of these inventions will be among those classified as "biological" by Heady (1949). The most important examples of such inventions are short-fallow and multi-cropping systems, all of which require more careful farming and more hours of labor per unit of output than do long-fallow systems. Some of the new seed varieties, for example, rice that requires the laborious Japanese method of wet-farming, are related examples.

Analytic Comparison of the Two Hypotheses

To recapitulate, the Malthusian invention-pull hypothesis is a reasonable description of the process that begins with exogenous inventions that are immediately "labor-saving" and "profitable." Such an invention can be one that "dominates" previous technology in the sense of using less labor for each and every level of output, or it can be an invention that uses less labor at the present level of output though it uses more labor than previous technology at lower output levels. It is reasonable that such inventions will be adopted immediately, and because they produce more output at the same amount of labor as before, they lead to further population growth.

The population-push hypothesis, in turn, is a good description of the place in economic-demographic history of inventions that produce the same output with less labor, or more output with the same labor, but *at higher labor and output levels* than are in effect at the time of invention. That is, in the population-push hypothesis, the key technological discoveries are *not* more "profitable" than the old technology at the time of invention, but rather are less desirable at the time of invention. The new invention becomes desirable later on, after population density has increased and total food "needs" have increased, according to the population-push hypothesis.

This brief analysis of the difference between the hypotheses focuses on (a) the properties of the key inventions, and (b) people's "needs" for food and leisure at the time of the inventions. Now, we know that some inventions are labor-saving at all output levels, for example, a better calendar, and implements such as bronze and iron sickles and scythes (see Curwen and Hatt 1953, especially 94). We also know that other inventions require much more labor than would ever be used with previous technology though the new inventions also can produce much more output per unit of land, for example wet-farming and double-cropping. Both types of inventions have been important in history, which implies that both the invention-pull and the population-push mechanisms have operated in history. The two hypotheses do not conflict with each other. Hence, they should not be seen as competitive explanations of premodern agricultural development, but rather as complementary.

As to the relative importance of the two mechanisms in history, there is at least one fact indicating that *both* were important: Even after much change in technology and after much population growth, the amount of work done on yearly crops by individual farmers in densely populated places is *not* higher by a different order of magnitude than in sparsely populated places. In both situations, farmers work most of the daylight hours during the harvest season and much less during most of the year. This suggests that invention-pull was not the whole story, because if it were, all inventions would be labor-saving and the work done would have become *less* as agriculture advanced. On the other hand, the fact that the amount of work per farmer has also not *increased* enormously suggests that the population-push mechanism is not the whole story either, because the technological changes it describes all require *more* labor than before. This demonstrates that *both* mechanisms must have been at work in history to an important degree.[9]

A word about more advanced agriculture: Neither of the two hypotheses describes the development of modern annual-crop and multi-crop agriculture in which output per farmer *rises*.[10] The invention-pull point of view is that the rate of exogenous inventions sped up for exogenous reasons. This comprehends the development of the internal combustion engine and many of the other components of farm machinery. But an increased rate of exogenous inventions has no logical connection with the invention-pull hypothesis. On their side, population-push theorists point to social and psychological changes that occur as people progress to more advanced agriculture. More economical social organizations with more division of labor evolve as people live closer together. Roads are built. Most important to Boserup (1965) and Clark (1967), however, is that changes in individual psychology take place, people becoming more willing to work hard over sustained periods. Together with the other social changes, this is the engine that eventually brings about a ''take-off'' far beyond subsistence and near-subsistence living, according to Boserup and Clark. But these changes are not inventions, or if they are inventions, there is no lag between invention and utilization. These changes are induced, just as in the United States new seed varieties are induced by market forces and by purposeful foundation or government research stimulated by foreseen needs. Of course there is a lag between the invention of the tractor and its use in India, but that is of the same nature as the delay between the invention of the forklift truck and its use in warehouses in India. The point is that after the passage from mostly-subsistence to mostly-market agriculture, neither the invention-pull hypothesis nor the population-push hypothesis has much to say that is distinctive and useful. The explanation of the development of business farming is like the explanation of the development of other business enterprises—

with regard to the effects of both the increase in demand and the increase in technical knowledge.

Early Biblical Period

Genesis makes very clear that the shift from food-collecting to tilling the soil was perceived as an increase in labor-intensivity. "Behold, I have given you every herb yielding seed, which is upon the face of all the earth, and every tree, in which is the fruit of a tree yielding seed—to you it shall be for food" (Genesis 1:29). But then: ". . . cursed is the ground for thy sake; in toil shalt thou eat of it all the days of thy life. Thorns also and thistles shalt it bring to thee; and thou shalt eat the herb of the field. In the sweat of thy face shalt thou eat bread, till thou return until the ground" (Genesis 3:17–3:19). According to the Bible, the technological shift in the Garden of Eden was caused not by population growth but by sin. Aside from that, however, the description is that of von Thunen (1966), Gourou (1965), Slicher van Bath (1963), and Boserup (1965).

The rest of the story in Genesis may be prototypical, at least for people in hot, dry, countries. If the tribe flourishes rather than being overcome by mortality, there come to be a few more members of the family and tribe than before, and the people then use a somewhat larger area of land for pasture, hunting, and gathering, all without a major decrease in product per person. Probably there is some gain in efficiency from their cooperative efforts in hunting and defense.

But if there come to be enough people in the tribe so that at the edges of their area the land is less bountiful, "personal income" will fall. When this happens the tribe will probably split, as with Abraham and Lot;[11] one group will move to different grounds. The group that moves is likely to have poorer prospects than the group that remains, and the movers will certainly incur a cost in moving. Hence the overall level of per-capita income apparently falls over the last part of this population expansion, or at least people will have to work harder on poorer hunting and collecting areas to sustain the same standard of living.

Overall judgment: The Biblical period is consistent with the population-push mechanism.

Other Hunting-and-Gathering Groups

A crucial element of the population-push hypothesis is that there is preknowledge of techniques that will increase aggregate output from the given land area. But there are at least some situations where such techniques are clearly not known to hunters and gatherers. One such situation was that of the Netsilik Eskimos in the 1920s and 1930s, whose situation "did not leave the Netsilik with much leisure" (Balikci 1968, 82). Life was very hard for the Netsilik by any material test. This does not fit the population-push hypothesis.

And before agriculture was invented, no one knew about it. Of course it is conceivable that in all societies agriculture was discovered before it was needed, but this hardly seems likely. The control of plant reproduction is nowhere near so obvious that anyone who could benefit from it would automatically know about it.

> All cultivated plants have been derived from wild varieties, and the first step in cultivating them consists in taking the seeds of the wild plants, sowing them in suitable soil, and by care and attention promoting their growth. . . . It may seem incredible to us that for countless thousands of years it never occurred to man to take this simple first step, but the very fact that he did not do so for so long emphasizes the magnitude of the discovery that eventually led him to take it. (Curwen and Hatt 1953, 15)

But the knowledge of agriculture was certainly available to *some* preagricultural groups *before* their population was pressing on its limits, and the knowledge came to be used as population grew.[12] The knowledge of agriculture has been shown to have diffused from one or a few discovery points in Eurasia—though also independently in the Americas, etc. Hence, some groups are likely to have learned of agriculture while they still had plenty of land on which to hunt and gather. It should not surprise us, therefore, that some or most hunting-and-collecting tribes live a comparatively easy life, as suggested in the examples adduced earlier.

Overall judgment: Some instances of hunting-and-gathering groups illustrate the invention-pull mechanism, and others illustrate the population-push mechanism.

Slash-and-Burn Agriculture

Slash-and-burn agriculture uses land more intensively than does collecting or hunting, but still not very intensively by standards of developed agricultural sectors today. As done today in the tropics, "the first trees are felled with axes, and when dry the vegetation is burnt; after the drop harvest the parch lies fallow and the forest regains control until it is once more burnt" (Gourou 1966, 31). The plot is then farmed for one, two, or three years in succession, and then the land lies fallow for up to thirty years but sometimes as little as two or three years. ". . . Between eight and twelve years are necessary to get a good cover of woody vegetation" (Gourou 1966, 38). Meantime, the agriculturalists work other land. The important point here is that a large area is needed to supply food for a group of people—up to thirty times as much as is cultivated in a single year.

Whether in earlier times practitioners of slash-and-burn agriculture generally knew of more "advanced" methods we cannot know for sure. But there is no reason to doubt that *present-day* slash-and-burn agriculturalists know about other techniques, as shown by the fact that the two systems coexist in some places (Gourou 1966, 107–8). The reason agriculturalists still prefer to continue using the slash-and-burn technique, according to Gourou (1966, 52), Clark and Haswell (1967, chapter 7), and Boserup (1965, 44–48), is that, for the quantities of food produced on the available land, slash-and-burn agriculturalists work fewer hours than if they were to use more intensive methods (at least, up to machine methods) to produce the same amount of food. Also, there is much evidence that when population density increases, people shift from slash-and-burn to more intensive shorter-fallow agriculture. One of the most persuasive pieces of evidence is that when population density *decreases*—perhaps due to an increase in tribal safety on low lands, an event exogenous to population growth—the process reverses and people go "back" to less-intensive longer-fallow methods (Gourou 1966, 107; Boserup 1965, 62–63).

Data on population and farming intensity among the Kikuyu in the Central Province of Kenya confirm the anecdotal reports and show clearly that higher population density is associated with less shifting cultivation and more settled farming: see table 3.2.

Other persuasive evidence comes from anthropological restudies. When one observes a society at only a single point in time, or over a very long sweep of history, one cannot be sure that it is not the change in agriculture technique that is the leading force, with population growth only following. But if one observes a society at a point in time, notes an increase in population taking place, and then observes a generation later that a shift in agricultural technol-

TABLE 3.2
Population Density and Land Usage, Central Province of Kenya, 1954

		% land under various forms of cultivation	
District	*Population per square mile*	*Settled agriculture*	*Shifting cultivation*
Kiambu	860	91.5	8.5
Nyeri	596	93.7	6.3
Fort Hall	499	89.7	10.3
Embu	351	68.3	31.7
Meru	236	66.7	33.3

Source: Barber 1970.

ogy occurred, this argues strongly that it was population growth that was the cause of the change in technique rather than the reverse—especially when the farmers tell the observer exactly these motivations for the change in method. Chan Kom, a village in Yucatan, Mexico, was studied by Redfield and Rojas in 1931, and again by Redfield in 1948. Population increased from about 250 people to about 445 during those 17 years. In 1931, there was unappropriated land available for anyone to farm (1934, 42). But by 1948 the situation had changed.

> So long as there remained to the south an unpopulated territory, it was possible to take care of the increasing numbers of people by the making of new settlements on that frontier. The people of a village would go farther and farther from their home community to find good land . . . the lands available to the village yield less than they did twenty-five years ago . . . as land becomes scarcer, it is planted again in a shorter interval after its last abandonment to bush.
>
> The average size of milpas [maize plots] is surely smaller now . . . about one-half as large as they used to plant.
>
> Four or five of the men have begun the development of such small tracts by planting fruit trees, tomatoes, beans, and other small crops, by building cattle corrals, establishing poultry on the tract, and, in a few cases, by digging wells.
>
> The people see the population press upon the resources. So far as they speculate as to remedies, they turn to the possibility of increasing resources. Don Eus sees a hope in diversified agriculture. (Redfield 1957, 54, 55, 57, 171, 172)

The changes in Chan Kom fit the population-push mechanism very well.

Another restudied village is Tepoztlan, in the Mexican State of Morelos. The picture one gets from the study in 1926–1927 (Redfield 1930) and restudy in 1943–1948 (O. Lewis 1951) is somewhat different but essentially consistent with that of Chan Kom. Unlike Chan Kom, in which only slash-and-burn agriculture was practiced, in Tepoztlan as of 1930 both slash-and-burn agriculture *and* no-fallow plow agriculture were practiced. In the former technique, a hole is made with a dibble or hoe for each seed; in the latter the ground is broken with a plow pulled by oxen, and the seeds are dropped into the furrow and then covered with the foot. Slash-and-burn requires much more land, but it *also* requires much more labor per unit of output—at least in Tepoztlan in the 1940s. Plow agriculture requires more capital in the form of oxen and plow. Plow culture began in Mexico only after the Spanish came; before that the plow was unknown. After the Spanish came there was also a *massive depopulation* of Mexico generally, and of Tepoztlan specifically (O. Lewis 1951, 26–30). Therefore, farmers must have adopted plow agriculture *not* because of increasing pressure of population on land, but simply because with the innovation one could get more output with less labor, even though using much less land. This conclusion is consistent with the existence of much unfarmed land in Mexico even until the recent very fast population growth. Hence, the shift after the Spanish came to a system of no-fallow plow agriculture is not consistent with the population-push view of history, but rather fits the invention-pull hypothesis quite well.

In the years between the Redfield and Lewis studies of Tepoztlan, population grew rapidly (O. Lewis 1951, 148). People responded with *an increase in slash-and-burn agriculture* in fields far away from the town, which contradicts the specific assertions of Gourou (1966) and Boserup (1965) about the sequence of shifts in technique. But it is also true that the daily trip to the milpa requires many hours back and forth; this trip increases the labor input so that it must be much greater per unit of output than in plow agriculture, and in this respect the shift fits the population-push hypothesis. Tepoztlan is also consistent with the population-push hypothesis in that knowledge of several techniques is available, and the agriculturalists choose the technique that maximizes their utility from production and leisure, given the land available to them and the indifference curves that reflect the number of children that they have.

Overall judgment: most slash-and-burn agricultural situations fit the population-push argument, but some fit the invention-pull mechanism.

Polynesian Short-Fallow Agriculture

Taro is the staple crop on the isolated Polynesian island of Tikopia, which Firth studied in 1928–1929 and again in 1952. As of 1952, the Tiokopians were worried about the press of population upon food resources because of population growth. "The taro resources of the people might possibly be increased by adopting a technique of irrigation and conservation. . . . But this would require . . . specific instruction by an external agency" (Firth 1939–1965, 50).

Firth implies that the Tikopians really do not know of a technological alternative that, even with increased labor, would expand their food supply greatly. Instead they look to birth control and suicide-migration by canoe to adjust population and food resources.

The physical isolation of this island is obviously a key element in its lack of alternatives, both for technological change and for migration.

Overall judgment: Tikopia's situation fits the Malthusian invention-pull hypothesis better than it fits the population-push hypothesis, in the sense that an increase in population cannot be handled by a shift to an already-known invention that will increase output though requiring more labor.

Shifts in Fallow Periods and Crop Rotations in Europe

The relevant highlights of the history of European farming from 500 to 1850 are as follows. Population reached its nadir, 19.3 million, near the beginning of the period (Clark 1967, 64). From then on the secular population growth was continuous, though not without major fluctuations around the trend. For the most part, then, we may associate changes in farming methods in the Middle Ages with increasing population.

A key change was from two-course to three-field rotation methods. In the former, "land was tilled or left fallow in alternate years." In the latter, ". . . winter corn (wheat or rye) was sown the first year, spring corn (barley or oats) the second, and in the third year the ground lay fallow" (Slicher van Bath 1963, 59). The three-course method increases total output per unit of land because more land is in production each year.

Slicher van Bath asserts that "it was nearly always at a time of increasing population that there was a changeover from two- to three-course rotation, for instance, in England in the thirteenth century . . ." (1963, 60). And in some places where it fitted farmers' needs, "both systems were running concurrently, or being alternated according to the crop: wheat in the three-course rotation and rye in the two course" (Slicher van Bath 1963, 60).[13] Boserup generalizes from this that "virtually all of the methods introduced in this period had been known before-hand" and awaited adoption until population density grew sufficiently (1965, 38).

Chayanov[14] (1925–1966) explored in great analytic depth and factual detail the workings of the push of population and consumer wants upon the behavior of Russian family-farmers at the turn of the century.[15] Chayanov investigated the "annual labor expenditure" of all the workers taken together on each farm, and found that the chief determinant, given any set of "production conditions," was "the pressure of family consumer demands on the workers" (p. 76), that is, the number of consumers in the family.[16] "This forcing up of labor intensity, buying increased annual agricultural income at the price of reducing labor unit payment, is achieved either by an intensification of work methods or by using more labor-intensive crops and jobs" (p. 113). It cannot be emphasized too strongly that Chayanov's conclusions are based, not on casual observation, but on the extremely detailed careful surveys of Russian agriculture that were made around the turn of the century by skilled, dedicated statisticians—surveys that still constitute perhaps the best available source of data on matters such as this. And though Chayanov's data, with a few notable exceptions, cover a single period, it is reasonable to assume that the cross-sectional differences recapitulate the changes over time as population density increased on the Russian peasant farm.[17]

Von Thunen described with wonderful precision the Belgian and Mecklenburg systems of cultivation, and clearly showed how the difference in techniques used was related to population density (1966, 85 ff). But details will be omitted because this segment of history belongs more to market than to subsistence agriculture.

But population-pushed changes in crop rotation and related work methods do not constitute the entire story of European agriculture from the Middle

Ages.[18] The development of the heavy plow and of horsepower to replace oxenpower were, according to some historians, equally important with the three-course rotation in the agricultural revolution. The heavy plow required iron for its blade, and the horse required both iron for horseshoes and the new chest-harnesses that were being perfected at that time. General use of both the heavy plow and the horse had to wait upon the increased supplies of iron that occurred in Europe at the beginning of the Middle Ages. When it became available, these innovations—together with the new harnessing and the three-course rotation—enabled European farmers to work profitably with the heavy soils of more northern lands than had previously been cultivated.

According to White (1962, chapter 2), the inventive knowledge underlying the availability of iron and the adoption of the heavy plow, new harness methods, and horsepower were *not* available before the Middle Ages, in direct opposition to Boserup's (1965) assumption. White further asserts that the three-field system was *also* invented in the Middle Ages. He cites the fact that "Charlemagne himself thought . . . the new pattern . . . as something so new and significant that he felt impelled to rename the months in terms of it" (1962, 69). White's account is very much one of new inventions pulling upward the size of the population, especially in Germany and Scandinavia (1962, 54), rather than of population pushing adoption of previously known methods.

New crops are still other exogenous technological advances that did *not* have to wait on further population increase in Europe for adoption. "The earliest type of technical change that came to modify medieval agriculture in Europe was in the introduction of new crops. Some of these changes were the precondition for changes of other kinds" (Dovring 1965, 631). The potato had the most dramatic impact.

> [O]n a pathetically small patch of ground one could grow in potatoes from two to four times as much food as one could in terms of wheat or other grains, enough indeed to feed a family of more than average size. . . . It was introduced [into Ireland] about the year 1600 and before the end of the seventeenth century had been generally adopted by the peasantry. By the end of the eighteenth century the common man was eating little else. . . . The unspeakable poverty of the country should, it would seem, have militated against any considerable population increase. Yet the population did increase from 3,200,000 in 1754 to 8,175,000 in 1846, not counting some 1,750,000 who emigrated before the great potato famine of 1845–1847.
>
> It was perfectly obvious to contemporaries, as it is to modern scholars, that this Irish population could exist only because of the potato. Poverty-stricken though it might be, the Irish peasantry was noteworthy for its fine physique. Clearly people were doing very well physiologically on their potato fare. Young people rented an acre or less for a potato patch. On the strength of this they married young and had large families. (Langer 1968, 11, 15)

Although Langer emphasizes the effect of potato cultivation[19] in increasing fertility, other writers (e.g., McKeown and Brown 1955) emphasize the potato's effect in reducing mortality, especially infant mortality due to malnutrition. Whichever is correct, there is little dispute that the ''invention'' of the potato and its diffusion throughout Ireland caused population to increase more than it would have otherwise.[20]

Overall judgment: There were some innovations and events during the Middle Ages in Europe that apparently illustrate the invention-pull mechanism, and others that apparently illustrate the population-push mechanism. The relative importance of these innovations and the dates of their inventions are subject to scholarly dispute, however. Therefore, an overall judgment is difficult to form—perhaps because more is known about this situation than about other situations discussed here.

Traditional Agriculture in China

Over almost 600 years from 1368 to 1957 the population of China increased from 65–80 million to 647 million.[21] But per person consumption did not decline secularly over this period, and perhaps rose. No fundamental shifts in mechanical technology took place.[22] Some new crops were introduced, but none had a revolutionary effect. Opening up new lands accommodated the largest part of the population growth.[23] Extension of water-control systems and double-cropping contributed less, and both of these methods had been well known before 1368. These facts are more consistent with the population-push mechanism than with the invention-pull mechanism.

Chinese history raises a puzzle. If the Chinese farmers were apparently able to increase total production under the pressure of more people, why did they not raise production *even faster?* One possible answer is that the parallel trends of production and population are just a coincidence. But this coincidence seems unlikely because the methods of raising production were known. Nor can one satisfactorily explain the relationship by the increase in labor alone, as Perkins shows (1968, 79–84); such an explanation would require that there are no *ceteris paribus* diminishing returns in agriculture, which there clearly are.

The most likely explanation why per-person consumption did not rise even faster, I judge, is that the Chinese farmers preferred not to trade more work for more output. This choice may (or may not) have been heavily influenced by the absence of consumer goods that would whet their desires. In any case, however, the outcome fits the population-push hypothesis.

The extent of change in the individual Chinese farmer's behavior as a result of ''population pressure'' may seem from the statistics greater than it actually was, because it was surely the young families just starting out who supplied much of the energy. If Chinese life was like Irish life in the eighteenth and early nineteenth centuries (Connell 1965, 428–29), it was the young just-married men and women who cleared uncultivated lands and settled there. The increase in output required of a mature father was much less than proportional to the number of persons in his nuclear family, especially after the children grew up.[24]

Overall judgment: The last six centuries of Chinese history suggest that the arrival of new knowledge—especially of seeds—was important. But population pressure was necessary for the innovations to be adopted.

Summary and Conclusion

Two apparently conflicting hypotheses—the invention-pull hypothesis and the population-push hypothesis—have been offered as explanations of demographic-economic growth in near-subsistence agricultural situations. The invention-pull hypothesis asserts that the diffusion of new methods begins immediately after invention occurs, and that the diffusion makes possible additional population growth which then takes place. The population-push hypothesis asserts that a pool of unused agricultural knowledge is available in each period, but that each more productive method requires more labor per worker. An increase in population is therefore necessary to force the adoption of the more productive methods, according to the population-push hypothesis. The population-push hypothesis sees population growth in a much more favorable light than does the Malthusian invention-pull hypothesis.

This chapter first demonstrates analytically that the invention-pull hypothesis refers only to inventions that are labor-saving relative to the methods in use. The population-push hypothesis refers only to inventions that are output-increasing but require more labor than is expended with the methods in use at the time of the new invention. Once this distinction is made, the two hypotheses are seen to be complementary rather than mutually exclusive.

The second part of the chapter reviews some historical and anthropological cases of economic-demographic change as they are relevant to the two hypotheses. Some cases are found that are well described by the invention-pull hypothesis, others by the population-push hypothesis. That is, some important inventions—such as the potato—have been immediately labor-saving, and therefore adoption began immediately after invention. Others—such as slash-and-burn agriculture—have been mostly output-increasing but require additional labor relative to the methods in use at the time of invention, and their adoption has awaited further population growth which requires additional output. This review confirms that both the invention-pull and population-push hypotheses have an important place in explaining economic-demographic history. Neither hypothesis, however, explains original inventions themselves, and neither describes the development of modern business farming.

From the standpoint of the human *future*, the thrust of the chapter seems quite positive. Considerable basic knowledge already exists from which the

LDCs can either draw directly when their needs and wishes (influenced by population growth or other forces) change so that the new practices are desirable, or which they can adapt for local use.[25] Institutional and communication blocks may stand in the way, of course, even if there is no lack of basic knowledge. But if enough people are motivated, institutions can and do change. The situation is at least subject to human control; this is the reassuring point.

Notes

1. The description of early-agriculture tenure systems is not accurate, but the abstraction should cause no trouble here.

2. This assumes a Cobb-Douglas production function with exponents of 0.5; this function is chosen for simplicity, but it is not far from the facts of the case.

3. It is apparently the rule in Africa that women work more hours on the farm than do men (Boserup 1970, 21). Even more noteworthy are the small number of hours worked by the men in both Africa and Asia while outside labor is hired to increase output (Boserup 1970, 21 and 25).

4. Illustrative numbers abstracted from various examples given by Clark and Haswell (1967, 26–27 and 47) and Kroeber (1948, 389–90). Somewhat higher population densities for hunting and fishing, and for ''pastoral and forestry,'' are given by Wiechel (cited by Jefferson cited by Hawley 150, 151).

5. Please note that the invention-pull hypothesis assumes only that diffusion *begins* immediately. Diffusion will take time to *complete*, of course, as learning takes place, and uncertainty and risk are reduced.

6. The invention-pull and population-push theorists generally assume away shifts in food quality, so that will also be done here. This assumption, however, runs some risk of invalidating the entire issue.

7. Please notice that such statements as ''labor-saving'' are comparisons relative to the agricultural technology *then in use*. To be labor-saving or capital-using is not an inherent property of an invention, but rather refers to the *difference* between a given invention and existing practice. Lack of recognition of this relativity has sometimes flawed discussions of technological advance.

8. Perhaps there is need to explain the difference in the sets of indifference curves associated with different ''needs'' or different ''standards of living.'' First, I assume that the same sort of alteration in the indifference functions comes from increased ''need'' induced by a larger number of persons (consumer-equivalents) in the family, and from increased income ''aspirations'' induced by a demonstration effect. The indifference curves are drawn in such fashion that an increased need *lowers the slope* of the indifference curve passing through any given output-leisure point. That is, increased need increases the amount of work the family is willing to supply in order to get an additional unit of output; the greater the family's need, the more sensitive is the labor supply to a change in the price of output.

9. The amount of work done on yearly crops is not, however, a very good measure for comparison of the two hypotheses in situations of more advanced agriculture. This is because long-run *investment* becomes progressively more important as agriculture

advances. The investment in slashing and burning in slash-and-burn agriculture is all used up after two or three years. But the stone clearing, stump pulling, digging of irrigation wells and ditches, polder-making, placing drainage tiles, and so on, that are necessary for more advanced agriculture are very long-lived investments—and they also require enormous amounts of backbreaking labor. Very little of this labor (which tends to support the population-push theory) shows up in the yearly time-budgets in settled agricultural regions. This means that data gathered about the labor spent on current farm operations in the context of advanced agriculture does not help discriminate between the population-push and invention-pull hypotheses. And another point about investment: its absence from Boserup's (1965) theorizing about the population-push hypothesis is an important lacuna in her scheme.

10. Part of the explanation clearly is that the *number of farmers* does not rise anywhere near as fast as total population, because of the development of the industrial sector. But this is because of the increase in agricultural productivity as well as because of the increase in industrial opportunities. There certainly have been increases in output per farmer holding, the amount of land constant, which is the phenomenon for which an explanation is sought.

11. Malthus also adduced this example (1803, 65).

12. Malthus read the history of Scandinavia after population increases in exactly this "anti-Malthusian" way: "The nations of the north were slowly and reluctantly compelled to confine themselves within their natural limits and to exchange their pastoral manners and with them the peculiar facilities of plunder and emigration, which they afforded for the patient, laborous and slow returns of trade and agriculture" (1803, 80–81).

13. From say, 1550 in Europe the pattern suggests that changes in agricultural technology were the result of changes in the nexus of prices and population density. The knowledge necessary for the changes was in existence long before, much of it in the Roman period when population density was higher; the methods were not new inventions at that time: "The high price of arable farm produce made it worthwhile to manure the land more richly. . . . In England and some parts of France, in the sixteenth century, marl and lime were put on the land for the first time since the Roman period and the thirteenth century (Slicher van Bath 1963, 205).

"The old monotony of cereal-growing in the countryside was broken down, and crops of other kinds began to take up more of the fields. The systems they esteemed so new, dated, in fact, back to the Middle Ages; the seventeenth and eighteenth centuries had brought them nothing different in principle. It was the great expansion of these systems that was revolutionary" (Ibid., 243–44).

14. I am indebted to James Millar for bringing Chayanov's extraordinary book to my attention.

15. These farms averaged 20%–50% of their income in money and the rest in subsistence in the various areas Chayanov studied (1925–1966, 121). This probably makes them as much "subsistence" farms as most of those in Asia today.

16. The pressure of population apparently worked its influence less directly, too: "In most parts of Europe . . . there were strong institutional obstacles to the introduction of the new techniques which were removed only under the pressure of population" (Habakkuk 1963, 612).

17. The above-cited data on European population-push adoption of labor-using innovations goes hand in hand with the well-documented population-pushed increases in investment in land reclamation, drainage, and irrigation discussed in the nonmonetized investment section of chapter 11 of *Economics of Population Growth*.

18. This following section is based on White (1962, chapter 2). I am grateful to Larry Neal for bringing it to my attention.

19. In England, increasing population led to the adoption of turnip husbandry and the accompanying creation of new wheat lands. "Under turnip husbandry the great sandy wastes in Norfolk were transformed into some of the best wheat land in England and the promoters of the reform are said to have, in effect, added a province to their country. The new methods spread very slowly in the first part of the [eighteenth] century but rapidly in the latter part, a remarkable fact when the notorious conservatism of those engaged in agriculture is remembered. The rapidly growing population provided the necessary stimulus; in the North, the agriculturists found new and lucrative markets springing up at their doors, in the South, London continued to grow in size and wealth. In both cases canals made easier the transport of agricultural products" (Buer 1926, 70).

20. Although mostly qualitative, Connell's history of the potato in Ireland is a satisfactory demonstration that the potato increased output on given land input with no increase in labor, and hence had a neat Malthusian invention-pull effect: ". . . the history of the potato in Ireland shows that it was of quite fundamental importance in *permitting and encouraging the rapid growth of population* in the sixty or seventy years before the Famine. It permitted the growth of population because, in early eighteenth-century Ireland, population had been pressing on resources: any substantial expansion of population implied a parallel expansion of the means of subsistence, and in large measure it was in an abundance of potatoes that the increasing number of people found its sustenance.

"It is not difficult to see how the potato lifted the restraints to the growth of population. When people had been living largely on grain, the substitution of the potato allowed their land to support at least twice as many people as before: when, as with the Irish before their general dependence on the potato, pastoral products had bulked large in the popular dietary, at least a quadrupling of the density of population became possible. At the same time, land which to a pastoral or grain-producing community had been of next to no economic importance became capable of yielding satisfactory crops of potatoes, and of allowing, therefore, a further measure of population-increase.

"It was not only through the substitution of the potato for the traditional crops that its influence was felt in relaxing the limits to population growth. There is evidence that, in the fifty and more years before the Famine, the potato itself was undergoing a process of substitution. Increasingly the traditional varieties were losing ground before new and more prolific types, which allowed a further increase in the density of the population of the areas where they were grown.

"The potato provided not only a prerequisite for the growth of population; it provided also a mechanism; it not only permitted, but encouraged increase. As potatoes were substituted for the traditional foodstuffs, a family's subsistence could be found from a diminished section of its holding. There tended to appear on every tenancy a margin of land that was needed neither to provide the peasant's subsistence, nor the landlord's customary rent. The tendency of landlordism was to force up rent until this margin had to be entirely assimilated with the section of the holding. . . .'' (Connell 1950, 159–60).

21. This section is drawn from Perkins (1968, particularly chapters 1 and 9). I appreciate Peter Schran's bibliographical advice on this topic.

22. ''. . . In China there were few improvements in 'best' technique in the six-century period [from 1368 to 1957] and little apparent spread of that 'best' technique from 'advanced' to 'backward' regions. The major innovations that did appear in the post-fourteenth-century period had to do with improved seeds and new crops from the Americas. Improved seed varieties were being discovered in China and brought in from abroad throughout these six centuries and in previous centuries as well. These seeds raised yields, reduced crop fluctuations, and contributed to the increase in double cropping. But there was no general movement of improved varieties from 'advanced' to 'backward' regions. If anything, the trend was in the opposite direction'' (Perkins 1969, 186).

Ho gives a slightly different emphasis: ''. . . It is partially true that for centuries there has been no technological revolution in Chinese agriculture, evidenced by the fact that the same kind of agricultural implements have been used by Chinese peasants of certain areas for centuries. Yet such a generalization requires qualification. During the Ming period there were significant improvements in agricultural implements, particularly in various kinds of water-pumps'' (Ho, Ping-Ti 1959, 169).

23. But this expansion of cultivated area was interrelated with the introduction of new types of crops, which is a technological change.

''In the absence of major technological inventions the nature of the crops has done more than anything else to push the agricultural frontier further away from the low plains, basins, and valleys to the more arid hilly and mountainous regions and has accounted for an enormous increase in national food production'' (Ho, Ping-Ti 1959, 169).

''Early-ripening rice aided the conquest of relatively well-watered hills. American food plants have enabled the Chinese, historically a plain and valley folk, to use dry hills and mountains and sandy loams too light for rice and other native cereal crops. There is evidence that the dry hills and mountains of the Yangtze region and north China were still largely virgin about 1700. Since then they have gradually been turned into maize and sweet potato farms. In fact, during the last two centuries, when rice culture was gradually approaching its limit and encountering the law of diminishing returns, the various dryland food crops introduced from America have contributed the most to the increase in national food production and have made possible a continual growth of population'' (Ibid., 184).

Population pressure was apparently necessary in bringing about this shift. For example, ''Mai Chu, governor general of Hupei and Hunan, 1727–1733, stated in a memorial that wheat was not grown extensively in Hupei, excepting in two northern prefectures. But after the serious flood of 1727 the peasants in low-land Hupei, under the persuasion of the provincial government, began to grow wheat widely'' (Ibid., 180).

''The repeated Sung exhortations, however, could not prevail over climatic and topographical factors; neither could they force the majority of rice farmers to adopt a more labor-intensive system of double-cropping in a period when land was still comparatively plentiful in the inland Yangtze region'' (Ibid., 178).

24. The history of Chinese agriculture after the Communist regime gained complete control is a slightly different story. Certainly, food production increased greatly, to the point of continued self-sufficiency, except for the disastrous ''Great Leap Forward'' episode, culminating in ten consecutive ''bumper harvests'' (Schran 1969; *Kwang Ming Daily*, in *Kayhan International*, Teheran, January 30, 1970, 2). The increase in agricultural production was accomplished without major technological change (though with a considerable increase in the use of fertilizer), and certainly not because of new discoveries, but rather due to a social reorganization which caused an increase in the amount of work done by agriculturalists. This certainly is consistent with the population-push hypothesis.

25. Soybean agriculture in India is an example. The same seeds and products used in Illinois cannot be used successfully in India. But soybean scientists know *how to learn* which changes are necessary to make a successful transfer.

References

Balikci, Asen. 1968. The Netsilik Eskimos: Adaptive Processes. In Richard B. Lee and Irven Devore, eds., *Man the Hunter*. Chicago: Aldine.

Baumol, William J. 1951. *Economic Dynamics*. New York: Macmillan.

Boserup, Ester. 1965. *The Conditions of Agricultural Growth*. London: George Allen and Unwin.

———. 1970. *Women's Role in Economic Development*. London: George Allen and Unwin.

Buer, M. C. 1926. *Health, Wealth, and Population in the Early Days of the Industrial Revolution*. London: George Routledge.

Chayanov, A. V. 1966. *The Theory of Peasant Economy*. Edited by D. Thorner et al. Homewood, Ill.: Irwin. First published in 1925.

Childe, V. Gordon. 1937. *Man Makes Himself*. London: Watts.

Cipolla, Carlo M. 1962. *The Economic History of World Population*. Baltimore: Pelican.

Clark, Colin. 1967. *Population Growth and Land Use*. New York: St. Martins.

Clark, Colin, and Margaret Haswell. 1967. *The Economics of Subsistence Agriculture*. New York: St. Martins.

Connell, R. H. 1965. *Land and Population in Ireland 1750–1845*. Chicago: Aldine.

Curwen, E. Cecil, and Gudmund Hatt. 1953. *Plough and Pasture*. New York: Collier.

Darity, William A., Jr. 1980. ''The Boserup Theory of Agricultural Growth.'' *Journal of Development Economics* 7: 137–57.

Dovring, Folke. 1965. Land and labor in Europe in the twentieth century. The Hague: M. Nijhoff.

———. 1966. ''Review of Boserup.'' *Journal of Economic History* 26: 380–81.

Firth, Raymond W. 1939, 1965. Primitive Polynesian economy. London: Routledge and Kegan Paul.

Gourou, Pierre. 1966. *The Tropical World. Its Social and Economic Conditions and Its Future Status*. New York: Wiley.

Hawley, Ames H. 1950. *Human Ecology*. New York: Ronald Press.

Heady, Earl O. 1949. "Basic Economic and Welfare Aspects of Farm Technological Advance." *Journal of Farm Economics* 31: 293–316.

Kroeber, Alfred L. 1948. *Anthropology*. New revised ed. New York: Harcourt, Brace.

Langer, William L. 1963, 1968. Europe's initial population explosion. *American Historical Review* 69: 1–17. Reprinted in *Readings on population*. David M. Heer, ed. Englewood Cliffs, N.J.: Prentice-Hall.

Lee, Richard B. 1968. "What Hunters do for a Living, or, How to Make Out on Scarce Resources." Pages 30–48 in R. B. Lee and Irvin Devore, eds., *Man the Hunter*. Chicago: Aldine.

Lee, Ronald. 1989. "Malthus and Boserup: A Dynamic Synthesis." In David Coleman and Roger Schofield, eds., *The State of Population Theory: Forward from Malthus*. Oxford: Basil Blackwell.

Lewis, Oscar. 1951. Life in a Mexican village. Urbana, Ill. University of Illinois Press.

McCarthy, Frederick D., and Margaret McArthur. 1960. The Food Quest and the Time Factor in Aboriginal Economic Life. In *Records of the American Australian Scientific Expedition to Arnhem Land*, Vol. 2. Melbourne: Melbourne University Press.

McKeown, Thomas, and R. G. Brown. 1955, 1968. Medieval evidence related to English population changes in the eighteenth century. *Population Studies* 9: 119–41. Reprinted in *Readings on population*. David M. Heer, ed. Englewood Cliffs, N.J.: Prentice-Hall.

Mellor, John W. 1963. "The Use and Productivity of Farm Family Labor in Early Stages of Agricultural Growth." *Journal of Farm Economics* 45: 517–34.

Nakajima, Chihiro. 1969. "Subsistence and Commercial Family Farms: Some Theoretical Models of Subjective Equilibrium." Pages 165–84 in Clifton R. Wharton, ed., *Subsistence Agriculture and Economic Development*. Chicago: Aldine.

Perkins, Dwight. 1969. Agricultural Development in China (1368–1968). Chicago: Aldine.

Pryor, Frederic L., and Steven B. Maurer. 1982. "On Induced Economic Change in Precapitalist Societies." *Journal of Development Economics* 10: 325–53.

Redfield, Robert. 1930. Tepoztlan—a Mexican Village. Chicago: University of Chicago Press.

———. 1957. A Village that chose progress. Chicago: University of Chicago Press.

Redfield, Robert, and Villa Rojas. 1934. Chan Kom: A Maya Village. Washington: Carnegie.

Sahlins, Marshall D. 1968. "Notes on Original Affluent Society." Pages 84–89 in Richard B. Lee and Iven Devore, eds. *Man the Hunter*. Chicago: Aldine.

Schmookler, Jacob. 1962. "Changes in Industry and in the State of Knowledge as Determinants of Industrial Invention." In National Bureau of Economic Research, *The Rate and Direction of Inventive Activity: Economic and Social Factors*, 195–232. Princeton, N.J.: Princeton University Press.

Schran, Peter. 1969. *The Development of Chinese Agriculture, 1950–1959*. Urbana: University of Illinois Press.

Schultz, Theodore W. 1964. *Transforming Traditional Agriculture*. New Haven, Conn.: Yale University Press.

Sen, Amartya K. 1959. "The Choice of Agricultural Techniques in Underdeveloped Countries," *Economic Development and Cultural Change* 7: 279–85.

———. 1966. "Peasants and Dualism With or Without Surplus Labor." *Journal of Political Economy* 74: 425–50.

Simon, Julian L. 1977. *The Economics of Population Growth*. Princeton, N.J., Princeton University Press.

Slicher van Bath, B. H. 1963. *The Agrarian History of Western Europe, A.D. 300–1850*. London: Arnold.

Thomsen, Moritz. 1969. *Living Poor*. New York: Ballantine.

Von Thunen, Johann H. 1966. *The Isolated State*. New York: Pergamon. First published in 1826.

White, Lynn, Jr. 1962. *Medieval Technology and Social Change*. New York: Oxford.

Woodburn, James. 1968. "An Introduction to Hadza Ecology." Pages 49–55 in Richard B. Lee and Irven Devore, eds., *Man the Hunter*. Chicago: Aldine.

[21]

Foreword

The following note went out with this paper in most of its forays seeking publication.

Referees were especially distressed by this paper. Here are a few excerpts from a three-page single-spaced damnation:

> The paper is more a debater's exercise than a scholarly espousal or defense of a position. It is replete with casual empiricism and logical non sequiturs. The paper avoids empirical testing where such is possible and either misstates or is in error on many factual points. It waits until p. 27 to cavalierly dismiss those propositions that are essential issues in any substantive consideration of its initial propositions ("no mention has been made ... etc."). The author essentially has dismissed central economic issues related to his discussion. The conclusions that a larger labor force yields increasing returns to idea-production totally ignores the costs of producing this information. The paper assumes that information tends to grow exponentially but makes little effort, other than dropping the names of the originators of paradigmatic scientific shifts, to consider the empirical evidence (de Solla Price, Machlup) on measures of scientific activity.
>
> The paper establishes only the loosest association among the terms, ideas, inventions, technical progress, and productivity improvements. Invention is a resource-using activity; thus considerations of its costs and of influences on its end uses cannot be dismissed. The paper is presented as an alternative to growth models, but its dismissal of economic factors is striking. The references are dated, often referring to the 1962 volume of the NBER or to literature of that period, with almost no attention to the extensive and diverse literature on the causes of technical progress. This includes, for example, works by Mansfield or Rosenberg, to take two very dissimilar traditions in the literature. It completely ignores comparative studies on the determinants of the level and rate of inputs and outputs in the many dimensions of idea-generation and technical progress (e.g., OECD studies, NSF's *Science Indicators*).
>
> Moreover, the entire discussion of the dependence of knowledge on the size of the population presupposes a "materialistic" outlook and an implicated investment in idea-generating skills. While the author's propositions have a certain heuristic value, they are historically empty. For example, note the statement calling out for verification on page 8, "compelling evidence on the contribution of additional people, ..." etc. Where is the evidence? My reading of what I take to be the relevant literature (e.g., R. Nelson, Arrow), but which is never cited by the author, is that it provides no support at all for the author's claims. It would seem to me that this is essential if one is going to take much of both the prior and subsequent analysis seriously. Moreover, there is no clear link between the general discussions on population size and presumed density as a function and as a stimulating factor in knowledge creation and the micromodel of invention.
>
> The argument clearly strains at being disingenuous. For example, the quotes from Coale on the shortage of people relate to specifically trained period, not to population per se. Indeed all these quotes suggest that there is at any time as new areas open up a shortage of people trained in that area, as in biotechnology, for example. But this has nothing to do with population.
>
> I am astonished, for example, by some of the statements, such as on page 25, "on the other hand productivity is increasing at an increasing rate as discussed by Solow (1957) and Fellner (1971)." Some of these quotes predate the "productivity slowdown" that has been a concern in delivered economics since the 1970s:

Several others suggested that the paper is "unfinished." They meant that there is no formal deductive proof of the central proposition. So what? Two of the best applied mathematicians in the country were unable to find closed proofs. And there is an approximate proof. Should the paper be judged on its economic content or its mathematical nicety? (Why, the latter, of course.)

2
A Micro-Model of Invention and its Relation to the Technical Progress Function

I. INTRODUCTION

Discussion of induced technical progress has been almost entirely at the level of the economy, the industry or the firm. That makes considerable sense because the available data are at those levels of aggregation, ranging from the Abramowitz–Solow–Denison tradition of work on the components of growth, to the Rostas–Verdoorn tradition of work on industries, to the Alchian–Arrow learning-by-doing tradition, and the industrial-organization and organizational-behaviour literatures on firms. But there has been little discussion and less formal analysis of induced technical progress at the level of the individual inventor and adapter. (I shall refer to an analysis of invention at this level as a micro-model, or a model of invention, to be distinguished from both a more aggregated analysis of technical progress, and from a macro-model of the economy as a whole that embodies a technical progress function.) Without a model of the actual actors, and their interactions with each other and with the body of existing knowledge, we are talking about a mechanism taking place in a black box, without any understanding of its mode of operation.

Therefore, it seems appropriate to offer a micro-model of invention before moving on to discuss macro-models. The little attention the topic has received has been devoted to the direction of advances in technology, whether affected by relative intensities of capital and labour, and whether influenced by demand in particular industries or autonomous (see, for example, the 1962 NBER volume edited by

Nelson). But the more important question from the point of view of both policy and growth theory concerns the determinants of the *total quantity* of technical progress and the rate of change in the level of technique.

The technical-progress functions that have been proposed in the literature – Kaldor's, Arrow's, Phelps's and others – vary greatly in their implications, and they would not be consistent with the same micro-models. Therefore, a micro-analysis can throw some light upon which of the contending technical-progress functions and accompanying macro-models is most plausible.

The aim of this chapter is to offer a model of the process of knowledge creation at the individual level, to see what it implies and how it fits with the aggregate evidence and the macro-models. Of course such a model is not likely to persuade everyone that it is reasonable, or even most people, though hopefully it will persuade *some*. And no one at all will think that by itself this model is adequate, or even more than a rough beginning. But it is hoped that this model will serve to initiate systematic discussion which will eventuate in a satisfactory micro-model of the process of technical progress, especially in relationship to population growth.

A major complication in the chain from invention to its effect on productivity and the standard of living is the relationship between invention and adoption of new techniques. At any one moment there is a large stock of useful techniques that have not been applied. But relatively few inventions ever get used – 1 in 1000, in Machlup's guesstimate. And the relationship between invention and adoption is not fixed, and there probably are diminishing returns to additional inventions in the short run. But in the long-run context of the present discussion, the number of potential appliers of knowledge should be proportional to the number of inventors, and therefore I shall assume that technical progress is a proportional function of advance in technology, without further discussion of the relationship between them.

Section II discusses the main theoretical considerations that may influence the relationship between technical progress and labour-force size and growth. Section III constructs a micro-model relating population to technical progress, and considers how it fits the various macro-models. Section IV discusses the results and qualifications of the. Section V concludes and summarizes. Afterword 2A discusses how the micro-model fits with the various macro-models. Afterword 2B discusses the prospects for continued advance in inventive activity.

This chapter may seem unfinished to the reader. Certainly, I have not found a way to make the argument as well as I would like. One source of difficulty is that the question at hand is rather different than those questions economics usually considers. Yet I think that the question is important, and the answer I suggest seems internally consistent even if the logic is not elegant. I hope, then, that you will read it in the spirit in which it is offered.

It is crucial to keep in mind that the unit to which the analysis refers is the entire human society, or at a minimum that chunk of human society which presently contributes substantially to increase in technology. In this respect, the chapter is in the same spirit as the rest of the book. Where countries are the units of analysis in empirical studies upon which I draw, that is solely because they are the best available approach to a sample of observations, in the absence of a sample of worlds.

II. ELEMENTS OF THE THEORY

Later chapters discuss technical-progress functions which contain such arguments as labour-force size, output, stock of knowledge and investment. But from the point of view of general policy questions, as well as social decisions about population growth, the key issue is not that of deciding *which* factor is the most important. Rather, the key question is whether *any* measure related to the size of the economy or the population has a strong effect on productivity. This behooves us to ask: Under which conditions might additional people *not* lead to increased productivity? These are some suggestions that have been made:

(a) Additional people dilute the stock of capital, even if they increase the stock of knowledge. Therefore, the trade-off between these two forces must be studied in the context of a full economic model, as is done in other chapters of this book.

(b) Some forces involved in technical progress are said to be 'inversely related to the rate of population growth' (Spengler, 1968, p. 115). A prominent example: faster growth and a larger population might lead to less education per person. But the data (Simon and Pilarski, 1979; Meeks, 1982; Miyata et al., 1982; Ram, 1982) suggest that this force does not operate strongly in the short run. And in the long course of history so far, it surely has not been much of a factor. Another possibility is that faster population growth reduces the rate of saving, and hence reduces the rate at which technology, embodied in capital, is brought into use. But the evidence on the population growth-saving relationship is very thin (see Simon, 1977). Therefore, neither of these matters is built into the models of this book.

(c) Another possibility is that additional people are so much like existing people that they are not likely to come up with any improvements that the existing population would not come up with. That is, people may be sufficiently homogeneous so that additional people do not produce additional variety in ideas. Evidence for similarity in people's thinking is found in the existence of independent inventions of the same idea; stochastic dominance is a recent example in finance, modelling of the consumer is an example in marketing, and DNA an example in biology; patent priority fights are additional evidence. This possibility implicitly assumes a limited base of existing knowledge which people can develop, and a limited range of other stimuli to people's imaginations.

(d) If there is a very obvious order in the value of potential projects, if people are clear-minded enough to perceive this order and if there is at least a fair amount of similarity in people's talents and interests, then there would be high duplication in work on the most important inventions.

The foregoing are arguments that have been made about why additional people might *not* lead to increased technology and productivity. Now let us add some remarks about why they *are likely* to have such effects.

Surely there is additional variety introduced by additional people. As Hayek puts it (1960, p. 29), 'the advance and even the preservation of civilization are dependent upon a maximum of opportunity for accidents to happen. These accidents occur in the combination of knowledge and attitudes, skills and habits, acquired by individual men and also when qualified men are confronted with the particular circumstances which they are equipped to deal with'. And it is clear that the more people there are, *ceteris paribus*, the more 'accidents' that can occur. It is also true that the '*ceteris paribus*' clause must not be ignored; the circumstances are crucial, as for example when Hayek also notes that 'Liberty is essential in order to leave room for the unforeseeable and predictable' (p. 29). Yet it seems to me that the more people there are, the more accidents, more variety, more advances in knowledge and productivity there will be.

Even if there are diminishing returns in knowledge production, in the very longest run an increment to knowledge now will have a more positive effect on income than any decrement to capital per worker due to additional people, on almost any assumptions. The question, then, must be: how *much* additional productive knowledge can we expect from additional people, and how long will it take to overcome the negative effects of capital dilution?

Furthermore, there are reasons to suppose that in the long run there are increasing returns to additional persons even in knowledge production itself. Kuznets makes an argument for increasing returns on two grounds: (a) the stimulating effect of a dense environment; and (b) 'interdependence of knowledge of the various parts of the world in which we human beings operate', (p. 328); for example, discoveries in physics stimulate discoveries in biology, and vice versa. And he discounts the possibility of diminishing returns because 'the universe is far too vast relative to the size of our planet and what we know about it' (p. 329).

Machlup suggests that 'every new invention furnishes a new idea for potential combination with vast numbers of existing ideas . . . [and] the number of possible combinations increases geometrically with the number of elements at hand' (1962, p. 156). It is this latter idea of an increasing number of permutations of elements of knowledge as the stock increases that seems most compelling to me, when put together with the idea of a reduced possibility of duplicate discoveries as the number of possibilities increases faster than the number of potential knowledge producers. And we shall see later that – contrary to intuition – duplication of intellectual effort is likely to be *less and less* of a constraint with the passage of time and with larger populations. Eventually we can expect the main constraint to be an individual's idea-production capacity alone, while the duplication factor will be negligible.

The divergence of views on this matter makes it important to investigate the process at the individual level, to build a model, and to speculate about reasonable parameters to see how they jibe with the aggregate evidence. A sound micro-model should help us decide which technical progress function is most to be preferred.

This model abstracts from the important issues of the social and economic framework within which the inventive activity is to take place, and the cost of the production of inventions. The former of these issues is discussed starting on p. 68, and the latter is discussed starting on p. 49.

III. A MICRO-MODEL OF INVENTION

At any moment there are L_t workers in the economy, all of whom are potential creators of new knowledge. These workers differ in their propensities to invent and innovate, and one could differentiate them in the model. But that would introduce complication without changing the conclusions.

Let us first notice that no matter what assumptions one makes about the composition of the 'original' population – about the homogeneity, and about the distribution of characteristics – an increment of people similiar in composition to the original people will increase the number of ideas by that same proportion *if* the original group and the incremental group are exposed to different but equally potent stimuli. That is, if people and stimuli are all that go into idea making, the function is homogeneous of degree one. There may be individual sluggards and individual big producers, but each kind will be found in each group. Critical-minimum-size groups may be necessary to produce some kinds of ideas, but this will be true in the same way for the original as for incremental groups. In brief, the only constraint or factor that might lead to diminishing returns to additional people in idea production (leaving aside education and capital for now) is the size of the stock of knowledge that is available in common to the potential idea producers. This means – somewhat surprisingly – that we do not need to know anything about the degree of similarity of additional people to existing people in order to know how additional people will increment the flow of ideas.

New technology is built upon the stock of technology and other stimuli, that is, the number of bits of information ($\Sigma_{t-\infty}^{t} J_t$), in the environment at moment t, resulting from events in all years up to the present *t*. This is the key idea and the fundament of this analysis. And there are two relevant aspects of the stock of knowledge that may be used for creating new ideas. On the one hand, when an idea is created, that idea is removed from the universe of possible new ideas still to be discovered. And if ten more people come along and re-discover the idea independently, nothing is gained; here we find the operation of a process of diminishing returns to additional ideas.[1] On the other hand, newly discovered ideas also add to the stock of elements that may be combined with other elements to create still other new ideas. Surely this describes the history of human economic and intellectual growth. Newton's and Einstein's, Smith's and Malthus's and Keynes's discoveries depleted the stock of those potential ideas, but opened up vast fields of possibility for future discoveries.[2] Discoveries about indexes and national income accounts removed those fish from the pond of potential discoveries in economics, but left their eggs to spawn large numbers of new fish which could not have previously hatched. The creation of new economic data – a result of more people and more income in a country – removes the opportunity to do this for the first time, but greatly enhances the possible number of other studies a contemporary economist can do. The research that required the brilliance of Adam Smith or John Graunt or William Petty can now be done routinely by us. And an article by Arrow or Becker or Markowitz or Schultz or Stigler can – fortunately or unfortunately – spawn a career industry.

New ideas arise not only from existing ideas but also are stimulated by observations of the natural and physical world, the effective variety of which increases as economic and social development takes place and as people are more mobile and thereby come into contact with more aspects of the world around them. But for simplicity here – and, I believe, without changing the nature of the argument – the analysis will proceed as if new ideas arise only from the combination of existing ideas, without reference to observations of the world itself.

The indulgence of the reader is asked with respect to the notation that will now be used. I have not been able to find a notation that expresses the necessary concepts and yet is clear and unconfusing. This difficulty arises from the fact that an idea that is the 'output' in one period is then a potential – but not necessarily actual – input to the production of other ideas in the next period. It is therefore hoped that the reader will have patience in following the argument through the notational difficulty.

Let $J_{j\bar{j}}$ be a new idea formed of the combination of two different idea stimuli, j and $\bar{j}$, coming from the set $j = 1,2,3,\ldots,M_{t-1}$ of stimulus elements existing as of the end of $t-1$. To be a new idea, this combination $j\bar{j}$ must never have occurred before, which also means that it is not itself found as an element in set $j = 1,2,\ldots,M_{t-1}$. (A fuller treatment would also consider the higher order combinations, $J_{j\bar{j}\bar{\bar{j}}}$, but here we may neglect them.)

The stock of technology M_t available at the end of any period t consists of the stock of knowledge at the beginning of the prior period M_{t-1} plus the sum of the new ideas created in that period, $\Sigma_{j\bar{j}} J_t$.

$$m_t = \sum_{t-\infty}^{t-1} \Sigma_{j\bar{j}} J_{t,j\bar{j}} + \Sigma_{j\bar{j}} J_{t,j\bar{j}} \qquad (2.1)$$

And each new idea is thereby added to the stock of stimuli available as building blocks for idea creation in subsequent periods. Notationally, each $J_{j\bar{j}}$ occurring in one period becomes a j in the next period.

We shall assume that during each period, each person i among the persons in the labour force L produces exactly one combination of j and $\bar{j}$, a random drawing without replacement (for that drawing) from M_{t-1}. In reality, people differ considerably in the numbers of ideas they create, but (as discussed earlier) this will be seen not to affect the model if we notice that a partition of the labour force into the same proportional divisions each year of idea producers (one idea) and non-idea producers (zero) would not affect the model (nor would a more continuous distribution).

It would also be realistic to assume that the flow of ideas per representative person increases over the years, both because more education probably leads to more productive ideas, and also because there is, to my knowledge, no evidence that scientific production is declining in output per person.[3] And we see ever-increasing flows of new products, and of such additional carriers of new information as magazines and journals. But this matter is left aside by the model.

Our ultimate aim is to learn how the number of potential idea-producing persons (the labour force) affects the growth of the stock of knowledge. For economic purposes we will want to know whether the additional ideas produced by additional workers will be sufficient to counter-balance the negative effect of additional persons on the supply of capital per person.

The potential number of ideas that might be discovered at time t is (dropping the time subscript of M)

$$N_t = M(M-1) - \sum_{t-\infty}^{t-1} \sum_{j=1}^{j=M} J_{t,j\bar{j}} \tag{2.2}$$

that is, the total number of combinations then possible less those that have already been discovered. We assume that if a person first hits on an idea that has *previously* (not concurrently) been discovered – the negative part of the right-hand side of the above expression – the person will simply 'throw the fish back' and find another hitherto-undiscovered idea, but one which may be concurrently discovered by another person. N_t is a simplified symbol for this concept.

The probability that a combination $j\bar{j}$ is a new idea, p_{new}, is the proportion of all possible $M(M-1)$ combinations that have not previously been discovered, that is, the ratio of undiscovered combinations to all combinations.

$$p_{\text{new}} = \frac{M(M-1) - \Sigma_{t-\infty}^{t-1} \Sigma_{j=1}^{j=M} J_{t,j\bar{j}}}{M(M-1)} \tag{2.3}$$

The probability of duplication or 'overlap' – that probability that a given new $j\bar{j}$ will be discovered by more than one person in the same period – is roughly the ratio of the number of people in the 'discovery' labour force, L_t, to the total number of possible undiscovered ideas, N_t, or L_t/N_t, and the probability of non-duplication,

$$p_{\text{nondup}} \approx \left(1 - \frac{L_t}{N_t}\right) \tag{2.4}$$

That is, a larger number of potential discoverers implies more duplication and a lower probability, p_{nondup}, that a given idea will be unduplicated. Therefore the total number of new ideas that will be discovered in a given period t, not counting duplicates or higher order overlaps more than once, is the number of idea producers multiplied by the probability that any given idea has not been previously discovered multiplied by the probability that a given idea is not discovered by more than one person concurrently.

$$\sum_{j=1}^{j=M} J_{t,j\bar{j}} = L_t p_{\text{new}}\, p_{\text{nondup}} = L_t \left[\frac{M(M-1) - \Sigma_{t-\infty}^{t-1} J_t}{M(M-1)}\right] \times \left(1 - \frac{L_t}{N_t}\right) \quad (2.5)$$

The number of new ideas discovered in t is a positive function of L_t. This may be seen by rearranging (2.5) as

$$\sum_{t=1}^{t=M} J_{t,j\bar{j}} = L_t\left(\frac{N_t - L_t}{N_t}\right)p_{\text{new}} = \left(\frac{L_t N_t - L_t^2}{N_t}\right)p_{\text{new}} \quad (2.6)$$

As long as $N_t > L_t$ (noting that p_{new} is not affected by L_t), then an increase in L_t means a larger increment to $L_t N_t$ than to L_t^2. But for two reasons this does not immediately imply that faster population growth and more people imply a higher standard of living in future years: (a) the number of people and of discoveries in t affects the stock of potential discoveries in two opposing manners – by creating more new J elements but using up more existing $j\bar{j}$ combinations. And (b), faster population growth implies less physical capital per person, *ceteris paribus*. Therefore, to understand the overall effect we must now analyse (a), and eventually take account of (b) in a complete macro-model simulation.

Intuitively we can seen that p_{nondup}, the proportion of ideas that are not duplicates, will increase each year because in successive years each new idea element can combine with an ever-larger number of existing stimuli-elements, as Machlup (1962) noticed. The number of j elements that is added to the set M each year is almost L_t, and therefore the number of new possible combinations is almost $L_t M_t$ – or better, $(L_{t-1} + \Delta L_t) M_t$, where the delta ($\Delta$) indicates the increment of population growth – whereas the number of possible duplications rises only from a bit less than L_{t-1} to a bit less than L_t, roughly ΔL_t. If ΔL_t is 2 per cent of L_t, then $L_t M_t$ is $50M_t$ as large as ΔL_t, a very large factor of multiplication no matter what number – a million, a thousand, or a trillion – one assigns to M_t. Given this very large rise in the ratio of to-be-discovered elements relative to the number of potential duplications, in a relatively short time the number of new ideas per period will approach the number of persons, as $\Sigma_{j\bar{j}} J_{t,j\bar{j}} \rightarrow L_t$. (We know this is not quite true because people do not work on ideas across the spectrum of possibilities, but cluster where the 'action' is. But if the *size of cluster* remains the same from year to year, we can replace 'idea' with 'cluster' in our thinking without changing the results.)

To put the matter another way, an additional person in year t has a chance of L_t/N_t of producing a duplicated idea ($p_{\text{nondup}} = 1 - L_t/N_t$), which is slightly greater than the previous person added to the group, that is, diminishing returns from this factor alone. In the next period, however, the number of potential combinations $j\bar{j}$ is approximately M times what it would be otherwise, which has a relatively large impact on reducing duplication. In this fashion, the analysis implies that there are increasing returns in technology creation from additional people until the process tapers off to constant returns. This suggests that additional people imply additional knowledge, without limits. And because an increment of technology has a cumulative effect in raising income through its effect on output and capital formation, a proportional increase in technology in t comes to have a more-than-proportional positive partial effect on income in $t + x$ where x = years after t.[4]

Assuredly, this analysis is far from realistically complete, but hopefully it takes the issue to a deeper level of understanding and to a higher level of precision than previously.

IV. COUNTER-ARGUMENTS AND QUALIFICATIONS

(a) Not all ideas that might be discovered have the same potential quality and value. If people came upon ideas only by chance, this non-equality would not in any way affect the workings of the model given above. But people prefer to produce high-value ideas rather than low-value ideas. If it were also the case that people could also identify the possible high-potential ideas with perfect accuracy, then – if there were no differences among people in interests and skills – every potential knowledge-producer would be working on the same potential idea at a given moment. If there were also a reasonably high likelihood that a random person would succeed in making the discovery of this highest value idea, then diminishing returns to additional persons would be sharp.

To obtain a satisfying understanding of this mechanism would require a fuller model. Such a model would not be easy to construct. More important, however, qualitative estimates of the relevant parameters are, to my knowledge, both non-existent at present and likely to be extraordinarily difficult to produce in the future. The best that we can do at present is to discuss the matter qualitatively and to try to compare the overall results against the aggregate facts, which I will do in that order.

Diminishing returns due to concentration of efforts on the same research project requires, first of all, that all persons have the ability to work in the same general area, and that intellectual mobility is total. But this is clearly not the case. The mature individual who shifts from one major area to another (e.g. from economics to biology or psychology, or the reverse) is rare, and even shifting between minor areas (e.g. public finance and population economics) is not very common. Furthermore, there is proliferation of areas within which people study and later work, so there may not even be a greater number of effective competitors than in the past; for example, Plato and Aristotle, and Bentham and Hume and Smith, took much of human knowledge as their playground, talked to others interested in all these subjects, and made fundamental contributions in all of them; this sort of behaviour is much less likely today. It might even turn out (if one were to examine membership lists of professional organizations over hundreds of years) that one's primary professional organization has grown no bigger, for example, the American Farm Economics Association or the Population Association of America now versus the American Economic Association at the turn of the century. If the size of 'non-competing groups' has not grown over the years, this would be enough to dispatch the worry of diminishing returns from increasing concentration on the idea with the highest potential value.

Second, diminishing returns from increasing concentration of workers requires ability among workers in a given field to spot the highest-value projects. Such perfect prevision is far from the rule; even the most eminent men disagree on which areas are most worthy of attention. Furthermore, there is ample evidence that many important ideas are not come upon even though the intellectual preconditions and the need for the idea are present. One example is dynamic programming, which could have been developed and used centuries before it was invented. Another example, according to Weinberg (1977, p. 6), is the set of 'the discoveries of the recession of distant galaxies and of a weak radio static filling the universe. This is a rich story for the historian of science, filled with false starts, missed opportunities, theoretical preconceptions, and the play of personalities'.

Third, people would have to be willing to practice a strategy of working on the project with highest potential but also greatest competition. If researchers are anything like Hotelling's spatial retail competitors, or Downs's political competitors, or several theorists' television-programme competitors, they will recognize that it can make sense to move away from the highest potential area of the market in order to face less competition. Certainly we see this in some areas of science: India and Brazil are of greater importance on the world scene than are Ceylon and Guyana, but some students (even those from the US or USSR) work on the smaller rather than on the larger of them.

With regard to the first three points above, it should be noted that we don't know much about how people pick topics to work upon. Some people are attracted by large concentrations of workers; others are attracted by empty areas. Some are influenced by the scientific literature; others – like Keynes in the 1930s – are influenced by the news and the events of the day. Some are influenced by ideas, others by physical objects. Some people like low-risk projects, others are less risk averse. About all we can safely say for sure – but this is important – is that there is great variety in people's topic-choosing behaviour, as may be seen from the fact that seldom will two members of an academic department be working on the same problem with the same tools and for the same purpose.

Fourth, concentration of workers on a given problem is only a cause of diminishing returns if the likelihood of any *one* person being successful is great enough so that the likelihood of *more* than one being successful is meaningfully large. And if this were really the case, then simultaneous duplicate production of important ideas would be seen frequently; it is not, in my observation.

Fifth, for concentration to be a cause of diminishing returns, communication among workers in the same general areas would have to be sufficiently slow so that a person who might work on a potential discovery would not be warned off by the just-previous success of another. Many of us have had the experience of contemplating working on an idea, checking the literature and the field of allied workers, and finding out that in fact it has been done. This is not counter-productive duplication, because the resources devoted to the initial insight are relatively small, and can often be redeployed on the basis of the knowledge of what the other person has already discovered. Given that the speed of relevant scientific communication is almost surely increasing, there is decreasing chance of duplication of work on the highest potential ideas (as well as lower potential ideas).

We are only interested in the above set of possibilities if *all of them* are each present to a high enough degree to *together* cause increasing duplication of effort with growing numbers of people. Therefore, an aggregate test is fair: the numbers of persons eligible to make discoveries have been increasing. But the rate of duplication of discovery of the greatest ideas shows no clear direction towards greater duplication. The Leibniz–Newton conjuncture is the last great incident I know of; and, has anyone argued that the circumstances surrounding the discovery of DNA indicate that too much talent was devoted to the task?[5] The key issue here is the concavity of $f(M)$ or $f(M,L)$ or $f(M,L,Y/L)$, upon which the number of duplications throw light, but there seems to be no increase in that concavity.

Another relevant test is the rate of investment in R&D: the very long-run trend is up rather than down, in percentage-of-GNP terms as well as in absolute terms. Of course this might reflect increasing supplies of potential investors. But it is also consistent with an increase in profitable research opportunities, and hence with decreasing duplication.

Still another line of evidence refers to the number of first-rate profitable opportunities for research, rather than to the rate of duplication itself. If the number is very large, then duplication of top possibilities is not a problem. Here are a few quotations that indicate the possibilities lying in wait for the idea producer:

Cancer researcher Cole: 'It's not so much a question of more money to look at the problem, as a lack of people and analytical tools for the job.' (Blakeslee, 1979)

Newton: 'I do not know what I may appear to the world; but to myself I seem to have been only like a boy, playing on the sea-shore, and diverting myself, in now and then finding a smoother pebble or a prettier shell than ordinary, whilst the great ocean of truth lay all undiscovered before me.' (quoted by Taylor and Wheeler, 1966, p. 187)

Bethe on nuclear fusion: 'Money is not the limiting factor: the annual support in the US is well over $100 million, and it is increasing steadily. Progress is limited rather by the availability of highly trained workers, by the time required to build large machines and then by the time required to do significant experiments.' (Bethe, 1976, p. 2)

It may also be useful to examine the lengths of time between discoveries that seem to be equally important landmarks in a given field. For example, one could list and measure the times between Ptolemy, Copernicus, Newton, Lorentz and Einstein. The decreasing intervals suggest that great discoveries in physics were not becoming increasingly hard to make.

When thinking about diminishing returns in technology production, it is important to distinguish whether the subject is technology in the small or in the large – that is, advances in technology with respect to a narrowly defined topic, or technology pertaining to productivity in a wide field or in the economy as a whole. Consider the interesting data in figure 2.1. There we see that the rate of technological progress with respect to any given type of particle acceleration has been much slower than the rate of technological increase in all types of particle accelerations taken together. Clearly there would be much more sharply diminishing returns to additional researchers working on any one type of acceleration than with respect to particle generators as a set. And there would be even less diminution of returns to additional workers in nuclear physics in all its breadth.

(b) The subject of the discussion so far has been the *quantity* of knowledge production. The reader may wonder whether the *quality* may decline even if the quantity does not. This is a difficult question. A more complete discussion of this topic, which concludes that it is indeed impossible to satisfactorily compare the value of later discoveries with earlier ones, is offered elsewhere (Simon, 1984). It may even be *logically* impossible to determine the value of later discoveries relative to earlier ones, because the later discoveries depend upon the existence of the earlier ones. This implies that part of the value of

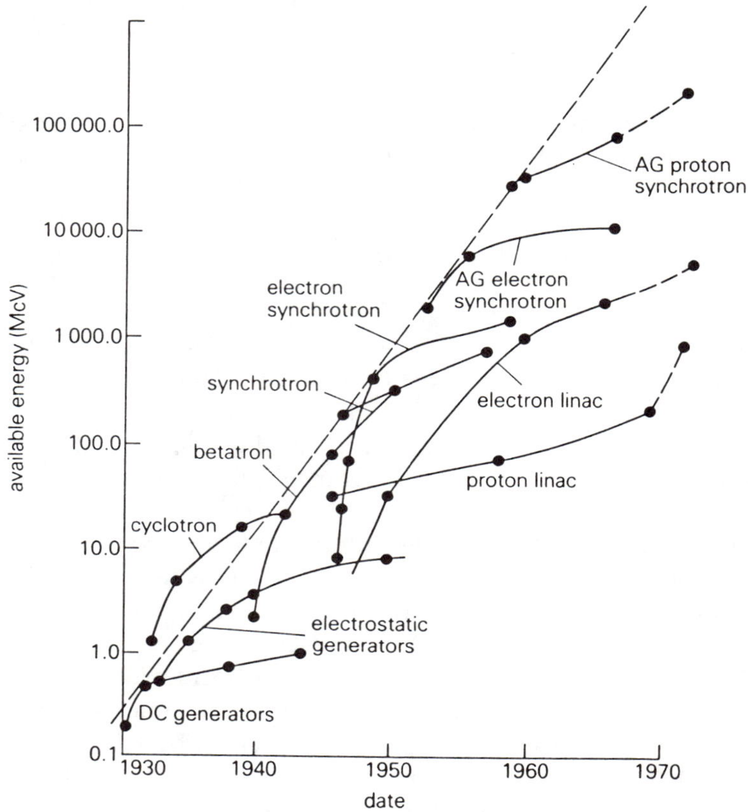

FIGURE 2.1 Energies achieved by particle accelerators from 1932 to 1968 (*Source:* Rescher, 1978, p. 177. Originally from M. Stanley Livingston, *Particle Accelerators: a Brief History*, Cambridge, 1969, p. 111.)

the later discoveries should be attributed to the earlier ones, and there is no meaningful way to make this partition. It is like the steps in a ladder: one can put a value on the benefits rendered by the first rung alone, but part of the benefit gained from the use of the second rung must be attributed to the first rung.

One possible avenue of inquiry is judgemental. We may ask questions such as: was Einstein's contribution less valuable than Newton's? Newton's less than Ptolemy's or Archimedes'? Some of this has implicitly been done in the lists that have been made of the 'great' discoveries by century (see the summary in Sorokin, 1937). But, of course, such lists are biased by difficulties in time separation between event and judges, as well as by the judges' (Western) cultural background.

A relevant fact is the relationship of the rate of knowledge accretion to the rate of productivity increases. The quantity of scientific literature has been doubling at a rate which has been fairly constant for a long time. De Solla Price (1961, p. 119) estimates that 'normal exponential growth' since 1660 has been a *constant* doubling every 30 years (whereas before that, 120 years were required for doubling). On the other hand, productivity has been increasing at an *increasing* rate, as discussed by Solow (1957) and Fellner (1970). This seems inconsistent with the idea that the 'quality' of scientific literature has been decreasing, or even remaining constant; rather, a constant doubling in the quantity of literature together with an increased rate of workplace productivity suggests an increase in economic productivity per unit of scientific literature (taking the latter as a proxy for all knowledge produced).

Of course, each and every fact and line of thought in this section is speculative at best. But this proves, more than anything, how ill-formed and uninvestigated is this topic. Under such conditions, however, any discussion, crude that it may be, may be a useful starting point.

As long as we think of knowledge as scientific knowledge in itself, we are not likely to reach a persuasive answer. But if we keep in mind that our interest here is in the output of economic welfare, we may be able to make some progress. We still will have major difficulties if we think in terms of GNP *per capita* as it is usually measured, because GNP measurement is itself affected by technological change in a variety of well-known ways. But it may be reasonable to examine the changes over time in a few key elements of economic welfare that seem reasonably comparable.

Consider grain output, for example. Its level of production technology in an economy is related to the level of other production technology, and the product is old enough so that it is not in a spectacular early-development period. Yet the rate of productivity increase has been increasing over the decades, and there seems no reason to doubt that the amount of human labour involved in grain production *per capita* will continue to diminish in the foreseeable future, and perhaps at an increasing rate (e.g. dropping 1 per cent of its manpower in the first period under discussion, 1.1 per cent in the second equal-length period, and so on – an infinitely sustainable process until the last farmer). This is at least measurable, and it is a reasonable proxy for the combined quantity and quality of technological knowledge. If the change in the level of productivity of all other products is similar to that of grain, this suggests that a given amount of product can be attained by an amount of work time that will diminish at an increasing rate, while leisure – a key element of economic welfare – will increase. There is an upper bound to the amount of leisure, of course. But if the amount of leisure is held constant and more types of goods are produced, economic welfare could continue to increase at an increasing rate.[6]

More generally, as stated earlier, it seems to me that comparative evaluation of advances in technology and productivity over the long run probably cannot be meaningful, as is discussed at length elsewhere (Simon, 1984).

(c) So far we have assumed that the rate of idea production (duplicated plus unduplicated) is the same for representative persons under all conditions. But we know – from statistical as well as casual evidence (de Solla Price, 1971; Love and Pashute, 1978) – that the production of technical-advance ideas is a positive function of *per capita* income. Including this effect of income on idea production in the model will only amplify the results shown without it.

(d) No mention has been made of the cost of producing technical knowledge. This does not imply that knowledge is costless. But the issue of the resources required is not germane here (see p. 49).

(e) There is a vast gap between the production and the application of technical knowledge, as Machlup emphasizes. But this, too, is not germane in the context of this model. The question of the extent to which knowledge should be thought of as a purchased commodity will be discussed later on pp. 48–9.

V. CONCLUSION

For hundreds of years economists and others have recognized that a denser population and faster population growth seem to be found where individual income is high and rising, though the simplest sort of theoretical reasoning suggested exactly the opposite conclusion. All the existing empirical evidence, however, is at the level of the economy or the industry. Still lacking – aside from Petty's simple suggestion – is an empirical or theoretical understanding at the micro-level of why a larger population and a bigger economy should lead to increased productivity. The task of this chapter is to propose such a theoretical model. The constituents of the model are the number of potential knowledge producers, the number of elements available in the environment to stimulate invention, and the probabilistic relationships between inventors and stimuli.

The model works out the trade-off between the forces that reduce the stock of ideas and the forces that increase the stock, under different conditions of population growth. The model shows that on assumptions that seem economically and psychologically reasonable, a larger labour force has increasing returns in knowledge production. The number of possible new combinations that result from the addition of a new idea element to the pool of knowledge is very large relative to the depletion of the pre-existing pool of knowledge by the discovery of that one idea. And the number of such possible new combinations that a representative additional person creates is very large relative to the additional possibilities of duplicated effort that result from the additional person. Hence the net result of an additional person is an increase in the total number of new ideas. And this effect will continue with the increases in total persons and total knowledge until duplication approaches zero, and unduplicated idea production for the representative person approaches the person's total capacity for idea production. Hence there are increasing returns in idea production to additional persons until convergence to constant returns.

As to the quality (or value or importance) of additional ideas with a larger rate of growth of the labour force and higher rates of increase of knowledge, there is no statistical evidence to suggest that quality is decreasing. On *a priori* grounds one might speculate, rather, that effective quality is increasing, because of the larger number of existing ideas and capital with which a new idea can interact and be fruitful. But it is logically impossible to evaluate the economic contribution of later ideas separately from the contribution of earlier ideas.

AFTERWORD 2A: WHICH MACRO-FUNCTION DOES THE MICRO-MODEL FIT?

Which macro-models in the literature best fit the micro-model set out above? Quite obviously, there is no warrant here for technical progress being driven purely exogenously, or being considered simply a function of time. And this model does not fit Arrow's learning-by-doing model (1.4), which could be written as (see chapter 5)

$$M_t - M_{t-1} = a_6(K_t^b - K_{t-1}^b) \qquad (2.7)$$

or as a more straightforward learning-by-doing model such as

$$M_t - M_{t-1} = a_7\left[\left(\sum_{t=0}^{t=\tau} Y_t\right)^b - \left(\sum_{t=0}^{t=\tau-1} Y_t\right)^b\right] \qquad (2.8)$$

The micro-model views technical progress as a function of human activity together with the stock of knowledge, perhaps in conjunction with the level of education; the learning-by-doing models are purely empirical in their origin, and no knowledge-producing mechanism is suggested for them. Everything said about learning-by-doing models pertains just as well to the Verdoorn model

$$\left(\frac{M_t - M_{t-1}}{M_{t-1}}\right) = a_1\left(\frac{Y_t - Y_{t-1}}{Y_t}\right) \qquad (2.9)$$

and the Kaldor model

$$\frac{M_t - M_{t-1}}{M_{t-1}} = f_1\left(\frac{K_t - K_{t-1}}{K_t}\right) \qquad (2.10)$$

Furthermore, the Verdoorn, Arrow and Kaldor models have different implications than those of the micro-model, as can be seen in table 1 (p. 20).

The macro-model best fit by the micro-model seems to be the basic function 6.6 in chapter 6 with income left out and using *M* rather than *A* here, which can be written as

$$M_t - M_{t-1} = f_5(L_{t-1}^{\phi} M_{t-1}^{\psi}), \qquad \phi, \psi < 1 \qquad (2.11)$$

In the limit of the micro-model this becomes

$$M_t - M_{t-1} = f_0(L^{\phi}_{t-1}) \qquad (2.12)$$

which may be viewed as equation (5.9) with $\psi \to 0$.

AFTERWORD 2B: CAN WE BE SURE TECHNOLOGY WILL ADVANCE?

Some ask: can we know that there will be discoveries of new materials and of productivity-enhancing techniques in the future? Behind the question lies the implicit belief that the production of new technology does not follow predictable patterns of the same sort as the patterns of production of other products such as cheese and opera. But there seems to me no warrant for belief in such a difference, either in logic or in empirical experience. When we add more capital and labour, we get more cheese; we have no logical assurance of this, but such has been all our experience, and therefore we are prepared to rely upon it. The same is true concerning knowledge about how to increase the yield of grain, cows, milk and cheese from given amounts of capital and labour. If you pay engineers to find ways to solve a general enough problem – for example, how to milk cows faster, or with less labour – the engineers predictably will do so. There may well be diminishing returns to additional inventive effort spent on the same problem, just as there are diminishing returns to the use of fertilizer and labour on a given farm in a given year. But old solutions spawn new problems, and the old diminishing-returns functions then no longer apply.

The willingness of businesses to pay engineers and other inventors to look for new discoveries attests to the predictability of returns to inventive effort. To obtain a more intimate feeling for the process, one may ask a scientist or engineer whether he/she expects his/her current research project to produce results with greater probability than if she/he simply sat in the middle of the forest reading a detective novel; the trained effort the engineer applies has a much greater likelihood of producing useful information – and indeed, the very information that is expected in advance – than does untrained non-effort. This is as predictable in the aggregate as the fact that cows will produce milk, and that machines and workers will turn the milk into cheese. Therefore, to depend upon the fact that technical developments will continue to occur in the future – if we continue to devote human and other resources to research – is as reasonable as it is to depend upon any other production process in our economy or civilization. One cannot *prove* logically that technical development will continue in the future. But neither can one so prove that capital and labour and milk will continue to produce cheese, or that the sun will come up tomorrow.

As I see it, the only likely limit upon the production of new knowledge about resources is the occurrence of new problems; without unsolved problems there will be no solutions. But here we have a built-in insurance policy: if our ultimate interest is resource availability, and if availability should diminish, that automatically supplies an unsolved problem, which then leads to the production of new knowledge, not necessarily immediately or without short-run disruption, but in the long run.

I'm not saying that all problems are soluble in the forms in which they are presented. I do not claim that biologists will make us immortal in our lifetime, or even that the length of human life will be doubled or tripled in the future. On the other hand, one need not rule out that biogenetics can create an animal with most of our traits and a much longer life. But such is not the sort of knowledge we are interested in here. Rather, we are interested in knowledge of the material inputs to our economic civilization.

A sophisticated version of this argument is that the cost of additional knowledge may rise in the future. Some writers point to the large teams and large sums now involved in natural-science endeavours. Let us notice, however, how much cheaper it is to make many discoveries now than it was in the past because of the existing base of knowledge and the whole information infra-structure. Kuznets could advance further with his research on GNP estimates than could Petty. And a run-of-the-mill graduate student can now do some things that Petty could not do. Additionally, a given discovery is more valuable now than it was then; GNP measurement has more economic impact now than in Petty's day. And it seems to me that the net present value in social terms of the discovery of agriculture was less than the net present value of something even as trivial as computer games. We could try reckoning the gain in gross social product to the few million people on earth when agriculture was developed, discounted even at 2 per cent per year. That is, say, $100 per person multiplied by say 10 million people at 2 per cent, gives an estimate of $3 billion. This is peanuts compared to the gain in gross social product from the transition to nuclear fission power, or the possible value of nuclear fusion. And agriculture was the only big discovery for thousands of years, whereas we came up with the transistor and nuclear power and lots more within a few decades.

One may say: let's calculate on a per-person basis. But why? The value of no other discovery or investment is figured that way. We will not be able to thrash that one out, but at the least, it is clear that there are a lot of open questions here.

NOTES

1 Even when there is duplication, the result is not pure waste. The double exposure increases the chances of the idea being accepted and put into use. And the two discoveries are likely to reveal somewhat different aspects of the phenomenon.

2 In a recent discussion of a nuclear power plant emergency, Royster commented, 'The experience should be humbling. It should give us pause. It should remind us of an eternal truth; the more we know, the more the mystery, the more we have to learn' (*Wall Street Journal*, 11 April 1979, p. 22).

3 This does not apply to the output of a *given* person over his or her career, but rather to a comparison of similar persons at the same ages in successive cohorts. For a review of relevant data in the physical sciences, see Rescher (1978).

4 I have implicitly been assuming that knowledge is permanent and does not obsolesce. To some extent knowledge does obsolesce, as we know it does from decreases in use of journals and books with the passage of time (e.g. Fussler and Simon, 1969); but note that some old knowledge remains in use by way of being embodied in newer ideas, an effect which does not show up in readership statistics, and from the diminution of patents kept in force (Nordhaus, 1969; but notice that these patent-maintenance data also simply show patents which were finally proven to have no use and be unprofitable, and hence are dropped). To this extent, the analysis must be modified. Obsolescence would seem to make additional people relatively more valuable because the essence of knowledge production is its external effect. But this needs further study.

5 It seems as if one could profitably classify discoveries into those that were foreseen by many (e.g. DNA) and those that were not (e.g. general relativity). Whether this is so, and what it might imply, is not obvious.

6 Life expectancy is an economic good at least as valuable as leisure and GNP goods. And I see no prospect of it increasing at an increasing rate. The reader may take this as a fatal objection to the argument - or may not. I think that the better position is that though GNP *per capita* might continue to increase at an increasing rate *as measured by the conventional methods*, this does not imply that human welfare is increasing at an increasing rate, and therefore arguments about life expectancy are not crucial in this context.

References

Bethe H A 'The Necessity of Fission Power.' *Scientific American*, 234, No. 1, January 1976.

Blakeslee A 'Which Foods Guilty in Cancer?' *Champaign-Urbana News-Gazette*, 21 June 1979, C-8

de Solla Price D *Science Since Babylon* (New Haven: Yale, 1961)

de Sola Price D 'Measuring the Size of Science.' *Israel Academy of Sciences and Humanities Proceedings*, 4, 6, 1971, 98–111

Fellner W 'Trends in the Activities Generating Technological Progress.' *American Economic Review*, 60, March 1970

Fussler H H, Simon J L *Patterns of Use of Books in Large Research Libraries* (University of Chicago Press, 1969)

Hayek F A *The Constitution of Liberty* (Chicago: University of Chicago Press, 1960)

Kuznets S 'Population Change and Aggregate Output.' In: Universities-National Bureau of Economic Research, *Demographic and Economic Change in Developed Countries* (Princeton: Princeton University Press, 1960)

Kuznets S *Population, Capital, and Growth* (New York: W W Norton, 1973)

Kuznets S 'Two Centuries of Economic Growth: Reflections on US Experience', *American Economic Review*, February 1977

Love D, Pashute L 'The Effect of Population Size and Concentration Upon Scientific Productivity.' In: Simon J L (ed.) *Research in Population Economics*, Vol. I (Greenwich: JAI Press, 1978)

Machlup F 'The Supply of Inventors and Inventions.' *Weltwirtschaftliches Archiv*, Band 85, 1960, Heft 2, 210–54. A shortened version appears in Nelson R R (ed.) *The Rate and Direction of Inventive Activity* (Universities–Princeton University Press, 1962, 143–70)

Meeks T J 'The Effect of Population Growth upon the Quantity of Education Children Receive: A Comment.' *Review of Economics and Statistics*, May 1982

Miyashita H, Newbold P, Pilarski A, Simon J 'The Effect of Population Growth upon the Quantity of Education Children Receive: A Reply.' *Review of Economics and Statistics*, May 1982, 352–5.

Nelson R R (ed.) *The Rate and Direction of Inventive Activity* (Princeton: NBER-PUP, 1962). See also the longer version in *Weltwirtschaftliches Archiv*, Band 85, Heft, 1960, 210–54

Nordhaus W D *Invention, Growth, and Welfare* (Cambridge: MIT Press, 1969)

Ram R 'Population Growth and Educational Expenditures: Some Further Reflections and Evidence.' Mimeograph, October 1982.

Rescher N *Scientific Progress* (Pittsburgh: University of Pittsburgh Press, 1978)

Royster V *Wall Street Journal*, 11 April 1979, 22.

Simon J L *The Economics of Population Growth* (Princeton: Princeton University Press, 1977)

Simon J L 'On the Evaluation of Progress and Technological Advance, Past and Future.' Xerox, 1984

Simon J L, Pilarski A 'The Effect of Population Growth Upon the Quantity of Education Children Receive.' *Review of Economics and Statistics*, November 1979, 572–84

Solow R 'Technical Change and the Aggregate Production Function.' *The Review of Economics and Statistics*, 39, 1957, 312–20

Sorokin P *Social and Cultural Dynamics* (Boston: Little Brown, 1937)

Spengler J J 'Agricultural Development is Not Enough.' In: Farnes R N *et al.* (eds) *World Population – The View Ahead* (Bloomington: Indiana University Press, 1968, 115)

Taylor E F, Wheeler J A *Spacetime Physics* (San Francisco: Freeman, 1966)

Weinberg S *The First Three Minutes: A Modern View of the Origin of the Universe* (New York: Bantam, 1977)

[22]

Foreword

The history of this article is a bit peculiar. My 1977 book, *The Economics of Population Growth*, included the results of some simulations of a macromodel with technological progress endogenous. The model's aim was to show that the standard result of growth theory – a faster rate of population growth implying a lower rate of growth of consumption – depended upon the absence of more people producing more knowledge.

Sometime later I came to wonder about the possibility of an "optimum" rate of population growth in the context of such a model. At first I thought that this was a wholly new idea. But after digging deeper into the literature on growth theory, I found that the same idea had occurred to other writers earlier, including Kaldor and Nordhaus and especially Phelps, though the idea was more implicit than explicit in Phelps's model of optimum research and development. And in sifting through this literature, I realized that the function I had earlier used is unreasonably responsive, whereas the function Phelps used could be admirably adapted to my purposes. I therefore went to work with the simulation method, broadening Phelps's function to include arguments for income and education. The simulations not only showed that the results converged to meaningful theoretical outcomes which had the properties of the "optimum" I sought, but also allowed intermediate-run (say, 30 to 200 years) assessments of the present value of different rates of population growth.

The reception of the paper by referees was horrendous. Mercifully, I cannot find them for publication.

About then, I asked Gunter Steinmann if he could solve the system analytically. And he did so, as is seen in the paper.

This version of our work is shown here because it is much shorter than other versions, and also because it is so neat compared to the simulations that even I find it more attractive than arriving at the same results by way of simulations.

The first journal to which the paper was sent accepted it, exceedingly speedily and without any revision required – both outcomes almost unprecedented in my prior experience.

The model in this paper is a centerpiece in my 1986 book on population growth and economic growth theory.

Reprinted from (and with the permission of)
Economics Letters 5 (1980) 177–182

PHELPS' TECHNICAL PROGRESS MODEL GENERALIZED

Gunter STEINMANN and Julian L. SIMON
University of Illinois, Urbana-Champaign, IL 61801, USA

Received 2 June 1980

We generalize Phelps' technical progress function and make it more realistic, by weakening assumptions and by adding education and income as influences on technical progress. The result retains the simplicity of Phelps' result, and reinforces the heterodox conclusion that higher population growth implies faster economic growth and higher consumption.

1. Introduction

Standard growth theory with exogenous technical progress indicates that population growth lowers the consumption level because of the diversion of output to higher steady-state investment. But Phelps' (1966) model of the research process with technical progress endogenous yields the conclusion that the rate of growth is faster, and the consumption level is higher, with a faster rate of growth of the labor force. [Kaldor's (1957) model and Arrow's (1962) model also yield this conclusion upon re-analysis, but neither author pointed out this result.]

This article extends Phelps' work to make it more realistic for the assessment of population growth's effects. It removes the restriction of homogeneity of degree one in the technical progress function, and it adds arguments to represent the effects of the income level and the education level upon the rate of technology increase. We find that even with these extensions we can arrive at a generalization of Phelps' conclusion which is consistent with steady-state growth under realistic conditions.

2. Phelps' technical progress function

Phelps proposed the technical progress function

$$(A_t - A_{t-1})/A_{t-1} = (A_{t-w-1}/A_{t-1})\, h(R_t/A_{t-w-1}) \,, \tag{1}$$

where

A = level of technology,
R = number of researchers,

and later

g = equilibrium growth rate of a subscripted variable,
K = the stock of capital,
L = labor force,
w = retardation factor,
Y = total output.

Phelps' makes $h(R_t/A_{t-w-1})$ a concave argument [1] because, he says, this assumption is necessary if 'an exponential growth of researchers will produce an exponential increase of the level of technology' (p. 134). The number of research workers, R, may be considered proportional to the labor force, and w is a 'retardation factor' to represent the delay in adoption of newly produced knowledge.

This function has the realistic properties that (a) more persons imply more knowledge, (b) there are diminishing returns at a given moment, and (c) a larger stock of knowledge leads to a larger increment of knowledge. Furthermore, it has the attractive theoretical characteristic that an exponential growth of researchers (or more simply for our purposes here, exponential growth of the labor force) produces an exponential increase in technical progress, and hence is consistent with the standard growth-theoretic notion of a steady state.

Phelps deduced from his model the golden-age equilibrium that 'consumption will grow at the rate $2\dot{L}$' where $\dot{L}$ is the rate of growth of the labor force; that is, per capita output (just as per capita consumption) consumption will grow at the rate of growth of the labor force, $(\dot{Y}/L) = \dot{L}$. He then goes on to derive an interesting golden rule for the amount of research, together with the amount of accumulation.

Phelps' function is more restrictive than it need be, however, even to satisfy his objective of golden-age steady growth. There are two directions in which this framework may be extended:

(1) There is no need to assume that the function is homogeneous of degree one. Even if there are increasing returns up to a high limit that we shall derive, the result is the constant golden-age rate of growth of A and of consumption per capita that Phelps sought.

(2) In Phelps' function there is no purely economic argument, and hence technical progress proceeds without depending upon capital or output. This clearly is not realistic. The function also should include an argument that represents the amount of 'tools' each potential knowledge creator is given, particularly the amount of education; this we may represent by the average level of output per worker

[1] In Phelps' continuous notation, the function is $\dot{A}(t)/A(t) = (A(t-w)/A(t))\, h(R(t)/A(t-w))$, where $\dot{A}$ = time rate of change of A.

(Y/L) which determines the average level of education. Furthermore, the total resources of an economy may influence its production of knowledge, in the manner that the total resources of the US permit it to make space flights whereas the total wealth and income of Sweden do not.

3. The extension and generalization

In order to make it analogous to a production function, Phelps' function may be written as

$$A(t) - A(t-1) = A(t-w)\,h(R(t)/A(t-w)). \tag{2}$$

The factor $A(t-w)$ is reasonably equal to $A(t-1)$ at all times. Hence the function boils down to (shifting to labor force, L, in place of R)

$$A(t) - A(t-1) = A(t-1)\,h(L(t)/A(t-1)), \tag{3}$$

or

$$A_t - A_{t-1} = A_{t-1}\,h(L_t/A_{t-1}). \tag{3'}$$

This may be re-written in the Cobb–Douglas form as

$$A_t - A_{t-1} = aA^{\Delta}_{t-1}L^{\gamma}_{t-1} \quad \text{where} \quad \Delta < 1, \quad \gamma < 1. \tag{4}$$

Implicit in Phelps' discussion is that $\Delta + \gamma = 1$ in eq. (4), as seen in Phelps' requirement that the function be homogeneous of degree one, and his statement that 'if the technology level should double we would require exactly twice the amount of research to double the absolute time rate of increase of the technology' (p. 135).

We shall index total resources by total income, and then write the more general function

$$A_t - A_{t-1} = bL^{\gamma}_{t-1}A^{\Delta}_{t-1}Y^{\phi}_{t-1}(Y/L)^{\psi}_{t-1}, \tag{5}$$

or

$$A_t - A_{t-1} = bL^{\mu}A^{\Delta}Y^{\epsilon} \quad \text{with} \quad \mu = \gamma - \psi \gtreqless 0, \quad \epsilon = \phi + \psi > 0. \tag{5'}$$

The implications of this function will now be explored with a simple model composed of the following output and savings equations:

$$Y_t = K^{\alpha}_t(A_tL_t)^{\beta} \quad \text{where} \quad \alpha, \beta = \text{constants}, \tag{6}$$

$$S_t = sY_{t-1}, \tag{7}$$

$$K_t = sY_{t-1} + K_{t-1}, \qquad 1 > s > 0. \tag{8}$$

Implicitly we have the short-run equilibrium condition that investment equals savings. Next, the exogenous labor-force growth

$$L_t = L_{t-1} + dL_{t-1} , \tag{9}$$

where d is a control variable in the analysis. The long-run equilibrium conditions are standard,

$$(A_t - A_{t-1})/A_{t-1} \simeq (1/A) \cdot (\mathrm{d}A/\mathrm{d}t) = \dot{A} = g_A , \tag{10}$$

$$(Y_t - Y_{t-1})/Y_{t-1} \simeq (1/Y) \cdot (\mathrm{d}Y/\mathrm{d}t) = \dot{Y} = g_Y , \tag{11}$$

$$(K_t - K_{t-1})/K_{t-1} \simeq (1/K) \cdot (\mathrm{d}K/\mathrm{d}t) = \dot{K} = g_K , \tag{12}$$

where g_A, g_Y, g_K are constants in equilibrium. We begin by rewriting (5′) as

$$\dot{A} = bL^{\mu} A^{\Delta - 1} Y^{\epsilon} . \tag{5''}$$

Taking logs and differentiating, we get

$$(1/\dot{A})(\mathrm{d}\dot{A}/\mathrm{d}t) = \mu\dot{L} + (\Delta - 1)\dot{A} + \epsilon\dot{Y} . \tag{13}$$

Using (10),

$$(1/\dot{A})(\mathrm{d}\dot{A}/\mathrm{d}t) = 0 . \tag{10'}$$

This with (13) yields the following relation between the equilibrium values of g_Y, g_A and g_L:

$$g_A = \frac{\epsilon}{1 - \Delta} g_Y + \frac{\mu}{1 - \Delta} g_L . \tag{14}$$

Eqs. (6), (7), (9), (10), (11), (12) plus the short-run equilibrium savings-equals-investment condition can be transformed and reduced into the well-known

$$g_A = \frac{1 - \alpha}{\beta} g_Y - g_L . \tag{15}$$

Eqs. (14) and (15) contain only the arguments g_A, g_Y and g_L plus constants. Therefore we can determine the equilibrium values of g_Y and g_A,

$$g_Y = \frac{1 - \Delta + \mu}{((1 - \alpha)/\beta)(1 + \Delta) - \epsilon} g_L , \tag{16}$$

$$g_A = \frac{((1 - \alpha)/\beta)\, \mu + \epsilon}{((1 - \alpha)/\beta)(1 - \Delta) - \epsilon} g_L . \tag{17}$$

For the special case of constant returns to scale in the production function (6), $\alpha + \beta = 1$, and we get the special results

$$g_Y = \frac{1 - \Delta + \mu}{1 - \Delta - \epsilon} g_L , \tag{16'}$$

$$g_A = \frac{\mu + \epsilon}{1 - \Delta - \epsilon} g_L . \tag{17'}$$

In this special case, the equilibrium value of the growth rate of per worker income

$$g_{(Y/L)} = g_Y - g_L$$

$$(= g_{(Y/P)} \quad \text{if} \quad g_P = g_L, \quad \text{where } Y/P \text{ is per capita income})\,,$$

$$g_{(Y/L)} = \frac{\mu + \epsilon}{1 - \Delta - \epsilon} g_L = g_A\,.^{2} \tag{18'}$$

Let us see what values of the parameters are possible, and acceptable for (18′) to be consistent with our equilibrium conditions. First, we know that the numerator, $\mu + \epsilon$, must be positive because $\gamma + \phi > 0$, and $\mu + \epsilon = \gamma + \phi$. Next, the denominator must also be positive, or else there could be no equilibrium with positive growth rates of L, A and Y. We can see in (5′) that $\Delta < 1$ or else $\dot{A}$ would increase with time, which violates an equilibrium condition. Furthermore, from (16′) and (17′) we know that $\Delta + \epsilon > 1$ implies $g_A < 0$ and $g_Y < 0$ for $g_L > 0$. This solution is not only economically meaningless, but some simulation calculations also show that, for all initial values $\dot{A}$, $\dot{Y} > 0$, the condition $\Delta + \epsilon > 1$ causes the system to explode because $\mathrm{d}\dot{A}/\mathrm{d}t$ and $\mathrm{d}\dot{Y}/\mathrm{d}t$ are positive. Hence for positive population growth a reasonable equilibrium exists only for $\Delta + \epsilon < 1$. What is most important, however, is that under these conditions there is an equilibrium.

Now to interpret our results. Given that both the numerator and denominator in eq. (18′) are positive, a higher rate of labor-force growth implies a faster equilibrium rate of growth of per capita income. And the mechanism is clear: We see in eq. (17′) that a higher rate of growth of the labor force implies a faster equilibrium rate of growth of technology, and the multiplier is the same as in eq. (18′). That is, more workers imply more technical change, and an increased rate of technical changes translates into growth of per capita income that is faster to the same extent. Phelps' model yields the same result because it is a special case of this model.

If, as Phelps assumed, $\gamma = \frac{1}{2}$, $\Delta = \frac{1}{2}$, $\phi = 0$, and $\psi = 0$ (the latter two being the exponents of variables not in his function) then (18′) reduces to Phelps' conclusion that the equilibrium rate of growth of per worker income equals the rate of growth of the labor force. If $\gamma > \frac{1}{2}$, $\frac{1}{2} \leqslant \Delta \leqslant 1$ and/or ϕ or $\psi > 0$, the equilibrium rate of growth of per worker income is faster than the rate of growth of the labor force, to the extent which is easy to figure from (18′) for any set of exponents. The same is true if $\frac{1}{2} < \Delta < 1$ and $\gamma \geqslant \frac{1}{2}$. If ϕ and/or $\psi > 0$, the positive effect of labor force growth is intensified, ceteris paribus.

In brief, either Phelps' function or our more general function has the important

[2] The general solution is

$$g_{(Y/L)} = \frac{(1-\Delta)((\alpha+\beta-1)/\beta) + \mu + \epsilon}{(1-\Delta)((1-\alpha)/\beta) - \epsilon} g_L\,. \tag{18}$$

implication that faster population growth implies a faster equilibrium rate of growth of the standard of living; this is exactly the opposite of conventional growth theory with technical progress exogenous. Our more general function also has the pleasant property for theory and theorists that a realistic model of technical change, and of the effect of population size and growth upon technical change, may be comfortably embodied in growth-theoretical models without upsetting the basic structure of that theory.

References

Arrow, K.J., 1962. The economic implications of learning by doing, Review of Economic Studies XXIX(3), no. 80, June, 155–173.

Kaldor, Nicholas, 1957. A model of economic growth, Economic Journal LXVII, Dec.

Phelps, Edmund S., 1966. Models of technical progress and the golden rule of research, Review of Economic Studies, April, 133–145.

[23]

Foreword

The second main line of theoretical analysis in my 1986 book on population growth and economic growth theory is a re-examination of the proposition implicit in Arrow's famous 1962 paper on learning-by-doing that more people do not imply a higher level of consumption. It turns out that Arrow's conclusion results from his use of equilibrium analysis, which is inappropriate for the purpose at hand. If one starts from first principles, one immediately sees that this is wrong, as can be seen in this analogy of haircutting: If Father Alpha has one son and Father Beta has twin sons, and both cut their sons' hair, both starting from the same level of skill, Father Beta will shortly have a higher level of skill than will Father Alpha due to more learning from more doing, leading to a higher level of consumption. (Inclusion of the role of capital in the analysis does not alter this conclusion.) The confusion arises from the fact that after the first haircut, the *rate of change* of skill will be the same for the two fathers, even though the *absolute* increases will be greater from week to week by Father Beta. This is a good example of how equilibrium growth rate analysis can bewitch and benight.

In light of this last remark, the reader may wonder why I wrote a book on growth theory. One reason is that nothing could have a prayer of altering belief in the standard growth-theoretic conclusion except another theory; empirical data alone will not suffice. Also, when the same framework is used for *short* periods to compare rate of increase – either of native births or of immigrants – the framework is not without meaning.

Referees insist that equilibrium analysis is the only acceptable way to view the problem, which of course leads them to accept Arrow's implicit conclusion and to reject ours; they have not been troubled by the fact that equilibrium analysis conflicts with the simplest model of what the relevant facts are. They also have been distressed by this "attack" upon Arrow. I have no rebuttal to that. The referees also objected with great vigour to my saying that Arrow's formulation misleads thought, and they seemed to take personally my criticism of him.

Prior to Steinmann joining in the effort, referees complained that the paper was "unfinished" and lacked "sophistication." Well, yes. Of course the main point was there, with sufficient argument to prove it. That is not enough, however, which seems to me a major problem with the economics publication system.

European Economic Review 26 (1984) 167–185. North-Holland

THE ECONOMIC IMPLICATIONS OF LEARNING-BY-DOING FOR POPULATION SIZE AND GROWTH*

Julian L. SIMON

University of Maryland, Baltimore, MD 21201, USA

Gunter STEINMANN

University of Paderborn, 4790 Paderborn, FRG

Received July 1983, final version received June 1984

In a comparison of two worlds that have different population sizes, but that are otherwise alike (including their capital–labor ratios and the initial per worker outputs), the larger world will come to have higher per worker output because of learning-by-doing. This conclusion is unlike the conclusion implicit in Arrow's model learning-by-doing, because Arrow looked at steady-state rates of growth rather than changes in the level of income from the starting point. (Arrow's analysis also is confused by using the capital stock rather than cumulative output as the measure of experience, though output is the variable used in the empirical analyses that are the basis of this line of work.)

1. Introduction

Following on the empirical studies of learning-by-doing by Wright (1936), Asher (1956) and others, and the summary and interpretation by Hirsch (1956) and Alchian (1963), Arrow combined the effect of experience with a macromodel to study the economic implications. That model followed Kaldor (1957) in making technical progress endogenous, though Kaldor's point of departure was Verdoorn's (1949) macro and industry data, rather than the firm-level data on which Arrow built and which lend themselves more obviously to a learning interpretation than to Verdoorn's data.

This paper contends that Arrow did not derive the most important implications of learning-by-doing, and that he also reaches some wrong conclusions. The conclusion which this paper reaches with a model like Arrow's are that population growth (and even more importantly, population size) may well have positive effects upon the rate of economic growth through their positive effects on the rate of technical progress, on reasonable assumptions about the likely capital–output ratios with different demographic structure, but negative effects with other capital–output ratio differences. This conclusion could have considerable implications for the understanding of

*We appreciate helpful readings of a previous draft by Mark Browning, Jonathan Cave, and Eytan Sheshinski.

population size and growth, and for the formation of social policy with respect to these forces.

Section 2 gives an intuitive explanation of the implications of learning-by-doing for evaluation of different *sizes* of population. This requires unraveling an apparent paradox in Arrow's analysis which leads to incorrect conclusions about this matter. Section 3 builds a learning-by-doing model at the micro-level referring to continuous processes such as shipbuilding. It then determines under which capital-dilution conditions a large population and faster population growth have positive and negative effects upon the standard of living. Section 4 offers some discussions. And section 5 summarizes the work and the conclusions. The appendix criticizes the concept of experience Arrow used, to make clear the reasons for the choice of concept used here.

A brief historical digression before beginning work: For Adam Smith, the source of technical progress was division of labor accompanying increases in population and demand. (Petty was just as clear on the division of labor, and he also took into account the invention of new ideas which Smith did not, to any significant degree). Perhaps because of modern evidence on the cessation of economies of scale at moderate outputs in most industries, interest of scale at moderate outputs in most industries, interest in division of labor seems to have waned. But it is worth noting that along with the increased manipulative skill that occurs in workers with increased division of labor, there is likely to be more learning-by-doing because some workers are paying more attention to each aspect of the operation (though of course this can have negative effects, too). Everett (1826/1970, p. 26) saw this clearly

> 'It is sufficiently notorious, that an increase of population on a given territory is followed immediately by a division of labor; which produces in its turn the invention of new machines, an improvement of methods in all the departments of industry, and a rapid progress in the various branches of art and science.'

2. Foundations of the analysis

The context of the paper is the more-developed world as a whole circa 1985, wherein technology advance necessarily occurs by its creation within that set of countries rather than by borrowing from another set of countries, as is the case for the less-developed countries. And implicitly we assume that the communication barriers within that more-developed world are relatively surmountable. Our perspective is like that of the economic historian in that we consider two scenarios, one of which may be considered the actual state of affairs with respect to population growth, and the other a counterfactual conditional rate of population growth starting at some chosen date. We then ask how history would be different with the counterfactual than with the actual, just as economic historians ask how American economic history would have been different if there had been no American Civil War and the consequent abolition of slavery, or how the countries of Africa would have fared if they had not gained their independence after World War II. In each case, the implicit assumption is that the history until the beginning of the counterfactual scenario is the same for the actual and the counterfactual scenarios. This means that our model is not intended to apply to less-developed countries which can adapt existing technology from the more-developed world, and it is not intended as a device for the comparison of larger and smaller countries at a given moment.

We must also emphasize that the perspective is the very long run. If one has a very high discount rate, it will always seem preferable to invest in more physical capital, which will embody already-discovered new techniques, from which the payoff will be immediate, rather than invest in additional children, from whom the earliest payoff is a quarter century in the future and much of the payoff comes decades and centuries later.

It should also be emphasized that the paper is not intended as the basis for policy prescriptions or for tests of hypotheses. Rather, its main intended value is as theoretical justification for discarding simple Malthusianism as the basis for policy decisions. As has often been said, it takes a theory to kill a theory. And simple Malthusianism, as developed somewhat as in the Coale–Hoover formulation, is the basis for the population aspect of the domestic and foreign policy of such countries as the United States. It is hoped that arguments such as are contained in this paper may serve as part of the re-examination of such policies, which seems have already begun.

All the empirical studies on which Arrow relied, and also most of those that have come afterwards (with exceptions to be noted below) related measures like 'the amount of direct labor required to produce an airframe and the (cumulative) number of airframes produced' (Alchian 1963, p. 680).[1]

[1]Here we should note that the empirical basis for the learning-by-doing function mostly comes from industry rather than economy-wide studies (Sheshinski's 1967 study is the exception). And this is as it should be, because the specific learning mostly takes place within firms, and across firms within the same industry. But an economy is an aggregate of industries. And unless there is reason to believe that the industries not yet studied follow entirely different processes than the industries that have been studied, or unless there is reason to believe that the economy is not essentially additive in this respect — and we know of no such persuasive reason to believe so — then it seems legitimate and reasonable to extrapolate from the industry level of analysis to the economy as a whole. This is what Arrow has done implicitly. And it is what must be done here if the issue is to be joined with Arrow, and if we are to go forward from this model rather than being locked into a wrong conclusion about the effects of population size and growth. As to whether the nation is too small to be the appropriate unit of analysis: the more-developed world as a whole, within which advanced technology and production methods are developed and applied, is the appropriate unit of analysis, and the model discussed here should be thought of as applying to that multi-country aggregate; individual countries are used in the empirical studies we refer to only because of their convenience as research observations and for thought experiments. We do not mean to imply that simply erasing the boundary lines between two nations would give rise to the processes modeled here (though in some industries such simple expansion could effect considerable increases in technique, for example in electricity and railroad networks).

$$H_N = H_1 N^{-b} = H_1 - H_1(1 - N^{-b}), \qquad N \geqq 1, \quad \text{where} \tag{1}$$

N = serial number of a particular unit of output,
H_N = hours of work per unit of output for serial number N,
b = constant.

Arrow (1962, p. 157) is very clear on this: 'The economic examples given above suggest the possibility of using cumulative output (the total of output from the beginning of time) as an index of experience'. We shall work with this concept rather than with cumulative gross experience with which Arrow worked. Our reasons for this choice, and the unfortunate results of the choice Arrow made, are described in the appendix.

We begin our intuitive description of the process at work by noting that a key difference between our models and that of Arrow boils down to a distinction between equilibrium and non-equilibrium analyses; the latter is appropriate for the issue under discussion here, which is analysis of the effects of population size rather than of steady-state growth patterns. This point may immediately be obvious to the reader when it is first raised in this section; if so, please skip to the formal and more general analyses in section 3. But experience has shown that this argument usually must be made at length for it to have a chance to persuade the reader. This is partly because there is an apparent paradox here. It is also because the main body of growth theory is framed in equilibrium terms, and therefore the reader is likely to come to this paper with a predilection to view the matter in an equilibrium context. We pray that you, the reader, will accept that, though equilibrium growth theory may be appropriate in some contexts, for most population-policy questions one wishes to either compare economies of different initial population sizes with the same rates of population growth, or economies of the same initial size with different rates of growth (or economies that differ in both size and growth rates). Such disequilibrium analysis leads to entirely different conclusions than does equilibrium analysis, as we shall see.

We must be crystal-clear about the nature of the empirical process on which the function is based, because a subtle shift in interpretation has caused a fundamental misinterpretation. It is all-important not to skim over the fundamentals of the process and rush into the formal model and manipulation in section 3, or else the value we think lies in our analysis, as distinguished from Arrow's, will be lost.

For the first unit made, the measured number of work hours spent on it is equal to H_1 in eq. (1), which is one of the two key values in the system. The process is assumed to start at this point, with H_1 given exogenously as a result of a variety of specified previous experiences. Successive units produced require amounts of labor equal to the amount in the initial unit less a proportion of that initial amount, the proportion depending on the serial number of the successive unit. To portray a learning-by-doing process one must therefore either know or be able to estimate from later data the original level of skill at which this particular process begins.

Assume that the good *i*, whose cumulative quantity produced up to period *t* is indexed by serial number $N_{t,i}$, is a normal good. It is reasonable to assume that the output of *i* in any period *t* is a proportional function of total income

$$N_t - N_{t-1} = gY, \tag{2}$$

and that total income is a proportional function of labor force size,

$$Y = hL, \tag{3}$$

where g and h are constants. The volume $N_t - N_{t-1} = ghL$ produced in t therefore is an increasing function of the population size. (It is all-important here to distinguish between, on the one hand, the volume produced in a given period t, and, on the other hand, the serial number N, which might be produced in any period t.)

Consider the moment when a given production process N begins with serial number $N=1$. For convenience, this takes place on January 1 of year $t=1$ in country Alpha. Assume population size is $P_{t=1}$, labor force size is $L_{t=1}$, and total national output for that year is $Y_{t=1}$. For those conditions, there will be X units of good i produced, so at the end of the first year (the beginning of year 2) the serial number is $N^{\alpha}_{t=2} = X$.

Now we assume instead that we are in country Beta and population size instead is $2P_{t=1}$, labor force size is $2L_{t=1}$, and consequently total national output is $2Y_{t=1}$. (Furthermore, the population and output have *always* been twice as large in Beta as in Alpha). From (2) and (3) we can expect that the end-of-year serial number will be $N^{\beta}_{t=2} = 2X$ rather than $N^{\alpha}_{t=2} = X$.

Now consider the rate of change of productivity A over the first period. Whatever the percentage change $(A_{t=2} - A_{t=1})/A_{t=1}$, the rate will be roughly twice as large for $2L_{t=1}$ as for $L_{t=1}$ (assuming that the change is small relative to the initial value, which one can ensure by making the period short, say a day rather than a year).

A point sufficiently elusive and easy to forget that the authors of the paper find themselves forgetting it each time they start to think about these ideas: The time required to produce a unit of any given serial number N is the same in both countries. The difference between the countries is that the unit with any given serial number is produced earlier in the country with the larger population, due to its larger demand. And therefore the larger country arrives at any given level of productive efficiency sooner than does the smaller country, and hence its efficiency increases faster in calendar time even though its efficiency is the same as in the smaller country at any given serial number.

This point may best be brought out by fig. 1, which shows the different dates at which given levels of efficiency are reached in countries of different size.[2]

To elucidate this point, let us write out the learning-by-doing concept in the greatest possible detail. Define the level of productivity A as the inverse of work time per unit, and using eq. (1)

$$A_N = \frac{A_{N=1}}{N^{-b}} = A_{N=1} N^b, \qquad (N \geqq 1),$$

$$= A_{N=1} + A_{N=1}(N^b - 1), \qquad (N \geqq 1). \tag{1'}$$

From (1′) it is quite clear that for two firms or economies α and β that produce, up to the same date, N^α and $N^\beta > N^\alpha$ units, the rate of change of productivity from the beginning to that date is greater for β than for α,

$$\frac{A_N^\beta - A_{N=1}}{A_{N=1}} > \frac{A_N^\alpha - A_{N=1}}{A_{N=1}}.$$

In Arrow's model, which works with cumulative investment rather than cumulative output, we do *not* find that the rate of change of productivity is a function of output or labor force in anywhere near the same way, because it is in the nature of any capital stock that it does not correspond in any simple additive way to all the capital produced since the beginning of time. (For more details, see the appendix.) And this is even more true in Arrow's model which includes obsolescence.[3]

Yet more important, Arrow's model invites one to write an experience function such as

$$\frac{A_{t+1} - A_t}{A_t} = \frac{aK_{t+1}^b - aK_t^b}{aK_t^b}, \tag{4}$$

[2]The parameter values which underlie fig. 1 are $H_1 = 100$ and $b = 1/3$. Therefore [see eq. (1)] $H_N = 100^{-1/3}$, $N \geqq 1$. It is assumed that the small country Alpha produces one unit per year and that the large Beta produces two units per year.

[3]The possibility of obsolescence does not cause difficulties in this paper's formulation, on reasonable assumptions.

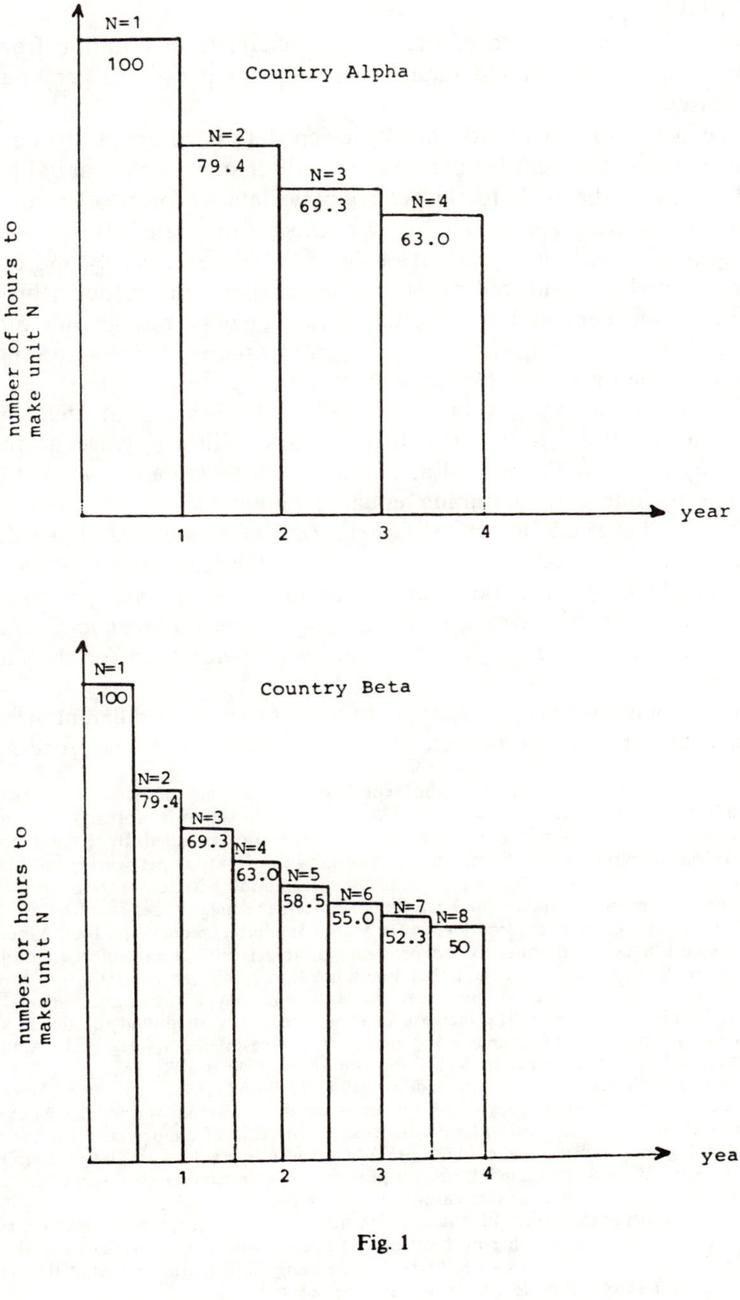
N=1
100
Country Alpha
N=2
79.4
N=3
69.3
N=4
63.0
number of hours to make unit N
year
1
2
3
4
N=1
100
Country Beta
N=2
79.4
N=3
69.3
N=4
63.0
N=5
58.5
N=6
55.0
N=7
52.3
N=8
50
number or hours to make unit N
year
1
2
3
4

Fig. 1

where the dates include any given period rather than one of the dates being the first period.[4]

We remind the readers here of the crucial difference in notation from A indexed by serial number and A indexed by calendar period, as per hour in our earlier discussion.

Given that a country's situation at any given date is compared to *its own* situation at some slightly earlier date, the rate of change of the capital stock may be expected to the *same* for larger country Beta as for smaller country Alpha, ceteris paribus. Hence in Arrow's model the rate of increase of productivity is essentially independent of the scale of the economy and of the population, though it will reflect short-run changes in output (through differences in investment and the capital stock). That is, though this model may lend itself to estimating the rate for a given process, it does not enable one to compare the results for two entities of different sizes.

To make the point as graphic as possible: If fathers cut their male offspring's hair monthly, a father with twin sons will get twice as much practice in any period, and his skill at any date will be higher, than that of a father with only one son (assuming equal beginning skill). This does not imply that in each period the twins' father's *rate of increase* of skill will be higher than that of the father of only one son; if the learning curve has the same exponent at all points, the rates will be the same in each period after the first. But the rate of increase of productivity *from the beginning* to any given later date will be greater for the father with twins than for the father with one son.[5]

There is an apparent paradox here: If two countries with different sizes of population and output are compared for a period starting *after* a process has

[4]Though Arrow does not write this function explicitly, he likens his model to Kaldor's, who writes the similar function $(A_{t-1}-A_t)/A_t=c(K_t-K_{t-1})/K_{t-1}$. In Arrow's words, 'The production assumptions of this section are designed to play the role assigned by Kaldor to his "technical progress function", which relates the rate of growth of output per worker to the rate of growth of capital per worker. We prefer to think of relations between rates of growth as themselves derived from more fundamental relations between the magnitudes involved' (p. 160). He also says that 'Verdoorn had also developed a similar simple model' (p. 160); Verdoorn differs in using output per year, but his independent variable is also a rate of change of the *current* magnitude. So there is little doubt that function (4) is a fair representation of Arrow's model. And in his empirical 'Tests of the "Learning-By-Doing" Hypothesis', Sheshinski (1967) estimated exactly this model where 'the increase in experience ... is attributed to current gross investment' (that is, the rate of change of productivity = investment/capital stock. Actually, Sheshinski estimated Kaldor's model in which the right-hand side is $c(K_t-K_{t-1})/K_{t-1}$ rather than Arrow's model in which the right-hand side would be $(K_t^b-K_{t-1}^b)/K_{t-1}^b$, though Sheshinski said that he was testing the learning-by-doing model — or in an alternative model, 'the change in experience is attributed to the rate of output' (that is, the rate of change of productivity = output/'cumulated gross output', where Sheshinski's empirical referent of the latter concept is unclear but is certainly not cumulated gross output since the beginning of the process, as is required for a reasonable portrayal of the learning-by-doing process).

[5]If one worries about the inequality in total employment of the two factors, the example could be changed to a society with one father-barber versus a society with two father-barbers, all with one child each. In the economy with two fathers, they exchange information on what they learn, and hence increase the rate of their learning; this is quite realistic.

begun, between the same dates in both, the rates of change of productivity over the period can be the same even though if the period begins *at the beginning* of the process, the rate of change of productivity of the larger country will be greater. For example, assume that Alpha produces one unit per period, and Beta produces two units per period. Between periods four and five, Alpha goes from serial 4 to serial 5, whereas Beta goes from 8 to 10. If A_1 — the level of technology of the first unit, the inverse of the numbers of hours required to make the first unit — is equal to 10, if $b=0.5$, and hence if $A_N=10N^{0.5}$, then for Alpha

$$\frac{A_{t=5}-A_{t=4}}{A_{t=4}}=\frac{A_{N=5}-A_{N=4}}{A_{N=4}}=\frac{10\sqrt{5}-10\sqrt{4}}{10\sqrt{4}}\simeq 0.414,$$

and also for Beta

$$\frac{A_{t=5}-A_{t=4}}{A_{t=4}}=\frac{A_{N=10}-A_{N=8}}{A_{N=8}}=\frac{10\sqrt{10}-10\sqrt{8}}{10\sqrt{8}}\simeq 0.414.$$

But from the beginning of the process to the end of period 5, the calculations are, for Alpha

$$(A_{t=5}-A_{t=1})/A_{t=1}=(10\sqrt{5}-10\sqrt{1})/10\sqrt{1},$$

and for Beta

$$(A_{t=5}-A_{N=1})/A_{N=1}=(10\sqrt{10}-10\sqrt{1})/10\sqrt{1}.$$

So Beta's rate of increase of productivity is faster than Alpha's when calculated from the beginning of the process.

3. Formal analyses of population effects through learning-by-doing

We define

H_N = work hours necessary to produce the Nth unit of a given type with serial number N,

h_N = cumulative work hours necessary to produce the series of units from 1 to N.

$$h_N=\sum_{1}^{N} H_N, \quad \text{or in continuous form} \tag{5a}$$

$$h=\int_0^N H_{N'} \mathrm{d}N. \tag{5b}$$

We exclude from our model any transfer of technical knowledge from other industries.

It is reasonable to assume that capital and labor force should remain the same throughout the production of a given product type, and this realistic assumption makes the analysis tractable.

$$K_{t=x}=K_{t=1}, \qquad L_{t=x}=L_{t=1}.$$

According to the learning-by-doing process an industry can produce the Nth serial-number unit faster than the $(N-1)$th serial-number unit because of the increased experience with the production of the good. The standard assumption for describing this process of experiencing and learning is

$$H_N=(H_{N-1})\gamma, \qquad 0<\gamma<1. \tag{1''}$$

H_N here is a function only of H_{N-1} and of the learning-by-doing parameter γ, which implicitly assumes a given labor force and stock of capital. But because we wish to compare worlds in which the industries or plants under discussion differ in these respects, we must broaden the H_N function. We do so as follows:

$$H_N=1/A(N)^{\gamma}K^{\alpha}L^{1-\alpha}, \tag{6}$$

and for $N=1$

$$H_1=1/A(1)^{\gamma}K^{\alpha}L^{1-\alpha},$$

and therefore

$$A=1/H_1K^{\alpha}L^{1-\alpha}.$$

When K and L are ignored, as in the standard literature, this reduces to $A=1/H_1$, and

$$H_N=H_1N^{-\gamma}=H_1-H_1(1-N^{-\gamma}).$$

That is, A is the level of technique in effect at the time of production of the first unit.

The Cobb–Douglas function with exponents adding to unity implies that in this model there are no diminishing returns to production of the first unit. (In another model there may be.) This assumes that the generalized skills brought to the plant by workers and engineers are the same in both cases, and that management chooses a satisfactory plant size (though not 'optimum' size, which would be a more complex intertemporal concept including differential learning speeds with different numbers of plants).

Next we calculate the cumulative time necessary to produce the first N units by substituting eq. (6) into (5b),[6]

$$h_N = 1/AK^{\alpha}L^{1-\alpha}\int_0^N \frac{1}{N^{\gamma}}\,\mathrm{d}N, \quad \text{or}$$

$$h_N = N^{1-\gamma}/(1-\gamma)AK^{\alpha}L^{1-\alpha}. \tag{7}$$

We now ask how many units are produced in various equal-in-length periods of time: $1, 2, \ldots, t$,

$$h_N = t.$$

We obtain from (7) the serial number at the end of period t (i.e., the cumulative output within all past period $1, 2, \ldots, t$),

$$N_t = \{(1-\gamma)At\}^{1/(1-\gamma)}K^{\alpha/(1-\gamma)}L^{(1-\alpha)/(1-\gamma)}. \tag{8}$$

In the same way we can calculate the serial number at the end of period $(t-1)$ as

$$N_{t-1} = \{(1-\gamma)A(t-1)\}^{1/(1-\gamma)}K^{\alpha/(1-\gamma)}L^{(1-\alpha)/(1-\gamma)}. \tag{8'}$$

From (8) and (8′) we can calculate the output produced within period t by simply subtracting N_{t-1} from N_t,

$$\begin{aligned} Y_t &= N_t - N_{t-1} \\ &= \{(1-\gamma)A\}^{1/(1-\gamma)}K^{\alpha/(1-\gamma)}L^{(1-\alpha)/(1-\gamma)}\{t^{1/(1-\gamma)} - (t-1)^{1/(1-\gamma)}\}. \end{aligned} \tag{9}$$

[6]At this point we ask a slight mathematical indulgence of the reader, arising from a discrepancy between reality and the calculus. The production process for products like airplanes and ships is markedly discrete; a serial number as found in the basic structural eq. (1) refers to a whole craft. But the standard mathematics is continuous. The serial number of the first plane is '1'. But if we write an integral with 1 at its starting point, then there is a confusion because of the apparent area under the integral between 0 and 1. There is no mathematically attractive way to deal with the problem without obscuring or even controverting the essential theme of the analysis, as we have found in a series of discussions with persons who have tried to overcome the problem elegantly. The only precisely accurate way to deal with the matter would be discretely with a representative set of numbers. But that lacks elegance, and might be less expressive to the sophisticated reader. Therefore, we shall simply write that the integral begins with 0. We hope it is clear, however, that this approximation is resorted to because of the built-in incapacity of a continuous integral to deal with the necessarily discrete real-life production processes that we seek to understand and model.

Dividing the output by the labor force we obtain the output per worker y_t in period t,

$$y_t = \frac{Y_t}{L_t} = \{(1-\gamma)A\}^{1/(1-\gamma)} K^{\alpha/(1-\gamma)} L^{(\gamma-\alpha)/(1-\gamma)} \{(t)^{1/(1-\gamma)} - (t-1)^{1/(1-\gamma)}\}. \tag{10}$$

Now we are ready to compare this industry's output per worker in two closed worlds I and II with different sizes of population but the same parameter values of A, α and γ. We shall first examine the case in which capital per worker is the same in the two worlds,

$$L_I > L_{II} \quad \text{and} \quad \frac{K_I}{L_I} = \frac{K_{II}}{L_{II}} \tag{11),(12}$$

By substituting (11) and (12) into (10) we get

$$\frac{y_{t,I}}{y_{t,II}} = \left(\frac{L_I}{L_{II}}\right)^{\gamma/(1-\gamma)} > 1 \quad \text{if} \quad 1 > \gamma > 0.$$

This says that output per worker is higher in each period when population size is larger, if capital per worker is the same in each world. This proposition is not surprising when we reflect that the larger population has no drawbacks in this model.

An increase in population can (at least temporarily) induce a fall in capital per worker. Let us therefore consider the case where the capital/labor ratio is lower in world I, to the extent that capital is no larger in total than in world II,

$$K_I = K_{II}. \tag{13}$$

By substituting (11) and (13) into (10) we get

$$\frac{y_{t,I}}{y_{t,II}} = \left(\frac{L_I}{L_{II}}\right)^{(\gamma-\alpha)/(1-\gamma)} \quad \begin{aligned} &> 1 \quad \text{if} \quad \gamma > \alpha, \\ &= 1 \quad \text{if} \quad \gamma = \alpha, \\ &< 1 \quad \text{if} \quad \gamma < \alpha. \end{aligned}$$

That is, if the learning-by-doing exponent is larger than the capital exponent, the larger population has a higher output per worker in each period; if not, not. And with representative parameters of 0.2–0.3 for learning-by-doing and 0.33 for capital, the smaller population would do better under this regime.

These two polar cases — full capital adjustment for additional persons, and no capital adjustment for additional persons — lead one to ask how much capital adjustment would be needed, with representative parameters, for the larger population to do better. We can calculate from (10) that the break point, $y_{t,I}=y_{t,II}$ is where

$$\frac{K_I}{K_{II}}=\left(\frac{L_I}{L_{II}}\right)^{(\alpha-\gamma)/\alpha}.$$

At that point the incomes per worker in worlds I and II will be the same in each period.

Other interesting questions may be raised about this model. For example, what if there are decreasing returns to labor in the first unit produced in larger plants, due to more confusion? One answer to this question is that management in the bigger world I would use plants the same size as in world II, but more of them. There might be less learning-by-doing in smaller plants, but this would leave the bigger world at least as well off as the smaller world, with some additional learning-by-doing produced in the additional plants and communicated among the plants.

4. Discussion

The model developed in this paper implies that the rate of growth of productivity increases with time, rather than being characterized by steady-state growth as Arrow concluded that it is. To show that this is so, we must return our thinking to the firm and industry level at which the learning-by-doing phenomenon actually takes place, rather than moving directly to the macro level by simple analogy to the firm, as Arrow did.

Once a given learning-by-doing process begins, the rate of learning may indeed be constant with continued production.[7] But another process that is identical in all economic details with the one previously under discussion, except that it comes along later, will operate in an environment of a bigger total market and total output (due in part to the earlier innovation) even if population size remains constant. Furthermore, price will be lower due to improved productivity. Therefore sales will be greater than before if the good is a normal one, and the rate of learning per unit of time will be faster for the later innovation than for the earlier one. To the extent that these innovations are representative of the economy as a whole, the rate of increase of productivity for the economy as a whole will therefore be increasing over time.

[7]Or it may decline with output [e.g., Barkai and Levhari (1973), Baloff (1966), and references cited therein]. Though the rate of learning in a given product situation may decrease, there may still be changes in the process which restart a high-rate learning process, and increase the overall rate of learning.

An increasing rate of growth of productivity implies that there is not a constant capital–output ratio, as may be deduced immediately from the well-known

$$s = v(n + \dot{A}), \quad \text{where}$$

s = savings ratio,
v = capital–output ratio,
n = population growth rate,
$\dot{A}$ = rate of change of A.

But this is in no way inconsistent with observed reality nor is it a ground for theoretical concern, despite the supposed 'stylized fact' of an observed constant K/Y ratio, because the monetary estimates of the capital–output ratio tell nothing about the physical capital–output ratio, as is shown elsewhere [Simon (1980)]. The observed constant K/Y ratio in value terms is simply an inevitable price response of competitive markets, and has no significance for long-run production relationships.[8] The relevant K/Y ratio — the physical ratio — probably is not constant in MDC's but rather secularly falling, though this proposition cannot ever be examined rigorously in its aggregate form.

One might wonder why larger economies do not grow faster than smaller economies, in light of the above analysis. In fact, Chenery and associates [e.g., Chenery and Syrquin (1975)] do observe economies of size in cross-national comparison of growth rates in LDC's. And the Rostas-tradition data show a strong effect of scale in individual industries [e.g., Clark (1967), West (1971)]. Additionally, to the extent that economies are open, there are forces that reduce the observed differences in growth among countries. Specialization (e.g., Sweden in autos, Holland in communications) can lead to larger markets than the national economy provides. And a considerable proportion of technical progress is not locally tied, but rather moves across national boundaries, and therefore the relevant conceptual unit for analysis of the sort given here is the Western industrialized world as a whole, with the relevant comparison being between imagined larger and smaller sizes of it. Hence there is no inconsistency between the observed data and the analysis given here.

5. Summary and conclusions

We have shown that, in a comparison of two worlds that have different population sizes, but that are otherwise alike (including their capital–labor

[8]It is still another problem with Arrow's model that despite its real-resource nature, he bases it upon the assumption of a constant K/Y ratio, despite the meaninglessness of the monetary K/Y ratio to describe the physical K/Y ratio in the long run and likelihood that the physical K/Y ratio is falling in the long run. But all this is not a central issue here.

ratios and the initial per worker outputs), the larger world will come to have higher per worker output because of learning-by-doing. This conclusion is unlike the conclusion implicit in Arrow's model, because Arrow looked at steady-state rates of growth rather than changes in the level of income from the starting point. (Arrow's analysis also is confused by the use of the capital stock rather than cumulative output as the measure of experience, though output is the variable used in the empirical analyses that are the basis of this line of work.)

If the total capital is the same for the two worlds, the larger world probably will have a lower output per worker than the smaller world, given likely parameters. But a capital–labor ratio so much smaller in the larger world is not a likely condition in any scenario. We have therefore figured the break-even point of capital–labor ratios.

There are no obvious pitfalls in moving from the industry-level micro-economics of the data and of the present analysis to an economy as a whole.

In brief, given likely conditions and parameters, the paper suggests that large populations will have faster economic growth and a higher standard of living, ceteris paribus. This proposition must, of course, be hedged by a great many ceteris paribus conditions, and certainly it is not to be taken as a policy prescription without a great deal of consideration of the special facts of a given country's situation, history, and preferences. Among those preferences, the discount factor is all-important; if the future is weighted insignificantly relative to the present, children will necessarily be an inferior choice compared to additional physical capital or even to additional immediate consumption. Again, our central aim is to show that the simple Malthusian system, from which endogenous knowledge is absent, should not be taken as the keystone of national policy decisions.

Appendix: Criticism of Arrow's measure of experience

This section is in the nature of clearing the ground for the foundation of the models built in the paper.

As noted in section 2, all the empirical studies that Arrow or we have found measure experience with the cumulative number of units produced. But because Arrow doubted the psychological generalization implicit in that concept (a concept which also avoids the necessity of having a measurement for cumulated output since the beginning of time), he shifted to a very different concept, with entirely different implications. 'I therefore take instead cumulative gross investment (the capital stock) (cumulative production of capital goods) as an index of experience' [Arrow (1962, p. 157)]. That is,

$$A_t = \frac{1}{H_t} = f(K_t) = \mathrm{d}K_t^b, \quad \text{where} \tag{A.1}$$

A_t = level of technique,
K_t = capital stock.

He also shifted from a serial-number concept to a time-period concept.

Arrow was aware of some of the limitations of the way that he constructed the model, and he decribed it as applicable only to the capital-goods industry. And other writers such as Wan (1971, pp. 226–227) have criticized Arrow's model on much the same grounds that we do.[9]

> 'Arrow's ... assumption is somewhat at variance with empirical studies where unit labor requirement is shown as inversely related to the cumulative output in a loglinear equation. Moreover, such studies are conducted on a plant basis. Arrow argued that cumulative output should be less suitable than cumulative investment as an index of experience, since the appearance of new machines should provide more stimulation for innovation while the cumulation of outputs (say, at a constant rate per unit time) appears to be rather uninspiring environment. One may take issue with Arrow on two counts: (a) repetitive operation leads to familiarity and expertise; hence, constant output rate is by no means an unfavorable situation for cost reduction, and (b) cumulated output as an index for experience is supported by observed evidence, whereas there is no empirical evidence of a similar dependency on cumulative investment.'

Our aim here is to show the confusion that is caused — both in general, and also more specifically for the understanding of the effects of different population size — by taking the capital stock rather than cumulated gross

[9]Though it seems clear that output rather than capital is the appropriate measure of learning-by-doing, it is less obvious than output alone as the appropriate measure. More specifically, by analogy with Alchian's (1959) distinction between the rate of output and the quantity of output, Pollak (1980) suggested that not only may the serial numbers of the units produced at time t in countries A and B affect the relative productivities in t within A and B, but also the time profiles of past production, because the learning acquired in earlier periods may have partially obsolesced. Though this may well be the case (it makes sense on some assumptions about worker retirement and replacement of older processes but not on the assumption that the learning-by-doing is embodied in accumulative step-by-step knowledge), this phenomenon would not change the results obtained later as long as the two economies are of the same proportional size in each period. This can be shown as follows. If the output in country A is $\ldots + Y_{t-3}, Y_{t-2}, Y_{t-1}, Y_t$, and the output history of country B is $\ldots 2Y_{t-3}, 2Y_{t-2}, 2Y_{t-1}, 2Y_t$, then if the obsolescence rate is r per year, the obsolescence-weighted sum of output for the two countries is

$$\sum_{i=-\infty}^{t} Y_i = \ldots r^3 Y_{t-3} + r^2 Y_{t-2} + rY_{t-1} + Y_t, \quad \text{and}$$

$$\sum_{i=-\infty}^{t} Y_i = \ldots r^3 2Y_{t-3} + r^2 2Y_{t-2} + rY_{t-1} + Y_t.$$

It is clear that the ratio of the r-weighted sums is the same as if $r=1$ and there is no obsolescence. We may therefore disregard this matter in further discussion, because there is no reason to make an assumption other than proportional size of the economies in each period.

output as the index of experience. One such confusion is that, even using Arrow's own assumptions, cumulated capital and cumulated output yield different conclusions, as may be seen in the following argument: In monetary terms, the capital–output ratio may be taken (and is so assumed by Arrow) to be roughly constant in this context. Hence the capital stock and one year's production are roughly proportional. So the capital stock can be considered as a proxy for incremental output rather than cumulated output. An incremental output is generally not proportional to cumulated output; if production in t and $t+1$ are equal, cumulative output is higher in $t+1$ than in t even though capital is constant.

Formally,

$$A=\left(a\sum_{i=-\infty}^{t} Y\right)_i^b, \tag{A.2}$$

where Y_t = output in period t, which can be rewritten

$$\frac{A_t-A_{t-1}}{A_{t-1}}=\left(\sum_{i=-\infty}^{t} Y\right)_i^b-\left(\sum_{i=-\infty}^{t-1} Y\right)_i^b\Bigg/\left(\sum_{t=-\infty}^{t-1} Y\right)_i^b, \tag{A.3}$$

where the right-hand side is always positive.

Now consider Arrow's function (A.1) from which can be written

$$\frac{A_t-A_{t-1}}{A_{t-1}}=\frac{K_t^b-K_{t-1}^b}{K_{t-1}^b}. \tag{A.1'}$$

If the capital–output ratio is a constant c, as Arrow assumes it is, then (A.1′) can be rewritten

$$\frac{A_t-A_{t-1}}{A_{t-1}}=\frac{(cY)_t^b-(cY)_{t-1}^b}{(cY)_{t-1}^b}=\frac{Y_t^b-Y_{t-1}^b}{Y_{t-1}^b}. \tag{A.4}$$

This is unequal to (A.3), as can be seen from the fact that if $Y_{t-1}=Y_t$, (A.3) will be positive but (A.4) will be zero. And (7) corresponds to the facts that Arrow cites, including the Horndal effect, whereas (A.4) does not.

Even worse are all the difficulties that flow from that most troublesome of all economic concepts to conceptualize and measure satisfactorily, capital. Most fundamental here is that the capital concept used in the Arrow model is physical, whereas the observed capital–output ratio that Arrow builds on is a monetary notion, and there is no necessary or likely correspondence between the two.

Arrow's definition of the capital stock also is not analogous to cumulated output in that it excludes old capital that has already obsolesced. This is important because it means that Arrow's model does not sum up experience since the very beginning of the learning process, which causes the paradox in interpretation of rates of productivity change discussed in section 2.[10]

In brief, the use of capital rather than cumulated output is a source of erroneous interpretation of the implications of learning-by-doing. When discussing the effects of population size, cumulated output leads to quite different conclusions than does the capital stock.

[10]Even cumulate output would have to be defined carefully because of the difficulty of estimating it for an economy or society as a whole. The entire transportation from, on the one hand, the firm or industry level with technical measurements to, on the other hand, the national economy value measurements can — and in this case does — cause the argument to lose its way, and later to be misinterpreted in empirical work by others.

References

Alchian, Armen, 1959, Costs and outputs, in: Moses Abramovitz et al., The allocation of economic resources (Stanford University Press, Stanford, CA).

Alchian, Armen A., 1963, Reliability of progress curves in airframe production, Econometrica 31, no. 4, 679–693.

Arrow, K.J., 1962, The economic implications of learning by doing, Review of Economic Studies XXIX (3), no. 8, 155–173.

Asher, H., 1956, Cost quantity relationships in the airframe industry, RAND Report no. R-291 (Santa Monica, CA).

Baloff, N., 1966, The learning curve — Some controversial issues, Journal of Industrial Economics XIV, 275–282.

Barkai, H. and D. Levhari, 1973, The impact of experience on kibbutz farming, The Review of Economics and Statistics LV, 56–63.

Brems, Hans, 1973, Labor, capital and growth (Lexington Books, Lexington, MA).

Chenery, Hollis and Moses Syrquin, 1975, Patterns of development, 1950–1970 (Oxford University Press, New York).

Cigno, Alessandro, 1984, Consumption and procreation in economic growth, in: G. Steinmann, ed., Economic consequences of population change in industrialized countries (Springer, Berlin, Heidelberg, New York, Tokyo).

Clark, Colin, 1957, Conditions of economic progress, 3rd ed. (Macmillan, New York).

Dixit, A.K., 1976, The theory of equilibrium growth (Oxford University Press, New York).

Eltis, Walter A., 1973, Growth and distribution (Macmillan, London).

Everett, Alexander H., 1826, New ideas on population, Reprinted in 1970 (Kelley, New York).

Hirsch, Werner Z., 1956, Firm progress ratios, Econometrica 24, 136–143.

Kaldor, Nicholas, 1957, A model of economic growth, Economic Journal LXVII.

Phelps, Edmund S., 1966, Models of technical progress and the golden rule of research, Review of Economic Studies, 133–145.

Pitchford, John D., 1974, Population and economic growth (North-Holland, New York).

Pollak, Robert A., 1980, Personal communications.

Rostas, Leo, 1948, Comparative productivity in British and American industry, Occasional Paper XIII (NIER, Cambridge, MA).

Sheshinski, E., 1967, Tests of the learning by doing hypothesis, Review of Economics and Statistics XLLX, 568–578.

Simon, Julian L., 1977, The economics of population growth (Princeton University Press, Princeton, NJ).

Simon, Julian L., 1980, A constant capital-output ratio is meaningless, Mimeo.

Solow, Robert, 1970, Growth theory: An exposition (Oxford University Press, New York).

Verdoorn, P.J., 1949, Factors that determine the growth of labor productivity, L'Industria, no. 1, 45–46, translated by G. and A.P. Thirlwall, in: Julian L. Simon and Julie DaVanzo, eds., Research in population economics, Vol. II, (JAI Press, Greenwich).

Wan, Henry Y. Jr., 1971, Economic growth (Harcourts, Brace, Jovanovic, New York).

West, E.C., 1971, Canada-United States price and productivity differences in manufacturing industries, 1963 (Economic Council of Canada, Ottawa).

Wright, T.P., 1936, Factors affecting the cost of airframes, Journal of the Aeronautical Sciences 3, 112–118.

[24]

Foreword

This is one of a set of empirical studies that I undertook in the 1970s to test, one by one, the key elements in the Malthusian analysis of the effect of population growth. (Others include the effect of density on the rate of economic growth, the effect on the construction of irrigation systems, the proportion of the labor force in agriculture, and the amount of education students receive.) My 1992 book compiles these articles. I chose to include this study anyway, as a sample, and because it arrived at a particularly neat set of results, and because it has gone almost wholly unnoticed.

The Effect of Population Density on Infrastructure: The Case of Road Building*

Donald R. Glover
University of Kansas

Julian L. Simon
University of Illinois, Urbana; and The Hebrew University

Introduction

The ill effects of population density are well known: less farmland per farmer and consumer, and more congestion. The positive effects of population density have been discussed less and studied almost not at all. This paper takes up one of the ways in which increased population density can be of economic benefit: higher density causes more available infrastructure per worker. More specifically, this paper studies the effect of differences in population density upon the amount of road construction. The effect of per capita income upon road construction is also discussed, but primarily it enters the study as a factor that must be held constant so as to understand clearly the effect of population density. The main conclusion is that higher population density is a significant cause of higher road density.[1]

To our knowledge, this topic has not been previously studied. The closest facet of the literature seems to be Fishlow's demonstration that population density was an important determinant of railroad building in the counties of the American Midwest just prior to the Civil War.[2] But Fishlow's primary interest was somewhat different from ours.

As to the importance of the phenomenon studied here, students of economic development are unanimous on the crucial role of transportation and communication—both of which roads represent—in the development process. For example: "Road conditions in Uttar Pradesh [India] are an important factor in the lack of tubewells, shortages of fertilizer, backward agricultural techniques, and failure to produce more remunerative crops for

* The authors gratefully acknowledge helpful suggestions by Nathaniel Leff and Charles Kindleberger.

[1] A similar analysis indicates a similar relationship in land building in agriculture: higher population density causes farmers to irrigate more land (Julian L. Simon, "The Positive Effect of Population Growth on Agricultural Saving in Irrigation Systems," *Review of Economics and Statistics* [in press]).

[2] Albert Fishlow, *American Railroads and the Transformation of the Ante-Bellum Economy* (Cambridge, Mass.: Harvard University Press, 1965).

market. All these conditions reflect the difficult supply lines to town centers that provide both a market and a source of inputs and technical help."[3]

Another example is the effect of a 15-mile farm-to-market road linking seven Indian villages which had previously had no transportation facilities available to them. "It was Chano's family...who showed us the road's importance. Unhulled rice in jungle villages was selling for about $1.50 for 83 pounds. Rice taken 12 miles in bullock carts on the new road to the only real town in the district, Jagdalpur (population about 15,000), brought twice as much."[4] And a highway example:

> In Costa Rica, before the Inter-American Highway was constructed, driving beef cattle on the hoof from grazing lands to San Jose often resulted in a 40 percent loss of weight, and imports were necessary to supply local needs. Now...it is possible to deliver truck-trailer units of cattle overnight, and Costa Rica is self-supporting in meat....[I]n Thailand, the Friendship Highway...has transformed partially unused jungle land along its hundred-mile route into highly productive and prosperous farms....Within three years the production of sugar cane, vegetables, bananas, and other fruits more than tripled in tonnage.[5]

Theory

The relevant theory is simple, and a verbal statement suffices. All other things (including per capita income) held constant, if there are more people in a given geographic area, it will cost less per person to construct a common facility such as a road. If the benefits per person are the same at different population densities (which is not an unreasonable assumption over a wide range of densities), and costs per person are lower, the benefit/cost ratio is higher at a higher population density; and there will be some population density that is high enough to make benefits outweigh costs. In the aggregate, increased population raises the rate of return on investment in roads. In empirical terms, then, it is to be expected that where population per unit area is higher, there will be more roads per unit area, *ceteris paribus*.

The theoretical effect of per capita income begins with the assumption that roads are surely a normal good. We may therefore expect income to have a direct effect on the amount of roads "purchased." We may also expect an indirect effect of income through an increase in the number of vehicles purchased. Hence, per capita income must be held constant in the analysis.

The appropriate function to test the effect of population density is:

$$\left(\frac{RDS}{LND}\right) = f\left(\frac{POP}{LND}, \frac{INC}{POP}\right),$$

[3] Wilfred Owen, *Distance and Development* (Washington, D.C.: Brookings Institution, 1968), p. 58.

[4] Anthony Chapelle and Georgette Dickey Chapelle, "New Life for India's Villagers," *National Geographic* 109 (April 1956): 572–95.

[5] Wilfred Owen, *Strategy for Mobility* (Washington, D.C.: Brookings Institution, 1964), p. 8.

where *RDS* = miles of road of all kinds, *LND* = square miles of land, *POP* = population, *INC* = national income, *RDS/LND* = total-road density, *POP/LND* = population density, and *INC/POP* = per capita income. Other symbols used in the paper are: *PVD* = miles of paved roads, *PVD/LND* = paved-road density, *UPD* = miles of unpaved roads, *UPD/LND* = unpaved-road density, i = country index, and t = time (year).

One must also consider whether higher road density may cause higher population density rather than the converse. That may indeed happen, but a higher road density would seem to affect population density through the distribution of people by migration much more than it would affect birth or death rates. And if the analysis is done (as here) with political units such as countries that are relatively closed to migration by law and geography, the effect of road density upon population density may be disregarded.

Farm-to-market roads constitute most of the world's roads. And congestion of the type found in urban areas is not found on such roads. Therefore we may assume that increased population does not lead to more roads because of a congestion effect, but rather constitutes an increase in transportation facilities to the representative citizen.

The Data

The units of observation are countries. In the various regressions, all countries were used for which road data were available except the island cities of Hong Kong, Singapore, and Malta.[6] Population and income data were less of a constraint. The quality of the road data is poor—probably even poorer than the population and income data, whose deficiencies are well known. Where errors in the road data were obvious, they were adjusted by interpolation; otherwise, they were used as published. Worry over bad data quality is reduced by the absence of reason to believe in systematic error. The effect of error, then, is simply to reduce the strength of observed relationships and to bias toward zero the parameter estimates. The means, medians, standard deviations, and rates of change over time of the variables may be seen in table A1 of the Appendix.

The main analysis employs total roads as the dependent variable. Paved roads and unpaved roads are also studied as dependent variables.

The total sample of countries is used in some of our analyses. In other analyses, the total sample is subdivided into per capita income groups in order to determine how the variables differ in their influences at different stages of economic development.

[6] Data on road mileage were obtained from publications of the International Road Federation. Data on national income were obtained from publications of the Agency for International Development, Organization for Economic Cooperation and Development, and the United Nations Statistical Office. Data on population and land area were obtained primarily from publications of the United Nations Statistical Office.

Economic Development and Cultural Change

The Results

Total Roads as the Dependent Variable

Our main method[7] is a cross-section in a sample of 113 nations at a single point in time, 1968. Consider first the linear regression:

$$\left(\frac{RDS_{i,1968}}{LND_{i,1968}}\right) = \underset{(t\,=\,-2.6)}{-.119} + \underset{\substack{(t\,=\,10.7)\\(\beta\,=\,.613)}}{.0025}\left(\frac{POP_{i,1968}}{LND_{i,1968}}\right) + \underset{\substack{(t\,=\,7.4)\\(\beta\,=\,.422)}}{.0003}\left(\frac{INC_{i,1968}}{POP_{i,1968}}\right), \quad R^2 = .65. \tag{1}$$

Population density and per capita income[8] are both significant in explaining road density, as the t-ratios show. The standardized (β) coefficients show that population density is somewhat more influential than is per capita income. And the R^2 of .65 suggests that the proportion of the variance explained is important. Collinearity presents no problem; the correlation between the independent variables is only .20.

The same relationship was also run in double logarithmic form in order to reduce the effect of the far-out observations on the various variables. The data are plotted in figure 1 for each of the five quintiles of per capita income (a device to hold income roughly constant). The relationship between population density and road density is clearly very strong.[9] The log-log regression produces convenient estimates of elasticities as follows:

$$\log\left(\frac{RDS_{i,1968}}{LND_{i,1968}}\right) = \underset{(t\,=\,26.8)}{-.380} + \underset{\substack{(t\,=\,18.1)\\(\beta\,=\,.704)}}{.726}\log\left(\frac{POP_{i,1968}}{LND_{i,1968}}\right) + \underset{\substack{(t\,=\,12.4)\\(\beta\,=\,.483)}}{.657}\log\left(\frac{INC_{i,1968}}{POP_{i,1968}}\right), \quad R^2 = .83. \tag{2}$$

[7] Tables A2, A3, and A4 in the Appendix present results for a more complete set of regressions than are discussed in the text.

[8] Kindleberger has shown that per capita income is strongly related to the densities of both roads and railroads across an international cross-section (Charles Kindleberger, *Economic Development* [New York: McGraw-Hill Book Co., 1965]).

[9] There would seem to be no problem of spurious correlation here. "The question of spurious correlation quite obviously does not arise when the hypothesis to be tested has initially been formulated in terms of ratios" (Edwin Kuh and John R. Meyer, "Correlation and Regression Estimates When the Data Are Ratios," *Econometrica* 23 [October 1955]: 400–416). The relationship of interest here is the effect of population density on the density of roads per square mile, for which the ratios in the regression are the appropriate proxies.

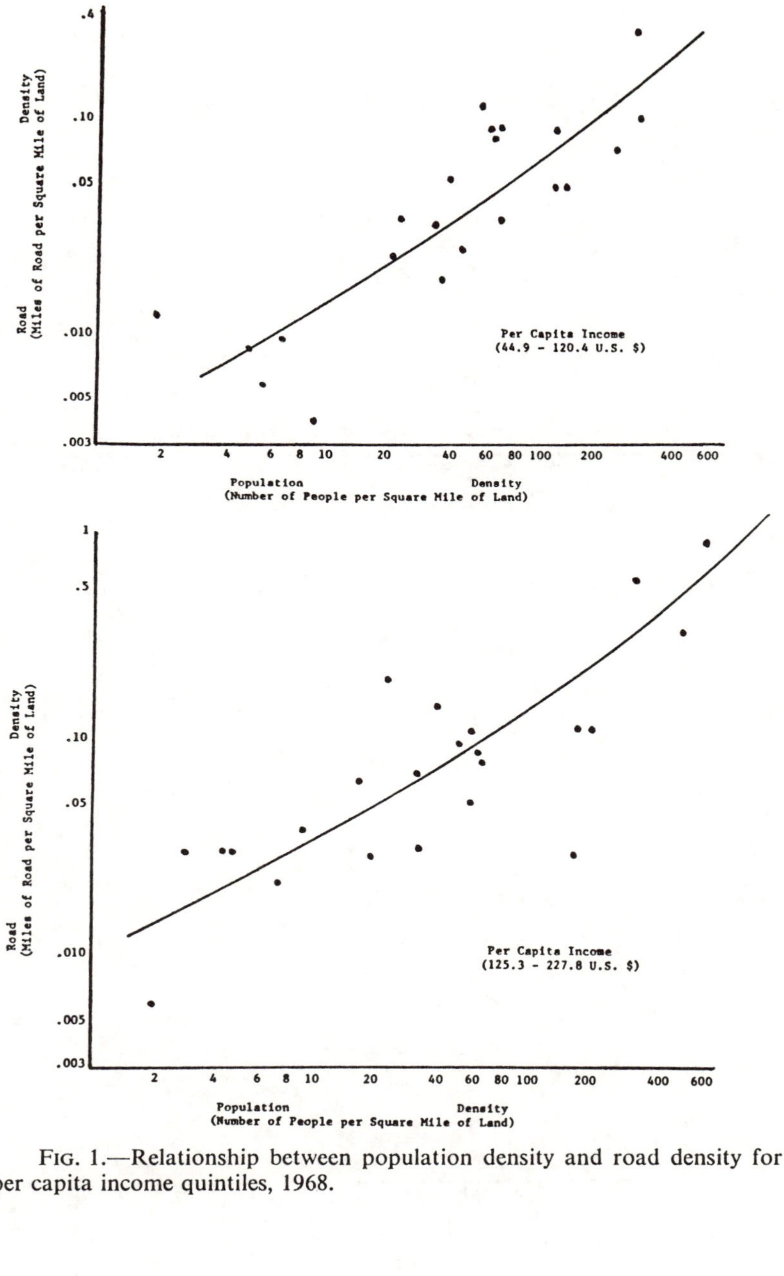

FIG. 1.—Relationship between population density and road density for per capita income quintiles, 1968.

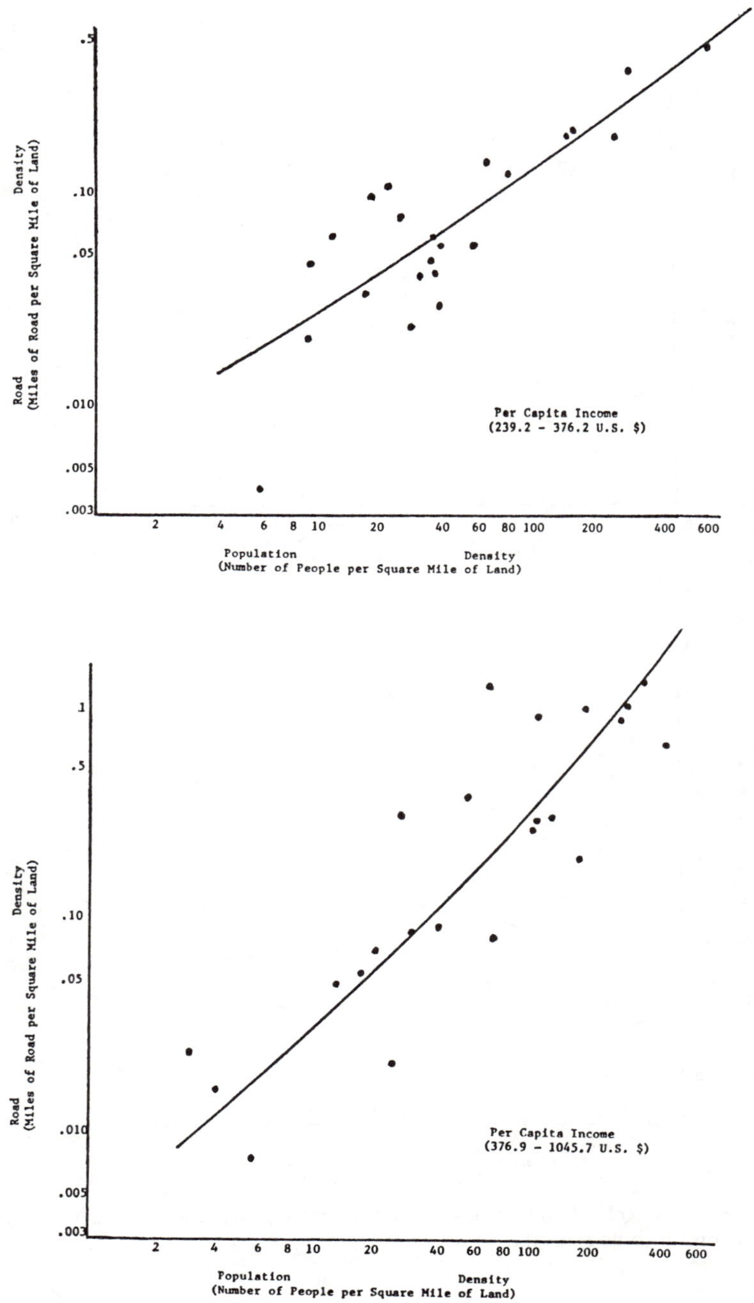

Road Density
(Miles of Road per Square Mile of Land)
.5
.10
.05
.010
.005
.003
2
4
6
8
10
20
40
60
80
100
200
400
600
Population Density
(Number of People per Square Mile of Land)
Per Capita Income
(239.2 - 376.2 U.S. $)
Road Density
(Miles of Road per Square Mile of Land)
1
.5
.10
.05
.010
.005
.003
2
4
6
8
10
20
40
60
80
100
200
400
600
Population Density
(Number of People per Square Mile of Land)
Per Capita Income
(376.9 - 1045.7 U.S. $)

FIG. 1

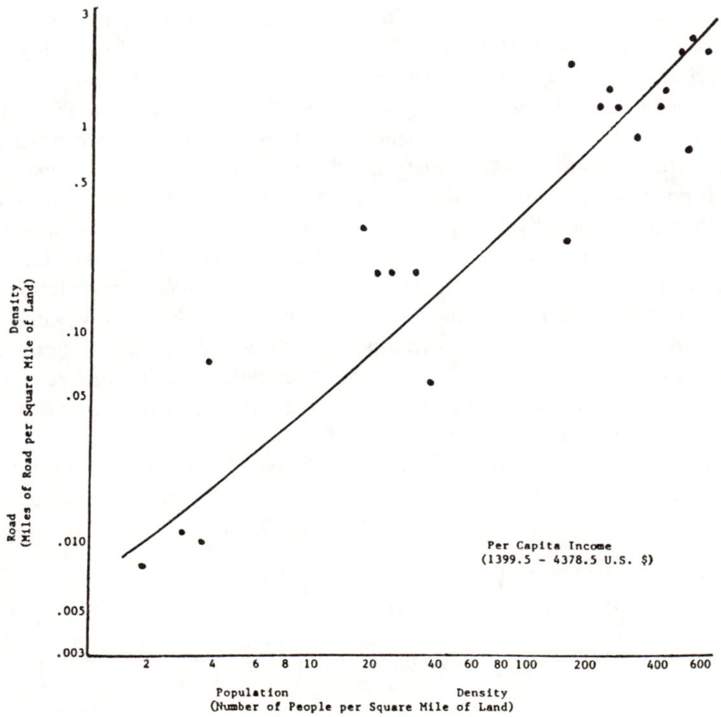

FIG. 1 (*Continued*)

These results seem (to the authors, anyway) impressive. The R^2 of .83 is exceptionally high for cross-national regressions, especially where only two independent variables are used; an R^2 so high suggests that one need not search further for additional variables to explain the variation in the dependent variable. The Student's *t*-ratios are extraordinarily high, and the elasticity of .73 of road density with respect to population density—a 1 percent increase in population causing a .73 percent increase in road density, or twice as large a population having almost one and a half times as many roads—indicates that the relationship is very meaningful in economic terms. And the "real" relationship must be even higher, because the estimate is biased downward due to measurement error. This regression is the main result of our study. We offer it as the basis for estimates of the effect of population growth on road density.

We also attempted to see what the series of observations within individual countries over time (1957–68) could tell us:

$$\left(\frac{RDS_{i,t}}{LND_{i,t}}\right) = a + b\left(\frac{POP_{i,t}}{LND_{i,t}}\right) + c\left(\frac{INC_{i,t}}{POP_{i,t}}\right), \text{ for each country } i. \quad (3)$$

Economic Development and Cultural Change

The median elasticity for population density is much the same as in the cross-sections (.614 in the linear form, but $t = .32$; .669 in the log-log regression, with $t = 1.3$). But the median multicollinearity between the independent variables was too high ($r = .932$) for their relative strengths to be evaluated, due to a common trend over time. And the median elasticity of per capita income was only .029. In addition, other reasons suggest that such time-series are not valuable in this case. (1) The estimates of population change are usually interpolations from at most two census observations within the period, making a mockery of yearly data. (2) The effect of population change (and also of per capita income) is likely to be felt only very slowly, a child influencing road construction perhaps only when he grows up. These factors also explain why regressions of first differences yielded a median R^2 of .14—meaning that the method of first differences is not useful here. All in all, we believe the individual-country simple time-series evidence is not to be trusted heavily.

A sample of the countries' experiences over time was also analyzed, with much better results. The dependent and independent variables are rates of change between the 2 years 1957 and 1968:

$$\left(\frac{RDS_{i,1968} - RDS_{i,1957}}{RDS_{i,1957}}\right) = \underset{(t = 0.8)}{.066} + \underset{\substack{(t = 3.9)\\(\beta = .448)}}{.984}\left(\frac{POP_{i,1968} - POP_{i,1957}}{POP_{i,1957}}\right) + \underset{\substack{(t = 1.3)\\(\beta = .151)}}{.019}\left(\frac{INC_{i,1968} - INC_{i,1957}}{INC_{i,1957}}\right), \quad R^2 = .22. \qquad (4)$$

This method is inherently free of many of the trend problems and other defects of simple time-series regressions,[10] and multicollinearity is observed to be very low ($r = .04$). The coefficients in this regression may be read immediately as elasticities. The results are (perhaps surprisingly) close to the individual-country time-series, though much more meaningful: population density shows a very significant elasticity of almost unity, while per capita income's effect is small.

Taken together, the time-series experiments suggest these judgments to us. (1) The strong effect of population density is confirmed. (2) The relatively weak effect of per capita income and the low R^2 suggest that the effect of some other important variable (or variables) is not being captured in the time-series analysis. That variable could be per capita income, and

[10] For an analysis of this method see Julian L. Simon, "The Demand for Liquor in the U.S., and a Simple Method of Determination," *Econometrica* 34 (January 1966): 193–205.

the reason for the effect's not being captured might well be the slowness with which per capita income's effect is felt. This would be consistent with our results from the "long run" and "fully adjusted" cross-section data where slow-acting variables have had time to play out their full effects and to show up in the data.[11] It would surprise us, however, if per capita income acted more slowly than changes in population, which renders this explanation less than satisfactory. Better data and/or a better explanation would be welcome here.[12]

Paved Roads as the Dependent Variable

The main cross-section regression using paved roads shows these results:

$$\log\left(\frac{PVD_{i,1968}}{LND_{i,1968}}\right) = \underset{(t\,=\,-34.3)}{-6.431} + \underset{\substack{(t\,=\,21.9)\\(\beta\,=\,.714)}}{1.166} \log\left(\frac{POP_{i,1968}}{LND_{i,1968}}\right)$$

$$+ \underset{\substack{(t\,=\,15.7)\\(\beta\,=\,.509)}}{1.095} \log\left(\frac{INC_{i,1968}}{POP_{i,1968}}\right), \qquad (5)$$

$$R^2 = .88.$$

The R^2 of .88—an extraordinarily large proportion of variance explained in a cross-section study with low collinearity ($r = .197$) and only two variables—gives the impression that searching for further explanatory variables would not be useful. The elasticities in the paved-roads regressions are even higher than in the total-roads regressions. This makes sense, because there is an increase in the quality as well as the quantity of a country's roads as income increases. This is reflected in an increased proportion of total roads that are paved, which is consistent with the higher elasticities in the paved-roads regressions.[13]

Unpaved Roads as the Dependent Variable

The basic cross-section regression using unpaved-road density estimates (total roads minus paved roads) yields results that support the findings for

[11] For a formal explication of the relationship of cross-section and time-series results when effects are lagged, see Dennis J. Aigner and Julian L. Simon, "A Specification Bias Interpretation of Cross-Section vs. Time-Series Parameter Estimates," *Western Economic Journal* 8 (June 1970): 144–61; or E. Malinvaud, *Statistical Methods of Econometrics* (New York: American Elsevier Publishing Co., 1966).

[12] The amount of measurement error—as measured by, say, the ratio of the average deviation between the observed and "true" values to the difference between the true value and the sample mean—must be much greater in the sample of observations over time than in the cross-section analyses because the overall differences among the levels of the countries in the cross-section are much greater than the changes in the levels within countries over the period 1957–68. This implies that the results in the time-series regression are more strongly biased downward than the cross-sectional results.

[13] A possible contributing reason is that the data for paved roads are likely to be more accurate than the data for total roads, a matter to be discussed shortly.

Economic Development and Cultural Change

total-road density and paved-road density:

$$\log\left(\frac{UPD_{i,1968}}{LND_{i,1968}}\right) = \underset{(t\,=\,-16.2)}{-3.508} + \underset{\substack{(t\,=\,10.1)\\(\beta\,=\,.626)}}{.585}\log\left(\frac{POP_{i,1968}}{LND_{i,1968}}\right)$$

$$+ \underset{\substack{(t\,=\,7.9)\\(\beta\,=\,.495)}}{.573}\log\left(\frac{INC_{i,1968}}{POP_{i,1968}}\right), \qquad (6)$$

$$R^2 = .58.$$

Population density explains more of the variance in unpaved-road density than does per capita income, as seen in the elasticities and β coefficients. But the elasticities are lower than for paved roads and total roads. A possible reason is the inaccuracy of the unpaved-road data. Unpaved-road data are the sum of the reported data for these three ill-defined categories: (1) gravel, crushed stone, or stabilized soil surface; (2) earth roads; and (3) unimproved roads. The data reported for these categories are often inconsistent from year to year. For example, Pakistan reported no mileage for unimproved roads in 1966; in 1967, 100,877 miles of unimproved roads were reported.[14] The effect of such error is to bias the parameter estimates downward.

The Influence of Stage of Development

It is reasonable to assume that population density will have different effects on road building at different stages of economic development. One relevant factor is that in poor countries unpaved roads are often built with contributed labor, making the process less dependent on income than if the roads must all be purchased with money. For example, in India road building involves matching contributions by the local district and the state or federal government. "Matching can be either in labor or in money [and] in many instances. . . villagers are too poor to afford the taxes required to permit a cash contribution."[15] Many roads are entirely local projects using local labor: "Our best [road] cost the Government nothing. It is 15 miles long, linking seven villages, and it was built in five days by a thousand farmers with their own tools."[16] This leads to the hypothesis that per capita income is less important relative to population density in poorer countries than in richer countries.

A second relevant factor is the tendency of contemporary rich countries, as they become richer, to pave some previously existing unpaved

[14] International Road Federation, *Highway Expenditures: Road and Motor Vehicle Statistics for 1958, 1959–1969, 1970* (Washington, D.C.: International Road Federation, 1959, 1971). The actual measure used for unpaved roads is the residual (total roads minus paved roads).

[15] Owen, *Distance and Development*, p. 66.

[16] Chapelle and Chapelle, p. 587.

roads. This may result in a sizable increase in paved roads, a relatively small increase in total roads, and a decrease in unpaved roads. This is in fact observed in contemporary rich countries over the period 1957–68. And the United States provides an example of such changes in the stocks of paved and unpaved roads. In 1949, total U.S. road mileage was 3.3 million miles, of which 16 percent (517,000 miles) was paved or "high typed surfaced."[17] In 1968, 41 percent (1.5 million miles) of the 3.7 million total miles of road was paved.[18] This represents an 11 percent increase in total road mileage, an increase of 194 percent in paved road mileage, and a 22 percent decrease in unpaved road mileage between 1949 and 1968.

To test the effect of the stage of economic development, the original cross-section sample of 113 countries was divided into three income subsamples: (1) 35 countries with per capita incomes up to \$200; (2) 47 countries with per capita incomes of \$201–\$700; and (3) 31 countries with per capita incomes of \$701 and above.

The elasticities for the unpaved-road–log-log regressions confirm the hypothesis that population density is relatively more important than per capita income in poorer countries than in richer countries (table A3). The respective population density and per capita income elasticities are .662 ($t = 7.4$) and .197 ($t = 0.7$) in the low-income countries; .656 ($t = 5.2$) and .804 ($t = 1.6$) in the middle-income countries; and .555 ($t = 6.6$) and .752 ($t = 4.5$) in the high-income countries.

The hypothesis concerning the substitution of paved for unpaved roads is confirmed by the elasticities for the unpaved-roads sample of changes over time in the high-income countries:

$$\left(\frac{UPD_{i,1968} - UPD_{i,1957}}{UPD_{i,1957}}\right) = \underset{(t = 2.3)}{.817} \underset{\substack{(t = -1.3)\\(\beta = -.171)}}{-2.520} \left(\frac{POP_{i,1968} - POP_{i,1957}}{POP_{i,1957}}\right) \underset{\substack{(t = -5.7)\\(\beta = -.770)}}{-.547} \left(\frac{INC_{i,1968} - INC_{i,1957}}{INC_{i,1957}}\right), \quad R^2 = .76. \tag{7}$$

These elasticities for unpaved roads with respect to both population density

[17] U.S. Department of Commerce, *Highway Statistics, 1950* (Washington, D.C.: Bureau of Public Roads, 1952), p. 126. "High type surfaced roads include bituminous penetration, sheet asphalt, bituminous concrete, portland cement concrete, vitrified brick, and block pavements of asphalt, wood, and stone" (U.S. Department of Commerce, *Historical Statistics of the United States: Colonial Times to 1957* [Washington, D.C.: Bureau of the Census, 1960], p. 456).

[18] International Road Federation, 1971.

and per capita income are quite negative, reflecting the substitution of paved for unpaved roads.[19]

Summary and Conclusions

Population density seems to have a significant and strong effect on total-road density in a cross-national sample—an elasticity of .7 or higher, despite bad data. Time-series analyses confirm this finding. The effect on paved-road construction is even stronger—an elasticity higher than unity. The effect on unpaved roads is somewhat smaller but still significant, an elasticity of approximately .6. These relationships can be interpreted causally because there is not much migration among countries (our units of observation). The results imply that an increase in population has a very positive effect on a country's infrastructure (road construction), on the reasonable assumption that increased congestion does not negate all the benefits of the additional facilities.

The stage of economic development does influence the effects of both population density and per capita income. At lower levels of income, per capita income is less important than population density in influencing changes in the stocks of roads since village labor can be substituted for money expenditures. At higher income levels, increased population density and per capita income cause the substitution of paved for unpaved roads.

[19] One may question why the elasticities in the unpaved-roads regressions for high-income countries are negative in the sample of changes-over-time data and positive in the cross-section data (tables A3 and A4). The explanation may lie in the fact that countries that are now rich, and years ago had incomes at least equal to the incomes of contemporary middle-income countries, first built unpaved roads and then paved them much later, whereas contemporary countries are more likely to build paved roads initially. For example, in 1904 paved road mileage accounted for less than .001 percent (144 miles) of total U.S. road mileage (2.1 million miles); per capita income was $294. By 1921, the percentage of total roads (2.9 million miles) accounted for by paved roads (35,874 miles) had increased to 1 percent; per capita income had increased to $682 (Highway Education Board, *Highways Handbook* [Washington, D.C.: Highway Education Board, 1929], p. 7; and U.S. Department of Commerce, *Historical Statistics of the United States: Colonial Times to 1957*, p. 139). But contemporary countries with similar incomes (and population densities as low or lower than the United States in earlier years) have higher ratios of paved roads to total roads. For example, in 1968, in Mexico, with a per capita income of $565, 57 percent of total road mileage was paved; in Syria, with a per capita income of $248, 61 percent of total road mileage was paved; and in Yugoslavia, with a per capita income of $481, 25 percent of total road mileage was paved. This suggests that contemporary incomes buy more paved roads than the same level of income bought years ago.

Donald R. Glover and Julian L. Simon

Appendix

TABLE A1

MEANS, MEDIANS, STANDARD DEVIATIONS, AND MEAN RATES OF CHANGE OF ROAD DENSITY, POPULATION DENSITY, AND PER CAPITA INCOME

Variable	Mean	Median	Standard Deviation
Cross-Section of Countries: Total Roads (Eq. [1], $N = 113$)			
RDS/LND..........	0.372	.096	0.596
POP/LND..........	108	37	147
INC/POP...........	\$662	\$290	\$844
Cross-Section of Countries: Paved Roads (Eq. [5], $N = 113$)			
PVD/LND..........	0.177	.046	0.437
Cross-Section of Countries: Unpaved Roads (Eq. [6], $N = 113$)			
UPD/LND	0.195	.050	0.357
Rate of Change 1957–68 for All Countries ($N = 64$)			
POP/LND..........	0.327	.333	0.213
INC/POP...........	1.501	.607	3.593
RDS/LND..........	0.425	.211	0.469
PVD/LND..........	1.654	.899	2.500
UPD/LND	0.091	.093	1.419

TABLE A2

EFFECTS OF POPULATION DENSITY AND PER CAPITA INCOME COEFFICIENTS FOR ROAD TYPES BY STAGE OF DEVELOPMENT: CROSS-SECTION LINEAR REGRESSIONS, 1968 (EQ. [1])

	DEPENDENT VARIABLE											
	Total-Road Density				Paved-Road Density				Unpaved-Road Density			
	β	Coefficient	t-ratio	R^2	β	Coefficient	t-ratio	R^2	β	Coefficient	t-ratio	R^2
All countries (N = 113):												
POP/LND....	.613	.0025	10.7	.65	.540	.0016	8.5	.58	.366	.0009	4.2	.18
INC/POP	.422	.0003	7.4		.438	.0002	6.9		.251	.00001	2.9	
Incomes up to $200 ($N$ = 35):												
POP/LND....	.705	.0016	5.7	.49	.532	.0002	3.6	.29	.681	.0013	5.3	.46
INC/POP	−.109	−.0005	−0.8		.066	.00006	0.5		−.138	−.0006	−1.1	
Incomes of $201–$700 (N = 47):												
POP/LND....	.550	.0016	4.8	.42	.811	.0009	9.8	.71	.330	.0008	2.5	.22
INC/POP	.308	.0010	2.7		.157	.0002	1.9		.316	.0009	2.4	
Incomes of $701 and above ($N$ = 31):												
POP/LND....	.740	.0037	5.6	.53	.788	.0031	6.6	.61	.231	.0006	1.3	.42
INC/LND....	.178	.00001	1.4		.024	.000001	0.2		.296	.00001	1.6	

TABLE A3

EFFECTS OF POPULATION DENSITY AND PER CAPITA INCOME ELASTICITIES FOR ROAD TYPES BY STAGE OF DEVELOPMENT: CROSS-SECTION LOG-LOG REGRESSIONS, 1968 (EQ. [2])

	DEPENDENT VARIABLE											
	Total-Road Density				Paved-Road Density				Unpaved-Road Density			
	β	Elasticity	t-ratio	R^2	β	Elasticity	t-ratio	R^2	β	Elasticity	t-ratio	R^2
All countries (N = 113):												
POP/LND	.704	.726	18.1	.83	0.714	1.166	21.9	.88	.626	.585	10.1	.58
INC/POP	.483	.657	12.4		0.509	1.095	15.7		.495	.573	7.9	
Incomes up to $200 ($N$ = 35):												
POP/LND	.830	.708	8.8	.71	0.875	1.226	11.2	.79	.786	.662	7.4	.62
INC/POP	.124	.341	1.3		0.184	0.828	2.3		.073	.197	0.7	
Incomes of $201–$700 (N = 47):												
POP/LND	.817	.814	10.1	.72	0.904	1.183	14.8	.83	.603	.656	5.2	.41
INC/POP	.181	.702	2.2		0.095	0.484	1.6		.190	.804	1.6	
Incomes of $701 and above ($N$ = 31):												
POP/LND	.048	.755	10.6	.81	1.062	1.157	12.2	.85	.903	.555	6.6	.61
INC/POP	.607	.863	6.1		0.394	0.848	4.5		.620	.752	4.5	

TABLE A4

EFFECTS OF POPULATION DENSITY AND PER CAPITA INCOME FOR ROAD TYPES BY STAGE OF DEVELOPMENT: SAMPLE OF CHANGES OVER TIME, 1957–68 (EQ. [4])

	DEPENDENT VARIABLE											
	Total-Road Density				Paved-Road Density				Unpaved-Road Density			
	β	Elasticity	t-ratio	R^2	β	Elasticity	t-ratio	R^2	β	Elasticity	t-ratio	R^2
All countries (N = 64):												
POP/LND	.448	0.984	3.9	.22	.096	0.652	0.9	.30	.047	0.365	0.5	.15
INC/POP	.151	0.019	1.3		.284	0.198	2.4		−.379	−0.150	−3.1	
Incomes up to $200 ($N$ = 13):												
POP/LND	.291	0.856	1.1	.30	.665	4.404	2.7	.42	.239	0.599	1.0	.43
INC/POP	.547	0.347	2.0		.087	0.124	0.4		.674	0.418	2.7	
Incomes of $201–$700 (N = 30):												
POP/LND	.347	0.812	1.9	.12	.079	0.574	0.7	.61	.300	1.005	1.6	.09
INC/POP	−.018	−0.002	−0.1		.314	0.218	1.7		−.009	−0.001	−0.1	
Incomes of $701 and above ($N$ = 21):												
POP/LND	.559	1.474	3.9	.74	.042	0.429	0.2	.04	−.171	−2.520	−1.3	.76
INC/POP	.427	0.054	3.0		.170	0.084	0.6		−.770	−0.547	−5.7	

[25]

Foreword

This is another exercise in checking out the supposed negative effects of population growth.

Douglas Love did this for a thesis in 1976. A paper by him containing the price results appeared in *Research in Population Economics* in 1977. But it took us 13 years, and about 20 rejections, before any journal agreed to publish the paper.

Ann Reg Sci (1990) 24:163–175

The Annals of
Regional Science

City size, prices, and efficiency for individual goods and services

Julian L. Simon and Douglas O. Love

College of Business and Management, University of Maryland, College Park, MD 20742-7215, USA
Department of Management, University of Nebraska, Lincoln, NE 68588-0491, USA

Received October 1989 / Accepted April 1990

Abstract. Studies indicate that the cost of living either is the same or rises slightly with the size of cities. This suggests – though it does not imply – that prices of goods and services are as high or higher in larger cities than in smaller cities. But is this really so? And if so, does this imply that costs of distribution (and of the production of services) are higher in bigger cities?

The relationship of prices to the sizes of cities is examined for 193 individual goods and services and for 23 broad groups. Price alone does not indicate efficiency. It is well-established that wages for the same work at given skill levels are higher in larger cities. Therefore, the total real inputs may be lower in a larger city, even if price is higher, which indicates better efficiency in larger cities. Study of individual goods and services, and of groupings of them, enables us to go beyond prices to learn which categories are offered more efficiently and which less efficiently in larger cities. We find that for most goods, economic cost decreases rather than increases with city size.

Introduction

Studies indicate that the cost of living either is the same or rises slightly with the size of cities. This suggests – though it does not imply – that prices of goods and services are as high or higher in larger cities than in smaller cities. But is it really so? And if so, does it imply that costs of distribution (and of the production of services) are higher in bigger cities?

Aside from the direct consumer interest in the subject, the question is of basic economic importance because of the light it throws upon the effects of population growth and size. Distribution of goods is not less important than their production, and hence the relationship of city size to efficiency of distribution is a key element in whether there are economies or diseconomies of urban growth and population increase.

Sveikauskas (1975) and Segal (1976) have shown that production is more efficient in larger urban areas. Alonso (1975) adduces data showing that less capital is needed per worker, *ceteris paribus*, in larger cities. Riefler (1930) and Stevens (1978) demonstrate that the cost of capital is lower in larger cities. Distribution costs can go a long way toward either completing this picture or confuting it.

The only body of research to date that bears upon these questions are the studies that examine the relationship between city size and the entire basket of goods and services that constitutes the Bureau of Labor Statistics' "family budgets," which usually are interpreted as "cost of living" [1]. These studies conclude either that there is no relationship (Shefer 1970; Attaran 1973; Langston et al. 1985) or that the cost of living is higher – but only slightly higher – in larger cities (Alonso and Fajans 1970; Haworth and Rasmussen 1973).

The cost-of-living studies tell little or nothing, however, about the comparative efficiency of various sizes of cities in providing services and distributing goods. An important reason for this lack of informativeness is that the cost-of-living indices are affected not only by differences in prices from place to place, but also by different *compositions of goods and services* from place to place – for example, different proportions for heating in the North and in the South.

This paper employs a unique database to examine the relationship of prices to the sizes of cities for 193 individual goods and services, and for 23 broad groups of them. Our aim is to determine which are more expensive and which are less expensive in bigger places. This helps to explain what makes some more expensive and others less expensive with increases in city size.

Price alone does not indicate efficiency, however. It is well-established that wages for the same work at given skill levels are higher in larger cities. Our results below also indicate this (see: Hoch 1972, 1976; Quinn and McCormick 1981; Hyman and Fearn 1978; Goldfarb et al. 1983). Therefore, the total economic inputs may be lower in a larger city even if price is higher, indicating better rather than poorer efficiency in larger cities, as we shall see in detail later. Study of individual goods and services, and of groupings, enables us to go beyond the price to learn which are offered more efficiently and which less efficiently in larger cities. We find that for most goods, economic cost decreases rather than increases with city size.

The Theory

Almost all manufactured goods sold in an American city in the latter part of the 20th century are made in factories outside that city.[2] The differences in retail prices of any good in cities of different sizes, therefore, do not reflect the effect of size of city on manufacturing productivity.[3] Rather, observed differences in retail prices must stem from: differences in retail labor productivity and wages paid to that labor; differences in retail overhead – rent in particular – and efficiency in utilizing overhead; differences in local transportation costs (intercity transportation tends to wash out across the sample of cities); and differences in

---

[1] A few authors (Attaran 1973; Haworth and Rasmussen 1973) have examined various sub-bundles, e.g., food at home, transportation, and shelter

[2] See Weiss (1972)

[3] Sveikauskas (1975) has shown that in the average manufacturing industry the level of labor productivity is 5.98% higher with each doubling of city size

the external environment that will be reflected mainly in the cost of purchased inputs, including power and water, specialized business services ranging from accounting to art work, and the cost of capital.

Some of these factors are clearly unfavorable to larger and more densely populated cities, e.g., wages and local transportation costs due to longer local distances and to congestion. Others are clearly favorable to larger cities, e.g., the cost of capital. Still others either vary in their effect with size or have not yet been studied and hence are presently unknown, e.g., the prices and wage-adjusted costs of power, water, and specialized business services.

For any given good, the relationship between city size and its price will be influenced by the relative properties of factors of production that bear negative and positive relationships to city scale. Services – which have been ignored implicitly until now – illustrate the matter: because labor is the dominant input and because the price of (skill-adjusted) labor is higher in larger cities, there is a particularly strong presumption that the price of services – for example, dental care – increases with city size. And unless there is reason to believe that internal or external economies of scale are present, one also would expect that there are no increases in productivity of a service with size of city after adjustments have been made for the differences in wages. Furniture and automobiles are, a priori, examples that run in the opposite direction than services because of the differences in inputs to their retail distribution process.

Data and method

Our method has two steps. First, we regress BLS price data for individual goods and services ("items" hereafter) on sizes of cities in order to describe the relationships. These results are summarized for 23 groups. We then estimate the differences in labor costs that we would have expected with increasing city size, based on the relationship between wages and city size and the proportion of total price that is attributable to local wages associated with retailing the good (or providing the service). This enables us to analyze the relationship of economic cost for particular items to size of city.

Elsewhere we shall adduce other independent variables to analyze the *causes* of the associations of price and city size.

Price data

The price data were gathered by the BLS in the fall of 1971 and published in 1973 (the only data of this sort that have ever been published). The data come from the 38 metropolitan areas for which average prices are published, a subset of the 56 urban areas that constitute the Consumer Price Index ("CPI" hereafter) "city sample," less Honolulu whose transportation costs differ from other areas. Prices of some items were not available for some cities, thereby reducing the sample sizes for those items.

---

[4] In some cases there were two or three specifications that differed only in the quality of the item being described. For example, there were three specifications for washing machines that can be summarized as "standard model," "semi-deluxe model," and "deluxe model." Each was treated as a separate item

For each of the 193 nonfood commodities and services there is a detailed specification[4] of characteristics and qualities that is used as an operational definition in data collection. The number of price quotations obtained in a given city depends on the item and the size of city, ranging from 4 to 30.

Though these data are not as recent as we would like, there is no reason to believe that the structure of the economy has changed since then in such a fashion that these data are not still relevant.

Population measures

We measured sizes of cities in several alternative fashions: total population size, population density per square mile, and population "potential." But because the results are similar for the various measures, only population size is discussed here. The data refer to SMSAs in 1970; "Chicago" is the Chicago-Northern Standard Indiana consolidated area, and "New York" is the New York-Northern New Jersey consolidated area.

Wage data

The wage comparisons should account for the quality or skill level of workers. Just as we want our price comparisons among cities to be for identical or similar items, we also want the estimated relationships between population and wages to be for the same worker quality or skill level. There are a variety of data sources with average wages for cities but only a few permit us to feel confident that we are comparing averages for the same quality of workers (Antos 1983).

We rely upon Eberts and Stone's (1986) skill-adjusted wage index for metropolitan areas, as well as our own estimates for more than 50 occupations, to determine the relationship between city size and wages. The Eberts-Stone index was constructed by specifying individual wages as a function of observed determinants of individual productivity – education level, experience, occupation, etc. By subtracting the predicted wage from the actual wage for each worker in the sample (May, 1974, *Current Population Survey*), Eberts and Stone netted out the portion of the actual wage that was related to the worker's skills. The resulting metropolitan wage index shows the differences in wage levels that remained after accounting for differences in the quality of labor among cities. Johnson (1983) used a similar method in a study of intermetropolitan wage differentials.

Our own wage regressions use Bureau of Labor Statistics wage survey data for various industries, including department stores. These data control for occupation within industry, and status (full/part time). Where appropriate, earnings are shown by other worker or job characteristics, including commission/no commission and male/female, for examples.

Groupings of goods and services

Individual regression equations with population size as the independent variable were estimated separately for each of the 193 goods and services considered. But we also grouped similar goods together for convenience and to give a better basis for understanding the connection of various characteristics of goods to the price-city size relationship[5]. The median results for the 23 groups, shown in Table 1, constitute the paper's main data.

Specification of regressions

All the results reported below are of the form

$$\log \text{price} = a + b \log (\text{population size})$$

Theoretically, the double-log formulation is more desirable in this situation than a simple linear specification on the grounds that it reduces the impact of outlying observations. Additionally, it has the convenient property of yielding results in the form of elasticities, the interpretation we seek in this study. But even more important than this theoretical justification or convenience is the fact that we obtain much the same results with linear regression, so the issue is moot.

Results

1. The statistical tendency of unadjusted prices

A sizable majority of items – 125 out of 193 – have higher prices in larger cities. When groups of items are considered, the same result is seen. Column 1 of Table 1 shows the number of individual items in each group with positive price elasticities and the number with negative elasticities (under the "+" and "–" headings) with respect to city size. The median elasticity and coefficient of determination for each group also are shown. Thus, for example, all three of the items making up the General Practitioner group had positive elasticities. For these three items, the median elasticity was 0.0635 and the median coefficient of determination was 0.244. Each of the three coefficients was significantly different from zero at the 0.001 level.

Few of the regression coefficients for individual items could be considered "statistically significant" by themselves, though far more fall into this category than would occur by chance. For example, by chance, we would have expected two coefficients to be significant at a 0.01 level but found 13 to be significant. Taken as a whole, the proportion of positive to total elasticities is most unlikely to occur by chance, as are the relative sizes of the positive and negative elasticities (see Table 1). There is virtually zero probability (less than 0.001) of obtaining as many

5 Price data were given for individual items, whereas data for payrolls, receipts, and percentage markons were for categories of goods rather than individual items. Since the data came from various sources, there was some variation in the definitions of the categories from one source to the next in terms of the specific goods included in each category. Even the price data were presented under categorical headings. The groupings used in this study were constructed so that they would correspond as much as possible with the groupings used in the data sources

Table 1. Summary of results for price regressed on population size

	Number of items in group with positive and negative coefficients + (1)	−	Price elasticity (median) (2)	R-squared (median) (3)	Payroll sales (4)	Wage elasticity Eberts-Stone sample (5a)	Labor cost associated with doubling of population size (4)×(5a) (6a)
General practitioner	3	0	0.0635	0.244	NA	0.043	
Motion picture adm	2	0	0.0486	0.177	0.210	0.043	0.0090
Dental care	3	0	0.0400	0.088	0.420	0.043	0.0181
Auto repair	2	0	0.0379	0.234	0.253	0.043	0.0109
Personal care serv	5	0	0.0377	0.145	0.478	0.043	0.0206
Women's apparel	10	3	0.0232	0.040	0.147	0.043	0.0063
Hshld text/clthg mat	13	3	0.0194	0.054	0.133	0.043	0.0057
Laundry service	3	0	0.0178	0.036	0.415	0.043	0.0178
Men's clothing	9	1	0.0135	0.044	0.157	0.043	0.0068
Girls' clothing	11	5	0.0116	0.025	0.133	0.043	0.0057
Boys' clothing	11	3	0.0107	0.018	0.133	0.043	0.0057
Women's Acc	10	4	0.0073	0.030	0.157	0.043	0.0068
Men's acc&frnshngs	10	5	0.0069	0.019	0.157	0.043	0.0068
Toilet goods	4	2	0.0046	0.013	0.144	0.043	0.0062
Footwear	9	9	0.0018	0.014	0.152	0.043	0.0065
Tobacco & alcohol	4	3	0.0004	0.017	0.092	0.043	0.0040
Furniture	3	4	−0.0011	0.007	0.150	0.043	0.0065
Sml hh appl/msc hswr	3	5	−0.0023	0.012	0.130	0.043	0.0056
Elec audio-vis appl	2	2	−0.0043	0.010	0.128	0.043	0.0055
Housekeeping supplies	4	8	−0.0054	0.021	NA	0.043	
Major household appl	3	6	−0.0106	0.054	0.130	0.043	0.0056
Auto tire & battery	1	2	−0.0111	0.087	0.160	0.043	0.0069
Eye care	0	3	−0.0214	0.075	NA	0.043	

NA – Data no available

as 125 positive signs of 193 trials where a plus or minus sign is equally likely.[6] Even this estimate overstates the probability of obtaining by chance the results shown here because it does not incorporate information about the sizes of the deviations of the coefficients from zero; the result is therefore all the more powerful. Hence this result may be considered to be statistically conclusive. This result agrees with the broad picture drawn by Haworth and Rasmussen (1973).

A large and important bias against larger cities should be noted here: there are many goods and services that are sold in larger cities that are not available at any price in smaller cities. (Examples include such services as specialized surgery, major league hockey, opera, and computer repair, as well as such goods

[6] This probability is obtained using a normal approximation to the binominal where $p = 0.5$ and $n = 193$:

$$z = \frac{125-(193/2)}{[(0.5)(0.5)(193)]^{1/2}}$$

Table 1. Continued

Decrease (−) or increase (+) in efficiency with city size (6a) − (2) (7a)	Wage elasticity Eberts-Stone subsample (5b)	Labor cost associated with doubling of population size (4) × (5b) (6b)	Decrease (−) or increase (+) in efficiency with city size (6b) − (2) (7b)	Wage elasticity category wage elasticities (median) (5c)	Labor cost associated with doubling of population size (4) × (5c) (6c)	Decrease (−) or increase (+) in efficiency with city size (6c) − (2) (7c)
–	0.052		–	0.052		–
−0.0396	0.052	0.0109	−0.0377	0.096	0.0202	−0.0284
−0.0219	0.052	0.0218	−0.0182	0.06	0.0252	−0.0148
−0.0270	0.052	0.0132	−0.0247	0.067	0.0170	−0.0209
−0.0171	0.052	0.0249	−0.0128	0.043	0.0206	−0.0171
−0.0169	0.052	0.0076	−0.0156	0.043	0.0063	−0.0169
−0.0137	0.052	0.0069	−0.0125	0.043	0.0057	−0.0137
0.0000	0.052	0.0216	+0.0038	0.132	0.0548	+0.0370
−0.0067	0.052	0.0082	−0.0053	0.079	0.0124	−0.0011
−0.0059	0.052	0.0069	−0.0047	0.043	0.0057	−0.0059
−0.0050	0.052	0.0069	−0.0038	0.043	0.0057	−0.0050
−0.0005	0.052	0.0082	+0.0009	0.043	0.0068	−0.0005
−0.0001	0.052	0.0082	+0.0013	0.043	0.0068	−0.0001
+0.0016	0.052	0.0075	+0.0029	0.043	0.0062	+0.0016
+0.0047	0.052	0.0079	+0.0061	0.133	0.0202	+0.0184
+0.0036	0.052	0.0048	+0.0044	0.043	0.0040	+0.0036
+0.0076	0.052	0.0078	+0.0089	0.156	0.0234	+0.0245
+0.0079	0.052	0.0068	+0.0091	0.073	0.0095	+0.0118
+0.0098	0.052	0.0067	+0.0110	0.043	0.0055	+0.0098
+	0.052		+	0.043		+
+0.0162	0.052	0.0068	+0.0174	0.076	0.0099	+0.0205
+0.0180	0.052	0.0083	+0.0194	0.043	0.0069	+0.0180
+	0.052		+	0.06		+

as Ferraris, luxury jewelry, fine art, and a wide assortment of crafts.) This implies an infinitely high price of these goods in places where they are not seen, or at least a differential equal to the cost of transportation time and outlay to go to a bigger city. These items do not appear in the BLS basket. Yet they are important enough to cause some people, and many businesses, to make their homes in larger places.

2. The economic importance

The elasticities are small when we think of them from the point of view of the effect of the possible growth of a city on the price of any item, e.g., perhaps a 0.007 increase – less than one percent – in the item's price if the size of the city were to double, on average. Even if we consider the effect in the context of a given person moving from a city of, say, 100,000 people to a city of 3,200,000 – five doublings – the effect would be only a 3.5% increase.

3. *Types of items*

The results for particular groups of items make economic sense. The items having the largest positive price elasticities with respect to city size – medical and dental care, auto repair, and personal care – are services for which wages make up most of the total cost. The items which show the opposite effect – lower prices associated with larger city size – are big-ticket items such as appliances, furniture, auto tires and batteries. (Autos show the same tendency in data we collected informally.) These are items for which wages are a relatively small part of total cost, as we shall see later, and for which inventory costs are relatively high and for which the rapidity of turnover possible in larger places is an important factor.

4. *Wages and city size*

The Eberts-Stone skill-adjusted city wage indexes are ideal for estimating the wage elasticities with respect to population size. Using their series, we obtain an elasticity estimate of 0.043, which is significantly different from zero at a 0.005 level. We also estimated a wage elasticity using the subsample of cities from the Eberts-Stone study that also were included in the BLS price study used here. We obtained an elasticity estimate of 0.052, which is significantly different from zero at a 0.0025 level. Using a single wage elasticity for all of the item and service categories would seem justified by the existence of reasonably efficient labor markets within cities. However, we also estimated wage elasticities for approximately 50 occupations within specific industries.

Almost all are as large as the elasticity estimate we obtained using the complete Eberts-Stone series. This makes a strong case for using the 0.043 estimate as a lower bound for the wage elasticity. This means that we can be confident in our identification of categories of goods that are provided more efficiently in larger cities. On the other hand, some of those categories that apparently are not provided more efficiently may be misclassified by using this lower bound.

5. *Efficiency and city size*

Given this wage-city size relationship, if we wish to evaluate efficiency – as measured by the ratio of market value of output to the total physical inputs – we must allow for the wage differential. Our procedure for estimating the relationship of efficiency to city size is as follows. For each group of items we estimate the labor cost of retailing the items of the group as a percentage of price. This measure is obtained by summing the payrolls of establishments of a particular type and dividing by the sales of those same establishments (column 4 of Table 1). These data are taken from the *Census of Retail Trade* and the *Census of Selected Services.*[7]

---

[7] The data used were the "Sales" and "Payroll entire year" columns of Table 1 on p. 7 of U.S. Bureau of the Census (1976a), and the "Receipts" and "Payroll entire year" columns of Table 1 on page 7 of U.S. Bureau of the Census (1976b)

We then multiply this quotient by the estimated elasticity of wages with respect to city size (which is taken to be the same for all goods, in columns 5 a and 5 b of Table 1). This yields the expected change in retail labor cost as a proportion of price associated with a doubling of population size (columns 6 a, b, and c of Table 1). We compare this expected change in labor cost as a proportion of price[8] with the estimated price elasticity (column 2 of Table 1) to determine for which goods and services distribution is more efficient in larger cities. Greater efficiency is indicated for the groups where column 6 exceeds column 2, because their prices do not go up as much with city size as would be expected based on the expected higher labor cost;[9] the result is seen in columns 7a, b, and c, where cases of greater efficiency are found for just under half of the categories.

We show columns 5–7 for three methods of estimating the wage elasticities. One method uses all cities included in the Eberts-Stone study (column 5 a). The second method uses a subsample of the Eberts-Stone sample consisting of those cities also included in the BLS price study used here (column 5 b). The third method uses wage elasticities corresponding to categories of items (column 5 c). For categories that had no wage data available, we used the lower of the two elasticities calculated using the Eberts-Stone data.

---

[8] The derivation of the change in retail labor cost as a proportion of price associated with a doubling of population size is:

Let W = wage per unit of labor
L = labor units per unit of retail output
P = price per unit of retail output
Q = quantity of retail output
POP = population

Then

$$\frac{\text{payroll}}{\text{sales}} = \frac{WLQ}{PQ} = \frac{WL}{P} \qquad (1)$$

and the elasticity of wage with respect to population size is

$$\frac{(\Delta W/W)}{(\Delta POP/POP)} \,. \qquad (2)$$

Multiplying (1) and (2)

$$\left(\frac{WL}{P}\right)\left(\frac{(\Delta W/W)}{(\Delta POP/POP)}\right) = \left(\frac{(\Delta WL/P)}{\Delta POP/POP)}\right) . \qquad (3)$$

Since we are considering a doubling of population we are left with

$$\frac{\Delta WL}{P} \,.$$

[9] Estimates also have been made for the expected change in floorspace costs as a proportion of space. But for most goods, payroll/sales is much larger than floor space rent/sales so this factor is not as important and will not be discussed here

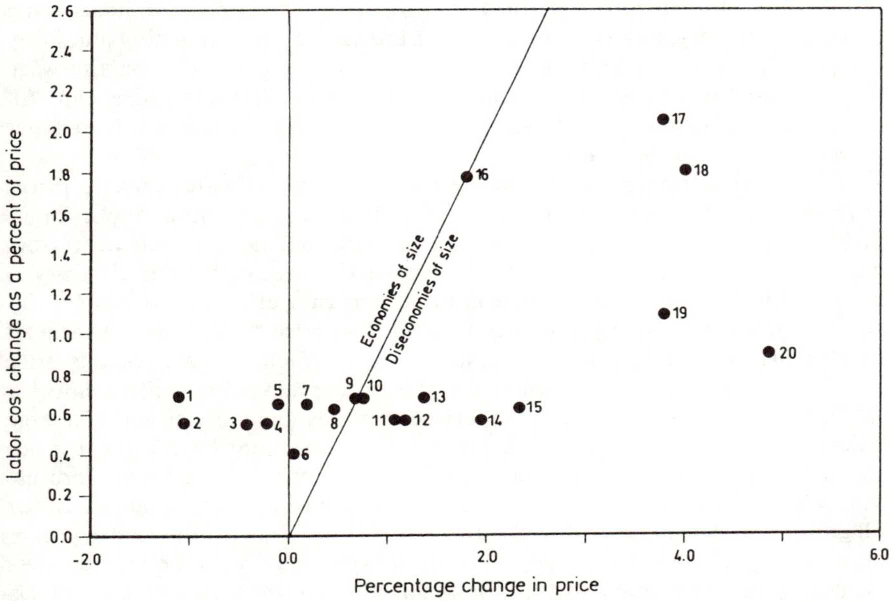

Fig. 1. Labor cost and price change associated with doubling of population size. 1 Auto tire and battery; 2 Major household appliances; 3 Electronic audio/visual appliances; 4 Small household appliances/Miscellaneous housewares; 5 Furniture; 6 Tobacco and alcohol; 7 Footwear; 8 Toilet goods; 9 Men's accessories and furnishings; 10 Women's accessories; 11 Boys' clothing; 12 Girls' clothing; 13 Men's clothing; 14 Household textiles/Clothing materials; 15 Women's apparel; 16 Laundry service; 17 Personal care service; 18 Dental care; 19 Auto repair; 20 Motion picture admission

We recognize that the observation errors in the price data, and the nature of the wage elasticities, render less than perfect the identification of the particular goods that are supplied more efficiently and less efficiently. Our main interest, however, is with the goods as an aggregate. Furthermore, by focusing on a wage-elasticity value that is a lower bound, we are more certain about those goods which we identify as being provided more efficiently. The fact that the results emerge as clearly as they do despite this source of error make the results more noteworthy.

Figure 1 shows graphically which types of goods are distributed more efficiently and which are distributed less efficiently in larger cities. The diagonal plots the line on which wage differences exactly account for price differences. To the left of the diagonal are those groups of goods that are distributed more efficiently and to the right are those groups that are distributed less efficiently with increases in city size.

Less efficient distribution with increasing city size is found for five groups of nonservice items,[10] consisting entirely of clothing and textile items; these are

[10] The service groups are: auto repair, dental care, eye care, general practitioner, laundry service, motion picture admission, and personal care services

fashion items for which it is particularly difficult to ensure that the items being compared for price in the various size cities are indeed equal in quality and fairly comparable. Women's accessories show mixed results depending on the wage elasticity used while the tobacco and alcohol category has a negative sign. All other nonservice groups – a majority – are distributed more efficiently in larger cities.

Of the five service groups for which payroll/receipts data are available, prices were found to go up more with city size than does labor cost (as a proportion of price) for four of the groups. Payroll/receipts data were not available for the eye care and general practitioner groups. Given that the median price elasticity is negative for the eye care group, there must be increasing efficiency with larger city size for these items. On the other hand, the median price elasticity for the general practitioner group is the largest of the 23 groups; given the value of this price elasticity and given the wage elasticity used here, any value of payroll/receipts for this group would indicate that these services are provided less efficiently in large cities. In brief, all of the service groups except eye care have positive price elasticities with respect to population size.[11] Furthermore, the results indicate that prices go up more with city size than the expected increase in labor cost for all groups except eye care and laundry service. These results for the service groups are puzzling. There is no reason, a priori, to expect services to be provided less efficiently in larger cities. In the case of professional services, one possible explanation of the results is that the relationship of "wage" to city size for professionals may differ substantially from the wage elasticity we use here. And of course, it is difficult to control for quality in services.

Summary and conclusions

This study investigates how the prices of a wide variety of individual goods and services – 193 items grouped into 23 classifications – are related to the sizes of cities. We also investigate the efficiency of the distribution of goods, and the production and distribution of services, by allowing for city-size wage differences in retail prices.

We found that more items have a positive relationship than a negative relationship of price to city size, and the median elasticity of price with respect to city size is about 0.007. This seems small, however, when considering population growth in any given city, and also does not seem economically important to a person moving even from a very small city to a very large city.

The efficiency with which goods and services are handled is more important from an economic point of view than is the raw price. Therefore we allowed for wages, the most important single element in the distribution of goods (other than the cost of production and transportation, which is much the same in all sizes of cities because goods are produced nationally rather than locally). We applied the

[11] The negative median coefficient for eye care, which contrasts with the positive median price elasticities found for dental care and general practitioner, may be explained by the inclusion of "dispensing of eyeglasses" along with "examination"

city-size wage differential to the wage proportion applicable to each group of goods, and then calculated an efficiency measure. We found that the majority of goods are produced relatively more efficiently in larger cities.

Most of the items with the largest negative relationships of efficiency to city size are services. The other negative-relationship groups are clothing and textiles, fashion items for which fair comparison among cities of different sizes is particularly difficult.

In short, efficiency in distributing consumer goods is greater in larger cities, with the possible exception of clothing and textiles. Services seem to show a contrary pattern, but there is no a priori reason to interpret the price data as showing less efficiency in the production of such services. Rather, the explanation may be in the particular income patterns of the professions, or in other unidentified nonefficiency factors.

References

Alonso W (1975) The economics of urban size. In: Friedmann J, Alonso W (eds) Regional policy readings in theory and applications. M.I.T. Press, Cambridge London

Alonso W, Fajans M (1970) Cost of living and income by urban size. Working Paper No. 128, Department of City and Regional Planning, University of California, Berkeley

Antos J (1983) Analysis of labor cost: data concepts and sources. In: Triplett JE (ed) The measurement of labor cost. The University of Chicago Press, Chicago

Attaran K (1973) Inter-metropolitan area budget cost determinants: an econometric analysis. Ph. D. dissertation, University of Southern California (unpublished)

Eberts R, Stone J (1986) Metropolitan wage differentials: can Cleveland still compete? Econ Rev (Federal Reserve Bank of Cleveland) Quarter 2:1–8

Goldfarb R, Yezer A, Crewe S (1983) Have regional wage diffentials really disappeared? Growth and Change 14:48–51

Haworth C, Rasmussen D (1973) Determinants of metropolitan cost of living variations. South Econ J 40:183–192

Hoch I (1972) Income and city size. Urban Studies 9:299–328

Hoch I (1976) City size effects, trends, and policies. Science 193:856–863

Hogan TD, Rex TR (1984) Results from a new database: intercity differences in cost of living. Growth Change 15:18–23

Hyman D, Fearn R (1978) The influence of city size on labor incomes. Q Rev Business Econ 18:63–73

Johnson G (1983) Intermetropolitan wage differentials in the United States. In: Triplett JE (ed) The measurement of labor cost. The University of Chicago Press, Chicago

Langston D, Rasmussen DW, Simmons JC (1985) A note on geographic living cost differentials. Land Econ 61:314–318

Quinn J, McCormick K (1981) Wage rates and city size. Indust Relat 20:193–199

Riefler W (1930) Money rates and money markets in the United States. Harper & Brothers Publishers, New York, pp 93–103

Segal D (1976) Are there returns to scale in city size? Rev Econ Statist 58:339–350

Shefer D (1970) Comparable living costs and urban size: a statistical analysis. J Am Inst Planners 36:417–421

Sieling MS (1982) Clerical pay differentials in metropolitan areas, 1961–80. Monthly Labor Rev, July, pp 10–14

Stevens J (1978) Demographic market structure and bank performance. Paper at the University of Illinois

Sveikauskas L (1975) The productivity of cities. Q J Econ 89:393–413

U.S. Bureau of the Census (1973) County and city data book, 1972. U.S. Government Printing Office, Washington DC

U.S. Bureau of Census (1976a) Census of retail trade, 1972. Volume 1: Summary and subject statistics. U.S. Government Printing Office, Washington DC
U.S. Bureau of the Census (1976b) Census of selected service industries, 1972. Volume 1: Summary and subject statistics. U.S. Government Printing Office, Washington DC
U.S. Burea of Labor Statistics (1967) Industry wage survey: Picture theaters, April 1966. Bulletin 1542. U.S. Government Printing Office
U.S. Bureau of Labor Statistics (1969) Industry wage survey: Laundry and cleaning services. Bulletin 1645. U.S. Government Printing Office, Washington DC
U.S. Bureau of Labor Statistics (1971a) Employment and earnings statistics for states and areas, 1939–1971. Bureau of Labor Statistics Bulletin 1370–9. U.S. Government Printing Office, Washington, DC
U.S. Bureau of Labor Statistics (1971b) Industry wage survey: Auto dealer repair shops, August 1969. Bulletin 1689. U.S. Government Printing Office, Washington DC
U.S. Bureau of Labor Statistics (1971c) Industry wage survey: Hospitals, March 1969. Bulletin 1688. U.S. Government Printing Office, Washington, DC
U.S. Bureau of Labor Statistics (1973) Average retail prices of selected commodities and services, 1971. Office of Prices and Living Conditions. U.S. Government Printing Office, Washington DC
U.S. Bureau of Labor Statistics (1975a) Handbook of labor statistics, 1975. Reference Edition. U.S. Government Printing Office, Washington DC
U.S. Bureau of Labor Statistics (1975b) Industry wage survey: Department stores, September 1973. Bulletin 1869. U.S. Government Printing Office, Washington, DC
Weiss L (1972) The geographic size of markets. Rev Econ Statist, LIV (3):245–258

[26]

Foreword

This paper was written under a pen-name because I lacked sufficient good material for this first volume of the series *Research in Population Economics* that I was editing, and I did not want it to look as if I was packing the volume with my own writings to the exclusion of others.

This was the first among several studies that examine the relationship of the total number of persons to the amount of knowledge produced; holding income constant, the relationship is generally proportional.

15

The Effects of Population Size, Growth, and Concentration on Scientific Productivity

WITH DOUGLAS LOVE

PREFACE

It would seem to be an obvious truth—even using only the sort of "common sense" described in the introduction to chapter 14—that more persons must mean more productive ideas. But even respected scholars have argued against the plain meaning of this proposition. One argument has been that the classical contributions of Greece arose from a tiny population, and that small inter-war Hungary produced a remarkable group of scientists; it is inferred that those populations were "sufficiently" large. But this line of thought stands up against neither simple logical analysis nor data showing that in those periods when Greece (and also Rome) had a larger population, discoveries were greater in number (Simon 1981, 201–02). Such arguments seem to me more a desperate attempt to protect an endangered theory than a worthy contender for belief.

This chapter is an empirical study of the effects of population size, concentration, and growth on scientific productivity as measured by the number of scientists in various countries who write professional articles. The most important finding is that, ceteris paribus, *a larger population implies more scientific activity. And scientific activity is roughly proportional to population size; that is, there is evidence for neither diseconomies nor economies of scale when the income level is allowed for.*

This essay was written under the pen name Lincoln Pashute—the first part being my middle name because I was born on Lincoln's birthday, and the second part being Hebrew for simple*—because it appeared in a volume of* Research in Population Economics *that I edited and that contained two other of my essays. I did not think it looked good for the series to have so many pieces by one author, especially the editor; it would look as if I could not get enough contributors—which was not far from the way it was.*

Published in *Research in Population Economics* 1 (1978): 127–42.
We appreciate the helpful correspondence with Francis Narin and Derek de Solla Price.

Theory

THE CENTRAL place of knowledge and the technological level in the economic process is now unchallenged. As Kuznets put it, "The greatest factor in growth of output per capita is, of course, the increasing stock of tested, useful knowledge" (1960, 328).

And, according to Kuznets, the amount of knowledge produced depends on the size of the population. Comparing a larger to a smaller population, or a faster-growing to a slower-growing population: If the bigger population educates and equips its people as well, or almost as well, as the smaller population, then the larger population implies more producers of knowledge. As Kuznets puts it, "Population growth, under the assumptions stated, would, therefore, produce an absolutely larger number of geniuses, talented men, and generally gifted contributors to new knowledge" (1960, 388).[1]

Kuznets's hypothesis, however, is neither self-evident nor universally accepted. Ansley Coale expresses the opposite viewpoint:

> [T]here is no warrant for the assumption that growth and knowledge is greater with a larger population. As I recall, Kuznets argued that knowledge grows largely through the presence of geniuses, or at least exceptionally gifted people, that the incidence of these is rare and proportional to population size and hence a larger population will have more important innovations.
>
> I think even the most cursory consideration of scientific or more general cultural history would bring to light too many counter examples to make this theory tenable. I have gifted and well-informed friends who seriously think that the intellectual heights achieved in classical Athens have never been equaled, and this was a community of a few thousand educated persons. The population of Florence at the time of the Renaissance was no greater than Trenton, New Jersey, yet Galileo was one of the key figures in the development of modern science; the Medicis and their fellow bankers were pioneers in the development of modern banking, including double entry bookkeeping; Dante is a figure in world literature rivaled only by Shakespeare and possibly Homer; Machiavelli is considered by some the godfather of political science, and in painting, sculpture, architecture, and engineering, the Florentines led the world. One could plausibly argue that this community of a hundred thousand persons did more for modern civilization in a few centuries than the United States has. Elizabethan London and Budapest between the two world wars (in fact, the Jewish community in Budapest) are other examples. In any event, scientific and technological knowledge . . . is shared by all national populations and Denmark, for example, does not suffer in terms of the knowledge to which it has

> access from being such a small country. (Personal correspondence, December 28, 1971)

Please notice that Coale is not simply arguing against a *proportional* increase in knowledge, but rather against *any* increase in knowledge as a result of additional population, that is, that the elasticity of knowledge with respect to population size is zero.

Since his original article, however, Kuznets has made clear (in lecture) his view that the bulk of technological advance comes from people other than the gifted and highly educated. This viewpoint is stated by Simon:

> "[T]echnological advance" does not mean "science," and scientific geniuses are just one part of the knowledge process. Much of technological advance comes from people who are neither well educated nor well paid—the dispatcher who develops a slightly better way of deploying the taxis in his ten-taxi fleet, the shipper who discovers that garbage cans make excellent cheap containers for many items, the supermarket manager who finds a way to display more merchandise in a given space, the supermarket clerk who finds a quicker way to stamp the prices on cans, the market researcher in the supermarket chain who experiments and finds more efficient and cheaper means of advertising the store's prices and sale items, and so on. (Simon 1977, 73–74)

Even if population size is a key element in the production of knowledge, the amount of knowledge that is produced may be influenced by other demographic and nondemographic variables as follows:

1. Knowledge and the educational system that supports its production is a consumption good as well as an investment. Hence the production of knowledge surely is a function of the wealth of a country. Furthermore, economic development causes knowledge production as well as being caused by the stock of knowledge. Both of these factors may be indexed by per-capita income or kilowatts of electricity produced per person.[2]

2. Population concentration may have a positive effect on the production of knowledge by way of a relatively high level of personal and intellectual interaction.[3] Or oppositely, there may be congestion effects.

3. Population size may imply decreasing returns to scale, as a larger number of people are working on the same knowledge basis; this, however, is not likely to appear in a cross-sectional comparison. Or there may be increasing returns because of "the interdependence of knowledge of the various parts of the universe in which we human beings operate" as Kuznets suggests (1960, 328). The coefficient of population size will indicate whether on balance there are decreasing or increasing returns to scale.

4. The fertility rate of population may also influence the amount of knowledge produced because, *ceteris paribus*, the number of child dependents may influence the allocation of national resources. Especially it is alleged by many that higher population growth means less education per child. (But see chapter 13.)

The amount of knowledge produced is difficult to measure well. Largely because at least some data are available, we will use scientific activity as a proxy for all knowledge production.

Our model for empirical test may be written as follows:

Scientific activity = f(population size, population concentration, child dependents, level of economic development)

The next section of the essay discusses previous studies that are relevant. Then we describe our method of estimation. Then we present our results. Lastly, we conclude and summarize.

Previous Work

The previous literature that is of interest here falls into three categories: earlier empirical studies that have examined Kuznets's hypothesis; other empirical studies that, while not explicitly noting the argument, provide information about the relationship between population and scientific activity; and finally, those studies that provide and evaluate empirical measures of scientific activity.[4]

In 1923, Hulme examined patent data in an effort to explain the variation in the number of scientific papers indexed annually in *The International Catalogue* over the period 1901–1913. These annual totals for the period show a doubling of "the output of original matter in science" between 1901 and 1910 but a general decline over the next three years (1923, 35).

Upon examination of the statistics of English patents and population for the same period, Hulme observed "that the decline in the output of scientific papers coincides with a flattening of the curves of population in England and Wales, and in Great Britain as a whole" (1923, 37). He also noted an association between the retardation in the growth of population that was general in Western Europe at that time, and "an irregularity in the movements of patent statistics throughout the leading industrial countries of the civilized world" (1923, 37). Hulme felt that the decline in the statistics of science over the three-year period could be accounted for by reference to economic events: "[A]n outward flow of capital coupled with the steady encroachment of taxation on the national income [lead] temporarily to a diminished output in science and invention and to a decline in the rate of growth of population'' (1923, 38).

Hulme's study is more interesting, however, for its place in the intellectual history of the subject than for its substantive results, because variation in the rate of population growth would not be likely to influence knowledge quickly enough to show up in Hulme's measurements.

Higgs (1971) related inventiveness to urbanization and to employment structure. Having postulated that inventive activity requires just two inputs, inventive talent and prior information, Higgs reasoned that the diffusion of technical knowledge depends on personal interaction which was available at a much lower cost for an urban than a rural population. (Note that the role of urbanization in Higgs's model is much like the part played by density in Kuznets's thesis.) Higgs's fundamental assumption was that the quantity of resources devoted to inventive activity, and hence the actual average number of inventions produced, varied directly with the expected rate of return on inventive activity. Results from regressions explaining the variation in inventions across states for each of the census years between 1870 and 1920 showed that ''in every case the regression coefficient of the urbanization variable [was] positive and highly significant.'' Furthermore, the size of the coefficient did not decline over time, as one would expect in view of the improvements in communications during the period (1971, 666). It is possible, however, that Higgs's finding is a result of the migration of inventors to larger communities, because of better wages or a larger intellectual community or other reasons.

Kelley tested Kuznets's hypothesis using the number of patents issued during the census years 1870–1920 as a measure of scientific activity. Having estimated regression equations incorporating population size and urbanization level as explanatory variables, he states that his results represent ''a limited amount of new evidence . . . which supports Kuznets's thesis that population size has been associated with increasing returns to scale in inventive activity'' (1972, 35).

Price has drawn graphs showing a fairly close linear relationship between the logarithm of scientific authors and the logarithm of total GNP across countries, but has reported a weaker relationship between the logarithms of the respective per-capita measures (1971, 110). When using electrical consumption rather than GNP as a measure of wealth, however, he has shown a log-linear relationship between wealth and scientific authors both on a total as well as a per-capita basis (1975, 27). His conclusion is that the share of scientific activity contributed by a country to the world total is very close to that country's share of the world's wealth.

These studies do not well test Kuznets's thesis. Only Kelley's study holds constant the education, training, and other quality variables of the population while considering variations in population size and scientific activity. Additionally, in some cases the concept of population concentration was not considered.

Method and Data

An empirical test of the effects of population size and concentration on scientific productivity was conducted by using data across countries. Two alternative empirical measures of scientific activity were employed:

$AUTHORS_i$ is the arithmetic mean number of scientific authors from country i listed in the annual volumes of *Who Is Publishing in Science* (*WIPIS*) for the years 1972 through 1975. *WIPIS* is a cumulation of the names and addresses of the first authors of papers published in journals covered by the various editions of *Current Contents*, the *Science Citation Index*, and the *Social Sciences Citation Index*. Thus for example, the 1974 edition of *WIPIS* provided a count of the geographical distribution of 270,841 publishing scientific authors from 159 countries.

$ARTICLES_i$ is the number of scientific papers published in the journals from country i that were covered by the *Science Citation Index* in 1973. These data are available for only a subset of the countries for which there is author data. They were not originally compiled for the purposes of measuring scientific activity and suffer several limitations in that capacity. Because these data are available for only forty countries, they will be used here only to verify results obtained from the author data.[5]

Three empirical measures of population concentration were used:

$DENSITY_i$ is the population per square kilometer of country i computed by dividing the 1971 population of the country (POP_i) by the surface area of the country. $URBAN_i$ is the percent of the total population of country i living in urban areas.[6] Although the definition of "urban" varies somewhat from country to country, it can be roughly defined as a place having more than two to seven thousand persons (Davis 1969, 17). $CITY_i$ is the percent of the total population of country i living in cities having population greater than 100,000.[7]

$CHILD_i$ is the percentage of the population of country i that is under age

15. It is used to control for effects that might be associated with the number of child dependents.[8]

The two empirical variables that were used alternatively to hold constant the education, training, and other capital investments (i.e., the level of development) that influence the proportion of potential contributors to knowledge in the population of each country are:

$\frac{GNP}{POP}$ i, per capita GNP of country i; and $\frac{KWH}{POP}$ i, the number of kilowatt hours of electricity produced per person in country i.[9]

One may test for increasing or diminishing returns either by (a) running the regressions with the dependent variable in per-capita terms, and examining the coefficient of population size to see if it differs from zero, or (b) using an undeflated dependent variable, and examining whether the population size coefficient differs from unity. The two approaches are logically identical when a log-linear model is specified. We chose the former because it seems more intuitively satisfying, and the t coefficients are more immediately interpretable.

The results presented below are from regressions run in logarithmic form, for ease of interpretation as elasticities and because the results may be easily compared against Price's work that uses per-capita income and electrical consumption as explanatory variables. For each of these log-linear regressions, the corresponding linear forın was also estimated (see appendix). But in every case except one, the coefficient of determination was lower for the linear form indicating a poorer fit.

The countries composing the sample used to estimate the equations shown in table 15.1 are listed in the appendix according to per-capita gross national product. Data for the number of scientific articles were only available for a subset of these countries, all but four having per-capita gross national products greater than the median of the original sample. Hence for purposes of fair comparison, results of regressions estimated from this subset of countries are shown in table 15.1 for both measures of scientific activity.

RESULTS

Total Population

The main result is that Kuznets's hypothesis is overwhelmingly confirmed: The amount of science produced is a positive function of population size. Furthermore, scientific activity is roughly *proportional* to the number of people.

TABLE 15.1

	Dependent Variable	Sample (See Appendix)	Intercept	Log POP	Log Urban	Log City	Log Density	Log GNP/POP	Log KWH/POP	Log Child	R^2
(1)	Authors/POP	All countries	− 2.767	0.110	−0.598			1.90		−0.282	0.82
			− 6.62	1.38	−2.74			12.62		−1.51	
				0.064	−0.222			1.048		−0.074	
(2)	Authors/POP	All countries	0.951	0.222							0.02
			4.42	1.22							
				0.13							
(3)	Authors/POP	All countries	− 3.314	0.096				1.603			0.79
			−12.95	1.15				18.06			
				0.056				0.886			
(4)	Authors/POP	All countries	− 1.596	0.115	0.171						0.41
			− 4.26	0.81	7.60						
				0.067	0.634						
(5)	Authors/POP	All countries	− 3.283	0.109	−0.667			1.965			0.82
			−13.45	1.37	−3.10			13.63			
				0.064	−2.475			1.086			
(6)	Authors/POP	All countries	− 2.600	0.098				1.558		−0.387	0.81
			− 6.05	1.20				17.36		−2.05	
				0.058				0.862		−0.101	
(7)	Authors/POP	All countries	− 0.418	0.056	−0.508				1.155	−0.499	0.80
			− 1.11	0.67	−2.22				11.60	−2.60	
				0.033	−0.189				1.002	−0.131	
(8)	Authors/POP	All countries	− 0.613	0.052		0.015			0.968	−0.569	0.79
			− 1.50	0.59		0.12			11.70	−2.63	
				0.031		0.009			0.839	−0.149	
(9)	Authors/POP	All countries	− 2.606	0.096			0.014	1.555		−0.390	0.81
			− 6.02	1.15			0.19	16.84		−2.04	
				0.056			0.010	0.860		−0.102	

TABLE 15.1 (Continued)

Dependent Variable	Sample (See Appendix)	Intercept	Log POP	Log Urban	Log City	Log Density	Log GNP/POP	Log KWH/POP	Log Child	R^2
(10) Authors/POP	High GNP subsample	– 3.137	−0.141	−0.631			1.928		0.172	0.82
		– 2.87	−1.97	−1.73			9.83		0.34	
			−0.145	−0.146			0.998		0.031	
(11) Authors/POP	Low GNP subsample	– 1.960	0.248	−0.413			0.130		−0.186	0.21
		– 2.38	1.82	−1.15			2.69		−0.78	
			0.271	−0.282			0.686		−0.112	
(12) Authors/POP	High GNP subsample	– 2.155	−0.150	0.367				1.227	−0.332	0.72
		– 1.62	−1.70	0.90				7.09	−0.54	
			−0.155	0.085				0.809	−0.059	
(13) Authors/POP	Low GNP subsample	– 0.239	0.150	−0.418				0.702	−0.200	0.33
		– 0.601	1.29	−1.52				3.97	−0.92	
			0.163	−0.285				0.759	−0.120	
(14) Articles/POP	Article subsample	– 3.556	−0.012			0.288	1.976		−1.011	0.73
		– 1.19	−0.08			1.75	5.53		−0.80	
			−0.007			0.181	0.749		−0.114	
(15) Authors/POP	Article subsample	– 1.124	−0.063			0.033	1.372		−0.856	0.82
		– 0.69	−0.73			0.37	6.98		−1.23	
			−0.055			0.032	0.782		−0.145	
(16) Articles/POP	Article subsample	– 4.040	−0.001			0.375		1.723	−0.458	0.72
		– 1.26	−0.01			2.13		5.27	−0.33	
			−0.001			0.236		0.789	−0.052	
(17) Authors/POP	Article subsample	– 0.994	−0.061			0.080		1.144	−0.649	0.78
		– 0.53	−0.65			0.78		5.97	−0.79	
			−0.053			0.076		0.788	−0.110	

Note: The numbers in each entry are, respectively: the unstandardized regression coefficient, the t value for the unstandardized regression coefficient, and the standardized regression coefficient.

This is confirmed by the results in table 15.1 taken altogether. The finding may best be expressed by a transformation of the regression on line 1 of table 15.1:

$$\log \text{AUTHORS}_i =$$

$$\underset{(-6.62)}{-2.767} + \underset{(14.01)}{1.110 \log \text{POP}_i} \; \underset{(-2.74)}{-0.598 \log \text{URBAN}_i} + \underset{(12.62)}{1.90 \log \frac{\text{GNP}}{\text{POP}}_i} - \underset{(-1.51)}{0.282 \log \text{CHILD}_i}$$

The fact that the coefficient of population size is greater than *zero* implies that a larger population leads to more scientific activity. This finding is of undoubted statistical significance, and linear regressions agree (not shown). The finding is consistent with Price's work (1971, 1975).

Effects of Scale

The all-countries sample results suggest faintly that a larger population—a proxy for a larger labor force—has a *more-than-proportional* impact on scientific activity. That is, the coefficient of total population size is positive, though hardly significant.

The coefficients of total population for the richer countries (the basic regressions 10 and 12) are negative, whereas the coefficients for the poorer countries (regressions 11 and 13) are positive—both sets approaching statistical significance; together, these samples suggest that the issue is in doubt. Of course it may be that there really are diseconomies to scale for the richer countries and economies to scale for the poorer countries but a resolution of the issue will require further research. (Another possibility is that there is much sampling error due to small amounts of total scientific activity in the poorer countries; a hint of this may be found in the low coefficients of GNP/POP.)

Data on the total number of *articles* (in contradistinction to the number of *authors*) are also available for forty countries, which tend to be higher-income countries. These data generally confirm the findings for numbers of authors, though they are less negative (regressions 14–17).

Linear regressions—which consistently have lower R^2 than the log-linear regressions—yield more negative coefficients than do the log-linear regressions, but in no case is the t ratio for a negative coefficient greater than 0.40.

The most judicious conclusion about the effects of scale apparently is that their presence is not strongly supported by the data, positive or negative.

Effects of Higher Fertility

All other things (and especially the number of adults) being held equal, an additional child has a negative effect on scientific activity; this is seen in all log-linear regressions except equation 10. In the linear regressions, however, three of the five coefficients for CHILD are positive, and none have t ratios greater than 1.25. This casts some doubt on whether there really is a negative effect. The effect in equation 1 persists when both KWH/POP *and* GNP/POP are in the regression, which is a basis for some confidence that CHILD is not simply a proxy for modernization (results not shown).

Population Concentration

The coefficients of URBAN, CITY, and DENSITY vary considerably with the specification of the model, and hence no conclusion is well founded at this time.

Overall Impact of Population Growth

Assume mortality is not a variable, and the effect of population concentration is unknown. What is the overall impact of additional children through the child-dependency and total-population influences?

The answer to the overall impact depends on the scenario one chooses to evaluate, and many such scenarios are possible—for example, steady growth at different rates, and one-time increments of fertility. And the net impact depends on the date at which the evaluation is made, for example, the immediate effect of a one-time addition of births is negative. The evaluation of various scenarios is beyond the scope of this article.

Summary

This is an empirical study of the effects of population size, growth, and concentration on scientific productivity as measured by the number of scientists in various countries who write professional articles.

The most important finding is that, *ceteris paribus*, a larger population implies more scientific activity. And scientific activity is roughly proportional to population size; that is, there is evidence for neither diseconomies nor economies of scale.

There is some evidence for a negative effect of population growth—as measured by the child-dependency ratio—on scientific activity. But this finding is far from solid at present, and requires further investigation.

There is no strong evidence for an effect of population density or urbanity upon scientific activity.

APPENDIX

Countries Comprising the Sample

Low GNP Countries	*High GNP Countries*
Afghanistan	Lebanon
Chad	Mexico*
Ethiopia	Jamaica
Indonesia	Portugal*
Malawi	Yugoslavia*
Nepal	Rumania*
Ceylon	Uruguay
India*	Chile*
Tanzania	South Africa*
Haiti	Bulgaria*
Sudan	Hong Kong
Uganda	Venezuela*
Madagascar	Spain*
Nigeria	Hungary*
Central African Rep.	Singapore
Kenya	Argentina*
Mauritania	Greece
Bolivia	Poland*
Liberia	USSR*
Thailand	Ireland*
Egypt	Italy*
Philippines	Czechoslovakia*
Ghana	Japan*
Jordan	East Germany*
Morocco	Israel*
Paraguay	Austria*
South Korea	United Kingdom*
Syria	New Zealand*
Honduras	Finland*
Ecuador	Netherlands*
El Salvador	Australia*
Southern Rhodesia	Belgium*
Tunisia	Norway*
Turkey	West Germany*
Algeria	France*
Colombia*	Denmark*
Iraq	Switzerland*
Zambia	Canada*
Guatemala	Sweden*
Malaysia	United States*

Countries Comprising the Sample (*cont.*)

Low GNP Countries	*High GNP Countries*
Dominican Republic	
Taiwan*	
Iran*	
Nicaragua	
Brazil*	
Peru	
Cuba	
Costa Rica*	

Note: ARTICLE SUBSAMPLE: An asterisk indicates those countries for which data were available for both scientific authors and scientific articles.

TABLE A15.1

	Dependent Variable	Sample (See Appendix)	Intercept	POP	Urban	City	Density	GNP/POP	KWH/POP	Child	R^2
(1)	Authors/POP	All countries	−69.501	−0.054	−0.434			0.128		1.234	0.75
			−1.31	−0.43	−0.92			11.01		1.09	
				−0.024	−0.069			0.968		0.081	
(2)	Authors/POP	All countries	84.286	0.104							0.00
			4.71	0.43							
				0.046							
(3)	Authors/POP	All countries	−29.742	−0.045				0.114			0.75
			−2.57	−0.37				15.81			
				−0.020				0.865			
(4)	Authors/POP	All countries	−72.658	0.104	3.476						0.31
			−2.45	0.51	6.12						
				0.046	0.553						
(5)	Authors/POP	All countries	−14.96	−0.054	−0.481			0.121			0.75
			−0.81	−0.44	−1.02			12.19			
				−0.024	−0.077			0.918			
(6)	Authors/POP	All countries	−86.907	−0.045				0.122		1.329	0.75
			−1.75	−0.37				12.50		1.18	
				−0.020				0.924		0.087	
(7)	Authors/POP	All countries	25.25	0.017	1.287				0.035	−1.453	0.59
			0.38	0.107	2.38				6.39	−1.06	
				0.008	0.205				0.579	−0.096	
(8)	Authors/POP	All countries	46.676	0.001		1.598			0.036	−1.667	0.60
			0.77	0.01		2.62			6.83	−1.25	
				0.001		0.203			0.598	−0.110	
(9)	Authors/POP	All countries	−81.90	−0.050			−0.013	0.122		1.257	0.75
			−1.63	−0.40			−0.85	12.45		1.11	
				−0.022			−0.046	0.923		0.083	

TABLE A15.1 (Continued)

Dependent Variable	Sample (See Appendix)	Intercept	POP	Urban	City	Density	GNP/POP	KWH/POP	Child	R^2
(10) Authors/POP	High GNP subsample	−183.77	−0.414	0.120			0.138		3.583	0.65
		−1.52	−1.10	0.100			6.95		1.12	
			−0.113	0.011			0.876		0.130	
(11) Authors/POP	Low GNP subsample	1.854	0.0149	−0.083			0.021		−0.006	0.17
		0.42	1.72	−1.11			2.33		−0.06	
			0.245	−0.273			0.589		−0.009	
(12) Authors/POP	High GNP subsample	−26.422	−0.056	2.576				0.033	−2.231	0.41
		−0.17	−0.12	1.81				3.82	−0.58	
			−0.015	0.237				0.539	−0.081	
(13) Authors/POP	Low GNP subsample	1.348	0.012	−0.062				0.014	0.046	0.42
		0.37	1.67	−1.44				5.13	0.55	
			0.194	−0.204				0.718	0.065	
(14) Articles/POP	Article subsample	−327.74	−0.094			0.996	0.151		4.667	0.46
		−1.33	−0.24			2.64	4.11		0.77	
			−0.031			0.349	0.643		0.127	
(15) Authors/POP	Article subsample	−165.96	−0.083			0.048	0.132		3.270	0.66
		−1.32	−0.42			0.25	7.04		1.05	
			−0.042			0.026	0.878		0.139	
(16) Articles/POP	Article subsample	114.36	−0.089			1.021		0.030	−3.941	0.27
		0.45	−0.20			2.24		1.84	−0.59	
			−0.029			0.358		0.316	−0.107	
(17) Authors/POP	Article subsample	132.66	−0.082			0.141		0.035	−2.482	0.40
		0.90	−0.31			0.54		3.67	−0.64	
			−0.042			0.077		0.569	−0.105	

Note: The numbers in each entry are, respectively: the unstandardized regression coefficient, the t value for the unstandardized regression coefficient, and the standardized regression coefficient.

Units of measure: POP, millions; URBAN, percent; CITY, percent; DENSITY, persons per square kilometer; KWH, millions; CHILD, percent.

Notes

1. It is interesting that the same commonsensical idea was expressed by Petty. "Even the arts are best promoted by the greatest number of emulators. And it is more likely that one ingenious curious man may rather be found out amongst 4 million than 400 persons."

2. See, for example, the studies by Price (1967, 1971, 1975).

3. "Creative effort flourishes in a dense intellectual atmosphere" (Kuznets 1960, 329).

4. Studies not discussed elsewhere in this article that provide or evaluate various empirical measures of scientific activity include: Baker (1966) (1971), Gottschalk and Desmond (1963), Keenan and Brickwedde (1968), Narin and Carpenter (1975), National Science Board (1973) (1975), Spiegel-Rosing (1972). Of particular interest is the work by Narin (1976), which includes a description of the historical development of the use of publication and citation counting techniques in the assessment of scientific activity.

5. The data for scientific articles are from table 6–7 of *Evaluative Bibliometrics* (Narin 1976, 151). The ARTICLES data suffer several drawbacks for the purposes of measuring scientific activity. The counting procedure allocates articles among countries according to the country publishing the *journal* in which the article appeared, rather than to the author's country of residence. The counts were made from the Corporate Index tapes of the *Science Citation Index*, which indexes articles in the physical and biological sciences. "The criterion for inclusion of journals in SCI is significance rather than proportional representation, or distribution of journals by national origin" (Narin and Carpenter 1975, 82). Furthermore, the data were available for only a subset of countries, most of which had gross national products per capita higher than the median for the original sample.

6. The data for the 1971 population of each country are from table 5, p. 127 of the 1974 United Nations *Demographic Yearbook*. The surface area data are from table 3, p. 108, of the same source.

7. Data for the percent living in urban areas as well as for the percent in cities having populations greater than 100,000 are the 1970 entries of table C, p. 113, in Davis (1968).

8. Data for the proportion of children are from table 3 of *Reports on Population/Family Planning*, Dec. 1974, and the United Nations *1972 Demographic Yearbook*, 1973 (New York: United Nations), table 6.

9. The 1971 per-capita GNP data are from the *World Bank Atlas*, p. 5. Data for electrical production are the 1971 entries of table 145, p. 392, in the *1975 United Nations Statistical Yearbook*.

References

Baker, Dale. 1966. "Chemical Literature Expands," *Chemical and Engineering News* 44: 84–88.

———. 1971. "World's Chemical Literature Continues to Expand." *Chemical and Engineering News* 49: 37–40.

Bonar, James. 1966. *Malthus and His Work*. New York: A. M. Kelley.

Davis, Kingsley. 1969. *World Urbanization 1950–1970 Volume 1: Basic Data for Cities, Countries, and Regions*. Population Monograph Series, No. 4, Berkeley: University of California.

———. *Revisions for Original Edition of "World Urbanization 1950–1970, Volume 1: Basic Data for Cities, Countries, and Regions."* Population Monograph Series, No. 4, Berkeley, Institute of International Studies, University of California, no date.

Gottschalk, Charles M., and Desmond, Winifred F. 1963. "Worldwide Census of Scientific and Technical Serials." *American Documentation* 14: 188–94.

Higgs, Robert. 1971. "American Inventiveness, 1870–1920." *Journal of Political Economy* 79: 661–67.

Hulme, E. W. 1923. *Statistical Bibliography in Relation to the Growth of Modern Civilization*. London: Butler & Tanner Grafton and Co.

Keenan, Stella, and Brickwedde, F. G. 1968. *Journal Literature Covered by Physics Abstracts in 1965*. New York: American Institutes of Physics, Information Division.

Kelley, Allen C. 1972. "Scale Economics, Inventive Activity, and the Economics of American Population Growth." *Explorations in Economic History* 10: 35–52.

Kuznets, Simon. 1960. "Population Change and Aggregate Output." Pages 324–40 in Universities-National Bureau Committee for Economic Research, *Demographic and Economic Change in Developed Countries*. Princeton, N.J.: Princeton University Press.

Narin, Francis. 1976. *Evaluative Bibliometrics. The Use of Publication and Citation Analysis in the Evaluation of Scientific Activity*. Contract NSF-C627, Report no. PB-252 339/7GA. Cherry Hill, N.J.: Computer Horizons.

Narin, F., and Carpenter, M. P. 1975. "National Publication and Citation Comparisons." *Journal of the American Society for Information Science*, 26.

National Science Board. 1973. *Science Indicators, 1972*. Washington, D.C.: National Science Foundation.

———. 1975. *Science Indicators, 1974*. Washington, D.C.: National Science Foundation.

Pilarski, Adam. "The Impact of Fertility on Hours of Work." *Research in Population Economics* (1978).

Price, Derek de Solla. 1967. "Nations Can Publish or Perish." *Science and Technology* 85–90.

———. 1971. "Measuring the Size of Science." Israel Academy of Sciences and Humanities Proceedings 4: no. 6, 98–111.

———. 1975. "Some Statistical Results for the Numbers of Authors in the States of the United States and the Nations of the World." Pages 26–35 in *Who is Publishing in Science, 1975*. Philadelphia: Institute for Scientific Information.

Simon, Julian L. 1977. *The Economics of Population Growth*. Princeton, N.J.: Princeton University Press.

———. 1981. *The Ultimate Resource*. Princeton, N.J.: Princeton University Press.

Spiegel-Rosings, I. S. 1972. "Journal Authors as an Indicator of Scientific Manpower; a Methodological Study using Data for the Two Germanies and Europe." *Science Studies* 2: 337–60.

PART V

IMMIGRATION

[27]

Foreword

The title "Immigration and Trade Are Dissimilar Phenomena" might be more evocative than the present title.

This paper has unsuccessfully sought publication since about 1980. Whatever its other problems – lack of either impressive formalism or extensive econometric work, for example – its counter-intuitive nature certainly must be important. Nobel prize winners have told me that it is certainly wrong and they will prove it by sending me counter-examples – though they never do. (Other Nobelists agree that the argument is sound, however.)

As I was pondering the lack of acceptance of the central idea of this paper by most of those to whom I have presented it, I found myself reading Albert Einstein's *Relativity* (1916). It is an explanation in simple prose intended for laypeople – in the words of the dust jacket, "explaining the theory in simple words that anyone with the equivalent of a high school education can understand." (The dust jacket may be correct in principle, but this reader, at least, finds it extraordinarily difficult even after hundreds of hours of reading.)

There is a provocative formal similarity between Einstein's problem and the problem under discussion here. Einstein's theory relates events that occur in different places; the same is true of trade and immigration theory. The source of the difficulty in both cases is that relating the separated events *seems* obvious and easy. In the case at hand, one can correctly say that a person is paid his/her marginal output both in the country of origin and the country of destination. But it is not agreeable to then hear that unless those marginal outputs are related in value terms, they cannot sensibly be compared. The only possible simple comparisons are necessarily inconclusive; the barter value of a haircut in bushels of wheat is not likely to be the same in the two countries, and the barter equivalents of a haircut in wheat and in dental services are likely to be unbalanced in different directions for those two goods. No recourse to a transformation such as the money values figured at the exchange rate can in principle wholly succeed; the inevitable flaw in that process is due to the differences in relative prices and quantities consumed in the various countries, differences which are at the heart of the phenomenon of international migration, it is argued here. The purpose of such work as that of Kravis et al. (1982) is to provide a useful, but necessarily partial, measure of the transformation that would be needed.

Perhaps because we are so accustomed to making exchange-rate comparisons for a variety of purposes, and because it is never enjoyable to recognize the inherent impossibility of this or any other measure providing a theoretically complete transformation, one does not feel comfortable with an argument that is based squarely upon this inherent impossibility, as is the case of this paper. It is, however, fatal to the understanding of the present argument to shrug this off and rush on to formal manipulations.

Einstein makes a similar point at the very start of his discussion, a point which is the keystone of his thinking and the point from which all of his theory of relativity departs.

> Lightning has struck the rails on our railway embankment at two places A and B far distant from each other. I make the additional assertion that these two lightning flashes occurred simultaneously. If I ask you whether there is sense in this statement, you will answer my question with a decided "Yes." But if I now approach you with the request to explain to me the sense of the statement more precisely, you find after some consideration that the answer to this question is not so easy as it appears at first sight.
>
> After some time perhaps the following answer would occur to you: "The significance of the statement is clear in itself and needs no further explanation; of course it would require some consideration if I were to be commissioned to determine by observations whether in the actual case the two events took place simultaneously or not." I cannot be satisfied with this answer for the following reason. Supposing that as a result of ingenious considerations an able meteorologist were to discover that the lightning must always strike the places A and B simultaneously, then we should be faced with the task of testing whether or not this theoretical result is in accordance with the reality. We encounter the same difficulty with all physical statements in which the conception "simultaneous" plays a part. The concept does not exist for the physicist until he has the possibility of discovering whether or not it is fulfilled in an actual case. We thus require a definition of simultaneity such that this definition supplies us with the method by means of which, in the present case, he can decide by experiment whether or not both the lightning strikes occurred simultaneously. As long as this requirement is not satisfied, I allow myself to be deceived as a physicist (and of course the same applies if I am not a physicist), when I imagine that I am able to attach a meaning to the statement of simultaneity. (I would ask the reader not to proceed farther until he is fully convinced on this point.) (1916, pp. 21–2)

The difference between Einstein and those who came before him is that he accepted this difficulty as a problem to be dealt with, rather than either not noticing its existence or closing his eyes to it.

Lest it be thought that I am making a laughably immodest comparison between the present work and Einstein's (and indeed, I have been reluctant to invoke his name because I recognize how pretentious it may seem), I note several enormous differences. First, I am attempting to *use* an insight; Einstein *discovered* it. And the discovery of that insight about the nature of simultaneity is the very heart of his work. Second, Einstein found a transformation (the Lorentz transformation) that solved the problem raised by his insight; this paper only argues that the problem raised is unsolvable in principle. And third, the matter at hand has none of the earthshaking importance of Einstein's work, of course.

These remarks are in no way intended to suggest that physics is a good model for economics. Rather, I agree with Hayek that physics is a poor model because of the simplicity of the systems with which physics deals, and the lack of the subjective element in that subject. But it should be noted that the physics that some take as the model for economics is Newtonian rather than modern physics, and perhaps the greatest philosophical difference between the classical and modern is the doing-away with property definitions in such circumstances as Einstein's pathbreaking case. This is the matter which makes Einstein relevant for the present discussion.

The paper does not conflict with the factor–price–equalization principle (though it suggests that that theory is in principle untestable). Just like Ricardian theory, factor–price–equalization theory refers to *goods that can be, and are, actually traded.* But immigration takes place when the goods at issue *cannot* be traded at long distance; that is, economic international migration takes place when movement of people, and movement of capital and movement of the produced goods, are not viable alternatives. Trade theory simply does not deal with internationally non-traded goods, and therefore there can be no conflict between it and the argument of this paper. The paper takes barbers as an example because haircuts cannot be sent by ship or plane. In contrast, trade theory deals with goods like haircutting kits, which *can* be traded. (For reasons given in the paper, the people who make haircutting kits may still have a reason to migrate, because their personal outputs are not internationally tradable in themselves, unlike the case of sculptors whose work has an international market.)

Ricardian trade theory throws no light on migration[1]

Introduction

Immigrants are thought to lower income in the country of origin and raise it in the country of destination because they transfer human capital from the former to the latter. The theory offered in this paper implies that this is not so.

An example of the use of this concept is found in the work on the brain drain by Herbert C. Grubel and Anthony Scott. They calculate that "On the basis of [T.W. Schultz's estimates of the value of human capital], US per capita income would be raised in the long run by the emigration of any person with less than two years of college education and lowered if the emigrant had more than two years of college" (1977, p. 31).[2]

Another example is given by Neal and Uselding (1972) who estimated the historical effect of immigrants on the United States' economy on the assumption that natives benefit from the human capital that immigrants bring with them. The implicit idea is that if a *native's* net contribution to the economy is zero – the social costs of educating the native offsetting the later benefits from that person – then immigrants must make a net contribution because the social costs of educating the person are borne in the country of origin. And this net contribution is implicitly identified with the Ricardian trade-like effect that immigrants are assumed to have. As Gallman puts it, following Neal and Uselding, "Thus one can compute the 'debt' of the United States to other countries, on account of immigration, in terms of the swings in the costs of child-rearing realized by Americans" (Gallman, 1977, p. 28).

This idea has been adopted widely, for instance Lerner and Roy (1984) apply it to an analysis of the immigration of scientists and engineers. In the essay "Economic Implications of Migration into the Federal Republic of Germany 1988–1992" by Geseck, Heilemann and von Loeffetholz (1994) the authors say that "the immigrants mean an inflow of human capital . . . for which Germany hardly had to invest in education or training" (see also Blitz, 1977; Krauss and Baumol, 1979; Hassan, 1988).[3]

The human-capital analysis reflects the standard view of economists that international trade and international migration are similar phenomena, to be analysed with the same general theory.[4] For example, these are the opening lines in the chapter on "The Economic Effects of Immigration" in the 1986 *Economic Report of the President* (p. 213):

> The movement of *people* between countries links national economies. Like international *trade in goods*, services, and financial claims, international *migration* connects domestic and international markets. The free flow of resources in response to market signals promotes efficiency and produces economic gains for both producers and *consumers*. The migration of labor, both domestically and internationally, represents such a flow of productive resources (italics added).

Froeb makes a similar comment:

> Economists generally like immigration because it permits the movement of an important resource, labor, from lower to higher valued uses. This movement increases wealth, so we are richer as a nation when we permit immigration and poorer when we prevent it (Froeb, 1995, p. 25).

The following jocular statements illustrate the parallel thinking about trade and migration: "Professors would quickly lose their zeal for open *trade* if universities found that their strained budgets could be relieved by dismissing high-priced *domestic* professors and importing cheaper (and better?) pedagogy" (McCracken, 1985, italics added), and: "Increased labor supply due to immigration enhances the welfare of the typical consumer . . . " (LaLonde and Topel, 1991, p. 167).

This idea apparently has not been challenged until now. The basis for the standard view is the Heckscher–Ohlin–Samuelson theory of factor-price equalization that considers movement of workers and movement of capital to be alternative routes to the same production end.[5] This paper suggests, however, that the analogy is not sound. International trade and international migration are theoretically different phenomena rather than similar. Trade theory is necessarily silent about migration, as is confirmed by its small place in texts on that subject. The gains from trade – at least the first-order Ricardian effects, which are the subject here – are quite unlike the gains from migration. Consumers do not obtain the same sort of gains from the international movement of people as they do from international exchange of goods, though there are important gains from immigration to the countries of destination through mechanisms other than trade-like effects. And the "explanation" of movement of people is different from the Ricardian explanation of movement of goods.

The reason for the existence of gains from trade is a continuing difference in the markets of the sort that the Heckscher–Ohlin theory is supposed to eliminate but in practice does not; in contrast, after an act of migration there is no such continuing difference which is relevant to the analysis and hence the Neal–Uselding effect does not exist. To put it differently, one cannot construct the sort of simple numerical example showing immediate gains to consumers consequent to the opening-up of migration of the sort Ricardo could show for the opening-up of trade between two nations.

Of course there are a variety of second-order effects that follow from both immigration and from opening-up of trade – for example, immigration-induced changes in technology – but these are not the subject here.

Physical capital is excluded from the analysis here for several reasons: (1) simplicity and clarity of presentation; (2) comparability with Ricardo's numerical demonstration; (3) the analyses of Yeager, Borts and Stein, and Berry and Soligo (mentioned below) show that the famous "triangle" net effect on natives in the two-factor model is very small.

Before beginning on the analysis, an analogy may show why it is implausible that there should be a trade-like effect. Consider a youth, whose schooling expenditures (and other "costs") have all been private, entering the labor force in his/her country of birth. No one believes that this event has large positive trade-like effects on the community; indeed, the common (but incorrect) Malthusian presumption is that the youth's entry has negative effects through diminishing returns. The entry to the same labor force of an immigrant youth is an identical event economically, so why should the effects now be expected to be positive? One can complicate the story with the foreign-born youth even going to school in the country whose labor force will be entered, or a native youth going to school abroad, with identical theoretical expectations. The label "immigrant" on one youth or another changes no relevant economic facts in the assumed cases, but somehow induces the expectation in economists of Ricardo-like trade effects.

I do not argue that it is impossible in principle to make the phenomena of trade and migration logically equivalent; a skilled economic logician can probably find a set of auxiliary propositions that can do so. My argument is that the Ricardian theory is not *useful* as a practical explanatory tool, which is consistent with the fact that it is not invoked in theoretical discussions of immigration except at the level of vague handwaving, as seen in the introductory quotations given above. This is unlike the case of the Ricardian analysis of trade.

The essence of the paper was put succinctly by Leland Yeager (in correspondence, 1 December, 1993): "An analysis assuming no international movement of factors of production cannot itself address the consequences of their movement". The reader who fully accepts that statement need read no further; the rest of the paper elucidates that idea with various rhetorical devices – a numerical example showing that the consequences of immigration are different from the consequences of trade, a set of analogies, and a variety of verbal analyses of the natures of trade and migration.

Yeager regards the central proposition as "trivial" theoretically because it does not lead to theorems or testable implications. I consider that an argument against a widely-held erroneous idea that affects policy discussion is not trivial in the larger context of economics. So much paper and ink is devoted to the subject because it proves to be exceedingly difficult to obtain assent to the central proposition.

Preliminary statement of the theory

To focus the discussion, let us consider first a numerical example of the most difficult case – an "occupationally unbalanced" migration wherein the migrants are not in the same proportion as the work force in the country of destination. (The case where immigrants are in the same proportion as the destination's work force is much easier to analyse.) Assume that just a single barber moves between countries ("US" and "India") which have only barber and chicken-farming sectors. The analysis proceeds in two stages, the first stage before the destination economy fully adjusts, and the second stage after it reaches its new equilibrium.[6]

In transition prior to new equilibrium

Assume that initially the "US" and "India" each have 400 worker-hours per week available to the economy and that they produce chickens and haircuts as in Table 1.

Table 1 Prior to migration

	US	India	Total
Haircuts	200	200	400
Chickens	600	400	1000

One worker-hour produces one haircut in both countries, but produces three chickens in the US and two chickens in India. One haircut is worth three chickens in the US and only two in India. Now let one barber migrate, shifting 40 worker-hours per week of barbering as shown in Table 2.

Table 2 After migration but before adjustment

	US	India	Total
Haircuts	240	160	400
Chickens	600	400	1000

In the first stage, the migrant barber forces down US haircut prices sufficiently to create demand for his services, but as yet no barbers have left the trade. The opposite happens in India. Production in the two countries is as shown in Table 2. Total world production is the same as prior to migration (the opposite of what happens following an opening-up of trade), so there is no *total* gain in *consumer* welfare. The barber is better off, however, because she/he is paid at a higher price than before – more than 80 chickens-worth though less than 120 chickens-worth – which explains why the migration takes place. And there must be some gain in consumer welfare for those who had already been living in the country of immigration, because of the increase in what the budget constraint will purchase; this gain is partially offset by the loss of purchasing power of native barbers. No one has shown how to compute a realistic estimate of such a gain, but the amount is unlikely to rival the computed deadweight gains from trade.

Another source of gains to natives during a transition period is from employer or transporter rents arising from exploitation of legal power (such as hiring an illegal alien who is in fear of being reported and deported; no one would hire illegals at the same wage as legals because of the business risks involved), imbalance in market knowledge (the new immigrant being unaware of employment opportunities elsewhere, and hence accepting a relatively low wage), or firm-specific capital (such as the owner speaking the language of an immigrant who does not speak English[7]). These rents – if they are to be considered so, rather than being considered to be entrepreneurial profits – are consistent with the behavior of firms in investing in the transportation and administrative costs in arranging immigration of selected persons abroad. The rents are conceptually similar to the gains from hiring discriminated-against minorities in Becker's model of discrimination economics. But they do not seem similar to gains from trade.

The fact that immigrants' education-and-skill-adjusted earnings begin below those of natives but come to equal or pass those of natives is consistent with the proposition that (except where the law serves to maintain them) these rents are transitory, a phenomenon that has no similarity in the case of trade in goods.

The most extreme cases are those of slaves and of babies sold for adoption, cases in which the Ricardian framework could apply as well as it does to trade in producer's and consumer goods respectively. But the natures of these exceptions illuminate and support rather than refute the general proposition of the paper, it would seem.

After the new equilibrium is reached

After some time, the shift in prices leads to occupational adjustments. There is no reason to expect the fully-adjusted occupational proportions to be different than before the migration. Hence the structure of production will be as shown in Table 3, and prices should therefore return to what they were prior to the migration. At equilibrium there is an increase of 20 chickens in total world production, but all the increase goes to the migrant barber, in connection with the higher price of haircuts that she/he gives in the US, and it constitutes an increase in his/her standard of living. But everyone else's standard of living is as before. So we distinguish three groups – the natives of the origin country who do not move, the natives of the destination country, and the immigrant. The first two groups do not benefit from the move, while the immigrant does; this lack of consumer benefit is quite unlike the Ricardian trade situation.

Table 3 After adjustment to the immigration

	US	India	Total
Haircuts	220	180	400
Chickens	660	360	1020

To repeat, trade-induced shifts in prices and production benefit consumers in both countries, whereas after equilibrium is reached the shifts due to international migration benefit only the migrant. And after full adjustment, international migration leaves prices as before, whereas trade in goods alters the price structure. (Capital has been omitted from the model, a matter discussed later.)

The entire process can be seen as a single stage if migrants come to the destination country in the same proportion as the existing labor force – not wildly different from reality in the US. Prices then simply remain unchanged, the total economy expands in proportion to the increase in population due to the migrants, natives' incomes are unchanged, and immigrants obtain a higher standard of living.

This discussion does not answer the question of why production of the tradable good is higher in the destination country. There are many possible explanations, just as in trade theory, the simplest in this case being that persons of higher-than-average competence in the origin country become the migrants. But this question is not part of the matter at issue here.

Ricardian trade theory refers to those goods which can be sold separately from the services of the persons who own the means of production of these goods – oranges, chickens, autos, computer programs. In contrast, the benefit which the migrant confers upon the person or organization that pays the migrant for her/his services cannot be delivered at a distance. That is, Ricardian trade theory deals by definition with internationally traded and transported goods, while international (economic) migration is a response to the fact that that person's output cannot be directly sold at a distance. It should not be surprising, then, for trade theory to be silent about the immigration that takes place.

The distinction between goods and services is not helpful in this context, I believe. What matters is whether the person in question can sell his or her output directly to a buyer in another country or not. If a computer programmer can market programs by mail, and deliver them by modem, the good is a tradable; if he cannot, it is not. It does not matter whether the person writes programs for an auto plant or for an airline; if the particular auto plant is in the same country and the programmer cannot work by mail for an auto plant in another country, his output is a non-tradable, even though the auto itself is a tradable. A barber cannot work at a distance, whereas a sculptor with an international reputation can; that is why I choose them as examples (and also because they are not complicated by selling their outputs to other than final buyers).

Please notice that both marketing and delivery of the goods must be possible across borders in order that the good be a tradable. Invoking the concept of transaction cost as an explanation – saying that the transaction cost of moving a barber from one country to another to give a shave is high – does not seem to me to be helpful here. For some products such as consulting the concept may be helpful, as well as for gravel and stone. But it does not serve to distinguish the main cases with which we are dealing here.

Standard trade theory does explain why migration *need not* take place under certain conditions. But it does not explain why the migration that actually takes place *should* occur. To put the point differently, people either migrate internationally or they do not. One class of people who (according to trade theory) do not immigrate are those engaged in the production of internationally traded goods; their wages are thereby equalized in all relevant countries (at least the wages are equalized in principle, though by another principle the equality of wages is not testable empirically) and they therefore have no motive to move. Another group of people choose not to migrate because their earnings are greater in the country of origin than in the country of destination. But some people do migrate internationally, even some whose skill in their professions is average in the country of origin. Factor-price-equalization theory provides no motive for these people to migrate. And most importantly, there is no gain to non-moving natives similar to the Ricardian wine-and-cloth increase in total production whose benefit is realized by native consumers.

This paper is not a criticism of trade theory in general or of factor-price-equalization theory in particular. Rather, it simply takes notice of the fact that basic Ricardian trade theory does not explain the international migration that takes place, and does not suggest that there are gains to non-migrant consumers.

The rest of the paper is simply an elaboration and explanation of the international migration that does occur, and an analysis of its effects, as is the memo which follows the paper. The reader who is satisfied with the foregoing argument may safely stop here.

Explanation

The logic of trade theory is sufficiently complex, and the definitions of important quantities and ground rules of the theory are sufficiently elusive, so that the argument easily loses its way when one attempts to deal with this issue formally. Therefore I shall elaborate with extremely simple (though realistic) examples of the simplest sort of migration, cases of individuals who work by themselves and for whom physical capital is unimportant.

Assume that migration between the US and India (just two countries for convenience) suddenly goes from being totally restricted to totally unrestricted. Assume, too, that trade in goods heretofore had been free. Along with the change in immigration policy goes the abolition of all occupational regulations that influence earnings, for instance barber licensing laws in the various US states that restrict entry to barbering and raise haircut prices. Still another assumption is that because of "transactions" costs, movement is not completely and instantly free among occupations. Let us consider the explanation of the immigration, and the analysis of its direct effects, in that order.

These are the events that would be expected: persons in India who produce goods that are freely traded internationally – for example, internationally-known sculptors whose work is sold in galleries in the United States and elsewhere – will not have economic reason to move, because their incomes would not be increased by moving; those sculptors can just as well produce their sculpture in India as in the US, and send it to the US galleries by ship. But persons who presently sell goods or services that are *not* traded internationally – for example, barbers in India, and Indian sculptors who presently do not sell their work abroad but believe that with personal access to US galleries and art buyers they will be able to develop a market in the US and worldwide – will flock to the US because they believe that with only a small alteration in their skills they can sell their services for vastly more than at present, as measured by the purchasing power of their incomes. The musician Ravi Shankar would move if he was at the time mainly in the business of giving concerts, but not if he was then mainly in the business of making records (assuming the marketing of the records would be the same no matter where he is living.)

Now about the effects: in the case of goods trading, consumers gain because they obtain more goods than when there is no trade. The classic statement is that of Ricardo who in the first sentence of his chapter on "Foreign Trade" wrote that "extension of foreign trade . . . will very powerfully contribute to increase the mass of commodities, and therefore the sum of enjoyments" (Irwin paperback edition edited by W. Fellner, 1817/1963, p. 67). And in his Portugal-and-England wine-and-cloth example (p. 71), Ricardo shows how the opening of trade enables England to obtain with the labor of 200 men the goods that heretofore required the labor of 220 men, while Portugal obtains with the labor of 160 men what previously required the labor of 170 men. The decrease in labor required for the same basket of goods implies some combination of an increased consumption of these goods, increase in consumption of other market goods, and increase in leisure. We can say, then, that the extension of trade increases the total goods produced and consumed in each country as well as in both countries taken together. This is proven by Ricardo without considering shifts in relative prices, though such shifts would certainly follow. And the system would remain in this equilibrium – unlike the situation after migration as discussed above.

But opening immigration to barbers produces no comparable gain to US consumers. There will be a temporary decrease in the price of haircuts. (There will be no price change if immigrants come to the US in the same proportion in all occupations; a similar statement cannot be made about any trade in goods.) During that initial period after the opening of immigration the same world total numbers of haircuts and other goods are produced as before, but there are as many more haircuts in the US as there are fewer in India. That is, opening up trade in *goods* is immediately beneficial to consumers because it increases total physical production from the same inputs. But immigration of barbers does not at first increase the quantity of total physical production, though it increases the *value* of the production – all this keeping in mind that we are so far considering only the immediate effects rather than any effects that may occur after an overall readjustment of the systems.

The absence of benefit to consumers from the migration is seen when we extend the illustration. Assume that the barber who migrates to the United States is accompanied by his entire set of clients in India, which happens to be a Maharajah or a group of internationally-known sculptors who decide to migrate for political and cultural reasons alone, and not at all for economic reasons. The barber will receive a higher income because he will be paid in the US by the clients at the US haircut rate rather than at the Indian rate. But the total number of haircuts that he will give, and that they will receive, will be the same in the US as had been the case in India. And no one else will be affected in India or the US, even by a change in the price of haircuts, which shows that there is no necessary gain to natives in the country of immigration through this channel. Also unlike the case with trade theory, no native importers and consumers gain the benefit (along with exporters and producers), but rather only the migrants.

After the initial stage, the two economies gradually adjust toward equilibrium. There is no reason (except capital dilution, which simply hampers the process) that the two systems should not return to the same structures of prices and production as before the migration. Per-person income in both instances therefore is the same as before. Only the immigrant benefits, moving from a lower-income to a higher-income country.[8]

The sale of an Indian antiquity in the United States is a case falling somewhere between ordinary goods trade and migration. On the one hand, there is no change in the structure of production in the two countries, unlike Ricardian trading; and there also is no overall change in the world's physical wealth, just as with migration. On the other hand, the antiquity itself is sold and moved, and a seller who remains in India earns from the transaction, which increases measured Indian income; in contrast, the barber's output cannot be sold apart from the location of the barber, and (except in the case of slavery, about which more will be said below) no one profits except the migrant, and hence measured Indian income is not increased by the migration (leaving aside remittances, which are not part of the main story.)

One similarity between the phenomena of trade and migration is that opening-up of both migration and trade enables resources to be put to work in higher-value uses than before the opening-up. The difference in value arises from the different price structures – the difference in price ratios among goods – in the two countries. And this arises from the more efficient production of the other (tradable) good in the destination country. But again, none of this immediate gain to immigration is obtained by natives of the US unless the services that flow from the migrant's human capital cooperate either with native physical or human capital so as to make that native capital more productive; this does not occur in the case of barbering. The barbers obtain approximately the difference in the value of their production in the two countries.

Notice that if you take a trip to India you will get a haircut cheaper than in the US, but internationally-traded sculpture will be no cheaper. (Of course if you buy sculpture which is not internationally traded, one could say that it is relatively cheap – but one could also just as well say that it is relatively expensive; given that it is not internationally traded, by definition there are not two prices in the two countries which one can compare to decide whether it is cheap or expensive.) It is crucial to emphasize this distinction between the trading statuses of a haircut and of internationally-traded sculpture. The very essence of the matter at hand is that immigration is a phenomenon which is involved with goods that are not traded internationally – the services of the immigrants – whereas trade theory focuses on internationally-traded goods. This is why trade theory has nothing to say about immigration. And this is the most likely source of misunderstanding in this matter, I believe, which is why I repeat it.

One more example may help: assume (totally contrary to fact, I hope) that you need a set of dentures. If you go to India, you may be able to have a satisfactory set made more cheaply than in the US. But if the denture maker migrates to the US, you will then pay her/him as much as you would pay a native US denture maker, and the immigrant pockets the difference. If someone finds a way to sell well-fitted dentures by mail-order, however, the price will come to be the same in both countries (in exchange-rate terms), and there will then be no reason for the denture-maker to migrate (assuming no differences in production methods, and so on.).[9]

So far there has been no discussion of differences in the amounts of human-made physical capital with which barbers and sculptors work in the two countries, or with differences in the natural endowments of the countries. Rather, we would expect barbers to move because of differences in the demand schedules for barbers at the moment of observation. And this differs from the explanation of why oranges or textiles flow from one country to another, the explanation in those cases having more to do with differential supplies of factors of production across countries than with demand.

We could reasonably say that before the opening-up of immigration the marginal physical product of barbers was the same in both countries but the marginal value products differed because the structures of relative prices differed in the two countries; barriers to migration being an important cause of the differences in structures. In the cases of haircutting and sculpture we could even drop the word "marginal" from the statement.

The purpose for choosing such simple examples is that we then do not need to worry about the complication of some people working for others and selling their wares in the form of services used as a factor of production. In the latter case the wage-worker's personal output is not an internationally traded good, though it may affect the output of internationally-traded goods to a greater or lesser extent; this complicates the issue and makes it more difficult to understand the nature of the mechanism at work.

This completes the restatement of the main argument – that there are no consumer gains from migration analogous to the consumer gains from trade in goods. This argument has two parts: first, the total amounts of various types of goods produced are not immediately affected by migration (though they *may* be later on), whereas the comparable magnitudes are changed by opening up trade. Second, the migrants obtain the benefit of the increase in the marginal value product that occurs immediately due to the international migration, and then they benefit from the increase in physical product that occurs later.

The next section contains speculation which the reader may forego and upon which the main argument does not depend, plus some additional explanations that may clarify the matter.

Discussion

1. Inevitably, some changes in relative prices due to the immigration of a disproportionate number of barbers, say, will persist for some time because of one key part of the argument adduced here – that some occupations need not immigrate because there are no gains to their immigration. Inevitably some distributional effect will occur, and it is especially obvious in the case of self-employed immigrants who work alone, for example doctors and domestics. The market for medical services in the United States in recent years has undoubtedly been affected by the influx of foreign physicians. And this is not welcome to US physicians; there will be an obvious loss to the previous sellers of that service who were previously sufficiently efficient to reap some producer surplus, as well as the more difficult-to-calculate loss to the previously marginal producers who are forced out of the business. (And the benefits gained by the immigrants are not an offset to the latter's loss, given that the context of our discussion is the welfare of natives.) During the time of adjustment the shift bestows some additional consumer surplus upon all consumers down to the marginal person who would not have bought at the old price. As to the size of such effects and their impacts upon consumers, considered relative to the gains from trade, I do not have an analysis to offer here. More work is called for.

After the systems reach equilibrium, however, and to the (considerable) extent that immigrants are distributed evenly throughout the occupations, and assuming that their consumption patterns are similar to those of natives, the wages and prices of goods will be exactly what they would be without immigrants, aside from the effects due to the temporary dilution of the stock of capital. That is, as occupations shift and the stock of capital returns to what it would have been in the absence of immigrants, the situation will be exactly what it would have been without the immigrants. The immigrants would then cause the economy to be larger, in proportion to the amount of immigration, but all other magnitudes would be the same.

2. One may question whether a barber's skills in India are sufficiently similar to those of barbers in the United States to make the analysis meaningful. Indeed, many barbers in India undoubtedly could not make the transition effectively because of their inability to handle other parts of the barber's trade than cutting hair and shaving beards, or because of difficulty in adjusting to different hair styles. But certainly there are many barbers who would have little difficulty making the transition, and it is they who would migrate. The very fact that many persons do choose to migrate, and make successful adjustments, disproves that cultural styles of work are so different that adjustment is impossible.

It may be pointed out that operating as a sculptor in India and selling in the US is not identical to operating in the US, because of differences in marketing capacities in the two locations. This is undoubtedly true for many sculptors, but it in no way vitiates the main argument. The argument uses the example of a sculptor who *can* operate equally effectively in both places, and there are some. But even if there were none, the theoretical example would make the point; the fact that there are actual examples is merely frosting on the cake. And the fact that there are only a *few* examples in no way damages the logic that the example is used to illustrate.

3. The difference between migration and trade in goods may be illuminated by considering some cases of the movement of people when the facts of ownership are

different than they ordinarily are in migration. The key, as Ethier notes (1984, p. 20) but does not explore, is that "labor movements have the distinction that they involve the migration of the owner of a factor service as well as the migration of the service itself", that is, property rights are different in the case of migration than in the case of international trade in goods. When babies are "sold" for adoption by parents in poor countries to couples in rich countries, the transaction is exactly like a trade in goods. The natural parents produce the baby at a lower cost (leaving the term "cost" vague for now) than can men and women in a rich country, and they reap gains from the sale; the buyers, too, reap gains in the sense that they pay less for the baby than if they purchased from a rich-country "producer." But if a child grows up and moves herself or himself, the parents then cannot sell the child and reap such gains (except through gift remittances), and the employer of the immigrant grown-up child pays as much for the labor as to a native worker, and hence reaps no gains from the "trade". Another example is the smuggling of people across borders by the "coyotes" on the Mexican–US border; the smugglers are collecting some of the gains from trade just as one would if one were trading in goods; the employer does not obtain any trade gains because she/he pays the alien a market-determined wage (unless the employer pays less because of the illegal's status and fear of being apprehended). Still another example is the sale of slaves, which also is like trade in goods; the slave owner pays less in purchase cost plus upkeep than the slave's marginal product, or else there would be no benefit in holding slaves; the difference between the sale of slaves and the movement of free people typifies the difference between the standard theory of trade and a theory of immigration that fits our purposes here.

Conclusion

This article aims to show that the Ricardian theory of trade has nothing to say about immigration that takes place, and immigration does not bring the same sort of benefits as does trade. People either immigrate, or they do not. Basic Ricardian trade theory explains why one group of people does *not* immigrate – those who make internationally-traded goods and whose wages therefore become (theoretically) equal in both countries. (Not only is this not very likely in practice, but in principle we can never know whether the wages really are equal.) Another set of people who do not immigrate are those whose earnings would be less in the rich country than in the poor country because their productivity is so low – well below the average in the sending country.

The people who do immigrate are those whose productivity is average or above in the old country, and who could earn more in the new country for that reason and/or because of the difference in price structures in the old and new countries. These are necessarily people whose earnings are not equalized in the two countries. (For example, sculptors who sell their sculpture on an international market and who can live and work anywhere will not migrate.) Trade theory says nothing about this latter group who do immigrate.

The core of trade theory is Ricardian, the thrust being that consumers are better off if there is trade than if there is no trade. Immigration does not make consumers better off in a Ricardian way. The gains to consumers from *trade* result from differences in the structures of production before and after trade – a supply-side phenomenon. The gains to immigrants result from differences in demand for labor in the two countries, and the supply structures are unchanged (except in size) in the before-migration and after-migration equilibria.

Immigration does, however, bring many other sorts of benefits not discussed here, as well as some costs (see Simon, 1989). These are the externalities that Harry Johnson notes are the forces that matter; Johnson's observation is in unusual accord with the theory presented here.

The subject of the paper, international migration, is far from identical theoretically to *domestic* migration. Relative prices differ much more between origin and destination in the former than in the latter case, and wages differ less (and can easily be compared in the same currency), a key matter for the analysis here. And the ratio of domestic migration going in one direction to that going in the opposite direction tends to be much higher than the comparable ratio in international migration to the United States.

Notes

1. I am grateful to Stanley Engerman, Milton Friedman, Herbert Grubel, Charles P. Kindleberger, Nathaniel Leff, Wallace Oates, Ivy Papps, Melvin Reder, Albert Rees, Paul Wonnacott, David Colander, and other participants in a Middlebury College conference on immigration for helpful comments on an earlier draft of this material, though it should be noted that some of them strongly disagreed with the argument.

   The central idea in this paper was presented in brief in Simon (1989, pp. 17–20).
2. One might wonder whether the schooling being paid for publicly or privately affects the valuation in the sending country; on most assumptions it does not. But in any case, there certainly is no effect on the country of destination, the focus of attention in this paper.
3. Nothing said here is intended to suggest that educated immigrants, even more than uneducated immigrants, are not economically beneficial. But the benefits arise from externalities rather than from a Ricardian trade-like effect.
4. Such clear-thinking economists as Gary Becker and Herbert Giersch have said this in public comment, adding that they think the central point of the paper is wrong and they can supply counter-examples. (But neither supplied those counter-examples, and at least one equally clear-thinking Nobelist does agree with the paper.)
5. An exception to the standard view was the assertion by Harry Johnson (1968, p. 80) that world or sending-country loss from brain drain must "hinge on a loss of externalities," which implies that gain must also depend upon externalities rather than an "internal" trade-like effect. This paper may be considered to be a proof of Johnson's assertion.
6. The numbers and some of the language in this example are adapted from a letter by Ivy Papps, who kindly granted me permission to do so, though his argument was different than mine.
7. Pertinent here is the joke about the Chinese waiter in a Jewish restaurant speaking broken Yiddish. When one of the patrons asked the owner about this phenomenon, the owner responded, "Sssh, he thinks he's learning English."
8. Perhaps it will help the reader's intuition to notice that there is an apparent paradox in thinking about migration. One the one hand, additional people (including immigrants) are (wrongly) considered to lower per-capita income in the country of destination and to raise it in the country of origin because of their effect through the stock of physical capital. On the other hand, immigrants are considered to lower income in the country of origin and raise it in the country of destination because they transfer human capital from the former to the latter. That is, the common presumptions that (a) natural population growth reduces income (by reducing output per worker), and (b) population growth from immigration increases income, directly oppose each other but refer to exactly the same type of event. And indeed, the theories of Borts and Stein (1966) and Berry and Soligo (1969) refer to the two events interchangeably.

   One might see this paper as merely an application of Borts–Stein and Berry–Soligo. But the connection to their work was not apparent to me until after many drafts, during which time its arguments had been disputed by almost every reader; hence, the thrust of the paper certainly is not obvious. Also, the B–S–B–S arguments focus on the role of capital, whereas this paper abstracts from it. And their arguments focus upon average income whereas this paper focuses on the separate experiences of natives and immigrants.
9. A newspaper story supports the supposition about the dentures: "WORTH A TRIP: CUT-RATE DENTURES LEAD TO THE OZARKS. Folks Hitch Up their RVs and Head for Missouri . . . The Russells live in Evansville, Why. Twice in the past month, they have made the two-day drive to this

little Ozark town so he could have work done at the Mid American Dental clinic, a big discount-denture operation here. 'Even with two trips, we saved money', Mrs. Russell says." (*Wall Street Journal*, Dec. 9, 1993, p. 1). Migration of the dentist, and mail-order dentures, can be seen as substitutes for migration of the patient, but there are barriers against these possibilities.

References

Albert R. Berry and Ronald Soligo, "Some Welfare Aspects of International Migration", *Journal of Political Economy* **77**, Sept./Oct. 1969.

Blitz, Rudolph C., "A Benefit–Cost Analysis of Foreign Workers in West-Germany, 1957–1973", *Kyklos*, 1977.

Borts, George J. and Jerome L. Stein, *Economic Growth in a Free Market* (New York: Columbia University Press, 1966).

James M. Buchanan and Richard E. Wagner, "An Efficiency Basis for Federal Fiscal Taxation", in Julius Margolis (ed.), *The Analysis of Public Output* (New York: NBER-Columbia U.P., 1970), pp. 139–162.

Ethier, Wilfred J., "International Trade Theory and International Migration" (xerox, 1984).

Frank, Robert H. "Are Workers Paid their Marginal Products?", *American Economic Review*, September, 1989.

Froeb, Luke M., *Vanderbilt Magazine*, Winter 1995.

Gallman, Robert E., "Human Capital in the First 80 Years of the Republic: How Much Did America Owe the Rest of the World?", *American Economic Review*, **67**(1): 27–31, May, 1977.

Geseck, Arne, Ullrich Heilemann and Hans Dietrich von Loeffetholz, "Economic Implications of Migration into the Federal Republic of Germany 1988–1992" in Sarah Spencer (ed.), *Immigration as an Economic Asset: The German Experience* (Stoke-on-Trent: IPPR/Trentham, 1994)

Grubel, Herbert G. and Anthony Scott, *The Brain Drain* (Waterloo, Ontario: Wilfrid Laurier Press, 1977).

Hassan, M. Kahir, "The Immigration of Third World Scientists and Engineers to the United States", *Pakistan Journal of Applied Economics*, **VII**(1): 43–58, 1988.

Johnson, Harry G., "In Search of an Analytical Framework", in *The Brain Drain*, Walter Adams (ed.), (New York: Macmillan, 1968), pp. 69–91.

Krauss, Melvyn B. and William J. Baumol, "Guest Workers and Income-Transfer Programs Financed by Host Governemnts", *Kyklos*, 1979.

LaLonde, Robert J., and Robert H. Topel, "Labor Market Adjustments to Increased Immigration", in *Immigration, Trade and the Labor Market*, edited by John M. Abowd and Richard B. Freeman, (Chicago: University of Chicago Press, 1991), pp. 167–200.

Lerner, J. and Roy Rustum, "Numbers, Origins, Economic Value and Quality of Technically Trained Immigrants into the United States", *Scientometrics*, **6**: 243–259, 1984.

McCracken, Paul W., "Light at the End of the Budget Tunnel", *The Wall Street Journal*, March 19, 1985, p. 28.

Neal, Larry and Paul Uselding, "Immigration: A Neglected Source of American Economic Growth, 1790–1917", *Oxford Economic Papers*, **24**: 66–88, 1972.

Ricardo, David, *The Principles of Political Economy and Taxation* (Homewood, Illinois: Richard D. Irwin, Inc., 1963).

Simon, Julian L., *The Economic Consequences of Immigration* (Boston: Basil Blackwell, 1989).

[28]

Foreword

This paper would not have been done without the last grant that I received from the federal government, in about 1979. There had only been two or three other grants before it during my entire work career, despite numerous applications. And this one happened because it did not pass through peer review, but was dispensed by Guillermina Jasso and Mark Rosenzweig when they were co-research directors of the Select Commission on Immigration and Refugee Policy. I am grateful to them for their courage in making the grant.

The mode of analysis is shaped to fit a very specific policy question: would present residents be made better off if additional immigrants are omitted? This dictated that a present-value analysis is needed, and that the relevant universe is the entire collection of immigrants rather than particular ethnic groups (the latter a subject which attracts researchers like moths to a flame). The policy orientation also explains why a theoretical framework is not needed.

The paper published here was drawn from my report to the Commission. This paper omitted lines of data from the tables (for the oldest immigrant groups, and for the immigrants who came in the years in [and after!] the survey) that I had to agree with the editor are not important to the analysis. But I worried to the editor that critics would jump on the omission if they were left out, and that therefore it would be better to include them. The editor's judgement prevailed, of course. And the critics did indeed jump on the omission, claiming that it invalidated the analysis.

These omitted data, together with the other data, are displayed in the summary Table F1.

There are two reasons why the data for the older immigrant groups are not relevant. First, applying any reasonable discount factor, economic events occurring 25 years and more in the future have little effect on current decisions based on present-value calculations. The second and decisive factor is that, on average, the oldest persons by then have children who are paying amounts into the system as taxes that balance what their parents withdraw as transfer payments; the immigrants' excess payments represent a one-time windfall to the equilibrium system. The only conceptual analytic alternative would be to include in the calculation the costs and benefits of the children when grown (and their children, and so on) on the ground that these streams of people are part of the consequences of the immigrants. But as a practical matter this is not feasible. (For an extended explanation, see Simon, 1989, 109–10.)

The nub of the explanation is that any average group of *natives* – including all, from the youngest to the oldest – may be considered to be in a dynamic equilibrium with respect to taxes and government expenditures; the in-payments from workers equal all the out-payments, including those for the non-working elderly and for children. But because a cohort of immigrants arrives without an accompanying group of non-working elderly (the few who come are not eligible for Social Security, though they do receive other forms of government transfers), an arrival cohort of immigrants is not in a dynamic equilibrium as are natives; instead, immigrants gradually move *toward* the same dynamic equilibrium as natives during the period that the working-age persons in the immigrant cohort grow older. The difference each year between the dynamic-equilibrium taxes and transfers of natives and the immigrants' taxes and transfers (putting aside public goods for now) constitutes the benefit to natives through the public coffers.

The windfall does not go on forever; the amount of windfall per year declines from the time of the arrival cohort's entry until the working-age persons in the first generation reach retirement (which in practice of course happens gradually), at which time the dynamic equilibrium is reached and there is neither windfall nor deficit.

TABLE F.1 Balance sheet of services used and taxes paid by families: Immigrants to the United States by year of entry of head of family, and natives, as of 1975

Immigrant cohort by year of entry and natives	(1) Total transfers (including medical) without Social Security ($)	(2) Total transfers (including medical) with Social Security ($)	(3) Schooling costs (and percent receiving service) ($)	(4) Total transfers plus schooling costs ($)	(5) Services used by natives (see "Natives" in col. 4) ($)	(6) Col. 5 – col. 4 ($)	(7) Total family earnings (and standard deviations) ($)	(8) Estimated tax paid on earnings (29% of col. 7)
1974	593	596	820 (63)	1,416	2,279	863	9,192 (10,688)	2,666
1973	396	445	755 (58)	1,200	2,279	1,079	11,387 (9,996)	3,302
1972	602	629	781 (50)	1,410	2,279	869	10,610 (8,383)	3,077
1971	512	517	716 (55)	1,233	2,279	1,046	10,826 (9,871)	3,140
1970	582	616	1,042 (80)	1,659	2,279	620	10,383 (7,295)	3,011
1965–69	721	873	1,068 (82)	1,941	2,279	338	12,247 (9,597)	3,552
1960–64	684	1,010	1,237 (95)	2,247	2,279	32	14,014 (11,310)	4,064
1950–59	631	1,055	1,237 (95)	2,292	2,279	–13	13,542 (10,309)	3,927
Natives	685	1,420	859 (66)	2,279			11,037 (10,377).	3,201
1976	388	394	(38)	—			— —	—
1975	217	248	(71)	—			— —	—
1920–49	358	2,587	—	—			7,740 (11,248)	—
Before 1920	369	3,459	—	—			2,184 (7,254)	—

This implies that the receipt of old-age benefits nowadays by immigrants who have been in the US for many years since their twenties or thirties should properly be considered part of an equilibrium system that includes their own children's generation. The children of retired immigrants support their parents with their taxes, just as the children of natives do for their parents. Hence the retired immigrants are no special burden upon natives.

The graph that follows the paper shows this effect diagrammatically. The difference between the old-age expenditures (E) due to Social Security (SS) in the immigrant and native cohorts until the immigrants reach age equilibrium accounts for the windfall.

TABLE F.1 (continued)

(9) Number of persons in labor force	(10) Taxes paid for pure public goods (20% of col. 8) ($)	(11) Taxes paid by natives (see "Natives" in col. 8) ($)	(12) Difference in taxes paid (col. 8 – col. 11) ($)	(13) Difference excluding public goods (80% of col. 12) ($)	(14) Net effect of immigrant cohort upon natives (cols. 6 + 10 + 13) ($)	(15) Alternate calculation of net effect of immigrant cohort upon natives per immigrant family, no allowance for public goods contribution (cols. 6 + 8 – 11) ($)	(16) Number of families in the sample
1.26	533	3,201	–535	–428	968	328	154
1.45	660	3,201	101	81	1,820	1,180	171
1.36	615	3,201	–124	–99	1,385	745	188
1.33	628	3,201	–61	–49	1,625	985	202
1.51	602	3,201	–190	–152	1,070	430	224
1.49	710	3,201	351	281	1,329	689	977
1.43	813	3,201	863	690	1,535	895	769
1.47	785	3,201	726	581	1,353	713	1,762
1.25							11,212
1.20	See text						50 See text
1.21							204
0.806							3,697
0.232							1,075

NOTE: Transfers include Unemployment compensation, Workers compensation, Veterans benefits, Public welfare, Supplemental Security Income, Aid to Families with Dependent Children, and Food Stamps.
SOURCE: Author's computations from Census Bureau 1976 SIE Survey.

Reprinted from (and with permission of) Population Council. Population and Development Review 10, No. 1 (March 1984).

Immigrants, Taxes, and Welfare in the United States

Julian L. Simon

Since the dawn of civilization, individuals and societies surely have recognized as economic fact that they benefit from adding to the group unattached persons in the prime of life. The young and the strong produce more than they consume; they support and protect the aged and the dependent children. In modern economic theory, this phenomenon was discussed by Neisser and then formalized by Modigliani and Samuelson.[1] All three writers argue that a faster rate of population growth leads to a higher rate of saving because young workers save in order to consume after they retire, and there is a higher proportion of young workers if population growth is faster. In an ongoing growth system the saving is in effect a system of transfers in each generation from the workers to the retired and to children, a process Samuelson compared to a chain-letter scheme. Although the context of Modigliani's and Samuelson's discussions was the private financial system, much the same principle holds for public tax-and-transfer systems, with obvious implications for social security systems.

If one adds to the analysis the transfers to children as well as to the retired, the gains from an ongoing growth system are less clearcut; Arthur and McNicoll made this criticism of Samuelson.[2] And indeed, in some societies such as Germany, the ratio of social transfer payments to children relative to the transfers to the retired is much larger than in the United States; this could invalidate the argument regarding rate of saving. Ultimately, it is an empirical question whether, under a society's transfer system, an additional baby born implies on balance a lower or higher proportion of a worker's income transferred to dependents outside the family through taxes than if the baby is not born.

The Neisser-Modigliani-Samuelson reasoning applies with even greater force to immigrants, because the newcomers are typically young men and women who arrive without elderly dependents[3] and with a relatively small number of children already born. Yet in the United States and elsewhere, immigrants are not generally greeted with open arms for their potential balance of transfers. Indeed, several objections to their influx are commonly offered.[4] First, it is often argued that the Malthusian capital dilution effect (the same amount of capital with more workers means less capital per worker) in a modern society outweighs the transfer effect, unlike the situation of early man when land (the main physical capital) was supposedly (though probably really was not) in very elastic supply. Second, it is said that the immigrants typically have characteristics that lead them to receive much more in services and to earn much less (thereby paying much less in the form of taxes) than do natives, so that the transfer balance is in fact negative. Third, immigrants are said to place an added burden on scarce natural resources. And fourth, immigrants are said to substantially increase native unemployment.

This article investigates the balance of transfers between immigrants and natives in a recent year in the United States. The results show that from the time of entry until about 12 years later, immigrants use substantially fewer public services (largely due to less use of Social Security because of the youthfulness of immigrant families) than do native families; after that, immigrant use becomes roughly equal to that of natives. On the contribution side, after about three to five years immigrant families begin to pay as much in taxes as do native families; subsequently, they pay substantially more. And the net balance of these two forces is positive in every year with respect to natives' incomes. In short, immigrants contribute more to the public coffers than they take from them.

The article does not address the issue of whether discriminating among groups of immigrants could increase native welfare through the public-coffers effect as well as through other channels. Discrimination by educational level would be beneficial, but would pose various practical and ethical questions. And discrimination by ethnic group seems to be sufficiently far from the spirit of contemporary America that it does not seem appropriate even to discuss it.

The various effects of there simply being more people are dealt with at booklength elsewhere.[5] Suffice it to say here that none of the individual effects except the impact through productivity growth is large, nor is their sum, relative to the effect discussed in this article; and the productivity growth effect goes in the same direction as does the effect discussed here.

The article also does not deal with the large number of other channels through which immigrants affect natives. The capital-dilution issue is discussed elsewhere,[6] in conjunction with the productivity-increasing effect of immigrants.

Finally, the article does not address the fact that the costs and benefits from immigrants are unequally distributed. Both costs and benefits are considered for the nation as a whole, whereas it is well recognized that many of the costs—such as pressures on educational systems—occur disproportionately in the locales of greatest immigrant location. This exercise demonstrates that benefits outweigh costs in the aggregate. This is not to deny the distributional problem.

The sample

The 1976 Survey of Income and Education (SIE), carried out by the Bureau of the Census, gathered information on the 1975 incomes and use of social services by 158,500 households, stratified in such a manner as to include more-than-proportional numbers of households with children living in poverty. The survey coverage is good: only 7,300 households refused to be interviewed. All households with foreign-born heads (about 15,000) constitute the main sample used here. A random subsample of about 11,000 native-American households, drawn from the entire sample, is used for comparison. Persons in private and public institutions such as nursing homes and hospitals were not included in the SIE survey.

The primary unit of analysis is the male immigrant together with the family he brings or acquires. This means that families with female immigrants married to male natives are excluded from the analysis. The logic is as follows. Imagine a male immigrant who marries a female immigrant and has children. It is reasonable to view the effects of the couple plus their children as the full effects of the male's and female's immigration. Now imagine that the same male and female had instead married natives who would otherwise have married each other, and that both families are now counted in the immigrant sample. Although total effect on natives' income is no greater than in the first assumption, the calculations on average would show twice as much effect; hence this would constitute double-counting. We can eliminate most of the misleading double-counting by counting only households headed by male immigrants.[7]

The family rather than the household or the individual seems the appropriate unit of analysis. One important reason for not focusing on individuals is that it is on the basis of family needs that public welfare, Aid to Families with Dependent Children (AFDC), and similar transfers are received; another reason is that children are attached to both parents (if present) rather than to just one of them. Furthermore, the earnings of the various members tend to be pooled by the family for consumption as well as for assessment of income taxes. The household (though in most cases identical with the family) is not such a longlasting unit with respect to other nonrelated earners, nor is income so likely to be pooled within it or transfers to be based upon it.

Associated with this reasoning is the decision to include single immigrant women as observations, but not married immigrant women. A single woman who immigrates and then marries an immigrant disappears as an independent economic entity, and her impact is then through the family unit. For a woman who remains single, the opposite is the case; hence for unmarried adults, both males and females are included as separate families without danger of double-counting.

Public services used by immigrants and natives

We begin by estimating the overall gross cost to US citizens of admitting average immigrants to the country. (Gross benefits and net effects are discussed

TABLE 1 Dollar values of transfer payments and services received in 1975 per person, by various entry cohorts and by natives[a]

Immigrant cohort by year of entry	Unemployment/ workmen's compensation, veterans' benefits (1)	Public welfare (2)	Supplemental security (3)	Aid to Families with Dependent Children (4)	Food stamps (5)	Social Security (6)	Medicare[b] (7)	Medicaid[c] (8)	Total, cols. 1–5 (9)	Total, cols. 1–6 (10)	Schooling costs for children aged 5–17[d] (11)	Total, cols. 1–8 and 11 (12)	Number of families (13)
1974	204	131	91	91	15	3	29	32	532	535	820	1,416	154
1973	238	47	63	6	7	49	23	12	361	410	755	1,200	171
1972	237	85	38	164	12	127	42	24	536	563	781	1,510	188
1971	261	189	16	13	17	5	2	14	496	501	716	1,233	202
1970	341	100	50	11	16	34	45	19	518	552	1,042	1,659	224
1965–69	339	191	86	18	12	152	48	27	646	798	1,068	1,941	977
1960–64	385	91	69	18	12	326	88	21	575	901	1,237	2,247	769
1950–59	301	122	31	50	11	424	76	20	515	939	1,237	2,292	1,762
Natives	288	108	46	45	11	735	167	20	498	1,233	859	2,279	11,212

NOTE: Puerto Ricans are not included in either immigrant or native category.

[a] Means weighted by sample probabilities to be unbiased estimates of the United States.

[b] At $592 per patient-year.

[c] At $126 per patient-year.

[d] At $1,302 per child-year of schooling.

SOURCE: Tables are based on the author's research for the Survey of Income and Education, carried out by the US Bureau of the Census.

in subsequent sections.) More specifically, we wish to estimate for the average immigrant in an entry cohort (a) the amount of each service used for each year after entry, and (b) the yearly total. (Some interpolation is necessary because some survey cohorts contain more than one year's immigrants.)

The estimate for immigrants as the average of an entire cohort is the most important for our purposes, because it is the relevant quantity bearing on policy decisions about the total number of immigrants to allow in; it tells us the gross cost to natives of the average immigrant family. (It may be useful for other purposes to know the quantities of services used by the various ethnic and occupational groups. Such investigations are not of central interest here, however.)

Table 1 shows the amounts of payments received by persons who have been in the United States varying lengths of time, and Table 2 shows proportions of cohorts receiving the payments. Columns 1–8 of Table 1 show the various transfer payments to natives and to immigrant entry cohorts ranging backward from 1974 to 1950. Results for families that arrived in 1976 and 1975 are not shown because their meaning is unclear, inasmuch as the data supposedly refer to the calendar year 1975.[8] Data for cohorts that arrived in 1949 or before are also excluded; they are not relevant to policy decisions concerning immigration because these older immigrants must now be seen as part of an ongoing system. Their children, and the economic impacts of those children, are an important part of the total effects of this cohort, but data on their children are not available; for the same reason, the 1950–59 cohort should not be considered an important part of the sample.[9]

The mechanism of this ongoing system requires amplification. To start, we are interested here in the resource flows due to immigrants that affect the

TABLE 2 Percents receiving transfer payments and services in 1975 among various entry cohorts and among natives[a]

Immigrant cohort by year of entry	Food stamps	Medicare[b]	Medicaid[c]	Schooling costs for children aged 5–17[d]
1974	15	4.9	25.6	63
1973	5	3.9	9.7	58
1972	8	7.0	19.1	60
1971	12	0.3	11.1	55
1970	10	7.6	15.7	80
1965–69	12	8.1	21.2	82
1960–64	8	14.7	16.9	95
1950–59	9	16.0	15.6	95
Natives	9	28.0	15.9	66

NOTE: Puerto Ricans are not included in either immigrant or native category.

[a] Means weighted by sample probabilities to be unbiased estimates of the United States.

[b] At $592 per patient-year.

[c] At $126 per patient-year.

[d] At $1,302 per child-year of schooling.

economic position of natives taken as a group. In other words, we want to compare the consumption of natives (including consumption of services) in two hypothetical situations, one with and one without a group of immigrants. We are not interested here in legal obligations, entitlements, equity, or the consumption of immigrants.

A simplified model may help. Consider a community of subsistence farmers in which there is a surplus of land and each farm produces the same output. Each family consists of three generations: a married couple, two children, and two retired adults. Children do not work until age 20, at which time they marry, have two children, and work for 20 years. At age 40 the couple retire and live until age 60. Each farm, then, always contains one working couple, two dependent children, and two elderly dependents—a stationary demographic system. The farm produces no surplus or saving; all production is consumed.

Consider, now, a newly married couple who move into the community. For 20 years, the production of this "immigrant" family need support only the couple and their children, leaving a surplus that the community can tax. During this period the immigrant family is an economic benefit to the natives as a result of their payment of taxes. After 20 years, when the immigrant couple retire, the family has come to have the same characteristics as an "equilibrium" native family, and the retirement consumption of the immigrant couple is paid for by their children. This illustrates the fact that there is a one-time benefit to natives during the first years that an immigrant couple is in the community, during which time they make no claims on the "social security taxes" contributed to the community coffers. In addition, the nature of the obligation between the immigrant couple and their children (which leads their children to support them) has no bearing on the consumption of natives.

Column 9 shows the totals for the five most important categories of welfare payment transfers aside from Social Security. The average family in each of the cohorts of immigrants since 1950–59 uses almost the same amount of such services or (in most cases) slightly more than do native families—ranging from $137 less to $148 more. But when Social Security payments are included,[10] we see in column 10 that immigrants receive a much lower overall level of welfare payments than do natives—ranging from $294 less to $823 less. In view of the consistency in composition from cohort to cohort, there is no question of the statistical significance of the smaller use of welfare transfers by immigrants than by natives.

Expenditures on education must be considered, too. The SIE sample does not show the total number of children per family, but it does show the number living at home. This latter number should be a satisfactory approximation for young families and for children under age 18. For the various cohorts, the average number of children per family aged 5 to 17 was multiplied by the 1975–76 average annual expenditure of $1,302 per student in public elementary and secondary schools;[11] the results are shown in column 11. Immigrants use substantially more educational services than do natives after a few years—$476 more per family for both the 1960–64 and 1950–59 cohorts.[12]

Next, we consider Medicare and Medicaid.[13] Columns 7 and 8 show the proportions of the various groups that use these services. The average cost per user of Medicare was $592 in 1975, and for Medicaid it was $126. (The average cost per person over age 65 was $205 for Medicaid, and a considerably larger proportion of natives than of recent immigrant cohorts are over 65, but there is no need for the present purposes to make an adjustment for this.)

Special assistance to refugees—which recently has amounted to $1,000 per person in cash plus some overhead to the assisting refugee organization, as well as some special programs—has been excluded from the analysis, because there is no way of knowing which families in our sample were admitted as refugees. If one wished to make a benefit-and-cost analysis specifically for refugees, it would be appropriate to deduct this sum, multiplied by the average number of family members, from the present value calculated for the family, as discussed below.

We are now in a position to estimate the average total amount of services used by the various cohorts, with results shown in column 12. There we see that the very recent cohorts use much lower levels of services than do natives—for example, $971 less per family for the 1973–74 cohorts considered together than for natives. The levels of services used by older cohorts are higher; they move upward and reach equality with natives some 10–15 years after arrival. Figure 1 plots the data on services used. A free-hand curve allows us to calculate the change in services with each additional year in the United States.

Native families are used as a benchmark because if immigrants were to use services and pay taxes in amounts equal to natives, the immigrants would have no effect on natives through the public coffers, because, on average, taxes paid equal the cost of services provided. In the overall cost-benefit framework employed later, personal services used by immigrants cannot simply

FIGURE 1 Cost of services used by various immigrant cohorts and by native Americans

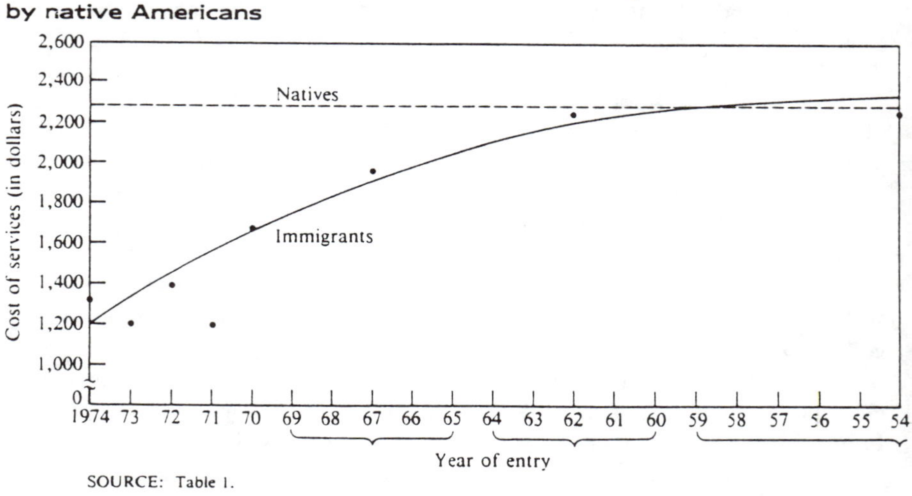

SOURCE: Table 1.

be compared with taxes paid by immigrants because the "overhead" of public goods must also be allowed for; the comparison with natives takes care of this.

Taxes paid by immigrants

To avoid confusion, it is important to avoid comparing the data on earning patterns in this article with earning patterns of immigrant males discussed by such writers as Chiswick and Blau.[14] They compare incomes of natives with those of immigrants while holding constant as many factors as possible other than immigrant–native differences, in order to understand the nature of the immigrant–native differences; by contrast, here nothing is held constant other than year of entry, because our aim is to assess the unconditional impact of that cohort on the natives' standard of living. Yet the broad patterns of family earnings data are clearly compatible with the other studies, including North's analysis[15] for the first six years in the country, based on Social Security data (which, however, refer to earnings of adult males rather than to family earnings).

Column 4 in Table 3, and Figure 2 based on it, show that the average immigrant family begins to earn about as much as the average native family somewhere between three and five years after entry, and subsequently earns more. (This finding uses an average for the 1970–73 cohorts.) This rapid approach to equality is heavily influenced, of course, by age and education composition and, especially, by the absence of retired family heads among the immigrants.

Inferences from earnings data about taxes paid by various immigrant cohorts, and by the representative native family, are tenuous though crucial. A key difficulty is that different proportions of overall taxes (not just income taxes) are paid by persons of different income levels,[16] which means that a

FIGURE 2 Family earnings by various immigrant cohorts and by native Americans

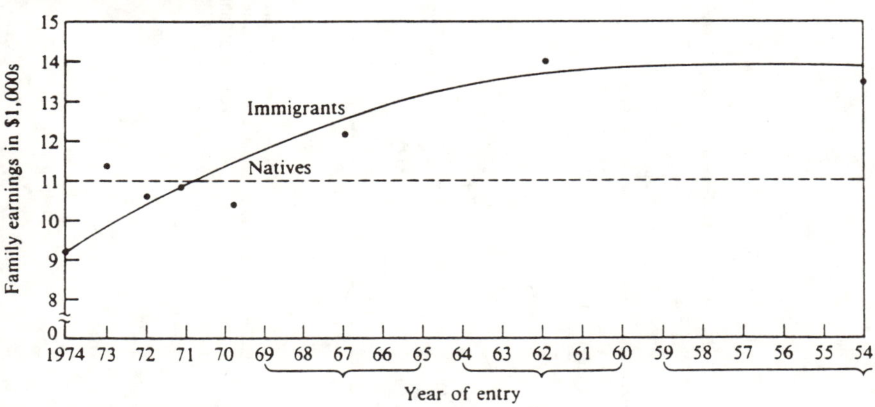

SOURCE: Table 3.

TABLE 3 1975 family earnings in US dollars and employment data for immigrants and natives[a]

Immigrant cohort by year of entry	Head's wages and salaries (1)	Spouse's wages and salaries (whether or not there is a spouse) (2)	Self-employment income (3)	Total wages and salaries[b] (4)	Total family earnings[c] (5)	Number of persons in labor force[d] (6)	Number of earners (7)	Number of persons employed (8)	Number of persons unemployed (9)	Estimated tax paid on wages: .29 × (4)[e] (10)	Estimated tax paid on earnings: .29 × (5)[e] (11)
1974	7,162	1,182	80	8,890	9,192	1.26	1.35	1.09	.131	2,587	2,666
1973	8,351	1,774	497	10,880	11,387	1.45	1.45	1.35	.071	3,166	3,302
1972	7,738	2,048	133	10,458	10,610	1.36	1.39	1.20	.165	3,043	3,077
1971	7,603	1,574	1,409	9,416	10,826	1.33	1.28	1.17	.115	2,740	3,140
1970	7,294	1,717	610	9,772	10,383	1.51	1.51	1.29	.168	2,848	3,011
1965–69	8,313	2,070	635	11,543	12,247	1.49	1.54	1.36	.13	3,359	3,552
1960–64	9,156	2,223	1,450	12,248	14,014	1.43	1.50	1.31	.112	3,564	4,064
1950–59	9,592	1,874	1,090	12,343	13,542	1.47	1.55	1.34	.117	3,592	3,927
Natives	7,503	1,614	722	10,164	11,037	1.26	1.37	1.18	.09	3,008	3,201

[a] Means weighted by sample probabilities.

[b] Total wages and salaries includes wages and salaries from other members of the household besides head and spouse, and hence column 4 should not equal the sum of columns 1–3.

[c] The figure for total family earnings may seem larger than warranted by the individual columns for head's and spouse's wages and salaries, and for self-employment income. The data do add up in a sample of individual records. The likeliest explanation is that the family earnings are top-coded to $75,000, and are entered directly, but the other categories are top-coded to $50,000.

[d] In principle, columns 8 and 9 should add to column 6. The discrepancies probably arise from different perceptions of the different questions.

[e] See text for origin of .29 multiplier.

proper calculation must be based on the entire income distribution of a cohort rather than just the mean.[17] Some light is thrown on the matter by the spreads of the income distributions in our data, which show somewhat smaller standard deviations relative to mean income for immigrants than for natives. This probably means that, for the same mean income, a group of immigrants—due to fewer very high incomes—pays somewhat less in taxes than does a group of natives. Nevertheless, we are not likely to go far wrong by assuming that taxes paid are proportional to mean income.

The total of taxes paid by immigrants—found in column 11 of Table 3—is the total receipts of the state, local, and federal governments—$771.9 billion in 1979, which we may approximate as 32.6 percent of the gross national product ($2,368.5 billion).[18] The taxes paid by the median-income earner are 85 percent of the taxes paid by the mean-taxes-paid taxpayer; that is, the rate at which taxes are paid by the person between the fifth and sixth deciles of income recipients—24.8 percent of income paid in taxes—is 85 percent of the mean 29.1 percent for all taxable incomes.[19] So even if immigrants are more concentrated near the mean than are natives, the effect on taxes paid will not be large.

In brief, although our estimates of taxes paid by immigrants and natives are rough, the inaccuracy is unlikely to be important in this context because the incomes, and hence the tax burden, of the two groups do not differ greatly from each other.

The net effect of immigrants on natives

Table 4 consolidates the relevant data on services used and taxes paid. Columns 1 and 2 show the total transfer payments and services used by immigrants in various years after entry (actually, by various entry cohorts during 1975) and by natives. Column 3 shows the differences between columns 1 and 2. If we make the reasonable assumption that the average family just pays for the average family's services used—an assumption that says no more than that government receipts equal the sum of government expenditures for various purposes—then column 3 indicates the net balance of immigrants with respect to services alone. In other words, it indicates the amount by which services used by an immigrant exceed or fall short of the amount paid for by the average taxpayer.[20]

Turning from services used to taxes paid, we first deal with government expenditures that are independent of the number of people, or that at least are pure public goods in the sense that the services they render to any person are independent of the services others obtain from them. The government expenditures that seem clearly to fit into this category are national defense ($85,552 million in 1975), international affairs ($6,922 million), and general science, space, and technology ($3,989 million), out of total outlays of $326,185 million, or 29.6 percent ($96,463 ÷ $326,185).[21] Federal government expendi-

TABLE 4 Overall balance sheet of services used and taxes paid by immigrants, United States, 1975

Immigrant cohort by year of entry	Services used by cohorts (Table 1, col. 12) (1)	Services used by natives (Table 1, col. 12) (2)	(2) − (1) (3)	Taxes paid by cohort (Table 2, col. 11) (4)	20% of taxes paid for pure public goods: .2 × (4) (5)	Taxes paid by natives (Table 2, col. 11) (6)	(4) − (6) (7)	(100%−20%) × (7) (8)	(3) + (5) + (8): Net effect of immigrant cohort on natives[a] (9)	(3) + [(4) − (6)]: Alternate calculation of (9)[b] (10)
1974	1,416	2,279	863	2,666	533	3,201	−535	−428	968	328
1973	1,200	2,279	1,079	3,302	660	3,201	101	81	1,820	1,180
1972	1,510	2,279	769	3,077	615	3,201	−124	− 99	1,285	645
1971	1,233	2,279	1,046	3,140	628	3,201	− 61	− 49	1,625	985
1970	1,659	2,279	620	3,011	602	3,201	−190	−152	1,070	430
1965–69	1,941	2,279	338	3,552	710	3,201	351	281	1,329	689
1960–64	2,247	2,279	32	4,064	813	3,201	863	690	1,535	895
1950–59	2,292	2,279	13	3,927	785	3,201	726	581	1,353	713

[a] Per immigrant family.

[b] Per immigrant family; no allowance for public goods contribution.

tures were 67 percent ($356.8 ÷ $532.8) of total government expenditures,[22] so the public goods categories constitute 20 percent (67% × 29.6%) of all taxes. Hence 20 percent of taxes paid by immigrants are shown in column 5.

Next we consider other taxes. The differences between the amounts of taxes paid by immigrants and by natives are shown in column 7 of Table 4. To the extent that immigrants pay less or more than natives, immigrants are taking from, or giving to, natives through the public coffers, allowing for the services they use.

We may summarize the logic of the tax calculation as follows: Benefit to natives = (taxpaid services used by the average native family less taxpaid services used by the average immigrant family) + (20 percent of taxes paid by the immigrant family as contribution to expenditures on public goods) + (80 percent of the difference between taxes paid by the average native family and the average immigrant family—a negative quantity in some cases).

A calculation is also shown in column 10 of Table 4 for the less realistic but more "conservative" assumption that there is no public goods element in immigrants' taxes that immediately lowers the tax burden of natives (or increases benefits from the taxpaid services).

We are now in a position to sum the effects on a year-by-year basis. This summary is shown in column 9 of Table 4. There we see that in every year following entry (until the immigrants themselves retire, at which time their own children are supporting them through the Social Security and Medicare system) immigrants benefit natives through the public coffers. And a calculation of the net present value of the stream of differences shows that immigrants are a remarkably good investment at any conceivable rate of discount, if we consider these partial effects only. At a 3 percent discount rate—roughly the long-run riskless rate adjusted for inflation in the West—each immigrant family was worth about $20,600 to natives around 1975, to be compared with the mean yearly native family earnings of $11,037. At 6 percent the 1975 value would be about $15,800, and at 9 percent it would be about $12,400.

When thinking of the totality of the economic effect of immigrants on natives, one must take into account, in addition to the calculations discussed here, both capital dilution (with a negative effect on natives) and productivity (with a positive effect on natives). Estimation of these latter effects as well as the totality requires a macroeconomic model, plus some key parameter estimates such as the proportion of the returns to existing capital that are captured by immigrants.[23] But based on the transfers estimated here, one may conclude that the average immigrant is an excellent investment for taxpayers on almost any reasonable set of parameter estimates.

Discussion

A major limitation of these data is that inferences about life-cycle behavior are drawn from a cross-section; the difficulty is widely understood. Furthermore, the subgroups observed in the cross-section—cohorts that came to the United States in different years—differ from each other in relevant characteristics.[24] Yet this analysis takes all the cohorts to be proxies for some portion of a single cohort's economic life—a cohort that has not yet arrived and whose composition is therefore not yet known.

In principle it would be possible to isolate the effects of various characteristics such as education, age, and perhaps ethnicity in past cohorts, and then to estimate the economic effects of a cohort expected to have a particular mix of these characteristics. But the cohort-wide data shown here should provide fairly accurate general guidance, partly because average education has not changed greatly from cohort to cohort (though age and ethnic compositions have changed). The general logical consistency in the pattern of the various cohorts substantiates that the cohorts that have arrived in the past are reasonably similar and offer a reasonable basis for prediction of the effects of future cohorts. And in any case, there is no reason to make such disaggregated estimates for a synthetic cohort until we know the composition of the cohort and know also that it is very different from past cohorts in these respects. (Without further investigation, however, we can say that policies leading to higher education and lower age of immigrants will be beneficial to natives.)

The public-coffers benefits to natives from immigrants at present derive overwhelmingly from the age composition of natives rather than from behavioral characteristics of immigrants; this may be seen in the importance of the Social Security effect.

In sum, our analysis shows that the net balance of taxes paid and services received by immigrants has a positive effect on natives in every year. In other words, immigrants contribute more to the public coffers than they take from them. When looked at by natives as an investment, similar to such social capital as dams and roads, an immigrant family is an excellent investment worth somewhere between $15,000 and $20,000,[25] even calculated with relatively high rates for the social cost of capital.

Notes

This paper is based on my report, "What immigrants take from, and give to, the public coffers," submitted to the Select Commission on Immigration and Refugee Policy, 15 October 1980.

I appreciate help of various kinds from Jeremy Atack, Francine Blau, Barry Chiswick, Susan Forbes, Guillermina Jasso, Mark Rosenzweig, David Simon, Rita Simon, Richard Sullivan, and DaNien Tzang.

1 Hans P. Neisser, "The economics of a stationary population," *Social Research* (November 1944): 470–490; Francis Modigliani, "The life cycle hypothesis of saving, the demand for wealth, and the supply of capital," *Social Research* 33 (Summer 1966): 160–217; and Paul A. Samuelson, "Optimum social security in a life-cycle growth market," *International Economic Review* 16 (October 1975): 530.

2 W. Brian Arthur and Geoffrey McNicoll, "Samuelson, population, and intergenerational transfers," *International Economic Review* 19 (1978): 241–246.

3 If the elderly do come, they do not qualify for public retirement funds.

4 These objections may be found most readily in flyers and fundraising letters of the

Federation for American Immigration Reform (FAIR) and the Environmental Fund, though it is often unclear whether the statements are directed toward illegal immigrants or all immigrants. Roger Conner, FAIR's executive director, summarizes these objections in a recent newspaper article (though focusing on illegals); Roger Conner, "Immigration in the era of limits," *Los Angeles Times*, 17 February 1980, Part VI, page 5. See also *The Wall Street Journal*, editorial, 7 October 1980, p. 24.

5 Julian L. Simon, "The economic effect of Russian immigrants upon the veteran Israeli population: A cost-benefit analysis," *The Economic Quarterly* 23 (August 1976): 224–253 (in Hebrew); and "The really important effects of immigrants upon natives' incomes," in *Conference on Immigration*, ed. Barry Chiswick (Washington, D.C.: American Enterprise Institute, 1982).

6 Simon (1982), cited in note 5. This article deals with the transfer effect in stylized fashion.

7 Comparisons have been made of married-couple families with (a) only the male an immigrant and (b) only the female an immigrant, to see whether including only males introduces bias. Direct comparisons holding entry date and/or age of immigrants constant are inappropriate because the female immigrant's native-born husband is, on average, several years older than the male immigrant. With this in mind, the comparisons do not indicate any major difference. Perhaps more convincing, adding to the general sample the families in which only the female is an immigrant does not much affect the results.

Because the numbers of male and female immigrants are not the same—the number of female immigrants in the childbearing ages, all in all, is somewhat greater than the number of males—the procedure is not perfect. But the numbers are close enough for most practical purposes.

8 George Gray of the Bureau of the Census, who was in charge of the SIE survey, said that there is no obvious explanation for the reporting of 1975 earnings and services used by the cohort that entered in 1976. The earnings could be earnings abroad, but the services could not be so explained. The likeliest explanation in his view is confusion on the part of the interviewers, who were not instructed specifically on this matter.

9 Additionally, discounting for a quarter century and more reduces the meaning of contemporary events attached to these persons.

10 Again, the fact that Social Security payments are "earned" is not relevant in this context. Whether a payment is "earned" or is "charity" refers to the legal and ethical obligations between persons. Our focus here is only on whether certain flows do or do not take place.

11 United States Department of Health, Education, and Welfare, *Statistics of Public Elementary and Secondary Day Schools* (Washington, D.C., Fall 1975), Table 2.

12 Persons in the institutional population among natives and within the various immigrant cohorts are not included in the SIE sample. We can be sure, however, that institutionalized persons are found in larger proportions among natives because the elderly constitute a large part of that subpopulation. But given that less than one percent of the population is in institutions—implying an average expenditure of perhaps $60 per person in total (even less for public expenditures)—the matter may safely be neglected.

13 United States Department of Health, Education, and Welfare, Publication No. (SRS) 76-03150, NCSS Report B-1 (12/75), *Medical Assistance (Medicaid) Finances Under Title XIX of the Social Security Act* (Washington, D.C., December 1975).

14 Barry R. Chiswick, "The effects of Americanization on the earnings of foreign-born men," *Journal of Political Economy* 86, no. 5 (1978): 897–921; and Francine D. Blau, "Immigration and labor earnings in early twentieth century America," in *Research in Population Economics*, Vol. 2, ed. Julian L. Simon and Julie DaVanzo (Greenwich: JAI Press, 1980).

15 David North, *Seven Years Later: The Experiences of the 1970 Cohort of Immigrants in the United States*, R & D Monograph 71, US Department of Labor, ETA (Washington, D.C.: ETA, 1979), p. 75.

16 Edgar K. Browning and William R. Johnson, *The Distribution of the Tax Burden* (Washington, D.C.: American Enterprise Institute, 1979).

17 The distribution can be partially estimated from these data (and I do so in the full report), but unfortunately the raw data are coded "$50,000 or more" for individuals and "$75,000 or more" for families despite the fact that the raw data included actual figures for the highest-income families (top-coding here is intended to avoid disclosure; it was also done for data on assets such as value of home, and liquid assets). Therefore, it is conceivable that two groups with the same calculated mean income from our data would actually pay different amounts of taxes because (a) distributions of families with the same mean income can pay different amounts of taxes, and (b) due to top-coding, the actual means can be different even though the calculated means are the same.

18 The White House, *Economic Report of the President* (Washington, D.C.: Government Printing Office, 1980), pp. 288, 203.

19 Browning and Johnson, cited in note 16, p. 51.

20 The average immigrant may here be considered to be like the average taxpayer, subject to adjustments mentioned in the text below.

21 *Economic Report of the President*, cited in note 18, p. 284.

22 *Economic Report of the President*, cited in note 18, p. 288.

23 Simon (1982), cited in note 5, develops such a model and it supports the conclusion that the average immigrant is a net economic benefit to society.

24 This can be seen in the background tables available from the author.

25 This is so even when calculated with relatively high rates for the social cost of capital. The amounts are in 1975 dollars, to be compared with mean yearly native family earnings of about $11,000 in that year.

The children of retired immigrants support their parents with their taxes, just as the children of natives do for their parents

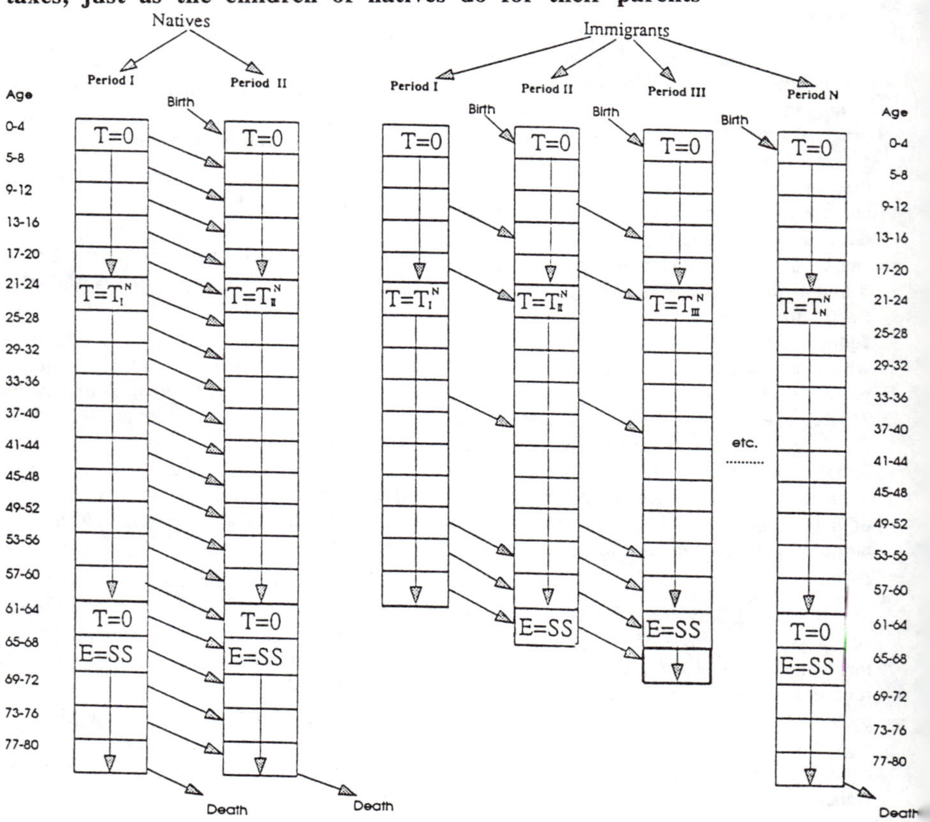

PART VI

NATURAL RESOURCES

[29]

Foreword

The key idea in this paper is composed of two propositions: (1) The elasticity of demand with respect to price is hypothesized to be greater for raw materials than for finished goods. (2) Proposition 1 explains the terms of trade being against natural resources. I have not gathered evidence to test the hypothesis about the elasticities, and it would not be easy to make fair and reasonable comparisons. But it should be worth the doing.

APPENDIX B

Are Natural Resources an Increasing Constraint upon Growth?

I. INTRODUCTION

Writers on economic growth from Jevons (1865) to Kaldor (1957) to Samuelson (1975) have mostly regarded natural resources[1] as a special kind of brake on economic growth. And in the case of economists such as Kaldor and Samuelson, resources have been seen as a qualification to the proposition that growth might continue forever in a benign fashion. Yet – curious behaviour for economists – this argument has not been formalized or even compared to the historical record, but has only been offered as an *ex cathedra* truism.[2]

Examined more closely, however, the proposition that natural resources are a special kind of brake on growth is far from obvious or unarguable. As many writers have pointed out, natural resources have had progressively decreasing importance in the global budget (Barnett and Morse, 1963) and in influencing the fates of particular countries, for example, Japan and Hong Kong (Bauer, 1981). This fact is not easily consistent with the conventional idea that the resource situation grows worse rather than better with increasing use of resources as history unfolds. And even casual inspection of the historical record shows that resource costs have not been rising, no matter what measurement you look at.[3] Yet more needs to be said on the subject to make the point convincing.

This appendix tackles the question as follows. After some clarification of concepts, the historical record is examined. We see long-term trends of falling cost of raw materials as far back as there is data (to 2500 BC in some cases). And we also have evidence on elasticity of substitution between raw materials and other productive inputs that makes sense of the falling costs. But there is no logical necessity that the future will see a continuation of this trend, just as there can never be such a logical necessity for any prediction. And many persons interested in this topic have opined – usually based on the assumption of fixity or finitude of resources plus Malthusian diminishing returns – that these benign trends will reverse in the future. Though a very long observed trend might itself be basis enough for a prudent forecaster to prefer its evidence to contrary theoretical speculation, the argument for a continued trend of cost reduction in natural resources would be stronger if there is also plausible theoretical reason for such a trend. Therefore, this appendix continues with a criticism of the standard argument for long-run increasing scarcity. It then proceeds to offer a theoretical framework which suggests that continuation of cost reduction is not impossible or implausible. This theoretical discussion begins with physical principles and then continues with economic arguments built upon those physical principles. The reader anxious to get to the new idea may skip the review section and jump to the end.

A central issue is how to characterize resources, of which copper and land and oil will serve as examples of different types. Resources clearly are a kind of capital upon which we draw. Natural resources *seem* different from factories and dams, however. And this is the nub of the seeming difference: we are accustomed to thinking that we augment our stock of non-resource capital by diverting some production from consumption to savings. But we do not usually think of augmenting our stocks of copper, land and oil in the same fashion; this seems to fly in the face of apparently commonsensical physical facts. I do not think that the appropriate physical interpretation of this apparent difference is as common sense has it, though.[4] I shall try to show that an economic interpretation leads to thinking of natural resources as quite analogous to other capital in respect to their stocks being augmentable, at a cost not greater than other capital, and at a cost that is not increasing with time but rather is decreasing. If this is so, then natural resources do not require special attention in the context of discussions of growth theory.

II. ABOUT THE CONCEPTS OF SCARCITY AND COST[5]

Before beginning on the main work, a few comments on key concepts seem needed, beginning with 'scarcity'. It is more congenial for economists than for physical scientists to consider cost – outgo in physical or money terms, relative to some other quantity – as the appropriate measure of scarcity, rather than an actual or hypothetical estimate of physical quantities. But not all economists are satisfied with such a cost concept. Nor is the appropriate cost index always obvious. Therefore, some discussion of cost and scarcity is needed.

Ask yourself: if copper – or oil or any other good – were much scarcer today than it actually is, what would be the evidence of this economic scarcity. That is, what are the signs – the criteria – of a raw material being in short supply? Upon reflection perhaps you will agree that a complete absence of the material will not be a sign of scarcity. We will not reach up to the shelf and suddenly find that it is completely bare. It is obvious that the scarcity of any raw material would only gradually increase. Long before the shelf would be bare, individuals and firms, the latter operating purely out of the self-interested drive to make future profits, would be taking steps to hoard supplies for future resale so that the shelf would never be completely bare. Of course the price of the hoarded material would be high, but there still would be some quantities to be found at some price, just as there always has been some small amount of food for sale even in the midst of the very worst famines.

The preceding observation points to a key sign of what we generally mean by increasing scarcity: a price that has persistently risen. More generally, cost and price will be our basic measures of scarcity. But there is often reason to question which measure of cost or price is more relevant in a discusion of resource scarcity.

In some situations market prices can mislead us. The price of a scarce material may not rise high enough to 'clear the market' – that is, to discourage enough potential buyers so that supply and demand come to be equal as they ultimately will come to be in a free market (or even in a satisfactorily adjusted socialist system). If the price is deliberately held down by the seller or by the government, there may be waiting lines or rationing, which may also be taken as signs of scarcity. But though lines and rationing may be efficient and fair ways of allocating scarce materials in the short run, in the longer run they are so wasteful that every sort of society tends to prevent them by letting the price rise enough to clear the market. Therefore we are not likely to see lines and rationing if there is a long-run (as contrasted to a temporary) scarcity of a raw material.

In general, then, if the scarcity of a raw material increases, its price will rise. But the converse need not be true; the price may rise even without a 'true' increase in scarcity. For example, a strong cartel may successfully raise prices, as OPEC did in 1973 even though the cost of producing oil remained unchanged. This suggests that the price in the market is not always the best measure of scarcity, and therefore we should also consider other measures.

Production costs come quickly to mind as an index of scarcity. We may measure the cost of a ton of copper by measuring the amount of workers' time necessary to produce it. But there are obvious difficulties with this approach. Capital equipment may be substituted for labour in order to economize on the use of workers' time; no allowance for the cost of the equipment is made in this approach. And some workers' time is more expensive that others'; an hour of a college-trained technician's time is worth more in the market than an hour of a pick-and-shovel man. Production costs measured in labour hours rather than in money may also be difficult to interpret because of changes in wage.

Another possible cost index is unit cost measured in payments for labour plus payments for capital. Barnett and Morse (1963) showed that, by this measure from 1870 to 1957 raw-material cost fell in much the same manner as do the other indices, but faster than in most indices. But this measurement also is not easy to make.

A more conventional approach is to compare the unit market price of, say, copper to the unit market price of some other good that seems to be unchanging – say, grain. But the cost of producing grain (and most other things) has also been changing over the years owing to changes in seeds, fertilizers, technology and so on. So if the cost of grain has been falling, then the cost of copper would be falling even if the relationship between the two prices – the terms of trade – has remained the same over the years.

A wrinkle on the terms-of-trade approach is to compare the price of copper to the price of a good whose production technology has changed little for a long time – say, a haircut. But the wages of barbers have gone up over the years, as can be seen from the fact that a barber in the US now has a much higher standard of living than did a US barber 100 years ago, because the wages of people in other occupations have risen owing to gains in technology and education. So this comparison, too, does not give us a 'true' or 'absolute' measure of changes in the price of copper.

Yet another approach is to examine the price trend of the source of the raw material – for example, the price of farmland instead of the price of grain, or the price of copper mines instead of the price of copper – relative to some other goods. But the price of the resource will rise if there is a technological improvement in production methods even if there is no change in the 'scarcity' of the product; the price of good farmland in the US rises when crop yields go up or when new machinery is introduced (though the price of poor farmland falls because it is no longer profitable to use such land at all).

And as yet we have said nothing about inflation. But allowing for price changes in a commodity due to changes in the general price level also raises a host of difficult questions.

How to choose among this welter of measures of public cost and price? We must accept the inevitable: there can be no 'true' or 'absolute' public measure of cost or price. Rather, different measures of cost give different sorts of information, useful for different purposes. But this we can say with assurance: the average cost of all consumer goods taken together – an index of consumer prices – has fallen over the years in more-developed countries, measured in terms of what an unskilled worker can buy; this is shown by the long-run increase in the standard of living. Therefore, if a raw material has remained at least level in price compared to the average of all (or of consumer) goods, its 'real' cost has fallen. And in fact the price of mineral natural resources has declined even more sharply than has the average price of other commodities, as we shall see shortly. Furthermore, all other measures of mineral costs have also declined over the long run. (See the next section. Also see Barnett and Morse, 1963; Simon, 1981. One may wish to compare Smith, 1979, though I do not feel that his work calls Barnett's conclusions in the same book into question at all.) Hence we can be quite sure that the cost of mineral natural resources has declined substantially, by any reasonable test.

A more personal – but often relevant – test of scarcity is whether you and I (and other people) feel that we can afford to buy the material. That is, the relationship between price and income may matter. If the price of food remains constant but income falls sharply, then we feel that food is more scarce. By a similar test, if our wages rise while the price of oil remains constant, our fuller pockets lead us to feel that oil is getting less scarce.

A related test of scarcity is the importance of the material in one's budget. One is not likely to say nowadays that salt has become appreciably more scarce even if its price doubles, because salt accounts for an insignificant share of our expenditures. (Once, though, salt was a precious commodity, which itself illustrates the process being described here.)

To restate the main theme: price, together with related measures such as production cost and share of income, is the appropriate test of scarcity at any given moment. What matters to us as consumers is how much we have to pay to obtain goods that give us particular services; from this standpoint, it couldn't matter less how much iron or oil there 'really' is in some natural 'stockpile'. Therefore, to understand the economics of natural resources, it is crucial to understand that the most appropriate economic measure of scarcity is the price of a natural resource compared to some relevant benchmark. Future scarcity is our interest. Our task, then, is to forecast future prices of raw materials.

III. RESOURCES AND THE SERVICES THEY PROVIDE

It is not capital itself – and the stock of natural resources clearly should be thought of as capital – that is of interest to us, but rather the services that we get from capital. For example, it is not the computer itself, but rather the computing services we get from it, and then the use of those computing services in the production of other goods, that affects us. Similarly, it is not copper or land or oil that matters to us, but rather the services that they render in the creation of final products. Therefore the relevant measure of the stock of capital is the cost of the services that we get from the capital. The market price of new pieces of capital is an upper-bound estimate on this cost of services because of progressive increases in productivity of capital, for example, the cost of computing services has fallen sharply over the years.

If it can be shown that the cost of the services we get from raw materials has fallen as fast as the cost of producer-good capital services, then it would seem reasonable to conclude that raw materials have not been an increasing bottleneck to the production of final goods. And if there has not been a trend toward greater bottleneck constraint in the past due to raw materials, then – in the absence of reason to believe that we are now at a structural turning point, a matter dealt with in section VIII – there is at least a *prima facie* case that raw materials will not constitute a greater constraint in the future than in the past. So, given that standard series of trends in capital prices do not show much difference from trends in final goods prices, and given that raw material prices have tended to fall at least as fast as prices of final goods, the evidence suggests that the economic element that supplies services on a continuing basis – that is, capital – is increasing as satisfactorily when we consider natural resource 'capital' as when we think about other capital. Of course this notion of capital is counter-intuitive, because one cannot easily imagine looking at an increasing stock of copper or energy the way one can look at an increasing number of trucks. But when we reflect how fuzzy are our economic notions about the nature of *any* capital, this notion of natural resource capital may seem easier to accept.

To (forgive me) ground the argument a bit more, let us consider farmland. As discussed in the footnote on p. 182 of appendix A, the valuation of farmland in the market is a neat function of the land's output, about 3.5 : 1 throughout history and geography (see Clark, 1957, pp. 637–51). And we shall see that the price of farm output has been falling throughout history relative to other goods. This suggests that there has not been an increasing scarcity of farmland. And given that total agricultural output has been expanding and price has been falling, there is no basis for thinking that the underlying land-related mechanism – the stock of agricultural land capital – has not been increasing its capacity as fast as other capital.

Or consider land for housing: the price of quality-adjusted housing has not been going up over the years, and floor space is the central service that we seek from housing and from land for housing. Of course the price of a housing acre in Manhattan has been going up, just as has a farm acre's price in central Illinois, but this by itself says nothing about the mechanism yielding land services.

So far nothing has been said about *why* the cost of raw materials has not been rising, or whether there is theoretical reason to believe that raw material costs may continue to fall in the future. These theoretical issues will be addressed in a later section.

IV. OBSERVED TRENDS IN RAW-MATERIAL SCARCITY

This section first considers trends in various indices of the cost of raw materials as materials, focusing on minerals. Then we shall dig a bit deeper into the trends in the cost of the services we get from raw materials in production. And last, we shall mention studies of natural resources in a production function to see how substitutable they are for other capital.

The historical cost record of raw materials is easy to summarize. Following on Barnett and Morse (1963), I have written about natural resources at length (1981), so I will be brief here: scarcity – as measured by the economically meaningful indicator of cost or price – has been *decreasing* rather than increasing in the long run for all raw materials except lumber and oil. Figures B.1 and B.2 show this effect for copper, which is representative of all the metals. And this trend of falling prices of copper has been going on a very long time.[6] The price of copper in labour time in the year AD 1 was about 120 times as great as it is in 1982 in the US. The price of iron was about 240 times as great then as now, and in 800 BC it was 360 times as great, while in 1800 BC it was 1620 times as great (calculated from data in Clark, 3rd edition, 1957, excursus, p. 652ff and Childe, 1942/1964).

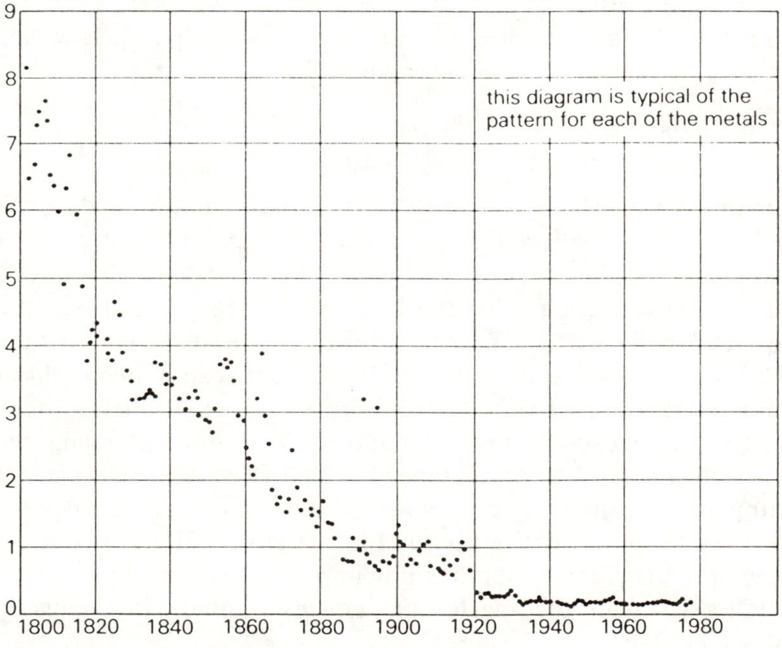

FIGURE B.1 The scarcity of copper as measured by its price relative to wages

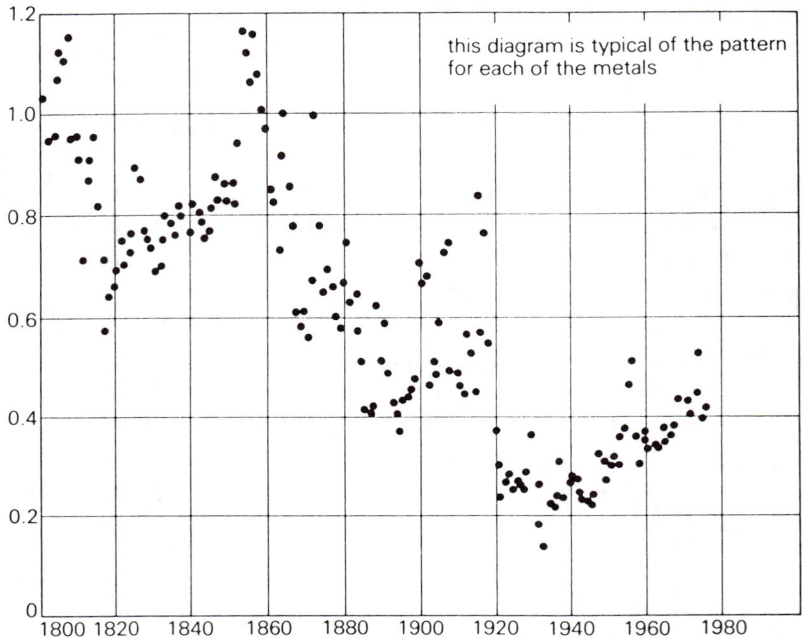

FIGURE B.2 The scarcity of copper as measured by its price relative to the consumer price index

Figures B.3 and B.4 show the trends for materials grouped together, in relation to non-extractive product prices and in relation to unit costs.

The available data are for the US, but the story is not essentially different for the LDCs. The price of raw materials in labour time in LDCs has not fallen as markedly as in MDCs, because income has not risen as markedly in LDCs, but the price surely has fallen *somewhat* in LDCs, too, because the world market price is much the same everywhere and income has risen somewhat in LDCs. And there is reason to suppose that the price of raw materials relative to consumer prices has fallen even more sharply in LDCs than in MDCs because the production of other goods has not improved as sharply in LDCs as in MDCs (though the matter of services tempers this judgement somewhat).

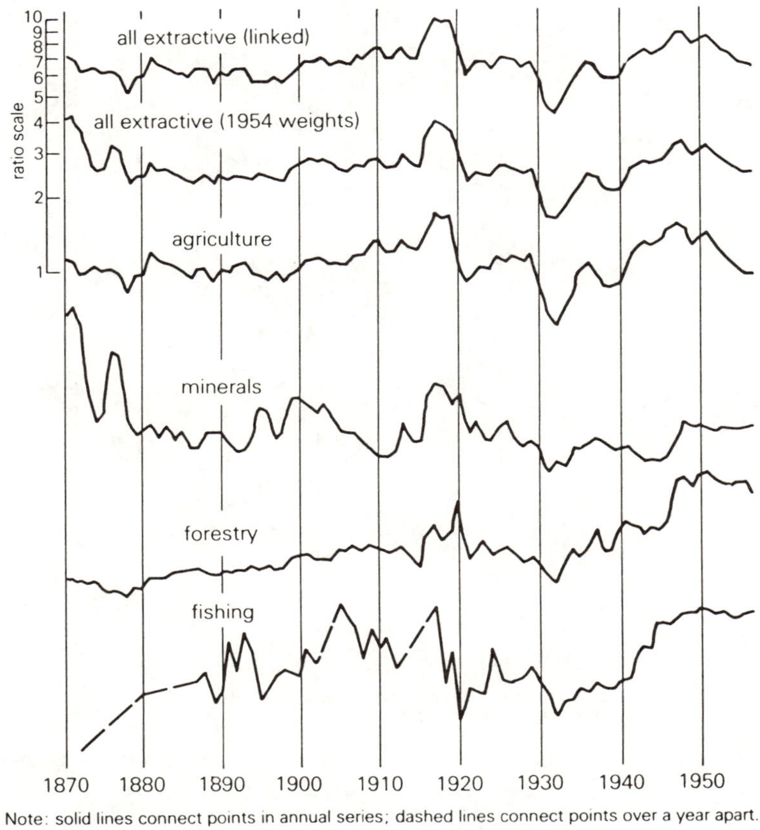

FIGURE B.3 Trends in unit prices of extracting products relative to non-extractive products in the US, 1870–1957
(*Source:* Barnett and Morse, 1963, p. 210)

Food is an especially important resource, and the evidence is especially strong that we are on a benign trend despite rising population. The long-run price of food relative to wages, and even relative to consumer products, is shown in figures B.5, B.6 and B.7. Famine deaths have decreased even in absolute terms, let alone relative to population, in the past century, a matter which pertains particularly to the poor countries. *Per capita* food consumption is up over the last 30 years (figure B.8). And there are no data showing that the

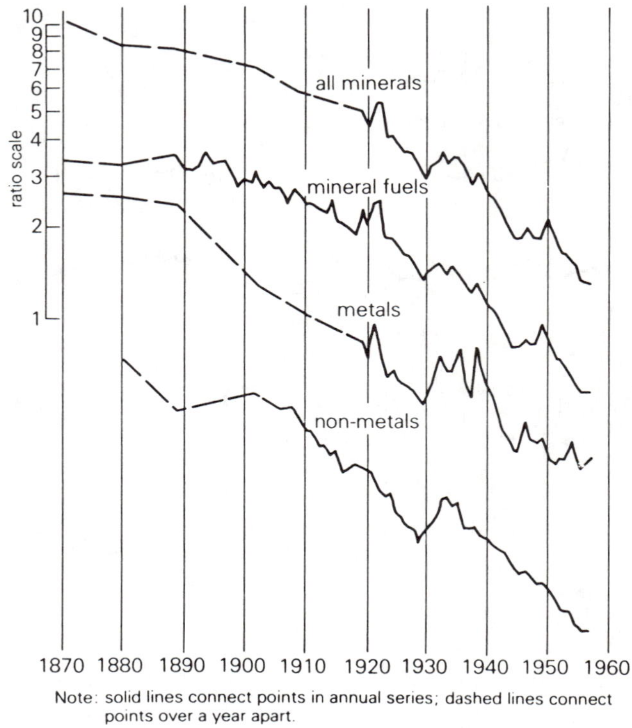

FIGURE B.4 US minerals: labour costs per unit of output, 1870–1957
(*Source:* Barnett and Morse, 1963, p. 181)

bottom of the income scale is faring worse, or even has failed to share in the general improvement, as the average has improved. Given the observed increase in mean income in the poor countries since the Second World War, and given also the observed lack of widening of the income distributions, there is *prima facie* reason to think that the bottom of the income scale is faring better with respect to food as well as other goods. Africa's food production *per capita* is down, but no informed person thinks that has anything to do with physical conditions; instead, it rather clearly stems from governmental and other social conditions.

There is now an empirical literature of considerable size estimating the substitution of natural resources and other input factors under

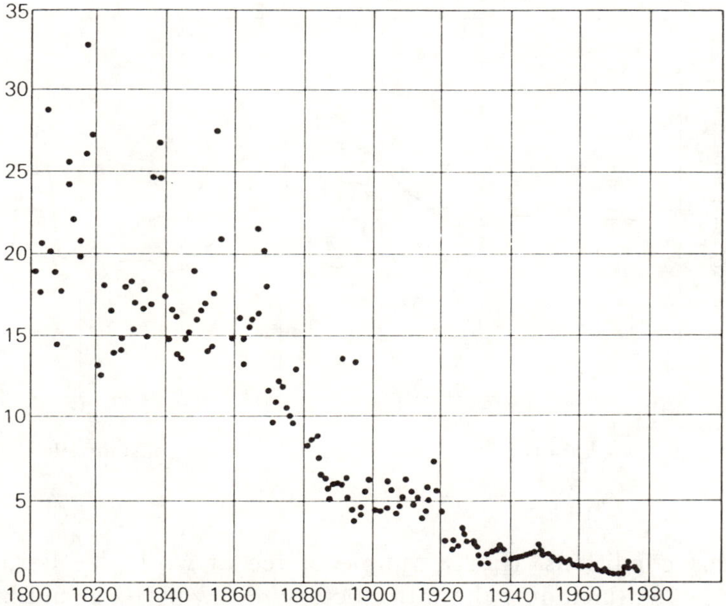

FIGURE B.5 The price of wheat relative to wages in the US

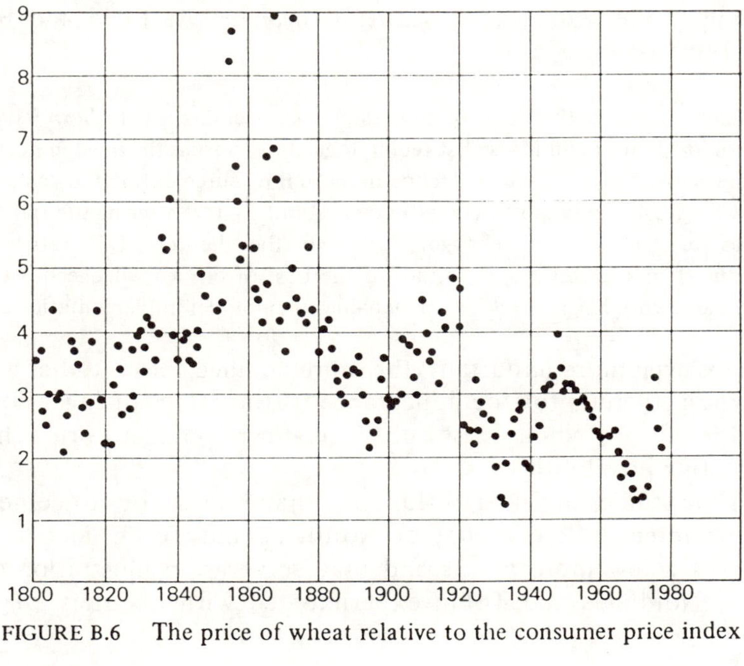

FIGURE B.6 The price of wheat relative to the consumer price index

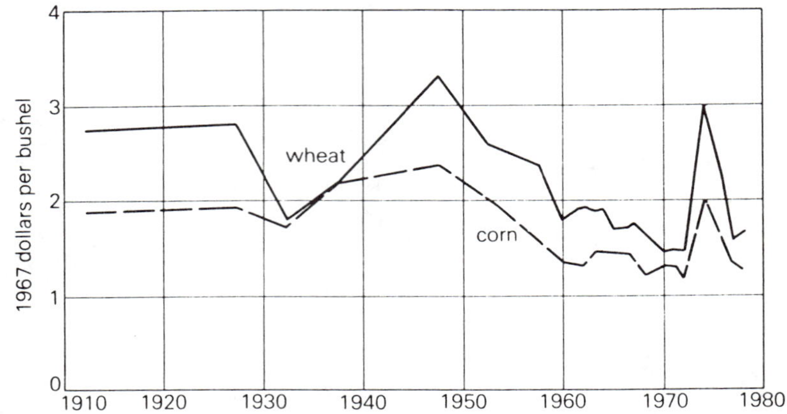

FIGURE B.7 Export prices of US wheat and corn in constant 1967 dollars

various conditions. (For a sample of recent work, see Berndt and Field, 1981, including the introductory review by Field and Berndt.) This literature is not directly relevant to the question at hand, however, because it does not relate such factors as population and income changes to the substitution process. As Field and Berndt (1981, p. 13) say:

> Finally, there is the issue of modeling technical change. In *Scarcity and Growth* Barnett and Morse list technological progress as the most important determinant of the secular decline in natural resource extraction costs and prices. Regrettably very little is known about factors altering the rate and bias of technological change. Although the theoretical literature on induced innovation is substantial, to the best of our knowledge this type of framework has not yet been amenable to empirical implementation.

Perhaps even more important, the more detailed these studies are, the less room there is for the appearance of the effect of invention and development of wholly new substitutes in response to price changes of existing possibilities.

Of the studies in this tradition, one that at least tries to come close to our interest here is that of Nordhaus and Tobin, and hence it deserves a few more words and may serve as an illustration of the genre. Nordhaus and Tobin experimented with a variety of three-

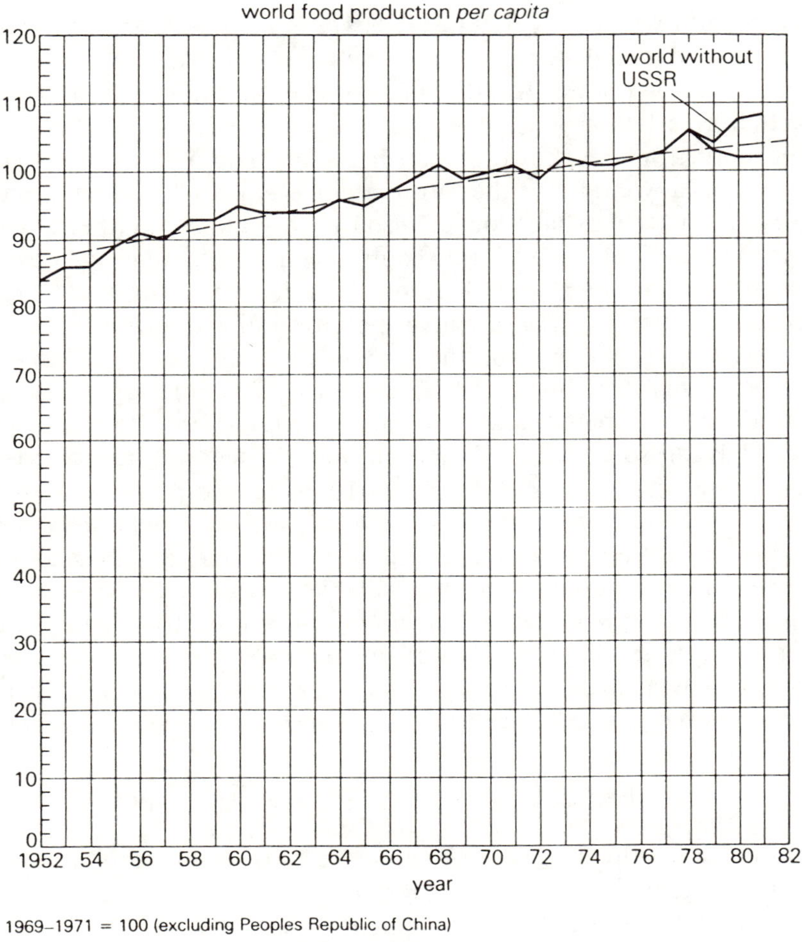

FIGURE B.8 World food production *per capita*
(*Source:* William J. Hudson, private communication)

factor (labour, capital, natural resources) production functions to find those that seem to explain best changes in the national product over time. Using a 'best fit' function, they estimated the elasticity of substitution between (a) natural resources and (b) a composite of labour and physical capital, regressing the ratio of the distributive shares on a function of the ratio of the inputs. The result was interpreted as an 'elasticity of substitution between neo-classical factors and resources of about 2 . . .' (1972, pp. 63–70). Also consistent with the observed facts is that technological change is natural-resource-saving relative to other factors of production. Irrespective of whether this latter or a high elasticity of substitution is the more important influence, however, Nordhaus and Tobin concluded that if 'the past is any guide for the future, there seems to be little reason to worry about the exhaustion of resources which the market already treats as economic goods'. (Of course some goods may not now be treated as economic, and therefore may have inappropriate prices placed on them. This is also true of pollution in many cases.)

A useful perspective on future raw-material scarcity is that of worst-case analysis. Singer (1981) offers rough calculations suggesting that: (a) given a reasonable time for transition – 100–200 years – we could rely on solar energy for all our energy needs at no worse than a doubling of present energy costs; (b) energy costs are now three-fourths of all raw material costs in the US; and (c) given our capacity to find substitutes for all the important non-energy raw materials in other raw materials that are available in vast quantities by any time measure, raw materials (including those used for energy) must be a bearably small proportion of our incomes even if (on his worst-case analysis assuming no major advances in technology) the prices of non-energy raw materials level off considerably higher than now.

V. SOME THEORY OF RESOURCE AVAILABILITY

In response to the suggestion that the facts of resource price trends are fundamental, Hardin (1982) responds, 'No, the facts are not fundamental. The theory is fundamental.' The 'theory' Hardin refers to is the Malthusian concept of diminishing returns. But that concept has two defects for our purposes here. First, if the concept is given content by specifying a period of the order of a human life expectation, give or take an expected length of life, that 'theory' fails completely in its predictive record; the trends have been downward throughout history despite forecasters having made dire predictions implicitly based on that concept since the beginning of recorded history and surely before.

Second, if instead of testing the 'theory' on the past they look to the future, Hardin and colleagues do not – as is their wont –

specify any observable (or even identifiable) time period during which prices will rise permanently to levels above what they are now, but simply say increased scarcity will happen 'sometime', then their theory is meaningless scientifically, according to the standard canon of scientific meaning, because a theory about 'sometime' cannot be tested, even in principle.

Hardin and similar thinkers certainly are correct, however, when they say that there is never logical entailment that past trends will continue their direction. Therefore we seek some structural knowledge of raw material scarcity. The matter will be considered first from a physical point of view, and then from an economic point of view. We shall not arrive at a theory supporting a uni-directional prediction for future trends. But I believe that we can safely conclude that there is no reason why past trends *cannot* continue.

The question that we wish to address theoretically must be kept firmly in mind: must the cost of one or more important raw materials rise in the long run? The doomsayers assert that there is theoretical reason to answer the question in the affirmative, that there is no escaping a rise in raw material cost in some very long run. Their reasoning is as follows: the reservoir of some raw material *X* is fixed, meaning that the reservoir cannot be increased just as the reservoir of authentic *Mona Lisa* paintings cannot be increased. (They have in mind, however, generic materials such as, say, copper and land and energy rather than one-of-a-kinds such as the *Mona Lisa* or Julius Erving; about those one-of-a-kinds there is no dispute.) Assume that the demand for the use of the material will (a) increase due to population growth or income growth or both, or (b) the reservoir will decline due to some of it being lost or otherwise unavailable, or (c) there will be both increased demand and decreased reservoir. Because (Hardin and like-minded writers assume) humankind first exploits the richest lodes and ores (that is, the lodes and ores cheapest to mine), successive mining operations will be successively more expensive; implicitly, those writers are assuming that eventually there will be either stationarity of technology or a growth in technology slower than the rate of decrease in richness of lode. Under those assumed conditions, cost must indeed increase.

Elsewhere (1981, chapters 1–3) I have said much more about the nature of technological forecasts and the variety in the forecasts made by various 'experts', so I will not repeat it here.

Certainly costs do increase during some periods, as reflected in real price rises at some times in history. And it is reasonable to suppose that during those periods the doomsday conditions hold (though price rises may sometimes be due to non-physical causes such as the formation of OPEC).

The optimistic cornucopian response to the pessimistic doomsayers is that technology to exploit the material will increase faster than the decline in richness of the reservoir. But whether this will be true or not is a matter of judgement; the history that it was so in the past is considered persuasive by the optimists but not persuasive by the pessimists. And there the matter has rested.

The only standard economic theory seemingly relevant has been Hotelling's theory of exploitation of particular exhaustible resources. That theory – which was originally intended to apply to a single mine rather than to a generic material – simply assumes the conclusion of exhaustibility and thereby formalizes the doomsday scenario sketched above. The ensuing body of theory has produced some lovely propositions which, however, are irrelevant if price will be falling rather than rising.

Stiglitz (1979) offered a theory in the neo-classical tradition which, on conventional assumptions, concludes there is no danger of resources being a brake upon economic development in the short term or intermediate term. Stiglitz's analysis is quite reasonable. It does, however, understate the optimistic outlook for raw materials because it concentrates on the substitution of capital for resources and gives short shrift to the substitution of one resource for another, the latter being the process which, in my view, is dominating, as we shall discuss shortly. It is perhaps for this reason that Stiglitz asserts that his analysis does not apply in the long run ('I am concerned here with the more immediate future', 1977, p. 37); that assertion provides a handhold which his critics can use to grapple with him.

Certainly it is correct, however, that there is never logical entailment that past trends will continue their direction. Therefore we will later seek some structural knowledge of raw-material scarcity.

Another sort of theory by economists is that of Georgescu-Roegen (1971) and Daly (1977), which expands on the assumption that energy is finite and that change in entropy should be taken into account in current economic decisions. The thrust of this theory, which they call 'neo-Malthusian', is to allocate the limited energy among generations and individuals in such fashion as to maximize a criterion of welfare which includes per-person income as well as moral well-being as measured by values specified by those writers.

It seems appropriate to illustrate the thinking of this school of thought because it is so different from the mainstream of economic thought. Unlike standard economic thought which takes tastes as given, these writers believe that the economist should choose goals for the society as well as provide intellectual machinery to help achieve goals. (Daly's book, *Steady State Economics*, is subtitled *The Economics of Biophysical Equilibrium and Moral Growth*.) As Daly puts it:

> The temper of the modern age resists any discussion of the Ultimate End. Teleology and purpose, the dominant concepts of an earlier time, were banished from the mechanistic, reductionistic, positivistic mode of thought that came to be identified with the most recent phase of the evolution of science. Economics followed suit by reducing ethics to the level of personal tastes. No questions are asked about whether individual priorities are right or wrong, or even about how they are formed. The same goes for collective priorities. Whatever happens to interest the mass public is assumed to be in the public interest. Our modern refusal to reason about the Ultimate End merely assures the incoherence of our priorities, both individually and collectively. It leads to the tragedy of Herman Melville's Captain Ahab, whose means were all rational, but whose purpose was insane. The apparent purpose of growth economics is to seek to satisfy infinite wants by means of infinite production. This is about as wise as chasing a white whale, and the high rationality of the means employed cannot be used to justify the insanity of purpose. Rational means simply make insane purposes all the more dangerous. Among our presumed 'infinite' wants is there not the desire to be free from the tyranny of infinite wants? Is there not a desire for finite wants, for only good wants? If the assumption of infinite wants includes the desire for finite wants (and how could it be excluded except as a moral commandment that 'though shalt want more'?), then we have a kind of liar's paradox – one of our 'infinite' wants is the want for finite wants! And even if wants were infinite, it does not follow that infinite production, even if possible, would be capable of satisfying more than a finite subset of our 'infinite' wants. Some logical cracks thus appear in one of growth mania's cornerstones. (1977, pp. 76–7)

Georgescu-Roegen shares this viewpoint, as seen in his comment on the paper of Daly's from which the above quotation was taken:

This paper represents an improvement on Daly's earlier pleas. One new point deserves special attention: it is the map in which the hierarchy of ends and means is correlated with the categories of disciplines that keep the human mind continuously on the run. To have a single element by which everything is in the last analysis guided or judged has been a need felt by all truly philosophical schools. All great philosophers have imagined, if not a religious God, at least a philosophical one as the ultimate criterion, not for what ought to be, but for what must be. There is an indisputable need for an ultimate end by which we can judge which of our actions are 'good' and which are 'bad'. We always need a criterion of some sort or other. To take a simple but appropriate example: if the price ratio of coffee and meat is, say, 5 to 2, and I spend my budget at a point where my marginal rate of substitution between those commodities is 7 to 4, that is 'bad'. The criterion of maximum utility for my preference structure tells me so. But why should we not also ask the further question: are my preferences good or bad? Daly's point is that for this question we must turn to the ultimate end. This paper thus strengthens the impression emerging from his previous writings that the essence of Daly's conception is not economic or demographic, but, rather, ethical – a great merit in a period in which economics has been reduced to a timeless kinematics. As a befitting commandment for the ultimate end of a religion that should help mankind to survive and lead a decent life, I would suggest 'Love thy species as thyself.' Such a religion would certainly bring about the amiable community for which Daly fights untiringly. But as intimated earlier, the most challenging enterprise is to establish any religious faith, any faith in an ultimate end. (Georgescu-Roegen, pp. 102–3)

Explicit here is a turning-back on the notion of exchange value as the guiding principle of the economy, and a return to the use value concept. As Georgescu-Roegen puts it:

[I]n order to arrive at the 'true' cost of any material commodity, we must know the true values of natural resources *in situ*, which constitute the first cost item. Some economists trained in the neoclassical tradition have occasionally spoken of the 'true scarcity value' of natural resources *in situ*. Yet, to my knowledge, the determination of these values is a problem totally ignored by all tints of economic theory. (1977, p. 99)

Georgescu-Roegen rejects auction-based prices as inadequate because future generations cannot now bid on an asset such as the *Mona Lisa* or on current natural resource supplies.

The Roegen–Daly view – and also the view of the *Limits to Growth* group, Ehrlich and most 'ecologists' and popular writers on these subjects – rests squarely on the assumption of finitude. That concept, however, not only is not self-evident, but upon close examination turns out to be vacuous. A detailed examination of that matter now follows.

Whether the moral point of view of Georgescu-Roegen and Daly causes acceptance of a finite view of resources, or vice versa, or whether both are influenced by a common third element, is unknown to me. But this set of views does lead deductively to the conclusion that government must control the allocation of natural resources in a much more active fashion than is the case with the standard framework of economic thought which takes tastes as given, and (separately) which does not put the assumption of finitude of resources at the centre of the analysis. More specifically, Daly advocates government control of births with a license system, maximum limits on income and wealth, and government quotas on the extraction of natural resources (1977, pp. 53–63).

Implicit in the analysis of Daly, Georgescu-Roegen and other economic entropists is that additional people do not affect humankind's welfare or destiny except in their roles as consumers of resources. Given the fixed stock of energy, there is no place in their system for the production of new knowledge to affect long-run welfare. Of course these writers might have brought the production of new knowledge into their system by considering it as a way of using a given amount of energy more efficiently from a welfare point of view, but they do not do so; re-distribution among income classes and over time, and limitation of numbers of people, are the devices they suggest for improvement of the human lot (e.g. Daly, 1977, p. 151ff.) '[B]y focusing on ... the ability of new technologies to tap new resources, economists fall into the trap of ignoring the ultimate finitude of the common denominator of all useful things, low-entropy, matter-energy, which is scarce in an absolute sense' (Daly, 1977, p. 25).

Economists have long discussed the role of substitution of one raw material for another, though this mechanism is not part of the conventional pessimistic scenario[7] considered earlier in Hotelling's analysis. Barnett and Morse pushed this argument furthest and, backed by their showing of the historical record of declining costs, suggested that substitution takes place at a rate that will lead to continued declining costs (actually in combination with discoveries of new lodes and new methods of exploiting raw material).

Goeller and Weinberg dug into the physical facts that make more concrete our understanding of the possibilities of raw-material substitutions. By examination of the materials in current use in our world economy, and of the physical possibilities of substitution among them, they conclude that – aside from energy, phosphorous and traces of copper, zinc and cobalt for agriculture – materials that are acceptably cheap and in supplies so large that they may be considered to be on a cost plateau are available to substitute for all the raw materials we now use. 'Society would then be based upon glass, plastic, wood, cement, iron, aluminum, and magnesium' (1976/1978, p. 4).

This does *not* ensure that costs will decline starting *now*; just the opposite. The materials to be substituted for are now cheaper to obtain and use than are their potential substitutes, else they would not now be used. But it does promise that there is some point at which rising costs of the presently used materials might reach the plateau costs of the substitutes. And from then on, any technological advance would produce declining costs.

The Goeller–Weinberg analysis suggests that costs can decline almost indefinitely (that is, for many, many generations, beyond any foreseeable planning horizon), but on one additional assumption: energy costs that do not increase in the long run. In their thinking, this assumption is met by nuclear power. It is here the questions arise, because the argument cannot be made in either direction with as much surety as for the other raw materials. Can nuclear-fission plants be built so that they will be politically acceptable? And will nuclear fusion become economical? Though one can be very sure – as I am – that one or another or both will happen long before major substitution of other raw materials is necessary – surely in the next 50 or 100 years, if not in the next 20 years – this judgement is reached on general intuition rather than upon a few clearcut arguable propositions.

If one assumes to the contrary that no nuclear energy will become available, and also assumes that biomass fuels and solar power and wind power and wave power and heat from below the surface of the earth (in such forms as geothermal energy) can never be exploited sufficiently to alter the long-run picture, then fossil fuels[8] are the only option left. And one could then reasonably argue that within some sensible planning horizon, fossil fuels will be sufficiently depleted to produce rising costs of energy. If so, the costs of other raw materials might rise, too. But please notice that considerations of the total energy available within our system – however that system is defined – have no part in the discussion; the second law of thermodynamics and the concept of entropy can only be red herrings here. This conclusion emerges both from a practical look at the length of the sun's life (say a billion years) relative to the length of human history and the life span of one human, as well as from theoretical considerations of the possible boundaries to our system in a time frame comparable to the sun's life or less.

So where are we left with respect to our original question about the inevitability of increasing resource costs, and resources as a brake upon economic development? The answer now seems straightforwardly negative. From Goeller and Weinberg alone we can say: several possibilities of (in the original sense of the word) practically inexhaustible sources of energy exist. And if one or more of these possibilities pans out, then at some point there will start to be indefinitely declining costs of other raw materials. And this conclusion is perfectly compatible even with present technology in raw-material exploitation and substitution. Beyond this, increases in knowledge might by themselves produce declining raw-material costs indefinitely; indeed, just that has happened throughout all of human history.[9]

In brief, it is not *logically* erroneous to assert that raw-material costs *must* eventually rise. But any one of many plausible possibilities *could* lead to indefinitely decreasing costs: (a) If there is a master resource by means of which refined resource *X* can be produced without increasing cost of obtaining *X* in the unprocessed state, then the cost of *X* may decrease. This would hold for fresh water if the energy to desalinate water were cheap and decreasing. And this would therefore also hold for arable land for the very long time during which desalinated water would be used to irrigate deserts, and as cheap energy would make it cheap to transport the water. The case of aluminium (say) would not be very different from the case of water because the richness of ore would decrease very slowly no matter how much were to be used. (b) If the cost of energy is level indefinitely even though not near zero, as seems to be the case with nuclear fission, then for raw materials such as aluminium for which energy is the main additional input, costs will decline if there is technological advance greater than the decline in ore richness. This seems not at all implausible for aluminium, iron and other metals, including those found in sea water or at the bottom of the sea. (c) If the material can be substituted for by other materials embraced by possibilities (a) and (b) above, and if technological change can improve the efficiency of such substitution over time, then X's cost can fall. And according to the Goeller–Weinberg analysis, this includes almost all raw materials. (d) If the material can be grown – as with food and wood – the notion of finiteness is obviously irrelevant except in the view of those who worry about the running down of both the sun and all other sources of energy after millions or billions or trillions of years. And the earth's land also is not a theoretical limit to production for a variety of reasons. For these reasons, the *possibility* of decreasing cost for some materials – even if not the *likelihood* – would seem easy to agree upon. And here, as throughout this discussion, only non-increasing costs and not decreasing costs are necessary to confute pessimistic predictions. And that requires only cost plateaus for energy costs and for the materials that can provide for our basic needs, substituting for those in use now.

VI. WHY HAVE MATERIALS PRICES FALLEN RELATIVE TO CONSUMER GOODS AND SERVICES?

The central notion of cost used until now in this appendix has been that of raw-material price relative to wages. There is no pure theoretical justification for this choice of definition but only a practical justification, to wit: if raw materials will be a decreasing proportional input (in value terms) into the mix of goods and services we use, and if wages in real terms will be going up (as we may expect them to, as long as there is technical advance and no constraint by natural resources), then, if raw-material prices will fall relative to wages, there is clearly no practical problem for consumers.

This section tries to go further, however, to speculate why raw-material availability has historically passed the much harder test of a fall in price of raw materials relative to consumer goods and services, the composite of which has itself been getting cheaper because of more efficient production. To repeat, however, it should be understood that even if this question is of theoretical interest, and even if it is of potential concern to investors in raw materials, it is not relevant to the question of whether raw materials will exert a constraint upon future growth.

There seems to be no logical *necessity* for the price of raw materials to fall relative to other goods. Without some other factor entering the situation, we would expect natural resources to become relatively more expensive due to exhaustion. And there is no reason to expect technology – for deeper digging, cheaper transportation and the like – to develop relatively more rapidly in natural resources than in other sectors of the economy. Nor does it seem likely that the higher degree of labour intensity (defined as the proportion of labour cost to selling price) in consumer goods would explain the matter. The following speculation, however, may be an explanation of the observed empirical trends.

Assume a static economy with, say, three goods – perhaps one consumer service, one good with a 20 per cent content of raw material X_1 whose ore gets progressively less rich as more of it is used, and the third with a 20 per cent content of X_2 whose ore content remains of almost constant richness for now. There will then be a progressive rise in the relative price of X_1 (and hence in the average of all raw materials) as labour is shifted from the consumer sector to the raw-material sector. Hence in a technologically stationary economy, with no substitution, the terms of trade will be in favour of raw materials; that is, raw-material prices will rise relative to consumer goods.

Nor does the existence of technological advance imply that the terms of trade must turn against raw materials. One might speculate (though it is not a demonstrated fact, to my knowledge) that the input of labour relative to capital is greater for consumer goods than for raw materials. And one might further speculate that technical advance works disproportionately in favour of goods whose labour input is relatively low, in the sense that technical advance tends to be capital-enhancing. But is the latter really true? The .services of writing, and singing, and doing arithmetic, have been made enormously cheaper over the years by the printing press, the phonograph an radio, and the computer.[10] Therefore, without some closer and more compelling analysis, technical advance as a general explanation of the fall in raw-materials prices relative to consumer prices does not seem to hold water.

If technical advance is not a satisfactory explanation, then a difference in likelihood of substitution seems the most plausible candidate. And indeed, intuitively there seems to be an important difference in this respect between raw materials and consumer (or producer) goods: raw materials are simpler in what we want of them in that there are few dimensions (often only one or two) on which we perceive them to matter; there are usually more dimensions that matter to us with consumer goods. For example, in construction, dried mud's benefit to us – rigidity – may be supplied by wood or concrete or iron or aluminium or stone or even other apparently dissimilar materials including water as ice or snow.[11] But a car or a geisha has many dimensions that interest us: for the car – shape, speed, gadgets, amount of noise, starting time and so on; for the geisha – shape (but different shape than the car), sound, grace and so on. This multitude of relevant dimensions makes it more difficult for a totally new consumer product to replace an old one than for a new construction material to replace an old one, as it was not simple for the car (especially with complementary roads) to replace the horse.

To repeat, the key to substitutability may lie in the relative *simplicity* of raw materials. Generally we want a raw material for a single property – rigidity, conductivity and so on – whereas we typically demand several properties of a consumer good. And the smaller the number of characteristics in which you are interested, the easier it is to find a substitute that has that particular characteristic or characteristics. This is also true of simple producer goods relative to more complex producer goods. It would be easier to find close substitutes (in the sense that the substitution would be little noticed) for iron nails and cotton fabric than for airplanes and violins.

An important reason why there are more dimensions relevant for a consumer good is that the final form of the good is affected by consumers' tastes, and therefore is influenced by human physiology, psychology and learning, whereas raw materials are not so affected. Original raw inputs are constrained only by physical interchangeability. As discussed earlier, Goeller and Weinberg have shown how, with respect to raw materials, there are very few relevant characteristics that affect interchangeability. And of course an increasing stock of knowledge increases the possibility of interchangeability (e.g. the knowledge of how to work with iron increases the possibility of its substitution for copper), and thereby reduces the cost of substitution.[12] And knowledge of physics increases possibilities for substitutions for copper in communications uses.[13]

More generally, it is relatively easy to find materials to perform purely physical functions compared to those materials that satisfy a taste. Consider how easy it is to find objects in a room to prop open a door, but how hard it would be to find a satisfactory substitute for your cello.

This explanation of why substitution propensity may be the answer to the question before us certainly is neither precise nor compelling. But luckily a compelling answer to this question is not vital to the general argument of this book, it being enough that the price of raw materials falls relative to *wages*. If this section at least asks the question in a fashion that someone else can answer better, it will be worthwhile.

VII. POPULATION GROWTH AND MATERIAL SCARCITY

So far the discussion in this appendix has proceeded without reference to various levels of population and rates of population growth, the very topic to which this book is addressed. It should be reasonably clear that population does not affect the qualitative discussion above about what will 'ultimately' happen in billions of years. But population certainly could affect the *timing* of changes in the direction of raw-material costs. It is this timing that we must consider.

The behavioural relationship between population (or more generally, demand) and resource cost is a key element. The relationship assuredly is not that which is suggested by the vulgar idea of a 'race' between them. More people certainly imply increased demand in the short run, and therefore higher costs than otherwise in the short run. But the long run is not just a sequence of short runs in this case, and hence it is fallacious to draw any conclusions from this short-run analysis. In the longer run, technology's advance comes from people, and technological advance is the sole factor responsible for the long-run declines in material cost.

The process by which increased demand due to more people and higher income causes advances in resource technology is only a special case of the general relationship between demand and technical advance analysed in chapter 14 of my 1981 book, where systematic empirical studies are presented. Here are some natural resource cases that illustrate the process:

(a) Tilton (1981) has reported studies analysing tin use in four applications – beer and soft drink containers, fruit and vegetable containers, solder applications and PVC plastic pipe. Though these studies do not address the question quantitatively, they suggest qualitatively that the price of tin affects technological change in tin-using industries (p. 14).

(b) Two historical vignettes: (i) Prices of copper and iron fell in early Babylonian history, as described earlier. (ii) Ivory used for billiard balls threatened to run out late in the nineteenth century. As a result of a prize offered for a replacement material, celluloid was developed, and that discovery led directly to the astonishing variety of plastics that now give us a cornucopia of products (including billiard balls) at a prices so low as to boggle the nineteenth-century mind.

(c) A contemporary example:

> When Northrop Corp. cranks out fighter planes nowadays, something out of the ordinary rolls down the assembly line: airplane parts cut from wide bolts of shiny black cloth. To the uninitiated, that might seem to signal a serious decline in the nation's defense industry. But the cloth – a blend of carbon fibers and epoxy – represents a technological leap. Once baked, pressurized and cooled, it yields rustproof wing parts, fins and rudders. Each is about half the weight of a comparable aluminum part – yet as strong as steel.
>
> The defense industry is not alone in its apparent fling with Seventh Avenue. In recent years corporations from coat to coast have dreamed up a dazzling array of new materials. (*Newsweek*, 1 February 1982, p. 56)

The cause of these advances in resources was evident to the writer of the story:

> Spurred by the oil shortages of the 1970s and a drive to lessen America's dependence on imported minerals and metals, scientists have developed sophisticated new plastics, ceramics and metallic products – all aimed at increasing energy efficiency – and tapping domestic raw materials. (p. 56)

And the outcome is better resources than we had to start with:

> Now scientists are developing ceramic parts that can withstand those temperatures and whose toughness puts the stuff of toilet bowls to shame. One new process developed by Corning Glass Works modifies the molecular structure of ceramic powder so that it expands instead of cracking – even at temperatures of up to 5,000 degrees Fahrenheit. The technology is in its infancy, but scientists are enthusiastic. 'This industry is about to embark on what happened to metallurgy when melting was first discovered,' says Raymond Bratton, manager of ceramic sciences at Westinghouse. (p. 57)

(d) Another recent example is the development of mines to produce copper, uranium, iron, lead, zinc, coal and even diamonds in Canada's Arctic where the ore is of very high grade. A newspaper report says: '[W]ith resources depleting in more-moderate climes, industry is turning increasingly to the far north.' In the past, this was impossible.

> At one time it all seemed nearly unattainable because of the vast distances and hostile temperatures of this cold desert ... Developing just some of these resources will require great leaps in understanding. Companies will need to find better ways to move the products of earlier exploration through long distances and thick ice. They will need to find ways to feed and house large groups of workers. 'The technological fallout ... will be tremendous,' predicts Charles Heterington, president of Panarctic. (*Wall Street Journal*, 5 February 1982, p. 1)

So we are likely eventually to have resources from the Arctic cheaper than if the threat of increasing scarcity had not induced development in the Far North. This typifies the process of increased demand from population and income leading to new and cheaper resources.

(e) Bernal in *Science and Industry in the Nineteenth Century* (1953) provides case studies of steel; electricity, light and power; chemistry, bacteriology and biochemistry; and the theory of heat and energy in the nineteenth century showing that innovations respond to economic demand. In the case of electricity, for example, 'The barrier, or rather the absence of stimulus to advance, was economic. Electricity developed quickly when it paid, not a moment before' (p. 131). And a large population size and density imply higher total demand, *ceteris paribus*, which is why Edison's first street lighting was in New York City rather than in Montana. It is also clear that countries with more people produce more knowledge, assuming income is the same, for example, Sweden versus the US. And Bernal shows how the power of final demand works indirectly, too. 'Once electric distribution on a large scale was proved feasible and immensely profitable, then came a demand for large efficient power sources' (p. 129), leading to the development of turbines. And the development of light bulbs led to advances in creating vacua, after the subject 'had stagnated for about two hundred years . . . Here was another clear case of the law of supply and demand in the development of science and technology' (p. 125).

On the related question of whether material well-being can be improved through there being more ordinary persons – not geniuses – who contribute to our knowledge in their everyday work, the story of electricity and power production is again illuminating. Bernal describes the 'stumbling progress of the first fifty years from 1831 to 1881 . . . the effort put into the development (1831–1881) . . . was small'. The people who made the necessary technical developments 'were not geniuses . . . and others no more gifted could have hit upon these ideas earlier if the field had attracted enough workers' (pp. 130–1).

(f) Soichino Honda, the inventor and founder of the Japanese motorcycle and car firm bearing his name, urges on us this slogan: 'Where 100 people think, there are 100 powers; if 1,000 people think, there are 1,000 powers (*Wall Street Journal*, 1 February 1982, p. 15).

NOTES

1 'Natural resource' can be a confusing term standing for a confused concept. Several ways of thinking about this concept can be appropriate in one or another context. In the present context, 'natural resource' shall mean material used to make goods at the earliest identifiable stage of cooperation with labour. For example, copper ingots are used at an earlier stage than copper wire, copper ore at an earlier stage than ingots and the earth containing the ore at an earlier stage than the ore. Of course the identification of the 'first' stage must be arbitrary, but that is not likely to cause confusion. Another way to think about these stages is with reference to the amount of value that has been added to the material at the beginning of a given work stage. This sort of definition helps us make a qualitative distinction between a plastic computer disk made from petroleum, and oil in the barrel

at the well-head, or oil in the ground. In most contexts there is little question of what is meant by natural resources: copper, oil, land, air, water are likely to be included; wheat, and trees grown on tree farms, are likely to be excluded because we clearly grow more of them. I shall not refer to any particular resource as sustainable or non-sustainable, exhaustible or non-exhaustible, because I do not think any such qualities are inherent in the nature of a particular material, but rather they depend on circumstances. For example, at one rate of fishing, the supply of fish in a body of water will decrease in the near future, and therefore may be called non-sustainable, while at another rate of fishing (perhaps together with fish-farming practices) the annual rate may continue unabated.

2 Samuelson may serve as the illustration because of his eminence in the economic profession. In the very last lines of a paper entitled 'The Optimum Growth Rate for Population', which is devoted to the analysis of saving and whose central argument implies that higher population leads to higher income, Samuelson concludes:

> Ultimately, positive exponential population growth will presumably bring back into importance the scarcity of natural resources ignored by the model .... For several generations people may benefit on a lifetime basis by having numerous children to support them well in their old ages, out of filial piety or by means of social security. And yet until the end of time their increases in population will cause the law of diminishing returns to be brought into play to leave all subsequent generations in a worsened situation. To the degree that childhood dependency is intrinsically less costly relative to old-age dependency, this dyshygienic temptation becomes all the more dangerous. (1975, p. 537)

The most interesting aspect of this quotation is that – following a long complex paper full of careful proofs – the assertion of resource drag is made without any reference to facts or theory, simply as if it is a known and accepted truth.

3 For the reader who may be wondering about the matter at this juncture, the recent technical literature and natural resource substitution (see, e.g. Berndt and Field, 1981) are mostly not relevant to the concerns of this chapter. More will be said about this later.

4 Popper's remark (1974/1976) is relevant: '[C]ommon sense, though often right (and especially in its realism), is not always right. And things get really interesting just when it is wrong'.

5 This section draws heavily upon my 1981 book.

6 Assume (a) income is measured by the amount (proportion) of time spent working for food; (b) food consumption is the same for all countries and periods with given proportion of population in agriculture; (c) 80 per cent

(it does not matter if the better estimate is 70 per cent or 90 per cent) of the population worked in agriculture in all ancient times; (d) the price of copper relative to wheat remained the same from 1800 BC to AD 1; (e) 10 per cent of US labour force was in agriculture in 1955 (6 449 000/62 171 000; *Historical Stats*, p. 127).

$$\frac{\text{price of copper in labour time in ancient times}}{\text{price of copper in labour time now}} = \frac{\text{\% in agric. then}}{\text{\% in agric. now}} \times \frac{\text{copper price/wheat price then}}{\text{copper price/wheat price now}}$$

7 Even as unworried an economist as Stiglitz writes that 'it is obvious that continued exponential growth is impossible, if only because eventually, at a strictly positive growth rate, the mass of people would exceed the mass of the earth' (1979, p. 37). My noting this comment of Stiglitz's does not mean that I am here advocating any particular rate of growth. What I wish to point out is that Stiglitz considers some absolute limits as worth mentioning (though he may only be paying the idea lip service). This suggests that physical limits may be a more binding constraint in the future than now, rather than viewing scarcity at any moment in the future as being of the same nature and of less severity than now.

8 The term 'fossil fuels' may be a misnomer. Coal and oil may be the result of methane gas deep in the earth rather than of fossils (Steele, 1982). If so, there are possibilities of vast supplies of methane to be exploited.

9 It is true that energy costs have been mostly falling rather than rising throughout history. But in the recent past, energy costs have been a sufficiently small part of total cost for many raw materials so that even rising energy prices would not have altered this conclusion.

10 Even geishas may perform before groups whose size may be magnified by telecommunications. Prostitution is the example that comes to mind of the good or service that is least subject to technical change and cost reduction, because there seem few possibilities for substitution on many of the relevant dimensions of sexual encounters, with little possibility for reduction in real resources used as inputs to the process.

11 Not only do the Eskimos build homes of snow, but a recent article about mining firms in the Canadian arctic says that they build – with ice-water piped onto gravel, which then freezes – ship docks, which are much cheaper to build with ice than with cement which must be shipped in at high cost (*Wall Street Journal*, 5 February 1982, p. 1).

12 The concept of dimensions may at first seem vague and not operational. But the concept can be made operational if one thinks in terms of purchase

specifications. Consider, for example, the list of specifications a purchasing agent would write for the building material to be used for a functional (not decorative) lamp-post, and the list of specifications that he or she would write for a perfume or a spouse. The difference is illustrated by comparing how much easier it is to delegate acquiring building materials than acquiring a spouse.

13 The replacement of copper intercontinental telephone wires by satellites, which sharply reduces the price of those communications sources, may be a well-known example by now. Optical fibres are another recent dramatic development in the centuries-long process:

> Gutenberg spent five years setting the Bible in type. Today the book, in electronic form, can be transmitted over ordinary copper telephone wires in less than an hour. The Bible can be sent in less than a second, however, through optical fibers, the very clear threads of glass that carry information as flashes of light instead of electric pulses.
>
> And enough text to fill 16 Bibles could be transmitted in a single second through a new type of conduit that is emerging from laboratories, the monomode, or single-mode optical fiber. 'Potentially, single-mode fibers represent as much an improvement over the optical fibers of today as today's fibers did over copper wire,' says Paul Fleury, director of the Materials Research Laboratory at Bell Telephone Laboratories, the research branch of American Telephone & Telegraph Corp. 'At present, commercial-mode fibers can be made that are 10 to a hundred times better than ordinary glass fibers,' he says. 'In the research stage, the fibers are 1,000 times better.' . . .
>
> Today's fibers are more expensive than copper, and monomode fibers are more costly still. But because of its higher capacity, glass is starting to supplant copper in long-distance communications and within major cities where the volume of telephone calls continues to swell but where the ducts that contain telephone wiring already are overcrowded with copper and cannot be enlarged.
>
> For similar reasons, monomode fibers are likely to be adopted soon, despite their price, although prices should drop. Monomode fibers cost between $2.30 and $5.50 per yard. But within five years, the price will decline to about 23 cents per yard, according to projections by Lightwave Technologies Inc., a monomode maker in Van Nuys, Calif. At very high transmission rates, the cost of monomode fibers already is competitive, Lightwave officials say. (*The Wall Street Journal*, 23 July 1982, p. 13)

References

Barnett H J, Morse C *Scarcity and Growth: The Economics of Natural Resource Availability* (Baltimore: Johns Hopkins, 1963)
Bauer P T *Equality, the Third World and Economic Delusion* (Cambridge, Mass.: Harvard University Press, 1981)
Bernal J D *Science and Industry in the Nineteenth Century* (London: Routledge and Kegan Paul, 1953)
Berndt E A, Field B C *Modelling and Measuring National Resource Substitution* (Cambridge, Mass.: MIT, 1981)
Child V G *What Happened in History* (Baltimore: Penguin, 1942/1964)
Clark C *Conditions of Economic Progress*, 3rd ed. (New York: Macmillan, 1957)
Daly H E *Steady-State Economics* (San Francisco: Freeman, 1977)
Georgescu-Roegen N *The Entropy Law and the Economic Process* (Harvard University Press, 1971)
Goeller H E, Weinberg A M 'The Age of Substitutability.' *Science*, 191, 1978, 663–89
'Is the Era of Limits Running Out? A Conversation with Garrett Hardin and Julian Simon, *Public Opinion*, March 1982, 48–54
Jevons W S *The Coal Question* (London: Macmillan, 1865)
Kaldor N 'A Model of Economic Growth.' *Economic Journal*, LXVII, December 1957
Nordhaus W D, Tobin J *Is Growth Obsolete?* (New York: NBER, 1972)
Popper K *Unended Quest* (La Salle, Illinois: Open Court Publishing Co., 1974/1976)
Samuelson P A 'The Optimum Growth Rate for Population.' *International Economic Review*, 16, December 1975, 531–8
Simon J L *The Ultimate Resource* (Princeton: Princeton University Press, 1981)
Singer M 'How the Scarcity Error Hurts America.' *Washington Quarterly*, Spring 1981
Smith V K (ed.) *Scarcity and Growth Revisited* (Baltimore: Resources for the Future and Johns Hopkins University Press, 1979)
Steele W 'The Methane Mystery.' *Mechanix Illustrated*, March 1982, 136
Stiglitz J E 'A Neo-classical Analysis of the Economics of Natural Resources.' Mimeograph, 1979
Tilton J E 'Prices, Innovation, and the Demand for Materials.' Mimeo, Penn State, 1981

[30]

Foreword

This paper claims to demolish one of the most honored papers in the history of economics. It is not surprising that referees offered the entire gamut of arguments to save Hotelling's idea, such as (1) the Hotelling idea is exceedingly interesting even if it does not square with the data, and (2) modifications can make the original idea square with the data being the opposite to what Hotelling originally assumed.

The perverseness of Hotelling's Rule

In their 50-year review, Devarajan and Fisher (1981) noted that Hotelling's famous 1931 article on exhaustible resources is unusual in being the sole origin of an entire formal "field" of economics. And after half a century, the literature it spawned appears at an ever more rapid pace (e.g. Farzin, 1984; Miller and Upton, 1985; Romer and Sasaki, 1985). This is interesting sociology of knowledge.

In my view, however, it is even more interesting sociology of knowledge that such a body of work exists at all, let alone flourishes, given that Hotelling's analysis has no descriptive or prescriptive power due to its being founded on a contrary-to-fact assumption.

Hotelling's Rule is not merely irrelevant for decision-making and for the understanding of decision-making; if that were so, it could be appreciated for its charm, and an attack upon it might decently be dismissed as bad form or lack of an aesthetic sense. But to the extent that it affects decision-makers, Hotelling's Rule is perverse, and imposes a cost because it is misleading; it focuses economists upon an analysis which leads to wrong conclusions for all known situations. And it wastes the time of economists who could be devoting themselves to more profitable activities. If valid, this is no small criticism, I trust. I belabor the point because of a tendency to justify formal analyses if they are "interesting" even if they are without reference to any conceivable actual situation.[1]

Hotelling's Rule may help illuminate a very different sort of situation than that about which he was writing, embargoed goods whether or not of an "exhaustible" natural resource, e.g. Bergstrom, Loury, and Persson (1985, and references therein), who arrive at solutions that may be viewed as special cases of Hotelling's Rule. But if their solutions might just as well be arrived at without reference to Hotelling's analysis, these studies or embargoes would seem to be scant justification for continued interest in Hotelling's Rule.

Everything said here has been noted by others, but in passing. What is new is a blunt rejection of Hotelling's Rule, and complete dismissal of the body of work built on it. (That there is not general agreement with this assessment is shown by the continued appearance of articles based upon Hotelling's Rule, despite Barnett and Morse's great book (1963) which should have laid Hotelling's rule in its grave. That book is not even cited in the mainstream Devarajan–Fisher review.)

The flaw in Hotelling's analysis begins (and can end) with the title of his article, which refers to a "resource" that is "exhaustible." It is crucial to be clear on what we are talking about; to rush on to technical matters without such classification and agreement dooms the discussion. We must first agree, I believe, that the appropriate definition of "exhaustible" must be an "operational" or "working" definition along the lines of Einstein's definition of time, rather than a "property" definition along the lines of pre-Einsteinian definitions of time. (A discussion of these types of definitions may be found in many places. My own view may be found in Simon and Burstein, 1985, ch. 2, or in Simon, 1970.)

Exhaustible resources are frequently classified into "renewable" and "non-renewable." The latter type was the subject of Hotelling's paper, "an industry in which the indefinite maintenance of a steady rate of production is a physical impossibility, and which is therefore bound to decline" (p. 139). Therefore, the "non-renewable" type of resource is the subject of the present discussion.

The term "exhaustible" has at least two different definitions in this context because of different references. For the oil-well owner who was the subject of Hotelling's formal analysis – though not the source of his interest, which was (in his opening sentence) "the world's disappearing supplies of … inexhaustible assets" – Hotelling's definition in the paragraph above is quite appropriate. In the context of the well-owner, the term "exhaustible" means that if pumping continues at a constant rate per period, there will come a time when (with the technology that is assumed fixed) no more oil will appear at the surface, or that it will appear in sufficiently small quantities that the value will be below the cost of production. (Oil is the strongest case for Hotelling because, unlike such resources as copper, oil is burned up and energy cannot be completely recycled.) The physical (in contrast to economic) nature of this definition causes no difficulty here because the depletion discussed in the definition is within the well-owner's control and is reasonably knowable with standard geological-engineering techniques.

For a society, however, or for humanity taken together, a physical definition of "exhaustible" is not helpful. For one thing, there is no generic commodity – including oil – that demonstrably cannot be produced at a constant rate indefinitely. Oil – by which we properly mean something that is viscous and burns – can be produced by growing plants, and hence is proximately limited only by the life of the sun. Georgescu-Roegen (and following him, Daly, and much of the environmental movement's writings) would like us to allocate our energy resources taking into account that eventual demise of the sun, and in their review, Peterson and Fisher (1977) say "The physical concept of entropy, as described by Nicholas Georgescu-Roegen (1971) is relevant here" (p. 692). But I hope that the reader will agree that such matters as the sun's lifetime, the possibility of other suns, whether or not the cosmos is or is not expanding, and so on, are not part of reasonable thinking here, for a variety of reasons that I hope need not be spelled out.

If one agrees that a physical definition of "exhaustible" will not serve, it is reasonable (and probably would be preferable even if a satisfactory physical definition were available) to turn to an economic definition. An appropriate working definition would seem to be: a natural resource whose cost or price[2] will rise with time as increments of the resource are used. The question whether cost (price) will indeed rise is crucial in both sorts of situations – in the social situation because it defines "exhaustible," and in the private firm's situation because it is the fundamental datum in the well-owner's decision-making.

Hotelling's analysis has two implications, one for managerial decision-making and the other for forecasting the prices of raw materials. The form of the future price curve, which is the heart of the forecast, is of interest to us here only as input to the decision-making, to which we address ourselves.

Consider the situation to which Hotelling first applied his analysis: the owner of a single mine in "free competition," i.e. a mine-owner whose sales are assumed to be too small to have an effect upon market price; this is the appropriate assumption in every conceivable case. If the market price is expected to fall or even to remain constant, the owner obviously would have no use for Hotelling's Rule or even for dynamic programming; s/he would sell as much output as possible just as soon as possible, subject only to the qualification of increasing production cost in the short run due to heavier use of facilities.

Next, consider a mine-owner who has sufficient monopoly power so that his/her sales affect the market price; Saudi Arabia as a whole might be such a case. If price is on a long-term decline which may be expected to continue in the future no matter what the owner's output decisions, then the optimizing decision is to set each year's output independently of future output decisions, as a first approximation. Or as a second approximation, a dynamic program embodying the effects of current sales on future price would yield an optimum set of price decisions for future periods. But in neither case would Hotelling's Rule be appropriate.

Now let us briefly review the evidence showing that the long-term course of raw materials is indeed downwards. The classical source is Barnett and Morse (1963), together with the series prepared at Resources for the Future which they analysed, covering 1870–1957. Their data, together with my analysis of individual resource prices in the United States from 1800 to 1976 (the period covered by *Historical Statistics of the United States*) plus scraps of evidence covering various commodities such as copper back to 1800 BC show that over the entire span of recorded history, the prices of all exhaustible raw materials (excluding industrial diamonds, for which I have not found data, and also those resources such as gold which are used as stores of values) have been constant or have declined relative to consumer goods, as shown in Figures 1 and 2.[3] A vivid demonstration of the disastrous outcome of following Hotelling's Rule is given by Anders, Gramm, Maurice, and Smithson (1980, Table 10.2), where they compare the actual prices of various "depletable resources" in 1975 to the prices that would have had to have prevailed if the resources had been bought in 1900 and the buyers had received a reasonable return on their investments (using a wide variety of rates of return). It is very clear that holding stocks of minerals starting in 1900 (or in 1800 or any other year) would have been an atrocious investment under any conceivable assumptions.

There has recently been discussion of alternative measures of natural resource scarcity (e.g. Brown and Field, 1978 and Halvorsen and Smith, 1984), but no measure proposed alters the basic conclusions concerning the trend in prices.

From the standpoint of human welfare as well as economic development, the trend in resource prices relative to the price of the most important good – human time – is even more important than relative to consumer goods. And the downward trend in resource prices relative to wages is even more marked than relative to consumer prices, especially in the advanced countries but also in poorer countries, as Figures 1 and 2 show.

The question may be raised whether a price rise for some years or decades – and there frequently are periods of increasing prices – may not constitute grounds for the application of Hotelling's analysis even if the secular trend is down.

Recent work by Smith (1979) and Halvorsen and Smith (1984) covering the years 1956 to 1974 for the Canadian metal mining industry, and Miller and Upton (1985)

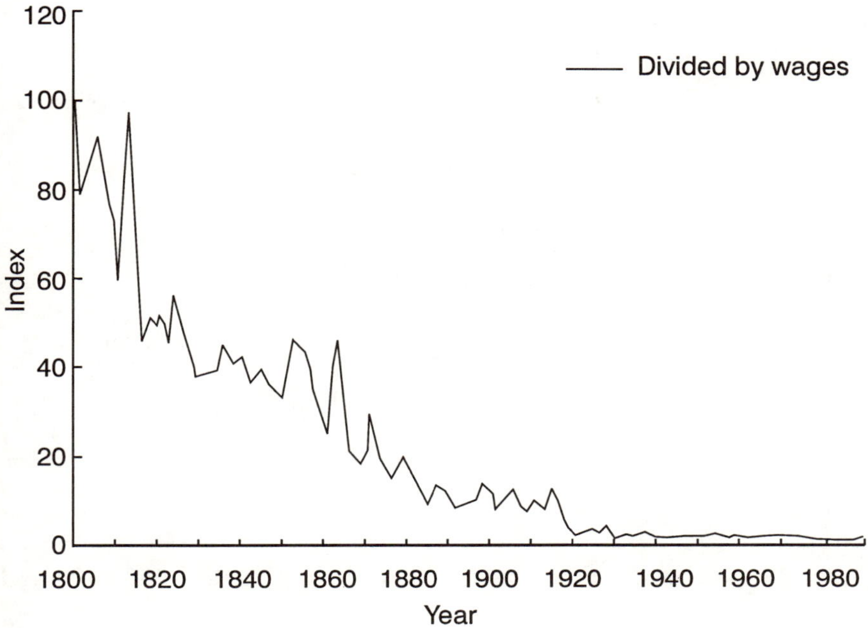

Source: Historical Statistics of the US, Washington: GPO, 1976

Figure 1 The scarcity of copper as measured by its price relative to wages

covering US oil and gas companies from the end of 1979 to the middle of 1981, illustrate analysis of trends using periods shorter – in some cases, much shorter – than the longest series available. This raises the difficult philosophical-statistical question about the appropriate length of series to use, balancing a greater volume of information versus (typically) less accuracy as one proceeds further back in history.

This seems clear: the number of incorrect forecasts based on too-short time series is enormous, surely much larger than the number of incorrect forecasts based on too-long time series or due to insufficient attention being paid to the most recent period. For the very shortest periods, the literature on random walks in security-price behavior would suggest that trend analysis of such periods is doomed to fail. And for the longest periods in the past, a forecast from one randomly chosen date to another randomly chosen date that price would fall would have had a far better-than-chance accuracy, which would seem to suggest that the longest secular trend should be the basis of a forecast, as long as that trend is monotonic. This does not deal with the issue of whether there may be temporary trend reversals, a matter that calls for investigation of auto-collinearity of adjusted series for raw materials. But even if one can predict upward price movements for a while based on past price movements, this would hardly seem a solid basis for resting one's thinking on Hotelling's Rule as a general matter, especially when such upward price movements may be expected to turn around sometime, based on the long secular trend.

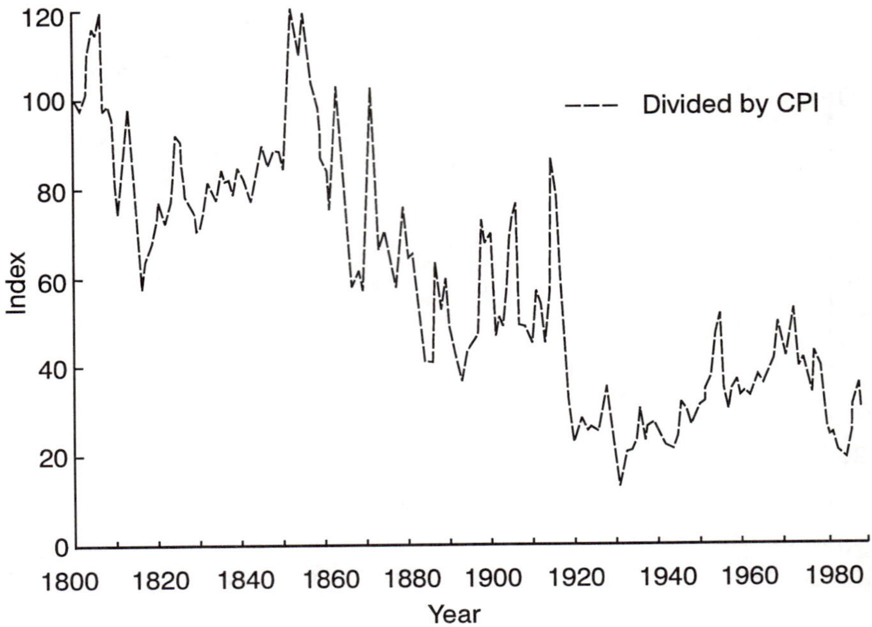

Source: Historical Statistics of the US, Washington: GPO, 1976

Figure 2 The scarcity of copper as measured by its price relative to the consumer price index

A related issue whether the analysis is useful if the future may be expected to be different than the past, to wit, that past trends do not forecast future trends; as Peterson and Fisher (1977, p. 706) put it:

> [W]e have no guarantee that the behaviour of extractive resource costs and prices will be the same over the next hundred years as it has been over the last hundred – indeed the work of Smith suggests that it may not.

It is always logically possible that a long secular trend will change direction. But if so, an explicit forecast is required. And if the forecast is other than the sort of environment assumed by Hotelling, which would lead to a smooth price rise of a particular form – a forecast requiring much stronger assumptions than even a change in historical direction – then the Hotelling analysis would not be useful; indicated instead would be a straightforward present-value analysis, as with any other kind of investment or manufacturing operation.

The analysis is much the same if it is intended for a country, even a dominant producer such as Saudi Arabia, or even a cartel with monopoly power such as OPEC. True, back in the 1970s some countries planned (or at least they *said* they planned) their oil production on the assumption that price would rise high enough in the future so that it would be a good investment to hold some oil in the ground; if they really took place, the behavior probably was motivated by the same ill-informed forecasts of rising prices that emanated from the doomsayers and such agencies as the US Department of Energy. But more recently, the behavior of all oil-producing countries, and of OPEC as a whole, clearly fits the model of sellers who do not assume that price will be rising enough in the future to make it worthwhile to withhold any output, or that they will even be rising at all.

One reason that Hotelling's Rule has reigned so supreme may be the absence up to now of a well-developed competing theory of resource prices. "No viable alternative paradigm exists," say Miller and Upton (1985, p. 24). But though a well-developed formal theory may not be available, the core ideas necessary for such a theory are not far from hand, and some formal analysis has begun to appear.

There is every economic reason to expect an actual or impending increase in price to trigger additional search for new sources (e.g. new oil fields) and new substitutes (e.g. oil from coal), as Barnett and Morse (1963), Nef (1977), and Rosenberg (1973) have described. And given the difficulty of the discoverer capturing a large portion of the returns to the discovery, and given the long-livedness of knowledge, prices will reflect the new knowledge.

Romer and Sasaki (1985) have set a model of endogenous technical advance in resource production into a competitive market situation, and shown that a competitive equilibrium exists. Here the resource is implicitly not finite in supply.

Simon and Steinmann (1986) have built a very-long-run model, using land as the resource example, showing how the price of the service (actually, the good that is produced) triggers a rise in the price of the resource, which then induces new discovery. The upshot of the model is that the price is lower in the long run if population growth or another pressure causes a run-up in the price in the short run, compared to no pressure being exerted upon demand.

Even if the resource is considered finite, a more difficult scenario than the one offered here, a discovery process could lead to a long-run fall in price. Baumol (1986) has observed that the effect of a given change in knowledge depends upon the "stock" of the resource that is augmented by a change in knowledge. (The appropriate concept of resource stock need not be troublesome in a discussion as abstract as this one.) He then sketches the system numerically and concludes that a drop in price indefinitely is feasible even if the stock approaches zero asymptotically. This notion could be a building block in a discovery-based formal theory of resource prices in which the outcome of the process will be a cost lower than if the scarcity had not increased or threatened.

Perhaps when the process of problem-induced solutions is understood in more detail, and then formalized, the field will drift in that direction and away from Hotelling's Rule as the "canonical model for modern theorists to build on" (Devarajan and Fisher, 1981, p. 71).

Notes

1. Marshall admonished us that "we are not at liberty to ... exercise ourselves on subtleties which lead nowhere" (quote by Skidelsky, 1983, p. 40).
2. We may leave aside the specifics of which price or cost concept is relevant except to note that it is a real price deflated relative to consumer prices to yield a "business price" of the sort that would be

relevant for business calculations. This is unlike a "welfare price" which would properly be considered relative to the price of human time.

3. The statement is also true for all important "renewable" natural resources such as food grains. The sole exception of lumber is explained by its transition from its early status as a nuisance to be gotten rid of by farm builders, to being an agricultural commodity. I am prepared to make a futures contract, taking the side that lumber prices will decline, as part of my more general standing offer. (See Simon, 1981, p. 27).

References

Anders, Gerhard, W. Philip Gramm, S. Charles Maurice, and Charles W. Smithson (1980), *The Economics of Mineral Extraction* (Praeger).

Barnett, Harold and Chandler Morse (1963), *Scarcity and Growth* (Baltimore: John Hopkins).

Baumol, William J. (1986), "On the Possibility of Continuing Expansion of Finite Resources," *Kyklos*, **39**, Fasc. 2, 167–79.

Bergstrom, Clas, Glenn C. Loury, and Mats Persson (1985), "Embargo Threats and the Management of Emergency Reserves," *The Journal of Political Economy*, **93** (February), 26–42.

Brown, Gardner M., Jr. and Barry C. Field (1978), "Implications of Alternative Measures of Natural Resource Scarcity," *The Journal of Political Economy*, **86**, (2), part 1 (April), 229–43.

Devarajan, Shantayan and Anthony C. Fisher (1981), "Hotelling's 'Economics of Exhaustible Resources' Fifty Years Later," *Journal of Economic Literature*, **XIX**, (March), 65–73.

Farzin, Y. Hossein (1984), "The Effect of the Discount Rate on Depletion of Exhaustible Natural Resources," *The Journal of Political Economy*, **92** (October), 841–51.

Halvorsen, Robert and Tim R. Smith (1984), "On Measuring Natural Resource Scarcity," *The Journal of Political Economy*, **92** (October), 954–64.

Hotelling, Harold (1931), "The Economics of Exhaustible Resources," *The Journal of Political Economy*, **39** (April), 137–75.

Miller, Merton H. and Charles W. Upton (1985), "A Test of the Hotelling Valuation Principle," *The Journal of Political Economy*, **93** (February), 1–25.

Nef, John V. (1977), "An Early Energy Crisis and Its Consequences," *Scientific American* (May), 140–51.

Peterson, Frederic M. and Anthony C. Fisher (1977), "The Exploitation of Extractive Resources: A Survey," *The Economic Journal*, **87** (December), 687–721.

Romer, Paul M. and Hiroo Sasaki (1985), "Monotonically Decreasing Natural Resource Prices Under Perfect Foresight," xerox, University of Rochester (February).

Rosenberg, Nathan (1973), "Innovative Responses to Materials Shortages," *American Economic Review*, **63** (May), 111–18.

Simon, Julian L. (1970), "The Concept of Causality in Economics," **Kylos**, 23, Fasc., 2, 226–54.

Simon, Julian L. (1981), *The Ultimate Resource* (Princeton: PUP).

Simon, Julian L. and Paul Burstein (1985), *Basic Research Methods in Social Science,* 3rd edition (New York: Random House).

Simon, Julian L. and Gunter Steinmann (1988), "Population Growth, Natural Resources, and the Long-run Standard of Living," xerox.

Skidelsky, Robert (1983), *John Maynard Keynes: Hopes Betrayed 1883–1920* (New York: Viking, p. 40).

Smith, V. Kerry (ed.) (1979), *Scarcity and Growth Reconsidered* (Baltimore: Johns Hopkins).

[31]

Foreword

An essential element of my thinking that is reflected in this article may be illustrated with how we describe the shape of the earth. Should one say "The earth is round"? I have exasperated my children by saying that I mostly regard the earth as flat, as is also appropriate for carpet-layers. Geophysicists consider it an elongated sphere. Airline navigators plotting a route from Europe to the United States sensibly regard the earth as round, but pilots flying from Denver to San Francisco had better view it as jagged, or else they will not view it for very long.

Taken altogether, the earth "is" not anything, and to say that it "is" anything falls into the snare of the word "is" mentioned earlier. The earth *equals* only the earth, and any descriptive adjective at best grasps only one aspect of the earth. In similar fashion, I recently read Benoit Mandelbrot, creator of the exciting new mathematical field of fractals, using the coast of Great Britain as his example; its length depends upon whether you measure it as the crow flies, or as a beachcomber would walk it, or in some other fashion.

This view of the world as deformed ex-chaos also leads to solid intellectual bases for prediction. An example of its fruitfulness: For some time now, following Harold Barnett, I have written about how our supplies of energy, land and other natural resources have been increasing rather than decreasing, contrary to all common sense and Malthusian diminishing returns. The central evidence for this proposition is that the prices of natural resources, relative to the price of our most precious commodity – the hours of our lives, as measured by the wage price – and also even relative to the price of consumer goods, have been decreasing rather than increasing. This has led to the prediction that this trend, which has been in operation over the entire span of history for which we can muster any data – and that includes almost 4,000 years for copper – will continue into the future indefinitely.

Unsurprisingly, not everyone agrees with this prediction. And naturally enough, many question the method by which this forecast is made. Simplifying dangerously, the answer boils down to the expectation that a trend will continue unless there is a persuasive theoretical reason to think that it will not. And in the case of resource availability such a persuasive theory does not exist; rather, the data square with a plausible theory that the problem of impending shortage mobilizes people to develop solutions that leave us better off than if the problem had not arisen. Furthermore, if statistical evidence is overwhelming, one may choose to believe that a trend will continue even despite persuasive theory to the contrary.

The underlying philosophical basis for this method and for the general proposition about trend continuation is that there is likely to be a positive correlation between contiguous observations, in consonance with the idea that the world as we know it departs from complete chaos, from complete randomness, as discussed in Chapter 6.

There is a certain amount of pulling oneself up by one's bootstraps in this way of thinking. It says that we may predict the future on the basis of past experience because the world is non-random, and we believe that the world is non-random because we have been able to predict successfully in the past.[1]

But the idea of non-chaos due to a single deformation is a structural vision that is not identical with the success of prediction; it is itself a hypothesis about the physical nature of the world and about a historical event. To the extent that this idea is sound, it buttresses the naked observation that prediction based on experience does better than random chance. And therefore the intellectual operation is not *just* a bootstrap operation, not just tautology and restatement.[2]

Notes

1. Hume supported his assumption that prediction is possible with a somewhat similar observation: "[I]f all the scenes of nature were continually shifted in such a manner, that no two events bore any resemblance to each other, but every object was entirely new, without any similitude to whatever had been seen before, we should never, in that case, have attained the least idea of necessity, or of a connexion among these objects" (p. 104). (Notice that though Hume says that we can never *learn* the nature of the physical connection among events, he does not deny that there is a connection.) And he makes a similar observation specifically with respect to social science. "[W]ere there no uniformity in human actions, and were every experiment, which we could form of this kind, irregular and anomalous, it were impossible to collect any general observations concerning mankind; and no experience, however accurately digested by reflection, would ever serve to any purpose" (p. 106).
2. This view fits with recent speculations by astronomers. Such physical corroboration, however, is not crucial for present purposes though it may make one feel more comfortable with the hypothesis.

FORECASTING THE LONG-TERM TREND OF RAW MATERIAL AVAILABILITY *

Julian L. SIMON

University of Maryland, College Park, MD 20742, USA

Keywords: Natural resources. Demand-cumulative. Evaluation. Forecasts of models of resource reserves. APPL-sector: Commodities. Trend curves – Evaluation.

1. Introduction

Will raw materials be more scarce, or less scarce, in future decades than at present? The actual outcome will have important consequences for our economic lives. And our *expectations* about the outcome will probably have even greater consequences than the outcome itself. Yet there are large and violent disagreements between two points of view, the 'doomsdayers' who expect us to 'run out' and who therefore forecast higher prices, and the 'cornucopians' who expect prices to be progressively lower as raw materials come to be more available rather than less available. My own forecast is simply stated: I am quite sure that prices of all natural resources will go down indefinitely.

The aim of this paper is to set forth what I believe should be the basis for such a forecast. The nature of this particular forecasting situation forces us to consider the very foundations of long-run economic forecasting, and indeed, of all forecasting.

My forecasting 'method' may be summarized as follows:

(1) Ask: Is there any convincing reason not to consider the percentage changes from year to year in the longest available data series on a resource's price to be a representative sample of the 'universe' from which the past, present, and future of this resource are drawn? That is, is there some convincing reason not to generalize from the sample already drawn to samples that will be drawn in the future?

If the observations had been those of secular constancy in the past, rather than secular decline, the sample-universe logic would seem more straightforward. But the constancy of an amount of change, or of a percentage rate of change, is based on the same foundation; predictions about a spacecraft circling the earth, and a spacecraft traveling away from the earth toward the stars, are on much the same footing.

Many persons assert we are now at a 'turning point in history' with regard to resources, which implies that the past is *not* a representative sample of the universe from which the next set of years to come will be drawn. If their reasoning is convincing to you, then my predictions will not be credited by you. (One of my arguments against such a turning point now is that such an assertion has been common in the past.)

(2) If you do not reject the past as a sample of the universe from which the next set of observations will be drawn, then we next ask if there is a reasonable 'theoretical' explanation for the observed

* A fuller version of this paper was presented at the Third International Symposium on Forecasting, Philadelphia, PA, 1983.

0169-2070/85/$3.30 © 1985, Elsevier Science Publishers B.V. (North-Holland)

trend. Such an explanation is not necessary for one to believe that the trend will continue. Few of us could explain why a spacecraft circles the earth or travels away from it, and people prudently did not await an explanation for the transmission of cholera before acting on the information that there was a geographic pattern connected with certain wells in London. But a theoretical explanation increases belief that the observed trend is not just caused by chance.

The explanation that the trend of decreasing cost results from market feedbacks causing new discoveries, substitutes, etc., accompanied by externalities which leave us better than before shortages arose, is persuasive to me. Of course one never can be sure that a theoretical explanation is sound; the test is your general wisdom and judgment.

(3) If the answer to (1) is 'no' and to (2) is 'yes' – or even if the answer to (2) is 'no' but the data in (1) are so many and so consistent that your statistical sense tells you that they are overwhelming – then you will extrapolate the observed trend with a monotonic function that seems to fit the data relatively well. That is the nature of my forecasting method. As I read Barnett and Morse (1963), which is the source of my general point of view on the history and future of raw material availability, this also is the forecasting method implicitly used by them. And it is the forecasting method used by many – but certainly not all – other makers of forecasts throughout the ages.

The paper will proceed as follows. Section 2 discusses appropriate ways to measure economic scarcity of raw materials. Section 3 provides some long-run history of raw material scarcity. Section 4 sets forth the Malthusian theory, which is at the heart of pessimistic forecasts of raw material scarcity, and explains why I do not find that line of thinking persuasive; it offers another way of thinking instead. Section 5 offers a very general argument about why trends can help predict; this takes us down to the foundations of scientific knowledge about the world we live in. Section 6 discusses the appropriate weights to put on long-ago data versus more recent information, which is much the same as discussing whether the longest-run trend should be believed rather than more recent 'reversals'.

2. Measurement of scarcity trends [1]

Economists generally view the expenditures in physical or money terms necessary to obtain a good, relative to some other quantity of expenditures, as the appropriate measure of scarcity. This is in contrast to measuring scarcity with an actual or hypothetical estimate of physical quantities that are thought to 'exist', as technologists are wont to do.

Two measures of cost are of particular interest here: The price of the raw material relative to consumer goods, and the price relative to wages. Each measure needs a further few words.

The price relative to consumer goods is the most popular measure, perhaps largely because of its similarity to an inflation deflator. But the average cost of all consumer goods taken together – an index of consumer prices – has fallen over the years in more-developed countries, measured in terms of what an unskilled worker can buy; this is shown by the long-run increase in the standard of living. Therefore, if a raw material has remained at least level in price compared to the average of all (or of consumer) goods, its 'real' cost has fallen. Therefore, even if raw material prices had not fallen as fast as consumer goods – as in fact they have – it would not be ground for alarm about resources exerting a braking effect on economic growth, or becoming an increasingly serious constraint.

The price of natural resources *relative to wages* is, in my view, the best measure of scarcity with respect to human welfare. This measure tells us how much of our most valuable resource, our own lives, that we must give up in order to obtain the resources. This bears considerable relationship to the

[1] This section draws heavily upon my 1981 book.

measure of the labor input time per unit of output that Barnett and Morse used, but it is easier to obtain, and is more comprehensive.

We should note that it is not really the natural resource itself that is of interest to us, but rather the services that we get from the resource. Just as it is not a computer itself, but rather the computing services we get from it, and then the use of those computing services in the production of other goods, that affects us, it is not copper or land or oil that matters to us, but rather the services that they render in the creation of final products. Therefore the relevant measure of the available resource is the cost of the services that we get from the resource. The market price of new pieces of capital is an upper-bound estimate on this cost of services because of progressive increases in productivity of capital, e.g., the cost of computing services has fallen sharply over the years.

3. Trends in resource scarcity

Now that we have arrived at some operational measures of scarcity, let's look at the record, in accord with the first step in my forecasting method. The historical cost record of raw materials is easy to summarize. Following on Barnett and Morse (1963), I have written at length elsewhere [Simon (1981)] about this matter, so I'll be brief here: Scarcity has been decreasing rather than increasing in the long run for all raw materials except lumber and oil, and even they have shown recent signs of becoming less exceptional. Figs. 1 and 2 show this effect for copper, which is representative of all the metals. And this trend of falling prices of copper has been going on a very long time. The price of copper in labor time in the year 1 A.D. was about 120 times as great as it is in the U.S. now. The price of iron was about 240 times as great then as now, and in 800 B.C. it was 360 times as great, while in 1800 B.C. it was 1620 times as great [calculated from data in Clark (1957, pp. 652ff) and Childe (1942/1964)]. Food is an especially important resource, and the evidence is especially strong that we are on a benign trend despite rising population [see Simon (1981, chs. 4–6)].

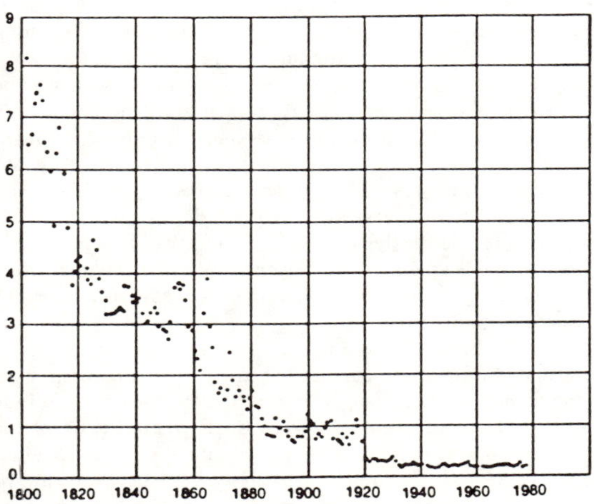

Fig 1. The scarcity of copper as measured by its price relative to wages (Source: Historical Statistics of the U.S.).

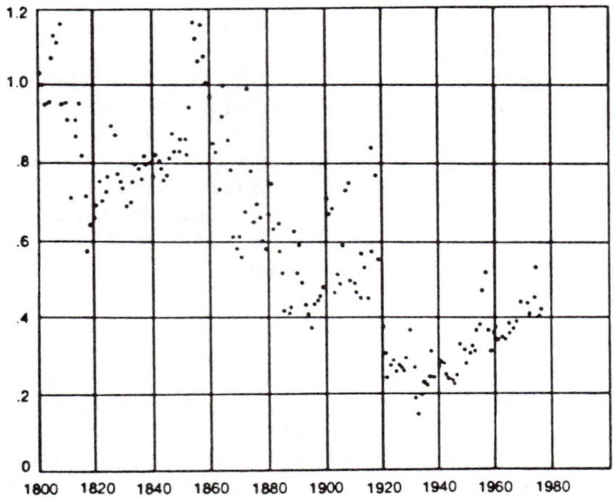

Fig. 2. The scarcity of copper as measured by its price relative to the consumer price index (Source: Historical Statistics of the U.S.).

4. Malthusian and other theories

Now let us move to the second step in my forecasting method, the theory. First let us consider contrary theories, because they cast light on the credibility of the theory I offer. The question that we wish to address theoretically must be kept firmly in mind: Must the cost of one or more important raw materials rise in the long run? The doomsayers assert that there is theoretical reason to answer the question in the affirmative, that there is no escaping a rise in raw material cost in some very long run. Their reasoning is as follows: The reservoir of some raw material *X* is fixed, meaning that the reservoir cannot be increased just as the reservoir of authentic Mona Lisa paintings cannot be increased. (They have in mind, however, generic materials such as, say, copper and land and energy rather than one-of-a-kinds such as the Mona Lisa; about those one-of-a-kinds there is no dispute.) Next they assume that the demand for the use of the material will either (a) increase due to population growth or income growth or both, or (b) the reservoir will decline due to some of it being lost or otherwise unavailable, or (c) there will be both increased demand and decreased reservoir. If humankind first exploits the richest lodes and ores, successive mining operations will be successively more expensive. Implicitly, those writers are also assuming that eventually there will be either stationarity of technology or a growth in technology slower than the rate of decrease in richness of lode. Under those assumed conditions, cost must indeed increase.

Certainly costs do increase during some periods, as reflected in real price rises at some times in history. And it is reasonable to suppose that during those periods the doomsday conditions hold (though price rises may sometimes be due to non-physical causes such as the formation of OPEC).

If the Malthusian concept of diminishing returns is given content by specifying a period of the order of a human life expectation, give or take an expected length of life, that 'theory' fails completely in its predictive record; as we have seen, the trends in scarcity have been downward throughout history despite forecasters having made dire predictions implicitly based on that concept since the beginning of recorded history and surely before.

If, instead of testing the Malthusian theory on the past, one looks to the future, but if one does not specify some observable (or even identifiable) time period during which prices will rise permanently to levels above what they are now, and, instead, one simply says increased scarcity will happen 'sometime', then the Malthusian theory is meaningless scientifically, according to the standard canon of scientific meaning; a theory about 'sometime' cannot be tested, not even in principle.

A very different theoretical viewpoint sees the process by which resources have become progressively more available as part of the broader story of the creation and adoption of new technology largely in response to increased demand and/or increased prices for the resources due to population growth. The relationship between technology and demand assuredly is not that which is suggested by the vulgar idea of a 'race' between them. More people certainly imply increased demand in the short run, and therefore higher costs than otherwise in the short run. But the long run is not just a sequence of short runs in this case, and hence it is fallacious to draw any conclusions from this short-run analysis. In the longer run, technology's advance comes from people, and technological advance is the sole factor responsible for the long-run declines in material cost.

The process by which increased demand due to more people and higher income causes advances in resource technology is only a special case of the general relationship between demand and technical advance. Here are two famous natural-resource cases that illustrate the process.

(1) Ivory used for billiard balls threatened to run out in the 19th century. As a result of a prize offered for a replacement material, celluloid was developed, and that discovery led directly to the wide range of plastics that now give us an astonishing variety of products (including billiard balls) at prices so low as to boggle the 19th century mind.

(2) England was full of alarm in the 1600's at an impending shortage of energy due to the deforestation of the country for firewood. People feared a scarcity of fuel for both heating and for the iron industry. This impending scarcity led to the use of coal.

Then in the mid-1800's Englishmen came to worry about an impending coal crisis. The great English economist, Jevons, calculated that a shortage of coal would bring England's industry to a standstill by 1900; he carefully assessed that oil could never make a decisive difference. Triggered by the impending scarcity of coal (and of whale oil, whose story comes next) ingenious profit-minded people developed oil into a more desirable fuel than coal ever was. By 1985 we find England exporting both coal and oil.

Another element in the story: Because of increased demand due to population growth and increased income, the price of whale oil for lamps jumped in the 1840's, and the Civil War pushed it even higher, leading to a whale oil 'crisis'. This provided incentive for enterprising people to discover and produce substitutes. First came oil from rapeseed, olives, linseed, and camphene oil from pine trees. Then inventors learned how to get coal oil from coal, a flourishing industry in 1859. About then, other ingenious persons produced kerosene from the rock oil that seeped to the surface, a product so desirable that its price then rose from $0.75 a gallon to $2.00. This stimulated enterprisers to increase the supply of oil, and finally Edwin L. Drake brought in his famous well in Titusville, Pennsylvania. Learning how to refine the oil took a while. But in a few years there were hundreds of small refiners in the U.S., and soon the bottom fell out of the whale oil market, the price falling from $2.50 or more at its peak around 1866 to well below a dollar.

In addition to a theoretical explanation of past trends, a forecast seems even more convincing if the future of the relevant variables is predicted as a function of an independent variable whose future magnitude is itself predicted with some confidence. Increases in natural resource availability have accompanied (and in my view, have been caused by) increases in population and total demand. It seems reasonable to forecast continued increases for population and total demand in the future.

Hence, this constitutes additional basis for forecasting continued increases in natural resource availability.

So, I believe that the first two steps of my forecasting method examination of the experiential data, and analysis of theoretical arguments and, especially, inquiry into a theoretical mechanism that explains the observed data, lead solidly to the third-step conclusion that it is reasonable to forecast a continuation of the observed trend, continued decline in resource prices and increase in availability.

I also said that even if there were no satisfactory theoretical mechanism to explain the observed data, it might well be reasonable to forecast a continuation of the trend observed in the data if the statistical evidence is sufficiently overwhelming. Critics who have not noticed the theoretical mechanism described above have sometimes said 'All you are doing is extrapolating', and they often call this 'mindless extrapolating', suggesting that extrapolating in the absence of theory has not scientific foundation. I disagree, and I wish next to argue that there is indeed a solid logical basis for doing so. This may be considered as a contribution to the debate about the scientific basis of induction which has raged ever since Hume.

5. Do trends predict? If so, why?

The main reason that I forecast increasing availability of natural resources is that such has been the trend throughout human history. But this then raises the question: Why is it reasonable to assume that a trend – even a long-run trend – will continue?

There seems plenty of casual evidence that the best first-approximation forecast of a social or economic or psychological state of affairs tomorrow is that it will be just as it is today. But *why* should that be so? Furthermore, a useful adjustment to this first-approximation forecast often is that the *rate of change* between tomorrow and today will be the same as the rate of change from yesterday to today. But why? That is, why should past trends be useful in prediction? At first thought the answer may seem obvious. But a second thought makes one wonder if the matter is as simple as it seems on first thought.

A related matter: You may improve a forecast of variable y – say, the type of car a family will own tomorrow – if you (a) know a relevant factor x, such as the family's income today, and (b) predict the family's income tomorrow on the basis of today's income. But *why* should one variable x help you predict another variable y?

The best way to begin, in my judgment, is just as we do in much other scientific work, by making assumptions. (These assumptions need not be true in an ultimate sense; all we ask of them is that they help us achieve our goals.) The key assumption I wish to make is that the world is not completely random, not totally disordered, that is, not in a state of maximum entropy, as the natural scientists would put it. Lack of complete disorder is the sort of picture that would emerge, for example, if the world were shapeless and void and then one enormous shock was inflicted on it, distorting it in innumerable ways. The result would be non-homogeneous and a lessened entropy; there would be 'form'. But there would not be order of the fashion of an orderly garden arranged according to someone's design. Someone once commented to me that 'God wrote a set of equations, and it is the scientist's job to discover them'. My view – the view that Einstein made most famous – is the opposite: man/woman the scientist writes a set of equations that more-or-less fit the uneven forms of the universe.

The fact that the assumption of inhomogeneity works in forecasting is a powerful reason to make the assumption. But for those who like to go to what they call 'first principles' – by which they often mean physical principles – there also seems to be cosmological evidence for his assumption, as a recent *Science* magazine review of the present state of astronomical thinking notes in its opening sentence 'To begin with, there is structure: the universe is obviously and grossly inhomogeneous' [Waldrop (1983, p. 1050)]. Physicists and mathematicians have recently begun to analyse various phenomena with a point of view similar to what I am suggesting here, with what is known as the theory of 'chaos'. (This seems an unusual choice of terminology. 'Chaos' is defined as 'constrained randomness' rather than the complete randomness that it seems to connote in common parlance. See *Newsweek*, July 18, 1983, p. 53.)

In a state of complete random disorder no prediction would turn out any better than any other prediction, except by chance. If all the materials of the world were scattered throughout the world in the same manner as random numbers are distributed in a random-number table, it would be just as impossible to make a better-than-chance prediction about any phenomenon as it is to predict the next random digit with better-than-chance accuracy. That is, no system of prediction of random numbers is better than any other. (If we could perceive a random world, it might seem like being in the middle of a well-mixed pile of sand of several colors.) But in fact many of our predictions clearly are much better than chance; they could not be so if the world was in a state of complete entropic disorder.

In passing, we might note that the assumption of non-disorder is much simpler and more 'parsimonious' than is an assumption that the universe follows a set of built-in equations, or has the sort of designed order that a logical thinking mind would develop.

Another way of defining complete disorder is that a given material or social element would then have no more similarity to the element next to it than to a random element far away from it. That is, in a totally disordered world, adjacent elements are – by definition – 'independent'. But if we assume that the world is not totally disordered, we are implicitly assuming that at least some adjacent elements are not independent of each other, and bear some similarity to each other. This is the assumption made so frequently in mathematics when 'continuity' is assumed. And *given this assumption, if one knows the properties of a given element and then predicts that the adjacent element has the same properties, one will be right more often than chance.* Furthermore, if the degree of similarity is the same among various adjacent elements, the higher the similarity between elements A and B, the better will be a prediction that C is like A (assuming A, B, and C are arranged in that order in a line). This is the process of 'extrapolation', predicting the unknown case from the known case.

Let us consider a homely example. You observe that the owner of the third house on the block owns a big new car. If you predict that the next-door neighbor in the fourth house also has a big new car, you will be right more often than if you make that prediction for randomly-chosen homeowners (on the assumption that the world, or rather the United States, is not in complete disorder). Furthermore, if you then observe that the fourth-house owner does have a big new car, a prediction that the fifth-house owner also has a new car is more likely to be correct than if only the fourth house and not the third house had a big new car. That is, the high degree of similarity between the third and fourth houses increases the chance of accuracy in a prediction that the fifth house would be like the fourth house.

The dimension on which one element is 'next to' another need not be geographic. Frequently the relevant proximity is in time. The number of minutes of daylight tomorrow may be predicted on the basis of the number of minutes of daylight today and yesterday. A patient's mental state tomorrow may be predicted on the basis of her/his mental state today. And the speed it takes a rat to traverse a maze in trial 22 may be predicted on the basis of its elapsed time in trial 21.

To summarize this section, why is it reasonable to assume that a trend will continue? The short answer is that continuity of state and continuation of trend are a basic feature – perhaps the most basic feature – of the world we live in.

6. How long should the base period be for a long-run forecast?

If you find that there has indeed been a trend during the relevant past, then it is often reasonable to extend that trend as the basis of your prediction. But the pattern of the past is often not consistent, in which case you must decide which parts of the past to pay most attention to.

In my view, the most important element in making sound long-run predictions from trends is to examine the sweep of history as far back in the past as possible, to ensure that what one thinks is a trend is not just a blip in history. For example, notice in fig. 2 how differently one would predict the course of future copper prices from 1970's evidence alone than from the evidence going back to 1800.

The main reason for looking at a longer rather than a shorter period is because the longer period contains more information. But the relevance of the information from various periods in the past is, of course, a most difficult question. It is generally reasonable to weight the recent past more heavily than the distant past, though never completely forgetting the distant past. The commonest source of error is extending an apparent trend during a short period of time – an uptrend in copper prices within the last three years, say – into a prediction for the long-run future – say, prices two decades from now. One of the many sad examples of fallacious short-trend extension was the conclusion by individuals and governments that the raw material scarcity that appeared in 1973–1974 would continue to get worse into the indefinite future. That conclusion was very costly in waste of social and personal resources. For excellent discussion of the accuracy of forecasts, see Ascher (1979) and Armstrong (1978).

7. Summary

To summarize: I forecast that prices of all natural resources will go down. My forecasting 'method' is as follows:

(1) Ask: Is there any convincing reason not to consider the percentage changes from year to year in the longest data series on a resource's costs to be a representative sample of the 'universe' from which the past, present, and future are drawn? That is, is there some convincing reason not to generalize from the sample already drawn to samples that will be drawn in the future?

(2) If you do not reject the past as a sample of the universe from which the next set of observations will be drawn, then we next ask if there is a reasonable 'theoretical' explanation for the observed trend. Such an explanation is not necessary for one to believe that the trend will continue. But a theoretical explanation increases belief that the observed trend is not just caused by chance.

The explanation I accept for the trend of decreasing cost is a set of market feedbacks resulting in new discoveries, substitutes, etc., with externalities that leave us better than before shortages arose.

(3) If the answer to (1) is 'no' and to (2) is 'yes' – or even if the answer to (2) is 'no' but the data in (1) are so many and so consistent that your statistical sense tells you that they are overwhelming – then it seems reasonable to extrapolate the observed trend with a monotonic function that seems to fit the data relatively well.

The appropriate economic measurement of raw-material scarcity is cost or price. The very longest trends throughout humankind's history exhibit decreasing rather than increasing scarcity for all raw materials except saw-logs and oil, and there are persuasive reasons to think that they, too, will show decreasing scarcity in the future. Malthusian diminishing returns theory does not fit these observed facts and is not compelling intellectually; a theory of endogenous invention is more persuasive, in my view. An explanation of the persistence and predictive power of trends was offered, and it is argued that, ceteris paribus, longer trends are a preferable basis than are shorter trends where the two conflict, because the longer trends contain more information.

References

Armstrong. J. Scott. 1978. Long range forecasting (Wiley. New York).
Ascher. William. 1979. Forecasting (Johns Hopkins University Press. Baltimore. MD).
Barnett. Harold J.. and Chandler Morse. 1963. Scarcity and growth: The Economics of natural resource availability (Johns Hopkins University Press. Baltimore. MD).
Childe. Gordon. 1942/1964. What happened in history (Penquin Books. Baltimore. MD).
Clark. Colin. 1957. Conditions of economic progress. 3rd ed. (Macmillan. New York).
Simon. Julian L.. 1981. The ultimate resource (Princeton University Press. Princeton. NJ).
Waldrop. M. Mitchell. 1983. The large-scale structure of the universe. Science. March. 1050–1052.

[32]

Foreword

The paper presents a formal model of the process which has advanced civilization and economy to where we are now: Growth in population and/or income causes problems of actual and threatened scarcity, as signaled by increased prices. That is, more people, and increased income, cause problems in the short run. This presents *opportunity* and prompts the *search for solutions*. In a free society, solutions are eventually found. And in the long run the new developments leave us *better off than if the problems had not arisen*.

5

Population, Natural Resources, and the Long-Run Standard of Living

WITH GUNTER STEINMANN

PREFACE

Douglass North began his Structure and Change in Economic History *by remarking on "the basic tension that has been and remains the center of economic history—that between population and resources" (1981, 13). That tension is the subject of this essay.*

North goes on to say that "the classical model provided no escape from its dismal implications, although as Ester Boserup has persuasively argued (1965), population sometimes acted as a spur to induce [actually, adopt rather than induce, in her model] new techniques (but she provides no theoretical bridge to account for the overcoming of diminishing returns to a fixed factor)." This essay provides such a theoretical bridge.

More specifically, this essay offers a formal theoretical explanation of the apparent paradox that even though we use natural resources, the supplies of the resources increase (as measured by the declines in their costs: the classic presentation is that of Barnett and Morse 1963, or see Simon, The Ultimate Resource, *1981).*

The key element in the model is that an actual or expected run-up in price of a raw material—land is the example of a raw material used in the paper because of its key importance in providing food—caused by an increase in demand provides incentive for people to seek new sources of the material (e.g., "waste" areas, and new continents), new ways of using the material more efficiently (e.g., irrigation, new seeds, and fertilizer), and substitutes for the material (e.g., hydroponics, rafts used as floating arable islands by the Aztecs, and plans to use ships in Tokyo Bay as floating office buildings; Wall Street Journal, *May 25, 1988, 1). When this key conceptual element is added to the Malthusian model in which more people imply increasing scarcity and a lower standard of living, the result is exactly the opposite of the Malthusian model: more people imply increasing availability and higher income.*

Published in part in the *Journal of Population Economics* 4 (1991).

Gunter Steinmann acknowledges financial support from the Volkswagen Foundation and a travel grant from the Fulbright Commission.

The essay first presents the key idea in a historical prose analysis, built on bare algebraic bones and displayed in a graph. Then it proceeds to a very abstract growth-theoretic analytic solution to the model. Lastly, it simulates outcomes under various conditions.

Can we be sure that this process will continue in the future? An interesting difference between short-run and long-run analysis is that—contrary to common assumption—the long run is much more predictable in these matters than is the short run. Indeed, it seems generally true for aggregate economic phenomena that the longer the time period, the more predictable the direction of the phenomena. The direction of the stock market is much more predictable for a ten-year forecast than for a ten-day or one-year forecast. The same is true for per-person income in almost any country, as well as for other measures of welfare. Relevant here is that the prices of natural resources relative to wages, and even to consumer goods, all show the same downward trend in the very long run, though the short run is extremely unpredictable. This is simply a realization of the Law of Large Numbers.

This essay originated in 1984 as a talk at the Population Association of America that outlined an early version of the model. I subsequently discussed it with Gunter Steinmann, with whom I had earlier collaborated on several papers, and suggested that he build a simulation of the model. He then suggested that it would also be possible to find an analytic solution to a stripped-down version of the model, and he quickly arrived at it. That solution revealed some shortcomings in the model, which together we corrected, and he solved the new model. Similarly with the simulation; the construction of the simulation revealed many alterations in the original model that were necessary to make the model tractable and to have it produce results that fit history, and we jointly worked out these alterations. (More discussion of that fitting process is in the essay.)

This is an opportunity for me to tell newcomers to the technique what everyone who has done a simulation already knows: It is a lot harder than it looks to build a sound simulation. One badly chosen variable, or one unrealistically chosen relationship, and the results will be nonsensical or wrong. The most famous slogan in computer analysis applies especially well here: GIGO—garbage in, garbage out.

SITUATED at a randomly chosen date in the past, a forecaster of the price of a randomly chosen raw material, for a randomly chosen future date (say, one or ten or one hundred years later) has had a remarkably good chance of being correct by predicting that the future price would be lower than the price as of the forecast date.[1]

So predictable a relationship calls for an explanation of its mechanism, rather than regarding it simply as an empirical regularity. Clearly it is not satisfactory to consider the phenomenon to be chance outcomes of a Malthusian "race" between, on the one hand, new provisions of the material, or substitutes for it, and on the other hand, the increased pressure on the provision of the material due to diminishing returns and to increased demand from the growth of income and population.

This essay studies the natural resources element in the theory of population growth over the very long run. The subject deserves attention because the "pressure" of human numbers on natural resources is a matter of concern for many people even though frightening Malthusian prophecies have been increasingly far off the mark with the passage of the centuries, as the following evidence shows:

1. *Decrease rather than increase in the cost of raw materials*. Figure 5.1 shows the relevant price—the ratio of the nominal price of a unit of the resource to hourly or daily wages—for three representative materials. (All other raw materials show similar behavior. Food is closer to the measure of the cost of services that we would like to portray than is copper, but this measure is the best that can be done for copper.) For general interest, figure 5.1 also shows the ratio of the nominal price of the resource to the nominal price of consumer goods, though this ratio does not show anything about whether raw materials have become more or less of a constraint upon economic development with the passage of time. (For more discussion of this idea, along with much other data on the matter, see Simon 1981.) The wage-ratio trends are nowhere near so dramatic in the poorer countries as in the United States, but they are in the same direction; this is implicit in the observed trends in real living standards, together with the observed trends in the ratio of raw materials prices to consumer goods prices.

2. *Diminution in the relative importance of agriculture and the rest of the primary sector*. This may be seen in value terms as a decreasing proportion of GNP, the classic demonstration being that of Barnett and Morse (1963). This is also indicated by the long-term decrease in the proportion of the labor force in agriculture in even the poorest countries, such as India, as shown by Clark (1957), Kumar (1973), and by the UNFAO *Production Yearbook*.[2]

3. *Decrease in the incidence of famine deaths, especially over the past century* (see Johnson 1970). Perhaps politically induced starvation (e.g., in the Ukraine in the 1930s) should be excluded from the proposition.

Over the span of human history that the model aspires to portray, the relevant variables differ in importance from era to era. We can only hope that the differences from stage to stage are not so great as to make the attempt useless or misleading. And of course this feature makes the model thoroughly inappropriate for any policy recommendations, though it does call into question the policy recommendation derived from very-short-run models which imply that having fewer people tends to improve the standard of living.

FIGURE 5.1a

The Scarcity of Copper as Measured by Its Price Relative to Wages

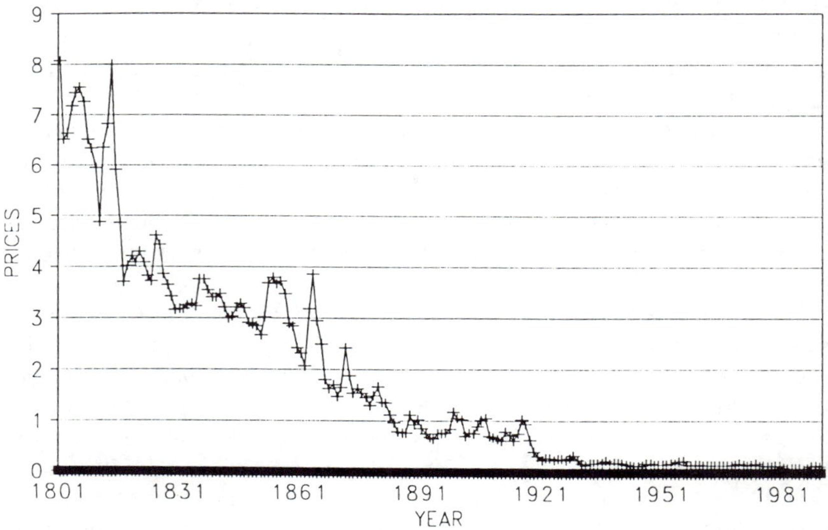

Source: Historical Statistics of the U.S.

FIGURE 5.1b

The Scarcity of Copper as Measured by Its Price Relative to the Consumer Price Index

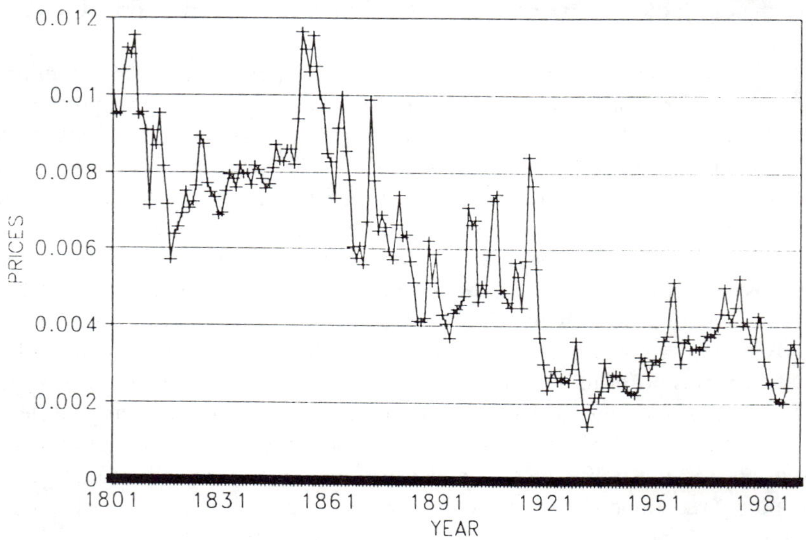

Source: Historical Statistics of the U.S.

FIGURE 5.1c
The Price of Oil Relative to Wages

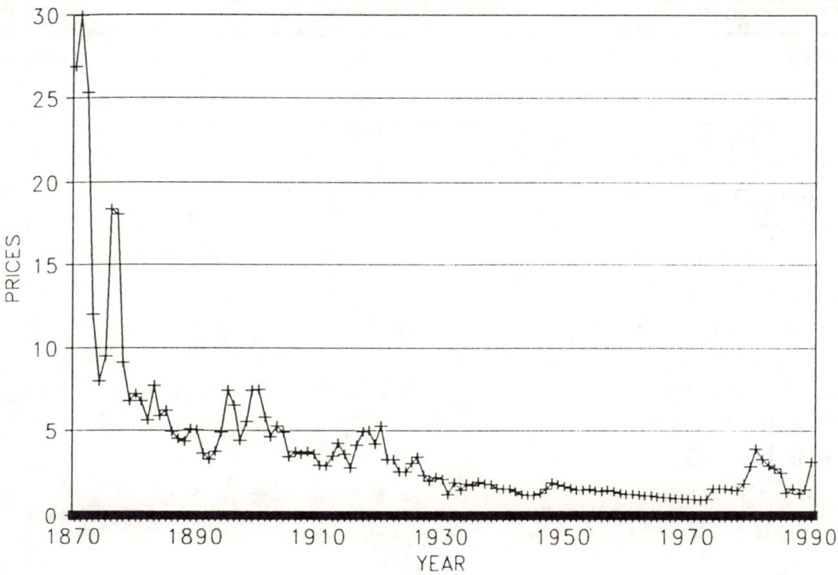

Source: Historical Statistics of the U.S.

FIGURE 5.1d
The Price of Oil Relative to the Consumer Price Index

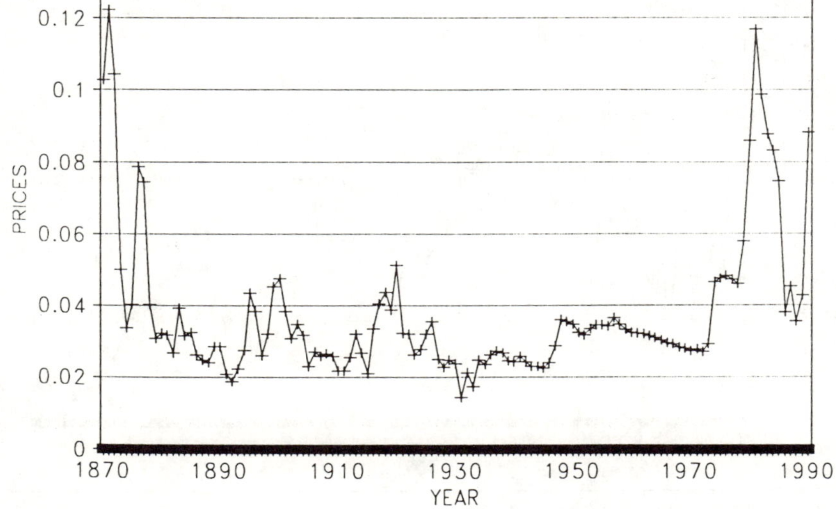

Source: Historical Statistics of the U.S.

FIGURE 5.1e
The Price of Wheat Relative to Wages in the United States

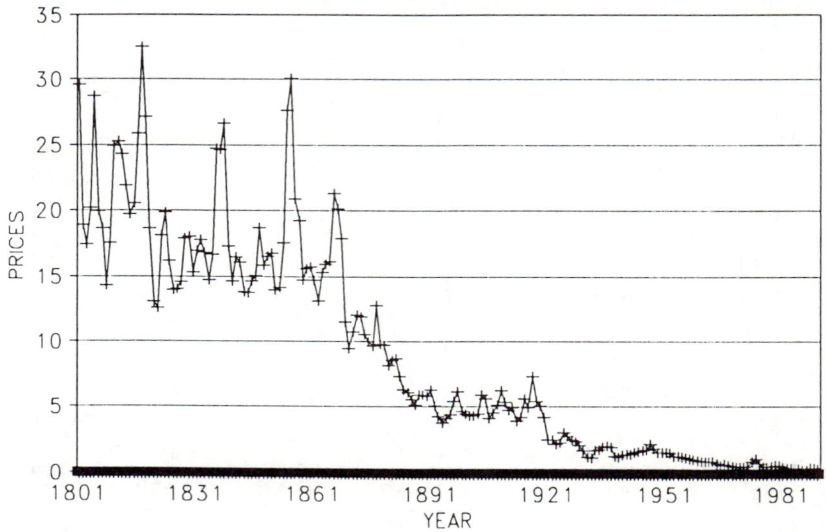

Source: Historical Statistics of the U.S.

FIGURE 5.1f
The Price of Wheat Relative to the Consumer Price Index

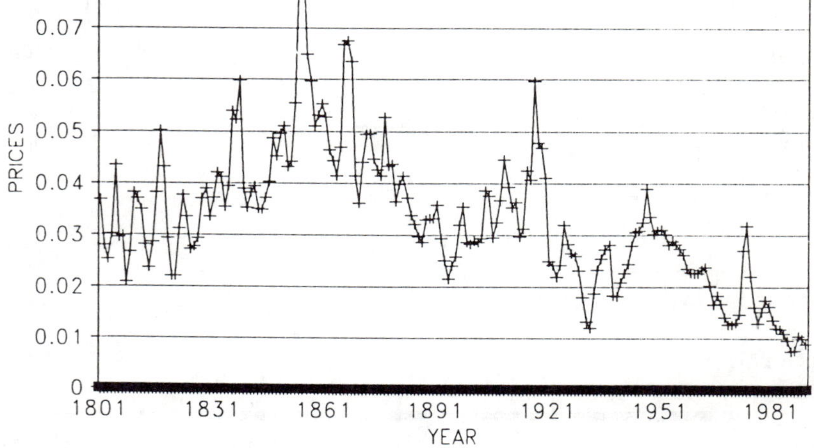

Source: Historical Statistics of the U.S.

Malthus's Model and Subsequent Thinking

Malthus's theory may be stated as follows:[3] Begin the operation of the model with the endowment of a given stock of natural resources. For simplicity we may, as did Malthus, consider these resources to be wholly fixed, renewable, and nondepletable; land is the canonical example. Population grows, and much faster than does the output of food (''output'' hereafter) because of diminishing returns (''geometric'' versus ''arithmetic'' rates) until it reaches subsistence. (Possibly some overshoot occurs, but this issue may be left aside.) At some time a new invention appears spontaneously that increases the effective stock of land and hence the output of food. The process then repeats itself endlessly because there is no mechanism that might cause the system to exit from this cycle. Population grows, but welfare does not. The food sector implicitly is the only sector of the economy; this is a reasonable simplification in a subsistence-agricultural context.

Let us write the Malthusian system as follows:

$$\text{Pop} = f(Q/\text{Pop}), \text{ positive and presumably monotonic} \qquad (1)$$
$$Q/\text{Pop} = f(A^*\text{Lnd}/\text{Pop}), \text{ positive and monotonic} \qquad (2)$$
$$dA = f(\text{Rand}), \text{ positive} \qquad (3)$$

where Q is total output, Pop is total population, Lnd is the stock of effective natural resources as measured by the physical quantity of land, A is the level of technique which (together with the stock of ''raw'' land) determines the amount of effective land, dA is the change in A from period to period, and Rand is a random exogenous increase in the stock of knowledge.

The course of economic welfare in Malthus's system depends entirely on the rate at which new technology fortuitously occurs. This is the probable origin of the notion of a ''race'' between the independently operating forces of, on the one hand, technology advance, and on the other hand, population growth. It is conceivable that the rate of appearance of new technology would be so fast that fertility could not keep up and income would therefore remain above subsistence for a prolonged period. But should autonomous technology ever falter in its rate of appearance, income would sink back to subsistence; there is nothing to keep income permanently raised above subsistence, in Malthus's system. This is why it is so ''dismal.''

Much modern work in population economics has followed Malthus in exploring the evolution of the economy with varying birth rates but resources either remaining constant (e.g., Day 1983, on chaotic fluctuations) or with declining resources (e.g., Cigno 1981).

Boserup (1965) controverted Malthus by making technique endogenous, though knowledge is still autonomous in her system. (Available knowledge is adopted when it becomes appropriate). In an earlier work (see chapter 3), Simon discusses the difference in the characteristics of inventions that fit

Boserup's system and those that fit Malthus's system, and thereby reconciles the two systems. (Also see Lee 1984). Boserup's system is very helpful in understanding earlier agricultural societies, especially primitive societies. But it does not fit well together with the important idea that new technology is induced by the demand for it.

Petty (1682/1899), Kuznets (1960), Kaldor in a very incomplete fashion (1957), and then—elegantly—Phelps (1966, though he does not state the implications of his model with respect to the effects of population growth), all portrayed technology as fully endogenous, as did Simon in earlier work (1977, chapter 4). But for those writers the only determinant of the rate of technological increase is the supply of minds (or trained minds in Phelps's case); there is no demand side in their models, and implicitly natural resources do not matter because there is no constraint on their systems. But the supply-side theory does not explain Malthusian crises and the recoveries from them.

Schmookler (1966), Rosenberg (1969), and lately North (1981) urge on us the importance of induced discoveries. True, the first two of those writers deal mainly with a more advanced economy than does Boserup. But we do not think that there is great disjunction betweeen Boserup's ideas and theirs, at least in the context we wish to address. And Sullivan and Simon studied agricultural inventions in England from 1541 to 1850 (measured by book titles and patents) which shows that food prices do have influence, along with population size and the existing stock of knowledge (chapter 16). But natural resources are not present in these formulations, either. (Also see Jones 1981.)[4]

Romer (1986) analyzed a model that takes an analogous view of the production of knowledge and produces similar patterns of continuing long-run growth. But his model deals with smooth secular trajectories rather than Malthusian cycles, and concentrates on demonstrating a competitive equilibrium rather than comparing the effects of different population-growth regimes.

Romer and Sasaki (1985) have placed a model of endogenous technical advance in resource production within a competitive market situation, and shown that a competitive equilibrium exists. Here the resource is implicitly not finite in supply.

Even if the resource is considered depletable, a scenario more difficult to master economically than the one offered here, a discovery process could lead to a long-run fall in price. Baumol (1986) has observed that the effect of a given change in knowledge depends on the "stock" of the resource that is augmented by a change in knowledge. (The appropriate concept of resource stock need not be troublesome in a discussion as abstract as this one.) He then sketches the system numerically and concludes that a reasonable rate of growth of productivity in the extraction of a natural resource such as oil could enable the effective supply to increase faster than demand due to population and income growth. In such a case, relative price might well fall even as the "real" stock of the resource diminishes toward a zero asymptote. Although the stock of land does not deplete, Baumol's calculations reinforce our general line of argument. Baumol's work differs from ours in not modeling a mechanism to explain the effect in question. However, Baumol's notion could be a building block in a discovery-based formal theory of resource prices in which the outcome of the process will be a cost lower than if the scarcity had not increased or threatened.

Steinmann (1989) offered a model that features the characteristics of long-run growth cycles. By implementing a production function for new technical knowledge, and the possibility of technical choices, into a neoclassical growth model, he was able to explain and simulate the historical experiences of recurrent and persistent Malthusian crises, technical revolutions, temporary escapes from Malthusian crises and, finally, unlimited and steady economic progress. However, his model is a one-sector model and does not deal with the sectoral shifts between agriculture and other industries.

Some writers have begun developing the macroeconomic consequences of the "new home economics" (e.g., Cigno 1988), but this line of work has not reached the analysis of natural resources.

Main Structure of the Model Offered Here

The task before us is to portray natural resources in such fashion that the model displays Malthusian crises in earlier times, while also showing how resources have become more available and less important with increasing knowledge and the long-term rise in income. Based on historical experience, the system should have the following properties: (a) Prices of resources should fall secularly relative to wages (and even relative to consumer goods, though this is not part of the system). (b) However, prices should turn upward in the Malthusian crises which should occur endogenously. (c) The rates of change of the population function and the price function should interact so as to produce Malthusian crises. (d) The Malthusian crises should become less severe and of shorter duration with the passage of time, perhaps becoming only inflection-point pauses in the upward trend as time goes on. (e) Q/Pop increases secularly. (Schultz's 1951 article on the growing unimportance of land goes directly to this point.)

In our structure, equation (1) may be as Malthus had it, though the function might be written to show the eventual transformation in which it becomes negative or no relationship at all.

Equation (2) is appropriate when the system begins, but as civilization proceeds, economic welfare depends less and less on the stock of natural resources, as indicated by the diminishing share in GNP. Therefore, we will need a two-sector model, and equation (2.1) acquires a subscript denoting that it applies to the food sector.

$$Q_{t,F} = f(A_{t,F} \cdot Lnd_t, Rand) \tag{2.1}$$

We shall not, however, distinguish between the level of technique being practiced in agriculture and in the nonfood sector at the same time. It seems reasonable to assume that the level of technique in the economy as a whole rises with the level of technique in agriculture; some support for this assumption is found in the close relationship between agricultural and nonagricultural wages; additionally, there may well not be any method, even in principle, to compare the rates of change of productivity in the agricultural and nonagricultural sectors that would be meaningful in this context. Therefore, $A_{t,F}$ refers to the "primary" sector of the economy. If so, we might write that the level of technique in use, multiplied by the land area, equals total output, on the assumption (for convenience only; the realistic contrary assumption would not affect the rest of this model) that the amount of work supplied remains the same under all conditions.

Now to specify the food-output equation for later use in steady-state analysis and computer simulation: The amount of food produced, and the sizes of the agricultural and nonagricultural labor forces, are jointly determined by a process wherein the proportion of total labor occupied in agriculture diminishes from the maximum of 95 percent (the initial condition) as food production per agricultural worker increases beyond the assumed maximum food-consumption per person of 150 percent of the initial level; the "surplus" labor shifts to the nonagricultural sector. When production falls below the maximum, labor shifts back to agriculture. For convenience, we let the total labor force L stand for total population.

$$Q_{t,F} = \min[Lnd_t^{\alpha F}(A_t^{\beta F} \cdot 0.95 \cdot L_t)^{\gamma F}, (1.5 \cdot Q_{0,F} \cdot L_t / L_0)] \qquad (2.2)$$

$$L_{t,F} = 0.95 \cdot L_t \qquad \text{if } Q_{t,F} < (1.5 \cdot Q_{t,F} \cdot L_t / L_0) \qquad (2.3)$$

In the simulation part of the work, we will need an additional constraint to keep a reduced agricultural labor-force from jumping upward all at once to 0.95 when food supply is temporarily devastated by the weather.

$$L_{t,F} = [Q_{t,F} / (Lnd_t^{\alpha F} \cdot A_t^{\beta F})]^{1/\gamma F} \qquad \text{if } Q_{t,F} = 1.5 \cdot Q_{0,F} \cdot L_t / L_0$$

$$L_{t,G} = L_{t,total} - L_{t,F}$$

A production function for the nonagricultural sector also is needed, though little discussion of it is necessary in the present context.

$$Q_{t,G} / L_t = g(A_t) \qquad (2.4)$$

or even $Q_{t,G} / L_t = b \cdot A_t$ where b is constant

Specifying (2.4) for analytical work:

$$Q_{t,G} = K_t^{\alpha G} \cdot A_t^{\beta G} \cdot L_{t,G}^{\gamma G} \qquad (2.5)$$

That is, the output of the economy outside of the agricultural sector depends on the work supplied, the capital, and the level of technology; A_t is assumed (strictly for convenience, with no change in the model needed if this assumption is not made) to be the same in the nonagricultural sector as in the agricultural sector. The sectoral outputs are expressed in real terms rather than value terms, but this abstraction should not cause difficulties and should prevent some confusion. In the simulation work, βG is set at unity while αG and γG sum to unity.

The change in knowledge and hence in the availability (stock) of resources (really, the level of technique in use) is far-and-away the pivotal and most challenging function in the model and requires extensive discussion to come in a later separate section, as does the distinction between the creation of knowledge and its adoption. For now we simply assert that the gain in technique from period to period, which we shall not presently distinguish from the gain in knowledge, depends on the stock of knowledge and on the price of resources. There is also a random element which depends on weather. This random element does not produce a crisis or a large rise in food prices when the "pressure" of population on food production capacity is relatively low, but when pressure is high, the random element triggers the Malthusian crisis that energizes the model, as discussed below with more precision.

$$A_t - A_{t-1} = m \cdot h[P_{t-x,Lnd} \cdot g(A_{t-1}), L_{t-1}] \qquad (3a)$$

where $P_{t,Lnd}$ is the price of land, and m is a multiplier which represents the economic and social climate for the development of new knowledge to take place, and is discussed later in a separate section. (This equation is written in discrete form because this best brings out the intuition it embodies, though the analysis will later be conducted intuitively.)

We next specify the technology function in a form that is more intuitively obvious on the l.h.s., and sufficiently precise for computation on the r.h.s.

$$A_t - A_{t-1} = m \cdot f(\tilde{N}_{t-x,Lnd}) \cdot g(A_{t-1}) \cdot L_{t-1} \qquad (3b)$$

with $\tilde{N}_{t-x,Lnd}$ the ratio between the price of land in period $t - x$ and the peak price of land before period $t - x$, and

$$f(\tilde{N}_{t-x,Lnd} > 1) > 0, \ f(\tilde{N}_{t-x,Lnd} \leq 1) = 0$$

Equation (3b) raises many questions. First, which price(s) should be on the right-hand side? Unlike the cases of most raw materials such as copper or coal, where the market prices clearly are the operative signals, the prices of both land and of its food output are likely to be signals to investments in land enhancement. In the short run, during which agricultural yields may be regarded as fixed, the prices of land and of food move together. But as yields increase, the price of a given quantity of food falls relative to a given quantity of land area.

One advantage of working with the price of land is that it is a closer analog to other raw materials, which are the general subject of this study, than is food. Also, the price of land is more easily thought of in real terms than are other raw materials because land can be valued in food equivalents, which constitute a meaningful system for long-run cross-nation comparisons (see Clark [1957]). While the price of food can be arrived at algebraically from land prices as constituted within this system, when derived in this fashion the food price seems much less meaningful than does the land price. Therefore, it would seem sensible to work with the price of land in the model rather than with the price of food. (We need not discuss whether the current or expected price should be chosen as the more relevant.)

The price of land may be expressed as follows:

$$P_{t,Lnd} = c \cdot (P_{t,F} \cdot Q_{t,F} / Lnd), \qquad \text{where c is constant} \qquad (4)$$

The rationale for this equation is Clark's law that the market value of a piece of land, everywhere and at all times (a major exception being the United States in the past two decades, though the price has been moving toward that value) has been about 3.5 to 4 times the value of a year's gross output. The actual multiplier used in equation (4) is of no consequence at all, however. The key aspect of the relationship is simply that the price of land is determined by the price of food and the output per unit of land, and not by the cost of creating the land, as Ricardo clearly taught us in his discussion of rents (1821/1963). But a multiplier of 3.5–4 makes sense in the long run because—given the owner's typical 50–50 share in a sharecropping arrangement—such a multiplier implies a return on investment of 12.5 percent to 14 percent, not at all high considering such costs to the owner as finding a tenant.

The price of food is negatively influenced by the supply of food per person, and positively influenced by the supply of nonfood goods, which is assumed here to stand for per-person income.[5]

$$P_{t,F} = k(Q_{t,F} / L_t, Q_{t,G} / L_t) \qquad (5)$$

The elasticity of the price of food with respect to the supply of food (μ) can be assumed to be greater than one for the length of period we are dealing with (a value of μ between 2.5 and 3 from European historical data is given by Abel 1978, 23; Gregory King gave data implying a sharply increasing elasticity with increasing price rise, as shown by Schumpeter 1954, 213, which is embodied in the simulation). We specify the price equation of food by

$$P_{t,F} = (Q_{t,F} / L_{t,F})^{-\mu} = (Q_{t,F} / L_t)^{-\mu} \cdot [(L_t - L_{t,G}) / L_t]^{\mu} \qquad (5a)$$

The relative food price decreases with higher labor productivity in agriculture, that is, with higher food production per head and higher ratio of workers engaged in nonfood production. By using the food-price equation (5a) and the production function of food (2.2) we can transform the price equation of land into

$$P_{t,Lnd} = \text{function } (L_t, A_t) \qquad (4a)$$

We may read from this equation that when technique is considered fixed for the moment, the price of land depends on population, and therefore [from (3b)] the change in technique depends on population size and the prior stock of knowledge.

We analyze this model in three ways. First, a causal graph allows inferences about the directional effects of the variables. Next, the steady-state analysis in the next section throws light on the relationships among the variables in the highly abstract and stylized context of growth theory. Then the simulation model allows us to analyze the relationships in a more realistic context, and permits us to learn about the quantitative and cyclical relationships among them.

Figure 5.2 portrays the equations and traces the directions of the effect of population growth in the shorter and longer run. We see in figure 5.2 that an increase in population has an unambiguous positive effect on the increment of technology, which then has some feedback effect in reducing the ''need'' for additional technology by reducing the prices of food and land. The change in food price that results from a one-time change in population size is theoretically uncertain. But we know empirically that it must eventually result in a drop in food prices; the price of food has been falling throughout history in terms of the labor time required to buy a quantity of food, which is the relevant measure here.

FIGURE 5.2

Circles Indicate the Effect of an Increment of People, Uncircled Effects Are Those of an Increment of Technology, and Dotted Lines Indicate Long-run Effects

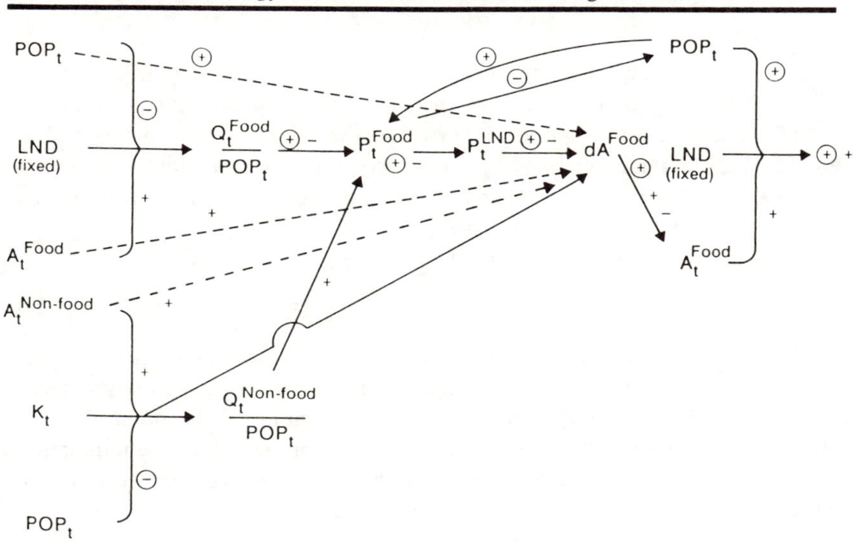

Steady-State Solution

To analyze the system in the highly abstract framework of equilibrium growth theory, we need to make some simplifying assumptions; this is the price for obtaining a solution that provides insights at a highly rarified level. The analysis is like a telescopic view into outer space, which necessarily reduces to invisibility many of the fundamental aspects of human life in our Earth world, and which may or may not reveal truths about the deep foundations of the system in which we are interested.

The steady-state analysis is carried out in continuous rather than discrete form. Although this reduces the intuitive link to the material, and courts the dangers that arise from working with ratios rather than absolute numbers, continuous analysis is unavoidable, and is here substantively identical to period analysis.

Let us assume for now that food consumption per person is constant. Given the range of variation of the human stomach among generations, and from bad times to good, and the range of body weights among persons in richer and poorer societies, this assumption is not very much at variance with observed reality, in the sense that the proportional deviation from reality is small compared to the proportional change in overall standard of living over the centuries in the richest societies.

$$Q_{t,\text{Food demanded}} = Q_{t,\text{Food supplied}} = c \cdot L_t \tag{6}$$

From (2.2) and (6), by taking the logarithms, differentiating by time and assuming constant rates of growth, we get[6]

$$\hat{L} = \beta F \cdot \hat{A} + \gamma F \cdot \hat{L}_F \tag{7}$$

That is, as the level of technique grows, the rate of growth of the labor force in agriculture can be less than the rate of growth of population without any reduction in food consumption per person, in the same spirit as equations (2.2) and (2.3). Or to put it another way, the improvement in agricultural productivity creates a "surplus" which enables the standard of living to increase by way of the production of nonagricultural goods.

We next specify and simplify the technical change function in

$$A_t - A_{t-1} = m \cdot \tilde{N}_{t-x,\text{Lnd}} \cdot A_{t-1} \tag{3b}$$

The size of the population that can supply and adapt new knowledge is omitted from equation (3b) for two reasons: Including it would present considerable analytical difficulty; and at the very beginning of the process, there probably was so much duplication in discovery that the size of the population mattered little. But including this element in the analysis would only reinforce our conclusions, as will be obvious upon inspection.

We get then the two alternative steady-state solutions:

$$\hat{A} = m \cdot \hat{P}_{Lnd} \qquad \text{if } \hat{P}_{Lnd} > 0 \quad \text{and} \tag{8a}$$

$$\hat{A} = 0 \qquad \text{if } \hat{P}_{Lnd} \leq 0 \tag{8b}$$

By substituting equation (6) and the price equations (4) and (5) into equation (8a), we derive

$$\hat{A} = m \cdot \hat{L} + m \cdot \mu \cdot (\hat{L}_F - \hat{L}) \tag{9}$$

Consumption per person can remain constant because the price of land increases with the output of land per acre, and the output of food per acre (upon which the price of land depends) rises with population. So we have quickly arrived at the fundamental characteristic of the system in which we are interested, the rise in the level of technique with the rise in population, to the extent that the economic and social system permits.

By substituting (9) into (7) we get

$$\hat{L}_F = \frac{1 - m \cdot \beta F \cdot (1 - \mu)}{\gamma F + (\beta F \cdot m \cdot \mu)} \cdot \hat{L} \tag{10}$$

The less the socioeconomic system permits and promotes change and improvement in knowledge—that is, the smaller is m—the less that the agricultural labor force can decrease while providing sustenance to the population, and (though it is not a part of this system) the more that work per person must increase in order to provide sustenance to the population. The possibilities may be divided into two cases, corresponding to different relative sizes of m. If

$$m < (1 - \gamma F) / \beta F \tag{10a}$$

then equation (10) leads to $\hat{L}_F > \hat{L}$. This condition cannot be satisfied in the long run. Consequently, economic development does not take place, and there is progressive immiseration toward a Malthusian low-level trap equilibrium; this is the source of the much-discussed low-level trap, rather than population growth per se (see chapter 7). If

$$m > (1 - \gamma F) / \beta F \tag{10b}$$

then we get $\hat{L}_F < \hat{L}\ (= \hat{Q}_F)$, that is, the escape from Malthusian crises. Furthermore, we can distinguish between two alternative results in this case. If

$$m > (1 - \gamma F) / \beta F \quad \text{and} \quad \mu > 1 \tag{10c}$$

then the absolute number of persons in agriculture is rising but the proportion of the total labor force in agriculture is falling, and economic development is taking place; this was the situation in the present-day rich countries for many decades. If

$$m > [1 / (\beta F \cdot (1-\mu)] > (1-\gamma F) / \mu \quad \text{and} \quad \mu < 1 \qquad (10d)$$

that is, relatively large m and small μ, then the absolute labor force is declining, which is the situation observed in all more-developed countries today, and which has been observed for a good many decades in the United States and elsewhere; despite the increasing population, the number of persons raising food falls.

We can also deduce the course of the output of nonagricultural goods per person, and of the standard of living. Let's assume for the sake of simplicity that the agricultural and the industrial production functions have the same output elasticities ($\alpha F = \alpha G$, $\beta F = \beta G$, $\gamma F = \gamma G$) and also constant returns to scale

$$\alpha F + \beta F + \gamma F = 1 \qquad (11)$$

and that the ratio of net investment (K) to industrial output (Q_G) is a constant s

$$dK = s \cdot Q_G \qquad (12)$$

Substituting (11) and (12) in (2.3) we get the steady-state solution

$$\hat{Q}_G = [(\beta F \cdot m) / (1-\alpha F)] \cdot \hat{L} + \gamma F \cdot \hat{L}_G \qquad (13)$$

We know that in the long run $\hat{L}_G \geq \hat{L}$. Therefore

$$\hat{Q}_G \geq [(\beta F \cdot m) / (1-\alpha F) + \gamma F] \cdot \hat{L} \qquad (13a)$$

and

$$\hat{q}_G \geq [(\beta F \cdot (m-1) - \alpha F \cdot \gamma F) / (1-\alpha F)] \cdot \hat{L} \qquad (13b)$$

The fraction on the right side of equation (13b) is positive if

$$m > (\alpha F \cdot \gamma F + \beta F) / \beta F \qquad (13c)$$

This condition is always fulfilled if condition (10b) is satisfied. The quantity of nonagricultural goods per person is increasing if the proportion of the labor force in agriculture is decreasing, and this is even more strongly the case when the absolute number of workers in agriculture is declining.

Numerical Simulation

Additional Hypotheses

The steady-state analysis indicates how a Malthusian crisis may come about due to a defective economic-social system, as indexed by a low value of m. But a steady-state analysis cannot show how a system moves through cycles of greater and lesser prosperity related to intermittent changes in the availability of raw materials. To do that, a simulation is necessary.

In addition to the structural equations, we specify a constant rate of population growth in each run. We equate population and labor force, ignoring differences in age distributions among populations. The total labor force is composed of agricultural and nonagricultural labor.

An exogenous rate of population growth is the key control variable. But this feature means that our simulation does not track human history as well as it might if population growth rose and fell with population ''pressure'' on the food supply—for example, the ''Malthusian'' contraction starting before the Black Death and the Malthusian expansion in the period around C.E. 1500. This exogenous-growth-rate characteristic of the model also is responsible for the proportion of the labor force in agriculture falling from a plateau earlier in our results than in history.

Fertility, mortality, and the population growth that is the difference between them could be treated as endogenous in a related model. But there is a puzzling absence of consensus at present concerning the Malthusian mortality effect (for example, see the analysis by Lee and Lindert of the English data developed by Wrigley and Schofield, and analyzed by Lee and by Lindert (Lindert 1983), and on the other side, Galloway (1985), which would make difficult the writing of acceptable population functions. The matter will therefore receive no further discussion at this point.

We assume that the production of food is influenced by random shocks from weather conditions (Z_t). The effects of the random shocks are assumed to decrease with higher technical knowledge. The equations (2.1.a) and (13) describe the production conditions and weather pattern.

$$Q_{t,F} = Lnd_t^{\alpha F} \cdot A_t^{\beta F} \cdot L_{t,F}^{\gamma F} \cdot Z_t \qquad (2.1a)$$

with

$$Z_t = 1 + \frac{Rand(w)}{(A_t / A_0)^{\lambda}} \qquad (13)$$

and

$$w_1 <= Rand(w) <= w_2$$

The parameters w_1 and w_2 show the maximum effect of bad (good) weather on food production $[-1 < w_1 < 0; w_2 > 0]$. The parameter λ measures the effect of improvements in technical knowledge on the relationship of food production to weather conditions. With a high value of λ, the weather conditions lose their impact on food production rapidly as soon as technical knowledge grows. On the other hand, with $\lambda = 0$, the effect of weather on production is independent of technical knowledge and does not diminish or disappear.

The most difficult technical decision is how to specify the technical progress function, including how to index the change in the price of land that enters the technical progress function. We assume

$$A_t - A_{t-1} = m \cdot [(\tilde{P}_{t-x,Lnd} - 1) + a_t] \cdot A_{t-1}$$
$$\text{if } \tilde{P}_{t-x,Lnd} > 1 \qquad (3c)$$

$$A_t - A_{t-1} = a_t \cdot A_{t-1} \qquad \text{if } \tilde{P}_{t-x,Lnd} <= 1 \qquad (3d)$$

with

$$a_t = 0 \qquad \text{if } F_t < F_{min}$$

$$a_t = a_{max} \qquad \text{if } F_t > F_{max}$$

$$a_t = a_{max} \cdot (F_t - F_{min}) / (F_{max} - F_{min}) \qquad \text{if } F_{min} <= F_t =< F_{max}$$

$$F_t = (A_{t-\epsilon 1}) \cdot (L_{t-\epsilon 2})$$

$[m \cdot (\tilde{P}_{t-x,Lnd} - 1) \cdot A_{t-1}]$ shows the technical response to high land prices in scarcity periods and $[m \cdot a_t \cdot A_{t-1}]$ indicates the technical stimulus stemming from higher population size and better technological knowledge.

m is the technical multiplier.

$\tilde{P}_{t-x,Lnd}$ is the ratio between the price of land in period $t - x$ and the peak price of land in the time before $t - x$.

F_{min} is the minimum level of the sizes of population and technological knowledge to produce new technological knowledge in the absence of food scarcity and, hence, without pressure to change technology.

$[m \cdot a_{max}]$ is the maximum rate of technical progress and is reached when sizes of population and technological knowledge exceed F_{max}.

ϵ_1 and ϵ_2 are parameters of the technical progress function.

We assume that the lag (x) between changes in the price of land and the technical change in question becomes shorter when the level of technical knowledge rises. We specify this hypothesis in the simulations by equation (14):

$$x = [1 + B / (A_t / A_0)^{\zeta}] \qquad (14)$$

The maximum length of the lag is $x = [1 + B]$ [if $A_t = A_0$]. The minimum length of the lag is $x = 1$ [if $A_t \rightarrow \infty$]. The parameter ζ shows the impact of an increase of technical knowledge on the length of the lag.

Numerical Specification of the Parameter Values

We use the following numerical values for the parameters in the simulations:

$\alpha = 0.33$, $\beta = 1.00$, $\gamma = 0.67$ in both sectors (production function exponents)

$\epsilon_1 = \epsilon_2 = 0.5$ (technical progress function)

Some simulation runs are shown in figure 5.3. The key comparisons are those between runs with otherwise-identical parameters that differ in the rate of population growth.

We shall not go into detail here about the parameter settings for the various runs, partly because of space (information is available in an appendix from the authors), partly because the particular specifications are not crucial to the argument (the findings are robust, the same results emerging not only from a wide range of parameters but also from models with other knowledge-production and food-production equations), and partly because they are not as close to realism as we would wish. As anyone who has built a cycling simulation knows, it is extremely difficult to find parameters that are sufficiently balanced so as to cycle and also approach realism. By analogy, it is much easier to prove that an airplane can remain airborne than it is to design a plane that will not uncontrollably head for the sky or the ground, or react violently to the slightest touch of a control. So it is with our analytic work and for a simulation like this one.

The key results that emerge from our simulation runs are as follows:

FIGURE 5.3a

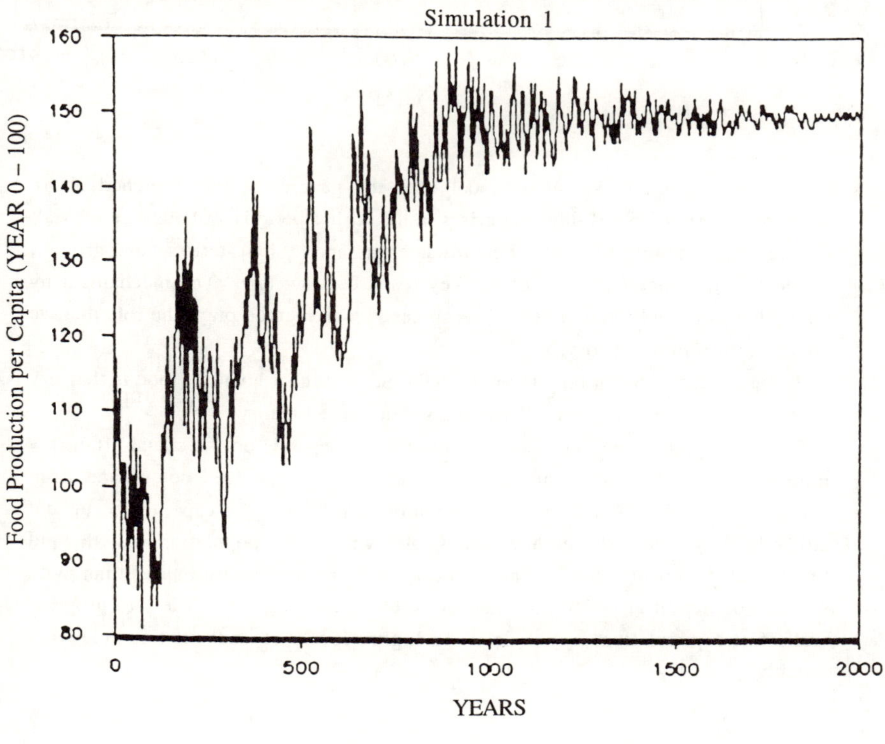

FIGURE 5.3b

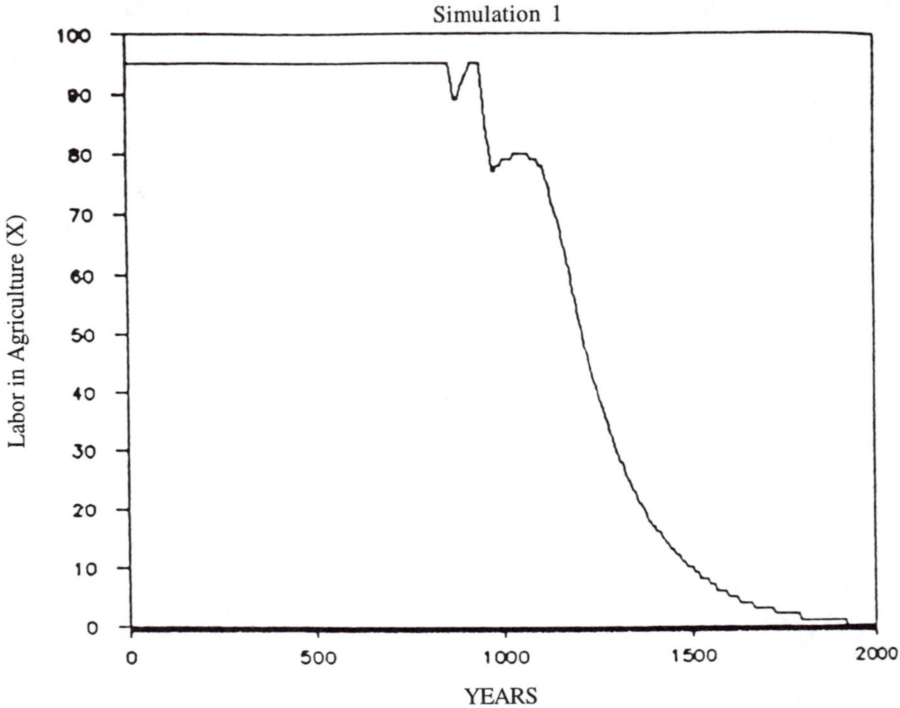

1. Most important is that a model with the general outline sketched above produces (a) short-run Malthusian crises in the earlier periods, (b) absence of Malthusian crises though still cyclical growth later on, and (c) long-term secular growth, all despite the apparent fixity of the key resource, raw land. The mechanism by which the stock of effective natural resources is incremented plays the role that we envision for it in our theory.

2. In all cases, slower population growth implies higher levels of food in the very short run, as is consistent with the simplest Malthusian theory.

3. The longer-run effect of population growth depends on the social-efficiency multiplier m. When m is sufficiently small, the society does not escape from subsistence living. When m is sufficiently large for an escape to occur but still relatively small, the escape comes later with faster population growth, and the level of consumption remains lower for a relatively long time than with slower population growth. But when m is sufficiently high for society to progress well, faster population growth leads to higher levels of consumption relatively quickly.

The Knowledge-Creation Function

The knowledge-creation function is the core of the model. There has been little or no historical work of which we are aware that helps us portray this process formally. Therefore, we shall now discuss the function specified earlier.

On the discovery side, response obviously is lagged, and posterity thereby gains more than do contemporaries from the occurrence of new problems. There are several reasons for the lag between the ''need'' revealed by the jump in price, and the onset and end of the responses. It takes time for ideas to be produced. It also takes time for ideas to be evaluated by the demanders and for the better ideas to shoulder aside the poorer ideas (which certainly is not done perfectly). Then it takes time for adoption of new ideas throughout the industry. Last, but perhaps most important, new ideas breed other new ideas, some of which have nothing at all to do with the original problem, and this process of self-perpetuating idea generation may go on almost indefinitely.

The response also is stochastic. We may think of the responses in the first, second . . . n years being drawn from a random distribution whose height is a function of the ''gap'' remaining as of that year, the results of the response only appearing some years after the time of the response. In that way, the cumulative response to the original gap will be large enough to leave the price lower than it would have been if the gap had never arisen. (In a simulation model, however, we make only the demand function stochastic, because that is enough to produce the random variation needed.)

The knowledge-creation function in the simulation model is stochastic to represent variations in weather conditions. There also are mechanisms that give reason to think that the function should be stochastic but that we have not included in the model for simplicity. Important among these is the Boserup-type effort-intensification process as population density increases. If this mechanism were included in the model, it almost would by itself require that the demand side be made stochastic, because if it were not, the constant pressure to remain at equilibrium would prevent the occasional appearance of unusual incentives for new developments. To illustrate, imagine a near-subsistence agricultural community where population is growing. Each year more effort is required to produce a ''satisfactory'' amount of food, and there is less and less unused capacity, both human and physical. Price, however, does not rise very much because of the additional effort. Then one year there occurs a chance catastrophe of some sort—drought, flood, depradation by another community, for example—and then price shoots far upward, much farther than it would if the same catastrophe had occurred at lower ''pressure'' on resources, that is, when the ratio of [A·Lnd/Pop] was lower. That large price rise then induces strong efforts to find ways to resolve the problem. And such efforts probably would be a more-than-proportional response to the gap between the pre- and post-catastrophe prices, perhaps proportional to the square of that gap. (The matter is taken up again in the discussion section below.)

The proposition that the technological response to price changes is more than proportional[7] to an increase in price from period to period is open to question. This proposition is important because if the system adjusts so smoothly as to prevent large price changes from occurring, and instead remains close to equilibrium values, the system could not develop the Malthusian crises that are a central phenomenon in the history that we seek to model. Natural catastrophes alone would not seem to completely fulfill this role of causing Malthusian crises, because they occur more frequently than do the worst of crises such as the famine prior to the Black Death, or the Irish famine of the nineteenth century.

There is no compelling reason in economic theory to suppose that the response to price changes is disproportionally large for large price changes. Perhaps there is a psychological mechanism having to do with thresholds that implies such a more-than-proportional response, but it, too, is not known to us, and even if it existed, its application to this situation would require substantiation. Yet there is evidence of large price spikes in the history of every extractive material.

If there is a more-than-proportional response function—and its existence must be an empirical question—it is likely to arise from the discontinuity of shifts in technique, as compared to the smooth transition from one level to another of application of the same technique. For example, one can gradually increase the land area planted, or gradually decrease the spacing of plants. As population density increases, families are likely to make such responses. But as the farmer increases intensity of cultivation with a given technique, the increments to additional effort grow smaller. Such conditions increase the likelihood that a given size of price rise will cause a shift to a new technology. (This process is modeled, though in terms of additional people rather than prices, in chapter 3). Even more to the point, a large price rise would seem more likely to induce a discontinuous shift to a new technique than would a small price rise. An analogy: A growing family may build additions to its original house for a while, but at some point it decides to move to a larger house. And twins may be more than twice as likely to induce the shift as one additional child. Some shifts are necessarily lumpy, and it therefore takes a major decision to cause them to happen.

It may also be that attention is disproportionate to the size of problems. Certainly there is a disproportionate amount of attention in the press to "crises," such as that given the rise in raw materials prices in the 1970s. Does anyone doubt that the number of column inches of space devoted to the price rises in the 1970s was much greater proportionately than the number of column inches devoted to the more moderate price rises that occur from time to time? And it seems as if the responses of governments, as well as of private individuals, were disproportionately affected by that press attention in the 1970s. (This is connected with the way in which experiences in the farther past seem to be underweighted in people's thinking relative to more recent experience, which certainly helps account for doomsday forecasts.)

It may also be the case that larger changes in price have disproportionately large effects on expectations about future prices, which then induce a disproportionately large effect on technical change. The continued existence of the cobweb corn-hog cycle would seem to prove that people do not learn in such fashion as to reach a stable equilibrium. And the evidence of various speculative bubbles—most recently documented in excellent detail with respect to the role of expectations in the farmland bubble in the United States from the 1950s to the 1980s by Hoch and Castle (1982)—makes clear that price behavior is often quite unjustified by the real economic situation.

There are still other avenues through which the process of problem occurrence caused by population and income growth, followed by new developments that tend to resolve the problem, bestows benefits upon the community. The new-knowledge response in agriculture contributes to technology in the nonagricultural sector, just as the development of the steam engine to remove water from mines contributed to many kinds of manufacturing and transportation. This effect will be reflected directly in the nonagricultural sector, in the system constructed above. In the model there also is an effect through the relative diminution of the agricultural sector, a connection that is not so obvious but that is a fundamental aspect of economic development.

Population growth is of central interest in this model, of course; we want to know the course of material welfare with different rates of population growth. A central aim of the analysis is to show that if population is stationary, and there are therefore no increases in the price of land, then the system will not move ahead and eventually produce higher incomes. This is another way of saying that we need more and bigger problems, rather than just having our problems solved, as the discipline of modern economics automatically takes to be our aim (and which is quite appropriate in the short run), because the process eventually leaves us better off than if problems were never to arise. This can be seen to follow directly from the system outlined here even without specifying the functions precisely.

Another way of using the system to arrive at the same point: If we run the model in reverse, we see that an exogenous decrease in the supply of resources, immediately causing a rise in price, eventuates in the supply of the resource being greater, the price lower, and resources being a smaller proportion of GNP, than if the exogenous loss of resources were not to take place. This is the history of humankind as we read it; if roots and rabbits had not gotten scarce ten thousand years ago, we would still be eating roots and rabbits, although maybe with some improved sauces.

The role of the economic and social system in the knowledge-creation function will be discussed briefly in the following section and at greater length in chapters 2 and 17.

The Effect of Economic and Social Systems

In the past few years, the element represented in the model by m, the institutional and cultural nature of the social and economic systems, has come to be regarded by many economists and historians as crucial. More specifically, the extent to which individuals are free to pursue economic opportunity, and the extent to which there is protection for the property that they purchase and create for both production and consumption, together with the presence of diversity and competition at all levels, seem to make an enormous difference in the propensity of people to develop and innovate. Clough (1951, 10) discussed the importance for the ''development of civilization'' of a social and political organization that will permit individuals to realize their total potential as contributors to civilization. What is implied here is that in a system where social taboos or political restrictions prevent large segments of a culture's population from engaging in types of activity that add most to civilization, the culture cannot attain the highest degree of civilization of which it is capable. Thus, the caste system in India, restrictions on choice of occupation in medieval Europe, and the anti-Semitic laws of Nazi Germany curtailed the civilizing process.

This factor seems to be the best explanation of the ''European miracle,'' to use Jones's term, in comparison to the recent centuries' histories of India and China. (See chapter 2 for more discussion) And it seems to explain why Hong Kong and Singapore are doing so well, and Africa is doing so poorly, right now.

The question of why societies have more or fewer social rigidities is outside of the scope of this paper, but we may note that population growth may cause a rigid structure to break up. This is Boserup's thesis (1965) applied to simple, small, societies, and Lal (1989) has made this case effectively for the history of India.

Including this general factor m also resolves some arguments about the effect of population growth, to wit: In circumstances where, due to adverse institutional and cultural conditions, there will be relatively little new creation of resources in response to the ''pressure'' and opportunity of population increase, the effect of more people may be quite negative for a long time, because total output will not rise much and per person output will fall; Africa's currently unfree countries make a good example, as did China at some times in her past, and (according to Lal) as did India for millenia until early in this century. But the United States, Europe from 1600 onward (especially the Netherlands, according to Toland), Taiwan, and some other countries, allow(ed) and even promote(d) freer and more rapid response. Hence, the negative effect of additional people in such places is short-lived and small, while the long run effect is positive.

The simplest way to build this factor into the model is with the multiplier m of the right-hand side of equation (3b). There may also be reason to use a multiplier in (4) and (5) to indicate that price response is nonexistent or muted in a nonmarket society, but we do not do so here.

Discussion

1. If one wished to construct a more comprehensive system, it would be possible to combine this model with a model developed earlier (chapter 8) to analyze the effects of population growth on income in less-developed countries for a somewhat shorter period, covering decades up to a century or two. The role of changes in hours of work as a function of ''need,'' as dealt with in the earlier model, and the role of economies of scale through increases in infrastructure as a function of population density, can probably be safely omitted from the present model, however, so as to render it less complex and the results easier to understand.

2. A major complication in constructing a system to track the course of economic civilization over the very long run is that, for millenia, the main response to increased demand for food was increased investment in land in the form of expanding the arable area rather than new advances in technology. The relative importance of the two responses has shifted over the centuries, with the increase in arable dominating early on (although bringing new land into production was intertwined with the development of ways of utilizing land that was not usable before, e.g., the heavy soils of northern Europe). In more recent years, perhaps largely in response to an increase in the cost of raw land, new technology (including technology for bringing raw land into cultivation, e.g., tractors) has dominated.

3. It is reasonable to inquire whether there is a theoretical reason to believe that the knowledge-production function must operate at a rate that will not only oppose the decreased availability of resources caused, *ceteris paribus*, by increases in population and income, but also will operate so strongly as to lead to increased availability in the long run. We have not found a persuasive and satisfactory theoretical argument to that effect, though one of us has sought one (Simon 1986, appendix 2). Our best-guess explanation is that the simplicity of raw materials—though it is not easy to define ''simplicity''—makes it easier to substitute for them than for consumer goods. That is, it is easier to find a substitute for copper than for a new car or an old Stradivarius, because when one wants to buy copper one wants it for just a single easily defined aim—to conduct electrical impulses, say—and anything else that does

this job is a satisfactory substitute. In contrast, many aspects of an automobile are of interest to a consumer—its speed, acceleration, looks, resistance to breakdown, resale value, and so on—each of which reduces the elasticity of substitution and hence makes it less likely that a new discovery will reduce the price. A related idea is that, for much the same reason, it is easier to routinize the production of raw materials than of consumer goods (though noting that farming is still extremely difficult to routinize because of the different treatment required by each field on a farm). With the passage of time, consumer goods are produced more cheaply relative to wages because of advancing technology; this is the heart of economic development. And the argument above suggests why the forces for advance in availability and cheapness may be even stronger for raw materials than for consumer goods. But the argument says nothing about the relative strengths of that force versus the forces of diminishing returns due to decline in richness of mineral lodes, and the increase in "pressure" on land. The net effect can be observed empirically, of course, but we have found no way to advance the matter theoretically.

4. One may deny the existence of the trends that we seek to explain, for example, that living standards have been rising, and that natural resources have been getting more available. But it is beyond discussion that even in the countries cited most often as "problems," such as Bangladesh, life expectancy has been rising significantly.

5. One may suggest that the propensities for sharp increases in mortality, and for price spikes due to weather or war or other exogenous shocks, do not increase during a period in which technique is stationary and population increases, that is, that there have not typically been "Malthusian crises." If this were so, then there would be no need to postulate a knowledge-creation function that responds disproportionately to pre- and post-catastrophe price differences. And indeed, such a function is not attractive to economists because it suggests that innovators and entrepreneurs do not respond smoothly and quickly to opportunities to innovate as they actually arise. A smooth function also implies that we do not need new problems for progress to occur. Indeed, as long as production cost is greater than zero, price increments have less than proportional impact on profits for a given quantity sold—though equal impact on total revenue. This suggests a smooth response.

The question is an empirical one. The evidence seems quite clear to us, but perhaps it is indeed open to doubt. Yet even if this objection is sound, only a minor change in the model would be needed, and a comfortable one at that. We could eliminate disproportionality, and simply assume that increasing tightness of supply of a resource, caused by population and income increase, spurs the search for new solutions, as may well have been the story of whale oil prior to the U.S. Civil War. Yet we continue to believe that disproportional reactions are important, even if they are not the whole of the story.[8]

6. Increases in knowledge arise costlessly in the model, though some im-

portant part of new knowledge uses resources at the cost of other uses, even in premodern times. For example, trying out a new seed requires at least extra effort if the seed is planted in addition to regular crops, and involves risk if it is planted as a substitute for other crops. But omission of this cost from the model does not seem to us a defect, for the following reasons: (a) Most important, to indicate a cost as a reduction in consumption during the period when it occurs would clearly have no effect on the operation of the model, and to make the cost a reduction in physical investment (in the larger model in which this cost segment must be embedded) also would probably make no difference, even though this model depends on the nature of the investment function used. (b) In the past, much, most, or perhaps practically all agricultural knowledge was produced without reduction in other resources, but rather simply by an increase in effort. And a considerable part of such ideas must have arisen purely "spontaneously" as "wonder," while following a plow or out hunting or lying in a warm bed in the morning. (Even physical investment on the farm tends to be not at the expense of other work because so much of it is done in the off-season.)

To put the matter in different words: The issue (as raised most sharply by Mark Rosenzweig in conversation) is the extent to which people should be assumed to maximize welfare subject to some constraint. Clearly, the question is not whether they "do" or "do not"; everyone agrees that a full maximization model makes no sense, as shown by the differences among behavior of persons. And we believe that in this model it is most appropriate not to be concerned about the cost of invention, because at most times and places the use of these resources has not meant less resources devoted to other investment or to consumption. (We are well aware of how hard this idea goes down with many competent economists. But we also recall how one of the great economists of our time, a Nobel prize winner whom we admire even compared to most Nobel winners, could not believe before the fact that the airlines would not voluntarily adopt an auction plan for dealing with oversales if it really were profitable for them to do so; after the fact, he was gentleman enough to admit that such was indeed the case.)

In this connection, it is instructive to recall Kuznets's statement when discussing "the processes by which new knowledge and new inventions originate": "(The) economic calculus is of limited application to a resource the returns from which are so wide-flung in space and time, and the identifiable costs of which are in such disproportion to returns when observable" (1977, 8).

7. If one does not feel comfortable looking at history in the fashion suggested by this model—its essence being that problems lead to improvements that leave us better off than if problems have not arisen—one may cast about for some other model to fit the history of the world. (While the absence of a more satisfactory competing model does not prove that this one is "correct,"

if this model provides some illumination it should have some claim to attention if there is no better competing model.) We do not, however, know of another model that performs as well or better than this one in fitting the indicated facts. Certainly the simple Malthusian model with autonomous technology, or any model with technology autonomous, utterly fails in this respect.

8. To write about the abundant possibilities of our physical world is not to declare oneself an across-the-board optimist. We have large reservations about whether our institutions will be sufficiently open and flexible to permit growth at the rate that physical and knowledge states permit. And effort might flag as people become more affluent. The latter is a story that Simon (1987) develops at length elsewhere.

9. The argument of this paper has implications for the effect of population growth on the prospects for war in the long run, by way of the change in the role of land and other natural resources. The central point is simple: To the extent that wars are about real turf, there would seem to be less rationale for such wars in the future as there occurs diminution of the importance of land for the production of goods other than esthetic enjoyment and sentimental attachment. This point is developed in chapter 20.

10. In Malthus's time, it would have been extraordinarily difficult for even the best-informed scholar to have effectively refuted Malthus's key idea, and to have demonstrated that we would not run out of resources in the long run. One then could not easily prove that one would soon be drinking coffee out of a paper cup using a plastic stirrer, and thereby replacing the glass and stone that had been in use for centuries. One could not then look down at the desert from an airplane (as one of us was looking down at the San Joaquin Valley, California, which was once a desert, when writing the first draft of this paragraph), and see the possibility of bringing water to that desert by modern transportation. (The best that one could have done would have been to look at the Bedouin in what is now Israel, and see their pitiful attempts to carry less than an ordinary kitchen-tap flow of water for many miles using all kinds of wooden channels and other contraptions, patently ineffective to conquer the desert.) But now we can see not only a history of change that promises great harvests, but we also can know that there is a large store of technology already in our hands able to create such changes; we do not even need to rely on any future development of technology. (This should calm the worriers who always ask how we can be sure that we will develop new ideas. Of course we will invent new ideas in response to new needs, but at this time we do not even have to rely on doing so.) All this experience and technical knowledge makes it possible for us to scientifically refute the idea of increasing resource scarcity, as we could not two hundred years ago.

11. One naturally wonders about the welfare implications of the model. Before making a brief comment on the matter, we would first like to emphasize that the primary purpose of the essay is to better understand history until

now, and not to serve as the basis for policy decisions. And even if we are pained at the tragedies of the past, we can give thanks on our own behalf, and on behalf of our descendants, that peoples in the past have propagated themselves to the extent that they set off the sequences of problems and solutions that have given us the long life expectancy and the high standard of material living that people in the richer countries now enjoy, and that people in the poorer countries can expect for their children or grandchildren even if not for themselves. And Malthusian crises are close to disappearing, with good luck never to be seen again. Therefore, the welfare implications of this system need never be debated.

If one wishes to pursue the welfare implications nevertheless, the question would be a difficult one in human terms though not in principle. Even if the long-run effect of a larger population and faster population growth is benign, the short-run effects of Malthusian crises are tragic. The appropriate method of evaluating these effects together would be to choose a discount factor and then assess the present values of the streams of economic welfare flowing from the several rates of population growth being considered. This general framework is shown for a somewhat similar problem in another article (Simon 1983).

12. The paper attempts to explain some key aspects of economic history with a small number of key factors. It will achieve its aims if (a) it is simple enough to highlight the mechanism it seeks to highlight; (b) none of the relationships runs grossly counter to the facts, as the reader takes the facts to be; and (c) it leads the reader to say that he/she better understands how things were the way they were. The paper fails if it does not achieve points (a) through (c); and if (d) there is another model that explains the same facts (or what the reader takes to be the main historical facts), as well or better than this model; or (e) if the main facts are not as they are assumed to be in the paper; or (f) despite not failing on principal characteristics, it does not leave the reader with the feeling of an enhanced understanding of the long sweep of history. It is not a failure of the model, in our judgment, if an element that the reader considers to be an important feature of the long sweep of history is omitted from the model. And in our judgment there is not even any reason to add such an element to the model unless it significantly improves the fit of the model to the stylized facts.

Summary

The physical nature of our world does not impose binding constraints that necessarily cause a reduction in the standard of living as population increases; though there always are ''limits,'' the constraints are relaxing rather than becoming tighter. This paper sketches a mechanism that, added to the Malthusian system, leads to entirely different conclusions than does the Malthusian system: Population growth creates new problems that in the short run constitute additional burdens but that, in the longer run, lead to new developments that leave us better off than if the problems had never arisen.

If all factors are fixed and there is no capacity to create new resources, additional people clearly cause economic disruption and resource scarcity. In such a system, additional people imply less output to go around. Hence, it is necessary to distinguish the effects of population growth in free market economies from the effects in economies where either there is central planning or the market does not operate effectively because of other social rigidities.

Notes

1. This essay benefited greatly from being presented in an earlier draft at a Population Association of America meeting in April 1984, to the Economic History workshop at the University of Illinois in November 1984, and to a seminar of the International Union for the Scientific Study of Population in New Delhi in December 1984. We appreciate valuable comments on earlier drafts from Stanley Engerman, E. L. Jones, and William McNeill.

2. Some persons have questioned whether the recent histories of Bangladesh and India disconfirm the trends shown in figure 5.1, and point instead toward immiseration. We think the data clearly show not. Consider (a) long-term trends in life expectancy—in India, up from 43.2 years at birth in 1960 to 51.8 years in 1980, and in Bangladesh, up from 37.3 years to 47.4 years (Ogaya and Tsuya 1988, 15); (b) proportion of labor force in agriculture—in India, down from 74.0 percent in 1960 to 69.3 percent in 1980, and in Bangladesh, down from 87.0 percent to 74.0 percent (Ogaya and Tsuya 1988, 35); and (c) primary school enrollment—in India, up from 61 percent in 1960 to 72 percent in 1980, and in Bangladesh, up from 47 percent to 63 percent (Ogaya and Tsuya 1988, 31).

3. Baumol's (1951) discussion of Malthus's system as the "magnificent dynamics" is an excellent formal treatment. The type of invention considered by Malthus is quite different from the type of invention considered by Boserup (see chapter 3).

4. This paragraph, and the paper as a whole, do not imply that economic forces account for all new inventions, even technical inventions. To a considerable extent we agree with Hayek that "man has been impelled to scientific inquiry by wonder and by need. Of these wonder has been incomparably more fertile." But Hayek does go on to note that "where we wonder we have already a question to ask" (1967). The need of the community, interpreted in the widest sense, often raises questions in thinkers' minds.

5. An increase in the model's A would therefore affect the price of food in both directions. But this complication is more apparent than real because any actual technical change occurs in one sector or the other, and hence its effect is unambiguous, while the only changes in which we are here interested are those in the natural resource sector where the effect of an improvement is to reduce the price of food. Specifying

the level of technique separately for the two sectors, as is possible though at the price of complexity, would eliminate this confusion. This boils down to the price of food depending on the level of technology in agriculture (negatively), the level of technology outside of agriculture (positively), and population (given that the supply of land area is fixed).

6. The equilibrium rate of growth of x is $_{x}$.

7. The question has been raised as to whether the mechanism works in reverse. Given the fact that the overall system being modeled is one of long-run secular change, one would be likely to assume that all mechanisms in the system are on an irreversible ratchet. But there does seem to be at least some evidence, as for example various cases cited by Boserup (1965), that indicate reversibility between population density and technical level, such as where decline in population has led to a technical "regression" to longer-fallow farming. And doomsday writers on nuclear war suppose such a regression, though involved with the destruction of modern equipment. The question is not crucial to the model, however.

Another point: Rashid has suggested (in conversation) that the function would not be monotonic, because at sufficiently high levels of distress, people are not able to respond to challenges. We accept the point, noting, however, that with respect to resources other than food, the function may well be monotonic.

Still another qualification: The discussion here is about changes in technique rather than discoveries of new technology. However, the distinction is not worth pursuing in this context, in our judgment.

8. A smooth reaction function is consistent with the idea that advance occurs even without population growth, because there are always disequilibria and opportunities. We expect cost-reducing discoveries in times of stationary population, but supply-enhancing discoveries in times of increasing population. (How does one classify a new source of energy?)

References

Abel, Wilhelm. 1978. *Agrarkrisen und Agrarkonjunktur: eine Geschichte der Land- und Ernhrungswirtschaft Mitteleuropas seit dem hohen Mittelalter*. 3. Auflage, Hamburg, Berlin: Pary.

Barnett, Harold, and Chandler Morse. 1963. *Scarcity and Growth*. Baltimore: Johns Hopkins University Press.

Baumol, William. 1951. *Economic Dynamics*. New York: Macmillan.

———. 1986. "On the Possibility of Continuing Expansion of Finite Resources." *Kyklos* 39, fasc. 2, 167–79.

Boserup, Ester. 1965. *The Conditions of Economic Growth*. London: Allen and Unwin.

Cigno, Alessandro. 1981. "Growth with Exhaustible Resources and Endogenous Population." *Review of Economic Studies* 48: 281–87.

Clark, Colin. 1957. *The Conditions of Economic Progress*. 2d ed. New York: Macmillan.

Clough, Shepard B. 1951, 1957. *The Rise and Fall of Civilization*. New York: Columbia University Press.

Day, Richard H. 1983. "The Emergence of Chaos from Classical Economic Growth." *Quarterly Journal of Economics* (May): 202–13.

Galloway, P. R. 1985. "Annual Variations in Deaths by Age, Deaths by Cause, Prices, and Weather in London 1670 to 1830." *Population Studies* 39: 487–505.

Hayek, Friedrich. 1967. "The Theory of Complex Phenomena." In *Studies in Philosophy, Politics, and Economics*, 22–42. Chicago: University of Chicago Press.

Hoch, Irving, and Emery Castle. 1982. "Farm Real Estate Price Components, 1920–78." *American Journal of Agricultural Economics* 64 (1): 8–18.

Johnson, D. Gale. 1970. "Famine." *Encyclopaedia Britannica*.

Jones, Eric L. 1981. *The European Miracle*. New York: Cambridge University Press.

Kaldor, Nicholas. 1957. "A Model of Economic Growth." *Economic Journal* 57 (December).

Kumar, Joginder. 1973. *Population and Land in World Agriculture*. Berkeley: University of California Press.

Kuznets, Simon. 1960. "Population Change and Aggregate Output." In *Universities-National Bureau of Economic Research, Demographic and Economic Change in Developed Countries*. Princeton: Princeton University Press.

———. 1977. "Two Centuries of Economic Growth: Reflections on U.S. Experience." *American Economic Review* 67 (February): 1ff.

Lal, Deepak. 1989. *Cultural Stability and Economic Stagnation: India, 1500 B.C.–1980 A.D.* London and New York: Oxford University Press.

Lee, Ronald. 1984. Paper at the Population Association of America, April.

Lindert, Peter H. 1983. "Some Economic Consequences of English Population Growth, 1541–1913." Xerox.

North, Douglass C. 1981. *Structure and Change in Economic History*. New York: Norton.

Ogaya, Naohira, and Noriko O. Tsuya. 1988. "Demographic Change and Human Resources Development in Asia and the Pacific: An Overall View." Nihon University Population Research Institute, March.

Petty, William. 1682/1899. "Another Essay in Political Arithmetic." In Charles H. Hull, ed., *The Economic Writings of Sir William Petty*. Cambridge: Cambrige University Press.

Phelps, Edmund S. 1966. "Models of Technical Progress and the Golden Rule of Research." *Review of Economic Studies* April: 133–45.

Ricardo, David. 1821/1963. *The Principles of Political Economy and Taxation*. 3d ed. Homewood, Ill.: Irwin.

Romer, Paul M. 1986. "Increasing Returns and Long-run Growth." *Journal of Political Economy* 94 (October): 1002–37.

Romer, Paul M., and Hiroo Sasaki. 1985. "Monotonically Decreasing Natural Resource Prices Under Perfect Foresight." Xerox. University of Rochester, February.

Rosenberg, Nathan. 1969. "The Direction of Technological Change: Inducement Mechanisms and Focusing Devices." *Economic Development and Cultural Change* 18 (1): 1–24.

Schmookler, Jacob. 1966. *Invention and Economic Growth*. Cambridge: Harvard University Press.

Schultz, Theodore W. 1951. ''The Declining Economic Importance of Land.'' *Economic Journal* 61 (December): 725–40.

Schumpeter, Joseph A. 1954. *History of Economic Analysis*. New York: Oxford University Press.

Simon, Julian L. 1977. *The Economics of Population Growth*. Princeton: Princeton University Press.

———. 1981. *The Ultimate Resource*. Princeton: Princeton University Press.

———. 1983. ''The Present Value of Population Growth in the Western World.'' *Population Studies* 37: 5–21.

———. 1987. *Effort, Opportunity, and Wealth*. Oxford: Basil Blackwell.

Simon, Julian L., and Richard Sullivan. n.d. ''Population Size, Knowledge Stock, and Other Determinants of Agricultural Publication and Patenting: England, 1541–1850.'' Chapter 15 below.

Steinmann, Gunter. 1989. ''Malthusian Crises, Boserupian Escapes and Longrun Economic Progress.'' In A. Wenig and K. Zimmermann, eds., *Population Economics*. Heidelberg and New York: Springer.

Steinmann, Gunter, and John Komlos. 1988. ''Population Growth and Economic Development in the Very Long Run: A Simulation Model of Three Revolutions.'' *Mathematical Social Sciences* 16: 49–63.

[33]

Foreword

Many environmental scares have turned out to be hoaxes on the public perpetrated by assorted interest groups, including academic disciplines. The species extinction scare must go this way some day. But until the time of writing this note, attempts to confront this idea have had little effect. The proponents of the scare have mostly simply ignored the data, successfully.

Species Loss Revisited

Julian L. Simon and Aaron Wildavsky

Note to Reader: Since completing the first draft of this article, a book edited by Whitmore and Sayer (1992) and sponsored by the International Union for the Conservation of Nature and Natural Resources (IUCN), has confirmed our central assertion here – from the pens of the very conservation biologists who have been most alarmed by the threat of species die-offs. Lengthy quotations have been included below documenting the consensus that there is no evidence of massive or increasing rates of species extinction. That book was originally conceived as a response to the questions raised by our predecessor article and by others since then.

INTRODUCTION

Species extinction is a key issue for the environmental movement. It is the subject of magazine stories with titles like "Playing Dice with Megadeath" with a subhead "The odds are good that we will exterminate half the world's species within the next century" (Diamond, 1990, p. 55.) Species "loss" also is a focal point for fundraising from the public. And the Congress is asked again and again for large sums of public money to be used directly and indirectly for programs to protect species and for "debt for Nature" swaps.

The central assertion is that species are dying off at a rate that is unprecedently high, and dangerous to humanity. The World Wildlife Fund, which publicizes this issue widely, frames the proposition as follows: "Without firing a shot, we may kill one-fifth of all species of life on this planet in the next 10 years."

The issue came to scientific prominence in 1979 with Myers's *The Sinking Ark*, and then was brought to an international public and onto the US policy agenda by the 1980 *Global 2000 Report to the President* (referred to hereafter as "GTR"). These still are the canonical texts.

GTR forecast extraordinary losses of species between 1980 and 2000. "Extinctions of plant and animal species will increase dramatically.

Hundreds of thousands of species – perhaps as many as 20 percent of all species on earth – will be irretrievably lost as their habitats vanish, especially in tropical forests" (US, 1980, I, 3).

In 1984 we reviewed the data on the observed rates of species extinction. We found that the scientific evidence was wildly at variance with the by-then-conventional wisdom and did not provide support for the various policies suggested to deal with the purported dangers. We also reminded readers that recent scientific and technical advances – especially seed banks and genetic engineering, and perhaps electronic mass-testing of new drugs – had rendered much less crucial the maintenance of a particular species of plant life in its natural habitat than would have been the case in earlier years. But the bandwagon of the species extinction issue continues to roll with ever-increasing speed.

Now we revise our presentation of the empirical and theoretical situations in light of the literature that has appeared in the 1980s. We find that our earlier conclusions remain sound and may be considered strengthened by the absence of new countervailing material coming to light since then.

These are the key questions: Are species defined with sufficient clarity so that different people can arrive at satisfactorily similar estimates? What is the history of species extinction until now? What are the most reasonable forecasts of future extinction? What will be the effects of extinctions (including resulting new additions) on species diversity? What will be the economic and non-economic impacts of the expected course of species diversity?

Society properly is concerned about possible dangers to species. Individual species, and perhaps all species taken together, constitute a valuable endowment, and we should guard their survival just as we guard our other physical and social assets. But we should strive for as clear and unbiased an understanding as possible in order to make the best possible judgments about how much time and money to spend in guarding them, in a world in which this valuable activity must compete with other valuable activities, including the guarding of valuable aspects of civilization and of human life.

The importance of the topic is clear from the far-reaching extent of the policies suggested. Edward O. Wilson and Paul Ehrlich actually ask that governments act "to reduce the scale of human activities." More specifically, they want us "to cease 'developing' any more relatively undisturbed land," because "Every new shopping center built in the California chaparral, every swamp converted into a rice paddy or shrimp farm means less biodiversity" (1991, p. 761).

DEFINING SPECIES

Before discussing rates of extinction, we must touch on an issue that complicates such estimates – the definition of a species. Referring to the "never-ending arguments about the definition of the species category," Ernst Mayr infers that "those who do not work with species but with cells or molecules may think that the species is an arbitrary and insignificant concept in biology." He argues otherwise. "What, then," Mayr asks, "is biological classification? Unhappily," he concludes, "No agreement on the answer to this question exists yet among biologists."

The *Encyclopaedia Britannica* defines species as "groups of individuals that resemble one another more than they resemble any others." But what constitutes "resemblance"? If we adopt the definition of "who mates with whom," we will reduce the number of species; if we give the more general definition that "Species are groups of organisms sharing many traits, or characteristics in common," the classifiers have a lot of room to raise or lower the number. If we use common DNA as a criterion, we guess the number of species would greatly diminish.

SPECIES LOSS ESTIMATES

The basic forecast for loss of species comes from Lovejoy:

> What then is a reasonable estimate of global extinctions by 2000? Given the amount of tropical forest already lost (which is important but often ignored), the extinctions can be estimated. . . . In the low deforestation case, approximately 15 percent of the planet's species can be expected to be lost. In the high deforestation case, perhaps as much as 20 percent will be lost. This means that of the 3–10 million species now present on the earth, at least 500,000–600,000 will be extinguished during the next two decades. (US, 1980, II, p. 331.)

This extract summarizes a table that shows a range between 437,000 and 1,875,000 extinctions out of a present estimated total of 3–10 million species. The table in turn is based on a linear relationship running from zero percent species extinguished at zero percent tropical forest cleared, to about 95 percent extinguished at 100 percent tropical forest clearing. The main source of differences in the range of estimated losses is the range of 3–10 million species in the overall estimate.

The basis of any useful projection must be some body of experience collected under some range of conditions that encompass the expected conditions, or that can reasonably be extrapolated to the expected conditions. But none of Lovejoy's references contain any scientifically impressive body of experience. The only published source given for his key table (US, 1980, Table 13–30, p. 331) is Myers's *The Sinking Ark* (1979).

Myers's summary may be taken as the basic source:

> As a primitive hunter, man probably proved himself capable of eliminating species, albeit as a relatively rare occurrence. From the year A.D. 1600, however, he became able, through advancing technology, to over-hunt ani-

> mals to extinction in just a few years, and to disrupt extensive environments just as rapidly. Between the years 1600 and 1900, man eliminated around seventy-five known species, almost all of them mammals and birds – virtually nothing has been established about how many reptiles, amphibians, fishes, invertebrates and plants disappeared. Since 1900 man has eliminated around another seventy-five known species – again, almost all of them mammals and birds, with hardly anything known about how many other creatures have faded from the scene. The rate from the year 1600 to 1900, roughly one species every 4 years, and the rate during most of the present century, about one species per year, are to be compared with a rate of possibly one per 1000 years during the "great dying" of the dinosaurs.
>
> Since 1960, however, when growth in human numbers and human aspirations began to exert greater impact on natural environments, vast territories in several major regions of the world have become so modified as to be cleared of much of their main wildlife. The result is that the extinction rate has certainly soared, though the details mostly remain undocumented. In 1974 a gathering of scientists concerned with the problem hazarded a guess that the overall extinction rate among all species, whether known to science or not, could now have reached 100 species per year. [Here Myers refers to *Science*, 1974, pp. 646–7]
>
> Yet even this figure seems low. A single ecological zone, the tropical moist forests, is believed to contain between 2 and 5 million species. If present patterns of exploitations persist in tropical moist forests, much virgin forest is likely to have disappeared by the end of the century, and much of the remainder will have been severely degraded. This will cause huge numbers of species to be wiped out. . . .
>
> Let us suppose that, as a consequence of this man-handling of natural environments, the final one-quarter of this century witnesses the elimination of 1 million species – a far from unlikely prospect. This would work out, during the course of 25 years, at an average extinction rate of 40,000 species per year, or rather over 100 species per day. The greatest exploitation pressures will not be directed at tropical forests and other species-rich biomes until towards the end of the period. That is to say, the 1990s could see many more species accounted for than the previous several decades. But already the disruptive processes are well underway, and it is not unrealistic to suppose that, right now, at least one species is disappearing each day. By the late 1980s we could be facing a situation where one species becomes extinct each hour (1979, pp. 4–5).

We may extract these key points from the above summary quotation:

1 The estimated extinction rate of known species is about one every four years between the years 1600 and 1900.
2 The estimated rate is about one a year from 1900 to the present.

No sources are given for these two estimates, either on the page from which the quote is taken or on pages 30–1 of Myers's book, where these estimates are again discussed.

3 Some scientists (in Myers's words) have "hazarded a guess" that the extinction rate "could now have reached" 100 species per year. That is, the estimate is simply conjecture and is not even a point estimate but rather an upper bound. The source given for the "some scientists" statement is a staff-written news report (Holden, 1974). It should be noted, however, that the subject of this guess is different than the subject of the estimates in (1) and (2), because the former includes mainly or exclusively birds or mammals whereas the latter includes all species. While this difference implies that (1) and (2) may be too low a basis for estimating the present extinction rate of all species, it also implies that there is even less statistical basis for estimating the extinction rate for species other than birds and mammals than it might otherwise seem.

4 This guessed upper limit in (3) is then increased and used by Myers, and then by Lovejoy, as the basis for the "projections" quoted above. In *Global 2000* the language has become "are likely to lead" to the extinction of between 14 percent and 20 percent of all species before the year 2000 (US, 1980, II, p. 328). So an upper limit for the

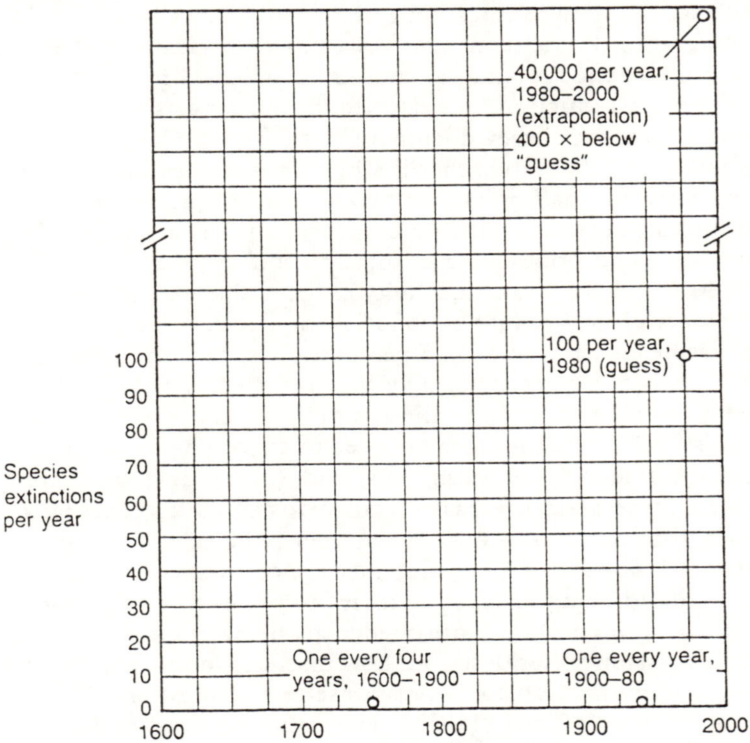

Figure 34.1 Myers–Lovejoy estimates of species extinction and their extrapolations to the year 2000
Source: N. Myers, *The Sinking Ark* (New York: Pergamon, 1979), and US CEQ and Dept of State (1980), The Global 2000 Report to the President, vol. 2 (Washington: GPO).

present that is pure guesswork has become the basis of a forecast for the future which has been published in newspapers to be read by tens or hundreds of millions of people and understood as a scientific statement.

The two historical rates stated by Myers, together with the yearly rates implied by Lovejoy's estimates, are plotted together in figure 34.1. It is clear that without explicitly bringing into consideration some additional force, one could extrapolate almost any rate one chooses for the year 2000, and the Lovejoy extrapolation would have no better claim to belief than a rate, say, one hundredth as large. Looking at the two historical points alone, many forecasters would be likely to project a rate much closer to the past than to Lovejoy's, on the basis of the common wisdom that in the absence of additional information, the best first approximation for a variable tomorrow is its value today, and the best second approximation is that the variable will change at the same rate in the future that it has in the past. And the uncertainty about the definition of species adds to the confusion.

Projected change in the amount of tropical forests implicitly underlies the differences between past and projected species-loss rates in Lovejoy's diagram. But to connect this element logically, there must be systematic evidence relating an amount of tropical forest removed to a rate of species reduction. We have found no reports of such empirical evidence. A recent survey document (Reid and Miller, 1989) says that "A useful rule of thumb is that if a habitat is reduced by 90 percent in area, roughly one-half of its species will be lost" (p. 35), and refers to a figure and an appendix, but no empirical studies are referred to, only speculation. The only empirical observation we found is by Lugo for Puerto Rico, where "human activity reduced the area of primary forests by 99 percent but, because of coffee shade and secondary forests, forest cover was never below 10 to 15 percent. This massive forest conversion did not lead to a correspondingly massive species extinction, certainly nowhere near the 50 percent alluded to by Myers" (1989, p. 28).

All this implies that there is no basis to choose between (a) Lovejoy's huge projected rates of extinction, and (b) modest rates continuing about the same as in the past – and this is the difference between the basis for recommending various national policies and not making any recommendations at all. (Again, this is not to say that no protection policies should be undertaken. Rather, it implies that other sorts of data to estimate extinction rates are needed as the basis for policy decisions.)

The discussion so far describes how matters stood when we wrote our 1984 article on the subject. In response to the questions we and others have raised, the "official" IUCN commissioned a book edited by Whitmore and Sayer (1992) to inquire into the extent of extinctions. The results of that project must be considered amazing. All the authors continue to be concerned about the rate of extinction. Nevertheless, they agree that the rate of *known* extinctions has been and continues to be very low. This is a sampling of quotations (with emphasis supplied), first on the subject of the estimated rates:

> . . . *60 birds and mammals are known to have become extinct between 1900 and 1950 (Reid, 1992, p. 55)*
>
> It is a commonplace that forests of the eastern United States were reduced over two centuries to fragments totalling 1–2% of their original extent, and that during this destruction, only three forest birds went extinct – the Carolina parakeet (*Conuropsis carolinensis*), the ivory-billed woodpecker (*Campephilus principalis principalis*), and the passenger pigeon (*Ectopistes migratorius*). Although deforestation certainly contributed to the decline of all three species, it was probably not critical for the pigeon or the parakeet (Greenway, 1967). *Why, then, would one predict massive extinction from similar destruction of tropical forest?* (Simberloff, 1992, p. 85)
>
> IUCN, together with the World Conservation Monitoring Centre, has amassed large volumes of data from specialists around the world relating to species decline, and it would seem sensible to compare these more empirical data with the global extinction estimates. In fact, these and other data indicate that *the number of recorded extinctions for both plants and animals is very small*. . . . (Heywood and Stuart, 1992, p. 93)
>
> *Known extinction rates are very low*. Reasonably good data exist only for mammals and birds, and the current rate of extinction is about one species per year (Reid and Miller, 1989). If other taxa were to exhibit the same liability to extinction as mammals and birds (as some authors suggest, although others would dispute this), then, if the total number of species in the world is, say, 30 million, the annual rate of extinction would be some 2300 species per year. This is a very significant and disturbing number, but it is much less than most estimates given over the last decade. (Heywood and Stuart, p. 94)
>
> . . . if we assume that today's tropical forests occupy only about 80% of the area they did in the 1830s, *it must be assumed that during this contraction, very large numbers of species have been lost in some areas. Yet surprisingly there is no clear-cut evidence for this*. . . . Despite extensive enquiries we have been unable to obtain conclusive evidence to support the suggestion that massive extinctions have taken place in recent times as Myers and others have suggested. On the contrary, work on projects such as Flora Meso-Americana has, at least in some cases, revealed an increase in abundance in many species (Blackmore, pers. comm. 1991). An exceptional and much quoted situation is described by Gentry (1986) who reports the quite dramatic level of evolution in situ in the Centinela ridge in the foothills of the Ecuadorian Andes where he found that at least 38 and probably as many as 90 species (10% of the total flora of the ridge) were endemic to the "unprepossessing ridge". However, the last patches of forest were cleared subsequent to his last visit and "its prospective 90 new species have already passed into botanical history', or so it was assumed. Subsequently, Dodson and Gentry (1991) modified this to say that an undetermined number of species at Centinela are apparently extinct, following brief visits to other areas such as Lita where *up to 11 of the species previously considered extinct were refound*, and at Poza Honda near La Mana where six were rediscovered. (Heywood and Stuart, 1992, p. 96)

> . . . *actual extinctions remain low.* . . . As Greuter (1991) aptly comments, "*Many endangered species appear to have either an almost miraculous capacity for survival*, or a guardian angel is watching over their destiny! This means that it is not too late to attempt to protect the Mediterranean flora as a whole, while still identifying appropriate priorities with regard to the goals and means of conservation." (Heywood and Stuart, p. 102)
>
> . . . *the group of zoologists could not find a single known animal species which could be properly declared as extinct*, in spite of the massive reduction in area and fragmentation of their habitats in the past decades and centuries of intensive human activity. A second list of over 120 lesser-known animal species, some of which may later be included as threatened, show no species considered extinct; and the older Brazilian list of threatened plants, presently under revision, also indicated no species as extinct (Cavalcanti, 1981). (Brown and Brown, 1992, p. 127.)
>
> *Closer examination of the existing data* on both well- and little-known groups, however, *supports the affirmation that little or no species extinction has yet occurred* (though some may be in very fragile persistence) in the Atlantic forests. Indeed, an appreciable number of species considered extinct 20 years ago, including several birds and six butterflies, have been rediscovered more recently. (Brown and Brown, 1992, p. 128)

And here are some comments from that volume on the lack of any solid basis for estimation:

> . . . How large is the loss of species likely to be? *Although the loss of species may rank among the most significant environmental problems of our time, relatively few attempts have been made to rigorously assess its likely magnitude.* (Reid, 1992, p. 55)
>
> *It is impossible to estimate even approximately how many unrecorded species may have become extinct.* (Heywood and Stuart, p. 95)
>
> While better knowledge of extinction rates can clearly improve the design of public policies, it is equally apparent that *estimates of global extinction rates are fraught with imprecision. We do not yet know how many species exist, even to within an order of magnitude.* (Reid, 1992, p. 56)
>
> . . . the literature addressing this phenomenon is relatively small. . . . Efforts to clarify the magnitude of the extinction crisis and the steps that can be taken to defuse the crisis could considerably expand the financial and political support for actions to confront what is indisputably the most serious issue that the field of ecology faces, and arguably the most serious issue faced by humankind today. (Reid, 1992, p. 57)
>
> The best tool available to estimate species extinction rates is the use of species-area curves. . . . This approach has formed the basis for almost all current estimates of species extinction rates. (Reid, 1992, p. 57)
>
> *There are many reasons why recorded extinctions do not match the predictions and extrapolations that are frequently published.* . . . (Heywood and Stuart, 1992, p. 93)

In the case of species extinction, as with many other public issues, there is a tendency – in both technical discussion and the press – to focus only upon the bad effects, and to exclude from consideration possible good effects of human activities. For example, Lugo notes that "Because humans have facilitated immigration [of species] and created new environments, exotic species have successfully become established in the Caribbean islands. This has resulted in a general increase in the total inventories of bird and tree species" (1989, p. 30). In tropical Puerto Rico where "human activity reduced the area of primary forests by 99%," as great a reduction as could be imagined, "seven bird species . . . became extinct after 500 years of human pressure . . . and . . . exotic [newly resident] species enlarged the species pool. More land birds have been present on the Island in the 1980s (97 species) than were present in pre-Colombian time (60 species)" (pp. 28 and 29).

Perhaps conservation biologists make mention of the extinctions but not of the newly-resident species because "there is a clear aversion to exotic [newly resident] species by preservationists and biologists (in cases such as predatory mammals and pests, with good reason!)" (Lugo, 1989, p. 30). This aversion to new species may involve the idea that humankind is somehow artificial and not "natural." Consider the language of Myers, who has played as important a role as any person in raising the alarm about species extinction: "[W]hereas past extinctions have occurred by virtue of natural processes, today the virtually exclusive cause is man" (1989, p. 42). If, however, it is species diversity that is at issue rather than only preserving species as they are today, then new species should count for as much as old ones.

Maintaining the Amazon and other areas in a state of stability might even have counterproductive results for species diversity, according to a recent body of research. Natural disturbances, as long as they are not catastrophic, may lead to discontinuity in environments and to consequent isolation of species that may "facilitate ever-increasing divergence" (Colinvaux, 1989, p. 103). Colinvaux goes on to suggest that "the highest species richness will be found not where the climate is stable but rather where environmental disturbance is frequent but not excessive." The same line of thought leads to possible benefits from interventions by humankind.

During the 1980s there has been increasing recognition that the rate of species loss really is not known. Myers now writes, "Regrettably we have no way of knowing the actual current rate of extinction in tropical forests, nor can we even make an accurate guess." And Colinvaux refers to the extinctions as "incalculable" (1989, p. 102). One would think that this state of affairs would make anyone leery about estimating future extinctions. Nevertheless Myers continues, "But we can make substantive assessments by looking at species numbers before deforestation and then applying the analytical techniques of biogeography. . . . According to the theory of island biogeography, we can realistically reckon that when a habitat has lost 90 percent of its extent, it has lost half of its species" (1989, p. 43). But this is mere speculation. And Lugo finds that in Puerto Rico, the "massive forest conversion did not lead to a correspondingly massive species extinction, certainly nowhere near the 50% alluded to by Myers" (1989, p. 28).[1]

Confirmation of the absence of scientific evidence for rapid species extinction is implicit in the nature of the "evidence" cited by, for example, Edward O. Wilson. He says that "the extinction problem" is "absolutely undeniable." But all he cites are "literally hundreds of anecdotal reports" (Charles C. Mann, "Extinction: Are Ecologists Crying Wolf?", *Science*, 253 (Aug. 1991), 736–8). The very reason for the scientific method in estimating rates is that anecdotal reports are of little value and often mislead the public and policymakers; that's why expensive censuses and other data-gathering instruments are mounted.

Some conservationists have become frustrated at their inability to document a rapid loss of species extinction that would justify calls for government regulation and funding; they also are annoyed at our writing about the actual state of the evidence. As a prominent conservationist responded to our article, "documenting degree of threat is often difficult, and economists and others who wish to downplay the risk of an extinction crisis can easily dispute this case or that case, casting doubt even on the claim that 5 percent of the world's birds are threatened" (Diamond, 1989, p. 41). Diamond therefore has suggested looking at the evidential issue in an entirely different fashion, one quite out of keeping with ordinary scientific practice. Normally, he writes,

> species are to be considered extant until proven extinct. . . . [But] For most species of the tropics or other remote regions – that is, for most of the world's species – a more appropriate assumption would be "extinct unless proven extant." We biologists should not bear the burden of proof to convince economists advocating unlimited human growth [an inaccurate description of one of the authors of this chapter] that the extinction crisis is real. Instead, it should be left to those economists to fund research in the jungles that would positively support their implausible claim of a healthy biological world. (p. 41)

This is an interesting twist, a "reversal of proof burden," as Western (1989, p. 33) puts it. It implies that it is enough for a warning to be sounded, a charge to be made, for the community to proceed as if the case has been proven. This intellectual strategy suggests that the biologists now despair of making their case with the usual tools of scientific inquiry and ask instead for support on the basis of non-evidential faith.

To go one step further: The conservationists premise their forecast of rapid species extinction on there being, now and in the future, a rapid rate of deforestation. We repeat that even if the rate of deforestation were indeed rapid, there would still be little or no basis for inferring a rate of species extinction of Lovejoy's projected magnitude. But their line of argument is rendered even less believable by the fact that the historical evidence does not support their projections of deforestation. (See chapter 33 by Sedjo and Clawson)

SOME OTHER ISSUES

1. Perhaps we should look backwards and wonder: Which species were extinguished when the settlers clear-cut the Middle West of the United States? Are we the poorer now for their loss? Obviously we do not know the answers. But can we even *imagine* that we would be enormously better off with the persistence of *any hypothetical* species? It does not seem likely. This casts some doubt on the economic value of species that might be lost elsewhere.

2. It is difficult to have a reasoned argument with biologists on species extinction. One reason is that they require an almost religious test of fealty and credentials before they will consider a person's testimony as relevant. The mention of a person's original training comes up again and again. In the recent survey volume that he co-edited, Western (1989, p. 33) writes: "The implications of an extinction spasm are also debatable, among both biologists and non-biologists," and Diamond (p. 37) says: "Our current concern with extinction is sometimes 'pooh-poohed' by nonbiologists with the one-liner 'Extinction is the natural fate of species'." In our view, the understanding of data is not the private province of any discipline, and the background of the analyst is not a test of the validity of the analysis. But as long as it is a criterion for biologists, the issue cannot be debated rationally.

Another difficulty is that conservation biologists' goals with respect to species diversity are not easy to understand. Sometimes they emphasize the supposed economic benefits of species diversity. For example, in its widely distributed 1990 fundraising letter (four letters received by the household of one of the present authors) The World Wildlife Fund asks, "Why should you care about the fate of these forests thousands of miles away?" and answers, "Because not only do they provide food and shelter to at least half the world's species of wildlife, these tropical forests are also the world's largest pharmaceutical factory – the sole source of lifesaving medicines like quinine, man's most potent weapon against malaria. Hundreds of thousands of people owe their lives today to these precious plants, shrubs, and trees. What would we do without them?" Diamond (1990, p. 59) answers similarly: "We need them to produce the oxygen we breathe, absorb the carbon dioxide we exhale, decompose our sewage, provide our food, and maintain the fertility of our soil."

But Quinn and Hastings say that "maximizing total species diversity is rarely if ever the principal objective of conservation strategies. Other aesthetic, resource preservation, and recreational values are often more important" (1987, p. 199). And Lovejoy says, most inclusively:

> What I'm talking about is rather the elusive goal of defining the minimum size [of habitat] needed to maintain the characteristic diversity of an ecosystem over time. In other words, I think the goals of conservation

> aren't simply to protect the full array of plant and animal species on the planet, but rather also to protect them in their natural associations so that the relationships between species are preserved and the evolutionary and ecological processes are protected. (quoted in Iker, 1982, p. 29)

This vagueness of goals makes it very difficult to compare the worth of a species-saving activity against another value. What are the relative worths of maintaining the habitat on Mount Graham, Arizona, for about 150 red squirrels who could be kept alive as a species elsewhere, for example, versus using 24 acres for an observatory that would be at the forefront of astronomical science (*New York Times*, March 8, 1990, p. A1)? There is much less basis here for a reasoned judgment in terms of costs and benefits than there is even with such thorny issues as electricity from nuclear power versus from coal, or decisions about supporting additional research on cancer versus using the funds for higher Social Security payments or for defense or even for lower taxes.

Policymaking is also made difficult by conservationists asserting on the one hand that the purpose of conserving is that it is good for human existence, and on the other hand that human existence must be limited or reduced because it is bad for the other species. "There are many realistic ways we can avoid extinctions, such as by preserving natural habitats and limiting human population growth" (Diamond, 1990, p. 59) is a typical statement of that sort – by the same writer who urges that humans should preserve the species because humans need them for existence!

Still another difficulty in conducting reasoned discussion of the subject with biologists is their attitude toward economists, whose trade it is to assess the economics of supporting public programs. One of the most noted of conservation biologists, Peter Raven, views economists as follows: "Perhaps the most serious single academic problem in the world is the training of economists" (1988, p. 229). We have plenty of complaints ourselves about the training of economists, but our complaint is that the fundamental truths about the subject get lost in technical escalations. The complaint of Raven and other biologists is more far-ranging: They believe that the fundamental structure of thought of economics is perverted because it leads to unsound social choices by omitting considerations the biologists consider crucial. But the conservationists do not render those considerations into a form that a calculus of choice can deal with. Herein lies a major problem for the issue at hand.

3. The view that the interests of humans and of other species are opposed leads to humankind being seen in a rather ugly light. "[O]ur species has a knack for exterminating others, and we're becoming better killers all the time" (Diamond, 1990, p. 58). A recent article is entitled "Extinction on Islands: Man as a Catastrophe" (Olson, 1989, p. 5).

4. It is quite clear that species are seen by many as having value quite apart from any role they play in human life, a value that is seen as

competitive with the value of human life. Raven writes, "Although human beings are biologically only one of the millions of species that exist on Earth, we control a highly disproportionate share of the world's resources" (1988, p. 212), suggesting that it is unfair that we "control" more resources than do eagles, mosquitoes, or the AIDS virus.

These beliefs lead to policy recommendations toward the human race that hinge upon values about the worth of humans versus the worth of other species. "[P]opulation buildup" is seen as part of a "dismal scenario."

5. It is not the case, as some have asserted, that we "wish to downplay the risk of an extinction crisis" (Diamond, 1989, p. 41). Rather, we want to make as clear as possible how great the risk is. We want to separate the available facts from the guesswork and the purposeful misstatements, in order to improve the public decision-making process. And we want to comment upon how society may reasonably take into account the economic and non-economic worths of species, in light of our values for human and non-human aspects of nature and other aspects of life on earth. More generally, we would like to move the discussion in the direction of thinking as well as we can about this problem that is indeed difficult to think about sensibly, though it is probably much easier to think about than the greenhouse issue, which is much less subject to experimentation and observational comparison because there is only one atmosphere, whereas there are many separated areas whose diversity can be studied.

SUMMARY AND CONCLUSION

The scare about species extinction has been manufactured in complete contradiction to the scientific data.

The highest proven observed rate of extinction until now is only *one* species per year. Yet the "official" forecast has been *40,000* species dying out per year in this century, a million in all.

It is truth that is becoming extinct, not species.

The argument that because we do not know how many species are being extinguished, we should therefore take steps to protect them, is logically indistinguishable from the argument that because we do not know at what rate the angels dancing on the head of a pin are dying off, we should undertake vast programs to preserve them. And it smacks of the condemnation to death of witches in Salem on the basis of "spectral evidence" by "afflicted" young girls, charges that the accused could not rebut with any conceivable material evidence.

If something is unknowable at present but *knowable in principle*, then the appropriate thing is to find out. This does not necessarily mean finding out by direct observation only. A solid chain of empirical evidence can lead to a reasonable conclusion. But there must be some reasonable chain of evidence and reasoning.

If something is *unknowable in principle*, at least with contemporary techniques, then there is no warrant for any public actions whatsoever. To assert otherwise is to open the door to public actions and expenditures on behalf of anyone who can generate an exciting and frightening hypothetical scenario.

Some say the numbers do not matter scientifically. The policy implications would be the same, they say, even if the numbers were different even by several orders of magnitude. But if so, why mention any numbers at all? The answer, quite clearly, is that these numbers do matter in one important way: they have the power to frighten the public in a fashion that smaller numbers would not. We can find no scientific justification for such use of numbers.

Some have said: But was not Rachel Carson's *Silent Spring* an important force for good even though it exaggerated? Maybe so. But the account is not yet closed on the indirect and long-run consequences of ill-founded concerns about environmental dangers. And it seems to us that, without some very special justification, there is a strong presumption in favor of stating the facts as best we know them, especially in a scientific context, rather than in any manipulation of them.

At a time when there appear frequent reports on the extraordinary possibilities of genetic engineering (for example, "Animals Altered to Produce Medicine in Milk . . . Scientists Say Rare Drugs Could be Manufactured with Relative Ease" [*The Washington Post*, August 27, 1991, p. 1]), it is beginning to seem ludicrous to justify extraordinary expense to protect an animal like the grey squirrel – which may not even be genetically distinct – on the grounds that its gene pool will be valuable for human life in the future.

Still, the question exists: How should decisions be made, and sound policies formulated, with respect to the danger of species extinction? We do not offer a full answer. One cannot simply propose saving all species at any cost, any more than one can propose a policy of saving all human lives at any cost.

Then we must also try to get more reliable information about the number of species that might be lost with various forest changes. This is, of course, a very tough task, too, one that might exercise the best faculties of a statistician and designer of experiments. One suggestion: if the population sizes of selected species could be measured in a series of periods along with experimental or non-experimental changes in habitats, extrapolation might teach something about conditions that would cause species to approach or reach extinction.

Lastly, policy analysis concerning species loss must explicitly evaluate the total cost of the protection, for example, cessation of foresting in an area. And such a total cost estimate must include the long-run indirect costs of reduction in economic growth to a community's health, as well as the short-run costs of foregone wood or agricultural sales (see Wildavsky, 1988, and Keeney, 1990). To ignore such indirect costs because they are hard to estimate would be no more reasonable than ignoring the loss of species that we have not as yet identified.

We summarize the situation as follows: There is now no prima facie case for any expensive species-safeguarding policy without more extensive analysis than has been done heretofore. But the question deserves deeper thought, and more careful and wide ranging analysis, than has been done until now. As children say, just saying so does not make it so.

NOTE

Additional criticism of the "bio-geography" theory of extinction rates has recently been reported in *Science* (Charles C. Mann, "Extinction: Are Ecologists Crying Wolf?", *Science*, 253 (Aug. 1991), 736–8), but further discussion is beyond the scope of this paper.

REFERENCES

Atkinson, Ian (1989): "Introduced Animals and Extinctions." In *Conservation for the Twenty-first Century*, eds. Western and Pearl.

Brown, K. S., and G. G. Brown (1992): "Habitat alteration and species loss in Brazilian forests." In *Tropical Deforestation* and *Species Extinction*, eds. Whitmore and Sayer, 119–42.

Colinvaux, Paul A. (1989): "The Past and Future Amazon." In *Scientific American*, May: 102–8.

De Beijer, J. R. (1979): "Brazil." *World Wood Review*, July, 38–9.

Diamond, Jared (1989): "Overview of Recent Extinctions." In *Conservation for the Twenty-first Century*, eds. Western and Pearl.

——— (1990): "Playing Dice With Megadeath." In *Discover*, April, 55–9.

Ehrlich, Paul and Anne Ehrlich (1981): *Extinction*, New York: Random House.

——— and Edward O. Wilson (1991): "Biodiversity Studies: Science and Policy." *Science*, 253, August 16, 758–62.

Fyfe, W. S. (1981): "The Environmental Crisis: Quantifying Geosphere Interactions." *Science*, 213 (3) July, 105–10.

Heywood, V. H., and S. N. Stuart (1992): "Species extinctions in tropical forests." In *Tropical Deforestation and Species Extinction*, eds Whitmore and Sayer, 91–118.

Holden, Constance (1974): "Scientists Talk of the Need for Conservation and an Ethic of Biotic Diversity to Slow Species Extinction." *Science*, May, 647–8.

Iker, Sam (1982): "Islands of Life In a Forest Sea." In *Mosaic*, September/October, 24–9.

Instituto Brasiliero Desinuol (1980): "Brazil," *World Wood Review*, July, 56–7.

Keeney, Ralph L. (1990): "Mortality Risks Induced by Economic Expenditures." *Risk Analysis*, 10, December, 147–8, 155.

Lugo, Ariel E., ed. "Diversity of Tropical Species." In *Biology International*, Special Issue–19.

Muthoo, M. K. (1978): "Brazil," *World Wood Review*, May, 51–3.

Myers, Norman (1979): *The Sinking Ark*. New York: Pergamon.

——— (1989): "A Major Extinction Spasm: Predictable and Inevitable?" In *Conservation for the Twenty-first Century*, eds Western and Pearl.

Olson, Storrs L. (1989): "Extinction on Islands: Man as a Catastrophe." In *Conservation for the Twenty-first Century*, eds Western and Pearl.

Persson, R. (1974): *World Forest Resources*. Stockholm: Royal College.

Quinn, James F., and Alan Hastings (1987): "Extinction in Subdivided Habitats." In *Conservation Biology*, 1 (3) 198–208.

Raven, Peter H. (1988): "The Cause and Impact of Deforestation." In *Earth '88 – Changing Geographic Perspectives*, 212–29.

Reid, W. V. (1992): "How many species will there be?" in *Tropical Deforestation and Species Extinction*, eds Whitmore and Sayer, 55–74.

Reid, Walter V., and Kenton R. Miller (1989): *Keeping Options Alive: The Scientific Basis for Conserving Biodiversity*. Washington: World Resources Institute, October.

Rohter, Larry (1979): "Amazon Basin's Forests Going Up in Smoke," *The Washington Post*, January 5, A14.

Roush, G. Jon (1989): "The Disintegrating Web: The Causes and Consequences of Extinction." *The Nature Conservancy Magazine*, Nov./Dec., 4–15.

Sedjo, Roger A. (1980): "Forest Plantations in Brazil and Their Possible Effects on World Pulp Markets." *Journal of Forestry*, 78, November, 702–4.

Simberloff, D. (1992): "Do species-area curves predict extinction in fragmented forest?" In *Tropical Deforestation and Species Extinction*, eds Whitmore and Sayer, 75–90.

Sommer, Adrian (1976): "Attempt at an Assessment of the World's Tropical Mist Forests." *Unasylva*, 28, 5–27.

US CEQ and Department of State (1980): *The Global 2000 Report to the President*, vol. 2. Washington: GPO.

US CEQ and Department of State (1981): *Global Future: Time to Act*. Washington: GPO.

Waldrop, M. Mitchell (1981): "Wood: Fuel of the Future?" *Science*, Feb. 27, 914.

Western, David (1989): "Conservation Biology." In *Conservation for the Twenty-first Century*, eds Western and Pearl.

——— and Mary C. Pearl (1989): *Conservation for the Twenty-first Century*. New York, Oxford: Oxford University Press.

Whitmore, T. C., and J. A. Sayer, eds (1992): *Tropical Deforestation and Species Extinction*. New York: Chapman and Hall.

Whittaker, R. H., and G. E. Likens (1975): "The Biosphere and Man." In H. Lieth and R. H. Whittaker eds, *Primary Productivity of the Biosphere*. New York: Springer.

Wildavsky, Aaron (1988): *Searching for Safety*. New Brunswick: Transaction Press.

PART VII

WELFARE ANALYSIS

[34]

Foreword

The economists say that this piece is philosophy, and the philosophers say it is economics – in both cases, reasons not to publish it. Philosophers have indeed written much on this topic, but (as is the case with natural resources and population growth generally) they never adduce any facts in their analysis, and they rest their analyses on assumptions that run counter to the facts.

Are there grounds for limiting immigration[1]

Introduction to the issue

Is there any "good" reason for a country such as the United States to deny entrance to persons who wish to immigrate but who simply are not desired as immigrants by some or most of the current citizens? The word "good" is written in quotes because various sorts of reasons – economic, moral, legal, ethical – might be offered as justifications of regulating immigration. I do not wish, by using an adjective referring to economics or morality or political philosophy or any other domain, to limit in advance the kinds of reasons that might be so offered by myself or by others.

The argument will assume without further justification that an individual has a right to his/her life, liberty, and property in the traditional Anglo-Saxon sense of freedom from the coercion of the state or other persons (except if a criminal act has been committed). Those who espouse legal traditions different from the Anglo-Saxon tradition as now exemplified by the US and Great Britain are not likely to accept this set of assumptions. I do not wish to join in argument with them about immigration on this occasion.

Let us also take note that the present international system is made up of real power monopolies referred to as countries (or sometimes ambiguously as nations), and any decisions made by a particular country hinge upon that fact. The question at hand does not encompass asking whether a world system without countries is better than a world system with countries, but rather takes as given a system of sovereign nations, practically all of which regulate immigration and/or emigration with respect to their own borders. The question is how the United States or a similar nation *ought* to behave about immigration given that fact and the assumptions in the paragraph above. Or to put it differently, what is it *sensible and moral* for the nation to do with its power of regulating immigration, consistent with the rights of the individual stated above?

To most persons, the question at hand is likely to seem almost frivolous. It seems obvious to most of those with whom I have discussed the matter that there *must* be sound grounds for a nation to regulate immigration; for many, the matter need go no further than taking notice of the fact that all nations do in fact exercise that power. But others challenge the morality of erecting barriers against the entrance of aliens into the United States or another country. The argument of the latter persons is that if one believes in a "great society" in which all people are to be treated equally, there is no logical reason to treat a person differently who stands on one side or another of a boundary line, that is, who holds one "citizenship" rather than another. And they point to the period of open borders in the United

States up to 1924 as evidence that such a policy need not be disastrous, or even more costly than beneficial. They also point out that only 75 years ago, it was considered uncivilized in the "advanced" countries for a government to restrict people's comings and goings across their borders for reasons other than health or pauperism (McNeill, 1976).

A crucial intellectual difficulty: who has a claim?

As with many other questions that seem too preposterous to warrant serious discussion, this one makes hard going. It may help to begin by identifying an intellectual difficulty in the economics of immigration, and indeed, throughout the economics of population size. Economic discussion customarily starts by assuming a fixed number of potential claimants to whatever resources exist or will be created in the situation under discussion, and proceeds to the allocation of scarce resources among alternative ends implicitly specified by the fixed group of individuals. As soon as the number of claimants is no longer fixed, but instead is a variable (perhaps along with other variables) whose value is to be decided in the course of the analysis, conventional economics is struck dumb and the analysis loses clarity.[2] Hence economic theory is not a rich source of ideas concerning the topic at hand.

Some economic consequences that arouse concern

It would seem reasonable that potential immigrants who would be a direct economic burden upon citizens through the public coffers should have no claim to be admitted. That is, no one has a legitimate claim to enter a society and free-load upon others by using more welfare services than taxes paid. But the data show (Simon, 1984; 1989; 1995) that, on average, immigrants are *not* burdens upon natives in this fashion, and therefore this is a much less restrictive condition than it might seem. Furthermore, it is a (surprising) fact that immigrants are *more* of a benefit nowadays with the existence of government welfare programs than in earlier eras when there were few or no such programs, because immigrants tend to contribute more to the public coffers in taxes than they take out in services (though this does not take into account indirect effects such as greater competition for housing or in the labor market).

Another common difficulty is the assumption that immigration implies a net cost to natives. But writers such as Walzer (1983, p. 47) put heavy weight on a supposed reduction of "wealth and resources" per native because of immigrants. More generally, much recent philosophical discussion about population has been based on the idea that resources are increasingly scarce with larger populations, e.g. Ackerman (1980).

The concern about homogeneity and "alien values"'

An issue to be mentioned only in passing is whether keeping the society homogeneous culturally or racially is a "good" reason for a nation to bar potential immigrants. For many, cultural homogeneity constitutes a reason to limit immigration. (Former Prime Minister of Great Britain Margaret Thatcher has voiced this argument and based her immigration policy on it). Such a consideration of taste is beyond the scope of this essay, though one could investigate the consequences for such social issues as economic freedom of restrictive policies based on cultural homogeneity. A related matter is a group's desire to "maintain their present way of life" (Walzer, 1983, p. 47). This issue involves so many weighty and worthwhile considerations on both sides of the matter that, like the boardinghouse issue in racial discrimination in the United States, it would have to be resolved by a judicial-like process, though the appropriate jurisdiction for such a judgment is not at all obvious. (Certainly the recent history of international tribunals does not offer much hope that such a forum could be very satisfactory.)

The concept of rights: not the place to begin

Which intellectual tools are best fitted to help us tackle the question this paper addresses? The legal-philosophical concept of rights – for potential immigrants, for natives, and for a country – comes quickly to mind. But I have concluded that arguments deduced from either natural individual rights, or from individual rights as derived from other sources, will not be helpful in this case, because any such discussion necessarily involves the question of who is to be allowed to share the right – persons outside as well as inside the nation's borders, or just those inside it. And to decide that question will require a theory of the state, which would (as I see it) inevitably be tautologous.[3]

Furthermore, the notion of a right of a *country* seems to have little standing in philosophical discourse, despite its casual use in common discussion and perhaps in international law. I will forswear use of such a concept both for that reason and because the use of such a concept appears to me unnecessary as well as confusing.[4]

Put another way, if there is to be useful discussion of rights in this case, it must be seen as similar to the discussion of other rules for the "great society," a discussion which considers pragmatically which rules provide the best framework for freedom, for the enjoyment of property and family, and for progress toward greater wealth and higher civilization, rather than considering which rights are "natural" or consistent with a theory of the state. (It seems to me that the natural rights approach, in conjunction with a common-law system, works best for situations concerning which there exists a great deal of experience, the kind of highly structured situation that one encounters in daily legal decision making.) If one accepts that natural rights are not an appropriate concept for this situation, one may also be willing to accept that discussion of abstract rights by itself will not immediately resolve the problem, no matter how enlightened the discussion.

One might also consider trying to deduce about rights, on the part of either potential immigrants or of present citizens, from other rights and privileges; an example is the privilege of a citizen to ask protection by her/his country when abroad, protection that a non-citizen may not ask. But I have not been able to make any headway with this approach; perhaps in other hands it would be more fruitful. Nor have I found relevant such related concepts as the "right" of a nation to require military service of a citizen but not of a non-citizen.

One of the drawbacks of hanging the issue on a discussion of rights is that the same basic assumption can lead to opposite conclusions. For example, Carens says he begins at the same place as Rawls – "the spirit of the moral point of view, i.e., that in reasoning about moral issues we should try to avoid being influenced by self-interested or partisan considerations" – but reaches a global view of immigrants' rights whereas Rawls draws a boundary around nations:

> Now clearly knowledge about one's citizenship (e.g., whether one is a citizen of a rich nation or a poor one, whether one is already a citizen of a particular state or an alien who wishes to become a citizen) is knowledge about "specific contingencies" that could "set men at odds." A fair procedure for choosing principles of justice must therefore exclude knowledge of these circumstances, just as it excludes knowledge of one's race or sex or social class.

This leads to a global view of the original position. The principles of justice apply in the first instance, to the world as a whole and only derivatively to nation states. Rawls' attempt to restrict the investigation of the principles of justice to members of a given society is not justifiable because such an approach presupposes the legitimacy of the autonomous nation-state. But the whole point of the original position is to provide a perspective from which to assess the legitimacy of social institutions. The legitimacy of the state as a social institution thus depends upon the extent to which it is compatible with the requirements of the principles of justice.

Before leaving the concept of rights, let us consider the possible role of what I shall call secular rights, those derived not from a conception of what is "natural" but instead from a conception of what is necessary for the governance of society under particular conditions. The Hayekian (also the libertarian) idea is that, in the proper governance of a modern "great society", all persons ought to be treated equally; it is as simple as that.[5] The Old Testament says the same about treatment of Jews versus foreigners or non-Jews. (Hayek adds, however [in correspondence] that this principle applies only to those who share the same moral values,[6] a qualification which I do not yet fully grasp and which I have not yet had the opportunity to explore with him, though the discussion below may discover what he has in mind.) Were this right not to be opposed by another potentially necessary pragmatic right, or by some consideration of ill consequences that may flow from this right, perhaps it would be enough to enunciate the right for the issue to be settled. But I believe that the discussion that follows compels us to think that there are opposing forces that cloud the issue. An example, to be considered now, is the right to be secure in one's property, and the associated right to transfer individual property to whomever one wishes, including descendants; this right is fundamental for libertarians and for Hayek.

The right of bequeathing property raises interesting questions. Does a small collective such as an agricultural cooperative have the right of bequeathing its property to whomever it wishes? May some persons be barred from joining the collective on the basis of their background? And what about a larger collective such as a town? Is there a private–public distinction here that leads to personal property having a different status from common property? At which point does one pass from a situation in which rights are accorded to an individual, or to a partnership into a situation of a group so large that it is not to be thought of in the same way?

A town in the United States may not prohibit any person from purchasing or renting a home on the basis of education or color or religion or other background characteristic. May the nation then do so? It would seem that the nation's right to exclude people on the basis of background characteristics requires that the nation be thought of as an entity fundamentally different to any other collective, private or public. This would require a compelling theory of the nature of a country-state if one is to make an argument about immigration on the basis of rights, and the theory would have to be different from the theory of the "night watchman" government, because that latter theory pertains to the city as well as to a nation, and a city is not permitted (in the US) to make an immigration policy. (Whether states such as Hawaii and Oregon and Colorado that wish to restrict immigration may do so is a matter which the courts have been considering lately.) These questions will not be pursued now, so as to hurry on to other matters. But I have the impression that it is next to impossible to construct a satisfactory argument for either closed or open borders on the basis of an argument to rights alone. (Yet the discussion will later come around the circle far enough that the reader may feel that it is really founded on a concept of rights.)

Arguing from the consequences of an immigration policy

Some non-problems first

There are three possible bases on which to evaluate immigration: natural law, contract law, and consequences. As I see it, the first two approaches do not work, so we must past on to the third and more general mode of analysis, asking: What *consequences* are likely to follow if an open-borders or a closed-borders policy is adopted? The question about secular rights discussed above also may be seen in this context, of course, in the following form: what will be the consequences for the system of rights if one or another rule is adopted with respect to immigration? But now we focus upon more direct economic and political consequences.

Before proceeding, however, we need some agreement about what is good and what is bad. Therefore we ask: Is there any overarching general principle that one can appeal to with some hope of gaining agreement? I hope that that the "Great Society" of Hayek is a goal toward which the US and the world are evolving and also (but not therefore) should aim at.

The Great Society implies 1) free mobility, and 2) do no avoidable harm to others. But these can be opposed to each other. Specifically, some feel harm from "cultural" changes induced simply by others changing the makeup of a community or country. (We can put ill economic effects aside as mostly not occurring.) US society has legislated against the introduction of such "cultural" harm being allowed to matter in public accomodations, hiring, and so on, and it is no longer subject to debate; it has been accepted as the "right" and moral thing to do. But this has not been extended to immigration. Nor does all the world have such rules, so it cannot claim universality and hence "natural law" status.

Now to specifics. As noted earlier, it would seem reasonable that an immigrant be required not to cause general economic harm to natives. This requirement is,however, different with respect to persons outside the nation and with respect to those who are citizens. Within a nation, it would be difficult to carry out this policy even if it were desired and acceptable, especially with respect to particular groups of migrants; for example, we make little or no attempt to prevent persons who may need public assistance from moving from one community to another. But the matter may well be different internationally, both technically and ethically. So it seems reasonable to require that a person has a reasonable probability, based upon his/her own capacities or the guaranteed help of others, not to become a public burden in the direct sense; this was even a requirement during the open-door days (toward Europe) of the US before 1924. We ought not tarry on this point, I think, because more difficult and controversial matters await us.

But what about indirect burdens, and burdens upon particular sub-groups within the society? An added person may cause added congestion in some areas. And an added person causes damage to some individuals by increasing competition in the labor force. It is impossible that an immigrant can enter without doing damage to *some* sub-group, and therefore no one could enter without being challenged by some groups or persons. Hence I submit that such indirect damage to one or another sub-group cannot be accepted as grounds for automatic disqualification.

And what about indirect negative consequences for the community at large, that is, the population within the nation-state? Here we must discuss which kinds of damage will and which will not be considered relevant. Should *any* kinds of effects that citizens consider to be ill-effects be considered to be disqualifying? The entrance of people with foreign racial characteristics is a key issue, of course. Here it would seem to me reasonable that damage to citizens' sensibilities should not be cause for barring a potential immigrant, because if a taste test be considered acceptable, there would be no reason why some citizens could not use such a test against other citizens in a form of unchecked democracy, with the sorts of majoritarian dangers that worried the framers of the US Constitution. But this is more in the nature of a personal opinion than a reasoned judgment. (It should be observed here that such notables as Margaret Thatcher do not necessarily agree with this point of view, as suggested by word and action.)

Racial exclusion arguments are often made on the grounds that race mixing leads to social tension and violence. It would seem unarguable that racial differences are *sometimes* the occasion for violence, but I have seen no evidence that the level of tension and violence in mixed societies is greater than in more homogeneous populations. Furthermore, there would seem to be a distinction between conflict that is personally unpleasant to some citizens and conflict that threatens the stability of the state as a whole.

One might argue that an infusion of a "foreign" racial group may lead to pressures to partition a nation into two or more nations. But unless one assumes a value for the existence of the state itself, in contrast to the continued existence of the state for the purposes of facilitating the economic and personal lives of the persons within it, then the argument of potential partition has no weight.

Some reasonable grounds for regulating immigration?

Alteration of the economic–political infrastructure

All agree that predictability of economic structure and rules is a necessary precondition for successful community economic life, because such stability is a precondition for the ability of an individual or an enterprise to influence its own fate secure from arbitrary manipulation by others. And such predictability requires a measure of continuity and stability in society's political institutions. We may think of a nation as having created an organization that conducts its business with some effectiveness, and this organization is a valuable asset, just as the firm's organization is for a business. The organization may not be "best" in some abstract sense, and it may well not be the result of "rational" design. But the fact that the organization survives indicates that, whatever its historical roots, it has some continuing value; citizens surely have invested much in dependence upon the continuation of that particular mode of organization.

What if the numbers (or types) of immigrants be sufficiently large as to quickly become a majority in some place or another, or large enough to combine with others to alter the fundamental fabric of the nation, and hence threaten the existence of that mode of organization? For example, consider – and this is not taking the argument to the point of absurdity – that a large country such as China were to threaten to inundate a much smaller country the size of Singapore with so many immigrants that the entire political complexion would be changed by means of democratic and constitutional process. And what if this were to be done for Chinese reasons of state, ideological or strategic? Should a nation simply accept the impending disruption or destruction of its economic life, even putting aside the question of social life and historical continuity?

Perhaps this possibility is what underlies Hayek's viewpoint about a "common system of basic moral beliefs." If it is reasonable to suppose that such a common system of values exists, one may also assume that there is no danger of alteration in the political–economic superstructure from a given group of immigrants. But discrimination among potential immigrants on such a basis clearly is fraught with difficulties and dangers.

It seems to me reasonable that if unlimited immigration presents a threat of this sort, a nation may reasonably put some limits upon its immigration, on the grounds of protection of property and economic life. This seems to me the only compelling argument in favor of limits upon immigration within the context of a "great society."

Having said this much, I wish to back off and take notice that this line of argument is not a general warrant for any arbitrary limits upon immigration that a nation wishes to impose (though the nation might, of course, find other warrants not included in the discussion here). Perhaps an appropriate way to think about the matter is that the burden of argument should be upon a nation to justify restrictions in terms of potential damage, rather than the burden being upon potential immigrants to show that the quantity of restrictions does not potentially inflict damage. And it would not be easy to make a strong showing that a potential immigrant cohort would be large enough, or would have the sorts of peculiar characteristics (other than lack of skills, which is discussed below) that would threaten to change irreparably the economic or political or social fabric of the society. Even if the volume of immigration were to be so large as to constitute a majority within five or ten years, it is not at all clear that this would threaten fundamental change, because of the demonstrated fact in the United States of successful absorption of immigrants no matter how foreign they may seem upon arrival. Perhaps a takeover of a small nation by a large one, of the sort discussed above, might be a real threat, but the world has never yet seen such an event, and therefore it would not seem reasonable to take strong steps to prevent its occurrence.[7]

Additionally, the required length of residence prior to acquiring citizenship and the vote – a procedure now in effect in the US, though under some attack by those who believe that all residents should have the right to vote[8] – might avoid the danger of democratic takeover, while allowing all who wish to enter, work and live.

Negative learning externalities

Another possibly relevant issue is what may be called negative learning externalities. People learn from one another on the job, and in the work place, and if the people with whom you work do not have a high level of technical skill and general economic culture, your performance is likely to suffer. Indeed, this – along with a defective economic–political structure – is the most plausible explanation of low individual productivity in countries with low average productivity. Therefore, one could object to massive immigration on the grounds that it would lower individuals' economic output. Indeed, it would make little economic difference if an individual were to work in the US in an environment with 99 per cent new immigrants from very poor countries, or work in the countries from which those persons came. Here it is important to note that the phenomenon under discussion is the learning relationship between people, and not complementarities of skill; the latter phenomenon suggests that highly-skilled technical persons benefit rather than suffer from there being more low-skill immigrants.[9]

As with the effects of massive immigration upon US political institutions, it is sure that people will worry much more about this phenomenon than deserved, and will use it as a smokescreen for other motives in restricting immigration. Yet the possibility must be mentioned. And if one begins with the premise of the sanctity of property, there is certainly a potential objection to immigration here. Perhaps the clear-and-present-danger doctrine is again the most reasonable response.

Some other considerations

Firstly, perhaps it will be illuminating to note that a nation controlling its borders *in extremis* is the opposite side of the coin from a group of people asserting autonomy for the region in which they live; without some possibility of keeping others out, effective autonomy is not meaningful.

Secondly, a more philosophically-based approach to this subject may be developed by beginning with an argument of Nozick's, even though he is addressing emigration rather than immigration (1974, pp. 173-4). He considers whether a person should be allowed to emigrate in light of a possible obligation for a citizen to contribute to the provision of social welfare for other members of society. He concludes in the negative, partly by reference to the ludicrousness of a nation being entitled to kidnap persons outside the country in order to compel such contributions.[10] The provision of social welfare does not come into the present discussion because, as we have seen, contrary to popular belief the average immigrant is a net contributor rather than a net recipient. But the more general notion that may be extracted from this line of thought is that a state surely should have the right to require that a citizen pay his/her contractual debts before leaving – delinquent taxes, for example, or debts owed to another citizen – even if it does not have the right to prevent emigration to extract payments that are not owed by contract or law. And this leads back to the idea that persons in any country have the right to protect themselves in elementary ways; the right of self-protection is asserted and delineated clearly by Locke (1690/1939). And though the concept of right may pertain to individuals and not to groups, there are situations in which individuals can only protect their rights if they do so in a corporate mamner, as is clearly the case with a police force, and it would seem to be the case with some aspects of emigration and immigration, too. That is, if some regulation of immigration is absolutely crucial to protect the basic interests of citizens, construed narrowly, this would not seem different from other actions of the "night watchman" government.[11]

Conclusion

Is there any persuasive reason for a country to bar a healthy, law-abiding person from immigrating? That is the question that this essay addresses.

Many believe it is in the natural order of things that movement across borders should be limited. But prior to World War I, it was thought uncivilized for nations not to permit free movement; passports mostly did not exist, though serfs had long been tied to the land and prevented from emigrating.

Arguments about immigration based on "natural rights" all seem to be inconclusive, in part because the concept of rights does not apply to countries as it applies to individuals.

Therefore, as with most other policies, we turn to judging the matter by considering its consequences.

The consequence most worried about is that immigrants constitute a financial burden on the public fisc. This worry usually runs contrary to the facts, however, and a variety of policies – many of them already in place – can prevent welfare burden in most cases.

Job displacement is another major concern. But a considerable body of recent research shows that immigrants do not have general negative consequences on labor markets; rather, the overall consequences are broadly positive. Some specific groups may be injured by a particular group of immigrants (mostly in wages rather than increased unemployment); the occupational prospects of physicians, for example, are vulnerable to immigrant doctors. But the considerations about a negative partial effect in the face of a positive general effect are the same as in the case of trade theory, and hence are not likely to be operative here.

The difficult questions – and therefore the possible justifications for controlling entry – arise with respect to externalities. Some externalities can be internalized by appropriate tax measures – for example the costs of school buildings and roads. But externalities such as schools having so many immigrant children that native children learn more slowly – an unlikely event, but one which must be considered in principle – cannot be easily internalized (though a voucher system might go a long way). It should be noted that other natives are not barred from entering a community on such grounds, however.

Societies which accept as legitimate that persons have greater private obligations to those more closely affiliated with them – an effective mechanism for supplying help to those who need it, but one which tends to be suspect in such societies as the Soviet Union, even within the family – might also embody the same principle in governmental actions. But it may well be that while this principle is constructive with respect to personal acts, it is destructive with respect to public action.

The most important externality is alteration in the economic and social system. If a large country were to flood a small country with immigrants for the purpose of taking it over democratically and then changing the system, this would threaten natives' property in their means of livelihood, because economic activities depend upon the social–political system. But such a possibility is quite unlikely. Furthermore, making the right to vote contingent upon citizenship which is awarded only after some passage of time may safeguard against this possibility. The same device should help ensure that at least the voting populace share basic civic values, a consensus which many writers argue is crucial for the satisfactory functioning of any society. Having non-voting residents with different values (at least at first) who might influence citizens – "foreign revolutionaries" – is a possible objection to immigration, but I do not know of any evidence to confirm (or deny) that this is in fact ever a realistic danger.

In short, the negative consequences of any level of immigration which is politically imaginable at present are at most speculative, rather than documented. Therefore, a policy which is both prudent and also consistent with these observations would be to increase immigration quotas in a series of increments of significant size – perhaps half a per cent, or one per cent, of total population at each step – to check on any unexpected negative consequences, and to determine whether demand for admission even exceeds the supply of places. (In this connection, note the current zero net immigration from Puerto Rico, whose population may freely move to the fifty states.)

So, where have we arrived? The main point is that it seems reasonable and acceptable for a given population of individuals, at the governmental level of the nation-state, to assert that they have a property right in their social and economic organization. This means that under some circumstances it may be appropriate for them to decide how many and which potential immigrants are allowed to enter. But it is ridiculously easy to concoct a supposed threat from immigrants to the economic stability and predictability of the nation-state, and this line of thought could be used to justify any restrictions upon entry that a country wished to enact. Therefore, there should be built into the constitution of the country sufficient safeguards against this power being used in situations other than those of clear and present danger. We ought also to recognize that to create such safeguards would be a very difficult task, one that goes beyond the bounds of this essay.

Notes

1. For helpful comments on this subject I am grateful to Frank Buckley, Ed Crane, Greg Lindsay, Ellen Frankel Paul, Burt Schorr, David Simon, Michael Simon, Alex Singer and Daniel Singer.
2. Only the utilitarians (e.g. Sedgwick) have attacked this issue frontally (see Simon, 1977, Chapter 18), and their analysis is no longer persuasive to me.
3. But see Walzer (1983, e.g. p. 52).
4. If one identifies a nation's rights with what international law allows – as Shue does – then the concept takes on some precision. But I think this is not what most persons have in mind when they talk about a nation's rights.
5. Some representative observations:

> There is. . . a fundamental difference between what is possible in the small group and in the Great Society. In the small group the individual can know the effects of his actions on his several fellows, and the rules may effectively forbid him to harm them in any manner and even require him to assist them in specific ways. In the Great Society many of the effects of a person's actions on various fellows must be unknown to him. It can, therefore, not be the specific effects in the particular case, but only rules which define kinds of actions as prohibited or required, which must serve as guides to the individual. In particular, he will often not know who the individual people will be who will benefit by what he does, and therefore not know whether he is satisfying a great need or adding to abundance. He cannot aim at just results if he does not know who will be affected.
>
> Indeed the transition from the small group to the Great or Open Society – and the treatment of every other person as a human being rather than as either a known friend or an enemy – requires a reduction of the range of duties we owe to all others. (Hayek, 1976, p. 90)

"To ask for protection against being displaced from a position one has long enjoyed, by others who are now favoured by new circumstances, means to deny to them the chances to which one's own present position is due." (Hayek, 1976, p. 95)

An objection to a global view is what Shue calls "priority for compatriots." He says it is "at the very least acceptable – perhaps necessary or even admirable," and in the name of this principle he respects "cosmopolitanism." But one can accept "priority for compatriots" as a principle for private actions, representing an emotional fact of human nature, and reject it as a principle for legal governmental action.

6. "My general principles clearly apply fully only between people who have a common system of basic moral beliefs. How far this justifies an exclusion of immigrants by the powers of the state I am simply not clear. But I certainly accepted it as fully justified of the inhabitants of the Tyrolese village in which I have now spent my summer holidays for some twenty-five years, [when they] several years ago refused to sell me a piece of land on the ground that they did not do so to foreigners." Letter, May 26, 1984, several obvious typographical errors corrected.
7. Carens makes a similar argument to mine in this section, and expresses similar reservations about whether it would ever apply.
8. Some writers – Walzer, for example – suggest that if delay in receiving citizenship were deemed necessary, it would be better not to admit the immigrants at all.

> One might insist, as I shall ultimately do, that the same standards apply to naturalization as to immigration, that every immigrant and every resident is a citizen, too – or, at least, a potential citizen. That is why territorial admission is so serious a matter. The members must be prepared to accept as their own equals in a world of shared obligations, the men and women they admit; the immigrants must be prepared to share the obligations. But things can be differently arranged. Often the state controls naturalization strictly, immigration only loosely.

> Immigrants become resident aliens and, except by special dispensation, nothing more. Why are they admitted? To free the citizens from hard and unpleasant work. Then the state is like a family with live-in servants.
>
> That is not an attractive image, for a family with live-in servants is – inevitably, I think – a little tyranny. (1983, p. 63)

And again,

> The determination of aliens and guests by an exclusive band of citizens (or of slaves by masters, or women by men, or blacks by whites, or conquered peoples by their conquerors) is not communal freedom but oppression. The citizens are free, of course, to set up a club, make membership as exclusive as they like, write a constitution, and govern one another. But they can't claim territorial jurisdiction and rule over the people with whom they share the territory. To do this is to act outside their sphere, beyond their rights. It is a form of tyranny. (1983, p.52).

There are several reasons why I reject this view. First, it is contrary to fact in the US that immigrants on average do dirtier work than natives. Second, a waiting period for citizenship has always been in force, with little or no complaint. Third, and most important, it forces the preferences of natives upon immigrants, telling them that even though they would prefer non-citizenship worker status to not entering, they are to be considered worse off in that status and natives would therefore be faced with "not an attractive image," that is, this notion is based on the tastes of natives, or more specifically, the tastes ascribed to them by Walzer.

Furthermore, this argument has been used cynically by anti-immigration organizations – for example, comparing illegal aliens to pre-Civil-War slaves – as a way of advancing their own desire for fewer immigrants. Hayek has this to say on the matter:

> those very groups within the existing states which are loudest in their demands for 'social justice', such as the trade unions, are regularly the first to reject such claims raised on behalf of foreigners. Applied to the international sphere, the complete lack of a recognized standard of 'social justice', or of any known principles on which such a standard could be based, becomes at once obvious; while on a national scale most people still think that what on the level of the face-to-face society is to them a familiar idea must also have some validity for national politics or the use of the powers of government. In fact, it becomes on this level a humbug – the effectiveness of which with well-meaning people the agents of organized interests have learnt successfully to exploit.(1976, p. 90)

9. William Poole suggested (in correspondence, July 22, 1986) that account should be taken

> of why Backwardia is backward. Per capita production in Backwardia might be low because of poor political and/or incentive systems. Once an individual moves to Richonia his output might immediately rise to the average level in Richonia. There is in this case no reason to expect that immigration will make Richonia more similar economically to Backwardia. . .It is often the case, for example, that foreign scholars coming to the U.S. are instantaneously more productive than in their native countries.

For example, the pay of German full professors does not depend on the quality of research and writing in their own country, but the incentive structure is different if one moves to the US. Change in behavior would then not be expected to depend upon whether a given immigrant German professor worked with native US professors or with other new-immigrant German professors.

If Poole's point has wide application, then the point under discussion is less important.

10. Locke made an argument strikingly like Nozick's.

> I desire them to resolve me by what right any prince or state can put to death or punish an alien, for any crime he commits in their country. 'Tis certain their laws, by virtue of any sanction they receive from the promulgated will of the legislative, reach not a stranger; they

speak not to him, nor, if they did, is he bound to hearken to them. The legislative authority, by which they are in force over the subjects of that commonwealth, hath no power over him. Those who have the supreme power of making laws in England, France, or Holland, are to an Indian but like the rest of the world – men without authority. And, therefore, if by the law of nature every man hath not a power to punish offenses against it, as he soberly judges the case to require, I see not how the magistrates of any community can punish an alien of another country; since in reference to him they can have no more power than what every man naturally may have over another. (1690/1939, pp. 406-407)

11. The reader might wonder how this line of argument relates to states such as the USSR requiring repayment of education costs before persons are allowed to emigrate. There might be a reasonable argument that emigrants ought to pay net costs of some sort before leaving, but the child's parents on average pay taxes in the amount of the child's education, and therefore there is no family net obligation. A state might make an argument on the basis of personal independence, but then it would have no grounds to collect taxes from parents to pay for children. Of course there might be some special circumstances, say a child receiving extraordinary educational or medical expenses, but this would not be a fruitful path down which to proceed here.

References

Ackerman, Bruce A. (1980), *Social Justice in the Liberal States,* New Haven: Yale University Press.

Carens, Joseph H. (1987), "Aliens and Citizens: The Case for Open Borders," *The Review of Politics*, **49**(2), Spring, 251-73

Hayek, Friedrich (1976), *Law, Legislation and Liberty*, Vol. II, Chicago: University of Chicago Press.

Locke, John (1939), "An Essay Concerning the True Original Extent and End of Civil Governnment," in Edwin A. Burtt (ed.), *The English Philosophers from Bacon to Mill*, New York: Modern Library.

McNeill, William H. (1976), "Human Migration: A Historical Overview," *Human Migration - Patterns and Policies*, Bloomington, Indiana: Indiana University Press.

Nozick, Robert (1974), *Anarchy, State, and Utopia*, New York: Harper Torchbooks.

Poole, William, personal correspondence, 22 July 1986.

Shue, Henry (n.d.), "Border-Crossings: National Autonomy and National Responsibility," xerox.

Simon, Julian L. (1977), *The Economics of Population Growth,* Princeton: Princeton University Press.

Simon, Julian L. (1984), "Immigrants, Taxes, and Welfare in the United States." *Population and Development Review*, **10**(1), 55-69.

Simon, Julian L. (1989), *The Economic Consequences of Immigration* , Boston: Basil Blackwell.

Simon, Julian L. (1995), *Immigration - The Demographic and Economic Facts* , Washington, D.C.: Cato Institute and National Immigration Forum.

Walzer, Michael (1983), *Spheres of Justice, A Defense of Pluralism and Equality*, New York: Basic Books, Inc.

[35]

Foreword

This is one of the very few papers I have written that I am now less sure of than when I wrote it. Hayek shook my faith in the sort of utilitarianism that underlies the work. Is it reasonable to aggregate people's welfare as this analysis does? I'm no longer satisfied that it is.

Cigarette advertising and the nation's welfare

The Federal Trade Commission is now [1964] holding hearings about whether cigarette companies should be required to post a "danger to health" warning on packs of cigarettes and in advertisements. These hearings are an out-growth of the recent report by the Surgeon General on the health hazards of cigarette smoking.

Some individuals and groups, including Senator Maurine Neuberger and Consumers Union, favor the proposed regulation. Some want cigarette advertising prohibited completely. However, no responsible person has suggested outlawing the manufacture or sale of cigarettes themselves.

People who oppose the warning proposal and the ban on advertising base their opposition on grounds of legality as well as of economics. This article will consider only the economics of a warning requirement or a ban. It will not consider other economic alternatives such as an increase in cigarette taxes.

I shall discuss the possible effects on cigarette use, and the consequent economic impacts, of these two proposals on the groups that have a stake in what happens. Mostly, I shall talk about the ban on advertising, because its effect is better understood. The effect of a warning requirement would probably be much less than an advertising ban, but of the same general nature.

Effect on cigarette consumption rate

Opponents of a warning to ban will say that forbidding cigarette advertising, or requiring a danger warning, will have "practically no effect" on consumption. Supporters of the warning, however, argue that advertising has a "substantial" effect in influencing people to start smoking, and in keeping them smoking. Where is the truth?

It is perfectly clear that advertising has the power to influence the purchase of *particular brands* of cigarettes. The $220 million spent annually for cigarette advertising is proof-positive of that. But we are not interested in the power of advertising to shift smokers from one brand to another. We want to know how cigarette advertising *as a whole* starts people smoking or keeps them smoking.

Neil Borden examined the role of cigarette advertising in the astounding growth of cigarette smoking starting about 1900, when the annual per capita consumption of cigarettes was 49. By 1962 the rate had risen to 3,958 cigarettes per capita. Borden did not say that advertising *caused* the rise in cigarette consumption. He argued that if the public had not been ready to take up cigarette smoking, advertising could never have caused such a large increase in consumption. Nevertheless, Borden concluded that advertising was an important factor in the size and speed of increase in cigarette smoking.

But we want to know the effect of advertising *now*, when cigarette smoking is a very prevalent habit. We want to know what would happen if advertising were banned, or if a warning were required.

Robert Basmann carried out an intricate statistical study of the rise and fall in cigarette advertising from year to year in the United States, and its apparent effect on cigarette consumption. He found that for each 1 percent change in total cigarette advertising, the number of cigarettes smoked changed 1/20 of 1 percent. In other words, the consumption of cigarettes *is* affected by the amount of advertising, but it takes a big change in the amount of advertising to make much of a difference in consumption. This is typical of an industry once it has become well established, but it may also result from the degree to which the smoking habit takes hold of people and the fact that nothing else is a good substitute for smoking.

What would happen if all cigarette advertising were cut off? An extension of Basmann's finding would suggest that if there had been no cigarette advertising last year, consumption would have been about 5 percent less than it was. If the ban on advertising continued, we might expect further decreases in the amount of consumption each year, but the absolute decrease would be less each year. These predictions are subject to many technical reservations, and they go far beyond the data. But they are the best that we can do at this time.

A required danger-warning in the ads would be a type of negative advertising. We cannot estimate how much the warning would cut smoking, but certainly the effect would not be as drastic as a ban on advertising, or no firm would continue to advertise. Our inability to come up with any better prediction is testimony to how little scientific knowledge we have about the effect of different forms of advertising copy. But it should certainly be possible to pretest ads that contain warnings, just as other ads are pretested, in order to obtain an estimate of the effect of a warning.

Now let us estimate the health effect of an advertising ban and the resulting reduction in cigarette consumption:

1. For each cigarette smoked, someone's life is shortened by 5 to 9 minutes. We shall figure 7 minutes per cigarette.
2. About 523 billion cigarettes were smoked last year. A decrease of 5 percent in consumption for just one year would mean an increase of human life in the United States of about 183 billion minutes, or 349,000 years of life. Remember, this is the amount of lifetime increased by a decrease of 5 percent in smoking for *just one year*.
3. People who are kept from starting smoking will live, on the average, 5 years longer than if they had started smoking.

Effect on employment and local economies

An estimated 225,000 people make a substantial part of their living in tobacco agriculture, earning approximately $600 million last year, of which about $450 million came from cigarettes. Some 31,000 factory workers earned $150 million last year from cigarette manufacture. In total, then, cigarette purchases put about $600 million into the pockets of workers and farmers. How will a ban or a warning affect them?

Notwithstanding the frantic reactions of Southern state officials, however, a drop in consumption would have no immediate effect on farm earnings, because of the government subsidy program. Unless the government removed the subsidy, the taxpayers at large, rather than the farm population, would take the loss. But let's assume that the subsidy would be cut.

If the subsidy were cut, the effect of a loss in earnings would probably be worse than the figures show, because the effect would be concentrated in a few states that are already economically backward. Many tobacco farmers are already poor and would find it hard to find new jobs.

Table 1 Consumption of tobacco products,[a] selected years, 1990 to 1962

Year	All tobacco (Pounds)	Cigarettes (number)	Cigars (number)	Pipe tobacco (Pounds)	Chewing tobacco (Pounds)	Snuff (Pounds)
1900	7.42	49	111	1.63	4.10	0.32
1910	8.59	138	113	2.58	3.99	0.50
1920	8.66	611	117	1.96	3.06	0.50
1930	8.88	1,365	72	1.87	1.90	0.46
1940	8.91	1,828	56	2.05	1.00	0.38
1950	11.59	3,322	50	0.94	0.78	0.36
1960	10.97	3,888	57	0.59	0.51	0.29
1961	11.15	3,986	56	0.59	0.51	0.27
1962	10.85	3,958	55	0.56	0.50	0.26

Note: Per person aged 15 years and over in the United States.
Source: U.S. Department of Agriculture, Economic Research Service.

For example, North Carolina is an agricultural state and almost half of its farm income comes from tobacco.

Using our estimates above, employment and earnings would be cut by 5 percent *at most* during the first year of an advertising ban. In subsequent years, the further cut in jobs and/or dollars would be less. I say "5 percent at most" because there is good reason to believe that an important proportion of smokers who quit smoking cigarettes, or young people who never start, would use other forms of tobacco instead. Table 1 shows that cigarettes largely *replaced* other forms of tobacco and did not create much *new* demand for tobacco. To the extent that smokers switch to pipe tobacco, cigars, chewing tobacco, and snuff, the damage to tobacco farming would be reduced, even though cigarette tobacco is a more expensive product than other types of tobacco.

Furthermore, some or many tobacco workers who are thrown out of work would get other jobs, so we are overestimating greatly when we assume that the equivalent of lost cigarette-industry wages would be lost to the economy as a whole. But we assume the worst, or close to it, for the sake of argument. Later we shall look at the potential effects on employment again, when we consider the overall picture.

Effect on cigarette companies

To understand the effect of a ban or a warning requirement on the cigarette companies, we must first understand the nature of advertising as a business investment.

When a firm spends a dollar in advertising a brand of cigarettes this year, the advertising bought with that dollar increases cigarette sales this year, but it also increases sales next year, and the year after, and in subsequent years. Customers get into the habit of buying a given brand, a habit that may continue for many years. To say it another way, a dollar of advertising may create some goodwill or brand-loyalty that persists long into the future, though each year the effect of that single dollar of advertising is less than the year before. Cigarette advertising is really an investment, just like an investment in a new machine that will produce for many years after it is bought.

Lester Telser studied the pre-World War II cigarette market in considerable detail. He found that only 15 to 20 percent of the advertising investment is used up in the year in which the advertisements appear. This means that for each dollar of sales created in the advertising year, much more than $3 of sales will be created in subsequent years. (However, because of the chaos in the postwar cigarette market, investment is probably used up faster than Telser's estimate.)

Therefore, even if all cigarette advertising were stopped tomorrow, the established cigarette brands would continue to sell well for many years, though at continually diminishing rates. During that time the cigarette companies would be recouping the investments they have already made. Furthermore, since all the firms would have to stop advertising, the investments already made would not be used up as fast, which would give the cigarette companies a better return on their invested dollars than they expected to earn when they made the investments.

The total effect, then, would be that in future years the sales of any brand would gradually decrease. But the gross profits on a brand would be at a very high rate for a while, because the firm would not be making any further investment in advertising. The cigarette companies would have a fine opportunity to "milk" their brands for profit.

The cigarette companies already know how to milk a brand after they cease advertising it. For example, substantial quantities of non-filter Old Golds have been sold in the last couple of years despite the fact that Lorillard practically quit advertising them.

If advertising were stopped, the cigarette companies would generate large amounts of cash each year, which they could either liquidate to stockholders or use to diversify. The former is not likely because of our tax structure and because no executive likes to liquidate himself out of a job. In the latter case, much of the capital would go to create new jobs in other industries.

Either way, I would guess that a cigarette stock would have a very solid value if advertising were banned. The same *type* of predictions would apply if a warning were required, but the effects would not be as sweeping.

Effect on advertising media

The advertising media have already been hit by the Surgeon General's report. Some radio and television stations have voluntarily restricted cigarette advertising to certain hours of the day, while others have cut it off completely. Some magazines and papers have always refused to accept tobacco advertising, notably the *Reader's Digest*. And now the cigarette advertisers have set up an authority to regulate copy and media.

A warning requirement would not hit the media as hard as a ban, of course. But a warning that really affected consumption would make advertising less profitable for the firms, and they would therefore advertise less.

Television would lose more than $120 million in advertising revenue, about 7 percent of its total revenue last year. But that would not represent a dead loss to television stations and networks. Television time is limited, especially on networks, and the time is therefore rationed among potential advertisers. If cigarette advertising were banned, the television time could be sold to other advertisers, though at a somewhat lower price.

Television stations are charged with the public interest to a greater extent than are other communications media, because they are given a free franchise for a channel. This franchise gives them some monopoly power. Therefore, the television people should be particularly slow to complain about the loss of cigarette advertising revenue if it is in the public interest.

Radio would lose an estimated $20 million in cigarette advertising revenue, less than 3 percent of its total revenue. Other advertisers would not replace this revenue. But radio stations also have a free franchise granted by the public.

The $34 million loss to general and farm magazines would be a complete loss, about 7 percent of their total revenue. The magazines would not find other advertisers to replace cigarettes, and some magazines would feel a considerable strain. But since it would hit them all, they could all be expected to reduce their editorial cost somewhat, without fear of losing advertisers or circulation to competition. This might cushion the impact somewhat.

The $18 million lost to newspapers would be only one-half of 1 percent of their advertising revenue.

Effect on advertising agencies

The advertising-agency business would take a beating if cigarette advertising were banned. Agencies would also be hurt if a warning were required, because in that case total cigarette advertising would decrease. Madison Avenue-type agencies would lose approximately $200 million billing of their total of perhaps $4 billion, about 5 percent of their total. (Actually, only 15 per cent of the $200 million – $30 million – stays with the agencies. The rest goes to the media.) Perhaps a thousand copywriters, account executives, and other agency people would be scurrying about looking for jobs, and the job market would be glutted for a while.

It is interesting to note that some major advertising agencies have said, after the Surgeon General's report came out, that they would refuse to handle cigarette advertising, because they now consider it immoral. Expectedly, none of those agencies now has a cigarette account. But their statements do mean something, nevertheless.

Effect on the economy as a whole

The total cigarette market is about $6.8 billion. Excluding taxes, the industry accounts for $3.6 billion, much less than 1 percent of the gross national product.

We have some evidence that Americans tend to spend a fairly constant percentage of their total yearly income, year after year. This suggest that a decrease in cigarette sales would lead to a compensating increase in other spending. If so, the effect on the economy as a whole would be lessened. Exactly how much the first impact would be, we cannot say. It would be somewhere between no effect and $180 million (5 percent of $3.6 billion).

On the other side of the ledger, the "multiplier effect" would magnify the ill effects of whatever decrease in spending does take place, by a factor of 2 or 3. This effect is due to the spending of money again and again by people in the business chain. In other words, if people saved half of the $180 million drop in cigarette sales, the drop in national income would then be between $180 million and $270 million.

In any case, a small yearly decrease in cigarette sales and cigarette advertising, made even smaller by a shift to other forms of tobacco, would not be even a drop in the bucket for the economy as a whole.

Cigarette smoking does affect the federal economy and the economies of the states and some cities, too, by way of taxes paid on cigarettes. Federal excise taxes amount to $2 billion, state taxes are above $1 billion, and municipal taxes are $40 million. These taxes are important to the tax-collecting bodies. But at first the loss would only be 5 percent of taxes that represent 2 percent of total government revenues. Furthermore, if taxes are not collected one way, they can be collected another way, at the same total cost to the public.

On the other hand, cigarettes may cost the economy far more than they contribute. Louis Lublin, a retired vice-president of Metropolitan Life Insurance, estimates that cigarettes cost the nation $10 billion annually in the lost services and earnings of men killed prematurely by cigarettes. My own estimate is a loss of more than $4 billion, based on 1.1 years of life lost by the average smoker before the age of 65, half of the men in the United States being smokers, and an annual payroll of $322 million.

In sum, then, we must balance the expected effects on health against the expected effects on employment and earnings.

Putting together our previous estimates, we can say that it takes a reduction of 880 cigarettes to produce a drop of one dollar in tobacco-worker's earning. And a drop of that many cigarettes means that someone's life expectancy goes up by 880×7 minutes = 104 hours. The drop in *both* consumption and earnings would be less in subsequent years. But they would stay in step with each other, so the same type of dollars-for-hours-of-life relationship would hold.

When we consider the $4 billion to $10 billion in earnings lost each year by men killed prematurely by cigarettes, it is clear that the country will gain more in live men's earning power than it will lose in revenue. And in fact, the gain in earning power for people kept alive by not smoking would be 10 to 20 times the loss in earning power of tobacco-industry workers.

Then, too, deaths caused by smoking decrease consumption spending. In the 104 hours lost by each dollar of cigarette-industry earnings, a live person would spend more than $20. This consumption spending is important to the economy.

This, then, is the decision that will eventually be made, if our assumptions are correct. Should the nation decrease employment temporarily to gain 104 hours of life per dollar of earnings lost? Should the nation reduce the tobacco industry revenue, gaining two dollars in earnings from live men for each dollar decrease in tobacco-industry revenue, and a gain of $10 to $20 in earnings of men kept alive for each dollar of tobacco-workers' earnings lost?

Conclusion

There is much to gain, little to lose, by stopping the advertising of cigarettes. My chain of reasoning goes like this:

1. Advertising *could* be banned without prohibiting smoking;
2. A ban on advertising would bring about no boomerang noneconomic ill effects and the economy's overall vitality would hardly be affected;
3. A prohibition on cigarette production could have harsh repercussions, as with the prohibition of alcohol in the twenties;
4. There are other commodities (e.g., contraceptives, medical services, liquor on radio and television, and many others) that are sold but cannot be advertised, so this would be no new precedent; and
5. Therefore, let's ban cigarette advertising.

Postscript

If the nation wishes to decrease cigarette consumption, raising the tax on cigarettes is an obvious alternative or additional measure that might be taken. There is no doubt that fewer cigarettes will be bought if the price is higher. However, the tax would take a larger proportion of some people's income than of others. And if the price of cigarettes goes up, people will smoke the butts closer to the end. The more of a cigarette that is smoked, the more dangerous it rapidly becomes. So an increase in taxation may not be a good alternative solution.

[36]

Foreword

The central idea in this paper came to me as I was dreamily looking out of the window of the car as my wife was driving through the Missouri Ozarks. My preoccupation with the issue addressed here began when I heard someone say that "science shows" that population growth is a bad thing.

DEMOGRAPHY© Volume 12, Number 1 February 1975

THE WELFARE EFFECT OF AN ADDITIONAL CHILD CANNOT BE STATED SIMPLY AND UNEQUIVOCALLY

Julian L. Simon
Departments of Economics and Business Administration, University of Illinois at Urbana-Champaign, Urbana, Illinois 61801; and the Jerusalem School of Business Administration, Hebrew University, Jerusalem, Israel

Abstract—There is no single calculable welfare effect of an additional person. Rather, there are many different judgments, which may be negative or positive. The welfare effect depends upon the particular economic situation the child will be born into, which point in his life-cycle one refers to, whether he is expected to have a positive effect upon his particular sort of economy and society during and after his lifetime, and most of all, on the kind of welfare criterion used. Furthermore, no matter which welfare criterion is used, the welfare effect of an added individual *summarized over time* is especially sensitive to the particular assumptions made.

Introduction

Analyses of the welfare economics of population growth generally make one or more of the following assumptions: (1) The criterion of social welfare at a point in time is per capita (or per consumer) income (e.g., Enke, 1966). (2) The effect of a given individual upon society is limited to his own impact during his own lifetime (e.g., Mirrlees, 1972). (3) Welfare is assessed at a single point in time, or at the same rate along a growth path, or without distinguishing between the various periods of the additional child's life-cycle (e.g., Phelps, 1968). Most of the older literature makes *all* of these assumptions (see Gottlieb, 1945).

It is the contention of this paper that a judgment about the magnitude and even the *direction* of the welfare effect of an added child depends upon each of these assumptions. That is, changing one or more assumptions to other reasonable assumptions often shifts the conclusion about the welfare effect from positive to negative or vice versa. Therefore, the aim of the paper is to map out the welfare effects of additional children under many different sets of assumptions.

From this welter of possible conclusions one can draw an important irrefutable conclusion: Analysis of the effect of population growth is complex and tenuous; it is *not* straightforward and clear-cut as it is too often presented in newspapers, television and professional journals by both laymen and specialists; any judgment is contingent on one's values and assumptions.

This general question is not one to which welfare-economics techniques can give any general answer. In this context the question of whether people should have more or less children is similar to the question of whether grocery stores should expand. One would never expect or try to deduce a general answer from welfare economics on the latter question; there are just too many if's and but's. Furthermore, the larger the number of if's and but's, the less possible it is to provide a general answer, or even manageably few answers, from welfare economics. This is unlike the question about whether a price ceiling on wheat is a good thing; with only a few if's and value assumptions, the economist can produce a general answer or two to such a question.

This is not to say that the economist is useless in the case of food-store expansion or family-size decisions. He has two useful functions: Firstly, he can sit with the decision-makers in a *particular* situation, determine which way all the if's and but's go in that particular situation, and help reach a situation-specific decision. Secondly, he can list the considerations that are relevant and that must be decided explicitly in *any* specific situation, e.g., the discount factor. But where there are many conditions that affect the answer, the welfare economist cannot produce a sound general answer about the better policy.

I do not mean to suggest that the various contradictory assumptions and values that will enter the discussion are morally indistinguishable. But it is not within the competence of economists or demographers to judge their relative morality. That must be left to the community, perhaps with guidance from philosophers, who are now busily arguing these ethical-moral questions (e.g., Narveson, 1967, 1973; Stearns, 1972; Brandt, 1972).

The term "welfare" as used in this paper refers to whether a given society is judged to be made better off or worse off on balance by a given action. That is, if one concludes that an additional child makes society worse off (or better off) under a given set of conditions, he is adjudging that there is a negative (or positive) welfare effect of the additional child.

The term "utility" refers here to the satisfaction that an individual gains from his life. With the exception of the parents of the additional child—whose utility *is* assumed to be affected by the number of children they have—utility is assumed to be a function only of the individual's own level of income (consumption). If an individual's utility were seen to be influenced one way or another by the number of siblings and the size of the community (aside from their effect on his income), the analysis would be even more complex and less determinate—which would only reinforce the central point of this essay.

The strategy of the paper is to disaggregate the problem in two directions. The first disaggregation is *over time*. Instead of asking for a single time-discounted value that summarizes whether welfare is higher or lower, considering all of the future periods together, welfare judgments will be discussed for a few separate segments of the future: (a) the added individual's childhood; (b) his adulthood; and (c) after the individual's death. Summary measures will also be considered critically.

The second kind of disaggregation is *by groups*. Instead of only a single criterion of welfare for the community as a whole, judgments will be shown about (a) the individual's welfare; (b) the welfare of his parents, (c) the welfare of all *other* persons excluding the added individual; and (d) some overall judgments, as well.

The paper begins with the simplest situation, that in which the individual has no negative or positive effects external to his own family and leaves no negative or positive inheritance of any kind to future generations. This situation (with the single complication that the additional child already has siblings) is briefly summarized in Table 1. Then the paper moves on to situations where there are externalities during his life and then to situations where there are continuing external effects after his death. The situations are analyzed with various welfare functions, under various

TABLE 1.—The Welfare Effects of an Additional Child, According to Some Different Criteria, in the Simplest Agricultural Situation (with Siblings)[a]

The Welfare Criterion and the Time Period in the Life-Cycle of the Additional Child	Indicated Welfare Effect
In Childhood	
1. Utility to parents	Positive welfare effect
4. Utility to older siblings	Negative welfare effect
6. Sum of utility of children in family if each utility function is concave and positive	Positive welfare effect
7. Sum of utility of children in family if shape of utility function is not assumed positive and concave	Indeterminate
8. Average utility of children in family	Negative welfare effect
9. Average utility of family including parents (parental utility including non-income-related utility from children)	Indeterminate
13. Per capita income (average utility) of community as whole	Negative welfare effect
14. Sum of utility of community as a whole if each utility function is assumed positive and concave	Positive welfare effect
15. Sum of utility of community as a whole if utility can be negative	Indeterminate
In Adulthood	
23. Sum of utility of older siblings	Negative welfare effect
25. Per capita income (average utility) of all children in family	Negative welfare effect
27. Sum of utility of all family's children if utility functions are assumed positive and concave	Positive welfare effect

Note: The aim of this table is to show that the judgment about the welfare effect of an additional child (with the complication of siblings) depends upon the criterion chosen.
Source: This table is drawn from Table 2, which shows a large variety of such situations and criteria. Row numbers correspond to those in Table 2; the welfare effects are excerpts from column b.

assumptions about the directions of the externalities.

The results of the analyses are summarized in Table 2. The text explains how only a few of the results in Table 2 are obtained. The material in the table should be considered as data on which the general conclusion of the paper is based. The main point of Table 2, and of the paper as a whole, is that the welfare effects of an additional person are very mixed and are largely indeterminate; the judgments must depend upon the particular economic conditions, the economic and value assumptions, and the choice of welfare criteria. The aim is to refute all analyses which purport to arrive at firm scientific conclusions about the welfare effect of population growth without noting the sensitivity of those conclusions to different welfare criteria and to the differing ramifications of additional people in various economic situations.

TABLE 2.—The Welfare Effects of an Additional Child with Various Factual Assumptions and Value Judgments

Assumptions about the Economic Situation

Welfare Criterion and Time Period in Additional Child's Life-Cycle during Which Welfare is Evaluated	a. Peasant Agriculture, No Labor Force Entry, No Externalities beyond the Family		b. Same as Column a, but with Older Siblings	c. Labor Force Entry, but No Other Externalities, All Markets Perfect. No End-of-Life Savings, No Creation of Knowledge or Economies of Scale	d. Same as Column c, except End-of-Life Savings Positive but Less Than Rate of Population Growth Contributed by Individual and His Children	e. Same as c, except Savings Equal to Contribution to Population Growth Rate	f. Same as c, except Savings Greater Than Contribution to Population Growth Rate	g. Schooling and Child-Service Externalities, but Paid for by Parents. Otherwise Same as c	h. Same as g with Respect to Externalities. Same as d Otherwise	i. Same as g with Respect to Externalities. Same as e Otherwise	j. Same as g with Respect to Externalities. Same as f Otherwise	k. Same as g but Externalities Not Paid for by Parents	l. Same as h but Externalities Not Paid for by Parents	m. Same as i but Externalities Not Paid for by Parents	n. Same as j but Externalities Not Paid for by Parents	o. Same as l (Negative Childhood Externalities, Positive Savings but Less Than Rate of Population Growth), and Positive Contribution to Knowledge and Economies of Scale Effect during Adulthood	p. Same as n (Negative Childhood Externalities, Savings Greater Than Rate of Population Growth), and Positive Contribution to Knowledge and Economies of Scale Effect during Adulthood
In Childhood																	
1. Utility to parents of additional person	+	directly by assumption	+	+	+	+	+	Same as column c	Same as column d	Same as column e	Same as column f	+	+	+	+	+	+
2. Additional person's own utility (assumed positive)	+	directly by assumption	+	+	+	+	+	Same as column c	Same as column d	Same as column e	Same as column f	+	+	+	+	+	+
3. Additional person's own utility (function not assumed positive or concave)	(?)	depends on family's income	±	±	±	±	±	Same as column c	Same as column d	Same as column e	Same as column f	±	±	±	±	±	±
4. Older siblings' utility (positive concave function assumed)	NA		(−)	−	−	−	−	Same as column c	Same as column d	Same as column e	Same as column f	−	−	−	−	−	−
5. All children in his family including him, consumption per child	NA		−	−	−	−	−	Same as column c	Same as column d	Same as column e	Same as column f	−	−	−	−	−	−
6. All children in his family including him, sum of utilities, function assumed concave and positive	NA		(+)	+	+	+	+	Same as column c	Same as column d	Same as column e	Same as column f	+	+	+	+	+	+
7. All children in his family including him, sum of utilities, his utility not assumed positive or negative	NA		(±)	±	±	±	±	Same as column c	Same as column d	Same as column e	Same as column f	±	±	±	±	±	±
8. Average utility of children in family	−		−	−	−	−	−	Same as column c	Same as column d	Same as column e	Same as column f	−	−	−	−	−	−
9. Average utility of family including parents (parental utility including non-income-related utility from children)	±		±	±	±	±	±	Same as column c	Same as column d	Same as column e	Same as column f	±	±	±	±	±	±

Table 2.--Continued

10. Other persons in community (i.e., beyond the family), per capita income	-	directly by assumption	-	-	-	-	-	↕	↕	↕	↕	-	-	-	-	-	-
11. Same as line 8, sum of utilities, positive concave function assumed	-	directly by assumption	-	-	-	-	-					-	-	-	-	-	-
12. Same as line 8, sum of utilities, concave function not assumed	-	directly by assumption	-	-	-	-	-					-	-	-	-	-	-
13. Community as a whole including the additional person and his family, per capita income	(-)		-	-	-	-	-					-	-	-	-	-	-
14. Community as a whole including the additional person and his family, sum of utilities, positive concave function	+		(+)	+	+	+	+					(±)	(±)	(±)	(±)	±	±
15. Community as a whole including the additional person and his family, sum of utilities, no assumed constraint on function	(±)		±	±	±	±	±					±	±	±	±	±	±
16. Community as a whole including the additional person and his family, expanded Pareto criterion, assuming positive and concave functions	+		±	+	+ aside from siblings	+	+	(+)	(+)	(+)	(+)	(±)	(±)	(±)	(±)	±	±
17. Utility of parents of added person	+		+	+	+	+	+	↕	↕	↕	↕	+	+	+	+	+	+
18. Utility of parents of added person, cumulatively through childhood	+		+	+	+	+	+					+	+	+	+	+	+
19. Added person himself, utility assumed positive, cumulatively through childhood	+		+	+	+	+	+					+	+	+	+	+	+
20. Added person himself, utility not assumed positive or concave, cumulatively through childhood	±		±	±	±	±	±					±	±	±	±	±	±
<u>In Adulthood</u>																	
21. Older siblings, total utility concave positive functions assumed	NA		(-)	-	-	-	-					-	-	-	-	±	±
22. Older siblings, total utility, concave positive functions, cumulatively through childhood and adulthood	NA		-	-	-	-	-	Same as column c	Same as column d	Same as column e	Same as column f	-	-	-	-	±	±
23. All family's children including him, per capita	NA		(-)	-	-	-	-					-	-	-	-	±	±
24. All family's children including him, per capita income, cumulatively	NA		-	-	-	-	-					-	-	-	-	±	±
25. All family's children including him, sum of utilities, assuming concave and positive functions	NA		(+)	+	+	+	+					+	+	+	+	+	+
26. All family's children including him, sum of utilities, assuming concave and positive functions, cumulatively	NA		+	+	+	+	+					+	+	+	+	+	+
27. All family's children, sum of utilities with no assumptions about utility function	NA		±	±	±	±	±					±	±	±	±	±	±
28. All family's children, sum of utilities with no assumptions about utility function, cumulatively	NA		±	±	±	±	±					±	±	±	±	±	±

Table 2.--Continued

Welfare Criterion and Time Period in Additional Child's Life-Cycle during Which Welfare is Evaluated	a Peasant Agriculture, No Labor Force Entry, No Externalities beyond the Family	b Same as Column a, but with Older Siblings	c Labor Force Entry, but No Other Externalities, All Markets Perfect. No End-of-Life Savings, No Creation of Knowledge or Economies of Scale	d Same as Column c, except End-of-Life Savings Positive but Less Than Rate of Population Growth Contributed by Individual and His Children	e Same as c, except Savings Equal to Contribution to Population Growth Rate	f Same as c, except Savings Greater Than Contribution to Population Growth Rate	g Schooling and Child-Service Externalities, but Paid for by Parents. Otherwise Same as c	h Same as g with Respect to Externalities. Same as d Otherwise	i Same as g with Respect to Externalities. Same as e Otherwise	j Same as g with Respect to Externalities. Same as f Otherwise	k Same as g but Externalities Not Paid for by Parents	l Same as h but Externalities Not Paid for by Parents	m Same as i but Externalities Not Paid for by Parents	n Same as j but Externalities Not Paid for by Parents	o Same as l (Negative Childhood Externalities, Positive Savings but Less Than Rate of Population Growth), and Positive Contribution to Knowledge and Economies of Scale Effect during Adulthood	p Same as n (Negative Childhood Externalities, Savings Greater Than Rate of Population Growth), and Positive Contribution to Knowledge and Economies of Scale Effect during Adulthood
29. All workers in same occupation, per capita income	-	(-)	-	-	-	-	Same as column c	Same as column d	Same as column e	Same as column f	-	-	-	-	±	±
30. All workers in same occupation, per capita income, cumulatively	-	-	-	-	-	-	Same as column c	Same as column d	Same as column e	Same as column f	-	-	-	-	±	±
31. All workers in same occupation, sum of utilities, assuming concave and positive functions	-	-	+	+	+	+	Same as column c	Same as column d	Same as column e	Same as column f	+	+	+	+	+	+
32. All workers in same occupation, sum of utilities, assuming concave and positive functions, cumulatively	-	-	+	+	+	+	Same as column c	Same as column d	Same as column e	Same as column f	+	+	+	+	+	+
33. All workers in same occupation, sum of utilities, no assumptions about functional form	-	-	±	±	±	±	Same as column c	Same as column d	Same as column e	Same as column f	±	±	±	±	±	±
34. All workers in same occupation, sum of utilities, no assumptions about functional form, cumulatively	-	-	±	±	±	±	Same as column c	Same as column d	Same as column e	Same as column f	±	±	±	±	±	±
35. Others in community (excepting only him and his family), per capita income	-	(-)	+	+	+	+	Same as column c	Same as column d	Same as column e	Same as column f	-	-	-	-	±	±
36. Others in community (excepting only him and his family), per capita income, cumulatively	-	-	±	±	±	±	Same as column c	Same as column d	Same as column e	Same as column f	-	-	-	-	±	±

Welfare Effect of Additional Child

Table 2.--Continued

37. Others in community, sum of utilities, functions assumed positive and concave	=		(=)	+	+	+	+	Same as column c	Same as column d	Same as column e	Same as column f	-	-	-	-	±	±
38. Others in community, no assumptions about functions	=		=	+	+	+	+					-	-	-	-	±	±
39. Others in community, no assumptions about functions, cumulatively	=		(=)	+	+	+	+					-	-	-	-	±	±
40. Community as a whole including him, per capita income	-		(-)	-	-	-	-					-	-	-	-	±	±
41. Community as a whole including him, per capita income, cumulatively	-		-	-	-	-	-					-	-	-	-	(±)	±
42. Community as a whole, sum of utilities, functions assumed positive and concave	+		(+)	+	+	+	+					+	+	+	+	+	+
43. Community as a whole, sum of utilities, functions assumed positive and concave, cumulatively	+		+	+	+	+	+					(±)	(±)	(±)	(±)	(±)	±
44. Community as a whole, sum of utilities, no assumptions about form of utility function	±		±	±	±	±	±					±	±	±	±	±	±
45. Community as a whole, sum of utilities, no assumptions about form of utility function, cumulatively	±		±	±	±	±	±					±	±	±	±	±	±
46. Community as a whole, expanded Pareto criterion assuming positive and concave functions	+		±	±	±	±	±					±	±	±	±	±	±
47. Community as a whole, expanded Pareto criterion assuming positive and concave functions, cumulatively	+		±	±	±	±	±					±	±	±	±	±	±
In Posterity																	
48. Community as a whole, per capita income	±	depends on number of children	-	-	-	=	+					-	-	=	+	±	(+)
49. Community as a whole, per capita income, cumulatively through childhood, adulthood, and posterity	±		±	-	-	-	±[a]					±	-	-	±[a]	±	±
50. Community as a whole, sum of utilities, function assumed positive and concave	+		+	-	±	+	+					-	±	+	+	±	(+)
51. Community as a whole, sum of utilities, function assumed positive and concave, cumulatively	+		+	±	±	+	+					±	±	±	±	±	±
52. Community as a whole, sum of utilities, no assumptions about utility function	±		±	±	±	±	±					±	±	±	±	±	±
53. Community as a whole, sum of utilities, no assumptions about utility function, cumulatively	±		±	±	±	±	±					±	±	±	±	±	±

a- Depends on discount rate.

Note: NA = not applicable;
+ indicates positive effect;
- indicates negative effect;
= indicates no effect;
± indicates indeterminate effect.

A circle in a cell indicates that the situation is discussed in the text. The table is intended to show only that there are both positive and negative effects for each economic situation. It is not intended to be an exhaustive set of analyses (and it could not be); rather each of the analyses is intended to be of special interest.

The strategy of the paper is like that of the mathematician who constructs counterexamples to show that a generalization does not hold. But in economics the counterexamples should be reasonable ones, rather than mere logical possibilities. Therefore, only criteria and situations that have some plausibility and social meaning are shown in Table 2, and they are only a sample of those that might be examined.

No Externalities beyond the Family during or after the Additional Child's Life

During His Childhood: No Siblings

We begin with the simplest situation worth considering, the kind of subsistence-agricultural community in which a child has practically no economic effects external to his family during or after his childhood, and in which there are until now no children in the family. We can quickly see that even in such a simple situation one can arrive at a variety of welfare conclusions about the addition of a child to the community, depending upon one's assumptions. Here are three such welfare-judgment possibilities.

(1) If an additional *first* child in a family has no effects external to the family during his childhood, then the welfare of all *other* persons in the society is unaffected by his birth—by assumption. However, by definition the welfare of his parents is increased by the occurrence of an event the parents desire.

Many writers on population problems choose to restrict the discussion to the effects on the welfare of those living now. If the welfare judgment is limited to the welfare of only those now living, the Pareto-optimum test immediately tells us that if, in this simplest situation, parents choose to have a child when they have none, the result is added welfare by the following simple reasoning: The parents are better off (by our definition of the situation); the rest of the community is no worse off (by our definition of the situation); and therefore the overall welfare increases.

(2) Now let us bring the added child himself into the discussion, as many people think is appropriate. To start with, the judgment about the welfare of the *child himself* depends upon one's assumption about the human utility function, together with the facts of the case. According to the assumption made by Meade (1955), Dasgupta (1969), Ehrlich (1968), and others, the welfare of a very poor child can be *negative* (Table 2, column a, line 3). But, of course, one can just as reasonably assume that the child's welfare is neutral or positive when he is very young. (Later, after he is old enough that one can reasonably impute choice to him, we can argue about his welfare in a different fashion, as will be discussed later.) But no matter what one assumes about the utility of life, by the test of *per capita income*, general welfare *falls* during this childhood period, because the same amount of product (assuming no increase in labor by the parents) is divided among more people (column a, line 13 in Tables 1 and 2).

(3) If one uses as a welfare criterion the *sum* of individual utilities, general welfare *rises* if the additional child's utility is positive. The same conclusion can be reached by a more economic and powerful approach, that of an expanded-Pareto optimum (an idea also suggested by Friedman [1972]): If a person whose utility is positive is *added* to the society, and if none of the existing people thereby have their positions altered for the worse, it is reasonable that this represents an increase in the society's utility. (The application of this criterion is unique to the very simple case under discussion, however; even the existence of brothers or sisters makes the criterion

inapplicable without further assumptions, as we shall see.)

Now for a side examination of a curious implication of the analysis for this simple situation: parents have *fewer* children than would maximize the total utility of the community. The reasoning is as follows. The parent continues to have children until he is at his own margin, indifferent between the birth and nonbirth of another child; the rest of the community is also indifferent by our definition of this simple situation. But at this margin an additional child would himself enjoy positive utility, by assumption; hence his birth would add his own utility to the community's utility, with no net utility change to his parents, yielding a positive effect on balance. Hence more children would increase total utility.

Despite the fact that families do not choose to have enough children to reach the point of zero net marginal social utility, one cannot know *how far* the laissez-faire outcome is from the margin without complete knowledge of people's welfare functions. Hence it seems that the only sensible course consistent with the foregoing conclusion is to let parents set their own limits on the number of children, subject to consideration of external costs and community values.

The inference that parents have too few children to maximize community utility applies only to the childhood period and may well hold only under the assumptions that (a) there are no other children in the family, (b) utility is positive, and (c) there are no externalities. It *might*, however, hold even if some of the foregoing assumptions were loosened in some ways.

With the foregoing analysis in hand, one may judge the welfare effects of contraceptive knowledge and of public health measures to reduce infant mortality. Consider contraception first. In a society where no one dies before old age, the ability to practice contraception increases the welfare of *parents* because it allows them to achieve the number of children that will maximize their (parental) utility. That is, ability to contracept increases parents' options, a Paretian basic welfare gain. If lack of contraceptive knowledge leads to more children than the couple wants *ex ante*, this *may* increase the total welfare of the family, and hence of the community. But to argue that people should be hindered from practicing contraception one must argue that (a) one knows the parents' and children's utility functions and (b) by overcoming the parents' "selfishness" one forces them to a higher level of community utility. (This is implicitly the position of the Catholic Church, as I understand it.) It seems to me that a person outside the couple cannot make such an argument satisfactorily, which implies that an outsider has no welfare grounds to hinder the practice of contraception.

Now consider infant mortality. If the main thrust of this section is correct—that in the simplest agricultural situation with no externalities welfare is maximized by there being at least as many children as parents desire, subject to community values and external costs—and if parents are able to control fertility accurately, then infant mortality is an unmitigated evil. This is because infant mortality must result in the parents often having more or less children than they desire, with consequently lower utility for the parents. Only by luck will the number of children they desire *ex ante* live to maturity. Even if parents are lucky enough to end up with the number of children they desire, they will have suffered the grief of children's deaths and extra child-raising costs that would not have occurred with a zero infant-mortality regime.

Furthermore, because people are generally risk-averse when it comes to the number of children and to the number of sons they have, the error will likely be on the side of achieving more children than were desired *ex ante,* as has been shown vividly by Heer and Smith (1968) and May and Heer (1968). Infant mortality might increase total utility by offsetting parental selfishness, but it might also reduce total utility by carrying the process beyond the point of diminishing total utility. Which is true cannot be known *a priori.*

Now let us consider the case in which the additional child's welfare is said to be *negative.* No judgment about the direction of the community welfare effect can then be made without assigning cardinal values to the individual utility of the additional child and that of his parents, which trade off if the child's utility is said to be negative (Table 2, column a, line 15). And if one considers even more complex welfare functions containing arguments of per capita income as well as of total utility or total population size (e.g., Meade, 1955; Votey, 1969), they will *a fortiori* also give indeterminate results in the absence of cardinal specification of the utility function.

During His Childhood if There Are Siblings

When a *second* or *subsequent* child is considered to be the additional child, the welfare effect becomes even more complicated (see Table 1 or column b in Table 2) because consumption by existing children will be reduced by the existence of an additional child. And unlike the parents, there is no reason to assume that the existing children desire the additional child. Hence, the welfare of the previous children is decreased on balance by an additional child (line 4). The overall welfare judgment must then depend upon the assumption one makes about the utility functions of the people involved.

If the individual utility function of each of the children is assumed positive at all consumption levels, and concave downward like this 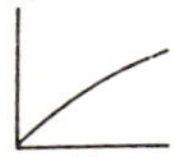 and if the utility functions of all the children are assumed to be the same, then the additional child increases total utility of the children in the family (Table 1, line 6). This conclusion follows from the mathematical fact that doubling the value on the x (consumption) axis is associated with *less* than doubling the value on the y (utility) axis when the function is concave downward. Hence the *total* utility is greater if one distributes a given amount of consumption among two or more persons with similar utility functions, rather than concentrating the consumption with one person. This is the same reasoning that underlies the conclusion that a more equal distribution of income increases utility, *ceteris paribus.*

If the children's utility functions can be negative at some consumption levels and/or have inflection points, the welfare effect of an additional child upon the children as a group depends on the economic facts and the specific utility functions and is indeterminate without cardinal specifications (Table 1, line 7). The effect on the family as a whole, and on the community, must also be indeterminate if the effect on the children is indeterminate (line 14).

Already we can see that even in the very simplest case, examined for only a single point in time, the evaluation is thoroughly messy and generally indeterminate. The reader who is convinced of this may quit reading at this point unless he is interested in the additional analyses for their own interest.

During His Adulthood: Subsistence Agriculture

During the additional person's adulthood in this simple world of no externalities, his welfare effect depends upon which reference group is being considered, just as it does during his childhood. An additional peasant in subsistence agriculture affects his brothers and sisters negatively by reducing their inheritance of land (Table 1, line 23), and therefore the expanded-Pareto criterion no longer applies. If, however, one assumes that the utility of all the siblings is positive and if all their utility functions are concave, the additional sibling would mean a net welfare gain to the people constituting the original nuclear family (line 27), and thence—by the expanded-Pareto criterion—to the society as a whole. But if one assumes that utility can be negative, no such conclusions can be drawn. Of course, the per capita income effect of an additional person is negative in adulthood in subsistence agriculture (line 25).

During His Adulthood if He Enters the Labor Market

Now let us leave idealized subsistence agriculture and move to the more interesting, but still simple, case in which the additional person enters the labor force but in which all markets are competitive and the individual is paid his marginal output (Table 2, column c). From the standpoint of average income, the *rest* of the community as a whole *benefits* from the added person's presence (lines 37, 39, 41, column c) as Berry and Soligo (1969) have shown; the nature of the benefit is exactly the same as the benefit that occurs when one country opens trade with another country. But assuming that the incremental person is a *worker*, the population of *workers* as a whole, and especially the workers in the trade he enters, will have lower wages because of him (line 31, column c). Furthermore, the average income of the entire community *including* the additional person will fall (line 42, column c). But if one assumes that all persons' utility functions are positive, concave downward, and similar, then the *sum* of the individual utilities in the community will be *higher* than before because total output will be greater (line 44, column c).

So again we see that, even for a single period—his adulthood—and in the simplest case of no externalities and no inheritances, the welfare effect of an incremental individual can be judged differently from different points of view. Furthermore, if one now wishes to *combine* the judgments about the welfare effects of the added person during his childhood and during his adulthood, the results are even more mixed and indeterminate.

We shall here end the story of the man who does not affect society beyond his family, either during or after his lifetime, with positive or negative savings of any kind, except by working in a perfect market.

Externalities during His Lifetime and before His Children's Adulthood

In societies that have advanced economically beyond family subsistence agriculture, an incremental child usually causes effects external to the family. These externalities can be distinguished into two sorts: those whose effects can be appraised and compensated for by way of markets and those that cannot. The former are treated in the next section, and the latter are treated in the section after that.

Where There Are Compensable Externalities

The main "compensable" externalities are in the labor market and in social-welfare expenditures, e.g., schooling. (I assume here that the society charges the full cost for all consumption products, including the cost of physical pollution prevention and removal. The nature of the effect of an additional worker's entrance into the labor force would be difficult to agree upon. But both the labor-force and social-welfare effects of additional children are calculable in principle even if we cannot now agree on how to calculate them. Standard welfare-economics arguments suggest that the total utility of all adults in a society at a given time will be maximized if families pay for all the services used in raising children and also for neutralizing any labor-market effect. That is, if one considers a median-income family with more than the average number of children, it would pay taxes to cover the "extra" child-raising services plus the labor-market effect of the "extra" children. The proof of the optimality of this policy is the same as that for other cases of external effects, as shown in a simple way by Coase (1960). As long as the parents pay the full market value of these external effects, a larger number of children produced by a family cannot be said to reduce the utility of the rest of the community. After the labor-force and social-welfare externalities are taken care of, in which case the utility of existing adults may be assumed to be maximized, the expanded-Pareto criterion may be applied again; after compensation no one except older siblings would be made worse off by the added person (Table 2, line 16, columns g–j). Hence, if the additional person's own utility is assumed to be positive, and putting siblings aside, parents stop having children before the community's welfare would be maximized, by the same argument as was given earlier. (If the added person's utility is not assumed to be positive, or if other children in the family are considered, no such conclusion can be drawn.)

A technical difficulty which turns into a major political problem arises with respect to compensable externalities, however. It is all very well to talk of parents paying *now* for the *future* effects of their children. But such payments would have to be discounted for futurity. The community would have to decide on an appropriate discount rate, because economic logic alone reveals none (or a multitude of them). Even if the community were to eventually arrive at agreement on such a discount rate, there would be major conflicts of interest. Old people without children would want a low discount rate and large sums paid immediately. Parents with many children would want the opposite. It might be suggested that the externalities be paid for as they occur; this might work for schooling and medical care, but it would not be feasible for the children's labor-force effect. So, because of this discount-rate problem, together with the difficulty of estimating the future effects of the children, it is quite possible that the community would not arrive at agreement on an externality-neutralizing agreement. If so, it would not be possible for an additional child to effect a Paretian welfare increase, and the total cumulative effect—in his childhood plus his adulthood—is Paretian indeterminate (Table 2, line 16, columns k–n). If externalities are not neutralized, the welfare effect by a total-utility criterion is also indeterminate during his adulthood and hence indeterminate for his life as a whole (lines 14 and 45, columns k–n).

Now let us consider the *per capita income* effect of an additional individual where there are externalities in child services and labor markets. The classical diminishing-returns analysis (same total capital and more labor yield a smaller average product) tells us that the effect is negative during the additional person's adulthood, as it was during his childhood. But in the more-developed world it is not only possible but likely Kuznets, 1960; Simon, 1975, Chapter 4) that after some time in the labor force an additional person will cause enough new knowledge and enough economies of scale that per capita income will be *higher* than it would otherwise be. (This *includes* the use of natural resources as raw materials in production and is supported by Barnett and Morse's [1963] finding concerning long-run natural-resource scarcities.) If so, by a per capita income welfare standard the additional person's effect is positive for at least the latter part of his adulthood (column o), and the effect may be sufficiently great to make his overall lifetime effect positive (Table 2, line 43, column o). But, given that per capita income is lower during his childhood because of him, to reckon the lifetime per capita income effect one would have to specify the effects for each year and choose a discount rate. A high enough discount rate could, of course, be chosen so that the later positive effect would matter little, and hence the lifetime effect would be negative. But with a lower discount rate the lifetime effect *might* well be positive if there are positive externalities from knowledge and economics of scale during the additional person's adulthood—as there is reason to believe there are. So a variety of possible welfare judgments are possible here.

Nonmarket Externalities and Community Values

Let us now consider externalities that realistically would not be compensated through taxes and subsidies, still confining the discussion to the lifetime of the additional person.

As Arrow (1970, p. 153) has made clear, there may be "a difference between the ordering of social states according to the direct consumption of the individual and the ordering when the individual adds his general standards of equity (or perhaps his standards of pecuniary emulation)." The latter states Arrow calls "values," in contrast to the former which he labels "tastes"; the "market mechanism . . . takes into account only the ordering to tastes." Hence it may be appropriate for the community, acting together, to make such laws—which may include taxes on or subsidies for children—as will achieve the sort of society that its members want. For example, someone might suggest that the community hold a referendum as to whether there should be a tax on parents of 100 shekels, say, for each child after the third. People might rationally vote for such a measure if they believe that a lower birth rate would increase the rate of economic development and if they put a positive value on economic development; or if they believe that infant mortality would decrease if each family had fewer children and they get disutility out of neighbors' children dying; or if they get disutility out of other people's children, e.g., because of the noise; or for other reasons. If people vote unanimously for the tax it would imply that each person would be willing to have fewer children if his neighbors also had fewer children.

Similarly, a community might have a positive value for a *larger* number of children in the community than people otherwise choose to bear, given their own tastes. Israel may be an example: Jews there may feel that the continuation of the historical tradition and the values of Judaism can be better served by more people rather than fewer, and they may be prepared to vote subsidies to children, just as a man may try to bribe his married son to have more children to carry on the family name. If people get positive utility out of their neighbors' children and vote accordingly, a subsidy on children would be indicated. Or people may believe that a larger population would contribute to economic growth within a short enough time span so that their subjective discount rate (which might be zero, as Ramsey [1928] believed it ought to be) would make the immediate social costs less than the discounted benefits; this is now the state of belief in Australia, as it was in western United States in the past.

The mechanism for decision—majority vote or monarchy or whatever—will depend upon the group's constitution. *Any* population policy may then be consistent with welfare economics, if voted in accordance with the constitution. The likeliest cause of distortion with respect to a *democratic* constitution is a population policy initiated and executed by bureaucrats who impose *their own* values upon the community while asserting that the rationale for the policy is the "scientific" finding that the policy in question is "provedly" better than noninterference and governmental neutrality with respect to parental decisions about family size. I believe that this danger is great because the officials or legislators may not recognize that their beliefs and values *are* values and beliefs and are not scientifically proven truths. As Weckstein (1962, p. 137) put it:

> There is a personal bias that colors one's view of the (relatively) poor which comes from appraising others' incomes against the standard of one's own aspirations. This bias is implicit in many conventional economic-welfare judgments, and it seems to me to be both indefensible and in fact without defenders. This is merely shoddy practice, not doctrine.

In the past decade so many scientists have made it clear that they favor lower birth rates that one can easily come to think that lower birth rates have indeed been shown to be scientifically better for society in every way, though in fact no such finding has been or could be scientifically arrived at because of the value considerations involved.

In brief, even where externalities are taken into consideration, the welfare effect of an additional child during his own lifetime depends upon so many considerations that, in general, the welfare effect must be said to be indeterminate.

Effects after the Added Person's Lifetime

Just as a person may affect his society for good or for ill during his lifetime, so may he have effects after he dies. Economists are accustomed to dismissing very-long-run effects because of their small weight in calculations made with interest rates of 5, 10 or even 15 percent. But society itself is more ambivalent about the long-run future and sometimes gives it relatively heavy weight, as the current environmental controversy shows. It may well be that the average man's total effects on posterity are more important than his total effects on his contemporaries—who are, after all, smaller in number than his posterity.

There are many sorts of effects one can have on posterity. The simplest and most surely positive is the savings that one leaves to his heirs; usually the savings exceed the debts, as we know from the fact that society's total capital generally grows over time. One may also leave knowledge behind him; the knowledge *might* be satanic, but usually knowledge is positive for the economy, as we know from the higher rate of productivity now than in former millenia. Still another effect is the children that the added person leaves. At first the effect of children seems very complicated. But consider that the effect of each child is expected to be the same as the effect of the added parent *aside from* his children. Therefore, the welfare judgment one makes about the added person is not changed by his having children—aside from their different positions in history, of course, which can be ignored unless there is special information about the course of history.

Another post-life factor is the delayed economies-of-scale effect associated with the creation of additional infra-structure and with changes in the nature of society—perhaps especially in less-developed countries. As an example, the population-density-induced changes in land-tenure laws and cropping systems shown to occur by Boserup (1965) can have long-run positive effects on productivity.

Let us now get more specific in welfare terms. If the added man leaves a positive net contribution to posterity and if he has no children—that is, if his contribution to subsequent economic growth exceeds his contribution to population growth, then his welfare effect on posterity is positive (Table 2, column p, line 50). If he does have children and he and his lineage add proportionately more to saving than to population growth, then the effect on per capita income of posterity is positive. If he and his heirs each leave something positive, but what they leave contributes less (marginally) to growth than this lineage contributes to population growth, the effect on posterity then is negative in terms of per capita income unless during his lifetime he contributes greatly in knowledge and otherwise. In such a case, the effect in terms of *total* utility is likely to be positive, however, given a reasonable distribution of income and no negative utilities. If the additional individual leaves a *negative* inheritance, then his effect on posterity is negative.

Each of the sorts of impacts classified above could be combined with impacts of the same *or* opposite sign in earlier periods; if the latter, the overall evaluation of the added man's welfare impact is indeterminate without numerical specifications of all impacts and an explicit choice of discount rates.

One might ask whether the possibility of a positive inheritance, and especially an inheritance proportionately as large as the population growth he causes, is just a theoretical nicety which may be disregarded. I think the answer is clearly "no"; the possibility of a positive inheritance effect may *not* be disregarded, though a negative inheritance for the *future* is assumed by such writers as Meade (1955) and Votey (1969). In less-developed countries, of which pre-20th century China is the best-documented example, per capita income remained at much the same level secularly over 700 years, though it sank seriously during some periods of rapid population growth. This suggests that the added person set in motion trains of events that increased saving temporarily; at some later time posterity was no worse off (by a per capita income test) for the added person's having lived earlier. On the other hand, it is also possible that in some places increased population keeps an economy in stagnation, preventing change and improvement.

In more-developed countries there is secular growth in per capita income. If the population had not grown to something like the present population size, contemporary per-person income would be far lower in more-developed countries than it now is. That is, people leave an amount of productive power to the next generation that is proportionally greater (perhaps two or three times greater) than the population increase they leave behind. This means that the added man could leave an inheritance considerably smaller than average and still leave proportionally more productive power than the population growth his lineage contributes.

This raises the question of whether the added man would contribute an inheritance anywhere near as great as the average person would contribute without him, i.e., whether the marginal contribution to posterity is far below the average contribution. First of all, there is no reason to suppose that he himself is less endowed with intelligence or chance in life than is the average person, unless one *assumes* that he is—and I can think of no special reason for assuming so. If his endowment is average, then the only factor causing him to lower the average inheritance would be the lesser physical and educational capital endowment per person at labor-force entry that population growth probably implies. Given that the average rate of inheritance in more-developed countries is much greater than the rate of population growth (in proportional terms), this classical capital-diluting effect could be of sizable magnitude without making the marginal inheritance smaller than the population growth contributed by the added person. Furthermore, there are very solid reasons to agree with Kuznets (1960), as noted earlier, that the knowledge and economies-of-scale effects lead to a higher per capita income before the end of his work life than if the additional person had not been born. If so, the average inheritance left at the time of his death will be *greater* than if he had not been born, which is a positive effect on posterity by any welfare test. Of course, this happy result is much less likely in a less-developed country than in a more-developed country, but this only proves once again the impossibility of making sound *a priori* welfare judgments about population effects without detailed specification of the conditions, assumptions, and criteria.

Summary and Conclusions

There is not one single calculable welfare effect of an additional person. Rather, there are many different reasonable judgments which may be negative or positive. The welfare effect depends upon the particular economic situation the child will be born into, which point in his life-cycle one refers to, whether he is expected to have a positive effect upon his particular sort of economy and society during and after his lifetime, and most of all, the kind of welfare criterion used. Furthermore, no matter which welfare criterion is used, the welfare effect of an added individual *summarized over time* is particularly sensitive to the particular assumptions made. Hence the conclusion is that the welfare effect of an additional child cannot be stated simply and unequivocally.

Acknowledgments

I am grateful to Louis Werner for several useful references to the philosophical literature, and I appreciate the suggestions as well as the patience of the referees.

References

Arrow, Kenneth Joseph. 1970. Social Choice and Individual Values (2nd ed.). New Haven: Yale University Press.

Barnett, Harold J., and Chandler Morse. 1963. Scarcity and Growth: The Economics of Natural Resource Availability. Baltimore: Johns Hopkins Press.

Berry, R. Albert. and Ronald Soligo. 1969. Some Welfare Aspects of International Migration. Journal of Political Economy 77: 778–794.

Blandy, Richard. 1974. The Welfare Analysis of Fertility Reduction. Economic Journal 84:109–129.

Boserup, Ester. 1965. The Conditions of Agricultural Growth: The Economics of Agrarian Change under Population Pressure. Chicago: Aldine Publishing Co.

Brandt, R. B. 1972. The Morality of Abortion. The Monist 56:503–526.

Carr-Saunders, A. M. 1922. The Population Problem: A Study in Human Evolution. Oxford: The Clarendon Press.

Clark, Colin. 1967. Population Growth and Land Use. New York: St. Martins.

Coase, R. H. 1960. The Problem of Social Cost. Journal of Law and Economics 3:1–44.

Dasgupta, P. S. 1969. On the Concept of Optimum Population. Review of Economic Studies 36:295–318.

Ehrlich, Paul R. 1968. The Population Bomb. New York: Ballantine.

Enke, Stephen. 1966. The Economic Aspects of Slowing Population Growth. Economic Journal 76:44–56.

Firth, Raymond William. 1939. Primitive Polynesian Economy. London: Routledge.

Friedman, David. 1972. Laissez-Faire in Populations: The Least Bad Solution. Occasional Paper. New York: The Population Council.

Friedman, Milton, and L. J. Savage. 1952. The Expected-Utility Hypothesis and the Measurability of Utility. Journal of Political Economy 60:463–474.

Gottlieb, Manuel. 1945. The Theory of Optimum Population for a Closed Economy. Journal of Political Economy. 53:289–316.

Heer, David M., and Dean O. Smith. 1968. Mortality Level, Desired Family Size, and Population Increase. Demography 5:104–121.

Jevons, W. Stanley. 1906. The Coal Question: An Inquiry Concerning the Progress of the Nation and the Probable Exhaustion of Our Coal-Mines. A. W. Flux (ed.), 3rd ed. London: Macmillan and Co. Limited.

Krzywicki, Ludwik. 1934. Primitive Society and Its Vital Statistics. London: MacMillan.

Kuznets, Simon. 1960. Population Change and Aggregate Output. 1960. Pp. 324–340 in Universities—National Bureau of Economic Research, Demographic and Economic Change in Developed Countries. Princeton: Princeton University Press.

May, David A., and David M. Heer. 1968. Son Survivorship Motivation and Family Size in India: A Computer Simulation. Population Studies 22:199–210.

Meade, James Edward. 1955. The Theory of International Economic Policy. New York: Oxford University Press.

Mirrlees, James A. 1972. Population Policy and the Taxation of Family Size. Journal of Public Economics 1:169–198.

Narveson, Jan. 1967. Utilitarianism and the New Generations. Mind: 76:62–72.

———. 1973. Moral Problems of Population. The Monist 57:62–86.

Phelps, Edmund S. 1968. Population Increase. Canadian Journal of Economics 1:497–518.

Ramsey, F. P. 1928. A Mathematical Theory of Saving. Economic Review 38:543–559.

Sen, Amartya Kumar. 1961. On Optimising the Rate of Saving. Economic Journal 71:479–496.

Simon, Julian. 1974. The Effects of Income upon Fertility. Chapel Hill: Carolina Population Center.

———. 1975. The Economics of Population Growth. Princeton: Princeton University Press. Forthcoming.

Stearns, J. Brenton. 1972. Ecology and the Indefinite Unborn. The Monist 56:612–625.

Votey, Harold L., Jr. 1969. The Optimum Population and Growth: A New Look. A Modification to Include a Preference for Children in the Welfare Function. Journal of Economic Theory 1:273–290.

Weckstein, Richard S. 1962. Welfare Criteria and Changing Tastes. American Economic Review 52:133–153.

PART VIII

MISCELLANEOUS

[37]

Foreword

The paper derived from hearing a representative of the CIA assert with confidence that population growth causes wars. This proposition is frequently found in print, but there is never any accompanying evidence that bears upon the subject either directly or indirectly.

This is what the reviewers for *Demography*, the official journal of the Population Association of America, reported on the paper:

> This manuscript cannot be published as is due to:
>
> - argument unfocused and hypothesis unclear;
> - selective and distorting use of history and situational information to support case;
> - no attempt at scholarly analysis, whereby discussion is not relegated to level of "belief," but remains at the level of argument and evidence;
> - treatment of Hitler is extremely distorted, discussion of Arabs and Israel incredibly naive, and the discourse on agriculture and the disclaimer on military expenditures is dilettantish.
>
> This is a very disappointing essay.

> This essay is so simple-minded, the analysis so superficial, the literature and data cited so sporadic, and the style so flip that it has no place in a scholarly journal. It may deserve a better fate than the *National Enquirer*, but just what that would be I know not.

Will anyone go on to read the article after absorbing those two reviews?

Lebensraum

PARADOXICALLY, POPULATION GROWTH MAY EVENTUALLY END WARS[1]

JULIAN L. SIMON
University of Maryland

Population growth may progressively reduce one of the motives for making war. Namely, population growth threatens shortages of resources, and especially land. Impending shortages cause a search for ways to mitigate the shortages. The discoveries eventually produce greater availability of resources than if population growth and pressure on resources had never occurred. The argument runs as follows: (1) Rhetoric about resource scarcity induced by population density has often contributed to international conflict, even if economics has not been the main motive in making war. (2) In the pre-modern era, war to obtain land and other natural resources may sometimes have been an economically sound policy. (3) Politicians and others in industrially developed nations believe resources may still be a casus belli. (4) Land and other productive resources are no longer worth acquiring at the cost of war.

Even the most hopeful persons do not foresee a world in which countries lack material reasons to make war, even in the most distant future. But perhaps if we separate ourselves from notions about land, territoriality, and population growth that have prevailed since the beginning of recorded history, we may envision such a time. With fewer reasons to make war, there may be fewer wars.

Adolph Hitler assaulted Europe (and, indirectly, the whole world) with perhaps the worst catastrophe in history, except for the Black

1. Some sentences in the essay are drawn from Simon (1981). I have not put these sentences in quotes because that practice seems to me a pretentious device that slows up the reader.

AUTHOR'S NOTE: I appreciate useful comments on an earlier draft by Colin Clark, Stanley Engerman, William McNeill, Larry Neal, and Gordon Tullock.

JOURNAL OF CONFLICT RESOLUTION, Vol. 33 No. 1, March 1989 164-180

Death, under the banner of a wrong doctrine about the relationship of population size to land area. He asserted the German "people" would be better off with more "living room," and should go to war in order to get it. If he (or many Germans) had understood that his reasoning did not make economic sense, perhaps—just perhaps—he would not have taken the world into war.[2]

The aim of this essay is not to analyze Hitler's "lebensraum" motives for going to war; other motives such as aggrandizement and military position surely were involved, too. The aim, rather, is to use that cataclysmic example to show the falsity of the doctrine that more land for a nation is worth the price of a war. The example of Hitler and World War II also is adduced to show that the lebensraum idea matters in human affairs, and that it therefore is worth rebutting.[3] This example and analysis are intended to illuminate a process that I suggest may progressively reduce one of the motives for making war: Population growth threatens shortages of resources, and especially land. Impending shortages often cause a search for, and the discovery of, ways to mitigate the shortages. The discoveries eventually produce greater availability of resources than if population growth and pressure on resources had never occurred.

I argue: (1) Rhetoric about resource scarcity induced by population density has often contributed to international conflict, even if economics has not been the main motive in making war. (2) In the premodern era,

2. Neal (1979) argues that trade advantages, too, did not provide a "rational" economic reason for Germany attacking Central European countries.

3. Interestingly, not only did Hitler assert Germany needed more land, but such a formidable antitotalitarian and free-market economist as Ludwig von Mises also said that Germany (and Italy and Japan) actually needed more land because they were "comparatively . . . over-populated."

> The German, Italian and Japanese nationalist justified their aggressive policies by their lack of *Lebensraum*. Their countries are comparatively overpopulated. They are poorly endowed by nature and depend on the import of foodstuffs and raw materials from abroad. They must export manufactures to pay for these badly needed imports.
>
> The Germans are doomed for ever to be "imprisoned," as they say, in a comparatively small and over-populated area in which the productivity of labor must be smaller than in the comparatively underpopulated countries, much better endowed with natural resources. They aim at fairer distribution of the earth's natural resources. As a "have-not" nation they look at the wealth of the richer nation with the same feelings with which many people in the Western countries look at the higher incomes of some of their countrymen.
>
> Italy's main problem is its comparative overpopulation [1947: 47, 73, 75, 76].

war to obtain land and other natural resources may sometimes have been an economically sound policy. (3) Politicians and others in industrially developed nations believe resources may still be a casus belli. (4) Acquisition of land and other productive resources are no longer worth acquiring at the cost of war.

RHETORIC ABOUT RESOURCE SCARCITY HAS HELPED MAKE WARS

Let us begin with some of Hitler's (1939) thoughts, as expressed in *Mein Kampf.* He first made clear the objective of "soil and territory as the goal of our foreign policy" (p. 944). He spelled out the logic of his war aims as follows:

> [W]e National Socialists must cling unflinchingly to our foreign-policy aims, that is to guarantee the *German nation the soil and territory* to *which it is entitled on this earth.* And this is the only action which, before God and our German posterity, would seem to justify an investment of blood: *before God,* since we are placed in this world on conditions of eternal struggle for daily bread, as beings to whom nothing shall be given and who owe their position as lords of the earth only to the genius and courage with which they know how to struggle for and defend it: before our German posterity, however, insofar as we spill no citizen's blood except that out of it a thousand others are bequeathed to posterity. The soil and territory on which a race of German peasants will some day be able to beget sons sanction the investment of the sons of today, and will some day acquit the responsible statesmen of blood and guilt and national sacrifice, even though they be persecuted by their contemporaries [pp. 947-948; italics in original].

The relationship of population to land area was central in his thinking. He wrote about "the German people today, penned into an impossible area" (p. 949) and specified it was land for settlement (presumably engaged in agriculture) that he had in mind:

> [W]e will find this question's solution not in colonial acquisitions, but exclusively in the winning of land for settlement which increases the area of the motherland itself, and thereby not only keeps the new settlers in the most intimate community with the land of origin, but ensures to the total area those advantages deriving from its united magnitude [p. 950].

On the other hand, Hitler did not give a plan for the utilization or expulsion of the existing Slavic populations in the area he eyed. As the editor of the English edition noted, "Hitler never indicates what the fate of the present residents is to be" (p. 948ff). It seems then that Hitler was truly concerned about the extent of Germany's land area *as land,* and he apparently had economic as well as military and "national importance" reasons for his desire for more land. But even if the lebensraum theme was purely cynical propaganda on Hitler's part, that argument surely affected the thinking of others (Germans and non-Germans, leaders and peoples) in the struggles that preceded World War II. Therefore, the lebensraum argument mattered.

ARE WARS REALLY MADE FOR ECONOMIC REASONS?

Let us digress to inquire whether economic motivation matters significantly in influencing whether nations go to war.

Wright (1968: 463) concluded that economic issues have not been the main cause of war, or even the dominant cause.

> In sum, studies of both the direct and the indirect influence of economic factors on the causation of war indicate that they have been much less important than political ambitions, ideological convictions, technological change, legal claims, irrational psychological complexes, ignorance, and unwillingness to maintain conditions of peace in a changing world.

Choucri (1974) suggests that "demographic" factors sometimes lead to conflict. However, the key demographic factor is the *relative* rate of increase in ethnic groups, rather than increase in population size or population density per se. This can be seen most clearly by listing the wars she considers "archetypical cases" of "population dynamics and local conflict": the Algerian War of Independence, 1945-1962; the Nigerian Civil War; the two wars involving Indonesia; the conflicts in Ceylon and El Salvador-Honduras; and the Arab-Israeli series of wars. None of these is a conflict undertaken to obtain more land or mineral resources so as to increase the standard of living of the group initiating the conflict. To argue that population growth causes conflict, one must show that two neighboring countries or groups, both of whom are growing rapidly, are more likely to come into conflict than two neighboring countries or groups neither of whom are growing rapidly. This has not been documented by Choucri. From her perspective, conflict could as easily be caused by one country or group *reducing* its growth rate relative to another country or group, as by one *increasing* its relative growth rate. In fact, many have argued that this was the case in France and Germany—that France's low birth rate induced the French-German wars.

Alexander Hamilton, in the sixth of the *Federalist Papers,* vividly asserted the multiplicity of motivations leading to war:

> The causes of hostility among nations are innumerable. There are some which have a general and almost constant operation upon the collective bodies of society. Of this description are the love of power or the desire of pre-eminence and dominion—the jealousy of power, or the desire of equality and safety. There are others which have a more circumscribed though an equally operative influence within their spheres. Such are the revivalships and competitions of commerce between commercial nations. And there are others, not less numerous than either of the former, which take their origin entirely in private passions; in the attachments, enmities, interests, hopes, and fears of leading individuals in the communities of which they are members. Men of this class, whether the favorites of a king or of a people, have in too many instances abused the confidence they possessed; and assuming the pretext of some public motive, have not scrupled to sacrifice the national tranquillity to personal advantage or personal gratification.
>
> The celebrated Pericles, in compliance with the resentment of a prostitute, at the expense of much of the blood and treasure of his countrymen, attacked, vanquished, and destroyed the city of the Samnians.

And Hamilton adduces other odious examples.

Kleinman (1980: 39-40) argues cogently that if ever a population change might have altered the propensity for war, it should have been the Black Death, by increasing the availability of land—but warring continued unabated.

McNeill sums up: "[E]conomic motivation comes far down on the list of the things that actually move men" (letter, February 20, 1982). But agreeing with McNeill does not warrant dismissing economic issues generally, or land and food in particular, as a cause of war.[4] Instead of discussing on a general level what "causes nations to go to war," we should acknowledge a variety of motives *of different persons,* and even for the same persons *at different times.* That is, when a nation is on the

4. Blainey (1973: 114) argues persuasively that "it is the problem of accurately measuring the relative power of nations which goes far to explain why wars occur. War is a dispute about the measurement of power. War marks the choice of a new set of weights and measures." But this view is not at odds with the argument offered here. It is the subject of disputes that is of interest here, and the subject can be economic or noneconomic.

brink of war, voices will be heard on both sides of the issue. Surely people fight for honor, excitement, and primitive territorial feelings. Some who are prowar will have economic issues in mind. Some of these will be people who expect to profit directly from the war, for example, some sellers and some soldiers. And others will think the nation as a whole can profit from the war by gaining land. Just how many there are in the latter category is an unanswered empirical question. To determine how important economic issues are, then, we need to know how many persons, and which groups, are motivated by such issues. Moreover, we need to know how sensitive war-or-peace decisions typically are, in order to guess how large a proportion of the population is necessary to have one position rather than another influence the outcome, and how particular groups influence that outcome. (Certainly a shift in a small proportion of the electorate has influenced national elections.) Even at different moments for the same person, economic issues have different importance. Would one not expect that, when two children are fighting over a basketball, providing a second basketball has some effect on the level of conflict?

McNeill states, "I do not think population growth is likely to end war. On the contrary I expect it to provoke violence as it has in the past. Consider El Salvador!" (letter, February 20, 1982). This is implicit agreement that land and economics *may* matter. If not, why should differential or increasing population densities—which are in fact *defined* with respect to land area—affect the propensity to make war?

WARS MAY ONCE HAVE BEEN PROFITABLE

Why would a country want a larger area? And how might increasing a nation's land area help that nation? It may seem self-evident that countries go to war in order to obtain additional agricultural lands to support their populations. Certainly there is plenty of historical evidence. For example, Childe asserted that land scarcity caused wars in prehistoric times (1964: 73, 155, 205, 238). The Bible has the Jews attacking the Canaanite tribes to obtain a homeland. The settlers of the Americas made war on the Indians to gain cropland and ranchland. The United States warred with Mexico and Canada to expand its area. Finally, blacks and whites fought for the land of Rhodesia.

> Zimbabwe's war wasn't just about voting rights and black men in parliament. "The war was all about land," says Moven Mahachi, Zimbabwe's minister for land resettlement. "People fought for land, they went to jail for land, they died for land" [*Wall Street Journal*, September 10, 1982: 1].

Of course, as discussed earlier, nations also have entered upon wars for reasons other than land. But it seems inarguable that the desire for more agricultural land has been a motive, and not a demonstrably irrational motive, for wars in the past.

We must distinguish between two situations in which nations have wanted more land: (1) Nations have wanted to conquer new lands in order to settle their own people on the agricultural land, or to exploit mines or other natural resources. This was the case with the Israelites and the Canaanites. It also was the notion underlying the Hitler passages quoted earlier; Hitler wrote about the lands to the east as if they were empty, or to be emptied. (2) Nations also have wanted new lands *along with* their existing populations *because of* their existing populations, to increase national size for greater power and/or for increased markets. I shall argue later that the logic in the second case is a derivative of the logic in the first case, and if the first case no longer makes sense, the second will not make much sense either. Let us discuss the two situations in that order.

HOW VALUABLE ARE LAND AND OIL WELLS TO A DEVELOPED NATION?

Would even a gift of additional land on its borders or elsewhere benefit an industrialized nation by way of increased agricultural opportunities? Let us consider the United States as a prototype of developed nations. Certainly there would be *some* benefit if the United States suddenly had a strip of empty land 50 miles wide that now is Mexico or Canada. This land would be additional "capital" some Americans could use in addition to their present land and other capital; it would expand some Americans' incomes and thereby increase the average income of the United States as a whole, besides increasing U.S. capacity to export food profitably.

But would there be *much* benefit from this addition to the United States? The surprising answer is no. Even with the vast size of U.S. agricultural land at present, only about 2% of the U.S. work force was employed on farms as of 1987.[5] Hence an increase in land area—even if it were to *double* the size of the United States—would change the occupational lives of only about 2% of the population. Furthermore, incomes derived from farming are not much higher than the average incomes of other Americans (though this would be hard to figure on a per-hour basis). Therefore, people who would otherwise not live on farms but who would till the new lands would not gain much by such an addition to U.S. agricultural land.

We could put the matter in another and more precise fashion by asking how much all U.S. cropland would be worth if a foreign buyer were to make us a fair offer for it, or if we would consider buying an equivalent amount of land from another country (but miraculously no further from us, so transportation costs can be ignored). Calculate this way: In 1984, 3.6% of the GNP came from farms, a little less than half of that (1.7%) came from crops, and the rest from livestock and products (U.S. Council of Economic Advisers, 1987: 268, 352). One of the great ratios in economics (derived from Clark, 1957) is that at all times and throughout the world—ancient Rome, 1960s India, Australia at the beginning of the century—the market value of a piece of agricultural land is roughly 3.5 times the gross value of a year's output; this constant is a sort of partial capital-output ratio. (Not relevant here is the value of urban land, and the value of farmland for tax purposes or for speculation on development and inflation, factors that much affect the price of some farmland in the United States.) So about 7% of *one year's* national income is all that U.S. cropland is worth to us as a nation. Thus land (i.e., *improved* cropland, not just virgin land, which is worth only a fraction as much as improved land) would not be worth fighting even a minor war for, let alone a major war. Two years' *peacetime* expenditures on defense would pay the whole bill.[6]

Another way to evaluate the land is Schultz's (1951: 726) method using the estimate that "20% of the cost of producing farm products is net rent." If so, .20 × .02 (something more than the proportion of GNP arising from crops) = .4% of each year's GNP. Capitalizing this rent by a factor of about 20 yields something like the estimate of 8% of *one* year's GNP as the value of the land in agriculture.

5. I acknowledge that some industrial workers make products used in farming. But these workers do not affect the argument, because they could continue as they are, selling their wares to "foreign" owners of the farmland. Readers wishing information on the "about 2%" assertion may write the author for documentation.

6. I am *not* advocating any particular level of expenditures for defense. The long-run argument has absolutely no bearing on short-run political decisions.

Data on the market value of farmland in the United States (U.S.D.A., 1981: 127) yield estimates more than twice as high as do the methods described above for the period about 1978-1981. However, farmland prices were then unusually high due to transient factors (compared to Clark's ratio), and a sharp fall has occurred since then. Even if the appropriate value was as high as, say, 20% of one year's GNP, rather than 7% or 8%, the thrust of the argument would not be affected.

What about agricultural exports, and the importance of agriculture on our balance of payments? The balance of payments is a short-run ephemeral matter; Japan has a whopping trade surplus without exporting much food. (I say "much" because, astonishingly, for a while Japan was exporting some rice, due to subsidies to farmers.) So exports and the balance of payments can be ignored here.

Back to the main theme: By this analysis, a developed country would be literally crazy to go to war just for agricultural land, even to obtain as much land as the United States. And less-developed countries are not in a position to start major wars without co-opting developed-country allies.

Oil may still be valuable enough to be worth fighting for. Fears about oil supplies clearly matter in political thinking, and population growth is involved in those fears, as is clearly shown in a speech by the U.S. undersecretary for economic affairs (and a well-known economist):

> I do see economic crisis in the 1980s unless we act decisively to avert it. I see economic events in the 1980s driven largely by two factors—rapid growth of world population and inadequate supplies of oil at existing prices [Cooper, 1980: 1].

Interestingly, Cooper consciously linked his statement to Hitler's thinking. After noting that world population would in the 1990s be twice what it was when he was born, he went on:

> Even at that time, some political leaders were complaining of congestion and calling for more *lebensraum* [p. 1].

And he then spells this out in detail:

> First of all, there will be population pressure against agricultural land. This will lead to domestic and international conflict such as caused the Central American football war more than a decade ago.

> Second, increased population growth will lead to greater urbanization and human congestion, which, in turn, will lead to political unrest, open conflict, greater terrorism, and possibly localized anarchy within many countries.
>
> Third, increased population will lead to vast increases in demand for food and paid employment to sustain life [pp. 1, 2].

In the future, however, when energy costs may again have fallen to a very small part of GNP for developed nations, even oil will not be a casus belli (see Simon, 1981). Indeed, the oil-generated crises foreseen in the 1980s have not come about so far, and there is now no sign that they will occur. (In my view, though, a decade is far too short a period to examine for evidence on such matters; a temporary alteration in the long-run trend can last for even a decade. A century is a better minimum safe period for observation, and several centuries provide safer evidence.)

Empty land and naked resources have been the subject so far. Let's now consider whether land with people on it is any more valuable or attractive than empty land. Again, the answer is negative. Consider an annexation by the United States of some of Canada or Mexico. U.S. citizens would not increase their capital per person if the Mexican and Canadian owners were to stay where they are and continue to take whatever "rents" the land provides. And there would be no other major economic benefit. Check with your intuition: If you are a citizen of the United States, how would you be better off economically if the U.S. jurisdiction suddenly included Canada and Mexico? Certainly, anyone who prefers that Puerto Rico not be part of the United States for economic reasons must logically say no to Canada and Mexico as well. Also, we see a calculation like this one actually in practice when we observe cities and towns not anxious to annex additional outlying areas; the principle is not different for the nation.

If agricultural land will not in the long-run future be a reason to make war, are there other land-connected reasons to attack another country to gain territory? Kings in the past have thought to conquer territory in order to farm its taxes exploitively. And cities are happy to annex areas that will improve their tax bases. But at the level of national conquest, nowadays, this would require taxing some areas within the enlarged country at different rates than other areas, or providing services at different levels to different areas, or both. Otherwise there would be no benefits through taxation for the conqueror. This sort of inequality would be very hard to sustain in a modern country unless the conquered persons were made serfs tied to the land.

Another possible land-connected reason to make war is access to larger markets to achieve economies of size in production. But customs unions and abolition of tariffs accomplish the same end just as well. More generally, tariff walls are decreasingly attractive as the numbers of producers of goods grow with increasing world development and improved transportation, and as each country needs reciprocity to sell its own goods.

What about military power as a reason for war? A larger population that comes with territorial acquisition implies larger potential armed forces. This certainly is a cogent argument, as long as one lives in a world where *other* countries might want to attack *you*.[7] But as the economic reasons for making war decline, the military reasons for making war to increase military power should also decline.

Another possible reason for wanting more land other than for farming is so that urban people feel less crowded in housing and other living space. However, there is no connection between the total land area of the country in which a person lives, or even the land area per person, and the sense of crowding, I surmise. The most important space element would be the size of a person's home in square feet of floor space. If each person were to have to him- or herself two rooms measuring 15 feet by 15 feet—a great many people patently do not feel crowded in luxury apartments with that much space, which is many times more space than Abraham Lincoln had in the log cabin in which he grew up—and if high-rise housing were built well below the height of the Sears building in Chicago or the World Trade Tower in New York, or even the Empire State Building, 155 million people could live on Manhattan Island and 1.59 billion within the land area of New York City, even leaving 20% of the land area for streets, parks, and buildings other than housing (calculation courtesy of David Simon). This example is inevitably hypothetical. And persons who have grown up in contemporary urban conditions might feel discomfort with such density of buildings. But perhaps the example is illuminating, even if extreme.

Still another nonreason for wanting to conquer another nation now is acquisition of its stock of assets. Perhaps in prehistoric times it made

7. Bertrand Russell (1929/1959: 169) put it thus:

> [I]t cannot be expected that the most powerful military nations will sit still while other nations reverse the balance of power by the mere process of breeding.

some sense for a nomad tribe to want to defeat and expel the inhabitants of a "city" in order to take over its dwellings and utensils. But today there would be no benefit in such a move. Though the physical stock of houses and factories of country A might be of value to the inhabitants of Country B if the assets could be moved to a place of country B's choosing (the way the Germans in World War II moved some Russian factory machinery), it is unlikely that any country today could profit much from such rapine. Without the transportation and communication sinews, and the mode of economic organization that has evolved together with the buildings and machinery, the physical assets are likely to be worth little to an invader. If the conquering country is as rich as the conquered, it already has a stock of assets with which its population already works. Exchanging all the old stock—or even part of it—for a new and strange stock of assets is not likely to increase the output of its citizens much, if at all. Keeping the conquered inhabitants in place and forcing them to work for you also is not very effective, as Hitler learned. Conquering and then exploiting by taxation is not impossible, but at least in the most recent case of the Soviet Union and Eastern Europe (where that may or may not have been part of the original motivation), it has not worked out that way (Wolf, 1985; but see Spechler and Spechler, 1987, for much lower recent estimates of the cost of "empire" because of revised oil-sale arrangements). In short, conquering an equally developed country by war is not likely to be a profitable business.

The notion of a poor population taking over the developed world, as dramatized in Raspail's *Camp of the Saints* (1975), is even less plausible. The uneducated poor have little capacity to operate the instruments of a modern society. A "horde" of them moving into and taking over a rich country might soon find shepherds sheltering themselves and their flocks in computer factories (a lesser use of the factory by a bit), which as shelter are not worth warring over. As someone once remarked, if Indians and Americans exchanged countries, in a few decades the United States would look more like India now, and India like the United States. This is simply because the stock of human capital embodied in the education, skills, and productive culture of a population is overwhelmingly important, as the post-World War II experiences of Japan and Germany demonstrated well. (On the other hand, if Indian newborns and American newborns exchanged educational upbringings at birth, the countries also would exchange appearances very rapidly.) Furthermore, the notion of the ragged poor being able to take over a rich country by violence, in the face of vastly superior weapons, is plainly ridiculous.[8]

It is true that it would be nice for a nation to have lots of open space with low tourist density close to its cities, and for that reason a country like the Netherlands or Israel may feel a desire for more land. With the decreasing cost of transportation, and the consequent opportunity for middle-class families to vacation in open desert, arctic tundra, or tropic jungle (or even space, in the future), this consideration simply does not seem to be a likely cause of future war.

Still another reason for wanting more nonfarm land is as a military buffer or staging ground. But, again, if war is not in the cards for other reasons, this reason would wither away.

The most complex reasons for wanting more land—and the most difficult to remove, because they are not economic—are the psychological reasons. The land area of a country (especially when more population accompanies the added land, as is the case after a conquest) has always symbolized more power. And power is heady. For modern nations, the satisfaction from possession of land may be in large part a simple confusion between individual ownership and national ownership. An individual who owns much land is rich because he or she can sell the land; the land is wealth to the individual. Today, it is not practical for a nation to sell land (unlike the Louisiana and Alaska purchases of the United States). Therefore, land does not represent wealth to a nation as it does to an individual. Simply drawing a boundary line to include additional area and people does not change national wealth at all.

LONG-RUN CAUSE: POPULATION GROWTH AND DENSITY

The history-reversing process that leads to this new vista of war and peace stems from the combination of increased income per person and

8. After this article was composed, I found that Shepherd (1986) has written about U.S.-USSR relations in quite the same spirit. Using rough calculations of such concepts as national income, investments, military spending, and possible return from plunder, he persuasively concludes there is no economic rationale for conquest or domination of either country by the other. Such "immobile" resources as farmland, forests, buildings, and coal mines are not even enough of a factor for him to consider in his reckoning (p. 29). For the special case he discusses, distance is a key element, and hence acceptance of Shepherd's argument does not imply acceptance of the argument expressed here, though the two arguments tend to support each other.

the accompanying decline in the proportion of persons working in agriculture. As discussed earlier, if only 3% of the income of a nation and less than 3% of its labor force is agricultural, then the quantity of agricultural land obviously is not important enough from an economic point of view to fight about. To understand the mechanism, however, we must go deeper.

Paradoxically, the long-run cause of this process is population growth. Additional people lead to actual or expected shortages and increased economic burdens in the short run. But these economic problems eventually lead to increases in technology, by way of both the "demand-side" increase in payoff to invention, as well as from the "supply-side" increase in potential inventors in the larger population (see Simon, 1981, 1986). There is no reason to expect that this process cannot continue indefinitely.[9] (The speed with which the response occurs may vary greatly from society to society, of course; the comparison between China and Europe as of say 1700 may serve as an example.)

Conventional thinking questions countries' capacities to feed increased populations, but productivity per farm worker has increased so greatly that a smaller *absolute* number of farm workers in developed countries produces larger amounts of food per consumer as well. A continuation of the present trend in the United States, say, carried to the same absurdity as doomsday scares, would eventually have just one person farming all the land in the United States and feeding everyone else.

Where will this benign trend stop? No one knows. As long as agriculture is pointed in this economically desirable direction, we need not be concerned about how long it can go on, especially as there are no obvious technological forces to stop it. While countries are still poor they cannot embark on a course of mechanization sufficiently intense to increase total output and at the same time reduce the total number of workers in agriculture. But at least the *proportion* of workers in agriculture falls, as is already happening in almost every developing country despite population growth. Eventually the absolute number of farm workers is likely to fall, too. This is not happening yet, but the

9. Those who fear population growth because they believe it leads to increased conflict—an example is Margaret Sanger (1938: 254, 420), who made the war issue a key element in her birth-control movement, along with eugenics—may be calling for policies that are counterproductive in the long run. By my argument population control as such may slow the trend toward greater resource availability and hence greater propensity for war.

poorer countries can expect eventually to experience the same trend that was at work in the past in the now-rich countries.

Nor is there a physical limit upon capacity. Should the need arise, processes such as hydroponics can produce incredible amounts of food in tiny compass of space, even without soil. This particular process is already commercially viable under special conditions. The Archer-Daniels-Midland firm in Decatur, Illinois, is now building a commercial facility to raise vegetables hydroponically under glass, in order to take advantage of water, CO_2 and heat byproducts from its food processing operations (Champaign-Urbana *News Gazette*, March 7, 1982, F5). Newspaper reports say there are about a dozen hydroponic farms on the outskirts of Washington, D.C., that sell vegetables profitably during the winter—without subsidy. In its early days, Israel developed successful experimental hydroponics agriculture because its planners worried about the capacity of its small territory to be self-sufficient in food. That line of development was not pursued simply because the rapidly increasing productivity of its farms, using conventional agricultural methods, was sufficient to resolve the food problem for the foreseeable future.

Difficulty would arise only if these new land-saving agricultural processes were to require so much labor as again to constitute a relatively large proportion of the population. We have seen that the trend has gone the other way. Nor is there convincing reason to believe that the trend will reverse in the future.

In the long run, land becomes relatively less important to farming, as Schultz pointed out in a more limited context several decades ago (1951), and as Liebig and Marx discussed from more technological points of view more than a century ago (Marx quoted by Meek, 1953: 17-18). In fact, all natural resources become less important for production as technology increases, because of our remarkable ability to substitute one material for another in production processes (e.g., aluminum in place of copper in electrical wiring, space satellites instead of copper telephone wires, and plastic shoes rather than leather). (See Goeller and Weinberg, 1976, for a full statement on this subject.)

CONCLUSION

Can it be true that some day war will lose enough of its attraction and become a much smaller threat than in the past and present? Or is this another utopian pipe dream? The answer depends upon the importance of economic considerations in national decisions. Ironically, all haters of war should pray that humans are very materialistic in their motives, as compared to their devotion to their religious or cultural heritage, or even to aesthetic values, because sound calculation of the economic benefit-cost ratio of war would result in the decision not to begin a war.

There is little reason to doubt that land for productive purposes will have steadily decreasing value to nations (as a proportion of GNP) with the passage of time, during which there will be population growth, technological growth, and increased income. In the same way, aside from its resale value, a piece of land is economically worthless to you and to me (as to most residents of rich countries) because we can earn less working the land than we can earn working with other capital. The same picture will increasingly emerge even for such resources as oil. This trend for oil works to remove, say, the cause of struggle between the United States and the Soviet Union in the Middle East. This trend does nothing to reduce the desire of many Arabs to make successful war on Israel, because that desire is motivated by hate and sentimental attachment to the land. Nor would this trend reduce the desire of many Israelis to hold on to the West Bank of what was Jordan before 1967 because of religious-historical-sentimental attachment to many places there, as well as because of military advantages and aesthetic appreciation of that area (as also was the case with other portions of land Israel conquered in 1967 but has since returned to Egypt).

In brief, to the extent economics matters, it is indeed realistic that the probability of war will decrease in the future. And in the long run, population growth speeds that process. Just how important economics is in national decisions is a matter that must be left to others to discuss.

REFERENCES

BLAINEY, G. (1973) The Causes of War. Glencoe: Free Press.

CHILDE, G. (1964) What Happened in History. Baltimore: Penguin.

CHOUCRI, N. (1974) Population Dynamics and International Violence. Lexington, MA: Lexington Books.

CLARK, C. (1957) Conditions of Economic Progress (3rd ed.). New York: Macmillan.

COOPER, R. N. (1980) "World economic crisis in the 1980s?" Address presented to the Alpbach European Forum, September 1.

ENGELS, F. (1953) "The myth of overpopulation," in Outlines of a Critique of Political Economy, reprinted in R. L. Meek (ed.) Marx and Engels on Malthus. London: Lawrence & Wishart.

GOELLER, H. E. and A. M. WEINBERG (1976) "The age of substitutability." Science 191 (4428): 683-689.

HITLER, A. (1939) Mein Kampf. New York: Reynal & Hitchcock.

KLEINMAN, D. S. (1980) Human Adaptation and Population Growth. New York: Universe.

MEEK, R. (1953) Marx and Engles on Malthus. Delhi: People's Publishing.

MISES, L. von (1947) Planned Chaos. Irvington-on-Hudson: Foundation for Economic Education.

NEAL, L. (1979, August) "The economics and finance of bilateral clearing agreements: Germany, 1934-8." Economic History Rev. (Second Series) 32 (3).

RASPAIL, J. (1975) Camp of the Saints. New York: Scribner.

RUSSELL, B. (1929) Marriage and Morals. New York: Horace Liveright.

SANGER, M. (1938) An Autobiography. New York: Norton.

SCHULTZ, T. W. (1951) "The declining economic importance of land." Economic J. 61 (December): 725-740.

SHEPHERD, W. G. (1986) The Ultimate Deterrent. New York: Praeger.

SIMON, J. L. (1981) The Ultimate Resource. Princeton: Princeton University Press.

SIMON, J. L. (1986) Theory of Population and Economic Growth. New York: Basil Blackwell.

SPECHLER, D. and M. SPECHLER (1987) "The economic burden of Soviet empire: estimates and reestimates," in D. K. Nelson and R. Menon, The Limits to Soviet Power. Lexington: Lexington Books.

U.S. Council of Economic Advisers (1987) Economic Report of the President. Washington: Government Printing Office.

U.S. Department of Agriculture (1981) Economic Research Service, Economic Indicators of the Farm Sector, Statistic Bulletin 674. Washington: Government Printing Office.

U.S. Department of Commerce (1986) Statistical Abstract of the United States, 1986. Washington: Government Printing Office.

WOLF, C. Jr. (1985) "The costs of the Soviet empire." Science (November 29): 997-1002.

WRIGHT, Q. (1968) "War: the study of war," in D. Sills (ed.) International Encyclopedia of the Social Sciences. New York: Macmillan-Free Press.

[38]

Foreword

It was only after I read Robert Axelrod's work on tit-for-tat that I had a framework for this additional – and particularly interesting – interpretation of the expectations I had previously labeled "cartel" in the duopoly simulation described in Volume One, Chapter 9.

Tit-for-tat expectations in duopoly simulation

The literature on the evocation of cooperation through a pattern of tit-for-tax (TFT) has emphasized *behavior*. That is, the *acts* of systematically replying with positive for positive, and negative for negative, have been shown to lead to cooperation more surely than do other response patterns (Axelrod, 1984).

The assumed mechanism is that such responses induce the *belief* that what one does will be matched by the other, and since one seeks positive acts by the other, one will find it in one's self-interest to do positive acts, and therefore actually perform them. But the expectations are only *inferred* in the research, rather than observed.

A simulation study of price competition in duopoly (Simon, Puig, and Aschoff, 1973) embodies the *expectations themselves*. Hence it offers a look at the effects of different patterns of expectations about the other's responses upon the extent to which the two competitors attain patterns of cooperation. The same is true of a simulation study of advertising competition in duopoly (Simon and Ben-Ur, 1982). Those studies were done for other purposes, and hence have some of the "double blind" protection against subtle and unconscious experimenter bias that medical research finds valuable. And both provide striking evidence that TFT expectations are effective in inducing mutually beneficial outcomes – high prices, and low advertising budgets, in the two cases.

In addition to throwing light upon the role of the expectations mechanism, the results also add a different sort of confirming evidence on TFT than has heretofore been adduced.

The overall structure of the price model is described in the Appendix. The crucial element for present purposes is that five different sets of expectations about the competitor's responses are combined with otherwise-similar sets of parameters in the series of runs. The five sets of expectations with which trials in each run are started – later revised as the firms "learn" about their competitors' responses – were are follows, as described in the original article:

In the case of the "tit-for-tat" setup (elsewhere called "Cartel"), the conjectured probabilities of a price raise, stay-same, or drop by competitor firm i' contingent on a price raise by firm i are 1.0, 0, and 0 respectively; the TFT probabilities of a raise, stay-same, or drop by firm i' contingent on firm i staying-same or dropping, are respectively 0, 1.0, 0; and 0, 0, 1.0. In the slightly (but crucially) different "Sweezy" set up – the difference is in not expecting the competitor to cooperate in raising prices – the conjectured probabilities of a price raise, stay-same, or drop by competitor firm i' contingent on a price raise by firm i are 0, 1.0, and 0 respectively; the "Sweezy" probabilities of a raise, stay-same, or drop by firm i' contingent on firm i staying-same or dropping, are respectively 0, 1.0, 0; and 0, 0, 1.0. For the other three initial set-ups, the sets of probabilities, in the same order as above, are: "Uncertainty": 0.33, 0.33, 0.33; 0.33, 0.33, 0.33; 0.33, 0.33, 0.33; "No-move opponent" or "Cournot": 0, 1.0, 0; 0, 1.0, 0; 0, 1.0, 0; "Partly-Sweezy": 0.5, 0,5, 0; 0.1, 0.8, 0.1; 0, 0.5, 0.5. (The probabilities for the sub-models ASYM, CONIG, CONKNOW, SEQCUT, and

SEQMATCH vary somewhat (see Appendix); for the SEQCUT and SEQMATCH models the probabilities refer to price levels rather than to price actions.)

But an actual firm's conjectured competitor-response function does not remain the same over time. The firm "learns" about its competitor's propensities. The model therefore revises the conjectured probabilities in light of the firm's experience with competitive reactions in the following fashion: consider any action-and-reaction pair, e.g. a price rise by i followed by no change on the part of i'. Assume i's prior probability estimate was 0.40 that the competitor i' would keep his price the same, conditional on i's price rise. Because i' actually did keep the same price, the next time i thinks about raising his price, i's probability estimate that i' will keep his price the same will be higher than 0.40. The *ex-ante* probability of the event that did occur, call it $L_{g,\ ex\ ante}$, is revised in accordance with the following rule:

$$L_{g,\ ex\text{-}post} = L_{g,\ ex\text{-}ante} + \mathrm{W}\,(1 - L_{g,\ ex\text{-}ante})$$

where W is a fixed constant between 0 and 1, usually 0.25. For example, if A's *ex-ante* period-t probability of the response that occurred was 0.40, A's estimate of the probability of that event *ex-post* period t will be

$$L_{g},\ ex\text{-}post = 0.40 + 0.25\,(1 - 0.40) = 0.55$$

The *ex-ante* probabilities of events that did not occur are lowered in total by the amount that $L_{g,\ ex\text{-}ante}$ is raised, and the total drop is distributed in proportion to their *ex-ante* sizes. Only the three probabilities of the competitor's responses contingent on the price choice that the firm actually did make are changed in each period. This scheme may be viewed as having some rough analogy to the Bayesian procedure.

The structure of the advertising model is sufficiently similar to the price model that it need not be described further here; the interested reader may consult the Simon–Ben-Ur article.

In the original studies the TFT expectations were labeled "Cartel" probabilities, which is a less accurate description than is "tit-for-tat".

Results

Table 2 (taken from Volume One, Chapter 9) shows that TFT reached much higher price levels, in a much shorter time, and with less instability, than did any other pattern of expectations. Cooperative behavior such as this may be bad for consumers and for the economy as a whole (as Axelrod noted, 1984, pp. 17–18), but that is not the subject here. If we focus only on what is good for the *participants* – which is the usual focus of studies of cooperation – we see that believing that the other party will practice TFT is a desirable and self-fulfilling forecast.

Table 1 (from Volume One, Chapter 9) shows that TFT produced much lower levels of advertising than did any other pattern of expectations. Again, this may or may not be good for the public, but that issue is not germane here.

Discussion

1. One may wonder why all the sets of expectations do not eventually evolve to the same price or advertising level(s), given that the model includes a mechanism through which each firm learns about the propensities of the other from actual behavior, and updates its expectations on the basis of the newly obtained information. The answer is that in the model, as in life, learning is imperfect, and people can get locked into their initial patterns of expectations. As we said in the original Simon, Puig and Aschoff (1973) article

> In some trials our competitors obviously fail to obtain a wide variety of experiences from which to learn because they lock into a repetitive series of interactions. This happens in life all the time. Assume that two of us are both mild-mannered fellows in the main. But if our acquaintance begins in a situation where one of us is snarling, we may continue to snarl back and forth without ever coming to learn that we are neither of us snarlers deep down. This lack of complete learning is responsible, we believe, for the influence of the initial conditions on the eventual price level.

2. Though our results show the effectiveness of the TFT pattern, we did not then interpret our results as throwing light upon the process of developing cooperation. Indeed, we tended to look upon the TFT expectations with distaste because they represent gouging behavior which is considered both unethical and illegal, and which the law properly discourages. It is to the credit of Axelrod that he generalized results like ours from a variety of sources into the discovery about the effectiveness of TFT in inducing cooperation.
3. The usual policy remedy for cooperative price-fixing is that there should be a larger number of competitors. There are many strands to the theory of this remedy. But in the present context, it is relevant that it is more difficult for there to be reliable interdependencies of expectations and responses when the number of competitors increases. The point can be illustrated with the results of an analogous simulation of triopoly that is discussed elsewhere (Simon and Puig, 1990); runs with similar sets of parameters produce lower price levels and less cooperation than in duopoly. It is not possible at this time, however, to determine how much of this differential effect may be attributed to the expectation-and-response mechanisms and how much to the other differences in the situations.

Summary and conclusions

Rich simulation experiments of duopolistic competition with respect to both price and advertising budgets show that tit-for-tat (TFT) expectations about the competitor's behavior result in closer cooperation than do other types of expectations. This tends to confirm the TFT evidence that derives directly from studies of behavior rather than expectations, and it illuminates the mechanism through which TFT works. This evidence, which is rather different than other kinds of evidence that have been adduced, also adds to the solidity of the general conclusion about the effectiveness of TFT.

References

Axelrod, Robert (1984), *The Evolution of Cooperation* (New York: Basic).

Simon, Julian L., Carlos M. Puig, and John Aschoff (1973), "A Duopoly Simulation and Richer Theory: An End to Cournot," *The Review of Economic Studies*, **XL** (3), July, 353–66.
Simon, Julian L. and Carlos M. Puig (1990), "Tripoly Simulations," xerox.
Simon, Julian L. and Joseph Ben-Ur (1982), "The Advertising Budget's Determinants in a Market with Two Competing Firms," *Management Science*, **28** (May), 500–519.

Appendix

Table 1 Effects of changes in initial conditions

Line	Market share	Comparison	Cost parameters c_1	c_2	c_3	Demand parameters d_1	d_2	d_3	Market share parameters s_1	s_2	s_3	s_4	Initial Figures Ad Budget: Firm A $A_i = 0.$ i - 1	Firm B $A_i = 0.$ $i = 2$	Total demand D_0	Final level of advertising budget: Uncertainty	Monopoly	Tit-for-tat (cartel)	Partly Sweezy	Sweezy	Rank of final advertising budget: Uncertainty	Monopoly	Tit-for-tat (cartel)	Partly Sweezy	Sweezy
4–1	MS–1		1.0	1.0	0	0.3	0.8	0.95	0.5	1000	0.9	0.6	3000	4000	400	24.2	24.2	50.0	24.2	24.2	3.5	3.5	1	3.5	3.5
4–2			1.0	1.0	0	0.3	0.8	0.95	0.5	1000	0.9	0.6	1*m*	1.2*m*	0.12*m*	19.6	19.6	21.4	16.1	23.2	3.5	3.5	1	5	2
4–3		4–a	1.0	1.0	0	0.3	0.8	0.95	0.5	1000	0.9	0.6	10*m*	12*m*	1*m*	15.3	15.3	9.3	21.8	43.6	3.5	3.5	5	2	1
4–4			1.0	1.0	0	0.3	0.8	0.95	0.5	1000	0.9	0.6	20*m*	22*m*	2*m*	30.7	30.7	6.8	12.7	36.4	2.5	2.5	5	4	1
4–5			1.0	1.0	0	0.3	0.8	0.95	0.5	1000	0.9	0.6	28*m*	32*m*	2*m*	24.2	24.2	9.9	13.1	48.3	2.5	2.5	5	4	1
4–6			1.0	1.0	0	0.3	0.8	0.95	0.5	1000	0.9	0.6	55*m*	60*m*	5*m*	26.7	26.7	18.7	26.7	26.7	2.5	2.5	5	2.5	2.5
4–7	MS–1		1.0	1.0	0	1.0	0.8	0.7	0.5	1000	0.9	0.6	1*m*	1.2*m*	0.12*m*	9.7	9.7	21.5	9.7	21.5	4	4	1.5	4	1.5
4–8		4–b	1.0	1.0	0	1.0	0.8	0.7	0.5	1000	0.9	0.6	10*m*	12*m*	1*m*	15.8	12.0	7.8	11.8	14.2	1	4	5	3	2
4–9			1.0	1.0	0	1.0	0.8	0.7	0.5	1000	0.9	0.6	20*m*	22*m*	2*m*	20.0	22.0	14.0	15.4	20.0	2.5	1	5	4	2.5
4–10			1.0	1.0	0	1.0	0.8	0.7	0.5	1000	0.9	0.6	28*m*	32*m*	2*m*	22.4	22.4	14.2	20.3	20.3	1.5	1.5	5	3.5	3.5
4–11	MS–1		1.0	1.0	0	1.0	0.7	0.95	0.5	1000	0.9	0.6	3000	4000	400	0.76	0.76	1.12	0.98	1.28	4.5	4.5	2	3	1
4–12		4–c	1.0	1.0	0	1.0	0.7	0.95	0.5	1000	0.9	0.6	1*m*	1.2*m*	0.12*m*	0.92	1.2	0.38	0.70	2.6	3	2	5	4	1
4–13			1.0	1.0	0	1.0	0.7	0.95	0.5	1000	0.9	0.6	28*m*	32*m*	2*m*	1.78	1.74	1.68	1.68	1.74	1	2.5	4.5	4.5	2.5
4–14			1.0	1.0	0	1.0	0.7	0.95	0.5	1000	0.9	0.6	55*m*	60*m*	5*m*	1.76	1.86	1.56	1.56	1.72	2	1	4.5	4.5	3
4–15	MS–11		1.0	1.0	0	0.3	0.8	0.95	0.5	10*m*	1.0	0.9	20*m*	22*m*	2*m*	15.0	15.0	4.8	7.5	8.7	1.5	1.5	5	4	3
4–16			1.0	1.0	0	1.0	0.8	0.7	0.5	10*m*	1.0	0.9	20*m*	22*m*	2*m*	15.4	15.4	6.8	15.4	9.8	2	2	5	2	4
4–17		4–d	1.0	1.0	0	1.0	0.8	0.7	0.5	10*m*	1.0	0.9	10*m*	12*m*	1*m*	8.4	8.4	3.7	7.0	7.0	1.5	1.5	5	3.5	3.5
4–18			1.0	1.0	0	2.0	0.7	0.95	0.5	10*m*	1.0	0.9	20*m*	22*m*	2*m*	23.6	23.6	6.8	21.5	23.2	1.5	1.5	5	4	3
4–19			1.0	1.0	0	2.0	0.7	0.95	0.5	10*m*	1.0	0.9	10*m*	12*m*	1*m*	19.4	19.4	1.8	18.0	21.3	2.5	2.5	5	4	1
																				Total Rank	46.5	47.5	79.5	69	42.5

Table 2 Prices at end of trial for various models and runs (please see explanatory notes at end of table)

										Initial probability set-ups														
										Sweezy			Partly Sweezy			Tit-for-tat (cartel)			No-move opponent			Uncertainty		
Run number	Basic model	Initial market share of firm α	Demand algorithm equation	Rate of change of probabilities	Discount factor	Price increment	Starting cost function	Starting price	Market share revision factor	α's price	Periods to stability	β's price	α's price	Periods to stability	β's price	α's price	Periods to stability	β's price	α's price	Periods to stability	β's price	α's price	Periods to stability	β's price
(1)	(2)	(3)	(4)	(5)	(6)	(7)	(8)	(9)	(10)	(12)		(13)	(14)		(15)	(16)		(17)	(18)		(19)	(20)		(21)
1	ASYM	0.30	3	0.25	0.60	0.06	normal	normal ($250)	0.66	$398	8	$398	(393)[b] (418)	91	(373) (396)	$398	8	$398	$415	187[a]	$393	$397	77	$397
2	ASYM	0.50	3	0.25	0.60	0.06	normal	$250	0.66	250	1	250	393	82	394	398	8	398	392	78	391	393	88	392
3	ASYM	0.70	3	0.25	0.60	0.06	normal	$250	0.66	398	155	395	418	179	394	714	165[a]	243	409	138[a]	383	389	156	389
4	ASYM	0.30	3	0.10	0.60	0.06	normal	$250	0.66	398	8	398	417	176[a]	376	398	8	398	434	(200) (NR)	389	414	165	392
5	ASYM	0.50	3	0.10	0.60	0.06	normal	$250	0.66	250	1	250	386	163	389	398	8	398	417	189	381	388	117	390
6	ASYM	0.30	3	0	0.60	0.06	normal	$250	0.66	316	4	316	(329) (370)	5	(329) (370)	398	8	398	(169) (190)	5	(169) (190)	(163) (183)	6	(163) (183)
7	ASYM	0.30	3	0.25	0.95	0.06	normal	$250	0.66	250	1	250	287	90[a]	(259) (294)	398	8	398	208	3	208	399	173[a]	379
8	ASYM	0.50	3	0.25	0.95	0.06	normal	$250	0.66	250	1	250	414	126[a]	382	398	8	398	251	(200) (NR[a])	258	364	104[a]	(328) (370)
9	ASYM	0.70	3	0.25	0.95	0.06	normal	$250	0.66	301	(200) (NR[a])	287	394	159	393	394	81[a]	(352) (398)	406	(200) (NR[a])	387	260	(200) (NR[a])	260
10	ASYM	0.30	3	0.25	0.60	0.02	normal	$250	0.66	394	23	394	400	148	393	394	23	394	400	142	400	400	104	400
11	ASYM	0.50	3	0.25	0.60	0.02	normal	$250	0.66	250	1	250	400	64	400	394	24	402	399	69	399	400	63	400
12	ASYM	0.70	3	0.25	0.60	0.02	normal	$250	0.66	265	15	264	398	74	398	265	11	265	398	81[a]	398	399	99[a]	398
13	ASYM	0.30	3	0.25	0.60	0.06	½ normal	$250	0.66	250	1	250	(290) (430)	7	(283) (400)	398	8	398	183	5	183	386	164[a]	382
14	ASYM	0.50	3	0.25	0.60	0.06	½ normal	$250	0.66	265	9	263	395	173	388	422	9[a]	374	(269) (428)	20	(273) (397)	(269) (429)	130	(274) (397)
15	ASYM	0.70	3	0.25	0.60	0.06	½ normal	$250	0.66	383	(200) (NR)	390	194	142	193	281	8	278	(264) (431)	30	(265) (400)	389	80	389

Run number	Basic model	Initial market share of firm α	Demand algorithm equation	Rate of change of probabilities	Discount factor	Price increment	Starting cost function	Starting price	Market share revision factor	Initial probability set-ups: Sweezy			Partly Sweezy			Tit-for-tat (cartel)			No-move opponent			Uncertainty		
										α's price	Periods to stability	β's price	α's price	Periods to stability	β's price	α's price	Periods to stability	β's price	α's price	Periods to stability	β's price	α's price	Periods to stability	β's price
(1)	(2)	(3)	(4)	(5)	(6)	(7)	(8)	(9)	(10)	(12)		(13)	(14)		(15)	(16)		(17)	(18)		(19)	(20)		(21)
16	ASYM	0.30	3	0.25	0.60	0.06	1/6 normal	$250	0.66	250	1	250	230	183[a]	234	398	8	398	162	7	162	135	12	135
17	ASYM	0.50	3	0.25	0.60	0.06	1/6 normal	$250	0.66	431	(200) (NR)	365	283	(200) (NR)	287	216	184	219	77	21	77	390	178	388
18	ASYM	0.70	3	0.25	0.60	0.06	1/6 normal	$250	0.66	339	(200) (NR)	343	162	174	160½	281	8	278	73	22	73	383	(200) (NR)	342
19	ASYM	0.30	3	0.25	0.60*	0.06	1/6 normal	$250	0.22	398	8	398	329	13[a]	533	398	8	398	351	12[a]	475	292	15[a]	597
20	ASYM	0.30	3	0.25	0.60	0.06	Zero	$250	0.66	250	1	250	396	48	396	398	8	398	152	8	152	0.79[d]		0.79[d]
21	ASYM	0.50	3	0.25	0.60	0.06	Zero	$250	0.66	0.66[d]		0.66[d]	0.74[d]		0.74[d]	283	(200) (NR)	285	0.66[d]		0.66[d]	0.74[d]		0.74[d]
22	ASYM	0.70	3	0.25	0.60	0.06	Zero	$250	0.66	0.66[d]		0.66[d]	0.74[d]		0.74[d]	0.84[d]		0.84[d]	0.66[d]		0.66[d]	0.70[d]		0.70[d]
23	SEQMATCH	0.30	3	0.25	0.60	0.06	5/4 normal	$250	0.66	250	1	250	385	135	385	385	135	385	(254) (346)	40	(254) (346)	(206) (327)	30	(207) (327)
24	SEQMATCH	0.30	3	0.25	0.60	0.06	normal	$250	0.66	221	4	221	(196) (258)	95	(196) (258)	358	140	358	(194) (258)	56	(194) (258)	(195) (257)	125	(195) (258)
25	SEQMATCH	0.30	3	1.0	0.60	0.06	normal	$250	0.66	208	6	208	316	142	316	358	140	358	183	11	183	264	78	264
26	SEQMATCH	0.30	3	0.50	0.60	0.06	normal	$250	0.66	221	4	221	244	(300) (NR)	244	(218) (268)	150	(218) (268)	(215) (268)	70	(215) (268)	(216) (268)	60	(216) (268)
27	SEQMATCH	0.30	3	0.10	0.60	0.06	normal	$250	0.66	221	4	221	(147) (219)	35	(146) (219)	(153) (220)	190	(153) (220)	(146) (208)	105	(147) (208)	(147) (207)	82	(146) (207)
28	SEQMATCH	0.30	3	0	0.60	0.06	normal	$250	0.66	221	4	221	(165) (219)	6	(165) (219)	398	25	398	(98) (130)	30	(98) (130)	(123) (159)	15	(123) (159)
29	SEQMATCH	0.50	3	0.25	0.60	0.06	normal	$250	0.66	250	1	250	(196) (258)	55	(196) (258)	357	34	357	(194) (258)	55	(194) (258)	(156) (222)	121	(156) (222)
30	SEQMATCH	0.30	3a	0.25	0.60	0.06	normal	$250	0.66	250	1	250	389	44	389	398	16	398	384	65	384	383	69	383

31	SEQMATCH	0.50	3a	0.25	0.60	0.06	normal	$250	0.66	250	1	250	383	70	383	398	16	398	406	63[a]	383	406	63[a]	383
32	SEQMATCH	0.50	3	0.25	0.60	0.06	normal	$250	(100% change)	99	35	99	(101) (120)	60	(95) (120)	154	(300) (NR)	154	99	34	99	135	(300) (NR)	152
33	SEQMATCH	0.30	3	0.25	0.60	0.06	½ normal	normal	0.66	(68) (77)	90	(68) (77)	(68) (77)	101	68 (77)	(72) (81)	111	(72) (81)	(66) (77)	85	(68) (77)	(66) (75)	170	(66) (75)
34	SEQMATCH	0.50	3	0.25	0.60	0.06	½ normal	normal	0.66	(68) (77)	90	(68) (77)	89	(300) (NR)	95	(68) (77)	90	(68) (77)	(68) (77)	90	(68) (77)	79	(300) (NR)	83
35	SEQMATCH	0.30	3	0.25	1.0	0.06	½ normal	normal	0.66	127	24	127	127	24	127	(186) (209)	25	(186) (209)	127	24	127	127	24	127
36	SEQMATCH	0.30	3	0.25	0.60	0.06	⅙ normal	normal	0.66	44	60	44	(39) (53)	65	(39) (53)	(41) (52)	65	(41) (52)	44	60	44	(41) (52)	65	(41) (52)
37	SEQCUT	0.30	3	0.25	0.60	0.06	normal	normal	0.66	220	4	220	384	278	384	358	205	358	270	(300) (NR)	270	207	15	207
38	SEQCUT	0.50	3	0.25	0.60	0.06	normal	normal	0.66	250	1	250	250	1	250	358	140	358	195	5	195	250	1	250
39	SEQCUT	0.30	3	1.0	0.60	0.06	normal	normal	0.66	(359) (404)	40	(359) (404)	(358) (404)	170	(358) (404)	(358) (404)	171	(358) (404)	221	3	221	(356) (404)	135	(356) (404)
40	SEQCUT	0.30	3	0	0.60	0.06	normal	normal	0.66	221	4	221	264	7	264	(353) (376)	22	(353) (376)	172	22	172	208	6	208
41	SEQCUT	0.30	3	0.25	0.60	0.06	½ normal	normal	0.66	189	(300) (NR)	189	142	(300) (NR)	142	134	(300) (NR)	134	135	(300) (NR)	127	189	(300) (NR)	189
42	SEQCUT	0.50	3	0.25	0.60	0.06	½ normal	normal	0.66	82	(300) (NR)	82	112	20	112	135	15	135	123	(300) (NR)	130	82	(300) (NR)	82
43	SEQCUT	0.30	3	0.25	0.60	0.06	⅙ normal	normal	0.66	(59) (66)	50	(59) (66)	(59) (67)	50	(59) (67)	(40) (57)	50	(43) (57)	(58) (66)	50	(43) (66)	(59) (66)	50	(59) (66)
44	SEQCUT	0.50	3	0.25	0.60	0.06	⅙ normal	normal	0.66	(59) (66)	50	(59) (66	53	34	53	(60) (67)	40	(60) (67)	(59) (66)	40	(59) (66)	(59) (66)	40	(59) (66)
45	CONKNOW	0.30	3	0.25	0.60	0.06	5/4 normal	normal	0.66	826	(200) (NR[a])	198	(301) (396)	163	(304) (441)	398	8	398	(291) (431)	115	(283) (440)	(279) (396)	77	(272) (432)
46	CONKNOW	0.30	3	0.25	0.60	0.06	normal	normal	0.66	398	8	398	(356) (402)	230	384	398	8	398	388	300[a]	(359) (406)	(359) (404)	127	387
47	CONKNOW	0.30	3	0.25	0.60	0.06	normal	normal	(100% change)	250	1	250	119	13	(106) (119)	398	8	398	103	(200) (NE)	100	(108) (121)	140	122
48	CONKNOW	0.50	3	0.25	0.60	0.06	normal	normal	0.66	250	1	250	187	30	187	398	8	398	221	2	221	221	2	221
49	CONKNOW	0.30	3	0	0.60	0.06	normal	normal	0.66	316	5	316	451	130	355	398	8	398	226	(200) (NR)	272	(172) (302)	40	(175) (296)
50	CONKNOW	0.30	3	0.25	0.60	0.06	A=normal B = ½ normal	normal	0.66	448	150[a]	372	401 (NR[a])	(100)	355	398	8	398	(403) (378)	176[a]	(355) (402)	293	(100) (NR[a])	323

Run number	Basic model	Initial market share of firm α	Demand algorithm equation	Rate of change of probabilities	Discount factor	Price increment	Starting cost function	Starting price	Market share revision factor	Initial probability set-ups: Sweezy: α's price	Sweezy: Periods to stability	Sweezy: β's price	Partly Sweezy: α's price	Partly Sweezy: Periods to stability	Partly Sweezy: β's price	Tit-for-tat (cartel): α's price	Tit-for-tat (cartel): Periods to stability	Tit-for-tat (cartel): β's price	No-move opponent: α's price	No-move opponent: Periods to stability	No-move opponent: β's price	Uncertainty: α's price	Uncertainty: Periods to stability	Uncertainty: β's price
(1)	(2)	(3)	(4)	(5)	(6)	(7)	(8)	(9)	(10)	(12)		(13)	(14)		(15)	(16)		(17)	(18)		(19)	(20)		(21)
51	CONKNOW	0.30	3	0.25	0.60	0.06	½ normal	normal	0.66	250	1	250	(363) (410)	59	394	398	8	398	189	170	(167) (196)	361	(200) (NR)	326
52	CONKNOW	0.50	3	0.25	0.60	0.06	½ normal	normal	0.66	250	1	250	(53) (60)	60	(53) (60)	398	8	398	195	4	195	(53) (60)	95	(53) (60)
53	CONKNOW	0.30	3	0.25	0.60	0.06	½ normal	normal	(100% change)	250	1	250	152	8	(135) (152)	398	8	398	91	43	(81) (91)	86	(200) (NE)	83
54	CONKNOW	0.30	3	0.25	0.60	0.06	⅙ normal	normal	0.66	250	1	250	165	(200) (NR)	167	398	8	398	(75) (85)	26	82	(63) (71)	30	68
55	CONKNOW	0.30	3	0.25	0.60	0.06	zero	normal	0.66	250	1	250	0.94[d]		0.94[d]	398	8	398	0.58[d]		0.58[d]	0.58[d]		0.58[d]
56	CONIG	0.30	3	0.25	0.60	0.06	normal	normal	0.66 (NR)	311	(200) (NR)	287	280	(200) (NR)	262	265	(200) (NR)	248	256	(200) (NR)	226	(257) (395)	30	(255) (418)
57	CONIG	0.30	3	0	0.60	0.06	normal	normal	0.66	(257) (306)	120	(276) (310)	(283) (352)	140	(288) (353)	(318) (473)	31	(306) (459)	226	(200) (NR)	272	(172) (289)	37	(175) (296)
58	CONIG	0.30	3	0.25	0.60	0.06	½ normal	normal	0.66	210	(200) (NR)	186	197	(200) (NR)	176	87	75	87	210	(200) (NR)	237	230	(200) (NR)	198
59	CONIG	0.30	3	0.25	0.60	0.06	⅙ normal	normal	0.66	(47) (63)	40	(47) (63)	(46) (60)	26	(46) (60)	(46) (64)	28	(47) (64)	(41) (51)	151	(41) (51)	(47) (64)	100	(47) (64)
60	CONIG	0.30	3	0.25	0.60	0.06	zero	normal	0.66	0.58[d]		0.58[d]	0.51[d]		0.51[d]	0.58[d]		0.58[d]	0.51[d]		0.51[d]	0.62[d]		0.62[d]

Notes:

The joint maximization price is approximately $397.

Many experiments were run whose results are not shown in the table.

(a) Indicates market share of one competitor approaching zero, and further trials not meaningful due to structure of model.

(b) Two prices within parentheses for a given firm indicate the approximate limits within which an apparently stable cyclical process is oscillating.

(d) Indicates price steadily declining apparently toward zero as a limit.

(NR) Indicates equilibrium not yet apparent as of period indicated in parentheses. Prices shown are those as of that period.

[39]

Foreword

A writer on Shakespeare explained how it is that Shakespeare was able to leap so far from his predecessors, his times, and his background: "Genius." That excellent non-explanation came to my mind when I read his first sonnet, the subject of this paper.

Culture and Society

Shakespeare, Procreation, and Progress

Julian L. Simon

It shocks and humbles me that a poet of long ago – even if the name is Shakespeare – could, in the span of fourteen lines and however long it took to write them, arrive at the heart of the demographic-economic vision for which moderns such as I had to struggle longer than a decade. It may be romantic, contrary to fact, and even counterproductive to think that Shakespeare arrived at this vision in a blinding flash. Perhaps he, too, struggled for it through many years before he compressed it into a few rhymes. But he got there without the help of the great predecessors who built the steps and lighted the way for us moderns, and without the data collected over two centuries that now provide the substratum for the idea.

Of course, Shakespeare's Sonnet 1 does not comprise a theory of the demographic-economic development of human enterprises. Yet the sonnet's themes express a vision that uncannily parallels a current theory of that subject. My aim here is to use the sonnet to illuminate this theory – to see the theory more clearly and show it to be more persuasive than it might otherwise appear. In connection with the exegesis, I will also argue that this parallelism is a reasonable reading of the sonnet. Even if the reader does not agree that there is a parallel, it is unarguable that the sonnet strikes sparks that light off rich meditation on the subject. Surely poetry serves a great purpose if it can set our thoughts afire, even if the direction of the thoughts was not the one intended by the poet. For a poem to just provoke fruitful misreading is a great achievement. And I trust that using a poem for its power to illuminate is neither foolishness nor fraud.

The "good" that Shakespeare wishes to advance is poetic truth, which is indistinguishable from beauty. This is the parallel to the natural resources and standard of living that are the subject of contemporary study of economic development. More about this shortly.

Let us examine Shakespeare's Sonnet 1. (This number may be more than a coincidence, just as it is not a coincidence that the ideas in Genesis come at the very beginning of the Bible.) Sonnet 1:

From fairest creatures we desire increase,
That thereby beauty's rose might never die,
But as the riper should by time decease,
His tender heir might bear his memory;
But thou, contracted to thine own bright eyes,
Need'st thy light's flame with self-substantial fuel,
Making a famine where abundance lies,
Thyself thy foe, to thy sweet self too cruel.
Thou that art now the world's fresh ornament
And only herald to the gaudy spring,
Within thine own bud buriest thy content
And, tender churl, mak'st waste in niggarding.
Pity the world, or else this glutton be,
To eat the world's due, by the grave and thee.

Shakespeare begins by assuming that "From fairest creatures we desire increase" – that is, that there should be more of such creatures. By "creatures" Shakespeare means people, our human species. That Shakespeare has such a demographic process in mind is clear from the third and fourth line – death preceded by birth and renewal. And we may suppose that Shakespeare is interested in the human race as a whole, not only in its most beautiful specimens. In *The Tempest* we read "How beauteous mankind is!"

If Shakespeare is indeed talking about people as if humans had a place different from that of other creatures in the scheme of things, the sonnet immediately takes its leave of those in contemporary society who believe that "other species have rights, too." These persons assert that when there is a conflict or trade-off between the increase of people and the increase of other species, the former must be constrained for the sake of the latter. As the eminent biologist, ecologist, and environmental activist Garrett Hardin put it: "If the space required to grow four redwood trees could be devoted to growing food for one person, we should say distinctly and bluntly that four redwood trees are more important than a person."

A recent debate, headlined in *The Washington Post* as *"A Cow is More Important Than a Hamburger,"* produced such statements as: "Other human beings certainly deserve my compassion, but laboratory rats and mice also deserve my compassion. The lives of laboratory animals mean a great deal to these animals just as our own lives mean so much to us." These thoughts do not square with Shakespeare's ordering of the species.

The sonnet's first line suggests that Shakespeare desires increase in the number of fair creatures for their own sake, just as many people look with satisfaction upon a populous, prosperous community. This sets him apart from many people in our age, for whom the increase of the human population is not a value in itself.

I do not suggest that Shakespeare called for an indiscriminate increase in people. Indeed, he mentions only the fairest, which we might interpret as the most talented. He might have agreed, though, that talent is spread widely, and that most people create a bit more than they use or destroy. And perhaps he would also have agreed that it is so difficult to predict where the bud of talent may sprout – he himself being a most powerful example – that the best way to increase the number of the fair is to increase the total number of people.

In the second line, Shakespeare gives yet another reason for desiring increase: survival of humankind. Many people today consider this idea "primitive" and logically unwarranted. Stabilization and zero growth of the population are seen as a value. And the prevention of births, even when the children are wanted by the parents, is a value so strongly held that Americans of this persuasion lobby their government to conduct taxpayer-financed programs to convince prospective parents in other countries (and even in the U. S.) that they should want and produce fewer children. Human increase, or even just the births of children who merely contribute to stabilization of the world's population, are of much less concern to many people than is mortal danger to those who are already alive. For example, a prominent newspaper recently carried an article entitled "Chinese Statistics Indicate Killing of Baby Girls Persists." This sounds terrible. But the article went on to report that "life expectancy is now sixty-nine years for Chinese women and sixty-six for men, an increase of twenty years over the past three decades." What better news could there be – unless one were to wish for fewer Chinese? Yet the story reads as if the small number of tragic cases of infanticide outweighed the large number of happy events that contribute to survival of the human species.

Shakespeare desires increase of fair creatures for their own sake.

Even for many among those who care about survival of humankind, survival of the race as a whole is subordinate to increase of their own ethnic or religious subgroup. And this preference is often more sentimental than a matter of seeking larger numbers to help them prevail in political conflict. In contrast, Shakespeare's only special plea is in favor of people who are "beautiful" and creative.

Let us turn now to Shakespeare's description of the mechanism for the advance of civilization, the most remarkable aspect of this sonnet. For Shakespeare, progress, rather than mere stability, lies within our power and possibilities; this is implicit when he writes of increase and abundance, rather than merely of maintenance and subsistence. Here is no pinched and dismal Malthusian vision of humanity's place on the globe, but an expansive and optimistic outlook of human dominion.

But then Shakespeare warns that humans may forego their opportunities by narcissistic preoccupation with their own luxurious living – taking from the common pot of humanity without putting back into it. "[C]ontracted to thine own bright eyes," Shakespeare tells us, humanity can make "a famine where abundance lies" by feeding our own "light's flame with self-substantial fuel."

We may fail to use our capital, the true nature of which is the human drive to create and improve and advance. Instead, humanity may devote its energies to consumption and self-satisfaction, thereby burying within its "own bud" its "content." I was taken aback by the combination of beauty and understanding of life with which these lines are suffused, surpassing in both respects other writings on the subject, whether scientific or artistic.

What is the nature of the "good" that might either be created in "abundance" or be made so scarce as to cause a famine? We must ask, with G. Wilson Knight and Mark van Doren (in the words of Knight): "What was he writing about when his deepest imagination was engaged?"

Truth and beauty are like natural resources that flow from knowledge.

Shakespeare certainly did not envision a process of economic development such as engages contemporary analysis of the subject, wherein we wish to increase the supply of consumer and investment goods, as well as natural resources, in order to live longer and better. Shakespeare cared about enhancing the world's stock of poetic truths such as he struggled to give us. Poetic truth is, of course, interrelated with – or perhaps identical to – the esthetic aspect of life Shakespeare calls "beauty," and which may be physical or artistic or spiritual. Knight argues forcefully that the sonnets are interpenetrated with the ideas of time (both past and future), material beauty, poetry, immortality, truth, nature, and art.

A key idea is the immortal "substance" of poetic beauty as "distilled" from the mere "show" of human beauty – "A liquid prisoner pent in walls of glass" (Sonnets 5, 6). This transmutation of physical beauty into poetic truth provides the best of reasons for Shakespeare to write poems about a particular beautiful young man. And indeed Knight writes:

> The poet knows well that his poetry is more than his ordinary self. It is 'the very part was consecrate to thee', his own 'spirit', 'the better part of me', to be contrasted with the element of 'earth' which is 'the dregs of life', bound for death. This 'better part' is a refined state of being, like the refinement of distilled essences.

From an economic point of view, the good we may call truth and beauty is conceptually no different than raw materials such as food as well as human-made goods such as services and manufactured products. As information and knowledge become an ever larger part of our economy, and tangible goods (especially natural-resource materials including energy) become an ever smaller share of inputs, there should be less and less difficulty in agreeing that truth and beauty – call it art, if you like – constitute a good that may be construed theoretically in ways similar to the ways we think of other economic goods. A key respect in which truth and beauty are like knowledge, and thereby like the supply of natural resources that flows from knowledge, is that our stocks of intellectual goods are not depleted by use, but will continue to enhance forever human life.

Shakespeare then proceeds to tell us that we may be wasting our chances, not only by gluttony and self-devotion, but also by attending to conservation rather than creation. He tells us that a society "mak'st waste by niggarding." This is a striking apprehension of the nature of civilization. It may be seen as parallel to the following sequence: Increase in population size and rise in the standard of living force upon us new problems that lead to the search for solutions (though great developments may also arise in a more spontaneous fashion). The solutions arrived at leave us better off materially, and perhaps with better social organizations, than if the problems had never arisen in the first place. (Hence we need our problems because eventually we will benefit from them.)

The resonance of the sonnet suggests that Shakespeare would have been sympathetic to this process. He would have felt at home with the notion that humanity not only needs to have its problems solved, but also needs to have bigger and better problems imposed upon it as a challenge to its creative powers – for the benefit of the human spirit as well as for the eventual benefit of future generations.

So I say with Shakespeare, "Pity the world, or else this glutton be, to eat the world's due, by the grave and thee."

Is it far-fetched to read a "theory of development" into Sonnet 1? I think not because for me, as for James Cook, "art is always concerning itself with more than it knows" (from undated letter). Hence the poem may be used as one uses a coppermine; convert it into a form that yields us a service.

Agreement with this argument may be found in an essay on a similar subject by the noted Shakespearean scholar Edward Hubler, who in fact entitles it "The Economy of the Closed Heart." He uses the word "economy" in a sense akin to my economic discussion here. Hubler begins: "There is no idea to which Shakespeare returns more often than to the doctrine taught by the parable of the talents. . . The idea is, of course, the concept of man's stewardship referred to in the discussion of plenitude." And "talents" means here both human talent and the monetary unit of wealth. Hubler writes that "in Shakespeare's view the open heart must give itself away in order to maintain its existence" and "the quality in the young man which most disturbed Shakespeare was the prudence of the closed heart." Hubler certainly agrees that the sonnet is about the utilization of a person's talent for the sake of others, as he writes:

> . . . the flower living to itself, and having therefore failed to fulfill its function, is incomplete, though it still has physical beauty; but if it should meet with infection (that is, if the expression of its function should be perverted), its odor (that is, its essence, its soul, its human utility as expressed in the deeds of the young man and the perfume of the flower) becomes worse than that of weeds, worse, that is, than that from which nothing was expected.

Hubler also emphasizes that "the distillation of essence is a symbol of procreation," confirming the link between procreation and usefulness crucial to my own argument.

Some readers may desire proof of the connection between what a poet had in mind and what we find in the poet. I find support for some such connection in Robert Giroux's *The Book Known as Q*, and secondarily in G. Wilson Knight's *The Mutual Flame*. Giroux's ideas are controversial, but within the realm of reasonable argument; that they be established fact is not necessary. And, of course, I do not claim that Shakespeare was setting forth a self-conscious theory of development that he hoped would instruct decision makers, as William Petty and Adam Smith did. The pertinent issue is whether the poet explicitly described a crucial aspect of the development mechanism as it acts through the long sweep of history. To ascertain whether this is so, we must dig into the purpose and the conditions of the sonnet's composition, difficult and controversial as that inquiry may be.

Let us assume that the object of the main batch of sonnets was the young Earl of Southampton and that Shakespeare was hired by Southampton's mother to persuade her son to marry Elizabeth Vere, the granddaughter of Lord Burghley, whom Giroux describes as "the most powerful person in the realm next to Queen Elizabeth." This business relationship is consistent with the tone in the first few sonnets, called by Giroux "impersonal." In such circumstances, what would be a sensible strategy for a man-of-the-world poet, who also has a high regard for his talent and a desire not to waste his rhymes on hackwork, yet who wishes to do the job he was hired to do in workmanlike and honest fashion? As Knight states, "Shakespeare, we must suppose, had some worldly wisdom: and we know that he possessed business instincts."

There is nothing worse than playing the whore in one's work and not even succeeding.

It seems reasonable that Shakespeare would not simulate paroxysms of adoration for the young man, commonplace as that may have been in the poetry of the times. The young man would know that Shakespeare did not have sufficient familiarity with him to be able to write such adoring words truly. Shakespeare explicitly rejects phony comparisons to the 'sun and moon, with earth's and sea's rich gems,/ With April's first-born flowers . . ." (Sonnet 21).

Advertising and other messages that seek to persuade must be credible if they are to be acted upon. Shakespeare knew this well: "Let them say more that like of hearsay well;/ I will not praise, that purpose not to sell" (Sonnet 21). There is nothing worse than playing the whore in one's work and not even succeeding: if you do your best work and fail, at least you have the work and your self-respect. So instead of phony appeals, Shakespeare musters the most believable array of arguments. He arrays the arguments in a battery, one after the other, all set forth with his full skill.

Another consideration probably influenced Shakespeare. If he wrote honest stuff rather than fake admiration and false paeans of love, the labor would be enjoyable rather than detestable. Knight writes that "Not only may we call them [the sonnets] sincere, but we may observe that sincerity is one of their leading themes . . .The jibes at any sort of artificiality are, as in the plays, where all exaggerated fashions are so regularly attacked, here also both strong and insistent." And "others employ 'strained touches of rhetoric', whereas his is made of 'true plain words'" (quoting Sonnet 82).

Is this motive of wanting to write honestly not consistent with our view of great talent – "genius" in

Giroux's word – and of what we can perceive of Shakespeare's nature from his work? This motive would likely have affected Shakespeare even if he thought that for a time the sonnets would be read only by Southampton. He could look ahead to publishing the material later in other ways, either as sonnets or reworked into other form in his plays, as he apparently used them in *The Rape of Lucrece* and elsewhere.

Imagine Shakespeare thinking about the task before him. To tell Southampton that the girl is attractive in person and personality would fail. Southampton knows the girl and is not interested in her, and Shakespeare is personally unacquainted with her. Shakespeare cannot write that the match is good business and sound politics; this is hardly fit subject for a poem, and furthermore, Southampton clearly has heard such advice from Burghley and from his mother. But there are other respectable reasons the poet can adduce. The first of the sonnets encapsulates many of them and weaves them into the full argument discussed earlier.

I do not contend that Shakespeare made his argument for the sake of the world; he may well have been writing to enhance his own situation. But his plea to the youth to marry for the sake of the world constitutes a powerful plea on behalf of the world. What matters here is that Shakespeare understood well the argument that he was making; it does not matter on whose behalf it was made, whether the world's or Shakespeare's.

It is not implausible that Shakespeare was capable of such a subtle analysis of the development of society and civilization. The idea of progress was not invented yesterday, and certainly was not foreign to the Renaissance period. A sound understanding of economic and social development does not require knowledge unavailable when Shakespeare lived. What was required was the ability to see farther and deeper than others. Shakespeare possessed such genius. Giroux gives precisely this one-word explanation for Shakespeare's ability to produce unexpected poetic and dramatic discoveries.

One last point: Is it reasonable to presume that Shakespeare would compose such sublime verse and subtle arguments to serve the very mundane aim of inducing a young man to marry? If indeed Southampton's family hired Shakespeare to persuade the youth, then *ipso facto* they had some appreciation of the artist and his art. And while it sometimes happens, there is no reason to assume that Southampton's family simply did the equivalent of hiring a great portrait painter to paint a picket fence. Such appreciation from a noble family and from the youth who eventually became Shakespeare's patron (if indeed this is what happened) could have produced a strong reaction akin to infatuation in a low-born and striving artist such as Shakespeare. As Giroux puts it: "Their first meeting also seems to have endowed the youth in his eyes with a superior, almost sacred character. The 'sacred' is not an exaggeration."

It is interesting to contrast Shakespeare's view of the course of civilization and productive economy with that of Bernard Mandeville who lived not much later. Mandeville also expressed himself in rhyme but he was clearly a social scientist by inspiration rather than a poet. (See for example the lengthy prose notes following the short rhyming pages of *The Fable of the Bees.*) Mandeville saw improvement and advance as inevitable; this progress will be brought about by the same selfish qualities that Shakespeare lamented, qualities Mandeville might also not have admired or enjoyed, but nevertheless saw as a constant element in human nature. In *King Henry V*, Shakespeare referred to the same mysterious phenomenon of social organization and spontaneous cooperation among insects Mandeville described in *The Fable of the Bees*. It is pleasant to imagine a meeting of the two men, each describing his vision and with the other instantly seeing the point and joining the other's vision to his own in a grand amalgamation.

Readings Suggested by the Author:

Giroux, Robert. *The Book Known as Q*. New York: Atheneum, 1982.

Hubler, Edward. *The Sense of Shakespeare's Sonnets*. Princeton, N.J.: Princeton University Press, 1952.

Knight, G. Wilson. *The Mutual Flame*. London: Methuen, 1955.

Simon, Julian L. *The Ultimate Resource*. Princeton, N.J.: Princeton University Press, 1981.

Julian L. Simon is professor of business administration at the University of Maryland. His books include The Economics of Population Growth; The Ultimate Resource; Theory of Population and Economic Growth: Effort, Opportunity and Wealth; The Economic Consequences of Immigration; *and most recently* Population Matters: People, Resources, Environment and Immigration, *published by Transaction.*

[40]

Foreword

This list arose out of teaching contemporary economic issues to an Executive MBA program – mature students mostly in business who wanted some structure for analysis of the policy questions we addressed. At various points in each discussion I'd asked "What number?" and they'd sing out "Number nine – Sellers respond powerfully to opportunities," and so on. This livened up the discussion.

In retrospect, the Bastiat–Hazlitt insight is the master element in policy analysis. Frederic Bastiat, whom Schumpeter called the greatest economic journalist of all time, in his famous essay "What is Seen and What is Not Seen" (1850/1964) taught that it is crucial for sound economic understanding to take account not just of the obvious and immediate effects of an economic event, but also the indirect and long-run effects as well. More recently, the American journalist, Henry Hazlitt, has built upon Bastiat's ideas to teach us what he calls "Economics in One Lesson" (1962, p. 17). This is how he states his lesson:

> The art of economics consists in looking not merely at the immediate but at the longer effects of any act or policy; it consists in tracing the consequences of that policy not merely for one group but for all groups.

Paying attention to the long run as well as the short run is particularly important in the study of population economics. A fundamental aim of all my work on the subject is to enlarge the time span within which the economics of population growth is commonly discussed, both by lengthening the horizon within which analyses of the future are made and by pushing the historical record back to earlier times than are usually adduced in the discussion. There is a single reason for both extensions: To understand and to take into account the slower-moving yet fundamental forces that, together with the immediate-action factors, connect population and economic welfare.

References

Bastiat, Frederic (1964), *Selected Essays on Political Economy* (Irvington-on-Hudson: Foundation for Economic Education).

Hazlitt, Henry (1962), *Economics in one Lesson*, (New York: Arlington House, second edition).

Some key elements in the economist's tool-box

1. The economy is an interdependent system, in which a change in one sector leads to responses elsewhere. Analysis that is too partial – that does not recognize the *important* responses to change that may occur – will lead to error. But analysis that tries to include too many factors is either too expensive or unmanageable. The art of the economist is to include *all* the important factors and *only* the important factors.
2. Exchange between voluntary partners benefits both of them.
3. The supply and demand schedules of the *groups* of sellers and buyers are the fundamental data. Given time, supply and demand forces (the tendency to exchange) are sufficiently powerful to overcome social, legal, and other barriers.
4. The supply schedule of an individual supplier depends only on variable costs in competitive markets.
5. Economies of scale derive from fixed costs or indivisibilities.
6. Demand is a function of tastes and the costs of substitutes in consumer markets.
7. Producers' demand for input is a function of the costs of substitutes and the effect on profits.
8. Supply and demand schedules are sloped, not horizontal or vertical. That is, elasticities never equal zero.
9. Sellers respond powerfully to opportunities to make profits. They search out opportunities, and get and combine much information with their other inputs.
10. There are fairly good substitutes for everything – and more are developed with the passage of time and advances in technology.
11. The hypothesis of profit maximization is a useful first working hypothesis in understanding economic behavior.
12. All analysis has a time dimension. The longer the time period, the larger and stronger the response to imbalance between supply and sales.
13. Present and future economic events are linked by the discount factor (the cost of capital).
14. Risk is always present, and the degree of risk influences the discount factor.
15. Price always matters, price changes lead to changes in conditions.
16. Prices are the signals that transmit information about opportunities and disequilibria throughout the economy.
17. The first alternative social control scheme one should consider for change of economic behavior is to employ prices as incentives.
18. An economist is an *evaluator*, a calculator of costs and benefits. Correct calculation of relevant costs and benefits leads to sound decisions.
19. The appropriate cost in an evaluation is the opportunity cost. Just which cost is the opportunity cost is exceedingly tricky.
20. Where there are external effects, the appropriate costs and benefits include the external effects.

21. The basic social welfare principle is that the social benefit per dollar should be the same in all investments. Resources should be transferred until the benefits per dollar are equal.
22. Sunk costs are sunk. The price you buy for should not affect the price at which you sell.

[41]

Foreword

The editors of *Journal of Economic Perspectives* were for a while enthusiastic about printing this bit of a black joke, but they found that their tolerance and sense of humor were not shared by other influentials in the American Economic Association publication establishment.

A step-by-step procedure for the guidance of gimlet-eyed referees

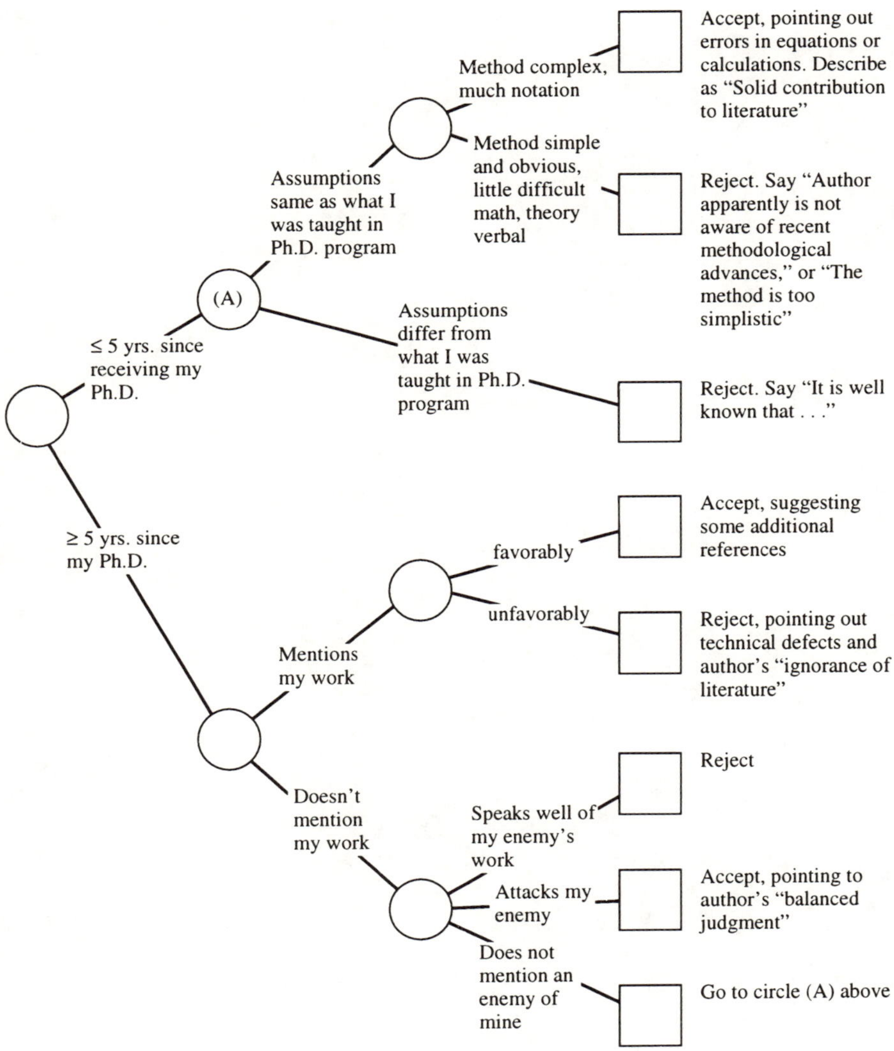

Appendix: Writings of Julian L. Simon

Monographs

How to Start and Operate a Mail-Order Business (New York: McGraw Hill, 1965); second edition, 1976; third edition, 1980; fourth edition, 1986; fifth edition, 1993; abridged paperback edition, 1984. Translated into Italian, 1989.

Basic Research Methods in Social Science (New York: Random House, 1969); second edition, 1978; third edition [with Paul Burstein], 1985.

Patterns of Use of Books in Large Research Libraries (with Herman H. Fussler), (Chicago: University of Chicago Press, 1969).

Issues in the Economics of Advertising (Urbana: University of Illinois Press, 1970).

The Management of Advertising (Englewood Cliffs: Prentice-Hall, 1971).

The Effects of Income on Fertility (Chapel Hill: Carolina Population Center, 1974).

Applied Managerial Economics (Englewood Cliffs: Prentice-Hall, 1975).

The Economics of Population Growth (Princeton: Princeton University Press, 1977). Translated into Chinese (Peking University Press, 1984.)

Research in Population Economics (edited), Vol. I (Greenwich: JAI Press, 1978).

Marketing Management (Tel Aviv: Dekel, 1978), in Hebrew. Largely drawn from previous works in English.

Advertising Management (Tel Aviv: Dekel, 1979), in Hebrew. Largely drawn from previous works in English.

Research in Population Economics (edited, with Julie daVanzo), Vol. II (Greenwich: JAI Press, 1980).

The Ultimate Resource (Princeton: Princeton University Press, 1981); second edition, 1994). Translated into French, Spanish, Portuguese, Norwegian, and Chinese, with options taken for translation into German and Japanese.

Research in Population Economics (edited, with Peter Lindert), Vol. 3, (Greenwich: JAI Press, 1981).

Research in Population Economics (edited, with Peter Lindert), Vol. 4, (Greenwich: JAI Press, 1982).

The Resourceful Earth: A Response to the Global 2000 Report (edited, with Herman Kahn) (New York: Basil Blackwell, 1984). Nominated for 1985 Mencken Award, Best Book Category.

Theory of Population and Economic Growth (New York: Basil Blackwell, 1986).

Effort, Opportunity, and Wealth (New York: Basil Blackwell, 1987).

The Economic Consequences of Immigration to the U.S. (Oxford: Basil Blackwell, 1989).

How do Immigrants Affect Us Economically? (Washington: Georgetown University, Center for Immigration Policy and Refugee Assistance, 1985). Short version of item immediately above.

Population Matters: People, Resources, Environment, and Immigration (New Brunswick, N.J.: Transactions Press, 1990).

Population and Development in Poor Countries (Princeton: PUP, 1992).

Good Mood: The New Psychology of Overcoming Depression (Peru, Ind.: Open Court, 1993).

Resampling Statistics (Boston: Wadsworth, 1993).

The State of Humanity (Boston: Basil Blackwell, 1994).

Scarcity or Abundance? A Debate on the Environment (with Norman Myers) (New York: Norton, 1994).

Professional articles

'Discipline and the Division,' *United States Naval Institute Proceedings*, **81** (10), Whole No. 632, October 1955, 1111–15.

'Direct Mail Testing Techniques: A New Approach,' *Direct Mail*, September 1962.

'Cigarette Advertising and the Nation's Welfare,' *Illinois Business Review*, **21**, May 1964, 6–8.

'What Marketing Science Now Offers the Advertiser' in L. George Smith (ed.), *Reflections on Progress in Marketing* (Chicago: American Marketing Association, 1965), 154–67.

'Are There Economies of Scale in Advertising?' *Journal of Advertising Research*, **5**, June 1965, 15–19.

'A Simple Model for Setting Advertising Appropriations,' *Journal of Advertising Research*, **II**, August 1965, 285–92.

'The Cause of the Newspaper Rate Differential: A Subjective-Demand-Curve Analysis,' *Journal of Political Economy*, **LXXIII**, October 1965, 536–9.

'The Professional Method of Finding Products,' *Direct Mail* (now *Direct Marketing*), **27**, 1965, 24–8.

'What Quantitative Methods Should be Taught in an Advertising Education?' *Occasional Papers in Advertising*, **1**, January 1966, 53–8.

'The Demand for Liquor in the U.S., and a Simple Method of Determination,' *Econometrica*, **34**, January 1966, 193–205.

'The Economic Effect of State Monopoly of Packaged Liquor Retailing,' *Journal of Political Economy*, **LXXIV**, April 1966, 188–94.

'Is the Statistic (Advertising/Sales) Useless for the Study of Economies of Scale and Other Purposes?' *Journal of Advertising Research*, **6**, September 1966, 37–43 (with George H. Crain).

'Expenditure Policy for Mail Order Advertisers,' *Journal of Marketing Research*, **IV**, February 1967, 59–61.

'How Many Books Should be Stored Where? An Economic Analysis,' *College and University Libraries*, March 1967, 92–103.

'Business Ethics, Business Ideology, and Business Behavior,' *Business and Society*, **7**, Spring 1967, 18–32.

'Some Principles of Practical Welfare Economics,' *Management Science*, **13**, June 1967, 621–30.

'The Spread of a Cost-Free Business Innovation: The Case of the January White Sale,' *Journal of Business*, **40**, October 1967, 385–8 (with Leslie Golembo).

'The Effect of Fixed-Wage Rises on Discriminated-Against Minorities,' *Industrial and Labor Relations Review*, **21**, October 1967, 96–7.

'The Effect of Competitive Structure Upon Advertising Expenditures,' *Quarterly Journal of Economics*, **LXXXI**, November 1967, 610–27.

'The Effect of Promotion on the Propensity to Consume,' *Kyklos*, **XX** (4), 1967, 950–61.

'Doctors, Smoking and Reference Groups,' *Public Opinion Quarterly*, **31**, Winter, 1967–68, 646–7.

'A Huge Marketing Research Job – Birth Control,' *Journal of Marketing Research*, **5**, February 1968, 21–7.

'The Effect of Economic Status and Traditional Culture Upon Economic Behavior,' *American Journal of Agricultural Economics*, **50**, May 1968, 448–51.

'An Almost-Practical Solution to Airline Overbooking,' *Journal of Transport Economics and Policy*, **II**, May 1968, 201–2.

'Investment Prospects in Economics – 1967,' *Economics Journal*, **LXXVIII**, June 1968, 476–9.

'What Does the Normal Curve "Mean"?' *Journal of Educational Research*, **61**, July–August 1968, 435–8.

'Class, Status, and Saving by Negroes,' *American Sociologist*, August 1968, 218–19 (with Rita J. Simon).

'The Price Elasticity of Demand for Cigarettes in the United States,' *American Journal of Agricultural Economics*, **50**, November 1968, 888–95 (with Herbert C. Lyon).

'The Effect of Income on Suicide,' *American Journal of Sociology*, **74**, November 1968, 302–3.

'The Health Economics of Cigarette Consumption,' *Journal of Human Resources*, **III**, Winter 1968, 111–17.

'The Role of Bonuses and Persuasive Propaganda in the Reduction of Birth Rates,' *Economic Development and Cultural Change*, **16** (3), 1968, 404–11.

'Some "Marketing Correct" Recommendations for Family Planning Campaigns,' *Demography*, **5**, (1), 1968, 504–7.

'Product Differentiation – A Meaningless Term and an Impossible Concept,' *Ethics*, **79**, January 1969, 131–8.

'Does "Good Portfolio Management" Exist?' *Management Science*, **15**, February 1969, B-308–19.

'Further Evidence on the Effect of Scale in Advertising,' *Journal of Advertising Research*, **9**, March 1969, 38–41.

'The Value of Avoided Births to Underdeveloped Countries,' *Population Studies*, **XXIII**, March 1969, 61–8.

'A Really New Way to Teach (and Do) Probability Statistics,' *The Mathematics Teacher*, **LXII**, April 1969, 283–8.

'The Effect of Advertising on Liquor Brand Sales,' *Journal of Marketing Research*, **VI**, August 1969, 301–13.

'How to Divide the Retail Advertising Budget Among Merchandise Divisions: A Scientific Program,' *Journal of Retailing*, **45**, Fall 1969, 37–45.

'The Effect of Income on Fertility,' *Population Studies*, **XXIII**, November 1969, 327–41.

'A Further Test of the Kinky Oligopoly Demand Curve,' *American Economic Review*, **59**, December 1969, 971–5.

'The Profitability of Mergers in Advertising Agencies,' *Bulletin of the Oxford Institute of Economics and Statistics*, **31** (2), 1969, 139–44 (with Harold W. Johnson).

'The New Proteins and World Food Needs,' *Economic Development and Cultural Change*, **17**, 1969, 520–26 (with David M. Gardner).

'The Middle-Class U.S. Consumption Function: A Hypothetical-Question Study of Expected Consumption Behavior,' *Bulletin of the Oxford Institute of Economics and Statistics*, **33**, February 1970, 73–80 (with Carl B. Barnes).

'Family Planning Prospects in Less Developed Countries and a Cost–Benefit Analysis of Various Alternatives,' *Economic Journal*, **80**, March 1970, 58–71.

'An Almost Practical Solution to Airline Overbooking: Reply,' *Journal of Transport Economics and Policy*, **V**, May 1970.

'Cross-Sectional Budget Studies, Aggregate Time-Series Studies, and the Permanent Income Hypothesis,' *American Economic Review*, **60**, June 1970, 341–51 (with Dennis J. Aigner).

'A Specification Bias Interpretation of Cross-Section vs. Time Series Parameter Estimates,' *Western Economic Journal* (now *Economic Inquiry*), **8**, June 1970, 141–61 (with Dennis J. Aigner).

'A Plan to Improve the Attribution of Scholarly Articles,' *American Sociologist*, **5**, August 1970, 265–7.

'The Per-Capita-Income Criterion and Natality Policies in Poor Countries,' *Demography*, **7**, August 1970, 369–78.

'The Concept of Causality in Economics,' *Kyklos*, **23** (2), 1970, 226–54.

'The Present Value of Unpaid Wages to Slaves in the United States,' *Journal of Economic Issues*, **5**, September 1971, 110–13.

'A Policy to Promote the World's Economic Development with Migration from LDC's to MDC's,' *Policy Sciences*, **2**, December 1971, 407–11.

'Toward Formal Evaluation of Scientific Research Projects: A Case Study in Population Control,' *Policy Sciences*, **3**, July 1972, 171–81.

'Analysis of Graduated Corporate Income Tax as an Anti-Bigness Device,' *Anti-Trust Law and Economics Review*, **6**, Winter 1972–3, 53–66.

'Does Economic Growth Imply a Growth in Welfare?' *Journal of Economic Issues*, **VII** (1), March 1973, 130–36.

'A Duopoly Simulation and Richer Theory: An End to Cournot,' *The Review of Economic Studies*, **XL**, 1973, 353–66 (with Carlos Puig and John Aschoff).

'Science Does Not Show That There is Overpopulation in the U.S.,' in Edward Pohlman (ed.), *Population: A Clash of Prophets* (New York: Mentor-New American Library, 1973), 48–62.

'Preparing and Launching a Research Study,' in Peter Rose, *The Study of Society* (New York: Random House, 1973), 54–66.

'Strategy and Segmentation of the Birth Control Market,' in M. McMillan (ed.), *Using Commercial Resources in Family Planning Communication Programs* (Honolulu: East-West Center, 1973) 34–50.

'Segmentation and Market Strategy in Birth-Control Campaigns,' *Studies in Family Planning*, **5**, March 1974, 90–97.

'Economic Effects of Population change,' *UNESCO Courier*, **27**, May 1974, 23–32.

'How Much Should an Airline Spend for Advertising? A Case Example,' *Journal of Travel Research*, **II**, Winter 1974, 10–14.

'A Calculation of the Black Reparations Bill,' *The Review of Black Political Economy*, **4**, Winter 1974, 75–86 (with Larry Neal).

'Interpersonal Comparisons Can Be Made – and Used for Redistribution Decisions,' *Kyklos*, **XXVII** (1), 1974, 63–98.

'SIMPLE: Computer Program For Monte Carlo Problem Solving,' *American Statistician*, November 1974, 163 (letter; with Dan Weidenfeld).

'The Effect of Population Growth on Agricultural Saving in Irrigation,' *Review of Economics and Statistics*, **LVII**, February 1975, pp. 71–9.

'The Welfare Effect of an Additional Child Cannot be Stated Simply and Unequivocally,' *Demography*, **12**, February, 1975, 89–105.

'The Mixed Effects of Income Upon Successive Births May Explain the Convergence Phenomenon,' *Population Studies*, **29**, March 1975.

'The Effect of Population Density Upon Infrastructure: The Case of Roadbuilding,' *Economic Development and Cultural Change*, **23** (3), April 1975 (with Donald R. Glover).

'Exploration and Puzzles in the Inter-relationships of Successive Births with Husband's Income, Spouse's Education and Race,' *Demography*, **12**, May 1975, 295–74.

'The Partial Effect of Income on Suicide is Always Negative: Reply,' *American Journal of Sociology*, **80**, May 1975, 1462–3.

'The Effect of Foster-Care Payment Levels Upon the Number of Foster Children Given Homes,' *Social Service Review*, **49**, September 1975, 405–11.

'How Much Is Your Customer Worth to Your Firm's Goal?' *Direct Marketing*, **38** (6), October 1975.

'The Effect of Money Incentives on Family Size: A Hypothetical-Question Study,' *Public Opinion Quarterly*, **38**, 1795, 585–95 (with Rita J. Simon).

'Population Growth May be Good for LDC's in the Long Run: A Richer Simulation Model,' *Economic Development and Cultural Change*, **24**, January 1976, 309–37.

'The Economic Effect of Russian Immigrants Upon the Veteran Israeli Population: A Cost-Benefit Analysis,' *The Economic Quarterly*, **23**, August 1976, 224–52 (in Hebrew).

'Probability and Statistics: Experimental Results of a Radically Different Teaching Method,' *The American Mathematical Monthly*, **83**, November 1976, 733–9 (with David T. Atkinson and Carolyn Shevokas).

'Income, Wealth, and Their Distribution as Policy Tools in Fertility-Control Campaigns in LDC's,' in Ronald Ricker (ed.), *Population and Development: The Search for Selective Interventions* (Baltimore: Resources for the Future and John Hopkins Press), 1976.

'The Auction Solution To Airline Overbooking: The Data Fit the Theory,' *Journal of Transport Economics and Policy*, **3**, September 1977, 277–83 (with Ganesan Visvabharathy).

'Graduate the Corporate Income Taxes to Abate Bigness Efficiently,' *Challenge*, **20**, November/December 1977.

'Is Population Growth Really Bad for LDC's in the Long Run?' *Agricultural Mechanization in Asia*, **8**, Winter, 1977, 13–20 (with Douglas Love).

'Choosing the Best Advertising Appropriation When Appropriations Interact Over Time,' in Jagdish Sheth (ed.), *Research in Marketing*, **I**, 149–67 (Greenwich: JAI Press, 1978) (with Haim Levy). Awarded prize as 'Best Theoretical/Empirical Research Paper,' AIDS National Conference, 1977.

'Population Economics in the 1980's: What Ought It to Be, and What Will It Be?' *Proceedings of IUSSP Conference*, Helsinki, August 1978.

'An Integration of the Invention-Pull and Population-Push Theories of Economic-Demographic History,' in Julian L. Simon (ed.), *Research in Population Economics*, Vol. I, (Greenwich: JAI Press, 1978).

'What Do Zielske's Real Data Really Show About Pulsing?' *Journal of Marketing Research*, **XVI**, August 1979, 415–20.

'The Effect of Population Growth Upon the Quantity of Education Children Receive,' *Review of Economics and Statistics*, **LXI**, November 1979, 572–84 (with Adam M. Pilarski).

'Additional People Improve the Standard of Living Through Knowledge Creation and Productivity Increases,' (Testimony given to the Select Committee on Population U.S. House of Representatives, June 2 1978), *American Demographics*, November/December, 1979.

'The Effect of Population Size and Concentration Upon Scientific Productivity,' in *Research in Population Economics*, Vol. I (with Douglas Love, and under pen-name of Lincoln Pashute).

'Economics Versus Racial Discrimination in the Provision of Birth-Control Services in the United States,' in *Research in Population Economics*, Vol. I (with Douglas Love, and under pen-name of Lincoln Pashute).

'Are We Losing Ground?' *Illinois Business Review*, **37**, April 1980, 1–6.

'Resources, Population, Environment: An Over-supply of False Bad News,' *Science*, **208**, June 27 1980, 1431–7.

'The Shape of the Advertising Response Function,' *Journal of Advertising Research*, **20**, August 1980, 11–30 (with Johan Arndt).

'On Firm Size and Advertising Efficiency: A Comment,' *Journal of Economic Literature*, **XVIII**, September 1980, 59–67.

'The Pain of Failing a Ph.D. Oral Exam, and an Unfortunate Confusion in Economic Thought,' *American Economist*, **XXIV**, Fall 1980, 43–6.

'The Fundamental Elements of Cataloging,' *Direct Marketing*, **43**, October 1980, 64–90.

'There Is No Low-level Fertility-and-Development Trap,' *Population Studies*, **34**, November 1980, 476–86.

'The Relationship Between Population and Economic Growth in LDC's,' in Julian L. Simon and Julie DaVanzo (eds), *Research in Population Economics*, Vol. II, (Greenwich: JAI Press, 1980) (with Roy Gobin).

'Population, Productivity, and Economic Growth in the Western World,' in I. Levenson and J. Wheeler (eds), *Western Economy in Transition: Structural Change and Adjustment Policies in Industrial Countries* (Westways Press, 1980) (with Larry Neal).

'Phelps' Technical Progress Model Generalized,' *Economic Letters*, **5**, 1980, 177–82 (with Gunter Steinmann).

'Environmental Disruption or Environmental Improvement?' *Social Science Quarterly*, **62**, March 1981.

'Unnecessary, Confusing, and Inadequate: The Marginal Analysis as a Tool in Decision-Making,' *American Economist*, **XXV**, Spring 1981, 28–36.

'False Bad News is Truly Bad News,' *The Public Interest*, **65**, Fall 1981, 80–90.

'Global Confusion 1980: A Review of the Global 2000 Report to the President,' *The Public Interest*, Winter 1981, 1–21.

'Strategies of Competition Among Organizations,' in William Starbuck (ed.), *Handbook of Organizational Design* (New York: Oxford, 1981) (with Thomas Friedland).

'The Really Important Effects of Immigrants Upon Natives "Incomes."' in Barry Chiswick (ed.), *The Gateway* (Washington: American Enterprise Institute, 1981).

'What Immigrants Take From and Give To the Public Coffers,' in *U.S. Immigration Policy As The National Interest*, Staff Report of the Select Commission on Immigration and Refugee Policy, Appendix (Washington GPO, 1981).

'Population Growth and Phelps' Technical Progress Model,' in Simon and Lindert (eds), *Research in Population Economics*, Vol. III, 1981, 239–54 (with Gunter Steinman).

'The Advertising Budget's Determinants in a Market with two Competing Firms,' *Management Science*, **28**, May 1982, 500–519 (with Joseph Ben-Ur).

'Are We Losing Our Farmland?' *The Public Interest*, **67**, Spring 1982, 49–62.

'Some Aspects of the Socio-Cultural Adjustment of Recent Soviet Immigrants to the United States,' *Ethnic and Racial Studies*, **5** (4), October 1982 (with Rita Simon).

'Global Food Prospects: Good News,' *Challenge*, November/December 1982, 40–48 (with William J. Hudson).

'How much Farmland Is Being Converted to Urban Use? An Analysis of Soil Conservation Service Estimates,' *International Regional Science Review*, **7** (3), 1982, 257–72 (with Seymour Sudman).

'Linguistic Confusion in Economics: Utility, Causality, Product Differentiation and the Supply of Natural Resources,' *Kyklos*, **35** (4), 1982.

'A Scheme to Promote the World's Economic Development With Migration,' *Research in Population Economics*, **4**, 1982, Editors: Julian L. Simon and Peter H. Lindert (Greenwich, Connecticut: JAI Press Inc.), 155–72.

'The Theory of Price-Changing and Monopoly Power,' *Journal of Post-Keynesian Economics*, **VI** (2), Winter 1983–84, 198–213 (with Edward Rice).

'Is It Sensible to Say That Natural Resources are Finite in Supply,' *Bulletin of the Atomic Scientists*, May 1983.

'"Population Pressure" on the Land: Analysis of Trends Past and Future,' *World Development*, **11** (9), September 1983, 825–34 (with William Reisler and Roy Gobin, pp. 825–34).

'The Effects of Population Upon Nutrition and Economic Well-Being,' *Journal of Interdisciplinary History*, **XIV** (2), Autumn 1983, 413–37.

'The Present Value of Population Growth in the Western World,' *Population Studies*, **37**, 1983, 5–21.

'Optimal Allocation of Space in Retail Advertisements and Mail-Order Catalogues: Theory and a First-approximation Decision Rule,' *International Journal of Advertising*, **2**, 1983, 123–9 (with Vithala Rao).

'Advertising's Sales Effect Can Be Measured and Evaluated Very Well,' *International Journal of Advertising*, 1983, 331–41.

'A Scheme to Improve Air Travel,' *Journal of Policy Analysis and Management*, **2** (3), 1983.

'Advertising and Economies of Scale: Critical Comments on the Evidence,' *The Journal of Industrial Economics*, **32** (2), December 1983 (with Johan Arndt).

'Immigrants, Taxes, and Welfare in the United States,' *Population and Development Review*, **10** (1), March 1984.

'Bright Global Future,' *Bulletin of the Atomic Scientists*, November 1984, 14–17.

'How to Choose the Optimum Advertising Investment,' *International Journal of Advertising*, **3** (4), 1984, 321–33.

'The False Religion of Farmland Preservation,' in John Baden (ed.), *Agricultural Land Preservation: Economics or Politics* (Lawrence, Kansas: University of Kansas Press, 1984).

'Some Observations on the Adjustment of Recent Soviet Jewish Immigrants to the United States,' *Crossroads*, **11**, 1984 (with Rita J. Simon).

'Regulation Improves Efficiency? In Airline Overbooking – Yes and Maybe,' *Research in Finance,* Supplement 1, 1984, 209–26.

'Research on Population and Productivity Growth,' in G. Steinmann (ed.), *Studies in Contemporary Economics, Vol. 8, Economic Consequences of Population Change in Industrialized Countries* (Berlin, Heidelberg: Springer-Verlag, 1984).

'Introduction' to *The Resourceful Earth: A Response to the Global 2000 Report* (New York: Basil Blackwell, 1984) (with Herman Kahn) 1–49.

'On Species Loss, the Absence of Data, and Risks to Humanity,' in *The Resourceful Earth: A Response to the Global 2000 Report* (with Aaron Wildavsky) 171–83.

The Economic Implications of Learning-by-Doing for Population Size and Growth,' *European Economic Review*, **26**, 1984, 167–85 (with Gunter Steinmann).

'On the Optimum Theoretical Rate of Population Growth,' *Jahrbucher für Nationalokomie und Statistik* (Stuttgart: Gustav Fischer Verlag, 1985) Vol. 200/5, 508–31 (with Gunter Steinmann).

'The Effect of Immigrants on Natives' Incomes Through the Use of Capital,' *Journal of Development Economics*, 1985, 75–93 (with A.H. Heins).

'Forecasting the Long-Term Trend of Raw Material Availability,' *International Journal of Forecasting*, **1**, 1985, 85–93.

'Social and Economic Adjustment,' with Rita J. Simon (ed.), *New Lives: The Adjustment of Soviet Jewish Immigrants in the United States and Israel* (Lexington, Mass.: Lexington Books, 1985).

'Disappearing Species, Deforestation and Data,' *New Scientist*, 15 May 1986, 60–63.

'The Price Effects of Monopolistic Ownership in Newspapers,' *The Anti-Trust Bulletin*, **XXXI** (1), Spring 1986, 113–31 (with Walter J. Primeaux and Edward Rice).

'What Do People Bring to the Stock Market (Besides Money)? The Economic Psychology of Stock Market Behavior,' in Benjamin Gilad and Stanley Kaish (eds), *Handbook of Behavioral Economics* (Greenwich: JAI Press Inc., 1986), 273–307 (with Randall Filer and Shlomo Maital).

'Population Growth and Economic Development: Policy Questions,' (a review article) *Population and Development Review*, **12** (3), September 1986, 569–77.

'Basic Data Concerning Immigration into the United States,' *The Annals of the American Academy of Political and Social Science*, September 1986, 12–56.

'Some Theory of Population Growth's Effect on Technical Change in an Industrial Context,' *Australian Economic History Review*, **XXVI** (2), September 1986, 148–58.

'Population Growth, Economic Growth, and Foreign Aid,' *The Cato Journal*, **7**, Spring/Summer 1987, 159–86.

'The Price of Citizenship – Auctioning Immigration Visas Helps Foreigners and Americans Alike', *Policy Review*, **39**, Winter 1987, 71–2.

'Demand, Cost and Prices in Duopoly,' *Energy Economics*, April 1988, 117–24 (with Joseph Ben-Ur).

'Re-Linking Fertility Behavior and Economic Security in Old Age: An Exchange,' *Population and Development Review*, **14** (2), June 1988, 327–31.

''Optimal Term Life Insurance – A Practical Solution,' *Insurance: Mathematics and Economics*, **7**, 1988, 81–93 (with Haim Levy and Neil A. Doherty).

'Paradoxes and Difficulties in the Evaluation of Progress and Technological Advance, Past and Future,' *Technology in Society*, **10**, 1988, 425–32.

'Cause e Conseguenze Demografiche Della Rivoluzione Industriale' ('Demographic Causes and Consequences of the Industrial Revolution'), in Piero Melograni and Sergio Ricossa (eds), *Le Rivoluzioni Del Benessere*, (Roma-Bari: Guis. Laterza & Figli Spa, 1988), 37–60.

'More on Immigrants' Earnings Over Time,' *Genus*, **XLIV** (1–2), January–June 1988 (with Richard Sullivan).

'Lebensraum: Paradoxically, Population Growth May Eventually End Wars,' *The Journal of Conflict Resolution*, **33**, March 1989, 164–80.

'Robinson Crusoe Was Not Mainly A Resource Allocator,' *Social Science Quarterly*, **70**, June 1989, 471–8.

'On Aggregate Empirical Studies Relating Population Variables to Economic Development,' *Population and Development Review*, **15** (2), June 1989, 323–32.

'A Generalization that Makes Useful the Dorfman-Steiner Theorem With Respect to Advertising,' *Managerial and Decision Economics*, **10**, 1989, 85–7 (with Haim Levy).

'Population Size, Knowledge Stock, and Other Determinants of Agricultural Publication and Patenting: England, 1541–1850,' *Explorations in Economic History*, **26**, 1989, 21–44 (with Richard J. Sullivan).

'Population Growth, Political Instability, and Economic Development,' in Herbert M. Levine (ed.), *World Politics Debated. A Reader in Contemporary Issues* (third edition) 1989, 533–8.

'The Population Establishment, Corruption, and Reform,' in G. Roberts (ed.), *Population Policy: Contemporary Issues* (Praeger, 1990).

'The Phony Farmland Scare,' *Washington Journalism Review*, May 1990, 27–33.

'The Theory of Binding Commitments Simplified and Extended, With Generalization to Interpersonal Allocation,' *Rationality and Society*, **2** (3), July 1990, 287–309.

'The Unreported Revolution in Population Economics,' *The Public Interest*, **101**, Fall 1990, 89–100.

'Great and Almost-Great Magnitudes in Economics,' *Journal of Economic Perspectives*, **4** (1), Winter 1990, 149–56.

'City Size, Prices, and Efficiency for Individual Goods and Services,' *The Annals of Regional Science*, **24**, 1990, 163–75 (with Douglas O. Love).

'The Case For Greatly Increased Immigration,' *The Public Interest*, **102**, Winter 1991, 89–103.

'A Theory of Effort as an Economic Variable,' *The Journal of Socio-Economics*, **20** (2), 1991, 105–23.

'A Solution for the Tenure Problem,' *Cato Journal*, **10** (3), Winter 1991, 835–8.

'Population Growth, Farmland, and the Long-Run Standard of Living,' *Journal of Population Economics*, **4**, 1991, 37–51 (with Gunter Steinmann).

'How to Add Junior Tenure-Track Positions at No Additional Cost to the University,' *Journal of Policy Analysis and Management*, **10** (3), 1991.

'Immigrants and Alien Workers,' *Journal of Labor Research*, **XIII** (1), Winter 1992, 73–8.

'Species Loss Revisited,' *Society*, **30** (1), November/December 1992, 41–6 (with Aaron Wildavsky).

'The Economic Effects of Immigration: Theory and Evidence' in Steven Globerman (ed.), *The Immigration Dilemma*, 1992, 128–46.

'The Economic Effects of Immigration,' *European Review*, **1** (1), 1993, 109–16.

'Do We Really Need All These Immigrants?' in Donald N. McCloskey (ed.), *Second Thoughts* (Oxford University Press, 1993) (with Rita James Simon).

'Probability and Statistics With Resampling Stats and Mathematica,' *The Mathematica Journal*, **3** (1), Winter 1993, 48–55 (with Peter Bruce).

'Origins of the Airline Oversales Auction System,' *Regulation*, 1194, Number 2, 48–52.

'Is Population Growth a Drag on Development?' in James Dorn and Alan Walters (eds), *The Revolution in Development Economics* (George Mason U. Press, forthcoming).

'The Effect of Immigration Upon Aggregate Native Unemployment: An Across-City Estimate,' *Journal of Labor Research*, **IV**, Summer 1993, 299–316 (with Stephen Moore and Richard Sullivan).

'Economic Thought About Population Consequences: Some Reflections,' *Journal of Population Economics*, **6**, 1993, 137–52.

'The Resampling Methods For Statistical Inference,' forthcoming in *Scientific American*.

'Why Don't States Income Converge? Effective Worker Pay Does Not Differ Among States,' *Economics of Education Review*, **12** (2), 1993, 105–16.

'Introduction,' in Julian L. Simon (ed.), *The State of Humanity* (Basil Blackwell, 1994).

'What Does the Future Hold?' in Julian L. Simon (ed.), *The State of Humanity* (Basil Blackwell, 1994).

'Trends in the Quantities of Education,' in Julian L. Simon (ed.) *The State of Humanity* (Basil Blackwell, 1994) (with Rebecca Boggs).

'Species Lost Revisited,' in Julian L. Simon (ed.), *The State of Humanity* (Basil Blackwell, 1994) (with Aaron Wildavsky).

'The Airline Oversales Auction Plan: The Results,' *Journal of Transportation Economics and Policy*, **XXVIII** (3), September 1994, 319–21.

'What Monty Hall Teaches about the Theory of Resampling: Some Difficult Problems, and the Computation of Sample Spaces,' *American Statistician*, forthcoming.

'The Reserves of Extracted Resources: the Historical Data,' *Non-Renewable Resources*, forthcoming (with Guenter Weinrauch and Stephen Moore).

'What's Happened to Airline Service?' *Consumer's Research*, February 1993, 15–17.

Incomplete list of fiction, book reviews, comments, newspaper and general periodical articles *(other than research; reprints and translations not included.)*

'Forbidden,' *Brooklyn Jewish Review*, Spring 1957 (fiction).

'Homebrew: A Man's Own Drink', *Cavaliar*, December 1958.

'Love Is a Baby', *December*, Fall 1960 (fiction).

'I Was Aboard the Exodus,' *Family Weekly*, 18 March 1961 (nonfiction) (with anonymous co-author).

'The Concept of Causality in Economics – Reply,' *Kyklos*, **XXIV** (4), 1971, 769–70.

'World Food Needs and "New Proteins": A Reply', E*conomic Development and Cultural Change*, **20** (3), April 1972, 558–9 (with David Gardner).

'Airline Overbooking – The State of the Art: A Reply,' *Journal of Transport Economics and Policy*, **VI**, September 1972, 254–6.

'How the National Income (of Israel) Will Be Divided in the Year 2000,' *Jerusalem Post*, Independence Day Issue, May 1976.

'Population Decline in Europe: Implications of a Declining or Stationary Population': Proceedings of a seminar held by the Council of Europe, Strasbourg, 6–10 September 1976. *Journal of Economic Literature*, **XVII**, September 1979 (book review).

'Wherein the Author Offers a Modest Proposal,' (on airline overbooking), *Wall Street Journal*, 10 January 1977, 12.

'Your Possibilities in Mail Order,' *Salesman's Opportunity*, February 1977, 36–7.

'Economic Implications of the Absorption of Soviet Jewish Immigrants,' *Scientists Committee of the Israel Public Council for Soviet Jewry*, News Bulletin No. 111, 15 June 1977.

'Untrue That Population Growth Harms Income in the U.S.,' *Intercom*, **6**, June 1978, 7–9.

'Interpersonal Welfare Comparison: A Reply,' *Kyklos*, **31** (2), 1978, 63–98.

'Comments on Telser's Paper,' in David G. Tuerck (ed.), *The Political Economy of Advertising* (Washington: American Enterprise Institute, 1978).

'Comment: Interactions of Economic and Demographic Household Behavior,' in Richard A. Easterlin (ed.), *Population and Economic Change in Developing Countries* (University of Chicago Press, 1980), 452–57.

'Economic Objections Fall Apart When Used Against Immigrants,' *Los Angeles Times*, 1 July 1980.

'Immigrants – Especially Illegals – Raise U.S. Incomes,' *Newsday*, 10 July 1980, 78 (similar to *LA Times* article above).

'And Now, the Good News: Life on Earth is Improving,' *The Washington Post*, 13 July 1980, E1–E2 (abridged version of *Science* article above).

'Losing Land?' *New York Times*, Op-Ed page, 7 October 1980, 23.

'Assuring the Future of U.S. Farm Land,' *The Wall Street Journal*, 10 November 1980, 23 (with Dale McLaren).

'Sorry, But Gloom Simply Won't Do,' *Next*, **11**, December 1980, 48–50.
'Reply,' *Science*, **210** (4476), 19 December 1980, 1296–308.
'Reply,' *Illinois Business Review*, **37** (10), December 1980, 3–4.
'Adding Up the Costs of Our New Immigrants,' *The Wall Street Journal*, 26 February 1981, 22.
'The Phantom 30,000 Acres of Lost Farmland,' *The Champaign-Urbana News-Gazette*, 17 May 1981, A–5.
'Cropland Acres and Quality Up,' *The Champaign-Urbana News-Gazette*, 9 June 1981, A–6.
'How Vietnamese Immigrants Fare in the United States,' *The Asian Wall Street Journal*, 25 June 1981, Commentary and Analysis section, 1.
'The Scarcity of Raw Materials,' *The Atlantic Monthly*, June 1981, 33–41.
'World Food Supplies,' *The Atlantic Monthly*, July 1981, 72–6.
'World Population Growth,' *The Atlantic Monthly*, August 1981, 70–6.
'The Doomsday Contagion: A Plague of Soothsayers,' *Bergen Record*, 25 September 1981, D–23.
'Rethinking the Population Explosion,' *Sh'ma* **12** (222), 13 November 1981, 163–4.
'Will We Run Out of Energy?' *Dialogue*, Number 56 – 2/1982, 16–20.
'Is the Era of Limits Running Out?' *Public Opinion*, **5**, February/March 1982, 48–57 (with Garret Hardin).
'Population Growth Is Good,' *Readers Digest*, March 1982, 115–17.
'World Population: Is More Really Worse?' *Families*, March 1982, 17–20.
'Is There An Answer to Malthus?' *Population and Development Review*, **8** (1), March 1982, 205–17 (transcript of William F. Buckley's *Firing Line* Show).
'Will We Get Enough to Eat?' *Today's Education*, **71**, April–May 1982, 43–5.
'Reply to Thomas Meeks,' *Review of Economics and Statistics*, **LXIV**, May 1982, 352–5 (with Hiroshi Miyashita, Paul Newhold and Adam M. Pilarski).
'Paul Ehrlich Saying It Is So Doesn't Make It So,' *Social Science Quarterly*, **63** (2), June 1982, 381–5.
'More is Beautiful,' *Population-UNFPA Newsletter*, **8** (7), July 1982, 2.
'The Farmer and the Mall: Are American Farmlands Disappearing?' *The American Spectator*, August 1982, 18–20, 40–41.
'This New Rule Would Hurt Bumped Air Travelers,' *The Wall Street Journal*, 17 August 1982, 26.
'Should We Heed the Prophets of Doom?' *Science Digest*, **90**, October 1982, 106–8.
'A Parable of Racquetball, Squash and Population Growth at U of I,' *The Daily Illini*, 20 October 1982.
'Growth Means Progress,' *Science Digest*, 91, April 1983, 76–81.
'In Favor of Immigration,' *Inquiry*, 6 May 1983, 18–23.
'The Global 2000 Juggernaut,' *Institutional Analysis*, Heritage Foundation, 13 May 1983.
'Gloomy Global Forecast Serves False Values,' *The Washington Times*, 25 May 1983, C-1.
'Human Ingenuity Overcomes Growth,' *USA Today*, 15 July 1983, 8A.
'Life on Earth Is Getting Better, Not Worse,' *The Futurist*, August 1983, 7–13.
'What is Really Eroding in America? *Christian Science Monitor*, 8 August 1983, 23.

'Why Is Soil Erosion Target Of Scare Tactics?' *Independent Daily Mail*, Anderson S.C., 11 August 1983.

'Special Report on Global 2000,' *About Issues*, **5** (9), September 1983, 24–5.

'U.S. Farmlands: The False Crisis,' *Heritage Backgrounder*, 14 September 1983.

'Global Deforestation,' *Resources for the Future*, Fall 1983, 4–8.

'Nine Myths About Immigration,' *Heritage Backgrounder*, Heritage Foundation, **326**, 1 February 1984, 1–14.

'Global Foresight Bills: The Danger of Centralized Data Sources,' *Heritage Backgrounder*, Hertitage Foundation, 24 February 1984.

'Don't Close Our Borders,' *Newsweek*, 27 February 1984, 11.

'Does Doom Loom?' *Reason*, April 1984, 31–4.

'Opinion,' *Population Today*, May 1984, 8.

'How Immigrants Affect Americans' Living Standard,' A Debate Between Julian Simon and Roger Conner, 30 May 1984, *The Heritage Lectures, No. 39*, pamphlet published 1985, 1–67.

'There Is No Crisis; Air, Water Are Safe,' *USA Today*, 12 July 1984.

'Treating People as an Asset,' *Heritage Backgrounder*, Heritage Foundation, 13 July 1984.

'Population is an Asset,' *The Baltimore Sun*, 29 July 1984.

'Don't Fear Job Loss – Simpson–Mazzoli, Act II,' *The New York Times*, 2 August 1984.

'Myths of Overpopulation,' *The Wall Street Journal*, 3 August 1984.

'People Are Not The Problem,' *The Washington Times*, 6 August 1984, C1.

'People Are No Threat to Health or Wealth,' *USA Today*, 6 August 1984.

'Do Aliens Make us Scofflaws?' *The Washington Times*, 14 August 1984.

'Truth Almost Extinct in Tales of Imperiled Species,' *The Washington Times*, 19 September 1984, 3C.

'Population Growth Can Be Good for Us,' *The Washington Post*, 10 November 1984.

'La Población, Un Recurso Inagotable,' *El País* (Malthus Section), 27 December 1984, 9.

'The War on People,' *Challenge*, March–April 1985, 50–3.

'Immigration – Debt Or Credit?' *The Washington Times*, 12 July 1985, 1D–2D.

'Let Some "Illegals" Come Temporarily To The US,' *The Christian Science Monitor*, 22 August 1985, 13.

'There's Really No Need To Control Our Borders,' *USA Today*, 24 September 1985, 10A.

'Why Do We Still Think Babies Create Poverty?' *The Washington Post*, 13 October 1985, B1 and B4.

'What About Immigration?' *The Freeman*, January 1986, 8–16.

'Auction the Right to Be an Immigrant,' *The New York Times*, 28 January 1986, 15.

'Flow of Immigrants Strengthens the USA,' *USA Today*, 3 April 1986, 6A.

'Immigration Benefits Our Country's Economy,' Scripps Howard News Service, in an unknown number of newspapers, July 1986.

'This Sea of Humanity Is No Threat at All,' *USA Today*, 17 July 1986, 8A.

'Anti-Growth Prophets Use Cracked Crystal Balls,' *Rocky Mountain News-Denver*, 29 December 1986, 47.

'Le mythe de la surpopulation,' *9eme Congrès International de la Famille – La fecondité de l'amour*, 1986, 71–9.

'World Bank: More Harm Than Good?' *The Washington Times*, March 1987.

'Can't Get on a Flight? There Should Be No Problem,' *The Wall Street Journal*, 9 April 1987, 32.

'Book review: *The World As A Total System*, by Kenneth E. Boulding', *Journal of Economic Literature*, **XXV**, June 1987, 739–40.

'Long Shelf Life For Bum Ideas,' *The Washington Times*, 28 July 1987, D4.

'Raise Immigration Quotas, Not Taxes,' *The Christian Science Monitor*, 29 July 1987, 11.

'"Batter's Slump" & other Illusions,' *The Washington Post*, 9 August 1987, C3.

'Now (I Think) I Understand The Ecologists Better,' *The Futurist*, September–October 1987, 18–19.

'China's Population Problem,' *The Asian Wall Street Journal*, 24 November 1987, 10.

'China's "Voluntary" Population Initiative,' *The Wall Street Journal*, 29 February 1988, 21.

'A Lesson in Job Creation,' *The Asian Wall Street Journal*, 27–8 May 1988, 8.

'Getting the Immigrants We Need,' *The Washington Post*, 3 August 1988, A17.

'Humanity doesn't Waste the Benefits Found in Trash,' *Chicago Tribune*, 27 February 1989, Section 1, 11.

'Comments on Review of *Theory of Population and Economic Growth*,' *Contemporary Sociology*, **18** (2), March 1989.

'Communism, Capitalism, and Economic Development: Implications for U.S. Economic Assistance,' *The Backgrounder*, No. 741, 8 December 1989 (with Stephen Moore).

'Le monde est-il surpeuplé?' *11eme Congrès International de la Famille – La fécondité de l'amour*, 1989, 345–53.

'Población Humana y Recursos Naturales: Los Datos Objectivos,' *Población, Desarrollo, Futuro*, 1989, 47–110.

'Bring on the Wretched Refuse,' *The Wall Street Journal*, 26 January 1990, A14.

'The Boon of Immigration,' *The Jerusalem Post*, 23 February 1990.

'Welcome The Invigorating Immigrants,' the *Hartford Courant*, 9 March 1990, C13 (with Rita J. Simon).

'Population Growth is Not Bad for Humanity,' *National Forum*, Winter 1990, **LXX** (1), 12–16.

'The Positive Worth of Waste: A Reply to Bromley,' *Social Science Quarterly*, **70** (4), December 1989, 989–91.

'Materials and Methods – Resampling States: a Computer Language and Program,' *International Statistical Education Newsletter*.

'The People Problem,' *The Sun*, 19 April 1990, 13A.

'Resources to Support All of Us?' *The Cincinnati Post*, 20 April 1990, 15A.

'Immigrants Made This Country,' *San Diego Tribune*, 24 April 1990, B–7.

'There Are No "Wrong" Immigrants,' *The Wall Street Journal*, 11 May 1990, A13.

Book review: *The Population Explosion*, by Paul R. and Anne H. Ehrlich, *Fortune*, 21 May 1990, 160 and 162.

'Injecting Capitalism,' *The Corporate Board*, May/June 1990.

'Immigration – A Boon to Israel,' A Special Report Prepared for the United Jewish Appeal, 14 June 1990.

'Little England's Missed Opportunity,' *Economic Affairs*, June/July 1990, 27–9 (with William McGurn).
'Why More HUDS May Lie Ahead,' *The Washington Times*, 17 July 1990, G1, G4.
Book review: T*he Coming Global Boom: How to Benefit From Tomorrow's Dynamic World Economy*, by Charles R. Morris, *The Washington Times*, 13 August 1990, F3.
'Migration Myopia,' *The Washington Times*, 24 August 1990.
'Comments on "Symposium on New Institutions for Developing Country Debt,"' Winter 1990, pp. 3–56, *Journal of Economic Perspectives*, **4** (4), Fall 1990.
'Letter From Jerusalem: Good Returns,' *Hadassah*, **72** (4), December 1990, 14–15.
'Energy Not Finite Resource Because Alternative Forms Perpetuate It,' *Anchorage Times*, 25 January 1991. Also in *Roanoke Times & World-News*, 10 February 1991, under title 'The Worriers Are Wrong: We aren't Depleting Energy, Other Resources.'
'Too Few People? Too Many Trees?' *Crisis*, **9** (2), February 1991.
'Muscle and Mind Should See Us Through,' *The Tablet*, 20 April 1991, 468–70.
'Europe's Costly Immigration Myths,' *European Wall Street Journal*, 24 April 1991.
'Shakespeare, Procreation, and Progress,' *Society*, **28** (5), July/August 1991, 58–62.
'Reply to Boomsma and Molenaar,' *Chance*, **4** (4), 1991, 30–31 (with Peter C. Bruce).
'Any Truth in the Balance?' *The Washington Times*, 17 February 1992, F–1.
'Getting State's Number in the Lottery Game,' *The Washington Times*, 18 March 1992, F–1.
'A Bet That Things Are Getting Better,' *The Sun*, 24 March 1992, 13A.
'Fleeing Haitians Deserve A Chance,' *Chicago Tribune*, 2 May 1992, 21.
'Population Control: Bush At Home In Rio,' *The Detroit News*, 31 May 1992, 3B.
'The Environmental Crisis That Isn't,' *Moment*, June 1992, 48–52, 61.
'A Tribute to Friedrich A. von Hayek, C.H.,' *The Mont Pelerin Society Newsletter*, **45** (2), June 1992, 12–14.
'The Extinction of Science,' *The Baltimore Sun*, 11 June 1992, 15A.
'Playing the Clown on Waste?' *The Washington Times*, 14 July 1992.
'Using Computer Simulation in Quality Control,' *Quality Progress*, August 1992, 129, 131, 133 and 135 (with Peter Bruce).
'Freer Skies Gave Us Better Service,' *The Wall Street Journal*, 14 October 1992, A1.
'A Sense of Siege,' *The Orange Country Register*, 6 December 1992, G1–2.
'Why Control the Borders?' *National Review*, 1 February 1993, 27–9.
'China's Family-Planning by Coercion,' *The Washington Post*, 10 March 1993, A19.
'If Only Clinton Would Read Hayek,' *Human Events*, 17 April 1993.
'The Nativists Are Wrong,' *The Wall Street Journal*, 4 August 1993, A8.
'The Media War Against Cheap Energy,' *Human Events*, 21 August 1993, 14.
'European Immigration: Problems and Opportunities,' *Swiss Review of World Affairs*, February 1994, No. 2, 4–6.
'Studies on Immigrants Prove They'd Rather Give Than Receive,' *The New York Times*, letter to the editor, 26 February 1994.
'More People, Greater Wealth, More Resources, Healthier Environment', *Economic Affairs*, April 1994.
'Más Gente, Mejor Para Todos,' *Nueve Revista*, No. 35, June 1994, 58–73.

Name index

Economists of the Twentieth Century

Monetarism and Macroeconomic Policy
Thomas Mayer

Studies in Fiscal Federalism
Wallace E. Oates

The World Economy in Perspective
Essays in International Trade and European Integration
Herbert Giersch

Towards a New Economics
Critical Essays on Ecology, Distribution and Other Themes
Kenneth E. Boulding

Studies in Positive and Normative Economics
Martin J. Bailey

The Collected Essays of Richard E. Quandt (2 volumes)
Richard E. Quandt

International Trade Theory and Policy
Selected Essays of W. Max Corden
W. Max Corden

Organization and Technology in Capitalist Development
William Lazonick

Studies in Human Capital
Collected Essays of Jacob Mincer, Volume 1
Jacob Mincer

Studies in Labor Supply
Collected Essays of Jacob Mincer, Volume 2
Jacob Mincer

Macroeconomics and Economic Policy
The Selected Essays of Assar Lindbeck
Volume I
Assar Lindbeck

The Welfare State
The Selected Essays of Assar Lindbeck
Volume II
Assar Lindbeck

Classical Economics, Public Expenditure and Growth
Walter Eltis

Money, Interest Rates and Inflation
Frederic S. Mishkin

The Public Choice Approach to Politics
Dennis C. Mueller

The Liberal Economic Order
Volume I Essays on International Economics
Volume II Money, Cycles and Related Themes
Gottfried Haberler
Edited by Anthony Y.C. Koo

Economic Growth and Business Cycles
Prices and the Process of Cyclical Development
Paolo Sylos Labini

International Adjustment, Money and Trade
Theory and Measurement for Economic Policy
Volume I
Herbert G. Grubel

International Capital and Service Flows
Theory and Measurement for Economic Policy
Volume II
Herbert G. Grubel

Unintended Effects of Government Policies
Theory and Measurement for Economic Policy
Volume III
Herbert G. Grubel

The Economics of Competitive Enterprise
Selected Essays of P.W.S. Andrews
Edited by Frederic S. Lee
and Peter E. Earl

The Repressed Economy
Causes, Consequences, Reform
Deepak Lal

Economic Theory and Market Socialism
Selected Essays of Oskar Lange
Edited by Tadeusz Kowalik

Trade, Development and Political Economy
Selected Essays of Ronald Findlay
Ronald Findlay

General Equilibrium Theory
The Collected Essays of Takashi Negishi
Volume I
Takashi Negishi

The History of Economics
The Collected Essays of Takashi Negishi
Volume II
Takashi Negishi

Studies in Econometric Theory
The Collected Essays of Takeshi Amemiya
Takeshi Amemiya

Exchange Rates and the Monetary System
Selected Essays of Peter B. Kenen
Peter B. Kenen

Econometric Methods and Applications
(2 volumes)
G.S. Maddala

National Accounting and Economic Theory
The Collected Papers of Dan Usher, Volume I
Dan Usher

Welfare Economics and Public Finance
The Collected Papers of Dan Usher, Volume II
Dan Usher

Economic Theory and Capitalist Society
The Selected Essays of Shigeto Tsuru, Volume I
Shigeto Tsuru

Methodology, Money and the Firm
The Collected Essays of D.P. O'Brien
(2 volumes)
D.P. O'Brien

Economic Theory and Financial Policy
The Selected Essays of Jacques J. Polak
(2 volumes)
Jacques J. Polak

Sturdy Econometrics
Edward E. Leamer

The Emergence of Economic Ideas
Essays in the History of Economics
Nathan Rosenberg

Productivity Change, Public Goods and Transaction Costs
Essays at the Boundaries of Microeconomics
Yoram Barzel

Reflections on Economic Development
The Selected Essays of Michael P. Todaro
Michael P. Todaro

The Economic Development of Modern Japan
The Selected Essays of Shigeto Tsuru
Volume II
Shigeto Tsuru

Money, Credit and Policy
Allan H. Meltzer

Macroeconomics and Monetary Theory
The Selected Essays of Meghnad Desai
Volume I
Meghnad Desai

Poverty, Famine and Economic Development
The Selected Essays of Meghnad Desai
Volume II
Meghnad Desai

Explaining the Economic Performance of Nations
Essays in Time and Space
Angus Maddison

Economic Doctrine and Method
Selected Papers of R.W. Clower
Robert W. Clower

Economic Theory and Reality
Selected Essays on their Disparities and Reconciliation
Tibor Scitovsky

Doing Economic Research
Essays on the Applied Methodology of Economics
Thomas Mayer

Institutions and Development Strategies
The Selected Essays of Irma Adelman
Volume I
Irma Adelman

Dynamics and Income Distribution
The Selected Essays of Irma Adelman
Volume II
Irma Adelman

The Economics of Growth and Development
Selected Essays of A.P. Thirlwall
A.P. Thirlwall

Theoretical and Applied Econometrics
The Selected Papers of Phoebus J. Dhrymes
Phoebus J. Dhrymes

Innovation, Technology and the Economy
The Selected Essays of Edwin Mansfield
(2 volumes)
Edwin Mansfield

Economic Theory and Policy in Context
The Selected Essays of R.D. Collison Black
R.D. Collison Black

Location Economics
Theoretical Underpinnings and Applications
Melvin L. Greenhut

Spatial Microeconomics
Theoretical Underpinnings and Applications
Melvin L. Greenhut

Capitalism, Socialism and Post-Keynesianism
Selected Essays of G.C. Harcourt
G.C. Harcourt

Time Series Analysis and Macroeconometric Modelling
The Collected Papers of Kenneth F. Wallis
Kenneth F. Wallis

Foundations of Modern Econometrics
The Selected Essays of Ragnar Frisch
(2 volumes)
Edited by Olav Bjerkholt

Growth, the Environment and the Distribution of Incomes
Essays by a Sceptical Optimist
Wilfred Beckerman

The Economics of Environmental Regulation
Wallace E. Oates

Econometrics, Macroeconomics and Economic Policy
Selected Papers of Carl F. Christ
Carl F. Christ

Strategic Approaches to the International Economy
Selected Essays of Koichi Hamada
Koichi Hamada

Economic Analysis and Political Ideology
The Selected Essays of Karl Brunner
Volume One
Edited by Thomas Lys

Growth Theory and Technical Change
The Selected Essays of Ryuzo Sato
Volume One
Ryuzo Sato

Industrialization, Inequality and Economic Growth
Jeffrey G. Williamson

Economic Theory and Public Decisions
Selected Essays of Robert Dorfman
Robert Dorfman

The Logic of Action One
Method, Money, and the Austrian School
Murray N. Rothbard

The Logic of Action Two
Applications and Criticism from the Austrian School
Murray N. Rothbard

Bayesian Analysis in Econometrics and Statistics
The Zellner View and Papers
Arnold Zellner

On the Foundations of Monopolistic Competition and Economic Geography
The Selected Essays of B. Curtis Eaton and Richard G. Lipsey
B. Curtis Eaton and Richard G. Lipsey

Microeconomics, Growth and Political Economy
The Selected Essays of Richard G. Lipsey
Volume One
Richard G. Lipsey

Macroeconomic Theory and Policy
The Selected Essays of Richard G. Lipsey
Volume Two
Richard G. Lipsey

Employment, Labor Unions and Wages
The Collected Essays of Orley Ashenfelter
Volume One
Edited by Kevin F. Hallock

Education, Training and Discrimination
The Collected Essays of Orley Ashenfelter
Volume Two
Edited by Kevin F. Hallock

Economic Institutions and the Demand and Supply of Labour
The Collected Essays of Orley Ashenfelter
Volume Three
Edited by Kevin F. Hallock

Monetary Theory and Monetary Policy
The Selected Essays of Karl Brunner
Volume Two
Edited by Thomas Lys

Macroeconomic Issues from a Keynesian Perspective
Selected Essays of A.P. Thirlwall
Volume Two
A.P. Thirlwall

Money and Macroeconomics
The Selected Essays of David Laidler
David Laidler

The Economics and Politics of Money
The Selected Essays of Alan Walters
Edited by Kent Matthews

Economics and Social Justice
Essays on Power, Labor and Institutional Change
David M. Gordon
Edited by Thomas E. Weisskopf and Samuel Bowles

Practicing Econometrics
Essays in Method and Application
Zvi Griliches

Economics Against the Grain
Volume One
Microeconomics, Industrial Organization and Related Themes
Julian L. Simon

Economics Against the Grain
Volume Two
Population Economics, Natural Resources and Related Themes
Julian L. Simon

Advances in Econometric Theory
The Selected Works of Halbert White
Halbert White

The Economics of Imperfect Knowledge
Collected Papers of G.B. Richardson
G.B. Richardson

Economic Performance and the Theory of the Firm
The Selected Papers of David J. Teece
Volume One
David J. Teece

Strategy, Technology and Public Policy
The Selected Papers of David J. Teece
Volume Two
David J. Teece

The Keynesian Revolution, Then and Now
The Selected Essays of Robert Eisner
Volume One
Robert Eisner

Investment, National Income and Economic Policy
The Selected Essays of Robert Eisner
Volume Two
Robert Eisner

International Trade Opening and the Formation of the Global Economy
Selected Essays of P. J. Lloyd
P. J. Lloyd

Production, Stability and Dynamic Symmetry
The Selected Essays of Ryuzo Sato
Volume Two
Ryuzo Sato

Variants in Economic Theory
Selected Works of Hal R. Varian
Hal R. Varian

Political Economy, Oligopoly and Experiment
The Selected Essays of Martin Shubik
Volume One
Martin Shubik

Money and Financial Institutions
A GAME THEORETIC APPROACH
The Selected Essays of Martin Shubik
Volume Two
Martin Shubik